ICTs and Sustainable Solutions for the Digital Divide:

Theory and Perspectives

Jacques Steyn
Monash University, South Africa

Graeme Johanson
Monash University, Australia

INFORMATION SCIENCE REFERENCE

Hershey · New York

Director of Editorial Content:	Kristin Klinger
Director of Book Publications:	Julia Mosemann
Acquisitions Editor:	Lindsay Johnston
Development Editor:	Julia Mosemann
Publishing Assistant:	Keith Glazewski & Milan Vracarich, Jr.
Typesetter:	Keith Glazewski & Milan Vracarich, Jr.
Production Editor:	Jamie Snavely
Cover Design:	Lisa Tosheff

Published in the United States of America by
Information Science Reference (an imprint of IGI Global)
701 E. Chocolate Avenue
Hershey PA 17033
Tel: 717-533-8845
Fax: 717-533-8661
E-mail: cust@igi-global.com
Web site: http://www.igi-global.com

Library of Congress Cataloging-in-Publication Data

ICTs and sustainable solutions for the digital divide : theory and
perspectives / Jacques Steyn and Graeme Johanson, editors.
       p. cm.
  Includes bibliographical references and index.
  Summary: "This book focuses on Information and Communication Technologies
for Development (ICT4D), which includes any technology used for communication
and information, researching the social side of computing, the users, and the
design of systems that meet the needs of "ordinary" users"--Provided by
publisher.
  ISBN 978-1-61520-799-2 (hbk.) -- ISBN 978-1-61520-800-5 (ebook) 1.
Information technology--Economic aspects. 2. Digital divide. I. Steyn,
Jacques. II. Johanson, Graeme.
  HC79.I55I285 2010
  303.48'33--dc22
                            2010016509

British Cataloguing in Publication Data
A Cataloguing in Publication record for this book is available from the British Library.

All work contributed to this book is new, previously-unpublished material. The views expressed in this book are those of the authors, but not necessarily of the publisher.

Table of Contents

Section 1
Foundations, Methodology and Terminology

Detailed Table of Contents

Section 1
Foundations, Methodology and Terminology

This chapter describes the field of Development Informatics as it has emerged in the past two decades, and highlights some of the strengths of its research and practices. It draws on the current literature and the expertise of the other authors of this book to help to define a set of basic terms. Any new intellectual domain is tied to some degree to the vagaries of its institutional alliances, to the perceived international status of its public forums, and to the criticism that on its own it lacks unique methodological rigour. These points are discussed candidly. Multidisciplinarity is the backbone of Development Informatics. The main virtues of Development Informatics are that it offers a platform for an evaluative critique to counterbalance the effects of relentless globalisation, that it comprises strong multidisciplinary teams, that it maintains an intellectual space to build on international momentum that has developed among theorists and practitioners, and that it opens up future imaginative possibilities for collaborative projects which involve communities in developing areas of participatory research and ongoing project evaluation in order to encourage self-sustaining entities.

This chapter argues for a shift of paradigm in the field of ICT4D. Since the inception of aid for development in the late 1940s with the introduction of the Marshall Plan, development has been dominated by emphasis on economic development, while development of other human characteristics have been neglected. The standard argument in ICT4D literature is that economic "upliftment" will result in social "upliftment". It is assumed that economics is the primary cause for social change. The author of this chapter challenges this assumption, and proposes that it is instead individual "upliftment" that influences social change that might (or might not) lead to economic change.

Chapter 3

Cristina Kiomi Mori, University of Brasilia (UnB), Brazil & Ministry of Planning, Brazil

In the past twenty years, there has been increasing involvement of governments, societies and communities in initiatives for bridging the digital gap, aiming economic and social development. These efforts are generally called 'digital inclusion' policies and projects. The expression 'digital inclusion' combines defining terms such as 'digital divide' and 'social inclusion', together with the assumptions, ideologies and value systems they carry. However, the comprehension of this expression varies among different agents involved. Identifying defining terms and analyzing their corresponding views is essential for improving scientific approach to any theme. This chapter scrutinizes definitions of 'digital inclusion', 'social exclusion' and related topics from specialized and academic bibliography, as well as from the field, in order to contribute qualifying academic and policy making debates. It proposes that the approaches to 'digital inclusion' are connected to concept views about society and social dynamics, State, market, civil society relationships and public policies. The notion of 'Information Society' and the purposes of disseminating digital information and communication technologies (ICT) are also present, thus framing 'digital inclusion' in different ways. The text concludes that scientific approaches must consider these aspects for addressing 'digital inclusion' as an object of analysis in a more consistent basis.

Chapter 4

Ricardo Ramírez, University of Guelph, Canada

This chapter calls for participatory monitoring and evaluation (M&E) of information and communication technology for development (ICT4D). The author describes the ontology of ICT4D as complex and unpredictable and favours an epistemology that is based on systems thinking and adaptive management as a foundation for participatory approaches. The M&E of ICTs faces a number of challenges including the lack of a unifying theoretical framework, the need to define users and purposes for each evaluation, the importance of agreeing on the type of causality that is expected, and the reality of short- term project durations.

Chapter 5

Chase Laurelle Knowles, Claremont Graduate University, USA

Since the conclusion of World War II, efforts to develop the so-called Third World have taken a variety of paths. In light of the multiplicity of competing theoretical lenses – modernization, post-structuralism, and dependency, to name just a few theories – the field of development is in a state of confusion. Consequently, it has been difficult for development informatics specialists to understand how best to harness the power of Information Communications Technology (ICT), as there is no clear goal in sight which ICT is supposed to be supporting. This chapter provides a brief historical overview of the field of development, with a special interest in the role technology has been understood to play in this context. A discussion of relevant scholarship points to the dual notions that the next wave of development informatics work will prize attention to cultural particularities, and as such, will necessitate a degree of participative technology design. By extension, a dynamic relationship between power and knowledge is affirmed, in line with scholars such as Schech (2002). Various strands of thought are ultimately synthesized into what is termed the mirror meta-principle, which stresses that culturally sustainable development informatics requires ICT to be participatively designed so as to support developing societies' economic and socio-cultural well-being and congruently "mirror" the economic and socio-cultural exigencies and traditions of developing societies. In this paradigm, the economic and socio-cultural patterns embedded into ICT need not be in line, or need to be moved into line, with the traditional Western ideology of modernization. With Heeks (1999), it is asserted that development informatics specialists' approach to the participatory process must remain grounded in real conditions.

Chapter 6

Jasmine M. Harvey, University of Loughborough, UK

The emergence of new information and communication technologies (ICTs) has generated much debate both in and out of academia in relation to theories ranging from economic advancement to imperialism. In the context of the 'low-income' economies, a dominant discourse associated with ICTs persists. The discourse of development predicts that nations which have joined the global market will use ICTs to harness global knowledge that will enable them to be competitive and therefore attain development. This has led to change in policy from international to local as ICTs are embraced as the next big development tool. Recently however, there have been reports of more failures of ICTs initiatives than success as professionals in the industry complain about unsustainability of the systems. A genuine issue is that so far analysis of this discourse has tended to be economically or technically deterministic, with little attention paid to social and cultural perspectives. In order to understand how the role of norms, practices and politics of people in particular communities play in this discourse in 'low income' economies, over 1000 semi-qualitative questionnaires were analysed from five geographical locations in The Gambia. A key conclusion that has emerged from the research is that there are different attitudes towards the ICTs in the different locations, which vary from full acceptance to rejection of ICTs. Such diverse reactions are underpinned by the religion and information ecologies in which gender plays a critical part. This result challenges the ICT4D agenda, and might be applied to reports of unsustainable ICT initiatives, especially in Africa.

Chapter 7

Andrew Thatcher, University of the Witwatersrand, South Africa
Mbongi Ndabeni, Rhodes University, South Africa

The digital divide is often conceptualised as inequalities of access to technology. While access is obviously a precursor to technology use, research consistently shows that the digital divide is not explained simply by access to technology; apparent in the evidence of digital divides within communities of equitable wealth or within the same geographical location. This chapter acknowledges the interplay between psychological as well as socio-economic factors as important in the adoption of technology. Within this approach, the authors construct a model based on the Technology Acceptance Model, the Theory of Planned Behaviour, Innovation Diffusion Theory, Hofstede's culture framework, and Social Cognitive Theory. The framework for the model is based on a combination of an extension of the Technology Acceptance Model, Innovation Diffusion Theory, and Social Cognitive Theory. The underlying theoretical assumptions are based on Social Cognitive Theory. While some aspects of these individual theories have already been applied to understanding the digital divide, this chapter develops a more comprehensive psychological model of e-adoption than currently exists in the literature.

Section 2
Social Inclusion and Bottom-Up

Chapter 8

Suely Fragoso, Universidade do Vale do Rio do Sinos (Unisinos), Brazil
Denise Cogo, Universidade do Vale do Rio do Sinos (Unisinos), Brazil
Liliane Dutra Brignol, Universidade do Vale do Rio do Sinos (Unisinos) & Centro Universitario Franciscano (Unifra), Brazil

This chapter discusses the success and failure of initiatives which provide access to Information and Communication Technologies (ICTs) as a means of promoting social inclusion. The authors believe that there is often a disparity between the supposed and the true needs and desires of the minority groups at the receiving end of digital divide initiatives. Observation of practices towards ICTs which are spontaneously developed by a minority group indicate that important achievements are being overlooked by formal evaluations of digital divide projects and policies. The observed practices are organized into six categories and a change of paradigm is proposed for further actions.

Chapter 9

Peter A. Kwaku Kyem, Central Connecticut State University, USA

There is a considerable debate about how the technological gap between rich and poor countries of the world can be bridged or eliminated. Technological optimists argue that Information and Communication Technology (ICT) can bring accelerated development to poor countries. Others question the viability of relying on ICT for development in low income countries. The ensuing debate has masked the digital divide problem and prevented a true discussion of how ICT can be deployed for the benefit of low income countries. On the other hand, confronted with the persistent failures of one-size-fits-all economic development models, low income countries can no longer treat modernization as the pivot towards which all ICT-related development efforts must gravitate. There is a need to drop the singular vision of development which is premised on the experiences of Western developed nations and rather restore local actors and their cultures into the actual roles they play in development processes that occur within localities. Accordingly, this chapter reviews the perspectives that currently shape the ICT for development discourse and offers the multiplicity theory to bridge the gap in development theory and promote a development strategy which incorporates activities of both local and global actors in the development of localities.

Chapter 10

Duncan Timms, University of Stirling, Scotland
Sara Ferlander, Södertörn University, Sweden

Although Sweden is generally considered to be at the forefront of the ICT revolution and to have high levels of social capital – interpersonal trust and participation – there remain areas and populations which are relatively disadvantaged. This chapter examines a number of efforts which have attempted to make use of ICT to enhance social capital in a Stockholm suburb which has been stigmatised in the press and which contains relatively high proportions of immigrants, single parents and the unemployed, all groups which are relatively excluded. An initial effort, based on the installation of a local community network, largely failed. A second effort, based on a locally-run Internet Café was more successful, with the café operating as a Third Place, both online and offline, bridging many of the divisions characterising the community. Despite its success in encouraging participation, trust and community identity, the IT-Café could not be sustained following the end of project funding and a change in personnel. The factors accompanying the success and failure of the Swedish undertakings provide lessons for other efforts to use ICTs in attempts to enhance social inclusion and community.

Chapter 11

Nitika Tolani-Brown, American Institutes for Research, USA
Meredith McCormac, American Institutes for Research, USA
Roy Zimmermann, American Institutes for Research, USA

Rigorous evaluations on the impact of information and communication technologies (ICTs) on learning outcomes in developing countries is sparse and often lacks the methodological quality necessary to guide policymakers towards sound, evidence-based practices. This desk study reviews research undertaken to date on the impact of ICTs on learning outcomes in developing countries. First, a series of in-depth, structured interviews with a range of stakeholders, including policymakers and academicians, researchers, users and developers of ICTs, was conducted, followed by a global literature review of published and unpublished evaluations on the educational impacts of ICTs. This study found that while qualitative studies often highlight the benefits of ICTs for learners and other stakeholders, there is little rigorous research to support a causal linkage between student learning outcomes and ICTs in the developing world. This study concludes that decision makers in developing countries are guided not by evidence or data but by intuition and other influences when choosing to invest in technology in an effort to upgrade the quality of instruction in their schools. Finally, recommendations for future evaluations are offered while considering important lessons learned from extant research.

Section 3
ICT4D and Economic Improvement

The chapter is about the importance of networking activities in building successful and sustainable international development cooperation (IDC) experiences. The reasoning starts from the consideration that, while society is going through a deep change process and is moving towards a network model (the so-called network society), international development cooperation still seems to adopt models and practices that were conceived for an industrial society. A brief review of the most common critics to IDC shows that increasing the level of networking and knowledge-sharing could contribute to effectively tackling the main inadequacies and challenges that IDC is facing. In turn, this would also help networking for development studies to find their place both in academic and in non-academic research and to be taken in greater account by policy makers. The concept of "networking for development", introduced in the central part of the chapter, is analyzed from different angles: first by defining the actors that should be involved and the mechanisms that should be put in place, second by reasoning on the added value of networking and on the ways to demonstrate its potential impact on IDC, and finally by mapping the relevance of the issue in a some donors' strategy.

Much rhetoric has been expended by researchers and advocates alike regarding the transformational effects of information communication technology (ICT) on economic and social conditions. Most such rhetoric posits very positive outcomes from the impending changes, economic development being just one of several. This research reports the findings of a three-year effort to determine whether such claims are actually being experienced in rural areas where access is often restricted because of public and private policies. The research findings highlight the importance of social conditions on the capacity of rural communities to effectively harness the potential of ICT for beneficial purposes.

Recent developments in information and communication technology (ICT) have affected all economic activities across the world. Although there is ample evidence for the direct impact of ICT on productivity, the spillover effect of ICT has so far not been sufficiently investigated, especially in the international context. This chapter discusses ICT and its spillover effects on labor productivity using an empirical growth model and panel data for 69 countries over the period 1992-2006. The results show that ICT and its spillover have positive impacts on productivity worldwide, but the effects are much stronger in developed countries than those in the less developed countries.

Chapter 15

Information and communication technologies are thought by some to offer a new solution to world poverty. It is argued that information and communication technologies (ICT) allow poor countries to 'leap-frog' traditional stages of development and become immediately engaged with the 'new economy'. Such an optimistic view requires appropriate government policies to facilitate this shift. Interventions required would include improving access levels and quality of telecommunication and electricity infrastructure, improved quality of education and numbers of those accessing education, and providing both direct and indirect support to encourage local firms to become engaged with the global economy. Ironically, these policies are consistent with current orthodox development policies currently pursued within the 'traditional' economy. This chapter therefore considers what exactly is new about ICT in terms of its potential impact on the poor.

Foreword

This book and its companion volume, *ICTs for Global Development and Sustainability: Practice and Applications*, are welcome initiatives of the Development Informatics (DI) research program at Monash University's South Africa campus and of IDIA – the International Development Informatics Association.

Monash University is Australia's largest institution of higher education. Based in Melbourne, it has long worked to become a truly international university. In addition to its six Australian campuses, Monash has campuses in Kuala Lumpur and Johannesburg, and a major study centre in Prato (Italy). It has strong strategic partnerships elsewhere in the world, notably with the prestigious Indian Institute of Technology Bombay (IITB).

In 2005 Professor Ed Wilson, then Associate Dean, Development in the Monash Faculty of Information Technology (and formerly founding Head of the School of Information Technology at Monash South Africa) took the initiative of bringing together IT academics from Monash Australia and South Africa, and from IITB, to think together about how far IITB's research approach in DI might be applicable to Africa. This collaboration occurred at an early stage in the relationship building between Monash and IITB which has culminated in the IITB-Monash Research Academy[1].

At that time the DI research program at IITB was centred in the Development Informatics Laboratory (DIL) of the Kanwal Rekhi School of IT. IITB is situated on a richly-treed campus in suburban Mumbai, alongside the large and serene Powai lake. It was here that the journey of exploration into the potentialities of DI for Monash South Africa began. The Monash research team was hosted by the inspirational founder of DIL, Prof. Krithi Ramamritham[2], (now Dean of R&D), his staff and students. There was a day-long agenda of presentations, discussions and technical demonstrations, including a presentation by the Monash team.

The academics in the Monash contingent were Dr Judy Backhouse (then Head of the School of IT at Monash South Africa), Dr Jacques Steyn (current Head of School) and myself (as immediate past Associate Dean, Research in the Monash Faculty of IT, and also as founding Chair of the Monash Centre for Community Networking Research).

From the quiet lakeside campus, and the streets of suburban Powai – crowded, bustling and brimming with life in uniquely Indian style – we set out for the back blocks of Maharashtra State in a lovingly beaded and decorated four-wheel drive, which routinely startled and delighted us by blaring a lively Indian tune as its reverse-gear warning signal. The notion of DI as a major focus for research and teaching at Monash South Africa was shaped in hours of discussion as the vehicle skimmed and bumped over the rural roads and tracks, punctuated by stops to photograph wayside temples and pale-coloured oxen with painted horns.

The purpose of the road trip was to visit some typical village based development projects with which IITB DI researchers were collaborating. Particular foci of the journey were the Farm Science Centre

Krishi Vigyan Kendra at Shardanagar, Baramati, central node of a multilingual advice network comprising both inputs from expert agronomists and peer-to-peer learning among farmers, and the Vigyan Ashram at Pabal where ICTs are part of a scheme to help the poorest people, especially young people, gain skills to set up micro-businesses within the rural economy.

The visit to India, and steady encouragement from Professor Ron Weber (Dean of the Faculty of IT) and Professor Tyrone Pretorius (Pro Vice-Chancellor, Monash South Africa) helped make Development Informatics at Monash South Africa a reality. Soon after the DI program commenced at Monash, including regular seminars for a wide range of stakeholders, IDIA (the International Development Informatics Association) was founded, led by Dr Jacques Steyn. Melbourne-based Associate Professor Graeme Johanson, Director of Monash's Centre for Community Networking Research, has been a tireless mentor for Jacques Steyn's program and also a pillar of IDIA. As mentioned, this volume on DI theory, and its companion volume on practice, result from the activities of IDIA. Dr Larry Stillman, (also Melbourne based, and Senior Research Fellow of the Centre) has likewise contributed strongly both to the Monash South Africa DI program and IDIA, especially through his active collaboration in the Digital Doorway initiative of the Meraka Institute of the South African government's Department of Science and Technology and the South African Council for Scientific and Industrial Research (CSIR).

There is a number of ways in which this book resonates with the learnings that the Monash researchers brought back from India.

Our visit to Mumbai and the rural villages of Maharashtra State was an exciting physical journey certainly, but it was also a journey into theory – like this book. The conceptual and philosophical maps that we Monash researchers brought to the exploration were, inevitably, limited – based on our own particular personal and disciplinary backgrounds, reading and previous research. Immersion – for however short a time – in the ideas and practical projects of our Indian colleagues both added to our knowledge, and helped us upgrade the organisation of that knowledge. We acquired new ideas and were stimulated to refine concepts and discover new conceptual links. This is the kind of stimulus to knowledge content and mapping that these two volumes, and not least this volume on theory, are also intended to provide.

The journey to India highlighted other ideas to which this book is faithful. Prof. Krithi Ramamritham explained to us that KReSIT, the school of IT to which the Development Informatics Laboratory belonged, dated back to 1998 when IITB identified the need to create IT R&D leaders trained 'to cut across their compartmentalized education and to combine technology expertise with domain knowledge to produce innovative solutions to real world problems'[3].

Himself an internationally recognised computer scientist, Prof. Ramamritham became convinced that for real world answers a genuinely interdisciplinary approach is required, where the social sciences and humanities work in synergy with the natural sciences. As a devoted Hindu, he is also keenly aware of the influence of tradition and the numinous in the daily lives of people. Consistent with that view, this book – chapter by chapter – reveals a convocation of researchers from a wide variety of backgrounds working in a truly interdisciplinary style.

Like other DI researchers, the chapter authors of this book might well have had an easier life staying within the comfort zones of their home disciplines, and working within less complex monodisciplinary research cultures. But this is not the way of DI researchers. They are individuals motivated to do something – however limited or humble – to lessen the destructive 'divides' in society – local, regional and global – that bring suffering to so many people, and also exacerbate the environmental degradation of the planet. DI researchers see in information and communication technologies a resource of unprecedented power to uplift the human condition.

The chapters of this book individually and collectively do what all good theorising does – they seek to identify and delineate – in whatever context – key factors, and the relationships among those factors, which if sufficiently understood can aid explanation or prediction, and thus serve as a basis for future thought or action. The theorising in the book proceeds at many levels, from micro to macro. At the IITB Development Informatics Laboratory such multi-level theorising was also very much in evidence.

In the remainder of this Foreword I would like to focus on perhaps the highest level of theory that implicitly or explicitly permeates programs like the one we witnessed in India, and every chapter in this book: namely the ethic of DI[4]. DI theorists and practitioners are all too well aware that technology, information and knowledge can be used for good or harm. To give just a few examples:

- Polio and other vaccines have helped sufferers globally. Yet weapons resulting from biotechnology are one of humankind's worst nightmares.
- Picasso's painting 'Guernica' memorialises the terror when aeroplanes were unveiled as technologies of massacre against entire civilian populations. Yet cognate advances in aeronautical engineering gave the world safe, affordable, mass inter-continental transport and helicopter rescue.
- The Internet has seemingly endless possibilities for human benefit, yet among the evils propagated through this medium are: child pornography, sexual violence, incitement to murder or oppression in the guise of religion or politics, hate sites, 'how to' crime sites, hacking and e-sabotage, e-scams and frauds, unregulated gambling.

Technology, information and knowledge can be used to develop and illumine lives, or to degrade and extinguish lives – and have been throughout history. Sometimes harm is accidental – an unforeseen or unwanted side-effect of some seemingly worthy application of technology – but too often it is deliberate. A recurrent theme in DI literature, including several chapters of this book, concerns DI initiatives that go wrong. Like the Hippocratic Oath in medicine, DI is a field where a credo concerning good versus harm is essential. Such a credo constitutes the axiomatic level of theory from which all the conceptual modeling, hypothesis building and testing, hermeneutic analysis and critique, or other modes of theorising in the field proceed. At IITB this reality was acknowledged in the very name of the Development Informatics Laboratory, whose acronym is DIL. In Hindi the word 'dil' means heart – and the message is that DI is a field where social justice and compassion are not optional, they are fundamental.

This axiomatic theory, the truth that must be held self-evident, for DI has at its core – I suggest – the concept of the good society.

What is a good society? It is most easily visualised by considering its opposite, the evil society. The evil society is the Hobbesian 'Bellum omnium contra omnes' – 'war of all against all'[5]. The notion of 'mutual obligation' or 'fair go' plays no role in this condition of society. Across place and time, gradations of the evil society all too often seem the default condition of the social system. Upliftment of the human condition over time is – sadly – far from inevitable. In the words of the social theorist Anthony Giddens, '"History" is not on our side, has no teleology, and supplies us with no guarantees'[6].

In contrast the good society recognises the legitimacy of self-interest, but always balanced by mutual obligation ('social contract', 'utopian realism'). Expressed in terms of Giddens' structuration theory[7], the patternings or institutions of society are shaped by the actions, small or large, of people in their daily lives. To the extent that a good society is one which is based on the enactment of mutual obligation this reality is incrementally and continuously constructed and re-constructed by the daily actions of its people. The good society embeds in its institutions expectations of behaviours that respect the rights of others as equal to one's own, a principle affirmed in both religious and secular visions of social justice.

Krithi Ramamrithan argued that the emphasis of DIL should be on 'allowing people to do what they do, where they do it, only better – enhanced by technology'[8]. By this, needless to say, he meant the good, mutually supportive – or at least unharmful – things that people do.

The concept of the good society was given renewed interpretation and present-day currency through the acclaimed book of that name written by John Kenneth Galbraith[9]. In it he advocated a 'humane agenda' containing the fundamental elements of economic growth; universal access to education; and protection for the young, old, disabled, and the environment.

DI theory affirms the value of people, individually and collectively, enacting mutual obligation at the local, regional and global levels, in both the immediate and longer terms. ICTs, being technologies through which people can share information, learn, create knowledge, foster collective memory, and renew culture are seen as potentially powerful agencies for the attainment of the good society

It was for me a privilege to participate in the establishment of the DI program at Monash South Africa, and the founding of IDIA. I express my appreciation for the invitation to write a Foreword for this thought provoking book, and warmly congratulate the editors, and the DI researchers from across the world who contributed to its content. I commend each chapter as a prism through which we can better envision DI's contribution to the good society.

Don Schauder

ENDNOTES

1   http://www.iitbmonash.org/
2   http://www.cse.iitb.ac.in/~krithi/2pagebio.html
3   Ramamritham, K. (2005) Personal communication, Mumbai, 9 Nov.
4   These thoughts were initially explored in Schauder, D. (2006) *Good versus Evil: The Internet and Society,* address to the IEEE Social Implications of Technology inaugural seminar, Melbourne, 18 Jul.
5   Hobbes, T. (1651) *De Cive,* re-printed by Kessinger Publishing, p.18 (available on Google Books)
6   Giddens, A. (1990) *The Consequences of Modernity,* Stanford Unversity Press. p.154
7   Giddens, A. (1984) *The Constitution of Society,* University of California Press. pp. 24-29
8   Ramamritham, K. *loc. cit.*
9   Galbraith, J.K. (1997) *The Good Society,* Mariner Books, 1997

Don Schauder *(BA DipLib Rhodes, MA Sheffield, MEd PhD Melbourne, FALIA, MACS) is Emeritus Professor of Information Management, and former Associate Dean (Research), in the Faculty of Information Technology at Monash University. He was a pioneer of Australian electronic publishing as founder of INFORMIT Electronic Publishing, and of community networking as co-founder of VICNET: Victoria's Network. He has been Director of several libraries, the first being the South African Library for the Blind and the latest RMIT University Library. As part of a Monash team he undertook commissioned research on knowledge management for the Olympics movement internationally. He served as a member of several advisory committees to the Government of Victoria on library and information policy, and of the Australian Government delegation to the UN World Summit on the Information Society. He is currently Honorary Chair of Monash's Centre for Community Networking Research (CCNR).*

Preface

The coming of age of the Personal Computer and the opening up of the Internet, particularly the World Wide Web, in the 1990s made possible reaching a much wider portion of populations. Technological determinists as well as social activists saw the potential of deploying networked computers to the general citizenry, and internet cafés and telecentres were established. Over the past almost two decades only a handful of very poor countries did not get onto this bandwagon. The past twenty years have also seen a convergence of different traditional media, or at the very least the spread of computing power to many other non-traditional computer domains, including domestic appliances, motorcars, mobile phones, entertainment, in short, incorporated into most traditional industries and products.

This book does not cover the entire range of computing, but focuses on Information and Communication Technologies for Development (ICT4D). ICT incorporates any technology used for communication and information - including paper! The "development" part indicates a focus on social development, which can mean many different things, depending on point of view, ideology and assumptions. ICT4D research may include investigating highly technological computer engineering topics, for example creating a network mesh using discarded food cans as antennae, as was done by the Meraka Institute in South Africa. Such research is necessary, but the focus in this book is not on such hardcore mechanistic aspects of ICT4D. Our focus is on the thus far neglected social side of computing, the users, and the design of systems that meet the needs of "ordinary" users, not on business systems, government systems, military systems, or such large enterprise systems, but on social systems. To distinguish this effort from hardcore ICT4D, we use the term 'Development Informatics'. Graeme Johanson's contribution (*Delineating the Meaning and Value of Development Informatics*) summarises different views on this new field.

The world is diverse, though with the smaller proportion of its population much more privileged than the majority, as indicated by buzz word such as *the divide*, and in our context, *the digital divide*. Efforts to deploy telecentres in more affluent communities (the *haves*) have not been as successful as hoped for, but in the poorer regions (the *have nots*), the situation is far worse. A good number of public ICT services are reportedly successful, but the majority seem to have been failures, with the most important reason for failure typically presented as a lack of economic sustainability of such centres.

Having personally observed more failures than successes over the past decade, the original impetus for this book set was an attempt to find reasons for unsuccessful projects by drawing upon experiences from all over the world. If projects are unsuccessful, or do not meet goals, an extraordinary amount of money is wasted that could rather be used for other purposes. The chapters serve as examples of trends and results that support informal conclusions drawn from personal experience over the past decade. The implications drawn in the Introduction from the chapters should not be viewed as committing the logical errors of over-generalization, cherry picking, or of composition. On the contrary, the chapters serve as points of illustration in support of informal observations.

It is claimed that since the 1960s more than 1 trillion US dollars has been donated as aid to African countries alone (Dambisa Moyo 2009 - *Dead Aid: Why Aid is Not Working and How There is a Better Way For Africa*). Worldwide, the figure must be astounding – perhaps as much as 2.3 trillion US dollars (Easterly 2006). Figures of support for ICT projects are lacking, but must be comparatively large. Yet despite all this money spent, a very strong case can be made that there is little to show for it.

This is not surprising, as there are no special theories of ICT for Development, and few models by which to measure success, while the dominant model seems to be biased toward a particular cultural-specific view of economics, namely neo-liberal capitalism. In fact, despite a large body of literature available, particularly on the Web, very little scientific or systematic research is done on ICT4D. Reasons for success or failure are not always clear or are not clearly understood, methodologies are often vague, metrics for success in many cases are lacking. Proposed models address only part of the complexity. This is to be expected from a young discipline which seems to be dominated by social activists at grassroots level, but it is sponsored by governments, non-government organisations (NGOs), donors and aid-givers, all of which are understandably anxious for a more accountable analysis of the benefits of expended resources, hence success stories seem to be exaggerated, if not fabricated, or ignore the negative impacts on other spheres of social complexity. The claimed success of mobile phones used by fishermen in Kerala comes to mind in this context.

The question whether ICT leads to growth (particularly economic growth) is still unanswered, and requires fuller research. It might be very difficult to determine ultimately, despite many sweeping and unfounded claims, as perhaps ICT effects are indirect. Saeed Moshiri and Somaieh Nikpoor (*International ICT Spillover*) investigate the economic effects of ICT, particularly spillover, which in essence refers to the much more difficult to measure secondary benefits, such as raising productivity through changes in organization, labour structure, and human resource management. They conclude that a 1% rise in the ICT investment rate will lead to 0.16% increase in economic growth in developed countries, but only 0.03% in developing countries. Similarly, the spillover effect is larger in developed countries than in developing countries. They further conclude that there is a positive correlation between ICT investment and economic growth, and wish to make a case that developing countries should invest in ICT, but caution against a technological deterministic view. If their view is accepted, this should affect ICT policies. But the figures are not been verified as yet.

That implementation of ICT does not automatically or necessarily have an economic effect on a community could be one implication of Kenneth Pigg's chapter in this book (*Information Communication Technology and its Impact on Rural Community Economic Development)*. The introduction of broadband into rural communities in the USA does not seem to have made any difference to local economies for a period of over a decade.

A further implication of Pigg's chapter is devastating news to social activists and technological determinists who wish to "uplift" the developing world by connecting it. In one of the most advanced countries on this globe, the USA, rural communities do not use broadband optimally, so the question is then, why would it make a difference to the poorer regions of the world? Is it only wishful thinking?

This also seems to be the case in other very highly developed countries. Sweden is one of the richest countries in the world, yet Duncan Timms and Sara Ferlander report in their chapter (*Social Capital and Third Places through the Internet: Lessons from a Disadvantaged Swedish Community)* that even in a Stockholm suburb a telecentre was unsuccessful for various reasons. Forcing technology onto communities does not result in its uptake (or appropriation) of that technology as foreseen by those in power (not only party politics, but any role players with power, including well-meaning NGO's) to enforce the technology.

Unsuccessful ICT projects are also found within communities which have been exposed to modern ICT for half a century of TV broadcast, of exceptional telecommunication services, compared to the rest of the world, and of a very high standard of living. If exposure to modern media indeed influences the uptake of, for example, internet technologies, as Pippa Norris (2003) proposes, making the adoption of new media technologies easier, then these two factors imply that the developing world will remain behind, possibly with a growing gap in the divide, for at least well into the second half of this century - except if some amazing technological breakthrough occurs. Connectivity, especially broadband, is just too expensive to have a 100% penetration into every community, and is much less likely in rural communities in the developing world. We have to be realistic about this. Secondly, there has not been much exposure to modern technologies among deep rural communities in the developing world, so culturally they are not ready for concomitant change. This has been demonstrated well by contributions covering regions such as in Peru and Chile in ICTs for *Global Development and Sustainability: Practice and Applications*, and in this volume The Gambia (Harvey). At least three issues will prevent uptake of ICTs in rural communities: cost of connectivity, cultural resistance to change, and cultural unreadiness for new media technologies.

The mission of many ICT4D programs seems to be to reduce poverty on the wrong side of the digital divide. Such a mission is based on many assumptions not always made clear in literature. Cristina Kiomi Mori (*'Digital Inclusion': Are We all Talking about the Same Thing?*) analyses variations of this issue and briefly presents the historical development of the notions of the divide and of exclusion versus inclusion. One's view of the divides is culturally biased. Even well-meaning social activists and donors often do not seem to realize their own cultural biases in their approach to ICT4D. Jasmine Harvey (*Cultural acceptance of ICTs: perceptions in practice*) reports on cultural variance in The Gambia, mainly due to religious views, and presents a case against technological determinism.

Suely Fragoso, Denise Cogo, and Liliane Dutra Brignol (*What Does it Mean, to Bridge the Divide? Learning from Spontaneous Practices towards ICTs*) show that the official views of what a community needs in order to overcome the digital divide may not be shared by the community itself. A top-down approach does not work, and neither can politics inform such decisions. Communities need to determine their own needs, while those in power (assuming they serve communities) should make tools available for communities to meet their own needs for the benefit of the greater society.

Peter Kwaku Kyem (*A New Development Opportunities Confront Old Paradigms: Exploring the Multiplicity Theory to Combat the Global Digital Divide*) finds the modernization approach of donors (such as the Washington Consensus) to be one-sided and simplistic, and argues for a more complex set of approaches to ICT4D. He concludes with an anti-technological deterministic stance that "technical solutions to the complex socio-political and cultural problems of development should never be pursued as ends in themselves". Kyem attempts to build a case for the need of a new perspective on development that he labels *multiplicity theory* as an attempt to overcome simplistic contemporary approaches. In brief, multiplicity theory is about bringing the psychological and social aspects into the discussions around ICT4D.

Andrew Thatcher and Mbongi Ndabeni (*A Psychological Model to Understand E-Adoption in the Context of the Digital Divide*) regard psychological as well as socio-economic factors as important in the adoption of technology, focusing on an inclusive Technology Acceptance Model that acknowledges "the interplay between the potential users, the specific technology, and the environment in which the interactions occur".

The importance of a more inclusive approach to human development is shared by Steyn (*Paradigm*

Shift Required for ICT4D) who exposes the assumptions of the economic globalization paradigm that underlies efforts to overcome the digital and other divides by implementing ideologically biased projects and promises. Economic globalization turns humans into economic machines (*homo economicus*), over-simplifying the complexity of human nature. It is proposed that psychological and social development should be priority, making use of ICT as tools, and that "development" should be defined culturally by local communities. Self-empowerment may indeed lead to economic "development", but that would be a consequence, and should not be the primary aim of ICT4D.

Fabio Nascimbeni (*Networking for Development: Cornerstone for Efficiency and Impact of ICT for Development Projects*) shows that international development cooperation projects still seem to adopt models and practices that were conceived for an industrial society, while societies are moving toward the network society. The digital divide is multi-faceted and multidimensional, and the simplistic industrial model not efficient. Nascimbeni is sympathetic to a paradigm that stresses the "appropriate use of ICT, knowledge sharing dynamics, social appropriation of technology, and more attention to the human side of the picture" as opposed to what could be called the dominant technological deterministic approach, as is evident from its assumption that connectivity alone would lead to development.

Chase Laurelle Knowles (*The Mirror Meta-Principle: Creating the Context for Culturally Sustainable Development Informatics*) offers a mirror theory, which holds that ICT4D systems should be participatively designed to reflect the economic and socio-cultural exigencies and traditions of local developing communities. Again a case is made for "community first", and more specifically, its local needs.

Scanning through ICT4D literature of reported case studies often raises more questions than it answers. Metrics for success are vague or absent. And there is a lack of consent on how the success or not of ICT4D systems should be assessed and evaluated. Ricardo Ramírez (*Participatory Monitoring and Evaluation of ICTs for Development*) suggests participatory monitoring and evaluation (M&E), which implies that measuring success should not depend on the implementers (or givers) only, but also on the receivers or users. Aid givers easily fall into the trap of measuring success by their own culturally biased criteria of success, and neglect to ask whether the target community have a similar view. To extend Ramírez's argument with a hypothetical case: if the mandate of the organization is to install a network, and the network is a technical success, that project can be deemed to be a success, even if the community does not use the network at all, or does not benefit from it. Success will be reported, as the network works technically. But for the community there may be no difference or impact at all.

Nitika Tolani-Brown, Meredith McCormac and Roy Zimmermann (*An Analysis of the Research and Impact of ICT in Education in Developing Country Contexts*) offer an overview of how ICT4D impacts on education in developing regions. They conclude that the perception that ICT always makes a positive difference is misplaced, and that in the real world the impact of ICTs on learner outcomes is much more complex and varied. ICT is not the magic bullet.

Matthew Clarke (*Understanding the Policy Implications of ICT for Development*) shows that ICT policies operate with the framework of 'traditional' neo-liberal economic theory, while the world has moved on to a new economy, which could perhaps be labelled *knowledge economy*. The implication is that development within the modern context is constricted by this old view. What is needed are ICT4D policies that consider the new economic realities of the new world.

In this book various authors are – from different perspectives - sympathetic toward the social and human side of ICT4D. This view is quite contrary to the dominant technological deterministic view of ICT4D and its economic globalization premises. Hopefully this book will encourage debate and intellectual discussion on ICT4D, particularly Development Informatics, which in some circles raises very political and sensitive issues. Too many divergent perspectives on the same practical development problems have confused and caused inertia. The dominant game of having to compete for research funds for development analysis does not lend itself to collaboration. A surprising number of very active participants in the ICT4D arena and high profile activists refused to contribute this book. They strongly believe that the discussion should take place not in an expensive book, but freely on the Web. Such passion is admirable, but in our view somewhat self-destructive. At this moment in publishing history, a compact book still focuses and distils more effectively than the endless Web. This book is intended to encourage intellectual discussions particularly among donor agencies with a social conscience, which would really like to make a difference, but which (perhaps) get the wrong guidance for policy-making.

A more systematic approach to ICT4D that exposes woolly assumptions, and that hopefully eventually will lead to a theory (or theories) of Development Informatics, is urgently required. Too much money is wasted on projects that keep on repeating the same mistakes -- money that could be put to good use. Let us keep the dialogue and theorising rolling, and listen with open minds, not blinded by narrow ideologies or fashionable theories. There is a real need for theoretical synthesis, rigorous case studies, policy models, and practical guidelines. ICT offers useful tools for self-development, and the social development of local communities, while "development" is not necessarily confined to the conventional notion of economic development. Personal and social development may result in more satisfied and happy citizens, who may or may not improve their economic status, but by expanding their minds they may become better equipped to carve out their own niches for themselves and their own spaces in this complex world.

ICTs and Sustainable Solutions for the Digital Divide: Theory and Perspectives focuses on broad themes of paradigms and theory. *ICTs for Global Development and Sustainability: Practice and Applications* focuses more on case studies from different regions of the globe.

Jacques Steyn
Monash University, South Africa

Graeme Johanson
Monash University, Australia

REFERENCES

Easterly, W. (2006). *The white man's burden. Why the west's efforts to aid the rest have done so much ill and so little good.* Oxford: Oxford Univ Press.

Moyo, D. (2009). *Dead Aid. Why aid is not working and how there is another way for Africa.* London: Allen Lane.

Norris, P., (2003). *Digital divide. Civic engagement, information poverty, and the internet worldwide.* Cambridge: Cambridge University Press.

Section 1
Foundations, Methodology and Terminology

Chapter 1
Delineating the Meaning and Value of Development Informatics

Graeme Johanson
Monash University, Australia

ABSTRACT

This chapter describes the field of Development Informatics as it has emerged in the past two decades, and highlights some of the strengths of its research and practices. It draws on the current literature and the expertise of the other authors of this book to help to define a set of basic terms. Any new intellectual domain is tied to some degree to the vagaries of its institutional alliances, to the perceived international status of its public forums, and to the criticism that on its own it lacks unique methodological rigour. These points are discussed candidly. Multidisciplinarity is the backbone of Development Informatics. The main virtues of Development Informatics are that it offers a platform for an evaluative critique to counterbalance the effects of relentless globalisation, that it comprises strong multidisciplinary teams, that it maintains an intellectual space to build on international momentum that has developed among theorists and practitioners, and that it opens up future imaginative possibilities for collaborative projects which involve communities in developing areas of participatory research and ongoing project evaluation in order to encourage self-sustaining entities.

THE GLARING GAP

In 2000 87% of the world's wealth was owned by 20% of the world's population, and 91% of Internet users were in OECD countries (amounting to only 19% of the world's population). It is tempting to link wealth and Internet usage. Both

these pairs of figures present very large divides to bridge (Pasquali, 2003: 219). The United Nations attempts to measure international development each year, bravely publishing cumulative figures, which are dependent on national governments for accurate data collection (International Telecommunications Union (ITU)). Apart from the CIA *World Factbook*, updated every two weeks online, the UN offers the only index of comparative,

DOI: 10.4018/978-1-61520-799-2.ch001

longitudinal data. Let us assume for the sake of argument that they are a rough guide to the comparative status of developing countries. The UN figures place 22 countries in the bottom category of 'Low Human Development' based on a range of measures, including life expectancy, levels of health, poverty, and literacy, and adoption of phones and the Internet. The poorest countries are all in Africa: in order they are Senegal, Eritrea, Nigeria, Tanzania, Guinea, Rwanda, Angola, Benin, Malawi, Zambia, Côte d'Ivoire, Burundi, Congo, Ethiopia, Chad, Central African Republic, Mozambique, Mali, Niger, Guinea-Bissau, Burkina Faso, and the poorest of all is Sierra Leone. In the period from 1995 to 2005 people in these deprived countries tripled their ownership of telephone mainlines, from 3 per thousand people to 9 per thousand people on average (still extremely low). In 2005 there were 48 cell or mobile phone subscribers per thousand people, far outstripping fixed phones, and they boasted 12 Internet users per thousand people on average. In contrast, for 'High Human Development' countries, the figures in the same categories in 2005 were 394 (mainlines), 743 (mobiles), and 365 (Internet). The figures for the third most developed country in the world, Australia, were: 564, 906, and 698.

It is hard to imagine a more eloquent summary statement of the huge problems which Development Informatics (DI) hopes to alleviate, than these figures presented by the UN. It also forms a fitting rationale for the aims of this chapter, which are to answer two basic questions: What is Development Informatics? and, What is its value?

In order to explore the first question, section two defines information, informatics, development, communications, ICTs, ICT4D, and related terms, using examples from the academic literature. It is hard to enumerate all of the disciplines that relate to developing regions. Section two describes the implications of multidisciplinarity, and differentiates Development Informatics from Community Informatics, and Organisational and Social Informatics, with which they are often linked. It plots the gradual evolution of Development Informatics as an area of study and research in its own right, and acknowledges that the scope is hard to delimit. The chapter points to the growing power of Information and Communications Technologies, which cannot be ignored by anyone. Finally, section three uses a brief content analysis of the other chapters of this book, and other academic sources, to show what authors themselves regard as the attributes of intellectual effort in this field.

To answer the second question – about the value of Development Informatics – fewer points are made in section four. There is a dearth of direct knowledge about how to deal with the pressing issues raised by our researchers in this text; everyone is struggling continually to understand the dimensions and implications of the issues. Most agree that there is a need to try to humanise the extensive commercial, political and technological forces which control development at the moment. Many researchers (some working in developing regions) feel a moral responsibility to use research to promote more equitable participation in the benefits of Information and Communications Technologies (Avgerou, 2008:142; Burrell, 2009:90). They are spreading fast everywhere, and their effects need to be monitored and evaluated.

Development Informatics provides a forum for reflective catch-up, along the lines offered by Critical Theory (Bohman, 2005). Towards the end of this chapter, the research-praxis nexus is addressed. Researchers tend to be depicted as dreamers, who do not converse with policymakers, who in turn are blinded by political ideologies. Then there are the practitioners who are so preoccupied with day-to-day necessities of project management, that they tend to overlook relevant research (Heeks, 2008:31). Development Informatics can offer a common discussion space to encourage potential interactions, and to jointly face up to collective challenges (United Nations Development Programme—UNDP, 2001:8).

If DI researchers use seven reflective questions as their guide to planning, they can test the relevance of their own work. Three of the questions are formulated by Heeks: what is the development goal at stake? What can be the role of information and communication in achieving that goal? Are there new technologies, or adaptations of them, which could deliver that role? (Heeks, 2008:32). Discussion in this chapter inspires four further important questions, to be added as follows: How can all stakeholders be involved in the achievement of the goal? Ideally is the goal the best that can be achieved in the circumstances, or can it be extended or improved? How can evaluation be integrated into the project from the beginning? What are the best ways of sharing the knowledge that is generated?

WHAT IS DEVELOPMENT INFORMATICS (DI)?

It is essential in this section to sort out some of the confusion around key terms. It defines DI, describes different current uses of the term, identifies the necessity for theoretical rigour, defines much-used terms in the field, suggests that DI may be the most straightforward term to adopt in a situation where several interchangeable terms are in vogue, and summarises the features of DI as singled out by other authors of this book.

Causes of Confusion

Unfortunately a good deal of confusion prevails about the term 'Development Informatics' (DI), partly because of the recency of its evolution, causing unfamiliarity (Heeks, 2006:2), partly because of its appropriation of ambiguous terminology, but also because of its unusual melange of multidisciplinary origins. Multidisciplinarity functions both as a strength and a weakness. There is resistance; for instance, the public forums of Information Systems vet development papers

which do not conform strictly with IS values and traditions (Avgerou, 2008: 134). Two commentators – including a Microsoft employee—noted recently: 'As with many multidisciplinary fields, the boundaries [of DI] are amorphous and the goals many' (Toyama, 2008: 22). This section aims to explore some of the boundaries and to determine, for example, whether there are any meaningful differences between 'DI', 'ICTD' and 'ICT4D,' and if so, what they mean.

Summary Definition of DI

By way of synthesis, I submit that DI studies:

- the use of meaningful content carried by merged computer networks and telecommunications technologies (Unwin, 2009b:42-43);
- to assist on a personal level with expanding choices, solutions for life problems, and know-how to assist with essential tasks, informed decisions, and learning and reflection (Colle, 2008:140; Walsham, 2005:20);
- to assist on a community level with the development of collective self-confidence, joint acquisition of information literacy skills, and effective applications for community improvement (Mbeki, 2009; Pitula, 2007);
- to assist on an organisational and societal level with promotion of information technology and applications to help to organise information and to structure knowledge, and to understand concomitant human behaviour and communications (Heeks, 2006:2; Unwin 2009b);
- in the overall hope of encouraging development of wealth, useful infrastructure, social growth, education, and a strong service sector; of providing basics such as food, shelter, clothing, drinking water, sanitation, and medical services; of advocating good government and good gover-

nance, and the rule of law; and of better-ing local manufacturing and agriculture (Ramamritham, 2005; UNDP, 2001).

In short, DI is a field of study, research, and training, which aims to advance development, to gain the commitment of local communities and their leaders in developing areas, to maximise beneficial uses of Information and Communications Technologies, for improving the quality of and choices in personal and collective lives.

Different Academic and Practitioner Backgrounds

Academics, students and practitioners are from a wide range of backgrounds. Diversity is easily demonstrated. Recently an Information Systems author wrote of DI as meaning good systems design and systems development for 'Community Informatics' (CI) (de Moor, 2009). A research group in the National Science Institute of South Africa uses DI specifically to mean the use of data from remote sensing for urban planning (Development Informatics Research Group, 2009). Noviciate students yearn for categories and labels for the field of study. Thus a US informatics student was confused (rather than enlightened) when sampling the listserv of CI researchers. He opines that DI is both too broad and too narrow at the same time: he objects that it is used to encompass any Information and Communications Technologies (ICTs) in any development context whatsoever, even if the two are not linked, and that there is a tendency to ignore interesting issues 'that do not correspond to the conventional development goals ([e.g.,] quality of life, games, social movements, etc.)' (Coward, 2009). In brief, he complains of projects of remote relevance and of a narrow interpretation of defining activities. Another postgraduate (Computer Science) student considers that visiting developing regions to understand requirements properly is fundamental to beginning useful research planning in DI (DeRenzi 2008). For him

observations 'on the ground' are the only point to begin; practice and research are inseparable.

Definitional precision is a preliminary requirement; the whole of DI melds several parts, using different research approaches, which have flourished independently for many years. One well-established DI researcher adopts a very pragmatic approach to scoping. He is impatient with post-modern theorising, and notes a need to avoid legacy jargon borrowed from other spheres of influence:

We research and do ... I'm not certain [that] 'underserved communities' does justice to what we do, especially as this is essentially a telco/ regulatory concept ... Donors and the private sector have probably dictated too much of what 'ICT4D' is... Basically I feel that if society deems a topic relevant, characterised by significant media attention, as well as government, civil society and commercial interventions, ... [then] it is worthy of study (Elder, 2009).

Practitioners sing a similar chorus: for them DI

strives to design practical, sustainable solutions that enable communities for self-empowerment, and evaluate[s] their effectiveness. Technically mainstream ICT solutions can be re-engineered to assist in overcoming constraints such as lack of energy, ... or illiteracy, or poverty (Steyn, 2008).

There is a danger of trying to differentiate terms for little purpose other than semantic sophistry or ontological obfuscation; the aim should be to nurture collaborative inputs and not to alienate like-minded efforts (Burrell, 2009:91; UNDP, 2001). In order to remove uncertainty, it will assist to reflect briefly in this chapter on precise meanings of key concepts—information, informatics, development, communications, Community Informatics, Social Informatics, Information and Communications Technologies, ICT4D, ICTD, and e-development. When used in combination, merged concepts make meanings more complicated, and can mislead.

Theory and Rigour

As the researchers in this book ably demonstrate, academic writings in our field insist on the virtue of evidence-based practice and the necessity for theoretical and methodological rigour. The problem derives from a wealth of riches; Walsham points out that there are many 'vast literatures to draw on' when development is under consideration. 'It would surely be foolish to ignore them.' (Walsham, 2006:13). Richard Heeks (2006:1) regrets that much research in the field of DI so far has been 'descriptive, not analytical'. The same judgement has been passed on Information Systems in Developing Countries (with yet another acronym, viz., ISDC) (Avgerou, 2008: 134). Heeks posits Structuration (Sociology), Actor-Network Theory (Science/Technology Studies, Community Informatics), Stakeholder Theory (Management Studies), and the Livelihoods Framework (Development Studies) as examples of suitable theories for DI to embrace (2006:2,4). From an Information Systems angle, Walsham favours Institutional Theory, Circuits of Power, Improvisation theories, Action Research, and Innovation and Diffusion theories (2006:13-14).

A common theme by no less than eight authors in this book is the lack of an empirical evidence-based link between the implementation of ICTs and constructive development outcomes in poor regions. Large-scale, international research into this link is inhibited by the expense of detailed analysis. The World Bank recently undertook an econometric study of the effect of phones and Internet access on GDP per person for 120 developed and developing countries. The average findings are remarkable: that 'for every 10-percentage-point increase in the penetration of broadband services, there is an increase in economic growth of 1.3 percentage points' in developing countries, and that the adoption of 10% more mobile phones in a developing country increases growth in GDP per person by 0.8% (World Bank, 2009b:7). There is no claim that economic growth equates with economic development, that such economic improvements are evenly spread over rural and urban areas, nor across each developing area; they are global statistics. More regional studies are required (Walsham, 2005:17), as is investigation into community benefits other than increases in GDP. The direction of the 'correlation' is uncertain. It is impossible to show cause and effect at present; the increase in ICT access and use may be caused by other forms of preliminary development, rather than vice versa.

Information

It is a long time since the futurist Joneji Masuda (1981:124) noted that 'information knows no natural boundaries' and predicted that the global gap between North and South in economics and knowledge would close because industrialisation and 'informationalization' would grow together worldwide hand-in-hand (ibid.:118,120). Around the same time, the prospects for development were predicated on the foundation of informatics as a fresh field of reflection:

Informatics will very probably be one of the dominant factors in mankind's development and progress during the decades to come (Granelli, 1984, quoted in Dosa, 1997:213)

Two decades later Heeks (2006:1) points out that too many practical actions have been undertaken in the absence of reflection and deep understanding. A suitable working definition of information in the development context can be taken from Dosa:

Information is typically defined as the composite of messages, including signs, data, facts and narrative, that a human being receives from the outside world and applies to information situations such as problems, tasks, decisions, learning, reflection or leisure (Dosa, 1997:186–7).

This definition carries overtones of Anthropology and Communication Theory, for individuals and groups, and conveniently invites inclusion of elements of Structuration and Information Systems by incorporating both formal and informal messages and structures in its ambit. In the context of development, the role of information is to assist in the collective application of a supportive system for well-informed decision-making for the benefit of all stakeholders (ibid.:247). In order to avoid prolonging this chapter, I equate information and knowledge for convenience, a conflation which will be contested by my Knowledge Management colleagues.

Informatics

German and French professors are credited with creating the word 'informatics', in 1957 and 1962 (Bernard, 2004; Widrow, 2005:5). Originally meaning the science of storing and processing information automatically, informatics was taken over by English, in its unerring acquisitive manner, to use it more loosely in numerous disciplines for many purposes, frequently in the medical and biological sciences. In English informatics is used now to mean research and study of the intersection of three inter-related themes: information technology and applications, information organisation and knowledge structures, and human behaviour and communications as they relate to the first two (School of Informatics, 2002).

Organisational and Social Informatics

Confusingly, the phrases 'Organisational Informatics' and 'Social Informatics' (O/SI) are also used to describe the combined study of all three themes. Organisational Informatics should be confined to the analysis of information within large organisations, e.g., in the form of Management Information Systems in large corporations or governments (McIver, 2003:40). The large scale, cost, and attrition rate of these systems makes them unviable in development contexts (Avgerou, 2008:137) – although multinational ICT companies claim to be trying to act in more socially-responsible ways by serving development needs (Kok 2005). Social Informatics focuses on the usefulness of ICTs for society as a whole. In this book, the association of informatics with development is our concern, whether it is for individuals, communities, organisations or societies.

Information, knowledge, ICT infrastructure and development stand out, and in combination they are changing the world rapidly. Their shotgun marriage has led to the need for coining several of the new terms under consideration. There is no precedent or pre-existing due process to stamp them with acceptable academic or practical cachet.

Development

Development is as relevant to disadvantaged groups in developed countries as to those in developing countries. Development Studies encompasses many backgrounds -- politics, governance, economics, sociology, anthropology, organisational management, and more (*European Journal of Development Research,* 2009; Hicks, 2006:3). The exact meaning of development is vigorously debated throughout this book – and the reader can observe its gradual revelation at will—but in the interests of conciseness, we need to lay out a common starting-point. As Tim Unwin observes, ideas of development began in Enlightenment Europe, and are 'commonly understood by those influenced by a European cultural background [as] involv[ing] concepts of 'progress' and of 'growth'.' (Unwin, 2009b:8). European tradition has been challenged recently because it is said to ignore indigenous autonomous social movements which might prefer individualism less and emphasise collectivism or 'irrational' formalistic ritualism more (Avgerou, 2008:141; Unwin, 2009b:11).

In the West development is measured typically by narrow economic indicators of national improvement, especially to serve the needs of governments, and multinational companies and agencies (King, 2005:73; World Bank, 2009a). It is no coincidence that for centuries economic growth and liberal democracy have been advocated in one and the same breath. The World Bank realised the potential of ICTs in the mid-1960s (Colle, 2008:145). From a simple economic perspective what matters is

the increased production of ICTs [which] contributes to output, employment and export earnings, while ICT use increases productivity, competitiveness and growth. ICT has the potential to make governments more efficient, more inclined to share information, more transparent and accountable. Governments can also use ICT to ... offer the poor economic opportunities (Qiang, 2003:2).

But there is much more to development than national economic or technological growth (Avgerou, 2008:135). Researchers in Development Studies were put off ICTs in the 1990s by the tendency to technological determinism (Toyama, 2008:25). As Unwin writes:

ICT4D should not principally be about achieving economic growth, but should rather be a moral agenda concerned with enabling equality of access to information and thereby helping to reduce global inequalities of opportunity ... My agenda ... is to get to grips with understanding precisely how ICT can make a difference to the lives of the poor and the marginalised. This does indeed in part depend on economic growth, but it is also to do with issues concerning access to information, about the ways in which people from different backgrounds communicate, and about the content needs that poor people have if they are to be able

to transform their lives and livelihoods (Unwin, 2009b:1,3).

Thus economic growth and the spread of information technology are just two in a range of important measures: others are the spread of other useful infrastructure, social growth, education, housing, health provision, and a strong service sector (Burrell, 2009:91). Ideally development involves good food, shelter, clothing, drinking water, sanitation, and medical services; widespread literacy; better management of enterprises; good government and governance, the rule of law; the redesign of old products, the creation of new products, and new systems for manufacturing and distribution; improved banking, insurance, transport, and media; and more productive agriculture (Colle, 2008:144; Feather, 2004:115–120; Unwin 2009a).

Communication

The fields of CI and DI are rich with texts about the importance of communication, historically and currently. Communication is depicted as much more inclusive and enriching than the one-way dissemination of information, or than the top-down imposition of information technologies. Thus Keeble points out that bridging the digital divide requires engagement, and not just simply access to ICTs. Virtual networked individualism (leading to social isolation) is starkly contrasted with the potential for development of collective self-confidence, the joint acquisition of information literacy skills, and effective applications for community life. (Keeble, 2007:112–117). Pasquali (2003:208) is emphatic about the clear benefits which flow from the proper use of ICTs for communication. Real communication will improve community if it is used progressively to promote human rights, if the technologies encourage bi-directionality (and they are not just designed to provide advantages to the transmitters), and if the institutions that control the communication are committed to promote pluralism, transparency, and democratic participation (Colle 2008:139). A note of warning is sounded in the chapter in this volume by Mori, who points out that there is a form of 'developmental determinism' apparent among researchers who are in opposition to entrenched technological determinism. She calls for a balanced partnership between the human and technical approaches.

ICTs

Pasquali (2003:198) makes the poignant observation that 'any society is a reflection of its communication networks'. Mention has been made several times of large-scale infrastructures, systems, and applications, all part and parcel of communications networks. They apply to the broad phrase 'Information and Communications Technologies' (ICTs), which mean the powerful connection of computer networks and telecommunications technologies. The World Bank defines them as hardware, software, networks, and media for collection, storage, processing, transmission and presentation of information in the form of voice, data, text and messages (Qiang & Pitt, 2003:1). Note that this definition excludes the creation of information and knowledge, and the re-use of it, surely an omission which is a bone of contention with advocates of the inclusive benefits of indigenous knowledge (Heeks, 2008:28-29).

Unwin connects ICTs for development with Critical Theory, putting a much more human face on them:

Unlike IT and ICT where the main focus is on what is and what can be achieved, ICT4D is about what should be done and how we should do it. ICT4D therefore has a profoundly moral agenda. It is not primarily about the technologies themselves, but is rather concerned with how they can be used to enable the empowerment of poor and marginalised communities ... This ... involves reflection on

behalf of all those who aspire to make the world a fairer and better place (Unwin, 2009b:43).

The key question, then, is not just whether ICTs are one useful tool in the pre-conceived development armoury, but if ICTs can actually transform the gamut of development goals, processes and structures (Heeks, 2008:27).

In a social context, it is important to enumerate a variety of specific component parts of ICTs: networked storage, the Internet, fixed-line phones, mobile phones, Blackberries, iPods, MP3 players, flash memory, mailing-lists, blogs, social networking websites, wikis, facsimile transmission, online chat, digital photography (still and moving), free-to-air and cable TV, downloaded software, downloaded text and music and films, community and commercial radio, CDs, DVDs (Colle, 2008:147; Johanson, 2008; Unwin, 2009a). Undoubtedly there are omissions from this selected list.

Acting together, ICTs present a formidable array of empowerment tools; they can also (justifiably) instill awe, fear and antagonism. Historical parallels are drawn between ICTs and the invention of writing and printing, and the attendant benefits to communities of quick communication and the ability to record and store vast quantities of useful knowledge, but ICTs are infinitely more pervasive and influential than their predecessors (Colle, 2008:140; Feather, 2004:208). No-one can opt out of the socio-political transformations which they introduce. They affect people living in less developed parts of the world just as much as in the developed world. For the first time in human history, the 'self' and 'society' are trapped together in one global milieu. In the words of the sociologist, Anthony Giddens, they produce 'the feeling of riding a juggernaut' (Giddens, 1991:22, 23, 28, 32).

Community Informatics, Social Informatics

One final definitional comment is required. Distinctions are drawn between Community Informatics (CI), Social Informatics (SI), and Development Informatics (DI) (Pigg, 2005). The difference between them is not always obvious, and lies in the subject of the Informatics, with its connection to a community, to society as a whole, or to developing communities and societies. Thus, research which evaluates the impact of the uses of public radio by a community of farmers would be an example of Community Informatics; a study which assesses the social values of Internet interactions generally (e.g., Web 2.0) would be an example of Social Informatics; and reviewing any benefits that might flow from the introduction for the first time of ICTs into a country at the 'bottom of the pyramid', would fit into the category of Development Informatics. It is possible to combine the three. By way of illustration, a project which analyses the uses of mobile devices (for sustaining cultural identity and social networks, finding jobs, transferring money, understanding and integrating into a host nation) by a diaspora of Chinese migrant labourers, spread across the globe, could be categorised in all three forms of informatics – dealing with a Chinese migrant community, Chinese society more broadly, and migrant development as a feature of global movements.

Recently Moeletsi Mbeki, executive member of the South African Institute of International Affairs, has suggested that a differentiation between nation and community is specious, and that the basis of equitable development and poverty alleviation begins in communities (Mbeki, 2009):

Achieving [community] begins with a sense of responsibility and reciprocity that does not require a formal constitution or expensive legal protocols to function. It relies, instead, on investing in the common cause... More than anything, the gap between the rich and the poor is the real enemy of the community [which] we desperately need to build a future for (Mbeki, 2009).

Three (and More's) a Crowd

It can be argued that there is no meaningful difference between 'DI', 'ICT4D,' and 'ICTD' (favoured by the UNDP). Can they co-exist peacefully? All of them – or just one of them --could be used as a means to encourage stronger links between technology and development studies, and between economics and informatics, and other groupings already suggested. Linkages must be our preoccupation. The full advantage of these links is only just beginning to emerge in published research (Heeks, 2006:3; Pitula, 2007; UNDP, 2001:3). It is a matter of explication. Arguments can be made for use of any one of the three on its own; it is preferable (and utilitarian) not to use all three at once. If as researchers we aim to just address those with inside knowledge, then multiple meanings are tolerable. But in fact we need to address multiple audiences with the most straightforward nomenclature possible; prevarication or ambivalence are unhelpful in such contexts.

Heeks (2006:2) expresses a preference for DI, because it removes some of the assumed dominant power of the technologies in reflective research. A problem with this view is that technology is also an integral part of 'informatics'. At the same time he acknowledges (Heeks, 2006:1) that the term 'ICT4D' carries the advantage that it brings together the contributing disciplines: library and information sciences for the 'I', communication studies for the 'C', information systems for the 'T' for technologies, and development studies for the 'D'. Nevertheless he regrets that the melding of the four elements in practice is not yet complete, nor is it immediately obvious in the grouped meaning derived from the use of the acronym itself (ICT4D).

Unwin (2009a) sees dangers in the inclusion of the '4' in 'ICT4D', in that it can imply two misdirected endeavours – the need of the private sector to impose its own exclusive commercial solutions for development, and the need of 'academics who have great ideas' to 'try them out' on developing areas in the manner of a carefree game. But presumably in normal usage the word 'for' can be used in a non-hegemonic way; for instance, we wear clothes 'for' warmth, modesty, and show, without them taking control of us, or diminishing us.

In this volume, Matthew Clarke, offers yet another name for DI, viz., 'e-development'. Perhaps the relationship between 'e' and 'development' requires a little more explanation than his juxtaposition alone permits. Perhaps it implies that ICTs dominate development. 'E' has been dropped too glibly in front of too many nouns recently, resulting in a loss of clarity and impact. In any case 'e-development' assumes that ICTs are integral to the full range of development activities and events, as does 'DI'.

DI is the shortest of the alternatives, and is the only one which requires research and reflection as an essential part of it.

Authors' Views of DI Issues

Twenty other themes in this exploratory book offer insights into DI issues which are identified as significant today. They are summarised here. As a word of caution, not all the authors devote the same amount of space to each theme. This analysis is based just on the frequency of a mention of a theme by the authors, not on the number of words which they devote to a discussion of it.

The most commonly-mentioned themes are about education, learning, and literacy (mentioned by eight authors), the implications of the digital divide (seven authors), better prospects for improved community health, and the importance of not destroying local identity by the introduction of ICTs (six authors each). The last point is reinforced by an expectation that the homogenising powers of ICTs need to be moderated by a respect for cultural diversity (five authors), including support

of local knowledge and taking a serious interest in local alternative adaptations of ICTs (two authors). In other literature the complete disappearance of local culture has been adumbrated (Law, 2006: viii; Unwin 2009a).

Five authors in this volume assume that improved local infrastructure for all services can accompany the adoption of ICTs. Four authors believe that ICTs reinforce pre-existing male gender bias in society; that they offer potential for beneficial knowledge sharing; that they require IT skills training, and guidance to relevant and useful knowledge content; that they are likely to lead to the reduction of poverty; and that they can improve social capital.

Four authors also severely criticise the naïve (but popular) assumption that ICTs enable developing countries to 'leapfrog' into the regimen of 21st-century knowledge economies quickly. As Nguyen (2008) shows, a problem with the advocates of this dynamic word is that they never explain its meaning properly in a development context (Nguyen:25, 117). Who is leapfrogging whom, or what, is never self-evident (Toyama, 2008:23).

Three authors express optimism that ICTs might improve rural development, the rule of law, and good governance. Two authors express the need for more focus by DI on the sustainability of development programs, and two see signs of improved business efficiencies, two of successful e-commerce projects, two of better leadership capacity, and two of constructive use of shared public e-spaces, such as community commons.

Single authors mention one strength or weakness. There is mention of increased trade and services, better democratic processes, e-democracy, more respect for human rights, and the value to developing regions of protecting their intellectual property. It is also asserted that ICTs perpetuate racism and ageism.

In brief, although several concerning observations are made about negative impacts of ICTs, overall they are outweighed by optimism for the betterment of developing lives. It is worth noting that development benefits nominated by our authors are not only material or tangible, but also moral, cultural and political, and related to individual aspirations and community choices for better quality of life, which fit well with current theories in Development Studies.

WHAT IS THE VALUE OF DI?

A number of advantages of a DI approach have been alluded to implicitly. In this section four valuable purposes of DI are set out more fully. Globalisation and its consequences seem irrevocable forces, which require tempering as much as possible by sound research and well-informed policy, by the improvement and spread of multidisciplinary studies which are dedicated to helping manage development issues, from human perspectives, and by encouragement of collaborative forums for all stakeholders to share knowledge, understanding, and constructive action.

Counter-Globalisation

The first value of DI involves its potential to dampen the detrimental influences of globalisation (Unwin, 2009b:18). Here there is insufficient space to engage in discussion of whether globalisation is a chimerical capitalist conspiracy, as some do, but to make bold to assert that globalisation is convenient shorthand for a bundle of observable activities and events that are well under way, as noted by several authors in this book. Some researchers even hold ICTs primarily responsible for globalisation (Law, 2006:vii). No-one can escape the transformations which globalisation causes. Features of globalisation that should concern us are: rampant free market capitalism, global warming and climate change, fear of terror, resource wars, weapons proliferation, endemic and preventable diseases, food insecurity, mass migration, impoverishment of political institu-

tions, lack of commitment to multilateralism in world affairs, poor governance, and the decline of the sovereign state (Sweeney, 2007:85–91; Unwin 2009a). In short, we live in a 'risk' society, full of insecurity, as described by Giddens, where change no longer conforms to expectations or predictions, and which is often beyond human control. Every world citizen is bombarded by popularised and recycled information in the mass media, carried by ICTs (Colle, 2008:144). Events in traditional space are separated from place, and local social systems, and are permanently 'switched on'. Global systems stretch time and space. ICTs are disembedding mechanisms; they comprise symbolic tokens and expert systems that separate human interactions from the particularities of locales (Giddens, 1991:6, 20-22, 24-25, 28).

Multidisciplinarity

The second value of DI stems from the level of multidisciplinary interest already invested in the field, and its focus on development problems. This is a large theme. There are other names for shared understandings; Avgerou calls them 'interdisciplinary macro-theoretical complexity' (Avgerou, 2008:142). The background disciplines and practical experiences of the authors of this book, and the range of themes which they address, show a breadth of knowledge, competencies and skills which is reassuring. Together they can achieve a lot. It is heartening when project designers and researchers ally with each other voluntarily (Dosa, 1997:243; Ramamritham, 2005). Heeks has studied ICTs for development for decades, and stresses the importance of 'multidisciplinary teams' and 'leadership':

Successful IT projects are led by hybrids that span the technical and organizational ... How to create these ICT4D champions remains a challenge. [Professionals] tend to self-create during ICT4D projects as leaders from any individual domain rapidly find themselves facing problems that only insights from other domains can solve (Heeks, 2008:31).

Unwin also calls for dedicated collaboration:

There is ... an urgent need for those involved in delivering ICT4D programmes to learn the distinct vocabularies, styles of discourse, practical agendas and means of validification that are adopted in fields other than their own immediate areas of specialism (Unwin, 2009b:5).

Walsham reinforces the points (Walsham, 2005:17).

The list of disciplines and fields of study represented in this book include many which can be applied helpfully to developing countries. They include: agriculture, architecture and urban planning, business management, community development, community informatics, computer science, conflict management, development studies, developmental psychology, economics, education, environmental design, evaluation, geography, human development, industrial psychology, information management, international development, journalism, knowledge management, media and communications studies, social policy, sociology, and systems design. The list of experience by our authors in non-academic organisations, civil society activities, and social movements is also apposite: an Amazon Forest NGO, Canadian First Nations, collaboration between universities and communities, community radio, e-health, e-government, e-inclusion, e-learning, international aid organisations, International Development Research Centre, internet provider, Geographical Information Systems company, lifelong learning co-operative, music editor, new media business, Peace Corps, print newspaper, research institutes, UNICEF Uganda, USAid, and World Vision.

Inevitably questions arise as to how such disparate interests can be co-ordinated constructively in future and how development overall can benefit

from their combined thrust. The next sections offer some suggestions.

Growing Dialogue

The third value of DI lies in the dialogue which it generates between researchers, practitioners, and policy-makers, in the field, and in related fields – already mentioned. The conversation needs to be extended in the academy and in projects on-the-ground (UNDP, 2001:5). Heeks regrets, for instance, that it has not extended from IS to Development Studies: 'IS tends neither to understand, nor to use the ideas of, development studies.' (Heeks 2008:31). Only in the past decade has the dominant development discourse advocated partnerships between all stakeholders (Unwin, 2009b:16), a refreshing trend. It enlivens the bodies of knowledge of all participants (Avgerou 2008:142), and guarantees the researcher 'a richer, more satisfying, more colourful experience' (Heeks, 2008:26).

A recent surge in interest in DI was stimulated by international commitment to the Millenium Development Goals (2000), which focus attention on the eradication of hunger and poverty, universal education and literacy, reversing major diseases and improving health care, environmental sustainability, and gender equality by 2020 (Colle, 2008:143; McIver, 2003:36). These themes 'assumed a new prominence, when the United Nations and G8 group of industrialized countries flagged ICTD as a global development priority' (UNDP 2001).

It has been suggested that the elimination of 'information poverty' should be an additional Goal (Accascina 2000:40), but in fact the Goals do embrace a DI ideal, 'Goal 8f' being devoted to 'make available the benefits of new technologies, especially information and communications' (UNDP, 2000).

Shortly after the Goals, the World Summits on the Information Society (2003, 2005) carried forward the role of ICTs in development further.

Managed by the International Telecommunications Union (ITU), the Summits aimed to bring together governments, businesses, and civil society to discuss how to share the apparent benefits of ICTs in the developed world with the developing world. Although UNESCO was said to be a less technological (and thus a better) UN unit to orchestrate the Summits than the ITU (Carpentier 2004), nevertheless a powerful Declaration and Plan of Action were agreed on. In somewhat grandiose language, part of the Declaration of Principles reads:

We, the representatives of the peoples of the world ... declare our common desire and commitment to build a people-centred, inclusive and development-oriented Information Society, where everyone can create, access, utilize and share information and knowledge ... We are aware that ICTs should be regarded as tools and not as an end in themselves. Under favourable conditions, these technologies can be a powerful instrument, increasing productivity, generating economic growth, job creation and employability and improving the quality of life of all ... We are resolute to empower the poor, particularly those living in remote, rural and marginalized urban areas, to access information and to use ICTs as a tool to support their efforts to lift themselves out of poverty (World Summit on the Information Society, 2005).

The DI banner continues to be displayed at annual international conferences and in journals. For instance, the conferences of the Community Informatics Research Network have included DI papers since their inception in 2004. For the past three years the International Development Informatics Association has held representative conferences. The International Federation of Information Processing holds a regular conference which is frequently cited as a source of DI papers (Walsham, 2006:8).

The most recent International Conference on Information and Communications and Development in Qatar hosted papers on the value of ICTs for democracy, health, literacy, small-to-medium enterprises, mapping, HIV-Aids education, Braille, banking, knowledge transfer, disaster management, sustainable communities, cinema, and conflict resolution, in Bangladesh, Cambodia, Ghana, India, Indonesia, Liberia, Nigeria, Malawi, Oman, Sierra Leone, Uganda, and other developing regions. It is not uncommon for conferences which do not focus on DI specifically to include papers related to DI; thus the 17th European Conference on Information Systems hosted approximately 11% of papers dealing with information have-nots (Brown, in press). The Association of Information Systems has a special interest group for developing countries (Heeks, 2008:30).

An analysis of the content of the *Journal of Community Informatics* for its first three years (2006–2008) indicates that 24% of contributions deal with international DI topics (Brown, in press). *Information Technologies and International Development* is dedicated to DI research. Many other journal titles commonly include DI contributions. A sample of the main titles is as follows:

- *African Journal of Information Systems,*
- *Development, Development and Change, Development in Practice, Development Policy Review,*
- *Electronic Journal of Information Systems in Developing Countries,*
- First Monday,
- *Information and Communication Technologies and Human Development,*
- *Information Development,*
- *Information Technologies and International Development,*
- *Information Technology for Development,*
- *International Journal of Education and Development Using Information and Communication Technology,*

- *International Journal of ICT Research and Development in Africa (from 2010),*
- *International Journal on Advances in ICT for Emerging Regions,*
- *Journal of Development Studies,*
- *Journal of Human Development and Capabilities; a Multi-Disciplinary*
- *Journal of Global Information Technology Management,*
- *Journal for People-Centered Development, Journal of International Development, Progress in Development Studies, Third World Quarterly,* and *World Development.*

Challenges Aplenty

The fourth value of DI is that this field presents many exciting challenges for researchers. As a new field of research, opportunities for original, creative projects abound. There is potential for much personal satisfaction from working in unfamiliar situations with unfamiliar constraints (Burrell, 2009:83). Three broad areas of challenge for DI are noted: to identify useful theory and knowledge, to engage constructively with all participants, and to devise realistic goals for action. It does not matter if together they are called development desiderata, a research agenda, or just the 'Big Challenges'.

In relation to the challenge of theory and knowledge, it may begin with adventurous researchers trialling new theories, outside their familiar territory (Walsham, 2006:16). Several authors address the need to harness disciplines and roles to achieve cross-cutting work teams (Avgerou, 2008:134; Walsham, 2006:16). For Heeks (2008:31) 'the key intellectual challenge' in DI is to manage multidisciplinarity, to bring together the three intellectual domains of Computer Science, Information Systems and Development Studies as a successful coalition. They are not natural allies, and over time they have teetered towards and away from each other spasmodically. As a core common objective, the collective aim

should not just be to advocate ICTs as a toolkit for development, but to use ICTs to transform development goals, processes and structures. A simple example of such a project would be one that starts

with a development goal, seek[s] to understand the role of information and communication in achieving that goal, then ask[s] which new technologies — if any — could help deliver that role (Heeks, 2008:32).

Presumably the researcher is involved in each stage of such a project.

Heeks expresses a very commendable desire for long-lasting knowledge which interprets major change in the world, rather than research which is used as a dispenser of stop-gap fixes with short life expectancy (Heeks, 2007:1). In a similar vein, Colle hopes that research ensures that solutions are effective (Colle, 2008:149–150), a point taken up by Walsham who advocates wider deployment of evaluation methodologies (Walsham, 2006:16). He would also like to see more use of participatory action research (Walsham, 2005:20). The final identified challenge in relation to knowledge is to find more effective ways to disseminate research results to key decision-makers in bureaucracies and privatised infrastructure services (UNDP, 2001).

The second area of challenge is to engage constructively with all participants in the development process. The aim is to ensure that the subjects of the research and development are involved as equal partners in the process along with the various managers -- creators, designers, planners, infrastructure providers, vendors, donors, funders, practitioners, and so on. Genuine involvement slows projects down (Stoecker, 2005), and it is a pity to have to acknowledge that 'social transformation is painfully slow' (Mbeki, 2009). Typically challenges in this category are expressed as: working with the poor as they adapt ICTs in their own situations for their own purposes, which is often not the original purpose of the ICTs (Heeks, 2008:30); stakeholder participation in the design of systems (Ramamritham, 2005); proof-of-concept of systems which can be sustained by individuals, social groups, and nations (Walsham, 2006:16); implementation of systems which are economically, culturally and socially sensitive to recipient needs (Walsham, 2006:16); and inclusion in projects of training to empower users to maintain and service their own systems (Accascina, 2000:40–41).

The final (and to me the greatest) area of challenge is to devise realistic goals for action. It may incorporate the previous area of challenge -- for example, alternative design approaches may prove to be best for some intractable development problems. Old technologies such as radio telephony, low-power television, and printed books still present good solutions in many contexts. The potential of open hardware standards, and open source software has not been not fully explored (Walsham, 2006,16). Heeks provides a challenging list of large-scale goals: to deliver the Internet to the five billion people who do not have it now, using mobile devices, radio and television; to enable money transfer on mobile phones, now accessible across 80% of the globe; and to ensure that ICTs provide local jobs in developing areas (Heeks, 2008:29). Another goal should be to demonstrate any causal link between the spread of ICTs and development. Improved communication between all groups with an interest in creating better multidisciplinary working teams is another highly desirable goal. It would be of great benefit to hold an ecumenical forum and workshop on the usefulness of the theories of DI, and theories for DI, rather than individual disciplines continuing to pursue narrow (yet sometimes parallel) theoretical and methodological meetings and publications separately.

Obviously much remains to be done, but as this chapter shows, there is an abundance of energy, constructive forums, and good will in the field.

CONCLUSION

The depressing global development statistics which show an enormous gap between developed and developing areas should not deter researchers from trying to find ways to alleviate the many attendant social, cultural, health, economic, political and other problems. DI is most likely to succeed when researchers, policy-makers, and project managers from different backgrounds work together (Colle, 2008:154). Solutions to development problems lie in Development Informatics, when it connects researchers, practitioners and policy-makers with leaders in developing areas to maximise beneficial uses for ICTs, for improving the quality and choices of personal and collective lives (UNDP, 2001:5). ICTs are here to stay; they must be integrated well into development processes and objectives. Global economic indicators show that development and the use of ICTs go hand-in-hand. On a national level, it is clear that ICTs have played a significant part in development in the past two decades in Korea, Taiwan, Brazil, India, and China (Heeks, 2008:31).

In presenting a case for the values of DI, a somewhat strident rhetorical tone has been unavoidable. DI achieves four important things. It provides an evaluative critique to counterbalance the effects of relentless globalisation, it offers multidisciplinary teams the opportunity to create imaginative responses to longstanding development issues, it maintains an intellectual discussion space (and publications) to build on international momentum that has developed among theorists and practitioners in the past 20 years, and it opens up many future possibilities for collaborative projects which involve communities in developing areas in participatory research and ongoing project evaluation in order to encourage sustainability (UNDP, 2001:19; Walsham, 2005:17,20). The potential advantages of DI are clear. To see more benefits actually emerge from DI requires serious ongoing dialogue and commitment to joint actions.

ACKNOWLEDGMENT

I am grateful for the help of Walter Brown, Tom Denison, Richard Heeks, Paul Plantinga, Don Schauder, Jacques Steyn, and Larry Stillman in the preparation of this paper.

REFERENCES

Accascina, G. (2000). Information technology and poverty alleviation, in SD Dimensions, Food and Agricultural Organisation of the United Nations (FAO), Rome. Retrieved September 2009 from www.fao.org/sd/CDdirect/CDre0055h.htm.

Avgerou, C. (2008). Information Systems in Developing Countries: a critical research review. *Journal of Information Technology, 23*, 133–146. doi:10.1057/palgrave.jit.2000136

Bernard, A. (2004). Philippe Dreyfus, in TechnoScience.net. Retrieved September 2009 from http://www.techno-science.net/?onglet=glossaire&definition=7447.

Bohman, J. (2005). *2009 from http//:plato.stanford.edu./entires/critical-theory*. Critical Theory. In Stanford Encyclopedia of Philosophy. Retrieved October.

Brown, W. (in press). *Leveraging Information and Communications Technologies for Development of the Bottom of the Pyramid ICT Market in South Africa.*

Burrell, J., & Toyama, K. (2009). What Constitutes Good ICTD Research? *Information Technologies and International Development, 5*(3), 82–94.

Carpentier, N., & Servaes, J. (Eds.). (2004). *Deconstructing WSIS: Towards a Sustainable Agenda for the Future Information Society*. Bristol, UK: Intellect Books.

Colle, R. D. (2008). Threads of Development Communication. In Servaes, J. (Ed.), *Communication for Development and Social Change*. New Delhi: UNESCO & Sage.

Coward, C. (2009). Second Recess, RSS feed, 11 March. Retrieved September 2009 from http://chriscoward.wordpress.com/2009/03/11/ict4d-ictd-or-what/.

de Moor, A. (2009). Moving Community Informatics research forward. *Journal of Community Informatics, 5*(1). Retrieved September 2009 from http://ci-journal.net/index.php/ciej/article/viewArticle/546/434

DeRenzi, B. (2008). Thoughts on Challenges in ICTD for Young Researchers. University of Washington. Retrieved October 2009 from www.cs.washington.edu/homes/bderenzi/.../derenzi_yrictd09.pdf

Development Informatics Research Group, Council for Scientific and Industrial Research. (2009). Knowledge generation for an efficient and competitive built environment. Retrieved September 2009 from http:www.csir.co.za/Built-environment/Planning_support_system/devinfo.html

Dosa, M. (Ed.). (1997). *Across all borders; international information flows and applications; collected papers*. London: Scarecrow Press.

Elder, L. (2009). Elder Musings, Monday, April 13, 2009. Retrieved September 2009 from http://eldermusings.blogs pot.com/2009/04/words-words-more-words-and-acronyms.html

European Journal of Development Research. (2009). Retrieved September 2009 from http://www.plagrave-journals.com/ejdr/about.html

Feather, F. (2004). *The information society; a study of continuity and change*. London: Facet.

Giddens, A. (1991). *Modernity and self-identity; self and society in the late modern age*. Stanford: University Press.

Heeks, R. (2006). Theorizing ICT4D Research. *Information Technologies and International Development, 3*(3), 1–4. doi:10.1162/itid.2007.3.3.1

Heeks, R. (2008). *ICT4D 2.0: the next phase of applying ICT for International development*. Computer.

Johanson, G. (2008). Flicking the Switch: social networks and the role of Information and Communications Technologies in social cohesion among Chinese and Italians in Melbourne, Australia. In *Proceedings, The Role of New Technologies in Global Societies: Theoretical Reflections, Practical Concerns, and Its Implications for China, Conference at the Department of Applied Social Sciences*. The Hong Kong Polytechnic University, HKSAR, China, 30th–31st July 2008.

Keeble, L. (2007). Community Informatics: building civil society in the Information Age? In Clay, C. J., Madden, M., & Potts, L. (Eds.), *People and places: an introduction towards understanding community*. New York: Palgrave Macmillan.

King, K. (2005). Knowledge-based Aid: A New Way of Networking or a New North-South Divide? In Stone, D., & Maxwell, S. (Eds.), *Global Knowledge networks and International Development; Bridges across Boundaries*. Oxford: Routledge. doi:10.4324/9780203340387_chapter_5

Kok, D. (2005). SAP invests in South African Technology Research Skills. Retrieved September 2009 from http://www.sap.com/southafrica/about/press/press.epx?pressid=4914

Law, P. L., Fortunati, L., & Yang, S. (Eds.). (2006). *New technologies in global societies*. Singapore: World Scientific. doi:10.1142/9789812773555

Masuda, J. (1981). *The Information Society as Post-Industrial Society*. Washington: World Future Society.

Mbeki, M., Vale, P. (2009). Community is the new state. *Mail & Guardian*, 27.

McIver, W. (2003). Community Informatics for the Information Society. In Girard, B., & Siochru, S. O. (Eds.), *Communicating in the Information Society*. Geneva: United Nations Research Institute for Social Development.

Nguyen, T. T. (2008). *Seeking Thachsanh's Rice Bowl: an Exploration of Knowledge, ICTs and Sustainable Economic Development in Vietnam*. Unpublished Doctor of Philosophy dissertation. Melbourne, Australia: Faculty of Information Technology, Monash University.

Pasquali, A. (2003). A brief descriptive glossary of communication and information (aimed at providing clarification and improving mutual understanding). In Girard, B., & Siochru, S. O. (Eds.), *Communicating in the Information Society*. Geneva: United Nations Research Institute for Social Development.

Pigg, K. (2005). An Introduction to Community Informatics and Community Development. *Journal of the Community Development Society, 1*(1), 58–73.

Pitula, K., & Radhakrishnan, T. (2007). A Framework and Process for Designing Inclusive Technology. In *International Conference on Software Engineering Advances (ICSEA 2007)*. Retrieved October 2009 from http://ieeexplore.ieee.org/stamp/stamp.jsp?tp=&arnumber=4299944&isnumber=4299877

Qiang, C. Z.-W., & Pitt, A. (2003). *Contribution of Information and Communication Technologies to Growth*. Washington: The World Bank. doi:10.1596/0-8213-5722-0

Ramamritham, K., & Bahuman, A. (2005). Developmental Informatics: Potential and Challenges. *Media Asia*, *32*(3), 165–167.

School of Informatics, University of Edinburgh. (2002). What does Informatics mean? Retrieved September 2009 from http://www.dai.ed.ac.uk/homes/cam/informatics.shtml.

Steyn, J. (2008). Book series, in IDIA International Development Informatics Association. Retrieved September 2009 from http://www.developmentinformatics.org/projects/book/index.html.

Stoecker, R. (2005). *Research Methods for Community Change: A Project-based Approach.* Thousand Oaks: Sage.

Sweeney, S. (2007). Globalization, Multiple Threats and the Weakness of International Institutions: a Community-centred Response. In Clay, C. J., Madden, M., & Potts, L. (Eds.), *People and Places: an Introduction towards Understanding Community.* New York: Palgrave Macmillan.

Toyama, K., Dias, M.B. (2008). Guest Editors' Introduction: Information and Communication Technologies for Development. *Computer*.

United Nations Development Programme. (2000). Millennium Development Goals (MDG). Retrieved September 2009 from http://www.undp.org/mdg

United Nations Development Programme. (2001). *Evaluation Unit. Essentials: Information and Communications Technology for Development. Synthesis of Lessons Learned, no 5. September.* New York: UNDP.

Unwin, T. (2009a). Blog. Retrieved October 2009 from http://unwin.wordpress.com/2009/04/27/reflections-on-ict4d-the-british-council-manchester

Unwin, T. (2009b). *ICT4D.* Cambridge University Press.

Walsham, G., & Sahay, S. (2006). Research on Information Systems in Developing Countries: Current Landscape and Future Prospects. *Information Technology for Development*, *12*(1), 7–24. doi:10.1002/itdj.20020

Widrow, B., Hartenstein, R., & Hecht-Nielsen, R. (2005). 1917 Karl Steinbuch 2005. In *IEEE Computational Intelligence Society Newsletter, August* (p. 5). Eulogy.

World Bank. (2009a). Data & Statistics. Retrieved September 2009 from http://web.worldbank.org/WBSITE/EXTERNAL/DATASTATISTICS/0,contentMDK:20535285~menuPK:1192694~pagePK:64133150~piPK:64133175~theSitePK:239419,00.html. Accessed in September 2009.

World Bank. (2009b). Information and Communications for Development 2009: Extending Reach and Increasing Impact. Retrieved September 2009 from http://web.worldbank.org/WBSITE/EXTERNAL/TOPICS/EXTINFORMATIONANDCOMMUNICATIONANDTECHNOLOGIES/EXTIC4D/0,contentMDK:22229759~menuPK:5870649~pagePK:64168445~piPK:64168309~theSitePK:5870636,00.html.

World Summit on the Information Society. (2005). Declaration of Principles; Building the Information Society: a global challenge in the new Millennium. Geneva, United Nations/International Telecommunications Union. Retrieved September 2009 from http://www.itu.int/wsis/docs/Geneva/official/dop.html

Chapter 2
Paradigm Shift Required for ICT4D

Jacques Steyn
Monash University, South Africa

ABSTRACT

In this chapter I argue for a shift of paradigm in the field of ICT4D. Since the inception of aid for development in the late 1940s with the introduction of the Marshall Plan, development has been dominated by emphasis on economic development, while development of other human characteristics have been neglected. The standard argument in contemporary ICT4D literature, based on the so-called Washington Concensus, is that economic "upliftment will result in social "upliftment". It is assumed that economics is the primary cause for social change. I challenge this assumption, and propose that it is instead individual "upliftment" that influences social change that might (or might not) lead to economic change. The more recent Post-Washington Consensus introduced a shift toward socio-economics, by addressing poverty, but is still based on a particular ideological brand of economics. There is a need to move away from such an economically biased approach to development, and from measuring success with economic metrics such as GDP. ICT4D projects are typically deployed within this economic paradigm. The alternative approach suggested here is to deploy ITC4D projects against a social and cognitive paradigm in which social networking and psychological enrichment would take priority over economic development. Within such a paradigm, the principle of least effort would be used for measuring success. This proposed new paradigm is a techno-utilitarian approach. In this regard Development Informatics could pave the way for designing new kinds of ICT systems that are socially relevant to remote communities (whether geographically or socially remote) by making life easier for individuals. It is envisaged that economic development would follow individual and social development. The focus on developing an individual by exposing such an individual to scientific knowledge, will enable that individual to make better choices, which will lead to changing that individual and his or her environment. As the individual changes, the surrounding society changes (which is not the same as progressivism). Social change may lead to a change in the components of society, one of which is economics. ICT is regarded to be a tool to make life easier, and focuses on the enlightenment of an individual within the social context in which such an individual lives, by facilitating the possible development of cognitive and psychological abilities.

DOI: 10.4018/978-1-61520-799-2.ch002

DIVIDES

There are different views of the role of ICT for development. Optimists regard ICTs as the solution to all problems, pessimists argue ICTs increase the divide, and realists see communities adapting new technologies (Polikanov & Abramova, 2003). Heeks (2008) presents a fair summary of current thinking in ICT4D. He provides an overview of how thinking about ICT4D has changed over the past few decades and suggests some approaches to address the failures of the past. In this context, according to him, an interdisciplinary approach between computer science, information science and development studies is required. Heeks points the road away from the failures of the past, of what he calls the first generation (version 1) of ICT4D, towards a reframing of many of the issues into an ICT4D 2.0 framework. This is admirable, and social activists would be happy if this could be achieved. However, there are still several assumptions not mentioned by Heeks, that we, as critical theorists, need to address. Not only the assumptions need to be reconsidered, but the paradigm underlying the programs implementing ICT4D.

A reader might object to so much emphasis on economic theory in this chapter. My reply would be that the standard justification for deploying ICT systems in developing regions is predominantly economic. The terms "development", "upliftment", "betterment", "bridging the divide" and others as used in the field have strong undertones of economic ideology, as will be shown in this chapter. A second reason for addressing economics is that the governments of by far the majority of poor developing regions do not have a large enough tax-based income to provide basic services such as water, energy and transport networks, and definitely not for ICT networks. They are dependent on foreign aid. However, despite the roughly USD2.3 trillion spent over the past half a century on aid (see e.g. Easterly, 2006), only the foolhardy could still believe that aid is successful.

Divides between social groups are typically measured with reference to economics. But the matter of divisions is much more complex. There are at least three types of digital divide that should be discussed in the context of development. Firstly, the operational divide concerns availability of ICT and access to ICT systems. This requires an infrastructure for ICT to operate, and devices for access. Secondly, the cultural divide refers to a social dimension where some groups may not have either technological or social access to dominant social networks (Castells, 2004a). Thirdly, political divides exclude some groups or individuals of communities. Castells points to Mulgan who observed that networks are also created to gain position of power, which of course leads to the dominance of some groups and consequently exclusion of others (Castells, 2004a: 23).

Ostensibly ICT4D is about overcoming the digital divide operationally. At least, that is what is often claimed in the media. However, ICT4D could also empower communities to overcome the other forms of divide. Equal access offers the ability to bypass political power structures. And whereas in the physical world dominant social structures are easy to observe, in the virtual world such barriers are less pronounced.

Making networks available operationally is not necessarily a neutral goal, as the justification is often to enable communities to join the trend toward globalization, which has a political agenda – the power-play of neo-colonialism in the form of globalization, corporatism and western culture. The donor group typically decides what is important for the receiving group, and that is politics. Among donors I include donor agencies, governments, NGO's, organizations such as the IMF, World Bank, UN, philanthropists and even social activists. The receivers are communities regarded as being on the wrong side of some divide in the context of ICT4D, typically the digital divide, which most often refers to remote communities, whether geographical or social, as well as to the so-called developing world, or the

South, previously known by other names, such as the Third World.

If one social group imposes ICT on another, even if it is supposedly or apparently for the good of the receiving group, it is implied that the receiving group is not involved in this decision. Even if a community is consulted, "insisting" by default that installing a telecentre is the answer is an argument from a position of power. And if one group decides on behalf of another, or enforces something, even if it is by power of knowledge, onto another group, this is domination through power, thus political. If this is a fair statement about the status of ICT4D, we need to contemplate the implications, and review our assumptions critically. This is what I will attempt to do in this chapter. The characteristics of the two groups, the donors and the receivers need to be investigated. And the underlying ethics of the process needs to be scrutinized.

DEVELOPMENT AND ICT4D

Development Studies as an academic discipline began in the second half of the twentieth century with the aim to address economic prospects for the "third world" after *uhuru* (or freedom from colonizers), or decolonization (Easterly, 2006). The notion of development embraces concepts such as "improvement". Since the inception of Development Studies, such improvement mostly meant economical improvement. The approach seems to be based on some form of social Darwinism, as interpreted from a progressivist bias.

Economic globalization was the dominant economic approach to macro-economics over the past few decades. That view influenced policies and implementation plans by governments and donor organizations, and in some cases even NGOs. As there is no clear theory or model that includes ethics on how technology should or perhaps rather could be applied to developing regions, ICT4D is often highly dependent on the globalization model,

even when implemented by well-meaning social activists as tools for social change.

The top rated academic journals (in the A ranked category) that deal with ICT and development related topics predominantly deal with economic matters concerning development. There are few exceptions, such as the *Journal of the Society for International Development* (SID), the *Journal Information Technology and People* and the journal *Development*. There are very few other ranked journals related to ICT and themes that resemble interest in social development. There is an abundance of non-ranked journals and websites dedicated to ICT4D. As it appears that by far the majority of literature seems to be reports that are written to keep donor agencies happy, generally speaking there is a lack of well-founded research in the field of ICT4D - it is unwise to bite that hand that feeds you. Such websites, and hyped media reports typically focus on the isolated success stories of ICT deployment in developing contexts, but fail to mention the worrying majority of cases that are failures.

For example, In the late 1990s the South African government introduced the Universal Services Agency (USA) to deploy telecentres. It was calculated that 4000 telecentres would be needed to serve the entire population. Plans were made to establish only about 100 telecentres. By year 2000 only 65 centers had been established, but only 40 had working telephone lines, and only 5 were actually online. By 2002 the government claimed 56 telecentres were in operation. Snyman and Snyman (2003) report that only 25 telecentres could be reached, while 7 had actually closed down. The government planned to address only 2.5% of the need, but in practice only 0.6% of the need was met. This does not indicate much of a success!

Another initiative by the South African government was to deploy MPCC's (Multi-Purpose Community Centres) in poorer communities. In 2006 the Department of GCIS (Government Communication and Information Services) claimed 62

MPCC's were in operation. Van der Vyver (2006) reported that their research showed that in fact only two were in operation – a mere 3%.

If claimed success stories are analysed, almost without fail the claims are biased toward some supposed economic benefit. One more example should suffice: the supposed success story of the use of mobile phones by the fishermen of Kerala. This flagship case of supposed success is the most commonly cited case I have come across in media reports and in more formal literature. It refers to the impact of ICT on the lives of fishermen on the Kerala coast of India. Jensen reports that "...a significant limitation to fish marketing is that while at sea, fishermen are unable to observe prices at any of the numerous markets spread out along the coast" and almost in the same breath that 70% of adults eat fish at least once a day (2007:881). The sympathy is with the fisherman's profit, regardless of the village that would go hungry if the fishermen rather land at another village which offers a better price that day. There is no mention of the local village market that will not operate – e.g. women who sell fruit when the fishermen sell their fish – if fishermen take their catch to a different market. Abraham (2007) did a follow-up study, and concluded that ICT benefits fishermen by bypassing middle-men and there is greater market integration (on supply-side). Neither Jensen nor Abraham mention anything about the benefits to the consumers, the final post on the demand-side. So we still do not know if ICT has benefits for the entire complex social system. Based on these articles, the only benefit is for the fishermen and the supply side of the market model. The "success" of the Kerala fishermen story is biased to economics, and based on a neo-liberal model of economics.

Over the past half a century two major approaches were implemented to "develop" economies not on par with highly developed economies: financial aid, and economic globalization. Aid has worked in some cases, and some aspects of globalization have worked in some cases. But overall, both approaches have failed. ICT4D has functioned within the context of these two approaches. It is thus important to consider aid and globalization to understand the current status of ICT4D.

The notion of "development", in the context of development studies, has been biased toward economic expansion since its inception – as demonstrated by the economic bias in academic journals. There are other senses of "development" that are rarely found in development studies, particularly in the context when ICT is included in the discussion. I refer to the notions of personal development, and of social development. It could of course be argued that economic development would benefit those two aspects, and I would not dispute that stance. But in this chapter I wish to argue that personal and social development should come first and would then lead to economic development, and not the other way around, as promoted by globalists. The focus should primarily be on personal and social development, and economic development would then follow. It seems to me that presently the horse is drawn by the cart.

Another word frequently used in development circles is "upliftment", which in this context typically means increasing spending money capacity. The World Bank, Jeffrey Sachs and many such "planners", as Easterly (2006) calls them, wish to reduce the number of people living on USD1 or USD2 per day. Such statements are misleading as living on some money refers to available spending money, and does not assign any monetary value to the fact that many such "poor" actually have enough to eat. A self-sustaining remote, rural farmer with USD1 spending money per day has a much higher quality of life than an inner city poor person having to live on USD1 per day.

Also, the question that is never addressed is: When will the poor have enough? Living on USD3 per day? Or USD30 per day? Once programs such as the MDG have succeeded to achieve their planned reduction in world poverty, and the poor then live on USD10 per day, will there then be a follow-up program to increase that too? Measuring development in terms of economics assumes we are *homo economicus*.

The sociological theories of Castells, Giddens, Derrida and Habermas are all attempts to interpret and understand the dominant current of modern societies. These thinkers differ on many aspects. Giddens and Derrida are basically structuralists, while Castells and Habermas are historical, with Derrida perhaps between the two extremes, as he argued that structure has a history, perhaps making him a post-structuralist. All these thinkers agree that a profound change has occurred in western capitalism, and that the economic view has become globally dominant. Castells moved from actors to the relations between actors, which is similar to Giddens, both focusing on the act of communication between subjects. For Castells relationships are mediated by technology. The role of technology is thus to be an enabler for the relations, and the space, Oldenburg's third place (1989, 2001) where this happens is no longer only the *agora*, a physical space away from home and work, but a virtual space, mediated by technology.

Globalization of social networks and communication channels occur in this third place. ICT makes this possible. Economic globalization is a different matter, focusing on economic development. Third place globalization focuses on social and psychological empowerment. The globalization with which I take issue is not social or communication globalization. The issue is with a specific model of economics that is forced onto all societies by a minority of very powerful players. Unfortunately it seems that ICT4D plays into the hands of these neo-liberal capitalists.

PHILANTHROCAPITALISM

The work of well-meaning promoters of development is to be admired, but reminds me of the saying: all roads to hell are paved with good intentions. The popularized work of Jeffrey Sachs (2005, 2008) comes to mind in this respect. He exemplifies this approach with the Millennium Villages established in Africa, and praises companies such as "Yara for fertilizer; Monsanto for high-yield seeds; Sumitomo Chemical for antimalarial bed nets...." (2008:322) and so forth.

Analize this, and notice the problems. Monasanto's seed do not reproduce seed that could be re-used. This means farmers now have to annually buy new seed, which is a much more expensive method they used to use, by harvesting their own seed from their own crop. Who benefits from this new "aid"? The corporation selling the seed; definitely not the farmer.

As Moyo (2009) points out, products as aid destroy local economies. Imported mosquito nets results in the small local mosquito net manufacturer going out of business and 150 people dependent on that income being devastated. So Sumitomo Chemical's philanthropy actually has quite the opposite effect than what Sachs claims. The imported inorganic fertilizer will have the same long-term devastation on the environment as it is already causing in many regions in the highly developed world. Diamond (2005) mentions that fertilizer run-off often pollute water, causing algal blooms (due to eutrophication). There is also the heavy-metal content of fertilizer that is not good for the long-term sustainability of the chemical mix of the soil, nor for areas affected by run-off. That Sachs in 2008 seems to not pay attention to such global problems is shocking, as the FAO report highlighting these dangers was released more than a decade prior to his book (Ongley, 1996). In his most recent book Sachs (2008:42) still argues that chemical fertilizers can alleviate the poverty trap. Sachs' excitement with this kind of aid is displaced, and does a disservice to the needs of the developing world.

This negative effect of aid is the result of simplistic, one-size-fits-all kind of approach to life that guerilla advisers typically promote. They rush into a country with their pre-conceived ideas of what the poor need, and those ideas are typically biased towards some form of economic globalization.

Sachs (2005, 2008) presents plans to reduce poverty by suggesting that the richest people and corporations pool together towards aid. To alleviate extreme poverty Sachs promotes the notion of holistic development by business philanthropists. Edwards (2008) and Ramdas (2008) are skeptical about corporate philanthropists. And the kind of aid is suspect too. As pointed out above with reference to Moyo (2009), the mosquito nets donated by Sumitomo Chemical caused more poverty than really helped the communities where they were distributed.

Bill Gates now argues for what he calls creative capitalism. Consider the statements he makes: "Capitalism has improved the lives of billions of people..."; "We need new ways to bring far more people into the system – capitalism – that has done so much good in the world."; "Some corporations have identified brand-new markets among the poor for life-changing technologies like cell phones" (Gates 2008). None of these statements are actually true. How is this "improvement" measured? Multinational corporations have benefited, but in real life the tax-paying middle class is no better off, and the poor in more traditional economies seem to be worse off (Moyo 2009, Saul 2009, Stiglitz 2002, 2006). The kind of philanthrocapitalism offered by the likes of Gates is highly suspect. Note how he measures success as the brand new markets established among the poor. The problem with philanthropism is not about the wonderful gesture by the rich wanting to make a difference. That is admirable. The problem is with the assumption that "development" or aid is tacitly defined ethnocentrically in terms of a particular economic worldview, exemplified by globalization.

ECONOMIC GLOBALIZATION

The economic approach to development promoted by both the Washington Consensus and the Post-Washington Consensus is based on the assumptions of *homo economicus*. This section focuses on the failure of economic globalization – the dominant paradigm behind ICT4D. I should explicitly state that I do not argue against the broad notion of globalization, with reference to sustainable ecology, global social networks, and positive and responsible global trade. With the latter I mean economics friendly to ecologically, socially and morally responsibility, which seems be opposite to how transnational corporates seem to behave. My argument is against the primacy of economic development at the cost of social and psychological "development".

Onis and Senses (2005) and Saul (2009) explain that the accumulation of economic surplus is in the hands of rentiers and transnationals. Less than 360 people combinely own more assets than 45% of the world population. Most countries earn less revenues than corporations. Of the thirty largest revenues in the world, the majority belong to corporations, not countries (Saul 2009: 190). Easterly (2006) and Saul (2009) show that money keeps on flowing out of developing regions to these corporations, reducing opportunities to create jobs for the unemployed in these regions.

Perhaps economic globalization in its present form of domination began with the colonial expansion of nations about five hundred years ago, and intensified through time. More specifically globalization is an economic drive that was driven economically by corporations, and politically by western governments only after World War II. In this restricted sense, economic globalization refers to the trend to privatize public enterprises, pressurize governments to deregulate commerce, and pressurize to remove barriers on international trade and financial flows (Broad & Cavanagh, 2006). This kind of globalization is known as the Washington Consensus (Onis & Senses, 2005; Saul, 2009), as it was driven from the headquarters of the International Monetary Fund (IMF), the World Bank, and the Treasury of the US government in Washington, USA. The term is used for the neo-liberal economic policies by these Washington-based institutions as framework for aid to developing regions.

The Washington Consensus promotes the following ten policies:

- Impose fiscal discipline
- Reform taxation – which basically means no tax for corporates, and an additional tax burden on the middle class
- Liberalize interest rates
- Increase spending on health and education
- Secure property rights
- Privatise government enterprises
- Deregulate markets
- Adopt a competitive exchange rate
- Remove barriers to trade
- Remove barriers to foreign direct investment (see e.g. Ferguson, 2009)

Reaction to globalization has come mainly from social activists, such as NGOs and citizen demonstrations, protests and even public riots (Saul, 2005; Onis & Senses, 2005; Stiglitz, 2006).

Corporations supporting the notion of developing the poorer regions explicitly state that technology such as mobile phones would bring those on the wrong side of the digital divide into the fold of the global economic community. Reports of organizations such as WSIS, Global Knowledge Partnership, World Bank, IMF, UN promote the incorporation of developing regions into the global economic fold. The economic argument among the ICT4D community is that these technologies will enable poor local communities to develop economically. By being connected to this global network, they will be able to find new markets for their produce. In its present form the ICT4D program thus fits neatly with the ideology of globalization.

ORGANICISM

The notion that "markets" drive an economy is based on a more general western cultural notion that reached its height in the 1800s. The idea that markets can regulate an economy implies that markets obtain the human property of "agent". This view holds that inanimate objects obtain a life of their own. It is found in the views of August Schleicher (1821-1868) on language as an organism, published in 1863 shortly after Darwin's theory of evolution, which was first published in 1859 (Darwin 1968). According to Schleicher, language as organism has its own *Sprachseele*, a form of vitalism.

D'Agostino explains organicism as follows: It is the view that:

"... human social institutions have aims, interests and dynamic propensities which cannot be reduced or accounted for in terms of the characteristics of the human beings who participate in them." D'Agostino (1985:148)

This view of inanimate objects obtaining and possessing life, is called organicism, which is a teleological view. Organicism holds to the view that cultural "objects" such as societies, language, markets, music, and many more are structurally independent of human agents. The structuralist movement of the 20th century was implicitly based on these notions, where "structures" were elevated to a supra-historical domain in which they "live". Since Levi-Strauss structuralists tacitly assume organicism as its basis. To a lesser extent it is also present in the structuration of Giddens. His theory of structuration holds that all human action is performed within the context of pre-existing social structures, implying that our free will as agents is restricted by social constraints. This does not imply unilateral determinism, as human agents can indeed change social structures. Nevertheless, the structures exist independently of the individual.

Organicism also underlies neo-conservative and globalist views of capital and the market. Saul (2009) does not label the assumption explicitly as "organicism", but he explains how globalism turned the abstract notion of money into an asset, a tangible asset, in its own right, contrary to what Hume and Adam Smith proposed. Money and economics get a life of their own.

Once organicism is assigned to social institutions, it is easy to fall into the trap of social Darwinism, where the path of development is pre-ordained. And the Nirvana state on this path is identified as western capitalism, meaning that all those other primitive societies not yet reaching this pinnacle must be developed to reach that state. Of course, the pretense is there that the colonial era is gone, so politically incorrect terms, such as "primitive" are no longer used. It was first replaced with "third world countries", and later with "developing countries", where the meaning "development" is restricted to changing local economies into a global economy, ruled by multi-national corporations. More recently the geographical "South" has been used as one pole on the bipole North-South. But "South" also usually includes India, and even China, which are in the northern hemisphere.

CRITIQUE OF ECONOMIC GLOBALIZATION

Bunge (1998) proposes that neo-classical microeconomics is a pseudo-science, as neoclassical economic theory has not changed much for more than a century, and remained uninformed by tremendous developments in the other social sciences. This theory is still caught up in the nineteenth century paradigm that assumes social systems have a life of their own. The assumptions of the neoclassical and neoliberal economic model are: markets are fully rational and free; they are well-informed and equally powerful; they are immune to politics. Economic globalization is an extension of neoclassical microeconomics, and these assumptions are also present in the economic globalization approach.

Broad and Cavanagh (2006) present five criticisms of economic globalization, offered

as myths. I base my discussion loosely on their conceptual categories. The main criticisms of globalism focus on:

1. Indicators and culture
2. Social Darwinism
3. Aid
4. Particular view of the market
5. Binary logic

Indicators and Culture

Among globalists such as Sachs (2008), it is assumed that poverty can be quantified and measured, and the metrics require that standard of living must be measured by money available for spending. Typically GDP (Gross National Product) is used as the metric. GDP is calculated as the sum of:

Consumer Spending + Investment made by industry + Excess of Exports over Imports + Government Spending.

The problem with this formula when used for developing regions is that growth typically shows only the local growth of the middle class. They're very seldom is growth among the poorer classes. So the middle class (only as households, not as individual income within households) and the rich have more spending money, chasing the consumer spending index upwards. It should be noted that the growth in middle class income is based on households which now typically have more than one breadwinner. Household income with single breadwinners has actually continuously declined since the 1970s (Saul 2009). The lack of considering any social stratification shows that GDP cannot be a good measure of success for developing regions.

Apart from this problem, figures showing supposed growth in the developing world are contaminated and skewed by the exceptional growth of the middle class in India and in China.

Media reports mention a new Indian middle class of 250 million people. Such a very large number of people in one country only skews the global development statistics, and gives the impression that globally there is an economic improvement, while in reality in many regions, particularly Africa, poor people actually become poorer. The "success" of globalization for developing countries, as promoted by Sachs, is suspect, to say the least. The Asian growth is not experienced by other regions, especially not by Africa. And even in Asia the poor remain poor, as it is only the educated middle class that now have more spending money, skewing the consumer spending index in the GDP formula.

Using GDP as criterion, many people who have a good quality of life according to the HDI (Human Development Index) would be regarded as poor. Anand and Sen pointed out that market mechanisms do not deal well with public goods (1994: 38). Some properties of HDI are: higher average life expectancy, lower infant and mortality rates, higher literacy rate (Anand & Sen, 1994), none of which is measured by GDP. Self-sustaining subsistence farmers may have enough to eat, may have fresh and clean water, and may actually be happy with their circumstances, yet, using western economic metrics, they would be regarded as poor. Alternatively GNH (Gross National Happiness) could be used (Saul 2009: 23). This concept was introduced as long ago as 1972 by Bhutan's former King Jigme Singye Wangchuck, based not on western Judeo-Christian ideology, but on the principles of Buddhism. Several indicators for measurement other than GDP are available, but reference to them are very scant in ICT4D literature.

Projects that appeal to alleviate poverty of those living on USD1 and USD2 per day are misdirected. The statistics are suspect, and have a bias toward a western capitalist model of economics.

Social Darwinism

Economic globalization assumes that all economic systems progress through time to the same goalposts. As globalization originated in the west, it comes as no surprise that the goalpost is defined as western capitalism. In economic development circles, the goal is to fast track "under-developed" economies to the same goalpost, which is globalized economies and corporatism. This progression from one economic stage to another is based on the view that cultural evolution follows the same path as biological evolution. It also confuses "change" with "improvement", and furthermore equates "improvement" being the change of other systems to becoming more like the target model system, thus progressivism.

The main assumption of social Darwinism is that cultures and societies progress through evolutionary stages. The old-fashioned Euro-American-centric view typically dominates this view. Conflated with the western corporate capitalist model, social Darwinism postulates that the developing world (which is typically regarded as inferior) needs to go through evolutionary stages to reach the pinnacle: that of corporate, western capitalism. In this evolutionary path, it is not only natural selection that offers the mechanism. Technological determinism is also dragged in. It is argued that the introduction of ICT into those poorly developed regions can speed up the "natural selection" toward progress, while progress is typically defined as increased market share. Technological determinists, such as McNamara (2000) regard ICTs as determinants of the sustainable development of individuals, communities and nations.

Social Darwinism, criticized by many, such as Gould (1996, 2006), Rose (2005) and Ehrlich (2000), is based on the assumption that cultural systems change in the same way as biological systems. Darwin's notion of evolutionary biological change is driven by the mechanism of "natural selection", and it is assumed by social Darwinists that societies change in the same manner. This assumption is misplaced as it overgeneralizes a mechanism that operates in a particular sphere (the biological) by imposing it on a very different sphere (the cultural). It transfers the properties of one system (a physical system) to another (a cultural system). The mechanism of "natural selection" does not even operate on all physical systems, so why would it operate on social systems? For example, "natural selection" did not operate on the level of the creation of matter in the early stages of the universe, and neither on the formation of stars. The biological selection process is a slow one. Cultural change, on the contrary, is very quick. Cultures can adopt and absorb new ideas literally overnight. There is no mechanism to explain cultural adoption, as there is for biological adaptation. Natural selection divides into species, while cultures do not divide, but assimilate. The only explanation for the assimilation is that that which is perceived to be of some benefit will be adapted. This is only in the conscious sense. Cars have been adopted from other societies that used them. Cellphones have been adopted from societies that first had them as useful tools by other societies. But many aspects are not consciously adopted. In this respect one thinks of values of other societies that silently "penetrate" a particular society. This "penetration" is not agent-like. It is the adopters who are agents, not the values, and they may adopt without being able to offer conscious reasons why they are adopting.

If this line of argument is acceptable, it means that societies will not of necessity adopt ICT systems because of some assumed pre-ordained evolutionary path from subsistence economies to corporate economies. It means that cultures will adopt ICT for their own purposes, if they indeed absorb ICT as enforced on them. After adopting ICT, they may wish to adapt it to meet their local needs.

A technology may be used for a purpose different to that envisaged. This reminds me of an observation reported by Jarred Diamond (2005:

285) among New Guineans when they got hold of a pencil. It was used for a variety of purposes, all excluding writing. Uses ranged from nose-rings to hair decoration. Similarly, ICT systems deployed by western agents in developing contexts may lead to uses other than the intended ones, including no use at all. This is already happening. Mobile phone uptake extends social networking opportunities, while not much economic activity happens as promoted by ICT4D evangelists.

ICT systems should be used by local communities as they see fit. Success should be measured not by metrics determined by givers, but by the local communities themselves.

Progress, Change and Progressivism

The basic tenet of Social Darwinism is typical of the Victorian mindset of progress, defined as improvement. The great proponent of this idea was Herbert Spencer (1823-1903), who was in fact also the first to coin terms such as "evolution" (which to him meant progress) and "survival of the fittest" (for which Darwin preferred "natural selection") - see Gould (2006) for a discussion on this. The amazing pace of development of the Industrial Revolution in England provided a backdrop for such thinking. Spencer saw change as improvement in many different aspects, ranging from biological systems and technological systems to social systems. In his mind there is progress from lower classed societies to higher classed societies, and of course his euro-centric view of the world put the English right on the pinnacle. During this era colonialism was also rife, and non-European societies were regarded as primitive, not yet advanced as far as the Europeans. Such societies were still far behind on the ladder of social evolution.

Today, in an era of supposed political correctness, in an era where people are generally regarded as equal, the notion of progress still underlies many development projects. The word "development" itself implies a change towards a more positive state. It is not a neutral term. In ICT4D "development" and "progress" are typically defined in terms of Western culture - its capitalist economic worldview, its organizational administration models, its popular music, product brand names, and so on. Add the notion of technological determinism to this mix, and ICT becomes a necessity to draw underdeveloped regions into the fold of modern consumerism. It is tacitly assumed that all cultures will actually reach the same state as western cultures, that in fact, they should. Cultures not sharing this view, are regarded as underdeveloped, or undeveloped, which in the world of being politically correct, is a euphemism for being savage or barbaric - words that are no longer used, but their concepts still seem to be present. The result is that much effort is spent to convince such cultures that they need to globalize, adopt the western model of economics, use ICT, and that then they would be well on the way to their development to the state in which the west requires them to be.

De-growth is a radical criticism of classic development's reliance on economism and progressivism (Latouche, 2007). This "program" wishes to reintroduce cultural inventiveness and creativity which have been blocked up by the totalitarianism of classic development. Its notion of thinking locally instead of globally fits in with the trend of growing neo-nationalism identified by Saul (2009).

Again, the implication for ICT4D is that once a giver has deployed ICT systems, the locals should use these tools creatively for their own purposes.

Another quite opposite view to the notion of progress would be that cultures do in fact change, but that there is no judgment that could be made on whether this change is positive. It just changes. The members of the culture would assign a value-judgment for themselves - they will decide whether it is positive or not. Of course, outsiders may also have a view, but this view cannot be enforceable. There is no particular reason to like

another culture. But the civil view would be that one would allow room for alternative views. If the path of "development" (i.e. change) of one culture differs from that of another, there should be no concern at all.

Similarly, technologies that are new to particular cultures may be adopted or adapted, or even rejected. When a new technology is made available, the particular society should itself decide what to do with it. This neutral stance to cultural change and the introduction of new technologies is in my view the most moral position.

Given such a neutral view, then why being involved in attempts to deploy ICTs in developing regions? My particular view is that technologies may make life easier in some or other way. For example, being able to pick up a phone and phone a migrant relative working in a distant region enables personal contact at much reduced effort. It is more personal, and more efficient than writing a snailmail letter. And a mobile phone has an advantage over a fixed line phone. As long as there is reception and one has a device to phone with, one can remain in contact regardless of the location. This makes life easier. Promoting ICT in regions not having them is also to expose local communities about possibilities. This should not be sales-talk, with the goal of convincing the communities of the qualities of a product. It is rather about investigating and determining the most pressing needs of a community along participatory lines, and then adapting and adopting a possible ICT solution by demonstrating how this could make life easier, leaving it up to the community to take this up or not – to adopt it or adapt it. The underlying framework should be based on techno-utilitarianism.

Aid

Broad and Cavanagh (2006) quote William Easterly's calculation that between 1960 and 2003 rich countries spent USD568 billion in aid to end poverty in Africa, yet poverty increased on this continent. African GDP per person between 1950 and 1980 rose by 1.8%, but between 1980 and 2000 when globalism was intensely promoted and applied, GDP fell by 6.2% (Saul 2009:103). Sachs of course is of the opinion that aid works, even though he states that economic growth in Africa has been the lowest of all regions since 1820 (Sachs 2005). Saul is cynical about statistics used for claims of the success of aid, referring to an American National Bureau of Economic Research report of 2000 that claimed that aid reduced extreme poverty (of living on USD1 per day) to only 350 million people, while in 2004 the World Bank gave this number as 1.1 billion, yet GDP is lower. The statistics differ radically, so which statement is to be believed? Saul concludes with the words of Krugman that economic statistics are a subgenre of science fiction (Saul 2009: 49-50). Easterly (2006) argues that aid for large projects does not help, and should be channeled to smaller localized projects. Moyo (2009) is even more outspoken on aid, and argues aid should be stopped.

Of course it is not aid as such that is problematic, but the kind of aid that is suspect. Financial aid with fine print negatively affecting the recipient country, benefiting some corporations of the donor country, seems to be common practice (Bond, 2006), and is immoral. Financial aid, and even products as aid granted without a detailed analysis of grassroots needs is also misplaced. Unfortunately guerilla consultants and advisers are to be blamed for improper advise to donors. "Experts" rush into a country for a week or two, make an assessment and recommendations, which when implemented devastate such a country (Stiglitz, 2002). Saul (2009: 104) relates an event when he shared an airplane trip to Thailand with an IMF representative flying to that country for a quick visit with the aim of assessing its economical and political position, which would affect how the IMF would treat that country, but not knowing much about the country at all. This kind of guerilla adviser does more harm than any good,

as it is impossible to make a proper assessment within such a short time. Yet, this is typically how advisers evaluate the needs of a particular country or region, also when it comes to ICT4D and it is symptomatic of any top-down approach. Some consultant advises a government to deploy a telecentre or MPCC without proper consultation with local communities, or research into the context and needs. The services are dropped down by government and expect them to work. They don't.

The kind of aid that should be offered should follow the wisdom of the ancient saying accredited to Laozi (in the west also known as Lao Tse or Lao-Tzu): "If you give a man a fish, you feed him for a day. If you teach a man to fish, you feed him for a lifetime." In this regard, Moyo (2009) argues that instead of donating mosquito nets, it would have been much better to assist the local mosquito net industry in their production, for example by offering micro-finance to expand the business, thereby employing more locals. Don't give fish or mosquito nets or ICT; enable local skills to deal with such matters. The matter of ICT is of course more complex, as it first requires an infrastructure that is typically absent in developing regions.

Perhaps aid should go directly into developing such infrastructures, as the Chinese now do in Africa. Aid should be used for developing alternative technical solutions. Perhaps global 24/7 connectivity is not as important as connectivity within a rural community.

Particular View of the Market

Economic globalization is dominated by a neoliberal view of economics - the Washington Consensus. During the decades when this view of economics ruled, instead of growth, there had been a worldwide decline in the world economy, unemployment rose, and the divide became larger. The only beneficiaries were the new managerial elite and technocrats, as Saul (2005) calls them. The main problem with this view of globalization is that it is reductionist, as it is based on a particular theory of economics, without acknowledging the cultural nature of economics as a human artifact. Onis and Senses (2005) point out the irony of one of the cornerstones of globalization. It was supposed to rule out corruption by being based on the notion of a free market that controls itself, yet as Saul (2005) points out, the lack of proper controls and government regulations almost certainly offers a breeding ground for corruption.

One of the results of globalization was to reduce government social responsibility, as the independent all powerful market was going to take over those functions through privatization programs. It may be time again that governments reassert themselves and reclaim their social responsibilities. As in times before globalization rendered them powerless, they again should develop social infrastructures, which in this case would include the development of ICT infrastructures to also reach remote communities.

Programs and projects that promote the deployment of ICT4D with the aim of incorporating developing regions into a particular view, especially if that view is further dominated by a particular view of the market, are doomed to fail. Many such projects also state they wish to be economically sustainable.

One implication of my proposal is that the dialogue on sustainability should be revisited. In ICT4D it is mostly economic sustainability that is promoted – a telecentre must become financially viable and sustainable. We should question why the same demands is not required for public transport, which in most countries runs at a loss, and is hugely sponsored by governments. If transport networks can be sponsored with tax money, why not communication networks? If ICT can be a very useful tool enhancing the cognitive and social quality of life of citizens, policies on ICT should not focus on sustainability, but on the good that will flow from such tools.

Binary Logic

There is a logical flaw underlying the assumptions of economic globalization. It promotes a particular economic model, and regards all other models as irrelevant. The Washington Consensus unilaterally forced down solutions that were regarded as the only proper medicine for "unhealthy" economies - while "healthy" was defined as a particular western capitalist model. There was no room for cultural variance, and absolutely none for any alternative economic models. The logic applied is a logic of exclusion: the model of the Washington Consensus is correct, all the other models are wrong.

By the same argument, ICT4D cannot be based on the notion of one size fits all. ICT, as neutral human artefact, can be used in many different ways by many different communities and cultures. For each the criteria of success would be different. One kind of ICT solution should not be elevated to the position of global solution, to the exclusion of other possibilities, methods and approaches. Economic globalization forgets that economics is a social and cultural construct, and cultural variance would by nature result in a variety of economic models.

Post-Washington Consensus

In the early 1990s the neoliberal orthodoxy foundation of the Washington Consensus was increasingly questioned among the intelligentsia, and toward the new millennium, by social activists. The Washington Consensus failed to explain the successes of regions (such as Malaysia and Brazil) that did not comply with perceived requirements of the World Bank and IMF, which hold that state interventionist strategies necessarily work against long-term public interest.

The standard position was gradually also modified, and resulted in what some call the Post-Washington Consensus, as it began to also include discussions on poverty and governance. Other more cynical commentators call it by other names, such as SIN (socio-institutional neoliberalism - Carroll 2009).

Important for the Post-Washington Consensus view was the pressure on government performance. Onis and Senses (2005) regard one characteristic of this new approach as one that recognizes the complementing roles of states and the market – whereas the neo-liberal view idealized markets. The new view also recognized that markets need to be regulated and accepted national developmentalism. But as Carroll points out, it seems to mold the "political terrain in the underdeveloped world towards the establishment and sustenance of liberal market societies" (Carroll, 2009: 448). It is thus still the same paradigm, with a bit of social consideration now added to the mix.

Onis and Senses (2005) argue that the Post-Washington Consensus is also a failure. They criticize the Post-Washington Consensus as not going far enough, as it does not address asset or wealth distribution, unemployment, ownership structures and the structure of power at the global level.

Although the Post-Washington Consensus at least revisits some notions of the Washington Consensus, which is a positive move, it is:

"a rather narrow and technocratic approach towards state–market interactions at both the national and global levels. It takes the existing power structure as predetermined. Hence, it fails to address the fundamental power relations and asymmetries of power that exist between classes at the level of the nation state, and powerful versus less powerful states in the global economy, although it is these very power relations that need to be challenged if key development issues are to be tackled in a comprehensive manner." (Onis and Senses 2005:286).

The World Bank reinvented itself by focusing on community development channeling funds to NGOs and governments. Kane suspects this to be an image exercise:

"Because of massive criticism, in recent years the Bank has been attempting to change its image but, in essence, continues as before to impose its same discredited economic recipe on countries throughout the globe." (Kane 2008:205). *"I believe it is important for radical, and not so radical, community workers not to be blinded or seduced by such posturing and help challenge people to see the reality behind the spin."* (Kane 2008: 206).

The apparent interest of the Post-Washington Consensus to alleviate poverty seems to be loaded with rhetoric, but lacking any action. It seems to focus on increased capital flows, aid, and market access for developing countries. But as Moyo (2009) argues, aid is one of the major causes of poverty, especially in Africa. Onis and Senses (2005) think that among neoliberal globalizers there is no willpower to investigate the causes of poverty. Only the ready-made one-size fits all solutions peculiar to a specific economic model seem to be recommend as remedy for poverty. The IMF's insistence on primary budget plus surplus opposes any notion of poverty alleviation as this approach leaves no room for social sector spending. A major factor in causing unemployment in developing regions is due to the interference of Washington Consensus players in the form of transnationals which are protected by the rules of globalization and after introduction dominate local markets as monopolies and oligopolies (Saul, 2009). These corporations do little for local development, and profits are channeled back to the global head office, while such institutions pay very little tax that governments would typically use for local projects.

Stiglitz (2006: 198-210) proposes six remedies to fix globalization.

- Corporate social responsibility – corporates should not be responsible only to shareholders
- Limiting the powers of corporations – the trend during globalization to create mo-

nopolies by closing down competition must be stopped
- Improving corporate governance – laws should be introduced to govern the behavior of corporates to be more responsible
- Global laws for a global economy – the local nature of laws result in corporations moving their head offices to where they would have the least legal hassles. If there are global laws, they cannot move anywhere to escape responsibility
- Reducing the scope for corruption - this is not only for the politicians in developing regions who are known for corruption; this is for corruption within corporations, as evident from the many corporate scandals over the past decade

The dominant approach of economic globalists, as aggressively promoted by the Washington Consensus as well as the post-Washington Consensus, has failed. ICT4D operates within this paradigm. If this paradigm does not work, we need another one.

ECONOMIC THEORIES: RATIONAL AND IRRATIONAL MAN

One of the basic tenets of economic globalization is that states should have less control over money matters. The assumption is that markets are rational, and can therefore self-regulate. This assumption has been around for almost a century now, and is promoted as being self-evident, and a universal truth. But it cannot explain the many stock market crashes and financial crises over the past century. Neither can it explain the growth of economies, such as Malaysia, Brazil, that are not based on the neoliberal assumptions of the Washington Consensus. Assigning to a market the property of being rational is based on the wrong assumption of organicism.

The dominant economic theory used by western capitalism is that of rational man, who makes rational decisions about economic matters and hence humans may be labeled *homo economicus*. This view is the foundation of economic globalism, an economic paradigm that originated with Adam Smith in the late 1700s and John Stuart Mill in the early 1800s. Man as an objective rational being is one of the Western myths which permeated all disciplines of thought during the age of reason. This view rests on a hosts of assumptions, the most important perhaps that logic is supra-historical, a Platonic ontological being detached from human brains. It therefore cannot account for cultural variance, not for logic as being content-dependent, nor for the modern neurobiological view of the individual plasticity of the brain which means that individual brains develop uniquely, implying that there is no universal logic.

That decision-making is an emotional matter has been demonstrated by neuro-scientists, such as Antonio Damasio (1994, 2004). Behavioral economists come to the same conclusion. Even our economic decision-making is irrational (Ariely, 2008).

That economics is not rational is shown by practical as well as theoretical evidence. George Soros, certainly one of the most successful financial investors reckons in *The new paradigm for financial markets: the credit crash of 2008 and what it means*: "Not only do market participants operate with a bias, but their bias can also influence the course of events." quoted in Ferguson (2009: 317). Ferguson concludes that this points to the irrationality and biases of investors.

The rise of behavioral economics as a discipline, and the results from its findings indicate that economical matters are not particularly rational. Among others, Dan Ariely shows that contrary to the conventional interpretation of economics as a rational enterprise,

"... we are really far less rational than standard economic theory assumes. Moreover, these ir-

rational behaviors of ours are neither random nor senseless. They are systematic, and since we repeat them again and again, predictable." (Ariely, 2008:xx)

The basic assumption of the economic globalization paradigm, and standard economic models that are biased toward western capitalism (which assumes that economics is rational), rests on weak evidence and reflects more about ideology than well-founded theory. Human behavior may show patterns, but these are not necessarily formally logical, nor rational in the sense that participants in the economy make "objective" rational choices among options.

Apart from these problems, the classic economic theory of Adam Smith of perfect markets is an idealization. In the real world nothing is ever perfect.

HOMO ECONOMICUS

Rational economics commodotizes people by calling them 'social capital'. The rights and obligations of people are conditioned by market parlance (see e.g. Carroll, 2009). This dehumanizes people.

The notion of *homo economicus* assumes at least two major fundamental premises, and basically makes two mistakes. It does not account for cultural notions of what trade is, and neither for the position that there is no objective logical system in the brains of humans. Decisions are not objectively rational, but culturally biased, and dependent on emotion. Anthropological studies since Edwin Boas, Claude Levi-Strauss, and briefly, a wide-range of cultural studies conducted since the early twentieth century, indicate that economical models are cultural, and as culture develops through time, must be historical in nature. The market economy is not the only possible custom. Many cultures follow a gift economy. If this is true, ICT4D shouldn't focus on economic

"upliftment", but on the social and psychological dimensions of people in communities.

One premise of the neo-classical paradigm of economics is that humans are money-making machines. Built on this premise is another: the particular method of making money should be western capitalism. Proponents of the second assumption have obviously not read the history of economics, neither contemporary cultural economics. Being products of western capitalist business schools, the capitalist status quo is dogma. There are many methods for making money, not only western capitalism. Money, of course, is merely a token to which some value is assigned. And instead of exchanging a basket full of eggs for half a ham, we could agree to exchange tokens. Adam Smith's insight was to verbalize that the marketplace would decide what value that token would have. The demand in the village market would determine how many eggs a ham would cost. If I get more ham for my eggs, I make "money". Does this make me a capitalist? No! Or perhaps, Yes! The answer will depend on which ideology of capitalism one adheres to, and within a particular ideology, which theory - there is no consensus on the characteristics of the notion of capitalism. The basic concepts used in economics, production, capital, labor, goods, traded, market and profits are all value-laden, and have often quite distinct meanings in different perspectives. Even non-capitalist ideologies (as defined by classic capitalism), such as Marxism, use these terms, often with different semantic properties.

The assumption of singling out a particular cultural model of economics is the driving force of globalization and corporatism. It is reductionist, by limiting complex human behavior to a single system, namely economics. It conveniently forgets economics is just one of the possible human enterprises, that it is a created social system with a history, that it changes through time, and that it is not an agent, or autopoietic biological system, to use Maturana and Varela's 1980 term. Without humans, there is no economical system. If this statement is true, it demonstrates that at least the human biological system and social system are prior to the economic system.

We are not *homo economicus*, and even if we were, we are not of the sub-species *homo economicus globalicus* – not that there is such a Latin word! We may indeed be *homo sapiens*, the thinking man, but we are also *homo socialis*. We cannot be reduced to one of our properties. We are a complex whole.

If this line of argument is acceptable, it is clear that ICT systems should not be designed only for corporate and organizational systems. The metaphors used for PCs show this bias: desk-top computer, files, directories, etc. All these metaphors show a bias toward office work. ICT systems should primarily be designed as social systems, or rather, as tools to enable humans to reduce effort in their social activities. Of course commerce would be one such activity. Of course ordinary people need to use organizational services, such as access to government information. But such systems should not be elevated to the position found in media propaganda, or views such as those that elevate mobile phones to the position of neo-modernist holy grail; the so-called e-commerce, and m-commerce systems that will enable the poor to become rich. The assumptions of globalization are particular cultural-historical notions, and it is immoral to force such a western view onto developing regions, as economic globalization then becomes just another form of neo-colonization.

Just enabling an inhabitant of a remote village to keep in touch with a migrant family member is already a major achievement, and a success story. Before the use of digital ICT the villager might have had to travel for a whole day to the nearest communication spot in order to send a letter, or message. Capitalists argue that ICT would enable the villager to save a whole day of labor, and not lose a day's wages. This may be true, but the principle of least effort turns this argument upside down. Even if the villager did not save money,

he would have been spared the discomfort and effort of traveling. It is ease of use that is the moral obligation; not saving money. Of course, if ease of use also saves money, that is a positive spin-off, but that would not be the goal.

The view that humans are economic machines is based on organicism, which assigns to economics a life of its own, independent from the social and cultural endeavors of humans. It turns economics into a supra-historical entity, that has an existence of its own apart from humans. From such a position it is then an easy step to argue that the economic model favored by the politically dominant culture must be the preferred and proper model. During the most recent history of humankind, this particular model was western capitalism, finding expression in economic globalization. Development programs were introduced against the framework of this paradigm. Within this paradigm ICT4D is just one development domain, focusing on technology.

But economic globalization has failed – with reference to its promises. Aid has failed. Most ICT4D projects have failed. It is time to stop, reflect and to introduce a new paradigm for "development"; a development not focusing on one cultural endeavor of humans, namely economics, but on humans as psychologically and socially whole and complex beings. Within such a framework economic "development" addresses just one of the possible sub-systems of human endeavors; what is to be developed is decided locally; and with reference to technology, it is a tool to be applied to the needs of local cultures, as determined by themselves.

TECHNOLOGY AND SOCIETY

Alampay (2006) links the information society to modernization and globalization. He explains modernization as societal development through a series of stages with different technological bases of production, and points out that this is a peculiar western concept. This view rests on social Darwinism, and exemplifies the dominant view in discussions on ICT4D.

The *ITU/UNCTAD 2007 World Information Society Report: Beyond WSIS* (Biggs et al 2007) does not argue the case for an information society, but merely assumes that there indeed is an information society. Its main concern is that "developing countries should not be left behind in the new Information Society." (2007: 13). WSIS promoted the establishment of a measuring system (an index) of ICT for Development (ICT4D). There was no argument supporting the view that we indeed live in an information era, nor making explicit its assumptions. That "developing countries should not be left behind" sounds like neo-colonialism, and it implies that some countries are ahead. It also assumes that the path of the west is the path all communities must follow, and that this path is the only proper path.

Castells (2004a) argues that it is misleading to talk about an information age to refer to contemporary societies, as all societies have been historically been "...based on information and knowledge as the source of power, wealth, and meaning..." (2004a:7). Castells revised his own original stance, admitting that he then ignorantly used the term information age for the new era. What is new is not the prevalence of information, but the technological tools to handle the information. Castells calls the new technological paradigm *informationalism*.

The information age in which we live is called thus because of the powerful tools we now have available to us to create, access and disseminate information. We invent technology to make life easier, and although social change may introduce new ways of doing things, this is not necessarily technological determinism (Heeks 1999, Grossberg, Struwig, Tlabela 1999). The goal of technology is to make life easier - the techno-utilitarian view.

ICT innovations ease effort as far as human cognitive endeavors are concerned. The role of ICT in a community is to facilitate handling information. ICT is a set of tools for extending the powers of the individual human mind in a social context. ICT is a tool set that enhances the total complexity of the mind and cultural endeavors, of which economics is just one among many. The one among many cannot be elevated to a superior position.

From a social roles perspective, humans have many roles. One set of roles may include to be a parent, an engineer, a feminist, a Muslim, a painter – all these things in one person (Sen 2006). Economics may play a role in the fulfilment of these roles, but only in a supporting manner. Economics does not define the roles, only reduce or enhance the ability to execute them. It may be easier for the parent to raise children with money; easier for the painter to obtain painting equipment and utensils. But economics does not take away these roles if there is no money. Humans are thus socially also complex, and ICT as a tool may facilitate performing these roles. ICT's primary task is thus to facilitate the cognitive worlds of individuals, as well as the worlds of their social roles. The measure of success should be on these worlds. And of course, economics is one small part of this world.

FOR THE GREATER GOOD... FOR THE GOOD OF THE PEOPLE

So if we should not deploy ICT systems in remote and rural communities for the sake of consumerism, corporatism, or globalization, why should we bother? I propose that the metric should focus on the principle of lesser effort. Does ICT make life easier? The metrics for assessing success in this regard would be determined by the local community. This approach is based on the utilitarian philosophy introduced in the late 1700s by Jeremy Bentham (1748– 1832). He had an interest in public morality as in his era there were many matters he regarded as socially unjust. In contrast to his contemporary philosophers, particularly the German romantics such as Immanuel Kant (1724 - 1804) whose philosophy remained in the intellectual study at the intellectual desk for an abstract ideal life, Bentham was a practical philosopher who tried to apply his ideas to real life.

A utilitarian view judges actions by their utility, while its popular maxim is *the greatest good for the greatest number of people*, which implies a democracy of some kind, not national, but down to village level. How can we determine what the greatest good is? It would be relative to different communities. People on the grassroots level need to decide for themselves what is good for them. What is good is defined with reference to their "happiness". The happiness approach I propose should allow for local decisions for the definition of happiness. There may be universal traits of happiness, but local communities should have the power to decide that for themselves. Some culturally biased definition of happiness cannot be enforced on local communities, especially if the enforcement is political – by the powerhouses, such as neo-colonizers, or despotic governments, which are typically ideologically driven.

That happiness is about saving effort is not such a new idea. As long ago as with Adam Smith, he suggested:

"The real price of everything, what everything really costs to the man who wants to acquire it, is the toil and trouble of acquiring it. What everything is really worth to the man who has acquired it, and who wants to dispose of it or exchange it for something else, is the toil and trouble which it can save to himself, and which it can impose upon other people. What is bought with money or with goods purchased by labor, as much as what we acquire by the toil of our own body." (Smith, 2003:43-44, first published in 1776).

The value of something is the value one assigns to it, and could be measured by how much toil and trouble (i.e. energy) one is prepared to spend to

obtain it. If technology assists us in reducing toil and trouble, we can reach happiness much easier. To save on toil or labor is to reduce effort, and in Smith's sense that has economic benefit. But I would go further than Smith. Reducing effort is not restricted to saving energy in the context of work, but in all spheres of life. Traveling by car instead of by foot for leisure also reduces effort. The effort saving I have in mind is about life in general, while Smith's toil or effort is just a component of the totality of the effort. The utilitarian view I propose is also not as abstract or hedonistic as that of Bentham, Smith and John Stuart Mill. My utilitarian view is specifically restricted to the use of technology, a techno-utilitarianism.

The utilitarianism of John Stuart Mill (1806 – 1873), seems to imply a kind of hedonistic happiness or pleasure meant for all, as utility is defined as the method to obtain happiness or pleasure. Dacey (2008) argues that happiness should rather be defined in terms of personal choice to live a meaningful life.

"... personal freedom of choice is the best policy not because all choices are equal, but because individual experiments in living are the best method for humanity to discover which choices are superior." (Dacey, 2008:180).

One can only discover which choices are superior if one has knowledge that can be used to make informed choices. The more information or knowledge one has about a matter about which one has to make a decision, the better that decision could potentially be. Choice of course does not lead to happiness. But an informed choice may lead to a better decision, which may result in happiness. For example, an ICT system that informs a farmer of a better method to spray against caterpillar to protect his pawpaws, may result in a better harvest, resulting in happiness (White African 2009). The content-poor situations of the developing world deny people living in such contexts access to information, and consequently good decision-making. ICT facilitates access to knowledge. ICT could play a huge empowering role by making various channels of communication available for such people to access information.

As humans we care for more than just happiness. We have other values as well. Of course, if life is made easier because we have to spend less energy or effort on some action, that may make us happy. Or we may just be relieved that we now do not need to spend a whole day traveling to the nearest fax machine to communicate, as such a service is available in my local village. The utilitarian position I propose is of the latter kind. The goal is not happiness in the classic utilitarian sense, but happiness that results from less effort. In this sense the utilitarian position I propose is restricted to the use of technology and tools. Technology can make life easier. As we have to spend less energy on an action, we feel "relieved", which is a positive emotion, and thus generates happiness. Technology enables us to spend less human energy on actions. This techno-utilitarian approach rewrites the "greatest good for the greatest number of people" as "the least effort for the greatest number of people". The moral imperative for deploying ICT systems in rural and remote communities is to enable communities to save human energy. This view of development fits in more with Giddens' *third way* – although he did not put it in these terms - than with a technological deterministic way.

There is no absolute or objective definition of what would be less effort. Properties of this notion would be both cultural, situational and personal. It would be cultural as there would be a historic component. A hunter-gatherer society would have a different set of properties for what they would regard as offering less effort than would be regarded by an agricultural society. It is also situational. Consider two agricultural villages, with almost exactly the same properties. One is on a transport network, the other not. For the village not being able to share the transport network, reducing travel effort would most likely be the dominant need. The community would

need to define the set of properties of what it would regard as reducing effort. And it would be personal. Freedom of choice is one of the highest human values, and choice in this context should always be personal.

The same approach would hold concerning ICT4D. If ICT is just a tool used for accessing and sharing knowledge, the kind of access (i.e. media modes, such as voice, text, image), and the knowledge content that enables empowerment that would result in happiness, would be local, and culture dependent.

The techno-utilitarian approach is a type of consequentialism as the moral worth of an action is determined by its outcome, in this case less effort. This position I restrict to the use of technology, and do not extend it to other spheres of human behavior. So as far as the implementation of a technology is concerned, I propose that we adhere to a consequentialist program, and that the yardstick by which its success should be measured is based on the principle of least effort. Dacey (2008) argues that consequentialism is the only method to judge the morality of actions. Nonconsequentialist theories assume an external set of criteria to judge the morality of actions – either a platonic ideal, or religious dogma, or in the case of globalization, of markets ruling human behavior, and I would add, ICT4D projects. They require an external judge, and cannot show the value of a moral by its intrinsic action. The only way to determine that intrinsic value is to discuss and debate assumptions socially. My view sits peacefully within such a framework.

The emphasis is not on effort itself, but the value attached to the effort, which is something quite different. Of course an individual may assign a value to his effort, but what I have in mind here is a saving on physical or mental effort. Access to and sharing of relevant knowledge saves effort. Relevant and appropriate knowledge would lead to better decision-making in all spheres of life, resulting in an easier life and in happiness. This is what ICT4D should be about.

CONCLUSION

Over the past half a century USD2.3 trillion was spent on aid, but there is little to show for this. The dominant paradigm against which such aid was offered to the developing world was economic globalization, which embraces corporatism and western capitalism, and more specifically a particular model, known as the Washington Consensus.

The reconceived Washington Consensus model, with its emphasis on attempts to alleviate poverty, and going under the banner of Post-Washington Consensus is also suspect, while philanthrocapitalism is a branch of this approach. This dominant paradigm is based on shaky assumptions. It neglects the importance of cultural differences, and assumes that one economic models must fit all cultures. It makes the mistake of assuming cultural Darwinism – that all cultures follow the same same path of cultural evolution, that the west has already reached this pinnacle, and that other cultures could be assisted to skip some intermediate stages and join the globalization bandwagon. It confuses change with progress, leading to progressivism. The program of attempts to bridge "divides" also suffers from this confusion. The larger philosophical framework against which these models operate is still based on Platonic ideals and forms, and its subsequent nineteenth century organicism in which a particular economic model becomes a suprahistorical entity with a life of its own. Against such a backdrop aid programs are managed by "planners" who "know the best answer", instead of allowing systems to evolve naturally from the bottom up in democratic fashion ("de-growth"), and locally according to the cultural needs of the locals. Aid actually disables, instead of enabling, as the method is upside down. Humans are not economic machines (*homo economicus*), and neither are markets rational.

Governments in developing regions are typically too poor to develop ICT infrastructures, especially digital ones such as computer and mobile phone networks. Corporations will not do this either, as the return on investment in rural areas is too small. This means that the billions of the rural poor will not be connected, except through aid. But, as we have seen, aid according to the current paradigm does not work. Aid for ICT4D will need to be deployed according to a very different paradigm. I proposed a value system in which technology is used to ease effort to make knowledge available, and to serve social needs. If an ICT system can reduce effort in any sphere in life, it is a success. ICTs should not be deployed primarily for economic reasons, but firstly for cognitive and social reasons. If local communities benefit economically as well, that is a bonus. The principle of least effort should be the guide.

What is regarded as effort cannot be decided by outside agencies, but should be determined by communities themselves. Development Informatics theoreticians and practitioners could then design systems that address those needs. These systems will not necessarily be the same as those developed for corporate use, or home use in highly developed economies. The systems will need a drastic redesign, focusing on particular local needs. Such systems would be local knowledge repositories of global knowledge, systems of communication, and focused on local connectivity to enhance social communications and relationships.

The role of Development Informatics in the arena of ICT4D is to create frameworks and systems to make this possible, and should be based on a techno-utilitarian approach with a focus on social and psychological development.

REFERENCES

Abraham, R. (2007). Mobile Phones and Economic Development: Evidence from the Fishing Industry in India. *Information Technologies and International Development*, *4*(1), 5–17. doi:10.1162/itid.2007.4.1.5

Adria, M., Bakardjieva, M., Poitras Pratt, Y., & Mitchell, D. (2006). *The Constructive Role of Researchers in the Social Shaping of Technology in Communities*. Paper presented at 3rd Prato International Community Informatics Conference. Retrieved December 2006 from http://www.ccnr.net/?q=node/123

Alampay, E.A. (2006). Beyond access to ICTs: Measuring capabilities in the information society. *International Journal of Education and Development using Information and Communication Technology, 2*(3), 4-22.

Anand, S., & Sen, A. (1994). *Sustainable human development: concepts and priorities*. New York: United Nations Development Programme.

Ariely, D. (2008). *Predictably irrational. The hidden forces that shape our decisions*. London: Harper.

Biggs, P., Kelly, T., Lee, S-H., Lozanova, Y., Nemoto, T., Sund, C., Hamdi, M., & Minges, M. (2007). ITU/UNCTAD 2007 World Information Society Report: Beyond WSIS.

Bond, P. (2006). *Looting Africa. The economics of exploitation*. London: Zed Books.

Broad, R., & Cavanagh, J., (2006). The hijacking of the development debate. How Friedman and Sachs got it wrong. *World Policy Institute*, 21-30.

Brooks, T. (Ed.). (2008). *The global justice reader*. London: Blackwell Publishing.

Bunge, M. (1998). *Social science under debate*. Toronto: University of Toronto Press.

Carroll, T. (2009). 'Social Development' as Neoliberal Trojan Horse: The World Bank and the Kecamatan Development Program in Indonesia. *Development and Change, 40*(3), 447–466. doi:10.1111/j.1467-7660.2009.01561.x

Castells, M. (2001). *The Internet Galaxy: reflections on the Internet*. Oxford, UK: Blackwell.

Castells, M. (Ed.). (2004). *The network society*. Northampton, MA: Edward Elgar.

Castells, M. (2004a). Informationalism, networks, and the network society: a theoretical blueprint. In Castells, M. (Ed.), *The network society: A cross-cultural perspective* (pp. 3–45).

D'Agostino, F. (1985). Ontology and explanation in historical Linguistics. *Philosophy of the Social Sciences, 15*, 147–165. doi:10.1177/004839318501500202

Dacey, A. (2008). *The secular conscience. Why beliefs belong in public life*. New York: Prometheus Books.

Damasio, A. R. (1994). *Descartes' error. Emotion, reason and the human brain*. New York: Avon Books.

Damasio, A. R. (2004). *Looking for Spinoza. Joy, sorrow and the feeling brain*. London: Vintage.

Darwin, C. (1968 / 1859). *The origin of species*. Harmondsworth, Middlesex: Penguin.

De Haan, A. (1999). Social exclusion: towards an holistic understanding of deprivation. In

De Haan, A. (2001). Social exclusion: enriching the understanding of deprivation. In World development report 2001 forum on inclusion, justice and poverty reduction. Retrieved October 2008 from http://www.sussex.ac.uk/cspt/documents/issue2-2.pdf

De Soto, H. (1989). *The other path: the economic answer to terrorism*. New York: Basic Books.

Diamond, J. (1987). The Worst mistake in the history of the human race. *Discover*, 64–66.

Diamond, J. (2005). *Collapse. How societies choose to fail or survive*. London: Penguin.

Easterly, W. (2006). *The white man's burden. Why the west's efforts to aid the rest have done so much ill and so little good*. Oxford: Oxford Univ Press.

Edwards, M., (2008). Philanthrocapitalism: after the goldrush. *OpenDemocracy* 20-03-2008.

Ehrlich, P. J. (2000). *Human natures. Genes, cultures and the human prospect.* New York: Penguin.

Ferguson, N. (2009). *The ascent of money. A financial history of the world.* London: Penguin Books.

Foucault, M. (1972). *The archaeology of knowledge.* London: Tavistock Publications.

Friedman, T. L. (2004). *The world is flat: a brief history of the twenty-first century.* New York: Farrar, Straus and Giroux.

Gates, B. (2008). How to fix capitalism. *Time, 172*(6), 24–29.

Giddens, A. (1984). *The Constitution of Society.* Los Angeles: Univ California Press.

Godin, B. (2008). The information economy: the history of a concept through its measurement, 1949–2005. *History and Technology, 24*(3), 255–287. doi:10.1080/07341510801900334

Gould, S. J. (1996). *The mismeasure of man.* New York: WW Norton.

Gould, S. J. (2006). The richness of life. (P. McGarr & S. Rose, eds.) S. London: Vintage Books.

Grameen Bank. (n.d.). Retrieved September 2009 from http://www.grameen-info.org/

Grameenphone (n.d.). Retrieved September 2009 from http://www.grameenphone.com/

Grayling, A. C. (2003). *What is good? The search for the best way to live.* London: Phoenix.

Grayling, A. C. (2006). *The heart of things. Applying phisolophy to the 21st century.* London: Phoenix.

Grossberg, A., Struwig, J., & Tlabela, K. (1999). Contextualising the global information revolution in a development arena: A case study. *Communicare, 18*(2), 81–103.

GSM World for Uganda. (n.d.). Retrieved September 2009 from http://www.gsm.org/cgi-bin/ni_map.pl?cc=ug&net=mt

Haidt, J. (2006). *The happiness hypothesis. Putting ancient wisdom and philosophy to the test of modern science.* London: Arrow Books.

Heeks, R. (Ed.). (1999). *Reinventing government in the information age. International practice in IT-enabled public sector reform.* London: Routledge. doi:10.4324/9780203204962

Heeks, R. (2008). ICT4D 2.0: The next phase of applying ICT for international development. *IEEE Computer,* 26-33.

Hongladarom, S. (2003). Exploring the philosophical terrain of the digital divide. *ACM CRPIT '03: Selected papers from conference on Computers and philosophy* (Vol. 37, pp. 85-89).

Honneth, A. (2007). *Disrespect: The Normative Foundations of Critical Theory.* Polity Press.

International Telecommunication Union United Nations Conference on Trade and Development. World Summit on the Information Society, *Geneva 2003, Tunis 2005.*

International Telecommunications Union (ITU). (2006). Telecommunication Development Report: ICT Statistics. Retrieved July 2006 from http://www.itu.org/statistics

Janneck, M. (2009). Recontextualising Technology in Appropriation Processes. In Whitworth, B., & De Moor, A. (Eds.), *Handbook of Research on Socio-Technical Design and Social Networking Systems* (pp. 153–166). Hershey, PA: IGI.

Jensen, R. (2007). The Digital Provide: Information (Technology), Market Performance, and Welfare in the South Indian Fisheries Sector. *The Quarterly Journal of Economics, 122*(3). doi:10.1162/qjec.122.3.879

Jubert, A. (1999). Developing an infrastructure for communities of practice. In B. McKenna, (Ed.), *Proceedings of the 19th International Online Meeting* (pp. 165-168). Hinksey Hill, U.K.: Learned Information.

Kane, L. (2008). The World Bank, community development and education for social justice. *Community Development Journal, 43*(2), 194–209. doi:10.1093/cdj/bsl043

Latouche, S. (2007). De-growth: an electoral stake? *The International Journal Of Inclusive Democracy, 3*,1. Retrieved September 2009 from http://www.inclusivedemocracy.org/journal/vol3/vol3_no1_Latouche_degrowth.htm

Lizardo, O. (2008). *Beyond the Antinomies of Structure: Recovering the Insights of Methodological Structuralism*. Paper presented at the annual meeting of the American Sociological Association Annual Meeting, Sheraton Boston and the Boston Marriott Copley Place, Boston, MA, Jul 31, 2008. Retrieved September 2009 from http://www.allacademic.com/meta/p239582_index.html

Maturana, H. R., & Varela, F. J. (1980). *Autopoiesis and cognition*. Dordrecht, Holland: D Reidel.

Max-Neef, M. A. (1982). *From the outside looking in. Experiences in 'barefoot economics*. London: Zed Books.

McConnaughey, J. W., & Lader, W. (1998). Falling through the Net II. New Data on the Digital Divide. NTIA Report. Retrieved October 2008 from http://www.ntia.doc.gov/ntiahome/net2/falling.html

McGowan, P. J., Cornelissen, S., & Nel, P. (Eds.). (2006). *Power, wealth and global equity. An international relations textbook for Africa*. Cape Town: UCT Press.

McNamara, K. S. (2000). *'Why be Wired? The Importance of Access to Information and Communication Technologies'. TechKnowLogia, March/April 2000*. Knowledge Enterprise, Inc.

Meredith, M. (2006). *The state of Africa. A history of fifty years of independence*. Johannesburg: Jonathan Ball.

Moore, D. (Ed.). (2007). *The World Bank development, poverty, hegemony*. Scottsville: University of Kwazulu-Natal Press.

Moore, S. K., & Gardner, A. (2007, June). Megacities by the numbers. *IEEE Spectrum, ▪▪▪*, 16–17. doi:10.1109/MSPEC.2007.295503

Moyo, D. (2009). *Dead Aid. Why aid is not working and how there is another way for Africa*. London: Allen Lane.

Narayan, D., Chambers, R., Shah, M. K., & Petesch, P. (2000). Crying Out for Change. *Voices of the Poor: Vol. 2. World Bank*. Oxford: University Press.

Narayan, D., Patel, R., Schafft, K., Rademacher, A., & Koch-Schulte, S. (1999). Can Anyone Hear Us? *Voices of the Poor: Vol. 1. World Bank*. Oxford: University Press.

Narayan, D., & Petesch, P. (2002). From Many Lands. *Voices of the Poor: Vol. 3. World Bank*. Oxford: University Press.

National Social Inclusion Programme of the UK. (n.d.). Retrieved March 2008 from http://www.socialinclusion.org.uk/

Norris, P. (2003). *Digital divide. Civic engagement, information poverty, and the internet worldwide*. Cambridge: Cambridge University Press.

Notley, T., & Foth, M. (2008). *Extending Australia's digital divide policy: an examination of the value of social inclusion and social capital policy frameworks*. Retrieved October 2008 from http://eprints.qut.edu.au/

NTIA. (1995). Falling Through the Net: A Survey of the 'Haves' and 'Have Nots' in Rural and Urban America. Retrieved October 2008 from http://www.ntia.doc.gov/ntiahome/fallingthru.html

Oldenburg, R. (1989/1997). *The Great Good Place*. New York: Paragon House.

Oldenburg, R. (2001). *Celebrating the Third Place: Inspiring Stories about the "Great Good Places" at the Heart of Our Communities*. New York: Marlowe and Company.

Ongley, E. D. (1996). Control of water pollution from agriculture - FAO irrigation and drainage paper 55. FAO (Food and Agriculture Organization of the United Nations). Retrieved September 2009 from http://www.fao.org/docrep/W2598e/w2598e00.htm

Onis, Z., & Senses, F. (2005). Rethinking the Emerging Post-Washington Consensus. *Development and Change, 36*(2), 263–290. doi:10.1111/j.0012-155X.2005.00411.x

Phahlamohlaka, J., Braun, M., Romijn, H., & Roode, D. (Eds.). (2008). *Community-driven projects: reflections on a success story. A case study of science education and information technology in South Africa*. Pretoria: Van Schaik Publishers.

Phelps, E. S. (1997). *Rewarding Work. How to Restore Participation and Self-Support to Free Enterprise*. Cambridge, Massachusetts: Harvard Univ Press.

Polikanov, D., & Abramova, I. (2003). Africa and ICT: a chance for breakthrough? *Information, Communication & Society, 6*(1), 42:56.

Ramdas, K. N. (2008). Philanthrocapitalism in denial. *OpenDemocracy*. Retrieved October 2008 from http://www.opendemocracy.net/article/globalization/philanthrocapitalism_in_denial

Renfrew, C., & Bahn, P. (2004). *Archaeology: theories, methods and practice*. London: Thames and Hudson.

Retrieved October 2008 from http://www.opendemocracy.net/article/globalization/visions_reflections/philanthrocapitalism_after_the_goldrush

Rose, S. (2005). *Lifelines. Life beyond the gene*. London: Vintage.

Rousseau, J. (1984). *A discourse on inequality*. London: Penguin. (Original work published 1754)

Sachs, J. (2005). *The end of poverty. How we can make it in our lifetime*. London: Penguin Books.

Sachs, J. (2008). *Common wealth. Economics for a crowded planet*. London: Penguin Books.

Saul, J. R. (2009). *The collapse of globalism and the reinvention of the world*. London: Atlantic Books. (Original work published 2005)

Sen, A. (2001). *Development as freedom*. Oxford: University Press.

Sen, A. (2006). *Identity and violence: the illusion of destiny*. New York: W.W. Norton.

Sengupta, A. (2000). Realizing the Right to Development. [Blackwell Publishers.]. *Institute of Social Studies, 31*, 553–578.

Singer, P. (1972). Famine, affluence, and morality. *Philosophy & Public Affairs, 1*(3), 229–243.

Smith, A. (2003). *The wealth of nations* (Classic, B., Ed.). Kruger, AB. (Original work published 1776)

Snyman, M., & Snyman, M. M. M. (2003). Getting information to disadvantaged rural communities: the centre approach. *South African Journal of Library and Information Science, 69*(2), 95–107.

Social Inclusion Board, Government of South Australia. (n.d.). Retrieved March 2008 from http://www.socialinclusion.sa.gov.au/

Steyn, J. (2009). ePost: Networking Remote Areas. In L. Stillman, G. Johanson, & R. French (Eds.), *Communities in Action: Papers in Community Informatics* (pp. 60-67). Cambridge Scholars Publishing.

Stiglitz, J. E. (2002). *Globalization and its discontents*. London: Penguin.

Stiglitz, J. E. (2006). *Making globalization work*. London: Penguin Books.

Stillman, L., Johanson, G., & French, R. (Eds.). (2009). *Communities in Action: Papers in Community Informatics*. Cambridge Scholars Publishing.

Tongia, R., & Wilson, E. J. (2007). Turning Metcalfe on his head: the multiple costs of network exclusion. *Telecommunications Policy Research Conference* (TPRC). September 2007. Retrieved October 2008 from http://web.si.umich.edu/tprc/papers/2007/772/TPRC-07-Exclusion-Tongia&Wilson.pdf

United Nations. (UN) (2000), Millennium Development Goals (MDGs). Retrieved October 2009 from http://www.un.org/millenniumgoals/

Van der Vyver, A. G. (2006). Personal communication.

Van Dijk, J. A. G. M. (2006). *The network society. Social aspects of new media*. London: Sage.

Warschauer, M. (2004). *Technology and social inclusion*. Cambridge, Mass: MIT Press.

Wenger, E. (1998). *Communities of Practice: Learning, Meaning and Identity*. Cambridge: Cambridge University Press.

Wenger, E. (2000). Communities of practice: The key to knowledge strategy. In Lesser, E., Fontaine, M., & Slusher, J. (Eds.), *Knowledge and communities* (pp. 3–51). Boston: Butterworth Heinemann. doi:10.1016/B978-0-7506-7293-1.50004-4

White African. (2009). Spray against caterpillar. Retrieved September 2009 from http://whiteafrican.com/wp-content/uploads/2009/06/Caterpillar.jpg

World Bank. (2006). World development indicators. Retrieved December 2006 from http://www.worldbank.org/data

World Development Report 2001 Forum on Inclusion, Justice and Poverty Reduction, prepared for the World Development Report 2001 Forum on 'Inclusion, Justice and Poverty Reduction'. Retrieved October 2008 from http://www.dfid.gov.uk/pubs/files/sdd9socex.pdf

World Factbook, C. I. A. (2009). Retrieved September 2009 from https://www.cia.gov/library/publications/the-world-factbook/

Chapter 3
'Digital Inclusion':
Are We All Talking about the Same Thing?

Cristina Kiomi Mori
University of Brasilia (UnB), Brazil & Ministry of Planning, Brazil

ABSTRACT

In the past twenty years, there has been increasing involvement of governments, societies and communities in initiatives for bridging the digital gap, aiming economic and social development. These efforts are generally called 'digital inclusion' policies and projects. The expression 'digital inclusion' combines defining terms such as 'digital divide' and 'social inclusion', together with the assumptions, ideologies and value systems they carry. However, the comprehension of this expression varies among different agents involved. Identifying defining terms and analyzing their corresponding views is essential for improving scientific approach to any theme. This chapter scrutinizes definitions of 'digital inclusion', 'social exclusion' and related topics from specialized and academic bibliography, as well as from the field, in order to contribute qualifying academic and policy making debates. It proposes that the approaches to 'digital inclusion' are connected to concept views about society and social dynamics, State, market, civil society relationships and public policies. The notion of 'Information Society' and the purposes of disseminating digital information and communication technologies (ICT) are also present, thus framing 'digital inclusion' in different ways. The text concludes that scientific approaches must consider these aspects for addressing 'digital inclusion' as an object of analysis in a more consistent basis.

INTRODUCTION

The present text consists of an attempt to define and explore the concepts of 'digital inclusion' and 'digital divide' from the perspective of the Social

Policy field. 'Digital inclusion' is an expression that combines terms such as 'digital divide' and 'social inclusion'. Each of these terms carries assumptions, ideologies and value systems. The purpose of this text is to bring and debate definitions on 'digital inclusion', 'social exclusion' and related topics from specialized and academic

DOI: 10.4018/978-1-61520-799-2.ch003

bibliography, as well as from the field. In doing so, it might contribute to qualify academic and policy making debates related to the use of information and communication technologies (ICT) for development.

Treating 'digital inclusion' from the field of Social Policies demands discussing issues that are usually taken for granted, or less discussed, if one views the question exclusively from a technological perspective. The central idea is to see how terms such as 'digital inclusion' and 'digital divide' can carry different conceptual views. These terms are embraced by quotation marks to reinforce the need to make explicit the ideas, interests and approaches that permeate them. As will be shown, there is a deep relation between these expressions and the contexts from which they emerge.

From a Social Policy theoretical framework, addressing 'digital inclusion' concepts demands considering 'social inclusion' and 'social exclusion' theories. The background section exposes notions that hopefully will clarify this debate.

The substantial core of this chapter are the many different views on 'digital divide' and 'digital inclusion' used in policy making and analysis. The main section presents what has been considered the most important definitions for addressing 'digital inclusion' from a Social Policy perspective. It describes and analyzes the context in which the terms 'social exclusion' and 'digital inclusion' emerge. It also presents how the mainstream approaches differ in their views of the concepts, and how this relates to public policies paradigms.

In the future trends section, some of the questions that may arise from the discussion of 'digital inclusion' as a multi-faced concept are presented. Finally, in the conclusion, the author's perspective is situated among the many controversial theories presented along the text. In doing so, the chapter tries to contribute to the scientific analysis concerning 'digital inclusion' and development.

BACKGROUND

As in any other field of thought, 'digital inclusion' concepts are influenced by interests, actors and value systems. Theoretical approaches on the theme vary according to different understandings about: (a) society and social dynamics; (b) State, market, civil society relationships and the role of public policies; (c) the purpose(s) of disseminating digital information and communication technologies (ICT), which are usually related to neologisms such as 'Information', 'Knowledge' or 'Network' Societies; (d) the reciprocal influence of each one of these aspects to one another, and how they connect to form different frameworks to approach 'digital inclusion'.

It is important to level some understandings about how this article will consider the above mentioned elements. Social sciences do not offer a monolithic block of theories, especially regarding public policies analysis. That is why the most important considerations about Modern and Post Modern social science approaches that form the article background are now explained in a very simple way.

Modern social sciences theories tend to treat society and social dynamics comprehension based on two main approaches. One of them sees social cohesion and integration as the main purpose of investigating social relations. This approach is present in Émile Durkheim's notions of 'social order' and 'anomie', considered the first steps of sociology as an academic field of thought. The French school of social theories is based on this view.

Another approach understands societies as a permanent struggle between actors. In this last case, there is a subdivision. The liberal perspective considers individual competition for economic resources as main engine of social relations. The Anglo-Saxon school of thought quite often uses this approach. On the other hand, there are Marxist perspectives, that see social classes dispute (capital *versus* labor) as of core importance for social analysis. As for Social democratic theories, they try to consider both views, focusing on the egalitarian distribution of resources in capitalist democracies.

Each Modern view is linked to distinct concepts on social equality, justice and freedom. They also differ in the understanding of how State, market and civil society are related to one another, and on how these elements should interact in ideal terms. Except from radical free market liberal approaches, for which governmental action is always negative, Modern social theories consider public policies an essential aspect for development in contemporary societies.

Post Modern social theories are also present in the theoretical debate. They intend to go beyond Modern social science views. It is difficult to classify Post Modern approaches in defined strings of thought. However, there are some common aspects identifiable in most of their analysis. One is the critique of 'rational-objective' Modern approaches. Post Modern views consider 'objectivity' and 'rationalism' as based in an Western European centered standpoint. This is an important issue to consider when analyzing public policies and 'digital inclusion' concepts.

Another common point in Post Modern approaches is the claim for a stronger role of culture and identity, and not only economy, in social dynamics theorization. These elements of analysis connect to concepts concerning social equality, justice and freedom. They also affect Post Modern understandings on State, market and civil society interactions. Global-local relations are stressed as an element of complexity in contemporary societies. Technology, communication and information are also brought as crucial elements for analyzing social dynamics. A combination of these Post Modern elements form different frameworks, and are used in optimistic and pessimist perspectives of the future.

Social Policy perspectives interact with Modern and Post Modern approaches. As will be shown, public policies have been categorized in paradigms that relate to social dynamics different concepts. Distributive, multi-relational, multidimensional and participatory policies are set up and implemented based on values and ideas.

Another polemic in the 'digital inclusion' theorization is about eras or stages of human development. Theorists debate the existence or the pertinence of naming the contemporary period an 'Information Society', a 'Knowledge Society' or a 'Network Society'. Assuming or rejecting these neologisms directly affects how one understands the dissemination, use and dynamics of digital ICT. 'Digital inclusion' projects and public policies are justified or attacked based on those views. Even among practitioners of the 'digital inclusion' field, there is no consensus about concepts and strategies, as they represent different interests, actors and value systems.

A scientific approach to 'digital inclusion' from the Social Policy field must consider this whole set of views, identifying their distinct frameworks and categories of analysis. In doing so, scientists can critically understand the different paradigms on 'digital inclusion' and recognize the place from where they speak in the academic spectrum.

Of course there is no intention of oversimplifying any of these theories. The purpose here is to set the tone with readers, trying to create a dialogue with the many comprehensions that will derive from the next pages.

THE MANY VIEWS ON SOCIAL/ DIGITAL/ EXCLUSION/ INCLUSION

How to Name and Define a New Issue: 'Digital Divide'? 'Digital Inclusion'?

It is important to briefly introduce the terminologies used in different languages to refer to what this text calls 'digital inclusion'. The term 'digital inclusion' easily connects to 'social inclusion'. That is not merely a phonetic or orthographic coincidence. As will be presented, the original expression to refer is 'digital divide' in English. There are also works using terms such as 'digital gap' and 'digital fracture' in other languages. However, the combination of 'digital divide' and 'social inclusion', forming 'digital inclusion', has gained popularity and strength. That indicates the need to analyze these concepts.

'Digital Divide': ICT Inequalities Show Up

The consensual view is that the expression *digital divide* is used for the first time in the United States. According to Lisa Servon (2002) the United States government used the term 'digital divide' in 1995. In that year, the National Telecommunication and Information Administration (NTIA) launched the first of four reports called "Falling through the Net". The document brought data that showed inequalities in access to telephone services, computers and Internet modems among United States citizens. The report was part of a diagnostic effort related to the administration agenda. Leading the so-called 'Knowledge Society' was one of the top priorities for Democrat president Bill Clinton (1992-1996 and 1996-2000). The national strategy was composed by a series of policies for wide dissemination of digital information and communication technologies (ICT) throughout the country.

The NTIA reports on 'digital divide' consolidated statistics on access to ICT by the population, to subsidize and legitimatize governmental policies. Each edition had a composed title in which the authors highlighted an aspect that they assigned as more relevant in the data presented. The first of these reports was called "Falling through the Net: a survey of the 'have-nots' in rural and urban America" (NTIA, 1995). The second was "Falling Through the Net: New Data on the Digital Divide" (NTIA, 1999). Both documents presented the concepts of 'have' and 'havenots' to refer to citizens with or without access to ICT.

The differences were so huge that 'divide' was the term chosen to express inequalities in ICT access.

According to Van Dijk (2005), for those who have English as a first language, the word *divide* refers both to a dispute or disagreement between parts, and also to a geographical division (as a water stream that separates two places). For the author, it is also a metaphor to refer to separation between social groups. Van Dijk compares the use of the expression 'divide' to the struggle for civil rights in the United States at the 1960's.

'Digital gap' is also used in English to refer to huge differences of access to ICT. That notion is similar, but does not mean the same as 'digital divide' in Dijk's opinion. For the author, *gap* is closer to the notion of 'gorge'. That was perhaps the reason for its use when the term 'digital divide' was translated into other languages. In French, for example, the most common translation for 'digital divide' are the expressions *fósse numéric* or *fracture numérique*; in Spanish and Portuguese, *brecha digital*.

'Digital Inclusion': Stressing a Social Perspective on ICT

Although 'digital divide' or 'digital gap' were the first terms used to refer to the difference between those with and without access to ICT, it is important to notice that official documents, reports and other texts in English also use terms like 'digital inclusion', 'eInclusion' and 'digital exclusion', especially in recent years.

Some theoretical approaches argue that the concept of 'digital inclusion' is essentially different from 'digital divide'. The latter would be focused on unequal access to ICT, whereas the first would be more comprehensive of the broad use of ICT in all aspects of social life (Foley, Codagnone & Osimo, 2008). This distinction would be the reason for European Commission and Organization for Economic Co-operation and Development (OECD) countries to start using 'digital inclusion' as an expression to refer to the human aspects of

ICT dissemination as a public policy issue, aiming the development of 'information societies'.

ICT dissemination through all aspects of human life does not directly relate 'digital inclusion' to 'social exclusion'. But 'digital inclusion' and 'digital divide' analysis frequently connect ICT access and use inequalities to economic, political, social, cultural, gender, ethnics, geographic and demographic aspects as central for understanding or explaining the issue.

'Digital Inclusion' Main Concepts

As seen above, 'digital divide' was used for the first time by the administration of one country – the United States – that considered it important to lead the so called 'Knowledge' or 'Information Society'. Entering or constituting this apparently new arena of social interaction through intensive use of ICT is one of the most important arguments in favor of 'digital inclusion'. This concept also brings the notion of advancing towards the future. The whole idea of a 'new era' is criticized, as will be further seen.

The term 'Knowledge Society' dialogues with the concepts of 'Information Society' and 'Network Society'. The distinctions among them will not be addressed in the present text. The point here is that full participation in the type of social dynamics related to the disseminated use of ICT among individuals or groups forms the argumentation basis for many different concepts of 'digital inclusion'.

A first outcome of this view is the notion of 'digital inclusion' as equal to economic development. ICT dissemination demands the production and consumption of related goods and services, contributing for market development. It also demands training skills in ICT use. A strong argument in favor of 'digital inclusion' is that workers need to continually update their skills, and also use new technologies in life-long learning. In this sense, 'digital inclusion' is an engine for increasing productivity, as well as promoting better job

opportunities. For many actors, 'digital inclusion' is almost essentially that.

A second outcome of the 'Information Society' view is the idea of 'social inclusion' through 'digital inclusion'. Together with the improvement in job opportunities assumption, it forms what has been called 'digital inclusion as panacea' concept. This perspective sees access and training in ICT as a solution for all social vulnerabilities and/or inequalities. Social policies specificities are taken for granted in this theory, and are substituted for technological determinism. These notions are object of belief and criticism among policy stakeholders and theorists, as will be further seen.

In dialogue with the concept of participation in the 'Network Society', there is also a perspective on 'digital inclusion' as a tool for multidimensional development. That has to do with the notion of using ICT in different aspects of human life. An enhanced view based on this assumption emphasizes the effective use of ICT in improving life conditions of disfavored individuals and communities. This last view stresses the need of participatory approaches in public policies as the only methodology to guarantee social appropriation of ICT.

These concepts have been briefly introduced to show that relationships between 'social exclusion' and 'digital inclusion' are very present to the ICT for development debate. How 'social exclusion' emerges as a concept in social sciences will now be examined in order to connect these views to broader frameworks.

The Long Debate on 'Social Exclusion' and Public Policies

It seems that 'digital inclusion' as an expression was created in analogy to 'social inclusion'. But is 'social inclusion' a consensual notion in social sciences? If one is to be 'socially included', 'inserted' or 'integrated', does it mean there are individuals that are 'excluded' from the conditions of belonging to society? Does each of the different social sciences approaches understand 'social exclusion' in that same way?

But social sciences view 'social exclusion' differently. Public policy approaches also relate to diverse understandings on social dynamics and on how issues must be addressed. Exploring this aspect is a step toward understanding the definitions of 'digital inclusion' and 'digital divide'.

'Social Cohesion': Classic Approaches and Derived Notions

The expression 'social exclusion' was first mentioned in social sciences works in the 1960's in France. A historical review on social integration theories, however, takes us back to Modern social science emergency. Martine Xiberras (1996/1993) states that classic social theorists like Durkheim, Simmel and Weber had approached the theme of 'social cohesion' or 'social order' in their writings as long ago as between the end of the 19th and the beginning of the 20th century. But those authors did not use the expression 'socially excluded' to refer to individuals not integrated to society.

According to Xiberras (1996/1993) this notion of classic social theorists was also used in 1930's, when the Chicago School started analyzing the urban industrialization phenomenon and its problems. They were concerned with the integration of immigrants and local communities into the dynamics of an industrialized city. Economic depression was then a central aspect of analysis, but the Chicago School perspective focused on individuals. A period of high economic development followed, and in the 1960's, that school studied the unequal benefits appropriation by different social groups. Their analytical tools were 'anomie' and other categories related to what social sciences call 'the Durkheimian matrix'.

Although varying in theoretical perspective, the last phase of the Chicago School view of integration was quite similar to the perspective of the French book "*Lês Exclus, un français sur dix*" (René Lenoir, 1974, as in Leal, 2004). According

to Leal (2004), Lenoir's piece focuses on prisoners, the mentally ill, disabled and aged, among other individuals that had been 'left behind' in a period of economic progress. The French author's view did not differ substantially from the analysis on 'marginality' that Latin America schools had at the same time. Caldeira (2005) argues that the difference from the Chicago School was that Lenoir – and most of Latin American theorists - blamed social dynamics for poverty situations, not individuals. However, it is not possible to extract from Lenoir's piece a theory on 'social exclusion' (Leal, 2004).

The Context in which 'Social Exclusion' Emerges as a Concept

'Social exclusion' and 'socially excluded' became current expressions, especially in the French school of social thought, after the economic crisis of the 1970's. The new terms were apparently similar to the previous notions of 'poverty', 'marginalization' and 'deviant behavior', but the approach had changed. The emergence of 'social exclusion' as a theoretical concept appears to be related to the new context.

Different schools of thought agree that, since the end of the Second World War, developed countries economies had more than thirty years of economic growth combined with social policies. Especially in Europe, governments focused on guaranteeing universal social rights to their national citizens. Public policies were based on Keynesianism as a theory for driving economy, and on Welfare/Social States as a paradigm for conducting social development.

According to Ianni (1992), after the 1970's economic crisis, a set of aspects combined demanding a shift in governmental approaches on public policies: the fall of the Berlin Wall in 1989; the end of 'real socialism' governments in Eastern Europe; and the controlled opening of the Chinese economy to capitalism since 1978. Another kind of economic paradigm was to substitute social-keynesianism as a developmental theory: economic neoliberalism.

The discourse for less governmental action in economy and other dimensions of social life gained strength. Governments deregulated productive activities on behalf of free market. Welfare State social policies were pointed out as deficit generators, and universal rights defense declined as legitimate basis for social protection. The consequences were public services and State support to citizens decline in countries where they once existed.

Capitalist production was restructured under these directions. Companies were allowed to hire employees under flexible rules, affecting labor rights. Deregulation of markets allowed for global production and financial flows. Worldwide dissemination of ICT infrastructure also relates to that context, as will be further detailed. ICT allowed for international corporations to reduce their costs. For workers, those changes caused unemployment, precariousness and increased labor vulnerability, affecting social security (Pochmann, 2002).

'Social Exclusion': The French School Approach

The new context took those used to the period of almost permanent employment and universal social rights by surprise. The French school of thought focused on the phenomenon of a large number of individuals in developed countries becoming unemployed, employed under precarious conditions and 'non-employable'. Along the 1980's and 1990's decades, authors analyzed the transformations in course as the emergency of a 'new social question' (Rosanvallon, 1998/1995) or a 'social question metamorphosis' (Castel, 1998/1995). The use of the term 'social exclusion' also became more frequent, especially among the French and Latin American schools of thought.

"L'Exclusion, l'État du Savoirs" (Serge Paugam, 1996, as in Demo, 1998) is one of the main efforts on 'social exclusion' theorization and paradigm definition of that period. For Paugam, 'social exclusion' as a category of analysis goes beyond traditional approaches. The concept does not refer to the opposition of interests, nor to the struggle for social recognition among groups or social classes. 'Social exclusion' would denote an individual's weakness and incapacity for presenting organized claims. Paugam argues that the term also reinforces an identity cohesion of the disfavored populations.

That approach opposes Modern liberal and Marxist's social sciences theories. Using the Post Modern argument of 'identity', it can be considered part of the 1990's decade search for new paradigms in a changing world. But the French school of thought had other theories addressing social changes.

In *"Les métamorphoses de la question sociale. Une chronique du salarial"* (1998/1995), Robert Castel questions the pertinence of the expression 'socially excluded'. In the author's opinion, the term 'exclusion' is vague and imprecise to designate the phenomenon he observes: the insistent presence of individuals 'fluctuating' in the social structure, unable to find a place in it. Castel refuses to use the term 'excluded' because, as he understands it, there is no one out of society.

For Castel, what happens is a process of dissociation. Due to the end of 'salarial society', a great quantity of individuals transits from stable work to an intermediated zone of social vulnerability, and from there to an even worse situation, which he calls 'defiliation'. In the first stage, the individual is in a situation of guaranteed solid social insertion. The second stage is characterized by work precariousness and fragility of social links. The last stage is dissociation, from which Castel sees a possibility of returning. For that to happen, a new cohesion status must come to substitute those of the 'salarial society' constituted in the Social-Keynesian period.

'Salarial society', for Castel, combined collective wealth and opportunities, security distribution, almost full employment, labor rights and Welfare

State social protection. That type of society ended its trajectory in the 1970's, generating the situation of 'defiliation' of a large quantity of individuals. 'Salarial society' was legitimated by the assumption that all individuals considered capable of working were in salaried and stable jobs. Most individuals were generating enough wealth both for the satisfaction of their own needs and social protection. That wealth was also sufficient for the protection of those considered non-capable of working, such as children, elderly, ill, invalidated, retired and others 'justifiably' non-employed. Like other French authors, Castel was also trying to contribute to a new way of addressing social cohesion in a context of deregulated economy.

Resuming the French School Perspectives

Despite Castel's claims on the imprecision of the term 'excluded', his thoughts are connected to a theoretical matrix of authors that use 'social exclusion' as a category of analysis. This may be called an 'integrationist' point of view that characterizes the situation of the 'excluded' as a break of social links. According to Leal (2004), many French authors share this approach, focusing on 'social exclusion', 'deviation' and 'inclusion'.

Leal argues that the common aspect of 'integrationist' theories is the idea of an 'inclusion/exclusion' path, along which individuals pass. In that path, there are vectors that enhance exclusion, precariousness or vulnerability. The end of the path is a state of total breaking – or 'anomie' – that characterizes 'social exclusion' or 'defiliation'. There is a dangerous threat to democratic societies in allowing that to happen, as it contributes to put in check the notion of cohesion. These views connect to Durkheim's thoughts on social order, sometimes combined with contemporary Post Modern elements, such as 'cultural identities'.

Anglo-Saxon Approaches: Focusing on Individuals

At almost the same time, different analysis appear in the United States to treat of the phenomenon that France called 'exclusion' or 'defiliation'. William Julius Wilson (1987, as in Demo, 1998) creates the concept of *underclass* to refer to individuals not integrated to society. According to Wilson, individuals get to that situation due to: (a) personal responsibility; (b) the fact that they inhabit areas of disfavored characteristics, like degraded neighborhoods and homes; or (c) a combination of those factors. *Underclass* situation is also linked to the absence of stable work. Wilson's approach is quite close to the Chicago School in considering the urban space and dynamics as central variables for explaining social stratification, inclusion and exclusion.

Bill Jordan (1996, as in Demo, 1998) is another representative of the Anglo-Saxon approach. For Jordan, the government role in social policies is to promote only equal opportunities to individuals. That is resumed in universal basic education, which would allow individuals to be capable of self-organizing themselves in institutionalized competitive groups, around economic interests. They should then be able to participate in social and political games. The best organized groups and individuals survive. The ones not able to demonstrate to the others that they deserve benefits, perish. From this perspective, the binomial exclusion/inclusion is considered positive, and essential to the constitution of associative identities that form competitive social groups.

The Multidimensional Approach to 'Social Exclusion'

The multidimensional view on 'social exclusion' dialogues to a 'human rights' approach on social dynamics. As Alfredo Bruto da Costa (1998) synthesizes, poverty is only one among the situations in which disruptions of social relations appear. In this sense, 'exclusion' relates to not having human rights attended. For Costa, individuals are only plentiful citizens when they can actually access a set of basic social systems. These can be grouped in five domains: social, economic, institutional, territorial and the one of symbolic references.

The social domain correspond to the relationships an individual is inserted in, being that groups, communities or social nets (family, neighborhood, local associations, friends, community, workplace). The economic domain is composed by resource generation (wage, social security, property), goods and services market, and savings system. The institutional domain is formed by public services and offices, and institutions related to political participation. The territorial domain emerged from the understanding that there are places where measures for global improvement are needed, including housing, social equipments and economic activities ('poverty islands' within countries, countries in a whole, migration issues). The last domain are symbolic references, related to the subjective aspects of exclusion (social identity, self-esteem, self-confidence, future perspective, initiative, motivation and sense of belonging to society) (Costa, 1998).

The multidimensional approach is related to the French school of 'social exclusion' analysis. However, Costa considers it different from 'integrationists' theories. The five different domains are in superposition, and the basic social systems are interdependent from one another. Different levels of access to the systems correspond to diverse degrees of exclusion. This theory also relates 'social exclusion' to human rights (civic, political, social and diffuse). A Social Policy perspective on rights and human dignity will now be presented to complete this view.

Human Dignity: Beyond Material Scarcity

José de Martínez Pisón (1998) argues that human rights as a category must be historically contextu-

alized. Different value systems have contributed to the development of 'human rights' notion and legitimacy. For Pisón, a central aspect in human rights discussion is the definition of 'human needs' beyond a 'minimum needs' approach.

For Potyara A. Pereira (2007/2000), public policies exist to attend rights, which correspond to the satisfaction of human needs. These comprehend the physical integrity and individuals participation in society. Therefore, it is not merely a question of material scarcity. Human beings must live in conditions that allow them to act as subjects, and to operate their critical thoughts against all forms of oppression. Pisón (1998) agrees that someone submitted to privations cannot decide and act freely. For him, autonomy refers to a level of agency (freedom of action) and a level of criticism (possibility of evaluating rules and transforming cultural practices). This last level requires cognitive capacities and larger social opportunities to become real.

Pereira (2007/2000) argues that human needs can be objectively defined. For that, a society must verify if the absence of attention to a certain aspect of human life provokes serious social damages or losses to individual dignity. These needs are to be prioritized, in positive or moral rights. In this sense, human rights attendance resume a lot of vulnerabilities and absences with which different schools of thoughts on 'social exclusion' are concerned. However, this approach considers human dignity a universal value. Pisón (1998) defends the view that the struggle for real universalization of the most basic rights is an irrevocable condition to be defended in contemporary society.

Criticisms from Civil Society Perspectives

'Social inclusion' can be also addressed in frameworks that criticize State action from a civil society prevalence perspective. These theories are usually present in Post Modern approaches to social dynamics and public policies. In short, they condemn homogeneous universal social service offers, and see dangerous technocratic control over citizens in social policies. For 'digital inclusion', the important point is that some of these approaches consider ICT as entirely embedded in that kind of control (Postman, 1993/1992). This view will be detailed further on.

Among civil society perspectives, there are also theories that understand new social movements as indicators of social problems and alternatives (Melucci, 2001/1982). And there are views that defend analyzing new social movements as strategical to force many different standpoints to be taken into consideration in public policies, as well as cultural identities and the right to difference.

Different Approaches, Different Public Policies

The many different approaches to how 'social exclusion' is conceived are reflected in the definition of public policies to overcome it. Graham Room (1995) analyzes the difference between French and English schools of thought in the study of disfavored individuals and groups. Room says that the British tradition is interested mainly in the wealth distribution aspects, focusing especially on poverty. The French school, on the other hand, prefers the relational aspects, and for this reason uses 'social exclusion' as central category. English tradition is essentially liberal, and sees society as a set of atomistic individuals, competing in the marketplace, propelled by economic interests. The French school has an elitist approach. It sees society as a set of hierarchized collectivities in the form of status, linked by mutual rights and obligations, rooted in a moral order that all individuals share. Room points to the social democratic vision as a third and different approach, based on egalitarian citizenship instead of traditional hierarchies.

Room's analysis helps in the understanding of why many Anglo-Saxon theories, like the *underclass* concept, blame the individual for the poverty and social weakness situation. The idea of *underclass* is also criticized for carrying the concepts of 'good' and 'bad' poor individuals. It supposes the existence of people who deserve social protection from public policies in the case of vulnerability, and those who are 'lost cases'. The French school of thought, in turn, bases its explanations on multi-relational and social cohesion theories. It is criticized for preserving social elites and tradition, rather than allowing for social equity.

For Marxist theorists, labor is the central category for analyzing social dynamics. They criticize French, Anglo-Saxon and social democratic views on 'social exclusion'. Pedro Demo (1998) sees the 'excluded' as a social force the 'included' individuals fear. From his perspective, 'social integration' and 'social equality' are unachievable in capitalism. Also, no distributive nor equal opportunities policies will ever be enough for promoting freedom to all individuals under the capitalist mode of production. The system logic does not allow for human rights being guaranteed universally, and capitalist societies will never achieve true democracy.

'Social Exclusion' and 'Social Inclusion' Concepts Move Forward

Generally speaking, liberal free market orientation is perceived of as having had a strong influence on public policies since the 1970's capitalist crisis, and responsible for a decrease in social protection. In the previous period, social democratic influence oriented distributive or 'integrationist' policies for compensating inequalities. Critical of both views, Marxist socialists have never believed the possibility of guaranteeing social justice under capitalism. However, they believe in contradictory aspects of social policies for the benefit of the labor classes.

Despite the theoretical differences between schools, 'social exclusion' has been absorbed as a category among theorists, and also by governments. In European Commission documents, for example, 'social exclusion' and 'social inclusion' have become frequently used. Once more strictly related to people with disabilities, the use of these expressions has been extended to many different situations, including immigrants, aged and other individuals in vulnerable situation.

'Digital inclusion' concepts carry these many views about 'social exclusion' and public policies to address it, as will be now presented.

'Digital Inclusion' in a Context of 'Social Exclusion'

How are the 'digital inclusion' and 'digital divide' concepts related to the 'social exclusion' and related theories developed above? First of all, it appears that there is no coincidence in the emergence of both concepts at practically the same period, during the 1990's decade. The development of ICT public policies was happening in the same context as the 'social inclusion' debate. This approach also helps understanding the different 'digital inclusion' concepts and the criticisms they receive.

ICT Dissemination and Governments

'Digital inclusion' emerged as an issue in a context of public policies deregulation. But it is important to remember that the United States, as well as France and other countries, had promoted the dissemination of ICT through government action in previous times. In the 1970's decade, the report "*L'Informatización de la Societé*" (Nora & Minc, 1978) was produced under request of French president Giscard d'Estaing. The document indicates the strategic importance of ICT dissemination well before the 1990's Internet boom. As Mattelart (2002/2001) puts it, developed nations have been treating ICT as a matter of political and economic relevance since the beginning of industrial economy.

The discussion about 'Information Society', 'Knowledge Society' or 'Network Society' that

appeared as a theoretical framework at the end of the 1990's decade did not always make reference to that. When analyzing the transformations concerning ICT in the 1990's, many theories consider technology evolution as a consequence of 'natural' development. This kind of approach is criticized as based on 'technological determinism'. Critical views argue that the dissemination of ICT was a consequence of deliberated action in the political and market arenas, moved by interests and intentionality.

Dissemination of ICT in a Market Driven World

The argument that 'digital inclusion' policies must be market oriented was – and still is – used to legitimate policies and practices of different actors involved in the implementation of initiatives: governments, companies, international/ multilateral agencies and non-governmental organizations.

Over the last twenty years, the massive spread of the consumption of ICT goods and services followed that orientation. Commercial Internet boom at the end of the 1990's is an example of that. Developed countries had long combined government and private investment in research and development of ICT for military use. They had also stimulated the development of audiovisual content and broadcasting companies. This allowed for the consolidation of huge corporations in those areas of business (Mattelart, 2002/2001). These companies had a great advantage while developing countries were almost forced to deregulate their ICT markets for accessing international loans under neoliberal hegemony.

On behalf of free market, State-owned telecommunications systems were privatized in practically all countries. The small number of large corporations with global presence gained the control of most telecommunications infrastructure and services in the whole world. These companies acquired smaller and medium companies, and merged. The process allowed for the concentration of not only capital and infrastructure, but also production, distribution and diffusion of contents, software, hardware and other goods and services related to ICT in the hands of only a few corporations (Mattelart, 2002/2001).

Criticisms of the 'Information Society' and Similar Concepts

In recent years ICT dissemination has been dependent on 'digital inclusion' debates. Among different schools of thought, arguments in favor of 'digital inclusion' are based on the assumption of the existence or rise of an 'Information Society', a 'Knowledge Society' or a 'Network Society' everyone must be integrated to.

For Michel Menou (2008), 'Information Society' and related theories have no ground basis. He rejects the assumption of linear progress in the History of mankind, present in many of these discourses. Menou is also critical of views that seem to believe there is a parallel virtual universe inhabited by special individuals that use communication and technology, completely separated from material universe where the rest of creatures live. The author discards the existence of an 'Information Society', based on the assumption that quantity of substantial knowledge has probably always been adapted to circumstances.

However, Menou considers there is an information explosion proportional to human growth as societies have developed. The increase in formal education during the past few centuries is an element that contributed to the information boom. By raising the number of new questions, it allowed for new knowledge gaps, to an extent that no one can cope with if selection is not wisely used. In Menou's view, information explosion has not yet reached vast areas of the planet. However, it has already increased social complexity, and confronted contemporary societies with many contradictions. He argues that the destruction of the planet is 'strangely coincident' to the advent of information explosion, science and technology application, and industry (Menou, 2008).

'Digital Inclusion' as Panacea for 'Social Inclusion'

The context in which 'digital divide' and 'digital inclusion' concepts became popular is the same in which the concept of 'social exclusion' is strongly debated. Not by chance, certain authors in the field of 'digital inclusion' perceive a technological utopism in governmental discourses also found in academic studies. In this view, access to ICT could answer for privations that the rest of public policies were not attending (Rodino-Colocino, 2006; Miranda, 2005).

One persistent notion about 'digital inclusion' sees ICT as a panacea for the solution of all social problems. This position is strongly backed in the need of qualifying workers in new digital technologies. From this perspective, developing ICT abilities would guarantee employment and continuous opportunity for individuals to build new capacities, especially through e-learning. Those benefits have been raised as essential requirements for workers to be adapted to the new flexible labor market.

Critical on that view, Marxist theorists see deregulation and destabilization of labor as always committed to favor capital over workers. Demo (1998) analyzes the post-1970's crisis configuration of global capitalism as promoting an extremely unequal society. This new stage of capitalism requires higher skilled workers, but qualified employees are not recognized and paid better wages. Intensive use of ICT and knowledge serve mainly to increase capitalist exploitation of the relative surplus value. On the other hand, Demo sees the increasingly qualified labor force as having a contradictory emancipatory potential. Higher skilled workers can better develop critical consciousness, leading to the overcoming of oppression and material poverty.

Free market defenders, in turn, consider labor flexibility a positive aspect of the new economy that allows for more free time to employees, and identify it with the idea of progress. This assumption dialogues with the 'digital inclusion' concept related to the notion of job opportunity. It also corresponds to the liberal notion that the individual is solely responsible for succeeding or failing in the marketplace.

ICT and Labor: Criticisms on the 'Digital Inclusion' as Panacea Concept

Under neoliberal economic orientation, business competition has increased (Ianni, 1992). Old companies were restructured and intensified use of ICT in their processes. New companies started up in a more flexible labor market, generating jobs more attuned to the new trends. Workers had to take temporary and/ or precarious jobs, if any. Many of the jobs closed in developed countries were opened up in developing ICT oriented countries, where wages could be enormously lower, without productivity loss (Cazeloto, 2008). The argument that ICT training was a necessary passport for a job was valid in those developing countries. Not so much in the developed ones.

As Rodino-Colocino (2006) states, a Seattle software programmer is no less qualified than a worker of same level in a Southeast-Asian country. Technological under qualification could not be blamed as the reason for the Seattle worker being unemployed, but transnational labor market competition could. That also led to an unfavorable environment for claims for labor rights and union organization. Employed workers were submitted to more strict labor discipline and had to accept lower wages.

Despite of this, one of the most prevalent arguments for job maintenance is 'digital inclusion'. This element is strongly present in common sense imagery, in government discourses and policies, and in some of the researchers segments. In

Demo's analysis of intensive use of knowledge in production, based on Marxist theory, ability to use ICT is actually an important employment factor in the labor reconfigured marketplace (Demo, 1998). But it is not the only one, as shown in Pochmann (2002).

Pochmann (2002) studied employment distribution for the period from the last years of 1990's decade to year 2000 in the city of São Paulo, Brazil. He criticizes the notion that individual ability with respect to intensive ICT and knowledge use are enough for getting or keeping a job. For him, economic and social developmental public policies should also be considered.

Pochmann's study demonstrates that most jobs created in São Paulo during the period he analyzes required very low qualification (Pochmann, 2002). They were mainly related to housekeeping services and private security. On the other hand, unemployment highest scores levels were among workers with better formal education degrees. In Pochmann's view, that situation was due to neoliberal direction in national governmental policies, oriented for the benefit of the financial market, not for economic development. As a consequence, the immense Brazilian social inequality levels increased. Pochmann also saw no evidence that the so-called 'e-economy' had any possibility of leading to 'social inclusion' under those circumstances.

Tragic Visions on ICT Dissemination

Before presenting this text's own view on 'digital inclusion' emergency context, the pessimistic visions on ICT dissemination will also be presented. Neil Postman (1993/1992) and Paul Virilio (1993, as in Cazeloto, 2008) have a very critical view on the integration of ICT in social relations.

Postman (1993/1992) analyzes the 'surrender of culture to technology' in a process he names 'technopoly'. For the author, the industrial use of machines initiated in the 18th century, in England, led to a 'technocracy'. By that time, tradition and technology co-existed. The latter gained strength as rationalization spread over many aspects of life on behalf of wealth generation. Postman sees the United States turned into a 'technopoly' by the end of the 20th century. 'Technopoly' is defined as the totalitarian control of 'technocracy' over social relations, in detriment of tradition and other means of individual and communitarian approaches.

Among many others aspects, Postman argues that computers create the illusion that decisions regarding social life are not under human control. Medical technology, computer technology, 'scientism' (the 'blind' belief in Science dominates other approaches) and invisible technologies have become sources of unchallengeable authority that characterizes the 'technolopoly'.

In a similar approach, Cazeloto (2008) recalls Paul Virilio to highlight what he sees as an uncritical present submission of humanity to information and communication technologies. Based on the assumption that acceleration and time saving are essential to capitalist development, the introduction of machinery has not been neutral, nor can be democratically controlled by society or governments. Cazeloto sees deep changes in capitalism throughout the second half of the 20th Century, based on two vectors: media saturation and informatization of everyday life. For him, 'digital inclusion' serves for intensifying these processes, benefiting a hierarchized cyberculture and its dependency on a 'megainfobureaucracy'. This last is the global ICT structure controlled by a supranational mode of global capitalist organization. For Cazeloto, economic and cultural aspects are in strict relation, and ICT play a central role in this new world dynamics.

Postman's approach and Cazeloto's review on Virilio are based on Post Modern notions which perceive ICT as totalitarian means of society control by a bureaucratic system, closed to participation and democracy, as well as destructive of traditional and local culture systems.

Understanding 'Digital Divide' from a Contextual Perspective

Since the notion of the 'digital divide' was introduced in 1990's, and in many academic and governmental studies since then, data presentation emphasized the differences or inequalities of access to ICT related to income levels, race, gender, generations and geographical localization. These approaches usually reached a 'dead end', presenting 'digital inclusion' as a mere reflection of social inequalities.

The present text argues that only the lack of a critical view concerning capitalist society could assign ICT access inequalities to be of such great importance. Dissemination of these technologies was, and still is, mostly and deliberately driven by market orientation, not by social equality paradigms. It would be actually impressive if ICT access had been equally distributed. ICT possession, use and development could not have been concentrated in ways substantially different from what consumer society allows for.

Researchers that perceive the existence of a market driven orientation in 'digital inclusion' public policies partially reach this same conclusion (Yu, 2006; Eubanks, 2007). Others consider it a central key to understanding the process, also claiming that social and non-economic dimensions must be taken into account for analysis (Spirakis, Manolopoulos & Efstathiadou, 2008).

'Digital Inclusion' and Public Policies Paradigms

Public policies concerning 'digital inclusion' have developed under different paradigms together with the many concepts about the purposes of ICT dissemination. Free market orientation affected the distributive paradigm in the historical development of 'digital inclusion' public policies. Distributive and multi-relational paradigms were connected in the 'beyond access' approach. Multidimensional and participatory policies have also been considered for addressing the issue.

Rejecting Digital Divide' as an Issue

By 2001 a remarkable shift related to free market orientation happened in the United States regarding 'digital inclusion' public policies. While the Clinton administration's approach to the 'Knowledge Society' was responsible for the 'digital divide' concept to appear and gain status, the George W. Bush administration cut 'digital inclusion' budgets at federal level. Theoretical defenders of this orientation, like Benjamin Compaine (2001), question if there is actually a 'digital divide'. In this view, it is not a matter of distribution, but consumer goods that should be treated strictly under market logic.

An example of this view was the speech by Michael Powell, the G.W. Bush nominee for the Federal Communications Committee (FCC). For him, assuming a 'digital divide' was something like talking about a 'Mercedes divide', nothing more than a myth. Powell's speech generated lots of criticisms among 'digital inclusion' practitioners and theorists at the time.

'Digital Inclusion' and the Distributive Paradigm

The distributive paradigm was actually under attack in the United States when the shift in federal administration affected 'digital inclusion' policies. Theorists were making a case for expanding the scope, not cutting budgets. They were trying to legitimate a new 'digital inclusion' paradigm, defending a 'beyond access' perspective. This movement engaged multi-relational elements to the distributive paradigm for approaching the issue.

For Van Dijk (2005), Warschauer (2006/2003) and other U.S. based researchers, the notion of 'have' and 'havenots', used in Clinton's administration reports to address the 'digital divide', allowed for a set of wrong consequences in the field of public policies. For these authors, 'digital divide' is not a matter of possession or access to computers and services, but of ICT use capability. They criticize governmental policies in most countries that were designed to cover only infrastructure and equipment distribution, leaving aside human and social factors.

Besides that, they see enormous inequality of access and abilities within the 'haves' side of the gap. The more privileged individuals get Internet band speeds and digital equipment of latest generation, leaving behind the disadvantaged 'haves'. In their view, the distributive paradigm is not enough to solve the problem, as it gets trapped in the logic of ICT market driven development (Yu, 2006; Spirakis, Manolopoulos & Efstathiadou, 2008).

Cognitive aspects and development of abilities were the core focus of 'digital inclusion beyond access' theories. In this sense, overcoming the 'digital divide' first concept - infrastructure and equipment dissemination, notably access to Internet and computers - was a restriction.

Shifting from an 'access to infrastructure' paradigm was really an important change in the concept of 'digital inclusion'. That same strand of thought also noticed that 'digitally excluded' individuals feel uncomfortable when dealing with ICT equipment and contents. Designed for a privileged elite, ICT would not correspond to the expectations and abilities of those who suffer from other types of social discrimination. These asymmetries would be a factor of deepening inequality between 'haves' and 'havenots', representing a lack of equal opportunities.

'Digital Inclusion' under a Participatory Paradigm

In dialogue with the above mentioned approaches, an apparently similar but different strand of thought emerges, calling for 'effective use' of ICT by poor, disfavored, excluded or socially marginalized individuals and collectivities. Michael

Gurstein (2003) named this approach 'Community Informatics'. It gathers a set of theorists and practitioners of 'digital inclusion' that argue for the participation of people to whom initiatives are directed to in the decision making process, implementation and evaluation of policies and project.

The 'effective use' string of thought bases its assumptions in 'digital inclusion' initiatives that have a participatory approach for introducing and promoting ICT appropriation in vulnerable communities. That does not mean there is an unanimous point of view about what would correspond to communities effective use of ICT. But as shown by Eubanks (2007), these processes must search for knowing and recognizing collectivities' expectations, challenges and, especially, making it possible for them to appropriate themselves of the many aspects related to the access and use of ICT in the contemporary world.

The main goal is allowing those communities and individuals to re-appropriate discourses, practices, contents, equipments and networks constitutive of 'digital inclusion' process by themselves. Participatory approaches stress the importance that communities must be able to transform these elements for the benefit of their own needs, with actual autonomy (Assumpção, 2001).

'Digital Inclusion' for Multidimensional Development

Under different public policy paradigms, governments are also looking for widespread use of ICT as a strategy for dealing with the multiple dimensions of 'social exclusion' as theorized by Costa (1998), or addressing human needs attention, as claimed by Pisón (1998) and Pereira (2007/2000). Public documents and reports are detailing the implementation and maintenance of ICT dissemination and use integrated with education, health, housing, culture, leisure and political participation for citizens in vulnerable situations (Besson, 2008; Foley, Codagnone & Osimo, 2008).

Another notion that is gaining strength is that ICT dissemination must be driven by common social interest, not by market forces. The *IT for Change* workshop report (2007) shows more widespread perception of the problems related to market driven ICT dissemination, especially among developing countries actors. As well as an apparent neoliberal decline in public policy orientation, community participation is becoming perceived as important. This participation refers not only to the implementation of ICT for development projects, but also in planning and designing the architecture and approach of interventions, as argued in 'Community Informatics' theoretical approaches.

Towards a Conclusion

From what has been presented, it can be concluded that 'digital divide' and 'digital inclusion' paradigms remain under construction. But the frameworks in which different approaches support their views are the same that have been developed in social sciences since long before. This chapter has shown relatively defined strands of thought on 'digital inclusion', their approaches, categories and concepts. One can argue that the statements made about each one of the identified strings and paradigms are not unanimous. That was really not the intention. Contributing to a theoretical overview and analysis on this field, taking into account Social Policy approaches, is an important step for present and future studies.

FUTURE TRENDS

While the scientific effort tries to clearly identify the main concepts and paradigms, blurring frontiers might be of strategical importance in the political arena. Future studies could address this issue, taking into account that public policies are elaborated and implemented within a complex system of political interests, actors and institutions. 'Digital inclusion' is also a field in which policy analyzers can deepen their studies, since no existing paradigm seems to have really found a whole set of models and elements to allow for 'normal science' in the Kuhnian sense (Thomas Kuhn, 1990/1962).

Besides good scientific paradigms, as a practice oriented field, 'digital inclusion' needs a better set of analytical elements to approach public policies. That should consider implementation, maintenance and evaluation of 'digital inclusion' policies specific needs. In this scope, conjuncture and structural factors shall always be considered, as this text has tried to reason.

As a small contribution for future studies, some questions can be raised. How distributive and multi-relational social policies paradigms can be used to analyze 'digital inclusion' policies implemented in different countries? In which ways social policies can be integrated and contribute (or deter) 'digital inclusion' processes? Which models of 'digital inclusion' public policies better approach attention to human rights? What elements and dynamics constitute these models? How economic, social and political dynamics involving the relationships between developed and developing countries are to be addressed in 'digital inclusion' studies? These questions are just a few that are in strong need of scientific investigation in this field.

CONCLUSION

'Digital inclusion' and 'social exclusion' concepts vary among analytical perspectives. Different theoretical understandings of society and its dynamics are behind different approaches to digital and social inclusion discourses and practices, public policies definition and implementation, and 'digital inclusion' projects around the world.

Disseminating ICT as means for reaching a better society is an apparent consensus among many theorists in favor of 'digital inclusion' initiatives. But they may not reveal the essence of the paradigms that support them, each one with different perspectives on equality, justice and freedom.

From what has been presented, it seems that only the 'community informatics' approach is capable of not getting trapped in the conceptual view that ultimately favors solely market interests. This approach also seems to be useful for finding some hope against perspectives that consider ICT dissemination as always embedded with totalitarian control of society by powerful socially uncontrollable market forces.

A critical approach also should not deny the strategic importance of ICT use in the process of overcoming situations of human indignity, for it would be denying to understand that reality is dynamic. Many 'digital inclusion' initiatives around the world, especially in developing countries, are showing that information and communication tools are very useful for achieving healthy human survival and individual autonomy.

It is obvious that offering ICT in substitution for food to a starving person is not considered. Beyond a restrictive analysis, one must consider the relevance and pertinence of ICT use in public policies administration and in the delivery of social services, as well as in social and political participation.

Despite each researcher's theoretical choice, scientific approaches must be considered as well as the working definitions presented here and elsewhere, in order to build more solid paradigms for addressing 'digital inclusion' as an object of analysis.

REFERENCES

Assumpção, R. O. (2001). *Além da inclusão digital: O projeto sampa.org*. Unpublished masters dissertation. University of São Paulo, São Paulo, SP. Retrieved December 22, 2008, from http://referencias.onid.org.br/media/arquivos/dissertacao_Rodrigo.pdf

Besson, É. (2008). *France Numeric 2012: Plan de développement de l'économie numérique*. Paris, Secrétariat D'État Chrgé de la Prospective, de L'Évaluation des Politiques Publiques et du Développement de L'Économie Numérique, Républic Française. Retrieved November 29, 2008, from http://francenumerique2012.fr/html/france_2012.html

Caldeira, F. (2005). *Exclusão social: uma aventura histórica pela busca de um conceito*. Paper presented in 4th Geography Week, FCT/Unesp, Presidente Prudente, SP.

Castel, R. (1998). *As metamorfoses da questão social: uma crônica do salário*. (I.D. Poleti, Trans.). Petrópolis: Vozes. (Original work published 1995).

Cazeloto, E. (2008). *Inclusão digital. Uma visão crítica*. São Paulo: Senac.

Compaine, B. M. (2001). *The digital divide: facing a crisis or creating a myth?* Cambridge, MA: MIT Press.

da Costa, A. B. (1998). *Exclusões sociais*. Lisbon: Gradiva.

de Miranda, A. (2005, November) *Technological determinism and ideology: questioning the 'Information Society' and the 'digital divide'*. Paper presented in 'The Future of Research in the Information Society' event, parallel to the World Summit on Information Society, Tunis, Nov 16-18, 2005. Retrieved November 29, 2008, from http://www.ces.uc.pt/bss/documentos/2006_11_13_alvaro_de_miranda.pdf

Demo, P. (1998). *Charme da exclusão social*. Campinas: Autores Associados.

Eubanks, V. E. (2007, September). Trapped in the digital divide: The distributive paradigm in community informatics. *Journal of Community Informatics* [Online], *3*(2). Retrieved November 29, 2008, from http://www.ci-journal.net/index.php/ciej/article/view/293/353

Foley, P., Codagnone, C., & Osimo, D. (2008). *An analysis of international digital strategies: Why develop a digital inclusion strategy and what should be the focus?* Research report. Tech4i2/Department for Communities and Local Government, London, UK Crown. Retrieved November 29, 2008, from http://www.communities.gov.uk/documents/communities/pdf/1000425.pdf.

Gurstein, M. (2003, December). Effective use: A community informatics strategy beyond the digital divide. *First Monday* [Online], *8*(12). Retrieved November 29, 2008, from http://www.firstmonday.org/issues/issue8_12/gurstein/index.html

Ianni, O. (1992). *A sociedade global*. Rio de Janeiro: Civilização Brasileira. IT for Change. (2007, January). *Development in the Information Society: exploring a social policy framework*. Workshop Report, Bangalore. Retrived May 17, 2009, from http://www.itforchange.net/media/wksp_reports/workshop_report_development_in_the_information_society_2007.pdf

Kuhn, T. S. (1990). *A estrutura das revoluções científicas* (Boeira, B. V., & Boeira, N., Trans.). São Paulo: Perspectiva. (Original work published 1962)

Leal, G. F. (2004). *A noção de exclusão social em debate: aplicabilidade e implicações para a intervenção prática*. Paper presented at the 14th Brazilian Association of Population Studies (ABEP) meeting, Caxambu, MG. Retrieved November 29, 2008, from http://www.abep.nepo.unicamp.br/site_eventos_abep/PDF/ABEP2004_42.pdf

Mattelart, A. (2002). *História da sociedade da informação* (Campanário, N. N., Trans.). São Paulo: Loyola. (Original work published 2001)

Melucci, A. (2001). *A invenção do presente: movimentos sociais na sociedade complexa*. (M.C.A. Bomfim, Trans.) Petrópolis: Vozes. (Original work published 1982).

Menou, M. (2008, April). *ImperialICTism: the highest stage of capitalism?* Keynote address [La Habana, Cuba, Foro Sociedad del Conocimiento: nuevos espacios para su construcción.]. *Info*, ▪▪▪, 2008.

National Telecommunications and Information Administration (NTIA). (1995). *Falling through the Net: a survey of the 'have-nots' in rural and urban America*. Washington, DC, U.S. Department of Commerce. Retrieved December 23, 2008, from http://www.ntia.doc.gov/ntiahome/fallingthru.html

National Telecommunications and Information Administration (NTIA). (1999). *Falling through the Net: defining the digital divide*, Washington, DC, U.S. Department of Commerce. Retrieved December 23, 2008, from http://www.ntia.doc.gov/ntiahome/fttn99/contents.html

National Telecommunications and Information Administration (NTIA). (2000). *Falling through the Net: toward digital inclusion*, Washington, DC, U.S. Department of Commerce. Retrieved December 23, 2008, from http://www.ntia.doc.gov/ntiahome/fttn00/contents00.html

Nora, S., & Minc, A. (1978). *A informatização da sociedade* (de Vasconcelos, P., Trans.). Lisbon: Sociedade Astória.

Pereira, P. A. (2007). *Necessidades humanas. Subsídios à crítica dos mínimos sociais*. São Paulo: Cortez. (Original work published 2000)

Pisón, J. M. (1998). *Políticas de bienestar. Un estudio sobre los derechos sociales*. Madrid: Universidad de la Rioja.

Pochmann, M. (2002). *e-Trabalho*. São Paulo: Publisher Brasil.

Postman, N. (1993). *Technopoly. The surrender of culture to technology*. New York: Vintage Books. (Original work published 1992)

Rodino-Colocino, M. (2006). Laboring under the digital divide. *New Media Society, 8 (487)*. Sage Publications, London, Thousand Oaks; CA and New Delhi. Retrieved November 29, 2008, from http://nms.sagepub.com/cgi/content/abstract/8/3/487

Room, G. (1995). Poverty and social exclusion: the new European agenda for policy and social research. In Room, G. (Ed.), *Beyond the Threshold: The Measurement and Analysis of Social Exclusion* (pp. 1–9). Bristol: The Policy Press.

Rosanvallon, P. (1998). *A nova questão social* (Bath, S., Trans.). Brasília: Instituto Teotônio Vilela. (Original work published 1995)

Servon, L. J. (2002). *Bridging the digital divide: Technology, community, and public policy*. Oxford: Blackwell Publishing. doi:10.1002/9780470773529

Spirakis, P., Manolopoulos, C., & Efstathiadou, R. (2008, May). *The socioeconomic aspects of digital divide*. Proceedings of the Bridging the digital divide in rural communities: practical solutions and policies Conference. Athens, Greece.

Van Dijk, J. A. G. M. (2005). *The deepening divide: Inequality in the Information Society*. Thousand Oaks, CA: Sage Publications.

Warschauer, M. (2006). *Tecnologia e inclusão social: a exclusão digital em debate* (Szlak, C., Trans.). São Paulo: Senac. (Original work published 2003)

Xiberras, M. (1996). *As teorias da exclusão: para uma construção do imaginário do desvio* (Rego, J. G., Trans.). Lisbon: Instituto Piaget. (Original work published 1993)

Yu, L. (2006). Understanding information inequality: Making sense of the literature of the information and digital divides. *Journal of Librarianship and Information Science,* 38 (229). London, Thousand Oaks, CA and New Delhi: Sage Publications. Retrieved November 29, 2008, from http://lis.sagepub.com/cgi/content/abstract/38/4/229

Chapter 4
Participatory Monitoring and Evaluation of ICTs for Development

Ricardo Ramírez
University of Guelph, Canada

ABSTRACT

In this chapter I call for participatory monitoring and evaluation (M&E) of information and communication technology for development (ICT4D). I describe the ontology of ICT4D as complex and unpredictable. I favour an epistemology that is based on systems thinking and adaptive management as a foundation for participatory approaches. The M&E of ICTs faces a number of challenges including the lack of a unifying theoretical framework, the need to define users and purposes for each evaluation, the importance of agreeing on the type of causality that is expected, and the reality of short- term project durations. In response to these challenges I review established and emerging approaches such as Utilization Focused Evaluation, Outcome Mapping and Most Significant Change that embrace participation. Participation is a term open to many interpretations; to clarify its meaning I offer several ladders of participation. I conclude with a reflection on the conditions necessary for participatory approaches to gain acceptance in this field. A major lesson in participatory M&E is to understand the methods and to go beyond and be vigilant of the conditions that enable their application.

INTRODUCTION

In this chapter I advocate a participatory monitoring and evaluation (M&E) approach to ascertain the benefits and risks of information and communication technology for development (ICT4D). I lean on the track record of participatory approaches in

DOI: 10.4018/978-1-61520-799-2.ch004

the fields of rural and international development. In both fields it has long been understood that the goals of interventions mean different things to different stakeholders, and this has implications in the evaluation field. I provide a theoretical justification for a participatory approach from a review of this field's ontology –the nature of what is 'knowable'- as well as from its epistemology – the nature of the relationship between the observer the knowable. I argue that ICT4D is characterized by complexity and that systems thinking provides us with the language to interpret it. I propose that constructivist approaches that embrace multiple stakeholder perspectives are necessary, and to be effective they in turn require stakeholder participation in the M&E process.

The field of M&E of ICT4D faces the following challenges:

1. *Theoretical framework*: Very few evaluation case studies are based on an established theoretical framework about development.
2. *Audiences and users*: A stakeholder analysis is necessary, including a differentiation early on between individuals and groups involved in a project –whose views need to be collected- versus the actual users of evaluation findings.
3. *Purpose*: A balance is needed between learning purposes of formative evaluation and impact assessments typical of summative evaluation. This balance is often not made explicit from the start leading to confusion in methodology.
4. *Causality*: An agreement on the assumptions about causality is important (attribution Vs contribution). The extent to which an activity is directly linked to an impact or result is debatable. It is not always clear that an ICD4D activity has been responsible for a measurable change, rather than the political, social or economic factors associated with it.
5. *Time dimension:* An agreement on the dimensions of change that will be measurable is needed from the beginning, including outputs, outcomes, and results or impacts. It is common for impact not to be evident during the lifetime of short projects.
6. *Multiple methods:* Context matters a great deal and there is no single methodology that fits all situations; a range of methods needs to be adapted to each context.

I address the above challenges and describe methods that embrace participatory M&E and that are taking root in the evaluation field and that merit testing in the context of ICT4D (Butcher & Yaron, 2006; Ramírez, 2007). The methods belong to an epistemology that embraces complexity, multiple voices and systems thinking.

Overview of Chapter Objectives and Structure

This chapter has four sections. I begin with a Background on ICTs, ICT4D and I review the ontology and epistemology of this field; I close the section with an example. The second section is a Response to the Challenges. I provide a brief review of systems thinking and adaptive management, two perspectives that embrace the complexity of this field. In the third section on Methodological Innovation I provide a brief review of participation, its promise and some of the critiques surrounding it. I continue with a brief mention of Key Evaluation Questions as a steppingstone to method selection, and I highlight some features of Outcome Mapping and Most Significant Change. In the Conclusion I focus on the conditions necessary for emerging and participatory approaches to take root in M&E of ICTs for Development.

BACKGROUND

Information and communication technologies (ICTs) have become yet another tool for poverty alleviation and improving livelihoods. A decade ago their potential began being touted as revolutionary. Their promise was to improve health services, extend educational opportunities, reduce costs and increase efficiencies for businesses and for society as a whole (Negroponte, 1995) and for rural development in particular (Richardson & Paisley, 1998). It remains a fact that the bulk of hardware and software is designed to suit the needs of urban, industrialized, modern business environments. Their relevance in rural, remote settings and their utilization for poverty alleviation purposes is often an add-on. It follows that their potential has also been qualified as they can exacerbate existing "divides" where the better off in society extend the edge they already have over the poorer ones (Bridges.org, 2001; Mansell & Wehn, 1998). The divides include age, education levels, social status, urban vs rural, religion, gender and income (Vehovar et al., 2006). Rural and remote areas have always been left behind when it comes to market driven expansions of infrastructure, and ICTs are no exception. Enabling access and sustaining it in these areas is an ongoing challenge because demand will never be as strong as in urban centres (Richardson et al., 2002).

Ascertaining the contribution of an ICT for development (ICT4D) initiative is challenging for the following reasons. The purposes behind an intervention may be multiple so the determination of relevant outcomes and results will be open to interpretation (Ramírez, 2001). The notion of "effective use" has been proposed to underline the conditions under which a community informatics strategy will deliver on its promise (Gurstein, 2003). In other words, ICTs on their own are not magic bullets. Their contribution to livelihood outcomes depend on other factors such as skills, additional infrastructures, relevant content, affordability and terms of access.

The range of contributing factors has been captured under the so-called readiness frameworks. Some of these focus on national elements for readiness (Bridges.org, 2001, Information Technologies Group, n.d.; Kirkman et al., 2002), others on regulatory requirements (Beardsley et al., 2002), and a few on sector-specific applications such as telemedicine (Jennett et al., 2003). In this context, it is not surprising that the determination of indicators and indexes is plagued with questions regarding relevance and scale (Barzilai-Nahon, 2006; Menou & Taylor, 2006; Minges, 2002; National Research Council, 1998; Partnership

on measuring ICT for development, 2005; van Dijk, 2001).

Such challenges are not unique to the ICT4D field. Dealing with multiple and interrelated objectives is common in other fields. Sustainability indicators are just as complex and dynamic (Pretty, 1994; Röling & Jiggins, 1998; Röling, 2003). In the natural resources field, watershed management is a case where multiple parties are involved, each with their unique perspective and indicators (Ramírez, 2001; Thompson & Guijt, 1999). In natural resource management the importance of embracing multiple perspectives has long been established (Guijt & Sidersky, 1996; Lee, 1993; Lee, 2001; Woodhill & Röling, 1998). An adaptive learning process for developing indicators has been developed as an effort to embrace the viewpoints of the different stakeholders involved (McAlpine & Birnie, 2006; Reed et al., 2006). The emphasis on listening to multiple voices and introducing them into research has begun spilling into the ICT4D world (Camacho et al., 2000; Ramírez, 2003; Srinivasan, 2006).

Ontology, Nature of the Beast

Ontology refers to the nature of what is 'knowable' (Guba, 1990). "Ontology is derived from the Greek word for *being* and it is the branch of metaphysics which concerns itself with the nature of things." (Snowden, 2005, p.2). The nature of the ICT phenomenon is particularly complex. The marriage of computer and communication has profound consequences in the way information is managed and processed (McLuhan, 1965). ICTs affect many parts of our lives. On the surface they change the way we communicate with one another and how we seek and process information. As Marshal McLuhan liked to say, the medium is the message. He went on to expand that to the notion of the medium as the 'massage' to underscore how it shapes every part of us, including the very language we use to think (McLuhan & Fiore, 1967). The new media influence how we perceive ourselves to the point of shaping our very identity (Turkle, 1984; Turkle, 1995). It follows that these new technologies have implications at many levels including the personal, technical, social and the political (Pacey, 1999).

It is also follows that the purpose of monitoring and evaluation will affect stakeholders differently. Each major stakeholder group derives particular benefits from tracking impact; be they different users of the services, services providers, governments and funders, private investors, or regulators. The benefits may be about planning, evaluating or replicating the investment (Ramírez & Richardson, 2005). "Since the decisions and the stakeholders involved differ, the type of measurement or estimates will need to be specific to their needs. At the same time, they need to be sufficiently relevant and consistent to support the agreements among them." (Ramírez & Richardson, 2005, p.301)

There have been numerous attempts to harness this complexity into an organized number of indicators and conceptual frameworks (for a detailed review see: Ramírez & Richardson, 2005). However, a fundamental perspective that has emerged is the notion of user participation in the very design of the technologies to be used in the first place:

" the approach to ICTs must be information centred, integral to its environment, integrated with development objectives, intermediated, interconnected, and indigenized." (Heeks, 2002, p.11)

" [information and communication technologies] ICTs have many revolutionary implications, but in order to achieve their full potential benefits it is necessary to focus on user-oriented and cost-effective applications rather than on technology-driven applications." (Mansell & Wehn, 1998, p.95)

In order to capture these requirements there is a need for an approach that acknowledges the multiple perspectives and dimensions involved;

in other words we need a new epistemology (Ramírez, 2003).

Epistemology, How to Learn about the Beast

Epistemology addresses the nature of the relationship between the inquirer and the known or knowable (Guba, 1990). Epistemology is about how we choose to relate to the ontology. The choice is influenced, among other factors, by our own value system and sense of identity, and by power relations. Participatory research, and participatory action research (Selener, 1997) are examples of methodologies that belong to an epistemology where the researcher believes in learning *from people* instead of treating them as passive subjects. The active participation of people leads to a collaborative understanding about a situation. This calls for a constructivist epistemology in contrast with an expert-driven or positivist one (Jiggins & Röling, 1997). While positivist researchers feel this compromises objectivity, I position myself in the constructivist paradigm. I have learned most through negotiation and an inter-subjective approach. I have found that a methodology that is negotiated with the research partners leads to clarity among all parties about the goals, methods for data collection, and in some cases to a joint analysis and interpretation of findings.

In the more technical field of information systems, the acknowledgement that multiple perspectives intervene is becoming recognized (Legris et al., 2003). From the conceptual side, researchers are beginning to grasp the fact that telecommunication services contribute to multiple social, economic, and livelihood dimensions that are interrelated (Hillier, 2000). As Ramírez and Richardson state:

In short what is being measured is a wide range of indicators that are chosen by the specific interest of each party as they are perceived to be of relevance to the subject matter. Policy makers may be satisfied with standard indicators of teledensity to satisfy universal access policies; commercial carriers will need to know the rate of return on investment; residential users will be mainly interested in the price and quality of service; while agencies involved in health and education may need to document the cost savings brought about by the use of the technology. There are multiple players and multiple targets, and measurement needs to embrace this complexity. (Ramírez & Richardson, 2005, p.301)

Example

The following example comes form the evaluation of a broadband demonstration project implemented by the Kuh-Ke-Nah Aboriginal network in northern Canada. The researchers focused on three complementary dimensions. The first were a set of community-wide measures of accessibility using indicators that were standardized by Statistics Canada and the International Telecommunications Union (ITU). This allowed for cross national and international comparisons. The second set focused on locally agreed sector action plans. These plans were developed through an engagement with local stakeholders to develop community visions of improved services in health, education, local government and economic development. The third component focused on changes in individuals' skills and knowledge levels. A feature of the approach was the integration of video testimonials to capture real-life stories from people where they explained how they were harnessing the technology (Ramírez & Richardson, 2005).

The background that I have described emphasizes the importance of engaging different voices in defining the goals of an ICT4D investment along with determining what constitutes evidence of achievement. This emphasis is cognizant of an ontology that is complex and dynamic, and it belongs to a constructivist epistemology (Guba, 1990; Lincoln, 1990). Constructivists find that the researcher is best able to document change as perceived by the different parties involved and affected by ICTs. They shape –construct- an understanding through inter-subjective views; as such it constitutes an alternative system of inquiry relative to the prevalent positivist one (Pretty, 1994).

RESPONDING TO THE CHALLENGE

I begin this section with a call to embrace complexity by adapting ideas from systems thinking and adaptive management. I then respond to the challenges to the M&E field that were listed in the Introduction (the lack of a unifying theoretical framework, the need to define users and purposes for each evaluation, explaining from the starts the assumed level of causality versus contribution and the challenge of short term project durations). The need for multiple methods is covered in the third section.

Embracing Complexity

Two theoretical foundations that embrace the complexity are systems thinking and adaptive management. They provide a basis on which to build M&E approaches that embrace the challenges inherent to the world of ICT4D, and that are fundamentally participatory. I begin with system thinking: a useful tool for learning about complex situations and for interdisciplinary research (Ackoff, 1969).

ICT4D deals with a range of problems. Some are simple and largely predictable (installing computers in a telecentre, training students to do on-line searches), others are complicated and required specialized skills (ensuring that telemedicine videoconferences have quality of service). Beyond that we face a third category: the complex problem. Complex problems are dynamic as the component elements will interrelate in ways that we can often not predict. An example of a complex problem is how people will interact with technology to make decisions on their health, their education or their employment. Complex problems are best approached with using a systems perspective (Patton, 2008).

Systems thinking is basically a way of exploring our world with full awareness of its inherent messiness, it constant change and its unpredictability. In this perspective, the interchange among factors means that one can expect to be surprised by what is referred to as emerging properties. This is common when societies and new technologies interact. As Chapman underlines: "Systems thinking is useful for tackling issues that are embedded in complexity, particularly where that includes human activity." (Chapman, 2004, p.35)

Systems thinking focuses on a holistic understanding rather than focusing on simplifying complexity by looking at component parts in isolation (Chapman, 2004). Conventional infrastructural projects rely on linear planning models, such as logical frameworks, to control predictable design and installation protocols. However, when technology is put to work in the context of social networks, contrasting cultural norms, and complex organizations, the certainty and predictability of linear planning is lost. Kay emphasizes the need to move away from our fascination with certainty:

Complex situations involve uncertainty and surprise. They give the impression that there is no right way of looking at them and no right answer to the problems they raise. The problem is really the singularity of our concept of the "right answer". Complexity defies linear logic as it brings with it self-organization and feedback loops, wherein the effect is its own cause... In essence, complexity is characterized by situations where several different coherent future scenarios are possible, each of which may be desirable, all of which have an inherent irreducible uncertainty as to the likelihood for their actually coming about. (Kay, 2008, p.3)

In the earlier example from the Canadian north we certainly had evidence of emerging properties and unexpected outcomes. The introduction of telemedicine and Internet-based education to remote communities, for example, received a positive level of acceptance by the elders beyond what we had originally expected.

For Kay (2008) systems thinking is about patterns of relationships that translate into emergent behaviours. It is a way of seeing and understanding complexity. It is a paradigm of relevance to the analysis of information and communication systems where multiple viewpoints intervene (Bennetts et al., 2000). Bennetts and colleagues underline that in systems thinking innovation is not seen as a linear process, but rather an emergent property of the interaction among complementary actors. Along with other authors (Bryden, 1994), they promote systems thinking as a relevant research perspective for ICT analysis.

A second and complementary theoretical foundation is adaptive management, a field that has a footing in the management of complex natural systems (Boyle et al., 2001; Jiggins and Röling, 2000, Lee, 1998). The notion of complex adaptive systems is beginning to take root in the business and economics literature (Davenport & Prusak, 1997).

Learning and adaptation jointly shape the concept of adaptive management and policy development proposed by Kai Lee (1993). According to Lee a process of ongoing negotiation among stakeholders is the best option to manage complex systems. While his work centres on natural resource management, the commonalities of that field with ICT4D has been established elsewhere (Ramírez, 2003; Ramírez & Lee, 2008). An underlying assumption is that natural resource systems on the whole are far too complex to allow for prediction of the impact of human intervention. This assumption applies to aspects of ICTs that are highly unpredictable, and that exhibit emerging properties in complex systems (Bar et al., 2000; Fink & Kenny, 2003; O'Reilly, 2005).

Kai Lee calls for a joint exploration among stakeholders of their interests. Each stakeholder, in turn, can provide indicators that capture relevant measures. He adds that the system is dynamic and highly unpredictable, hence the indicators serve to track how the system responds to a management strategy; he calls it 'system feedback'. Lee's account of the negotiations for the management of the Columbia River Basin provides an example of this approach. Biologists, hydroelectric damn engineers, cottagers, Aboriginal groups and environmentalists came to together to agree on how to manage the massive watershed (Lee, 1993; Lee, 1995; Lee, 1998). One lesson learnt was that when multiple parties agree to collaborate using commonly agreed indicators, a new language develops (Lee, 1993; Glasbergen, 1996).

This example is of interest in the world of ICTs, where different terminologies abound. The translation of these concepts into the world of ICT4D is only just starting. There is a need for on the ground testing to verify their relevance and combine them with monitoring and evaluation (Andrew & Petkov, 2003; Ramírez, 2007).

Theoretical Framework for Development

The bulk of existing ICT4D research to date has been biased towards action, rather than knowledge; it has been mainly descriptive rather than analytical; and it has lacked rigour (Heeks, 2007a). In response to this trend, Heeks advocates for research that is grounded in an identified theory. He flags the prevalence of theories based in library and information sciences, communication studies, and information systems; and he calls for further integration with development studies.

By making one's development framework explicit, one has to revisit goals and assumptions that are otherwise left unchallenged. In the broad international development context several frameworks are prevalent. The Millenium Development Goals (MDGs) is an attempt to outline a set of priorities

across major development sectors[1]. The Human Development Index (HDI) is another framework that development programs use as a yardstick to gauge their progress[2]. A complementary and more people-oriented framework developed by Amartya Sen is based on rights and capabilities (Sen, 2005).

Some theoretical frameworks are associated with more specialized aspects of development. In the field of Communication for Development there have been ample debates as to the overall concept of development to be pursued. Communication initiatives, just like ICT4D ones, are part of an overall theoretical framework for development. For decades, the dominant framework was the *diffusion of innovations*, while today the shift has moved towards perspectives that focus more on *social change* (Alfaro Moreno, 2006; FAO, 1994; Waisbord, 2001).

In other more specific sectors, for example, the authors of an Irish study on the social impact of ICTs chose to focus on their *communicative* aspect as opposed to their *instrumental* one (O'Donnell & Henriksen, 2002). In the UK, research on the educational outcomes of ICTs focused on finding an integrative theoretical framework to confront a tendency to have research fragmented by specialist concerns (Underwood, 2004). These examples signal the need to find holistic frameworks that acknowledge the complex nature of ICT4D interventions.

The sustainable livelihoods framework integrates five types of assets (financial, physical, natural, social and human) with issues of risk and vulnerability (Carney et al., 1999; Gilling et al., 2001; Scoones, 1998). In contrast with the MDGs or HDI, it pays attention to process dimensions (Wright, 2008). This framework has begun to be linked to ICTs research and evaluation (Barroso, 2007; Chapman et al., 2005; FAO et al., 2002; Parkinson, 2005; Parkinson & Ramírez, 2006). There have also been attempts at combining elements from the livelihoods framework with Sen's rights and capabilities that merit further attention

(Alampay, 2006; Grunfeld, 2007). Chapman explains the cross-sectoral features of the livelihoods framework:

A notable feature of livelihoods thinking is that it promotes an approach to development problems that transcends individual sectors. Building cross-sectoral, multi-disciplinary partnerships is a complex challenge. Success will ultimately depend upon the establishment of effective systems of information and communication which facilitate multi-level knowledge partnerships between different stakeholders in rural development strategies. (Chapman et al., 2005, p.vi)

The development industry is beginning to shift away from a narrow focus on linear, performance-based approaches, to a wider array of methods. A renewed attention to process and to long-term perspectives is on the agenda. This creates an opening for a combination of evaluation methods and for a more prominent role for development beneficiaries (Wright, 2008).

Defining the Evaluation Users and Purpose

The second and third challenges listed in the Introduction are about purpose and users. A key starting point in evaluation is to clarify its purpose. Who is the evaluation for, and how are the users going to utilize the findings? These simple questions are at the heart of utilization focused evaluation (UFE) (Patton, 2008). A characteristic of UFE is the definition of the actual individuals who need the evaluation: not vague categories such as "policy makers" but rather specific names of people and their positions: Jayne Smith, Director of Research. A second feature is the definition of specific decisions she has to make that are dependent on the evaluation findings. In Michael Quinn Patton's experience, these two questions set the stage for the definition of evaluation questions.

Engaging decision makers in defining evaluation questions is desirable. From a participatory perspective, the active engagement of decision makers from the early stages of the evaluation enhances their buy-in since the process responds to their particular needs. Those needs guide the balance between learning objectives (formative evaluation) and impact assessments (summative evaluation).

Causality and Time

Among the challenges mentioned in the Introduction to this chapter, causality is of particular importance. The debate centres on the notion of attribution versus contribution. Attribution refers to the assumption than an ICT activity will lead to a predictable outcome that in turn will lead to a measurable result. This perspective or theory of change is based on a linear and causal effect mindset that is rooted in result-based management (RBM). In many international and national bureaucracies, RBM and its sister tool logical framework analysis (LFA), are required planning instruments to apply for funding.

The LFA follows a hierarchical sequence linking a high level, overall *purpose* of a project all the way to the specific *activities* to be delivered. At the lowest level of the hierarchy there will be *activities* (e.g. training sessions) that will lead to measurable *outputs* (e.g. number telehealth facilitators trained). These in turn are expected to provide *outcomes* (e.g. funds saved from reduced medical travel for specialist consultations). The collection of *outputs* will enable the *outcomes* to become evident (e.g. a coordination of equipment, financing, human resources). Beyond that it is expected that the *outcomes* will lead to the overall *purpose* often worded in terms of *results* or *impact* (e.g. improved health status of a population). In other words, the LFA is based on the notion of attribution or direct causality.

Coupled with the causality challenge is the issue of time. A challenge encountered in practice is that many projects only last 2-3 years and they tend to yield evidence mainly at the *output* and *outcome* level. Ramírez explains this further:

It is therefore not surprising that evaluation reports often confirm Outputs being achieved in quantitative terms, as well as a number of Outcomes through a combination of qualitative and quantitative findings. However, the extent to which Results may become measurable in the longer term is tempered by the short duration of the projects combined with the inevitable influence by other factors. In other words, the direct causality between the project investments and the overall Results is elusive. At best the contribution of the investment is evident, rather than its attribution. (Ramírez, 2007, p.86)

The contribution view acknowledges the many other factors outside the control of a project that shape the results. In this perspective, the focus is placed on the *outcomes*. While *results* remain important, their achievement is not sought as evidence that the project itself was responsible for the change. In addition, unexpected *outcomes* are embraced. The emergence of innovations is seen as evidence of socially negotiated solutions where people use technologies, often in ways that planners never considered. These challenges to evaluation have already been recognized in the evaluation field (Parks et al.; 2005, Rogers, 2008), in the communication for development field (Figueroa et al., 2002) and in ICT4D evaluation (Myers, 2004). Parkinson and Ramírez elaborate on this on the basis of research in Colombia:

In ICT-for-development projects, there is very rarely a direct causal link between the intervention and the benefit realized, and the benefits themselves may be very hard to predict, especially when ICTs are introduced in an open-ended manner, such as through a telecentre. A child may use a telecentre to research a homework project; an older woman may use it to communicate to her son working overseas. Different users may value their use for distinct reasons, not always in line with the expectations of the project designers. As has been commonly found in other development projects, there may be unintended negative consequences with the introduction of a telecentre. (Parkinson & Ramírez, 2006)

METHODOLOGICAL INNOVATION

In this third section I review the emergence and evolution of participation in research. I continue with a brief review of key evaluation questions as a first step in the definition of relevant methodologies. I continue with an elaboration of emerging methods that hold promise for participatory M&E of ICT4D.

Heeks (2007b) suggests the following six questions to guide impact assessment of ICT4D:

- Why: what is the rationale for impact assessment?
- For whom: who is the intended audience for the impact assessment?
- What: what is to be measured?
- How 1: how are the selected indicators to be measured?
- When: at what point in ICT4D project lifecycle are indicators to be measured?
- How 2: how are impact assessment results to be reported, disseminated and used? (p.2)

Under "How 1" he adds that "… a key element here will be the extent of participation of project users in measurement (and in more upstream processes such as selection of indicators)." (Heeks, 2007b: 2) The guiding questions are a useful map for methodology selection and the reference to participation provides an entry point into the different meanings of the term.

The Emergence and Evolution of 'Participation'

In the international development field, the focus on 'community participation' became a hallmark of poverty alleviation projects by the 1980s. The shift from the diffusion of innovations approach, to a more critical, structural critique responded to a move away from the modernist perspectives of the 1950s and 60s, to the dependency theories that came from the South (Escobar, 1995). The literature on participation grew and became associated with action research and social movements (Selener, 1997). The emphasis on making the voices of the poor heard was advanced by practitioners and academics (Chambers, 1997).

During the 1990s, with the advent of globalization and liberalization, attention shifted from an initial focus on empowerment and capacity development, to the efficiency and effectiveness of project interventions (Cornwall, 2002). Participation was then associated with decentralization efforts and with attention to beneficiaries as 'clients' that can demand services. While participation became a 'must have' approach, it was also institutionalized. Criticism has since grown about its limitations and abuse (Cooke & Kothari, 1998; Mosse, 1993; Quaghebeur & Masschelin, 2003). A common critique stems for the tendency to institutionalize participatory approaches to suit funding requirements, to the expense of local dynamics. This leads to a legitimization of power differences. There remains, however, more criticism in academic circles relative to practitioner ones, where the potential of enhancing ownership and creating capacity remains a priority (Grunfeld, 2008).

While many of these critiques are valid, there is also room for a qualification. What is exactly meant by the term? Is it necessary all the time? What level of participation are we talking about?

There are varied definitions of participation: "…definitions of participation range form assisting people to exercise their democratic rights to a means of obtaining views from different stakeholders" (Kanji & Greenwood, 2001, p.7)

Participation: enabling people to realize their rights to participate in, and access information relating to, the decision-making processes which affect their lives. Democratic institutions and access to information about governments' policies and performance are necessary to enable people to participate in the decisions that affect their lives. They also need to be able to form organization, such as unions, women's groups or citizens' monitoring groups, to represent their collective interests. (DFID, 2002: p.24 as quoted in Kanji & Greenwood, 2001)

A method that is often associated with participation is stakeholder engagement. It can take place during different stages of a project: defining the agenda; development of a proposal; preparatory phase; implementation; analysis of results; and/or dissemination and action (Kanji & Greenwood, 2001).

At each stage there can be a different level of participation. The levels are described through "ladders of participation". Table 1 provides examples from three different sources.

The ladders show a continuum from self-mobilizing all the way to totalitarian control. In a more recent variation there is attention to the evolving roles and relationships between outsiders and local people who gradually take ownership and shift upwards along the ladder towards more self-control (Chambers, 2005).

An Achilles Heel in participatory work is the tendency to exaggerate what was accomplished: suggesting that a process of collective action occurred when in fact the activity was simply a consultation (Ramírez, 2008). Heeks (1999) has added his concern in the field of information systems. He proposed three key questions to avoid some of the pitfalls described above:

Table 1. Three ladders of participation

Arnstein (1969)	Pretty (1994)	Kanji & Greenwood (2001)
Citizen Control	Self-mobilisation	Collective action
Delegated power	Interactive participation	Co-learning
Partnership	Functional participation	Cooperation
Placation	Participation for material incentives	
Consultation	Participation by consultation	Consultation
Informing	Participation in information giving	
Therapy	Passive participation	Compliance
Manipulation		

1. What is the political and cultural context? The context matters and may determine if participatory approaches are viable or not.
2. Who wants to introduce participation and why? The motivations by the proponents need to be clear to avoid a transfer of work-loads and to make sure it provides a venue for increased ownership.
3. Who is participation sought from? Do they want it and can they participate? The actual interest, willingness and ability to partici-pate by different parties cannot be taken for granted (Heeks, 1999).

What matters most is to be sincere about the type of participation that is possible at every stage of the research. Doing a consultation and yet suggesting it represents social mobilization will damage the reputation of any participatory approach.

The evaluation literature has begun to recog-nize the advantages of emergent practices that embrace collaborate models. Evaluations that engage intended users in the research process lead to personal learning among them. This in turn leads to more direct application of the evaluation findings to program practices. It also enhances the users' confidence in using the findings. In addition, participatory approaches reduce power differentials between evaluators and program practitioners, and this in turn leads to more ne-

gotiated decision making and learning (Shulha & Cousins, 1997).

Developing Key Evaluation Questions

Heeks' six questions (listed at the start of this Section) focus our attention on the basic *why, for whom and what* dimensions of evaluation. We need to attend to these in the form of key evaluation questions (KEQ) before we can select methods. A set of clear KEQs will guide us in the selection of our methodology.

It is only possible to define relevant method-ologies once the research questions are set. The following are main categories of key evaluation questions: impact, outcomes, approach or model, process, quality and cost effectiveness (Dart, 2006)

Examples

*   *Impact:* to what extent is it likely that youth who play computer games will earn higher marks in class?
*   *Outcomes:* to what extent did girls who completed an on-line literacy tutorial change their reading habits?
*   *Approach/model:* how does a self-directed course compare with the standard teaching guidelines?

- *Process:* to what extent were parents and students engaged in the design of the course?
- *Quality:* what was the quality of the learning outcomes?
- *Cost effectiveness*: what is the expected cost benefit of the pilot course? (adapted from Dart, 2006)

Dart (2006) suggests the following generic matching of evaluation questions and methods:

- *Impact:* Contribution analysis, data trawl, expert panels, Gender Evaluation Methodology (GEM)
- *Outcomes:* Outcome Mapping (OM), Most Significant Change (MSC), GEM
- *Unexpected outcomes:* OM
- *Approach/model:* Comparative studies
- *Process:* Interviews, focus groups
- *Quality:* Audit against standards
- *Cost benefit:* Economic modeling

Emerging Methods to Test in ICT4D

Among the above examples there is reference to recent methods with promise. They merit to be tested in the context of ICT4D. In doing so we do not need to throw out the baby with the bathwater: conventional methods have value for specific purposes. For example while linear planning tools such as results-based management and logical frameworks have limitations, they do capture the logic between activities, outputs and outcomes. There are suggestions for a combination of logframes with emerging methods such as Outcome Mapping (Roduner & Schläppi, 2008; Ramírez, 2007)

Outcome Mapping (OM) is one method that centres on *outcomes* (Earl et al., 2003). It acknowledges that project activities can be linked, for example, to how people change what they do as a result of a training event. In OM, the people who are directly involved in an activity are de-

scribed as *boundary partners*. OM focuses on documenting their changes in behaviour. Earl and colleagues explain that a boundary partner, upon returning from a training event to her own work environment or community, will face a myriad of other factors that may enhance or limit the extent to which she can apply the newly acquired skills and knowledge. In OM, the emphasis is on the contribution of an activity, not its attribution. OM focuses on *change markers* that function as indicators of behavior change. When they are developed in a participatory manner, the interested stakeholders can define and adjust those markers as their own perspectives and behaviours evolve.

In the ICT4D world the value of narrative is gaining recognition as a way to capture the complex and dynamic effects of technology and services. Stoll et al. (2002) recommend collecting first-hand stories from people about how they make use of the technologies. This allows relevant data to emerge, without the need to predict (Stoll et al., 2002). Most Significant Change (MSC) is based on people's rich memories and personal knowledge of their context (Dart & Davies, 2003). Most Significant Change (MSC) uses narrative as its main data source. In MSC, domains of change (relevant categories of issues) are selected along with criteria to identify the stories that are worthy of selection. Story telling is relaxing; it is based on traditions of dialogue (Dart & Davies, 2003). As with OM, Dart and Davies underline that MSC is meant to be combined with other methods. This methodological pluralism responds to the range of key evaluation questions listed above.

From a participatory point of view, UFE, OM, MSC call for the active engagement of a number of parties. UFE emphasizes the need to define users and to have them determine what it is that the evaluation is needed for. In both OM and MSC, stakeholders who are able to determine change markers, will have a sense of ownership over the changes and a stake in documenting them.

It is clear that context matters and there is no one-size fits all approach; a range of methods need to be adapted to each situation. Regardless of the methodological combination, the participatory dimension underlines the importance of ownership. An evaluation that responds to a specific set of decision makers will end up being used. Users will be able to adjust the process as they uncover the specific data they need to inform their decisions. As was described above, participation can take place at different levels and at different stages. One type of participation is not superior over another; what is important is to be transparent about the level that is sought or achieved.

Example

An evaluation of an e-government project in the Oxford County library network in Ontario, Canada provides a case where of some of the above methods were introduced (Ramírez et al., 2000). The example also highlights some of the organizational conditions necessary for participatory evaluation to thrive.

During all of 1999 the Oxford County Library (OCL) and Human Resources Development Canada (HRDC) collaborated in the implementation of the Rural Resources Partnerhsip (RRP) project. The purpose of the project was 1) to offer information on HRDC Income Security and Canada Pension Plan services through the OCL branches across Oxford County, 2) to offer extended hours of operations for the libraries, 3) to involve high-school co-op students working as interns in delivering the services. It is expected that the RRP will serve as a pilot project with applicability to the future delivery of a wider range of government services. (Ramírez et al., 2000, p.1)

The Oxford County library already had a track record as a pioneer in ICTs and they were keen to attract more services to make use of their expanded bandwidth. As researchers we were invited to develop the evaluation questions with the participation of the Chief Librarian and his

team, and with the HRDC, the federal agency funding the project and delegating the government services to the library. Both parties were interested in documenting how the pilot project worked in order to expand the approach to other rural municipalities. Without utilizing UFE language we were inadvertently using the same principles: a focus on specific users and their needs.

The objectives of the evaluation were to assess the extent of community awareness of the new services; the level of utilization of library services; the satisfaction of RRP program participants; the level of skills/knowledge and attitudes of student participants; the satisfaction of the library client base, and the extent of community acceptance.

We chose several methods on the basis of the key evaluation questions. Our data collection tools included the following: a user survey of library patrons was applied over four different dates; this was complemented with a random telephone interviews of households. We held focus groups with library patrons, and others with library staff. Last, we completed before and after knowledge and skill questionnaires with the co-op students.

The focus groups with library staff resembled the MSC method in that we sought to uncover the changes that the new e-government services had brought to the staff. In hindsight, the student knowledge and skill questionnaires could have been greatly enhanced had Outcome Mapping been available as a method to make behavioural changes explicit.

Was our an example of a participatory evaluation? - Only to a limited extent. We achieved high levels of interaction with most of the users of the evaluation: the Chief Librarian and the HDRC representatives were engaged and very keen on utilizing the report. As evidence of that, the library staff along with some municipal officer presented a paper at an international conference summarizing the evaluation process[3]. On the other hand, the extent to which patrons and library staff participated in the evaluation was limited to participating in focus groups and responding to surveys; a dimension that we did not consider to be participatory. We did, however, make sure we presented our findings to the library staff as our findings were of interest to them as evaluation users.

CONCLUSION

Throughout this chapter I have advocated for participatory monitoring and evaluation of information and communication for development initiatives. I have explained the complex nature of ICT4D and I have expressed my preference for a constructivist epistemology. I have argued that these initiatives affect us all in multiple* ways and that we simply have no choice but to embrace multiple voices and build an inter-subjective understanding of change. I have argued that the change that is brought about by ICTs is best captured through a contribution perspective, instead of a linear, attribution one. I have leaned on systems thinking and adaptive management as approaches that invite multiple voices and embrace the dynamic, every changing nature of ICT4D. Finally I have provided a glimpse of Utilization Focused Evaluation, Outcome Mapping and Most Significant Change as an approach and as two methodologies that provide a course of action for participatory evaluation.

I have come to the realization that there is ready supply of participatory methods in contrast with the conditions that enable one to apply them. I turn my attention to these conditions as they dictate the possibility of applying the methods much more often than any theoretical consideration. The attention to context is recognized in evaluation literature, especially in studies that focus on evaluation utilization (Shulha & Cousins, 1997).

Above all, the culture of the organizations involved is of paramount importance. If they are willing and able to learn, to do course correction on the basis of feedback, and to embrace mistakes as a way to improve their services, then there is

room for an evaluation that is participatory – or at best that uses participatory methods. Byrne emphasizes the influence of organizational cultures:

To achieve its potential, it is crucial that M&E is fundamentally linked to and part of broader processes of organisational learning and development...PM&E practitioners and writers all emphasise the importance of evaluation and learning processes being integral to wider organizational processes and practice. Although this seems obvious, factors that militate against it include professional silos, the artificial division of related responsibilities, weak capacity and understanding, little attention to refection and learning from experience (i.e. to experiential knowledge), dominant professional and knowledge hierarchies, and inadequate higher-level support. (Byrne, 2007)

In both the examples provided in this chapter, the Kuh-Ke-Nah Aboriginal Network and the Oxford County Library, the organizations hosting the evaluation were sincere about learning from the process. Both had developed a trustful relationship with their respective funders, who in turn were also keen to learn rather than judge. This explains why we as researchers were invited early on to prepare an evaluation methodology as the projects were being developed – a rare situation indeed.

In both of these evaluation experiences we enjoyed many of the factors that are recognized as facilitating participatory monitoring and evaluation (PM&E):

- Open and safe space for people to participate and voice their own views and concerns;
- Enabling policies and necessary financial support, to enable and legitimate in particular the involvement of less powerful stakeholders;
- Capacity, including for creativity and flexibility;

- Incentives to reward staff for innovation, learning and adaptation;
- Support and facilitation from able and creative intermediary institutions;
- Adequate time;
- Openness to and reward of risk-taking;
- Institutional openness and willingness to participate fully;
- Leadership and champions, for PM&E to be both effective and sustainable;
- Senior-level staff involvement and commitment, including informed initial buy-in, so resources and support for evolving process and findings are sustained. This is particularly important as PM&E often unleashes uncomfortable, deeper questions about organizational practice, processes and priorities;
- Strong and sustained management support, including dedicated human and financial resources;
- Clarity about roles and responsibilities from the start;
- Supportive networks for mutual exchange of experience and learning;
- The support of relevant interest groups, internally and externally; and
- A firm grounding in local context and culture. (Byrne, 2007)

In both cases, the implementers had committed to the evaluation and had budgeted the resources from the start. There was a long-term view about the benefits from learning systematically about the pilot project. The project leaders in each agency were the main users and they had very clear needs to fulfill. As with other participatory approaches, we benefited less from methodology and more from the conditions in place: dedicated champions in place who were sincere in their desire to serve, to learn and to improve their community (Quarry & Ramírez, 2009).

A major lesson in participatory M&E is to understand the methods and to go beyond and be vigilant of the conditions that enable their application. If the conditions are not there, any effort and participation will be disappointing. On the other hand, when the conditions are right, there are few limits to innovation and engagement.

REFERENCES

Ackoff, R. (1969). Systems, organizations, and interdisciplinary research. In Emery, F. (Ed.), *Systems thinking* (pp. 330–347). Middlesex, England: Penguin Books.

Alampay, E.A. (2006). Beyond access to ICTs: Measuring capabilities in the information society. *International Journal of Education and Development using Information and Communication Technology (IJEDICT) 2*(2), 4-22.

Alfaro Moreno, R. (2006). *Otra brújula: Innovaciones en comunicación y desarrollo*. Lima, Peru: Calandria.

Andrew, T., & Petkov, D. (2003). The need for a systems thinking approach to the planning of rural telecommunications infrastructure. *Telecommunications Policy, 27*(1-2), 75–93. doi:10.1016/S0308-5961(02)00095-2

Bar, F., Cohen, S., Cowhey, P., DeLong, B., Kleeman, M., & Zysman, J. (2000). Access and innovation policy for the third-generation internet. *Telecommunications Policy, 24*, 489–518. doi:10.1016/S0308-5961(00)00047-1

Barroso, M. (2007, 25-27 October). *Waves in the forest - Radio communication and livelihoods in Brazilian Amazonia*. Paper presented during the World Congress on Communication for Development. Rome.

Barzilai-Nahon, K. (2006, November-December). Gaps and bits: Conceptualizing measurements for digital divides. *The Information Society, 22*(5), 269–278. doi:10.1080/01972240600903953

Beardsley, S., von Morgenstern, B., Enriquez, L., & Kipping, C. (2002). Telecommunications sector reform - A prerequisite for network readiness. In Kirkman, G., Sachs, J., Schwab, K., & Cornellius, P. (Eds.), *The Global Information Technology Report 2001-2002: Readiness for the networked world* (pp. 118–136). Oxford, UK: Oxford University Press.

Bennetts, P., Wood-Harper, A., & Mills, S. (2000, April). A holistic approach to the management of information systems development: A review using soft systems approach and multiple viewpoints. *Systemic Practice and Action Research, 13*(2), 189–205. doi:10.1023/A:1009594604515

Boyle, M., Kay, J., & Pond, B. (2001). Monitoring in support of policy: An adaptive ecosystem approach. In Munn, T. (Ed.), *Encyclopedia of Global Environmental Change* (*Vol. 4*, pp. 116–137). London: John Wiley and Sons.

Bridges.org. (2001). Spanning the Digital Divide: Understanding and Tackling the Issues. Retrieved October 6, 2008 from http://www.bridges.org/publications/65

Bryden, J. (1994). Towards sustainable rural communities: From theory to action. In Bryden, J. (Ed.), *Towards sustainable rural communities: The Guelph Seminar Series* (pp. 211–233). Guelph, Canada: University of Guelph School of Rural Planning and Development.

Butcher, G., & Yaron, G. (2006). *Scoping study: Monitoring and evaluation of research communication*. Prepared for the Research Communication M&E Steering Group, London. Retrieved December 5, 2008 from http://www.healthlink.org.uk/PDFs/scoping.pdf

Byrne, A. (2007, November). Working towards evidence-based process: Evaluation that matters. *Mazi, 13*. Retrieved December 5, 2008 from http://www.communicationforsocialchange.org/mazi.php?id=13

Camacho, K., Villalobos, V., & Shrader, E. (2000). Building an ICT Evaluation Framework: IDRC Workshop Proceedings. El Tirol, Costa Rica. Retrieved February 9, 2005 from http://www.bellanet.org/leap/docs/Building_an_ICT_Evaluation_Framework.doc?OutsideInServer=no

Carney, D., Drinkwater, T., Rusinow, K., Neefjes, S., Wanmali, S., & Singh, N. (1999, February). *Livelihoods approaches compared. A brief comparison of the livelihoods approaches of the UK Department for International Development (DFID), CARE, Oxfam and the United Nations Development Program (UNDP)*. FAO E-Conference and forum on Operationalizing Participatory Ways of Applying a Sustainable Livelihoods Approach. Rome: FAO.

Chambers, R. (1997). *Whose reality counts? Putting the first last*. London: IT Publications.

Chambers, R. (2005). *Ideas for development*. London: Earthscan.

Chapman, J. (2004). *System failure: Why governments must learn to think differently*. London: Demos.

Chapman, R., Slaymaker, T., & Young, J. (2005). *Livelihood approaches to communication and information in support of rural poverty elimination and food security* [ODI]. London, Rome: DFID and FAO.

Cooke, B., & Kothari, U. (1998). *Participation: The new tyranny?* London: Zed Books.

Cornwall, A. (2002). Making spaces, changing places: Situating participation in development. *IDS Working Paper, vol. 170*. Sussex, UK: Institute for Development Studies.

Dart, J. (2006). *Key questions for evaluation*. In Evaluation in Practice Website. Retrieved October 9, 2008 from http://www.evaluationinpractice.wordpress.com/2008/01/questionschoices.pdf

Dart, J., & Davies, R. (2003). A dialogical, story-based evaluation tool: The most significant change technique. *The American Journal of Evaluation, 24*(2), 137–155.

Davenport, T., & Prusak, L. (1997). *Information ecology: Mastering the information knowledge environment.* New York, Oxford: Oxford University Press.

Earl, S., Carden, F., & Smutylo, T. (2003). *Outcome mapping.* Ottawa: IDRC.

Escobar, A. (1995). *Encountering development: The making and unmaking of the Third World.* Princeton, NJ: Princeton University Press.

FAO. (1994). *Communication: A key to human development.* Rome: Communication for Development Service, FAO.

FAO. ODI, & DFID. (2002). A Livelihoods Approach to Information and Communication: A proposal. Retrieved February 9, 2007 from http://www.livelihoods.org/info/linksevents_sub/linksevents_FAO_ICTs.html

Figueroa, M., Kincaid, L., Rani, M., & Lewis, G. (2002). *Communication for social change: An integrated model for measuring the process and its outcomes.* New York: The Rockefeller Foundation.

Fink, C., & Kenny, C. (2003). W(h)ither the Digital Divide? *Info, 5*(6), 15–24. doi:10.1108/14636690310507180

Gilling, J., Jones, S., & Duncan, A. (2001). Sector approaches, sustainable livelihoods and rural poverty reduction. *Development Policy Review, 19*(4), 303–319. doi:10.1111/1467-7679.00136

Glasbergen, P. (1996). Learning to manage the environment. In W. Lafferty & J. Meadowcraft (Eds.), *Democracy and environment: Problems and prospects.* (pp. 175-193). Chettenham: Edward Elgan.

Grunfeld, H. (2007). Framework for evaluating contributions of ICT to capabilities, empowerment and sustainability in disadvantaged communities. Paper presented at the *CPRsouth2 Conference.* IDRC. Chennai, India, Dec. 15-17.

Guba, E. (1990). *The paradigm dialogue.* Newbury Park, CA: Sage Publications.

Guijt, I., & Sidersky, P. (1996, December). Agreeing on indicators. *ILEIA Newsletter, 12*(3), 9–11.

Gurstein, M. (2003, December). Effective use: A community informatics strategy beyond the digital divide. *First Monday 8*(12). Retrieved April 23, 2007 from http://www.firstmonday.dk/issues/issue8_12/gurstein/index.html

Heeks, R. (1999). The Tyranny of Participation in Information Systems: Learning from Development Projects. *Working Paper No. 4.* Retrieved February 9, 2005 from http://www.sed.manchester.ac.uk/idpm/publications/wp/di/di_wp04.htm

Heeks, R. (2002). I-development not e-development: Special issue on ICTs and development. *Journal of International Development, 14*(1), 1–11. doi:10.1002/jid.861

Heeks, R. (2007a). Theorizing ICT4D research. *Information Technologies and International Development, 3*(3), 1–4. doi:10.1162/itid.2007.3.3.1

Heeks, R. (2007b). *Impact assessment of ICT4D projects: A partial review of frameworks.* Unpublished paper prepared for the Investigating the Social & Economic Impact of Public Access to Information & Communication Technologies (IPAI) project.

Hillier, J. (2000). Going round the back? Complex networks and informal action in local planning processes. *Enivornment and Planning A, 32,* 33–54. doi:10.1068/a321

Information Technologies Group. (n.d.). *Readiness for the networked world: A guide for developing countries*. Cambridge, MA: Center for International Development. *Harvard University.*

Jennett, P., Yeo, M., Pauls, M., & Graham, J. (2003). Organizational readiness for telemedicine: Implications for success and failure. *Journal of Telehealth and Telecare, 9*(Suppl. 2), S2: 27-39.

Jiggins, J., & Röling, N. (1997). Action research in natural resource management: Marginal in the first paradigm, core in the second. In C. Albadalejo & F. Casabianca (Eds.), *Pour une méthodologie de la recherche action.* (pp. 151-169). Versailles: INRA/SAD.

Jiggins, J., & Röling, N. (2000). Adaptive management: Potential and limitations for ecological governance. *International Journal of Agricultural Resources. Governance and Ecology, 1*(1), 28–43.

Kanji, N., & Greenwood, L. (2001). *Participatory approaches to research and development in IIED: Learning from experience*. London: IIED.

Kay, J. (2008). An introduction to systems thinking. In Waltner-Toews, D., Kay, J., & Lister, N.-M. (Eds.), *The ecosystem approach: Complexity, uncertainty and managing for sustainability.* New York, Chichester: Columbia University Press.

Kirkman, G., Osorio, C., & Sachs, J. (2002). The networked readiness index: Measuring the preparedness of nations for the networked world. In Kirkman, G., Sachs, J., Schwab, K., & Cornellius, P. (Eds.), *The Global Information Technology Report 2001-2002: Readiness for the networked world* (pp. 10–29). Oxford, UK: Oxford University Press.

Lee, K. (1993). *Compass and gyroscope: Integrating science and politics for the environment*. Washington, D.C.: Island Press.

Lee, K. (1995). Deliberately seeking sustainability in the Columbia River Basin. In Gunderson, L., Holling, C., & Light, S. (Eds.), *Barriers and bridges to the renewal of ecosystems and institutions* (pp. 214–238). New York: Columbia Press.

Lee, K. (1998, September 16-19.). *Appraising adaptive management*. Adaptive Collaborative Management of Protected Areas: Advancing the Potential. Cornell University, Center for International Forestry Research.

Lee, M. (2001). A refusal to define HRD. *Human Resource Development International, 4*(3), 327–341. doi:10.1080/13678860110059348

Legris, P., Ingham, J., & Collerette, P. (2003). Why do people use information technology? A critical review of the technology acceptance model. *Information & Management, 40*(3), 191–204. doi:10.1016/S0378-7206(01)00143-4

Lincoln, Y. (1990). The making of a constructivist. A remembrance of transformations past. In Guba, E. (Ed.), *The paradigm dialogue* (pp. 67–87). Newbury Park: Sage Publications.

Mansell, R., & Wehn, U. (1998). *Knowledge societies: Information technology for sustainable development*. Oxford: Published for and on behalf of the United Nations by Oxford University Press.

McAlpine, P., & Birnie, A. (2006). Establishing sustainability indicators as an evolving process: Experience from the Island of Guernsey. *Sustainable Development, 14*(2), 81–92. doi:10.1002/sd.301

McLuhan, M. (1965). *Understanding media: The extensions of man*. New York: McGraw-Hill Book Company.

McLuhan, M., & Fiore, Q. (1967). *The medium is the massage*. New York, London, Toronto: Bantam Books.

Menou, M., & Taylor, R. (2006, November-December). A "Grand Challenge": Measuring information societies. *The Information Society, 22*(5), 261–267. doi:10.1080/01972240600903904

Minges, M. (2002). *Counting the Net: Internet Access Indicators.* Geneva: ITU.

Mosse, D. (1993). *Authority, gender and knowledge: Theoretical reflections on the practice of participatory rural appraisal. Network Paper (Vol. 44).* London: ODI.

Myers, M. (2004). *Evaluation methodologies for information and communication for development (ICD) programmes.* London: DFID.

National Research Council. (1998). *Internet counts: Measuring the impacts of the internet.* Retrieved February 9, 2005 from www.bsos.umd.edu/cidcm/wilson/xnasrep2.htm

Negroponte, N. (1995). *Being digital.* New York: Routledge.

O'Donnell, d., & Henriksen, L.B. (2002). Philosophical foundations for a critical evaluation of the social impact of ICT. *Journal of Information Technology, 17*(2), 88–99.

Pacey, A. (1999). *Meaning in technology.* Cambridge, MA: The MIT Press.

Parkinson, S. (2005). *Telecentres, access and development: Experience and lessons from Uganda and South Africa.* Warwickshire, UK; Kampala; Ottawa: ITDG, Fountain Publishing, IDRC.

Parkinson, S., & Ramírez, R. (2006). Using a sustainable livelihoods approach to assessing the impact of ICTs in development. *Journal of Community Informatics, 2*(3). Retrieved October 7, 2008 from http://ci-journal.net/index.php/ciej/issue/view/15

Parks, W. with Felder-Gray, D., Hunt, J., & Byrne, A. (2005). *Who measures change? An introduction to participatory monitoring and evaluation of communication for social change.* New Jersey, USA: Communication for Social Change Consortium.

Partnership on measuring ICT for development. (2005). *Core ICT Indicators.* Beirut, Lebanon: United Nations - ESCWA.

Patton, M. (2008). *Utilization-focused evaluation, 4th.* Thousand Oaks, CA: Sage Publications.

Pretty, J. (1994). Alternative systems of inquiry for a sustainable agriculture. *IDS Bulletin, 25*(2), 37–48. doi:10.1111/j.1759-5436.1994.mp25002004.x

Quaghebeur, K., & Masschelin, J. (2003, 27-28 February). *Participation making a difference? Critical analysis of the participatory claims of change, reversal and empowerment.* Paper presented at the workshop on Participation: From tyranny to transformation? Exploring new approaches to participation in development. University of Manchester.

Quarry, W., & Ramírez, R. (2009). *Communication for another development: Listening before telling.* London: Zed Books.

Ramírez, R. (2001). Understanding the approaches for accommodating multiple stakeholders' interests. *International Journal of Agricultural Resources. Governance and Ecology, 1*(3/4), 264–285.

Ramírez, R. (2003). Bridging disciplines: The natural resource management kaleidoscope for understanding ICTs. *The Journal of Development Communication, 14*(1), 51–64.

Ramírez, R. (2007, March-April). Appreciating the contribution of broadband ICT with rural and remote communities: Steppingstones towards an alternative paradigm. *The Information Society, 23*(2), 85–94. doi:10.1080/01972240701224044

Ramírez, R. 2008. A 'meditation' on meaningful participation and engagement. *The Journal of Community Informatics 4*(3). Retrieved 1 June 2009 from http://ci-journal.net/index.php/ciej/article/view/390/424

Ramírez, R., & Lee, R. (2008). Service delivery systems for natural stakeholders: Targeting information and communication functions and policy considerations. *Agronomía Colombiana, XXV*(2), 357–366.

Ramírez, R., Murray, D., Kora, G., & Richardson, D. (2000). *Evaluation Report: Rural Resources Partnership for Oxford County Library and HRDC*. Guelph, Canada: University of Guelph.

Ramírez, R., & Richardson, D. (2005). Measuring the impact of telecommunication services on rural and remote communities. *Telecommunications Policy, 29*, 297–319. doi:10.1016/j.telpol.2004.05.015

Reed, M., Fraser, E., & Dougill, A. (2006). An adaptive learning process for developing and applying sustainability indicators with local communities. *Ecological Economics, 59*(4), 406–418. doi:10.1016/j.ecolecon.2005.11.008

Richardson, D., & Paisley, L. (1998). *The first mile of connectivity: Advancing rural telecommunications through a communication for development approach*. Rome: FAO.

Richardson, D., Ramírez, R., Aitkin, H., & Kora, G. (2002). Sustaining ICTs for rural development. *INASP Newsletter, 20*, 5.

Roduner, D., & Schläppi, W. (2008). Logical framework approach and outcome mapping: A constructive attempt of synthesis. *Rural Development News, 2*, 9–19.

Rogers, P. (2008). Using programme theory to evaluate complicated and complex aspects of interventions. *Evaluation, 14*(1), 29–48. doi:10.1177/1356389007084674

Röling, N. (2003). From causes to reasons: The human dimension of agricultural sustainability. *International Journal of Agricultural Sustainability, 1*(1), 73–88. doi:10.3763/ijas.2003.0108

Röling, N., & Jiggins, J. (1998, September 16-19, 1998). *The soft side of land: An incomplete exploration of the implications of seeing ecological sustainability as emerging from human learning and inter-action*. Paper presented at the Symposium on Adaptive Collaborative Management of Protected Areas. Cornell University and CIFOR.

Scoones, I. (1998). Sustainable rural livelihoods: A framework for analysis. *IDS Working Paper, vol. 72*. Brighton, UK: IDS.

Selener, D. (1997). *Participatory action research and social change*. Quito, Ecuador: Global Action Publications.

Sen, A. (2005). Human Rights and Capabilities. *Journal of Human Development, 6*(2), 151–166. doi:10.1080/14649880500120491

Shulha, L. M., & Cousins, J. B. (1997). Evalution use: theory, research, and practice since 1986. *Evaluation Practice, 18*(3), 195–208. doi:10.1016/S0886-1633(97)90027-1

Snowden, D. (2005). *Multi-ontology sense making: A new simplicity in decision making*. Singapore: The Cynefin Centre.

Srinivasan, R. (2006). Where information society and community voice intersect. *The Information Society, 22*, 355–365. doi:10.1080/01972240600904324

Stoll, K., Menou, M., Camacho, K., & Khellady, Y. (2002). *Learning about ICTs' role in development: A framework towards a participatory, transparent and continuous process*. Ottawa: IDRC.

Thompson, J., & Guijt, I. (1999). Sustainability indicators for analysing the impacts of participatory watershed management programmes. In Hinchcliffe, F., Thompson, J., Pretty, J., Guijt, I., & Parmesh, S. (Eds.), *Fertile ground: The impacts of participatory watershed management* (pp. 13–31). London: IT Publications.

Turkle, S. (1984). *The second self: Computers and the human spirit*. New York: Simon & Schuster.

Turkle, S. (1995). *Life on the screen: Identity in the age of the Internet*. New York: Simon & Schuster.

Underwood, J. (2004). Research into information and communication technologies: Where now? *Technology, Pedagogy and Education, 13*, 135–145. doi:10.1080/14759390400200176

van Dijk, J. (2001, 15-17 November). *The ideology behind "closing digital divides": Applying static analysis to dynamic gaps*. Paper presented at the IAMCR/ICA Symposium on the Digital Divide. Austin, Texas: University of Texas.

Vehovar, V., Sicherl, P., Hüsing, T., & Dolnicar, V. (2006, November-December). Methodological challenges of digital divide measurements. *The Information Society, 22*(5), 279–290. doi:10.1080/01972240600904076

Waisbord, S. (2001, May). Family tree of theories, methodologies and strategies in development communication: Convergences and differences. Retrieved 5 December, 2008 from http://www.comminit.com/stsilviocomm/sld-2881.html

Woodhill, J., & Röling, N. (1998). The second wing of the eagle: The human dimension in learning our way to more sustainable futures. In Röling, N., & Wagemakers, M. (Eds.), *Facilitating sustainable agriculture: Participatory learning and adaptive management in times of environmental uncertainty* (pp. 46–71). Cambridge: Cambridge University Press.

Wright, K. (2008). *What role for evaluation in the context of performance-based management? INTRAC Briefing Paper No. 22*. Oxford, UK: INTRACT.

ENDNOTES

[1] Eradicate extreme poverty and hunger; Achieve universal primary education; Promote gender equality and empower women; Reduce child mortality; Improve maternal health; Combat HIV /AIDS, malaria and other diseases; Ensure environmental sustainability; Develop a global partnership for development.

[2] Every year the United Nations Development Program publishes the indexes for every member state.

[3] Moore, J.; Ramírez, R.; Coghlan, S.; Oliphant, D. & Whiteford, K. 2001. Community Network as a Learning Organization: An outcome of academic and community collaboration. Paper presented at the II Global Congress of Citizen Networks, Buenos Aires, Argentina. December 5-7.

Chapter 5
The Mirror Meta-Principle:
Creating the Context for Culturally Sustainable Development Informatics

Chase Laurelle Knowles
Claremont Graduate University, USA

ABSTRACT

Since the conclusion of World War II, efforts to develop the so-called Third World have taken a variety of paths. In light of the multiplicity of competing theoretical lenses – modernization, post-structuralism, and dependency, to name just a few theories – the field of development is in a state of confusion. Consequently, it has been difficult for development informatics specialists to understand how best to harness the power of Information Communications Technology (ICT), as there is no clear goal in sight which ICT is supposed to be supporting. The following chapter provides a brief historical overview of the field of development, with a special interest in the role technology has been understood to play in this context. A discussion of relevant scholarship points to the dual notions that the next wave of development informatics work will prize attention to cultural particularities, and as such, will necessitate a degree of participative technology design. By extension, a dynamic relationship between power and knowledge is affirmed, in line with scholars such as Schech (2002). Various strands of thought are ultimately synthesized into what is termed the mirror meta-principle, which stresses that culturally sustainable development informatics requires ICT to be participatively designed so as to support developing societies' economic and socio-cultural well-being and congruently "mirror" the economic and socio-cultural exigencies and traditions of developing societies. In this paradigm, the economic and socio-cultural patterns embedded into ICT need not be in line, or need to be moved into line, with the traditional Western ideology of modernization. With Heeks (1999), it is asserted that development informatics specialists' approach to the participatory process must remain grounded in real conditions.

DOI: 10.4018/978-1-61520-799-2.ch005

INTRODUCTION: DEVELOPMENT AND INFORMATION COMMUNICATIONS TECHNOLOGY

Deep socio-cultural contextualization of the theories and practices of development informatics has often proved elusive. One does not need to look far to understand the reason for this: the mother traditions of information science (IS) were computer science and management. In turn, the majority of IS research has been conducted in a positivist fashion and encouraged to adopt a myopically technological focus at times (Rose, 1998). While these practices have produced some very fine research, this does not negate the fact that more socio-culturally interpretive and historically grounded methodologies have frequently been ignored. The focus on pure technology "for technology's sake" has led to a lack of understanding as to the practical and theoretical implications of Information Communication Technology (ICT) within broader society. This situation is problematic enough when one is simply attempting to study and work with ICTs within their socio-cultural – mainly Western – milieu of origin. As the field of development informatics can attest, it becomes vastly more complicated when one is dealing with a "technology transplant," wherein someone or some group of persons is attempting to funnel ICTs into an impoverished society in which the use, and perhaps even the idea, of ICTs are decidedly foreign.

The core question is, therefore: What intellectual underpinnings can help us create the potential for culturally sustainable ICT use in the developing world? Conventional advice would lead us to believe that success in this endeavor is tied to the fulfillment of two common sense conditions. First, the ICT systems must be economically and technologically self-supporting. The presence of ICT should be a sovereign tool which encourages independent agency, and not engender greater dependence on the source of those ICTs. Second, the ICTs must be in synch with the cultural context of the use community which is attempting to adopt them. This means that there is not a breakdown between technology design and actualization, in which the introduction of ICT creates dissonance between the developing society's cultural norms and those of the environment in which the ICT was created (Heeks, 2002). Once these two conditions are satisfied, the potential exists for technology use to become a routine, embedded social practice. And such social practices may evolve into stable institutionalized features of life – in other words, they may become social norms – should they spread through space and time (Rose, 1998). It is this successful transformation of ICT from exotica to norm that intrigues many practitioners and academics in fields as disparate as information science, sociology, anthropology, and public policy, to name just a few.

The problem with the commonly accepted development informatics mantra – solve all the issues surrounding material logistics, culturally harmonize the innovation, and 'off things should go' – is not the advice per se, but the fact that it is often book-ended with assumptions of Westernization. The goal, more or less, has been to remake the entire world into the First World – which, like it or not, is basically the Western world. Problematically, this requires most developing territories to be either converted or coerced into behaving like the West, as opposed to adapting Western methodologies to their socio-cultural constraints. The exchange of explicit for implicit colonization is, unsurprisingly, often resisted strenuously, and comprises one of the factors contributing to the many failed decades of development. Even the greatest advocates of "development" have found it impossible to paper over the conflict. By 1990 the World Bank argued that,

"The postindependence development efforts failed because the strategy was misconceived. Governments made a dash for 'modernization,' copying, but not adapting, Western models. The result was poorly designed public investments in industry;

too little attention to peasant agriculture; too much intervention in areas in which the State lacked managerial, technical, and entrepreneurial skills; and too little effort to foster grassroots development. This top-down approach demotivated ordinary people, whose energies most needed to be mobilized in the development effort... (original emphasis) (qtd. in Mabogunje, 2000, p. 14007)

Indeed, much of First World thinking concerning "development" has not been the value free intellectual panacea which it is often made out to be: it assumes the values of Western modernism (Brubaker, 2007; Jasanoff, 2002; Santa Ana et. al., 2006). Axiomatically, the intellectual framework in which development informatics efforts are conceived proves similarly flawed. But where informatics is concerned, the pre-existing value judgments about what is socially, culturally, and politically "right" in developing territories are compounded by the fact that technology itself is also imbricated with a particular set of values. There is a mismatch between the – again, usually Western – socio-cultural context in which technology is designed, and those of developing nations in which it ends up (Hasan et. al., 1999; Heeks, 2002; Hill et al, 1998; Fredland, 2000; Kamppinen, 1998). With this in mind, it makes sense to wonder if the reason there is a jungle of academic theories and a landscape littered with failed political policies is that well-meaning theorists and practitioners have been trying to solve the wrong problem: How do "we" turn "them" into the West? In doing so, they may be blinded to the empirical realities of the development which is taking place. An assessment of current world trends shows that developments as such *are* taking place, just not along the socio-cultural lines many would like to see. Of real importance for the ICT researcher are alternative development paradigms of highly arguable validity – for example, transnational Islamism as propagated by al-Qaeda, or sub-state Islamism as instantiated by Hezbollah – have done a great job of integrating ICTs into their activities (Brachman, 2006; Knowles, 2008). This while many "legitimate" ICT development projects lie in the ashes throughout the greater Islamic Middle East precisely because they are culturally unsustainable! Clearly, to paraphrase Harrison and Huntington, the culture using the technology makes a difference (2000). Another way to say this is that whether or not a particular socio-cultural group has been able to tailor technology use to its individual situation is a key factor in deciding whether ICT is absorbed or rejected by a group.

With this stated, it is important to stress that the successful transfer of ICT to impoverished regions is not entirely dependent on socio-cultural concerns. To the contrary, it is absolutely contingent upon resolving issues of material poverty: computers are useless if one doesn't have electricity, having the option to text from one's cell phone is of little use when one is illiterate, and the existence of the Internet in urban centers is worthless if one is mired in rural poverty. Yet it must be noted that if one has no interest or need of the type of computer or cell phone that has been provided, than such logistical concerns are irrelevant. Consequently, I will indulge in the luxury of allowing my colleagues to explain further the technical pressures on ICT in developing nations.[1] Instead, I will focus on the task of elaborating the socio-cultural exigencies surrounding the transfer of ICT into a development context. There will be three components to this explanation. First, I will provide a short overview of the history and theories behind development since World War II. Second, I will use this information as a backdrop to explain how concepts of Western modernity intersect with technology in a development context. Third, by way of a constructive move, I will suggest that pre-existing, disparate trends of thought regarding development informatics' theoretical underpinnings point to the existence of a "mirror meta-principle." In brief, the argument indexed by the mirror meta-principle contends that development informatics is essentially a problem of technology design. Rather than seeking to present a totally new concept, the meta-principle seeks to synthesize concepts from both informatics and development scholarship which together give shape to the "next wave" of theoretical and practical efforts. I conclude that a methodology which realistically combines elements of community informatics and participatory design can help create the context for a culturally sustainable development informatics, although the latter will still be effected by larger processes of social change. The ultimate goal of this chapter is hence to provide a preliminary theoretical organization of the currently chaotic knowledge narrative with which development informatics specialists must work. It is hoped that this work will facilitate scholars' and practitioners' efforts to gain a sense of where the field's strong and weak points are – and consequently, to move forward with a renewed understanding of the challenges ahead.

HISTORICAL OVERVIEW OF POST-WWII DEVELOPMENT EFFORTS

It is imprudent to begin dispensing advice on the historically complex and politically charged topic of contemporary development without a thorough understanding of the tortured road this policy field has already traveled. During the age of colonialism, the aim of imperialistic European states was to take advantage of their non-European territories for economic profit. It was assumed that the hapless colonized territories were either unable or unwilling to maximally exploit their own resources; it was also believed that European activity toward this end was not only materially, but ethically beneficial for the world at large (Wallerstein, 2005). This justification for Western profiteering began collapsing in 1945, with the strengthening of the anti-colonial collective will in Asia, Africa, and Latin America. Concomitantly, it was widely believed that the global South could achieve a level of prosperity equivalent to the North's with

the benefit of an appropriate policy toolkit. Latin American thinkers labeled this ideology "developmentalism," and it would subsequently appear in various forms throughout the world (Wallerstein, 2005). Subsequently, the economic development (per the United States' terminology) or socialist expansion (as the Soviet Union liked to call it) of Southern states became a pawn in the Cold War, as both sides struggled to gain allies. A new "expert" class of development advisors would emerge – most connected with the United Nations and/or the so-called Bretton Woods institutions (usually cited as the International Monetary Fund, World Bank, and World Trade Organization). Additional theories regarding the relationship between the prosperous, economic "core" and the unfortunate, dilapidated "periphery" would appear courtesy of the Economic Commission for Latin America, which advised "import-substitution industrialization" as one solution. And the Southern intelligentsia held forth on how devastating traditions of "dependency" had to broken if the South was ever to develop.

Reflecting said experts' optimism about the possibilities for economically revivifying the Third World, the United Nations announced that the 1970s would be known as the "decade of development." Stagflation and devastating Organization of Petroleum Exporting Countries (OPEC) price hikes ensured, however, that such was not the case. What happened instead was that oil-exporting states managed to accrue immense amounts of surplus capital. This capital habitually snaked its way into American and German banks, which – of course – were eager to put the overflow funds to good use. Fortunately or unfortunately, depending on if one was a high-level Northern banker or the average Southern tax payer, the non-oil-exporting South was suffering balance of payment difficulties. These were the result of a coincidence between a steep cost increase in their imports and a dismal drop in their exports' economic value. After having surveyed the dismal fiscal landscape, the aforementioned banks concluded they could solve the problem of Northern remuneration and the insolvent South's liquidity ailments in one swift stroke: the solution was to make enormous loans to the Third World, the principle on which the banks intended to charge cumulative interest (Wallerstein, 2005). It was at this point that developmentalism became a free-for-all, as the "debt crisis" engulfed state after suffering Third World state.

Perhaps deservedly so, given its poor track record, developmentalism went out of fashion during the 1980s. Nipping on its heels, however, was neo-liberal globalization. Most globalization advocates bitterly condemned centralized state planning as inefficient. They explained the failure of the previous decade's loans as a case of the money not coming with enough strings attached: states which wished to receive loans would henceforth need to tighten their wasteful bureaucratic belts, aggressively privatize formerly nationalized industries, and encourage the rise of entrepreneurialism if they wanted to experience financial privilege. Developing nations were encouraged to forget the much-hallowed import-substitution model of economic advancement, and capital controls along with it; the experts now pushed impoverished states to make themselves into magnets for cheap export production, and to allow capital to flow freely through their borders. The collapse of the Berlin Wall, the rise of the so-called Asian Tigers, the formation of the European Union, and the US' phenomenal economic boom, as well as the worldwide spread of democratic forms of government and instantiation of neo-liberal economic policy made the peace and prosperity promises of globalization seem all but assured.

Regrettably, this second wave of optimism also went the way of developmentalism. It is not difficult to see why in retrospect. A quick overview of the disasters the global citizenry has witnessed since the mid-1990s must include the 1997 currency crisis (which engulfed the entirety of East and Southeast Asia, not to mention Brazil

and Russia), spectacular protests against the dictums of the World Trade Organization, the rise of transnational terrorist organizations like Osama bin Laden's Al-Qaeda, and a surge in powerful transnational organized crime (many of these criminals, like Russian gunrunner Viktor Bout, actively aided terrorists, genocidal warlords, and the like). There was continued unrest and "ethnic cleansing" in the Balkans, 9/11, massive bombings in Madrid, London, Istanbul, Mumbai, and Pakistan, disastrous US-led wars in Afghanistan and Iraq, nuclear fiascos with Iran and North Korea, ongoing misery between Palestine and Israel, genocides in Rwanda and Darfur (to name, sadly, just a couple of the many major killing sprees), and the 2008 collapse of the US' financial sector – an economic tragedy which rapidly infected the rest of the world. Although it is probably too close to historical events to pass resounding final judgment, neo-liberal globalization seems to have given the world not peace and prosperity, but a radicalized political contingency and rapidly growing gap between the rich and the poor (Juhasz, 2007).

Thus, despite the immense sums of financial and human capital poured by both the South and the North into improving the lot of impoverished states since 1945, one might wonder whether things have not actually gotten worse. The world system is still polarizing, the South is continues attempting to improve its economic situation, and the North remains rightly worried about the security threat to the state system embodied by an enraged underclass which is adding new – formerly middle class – members by the day (Wallerstein, 2005). This has spurred initiatives such as the United Nation's much-ballyhooed Millennium Development Goals. Long on good public relations sound bites and short on solid strategies and actionable commitments from the world's wealthiest nations, the Goals aimed to lower the number of poor persons by 50% between 2000 and 2015. Within months it became clear that this was a patently unrealistic goal, so in 2003 the target date was extended to 2025. Given the absence of any solid strategies or commitments from the globe's wealthiest nations, and the severe economic downturn in 2008, even this seems to be a fantasy goal. Barring an extraordinarily gracious and, as of now unforeseen, twist of fate, we can be sure that at least one or two more generations will suffer extreme poverty (Steyn, 2007). And a decade into the "new" millennium, with the high hopes of developmentalism and globalization resigned to a forgotten corner in history's attic, there is also no widely accepted intellectual roadmap to guide subsequent efforts. The only thing that everyone seems to agree on, in fact, is that somehow subsequent efforts must be made. Because informatics will no doubt play a lynchpin role in such activities, it is crucial the field not be working in a theoretical void, without a clue as to what could finally allow the relationship between technology and development to turn a successful corner.

THE RELATIONSHIP BETWEEN DEVELOPMENT, CULTURE, MODERNITY, AND TECHNOLOGY

The task of this next section is to hammer out a preliminary intellectual framework into which ideas regarding ICTs and development may be dropped. This requires paying careful attention the philosophical and cultural orientations that underpinned the attempts at development just outlined.

As was already pointed out during this chapter's introduction, development paradigms have historically shared a common ideological framework. They assumed – perhaps subconsciously and implicitly, due to the pressures of political correctness – the Westernization of developing states. It is necessary to revisit this statement before moving on, because it calls up significant issues which cannot simply be glossed over with a flip jibe about the evils of Western ethno-centrism. In fact, it is more correct to say that the logical flaw

embedded into these theories was the conflation of development with the West's epistemological modernization; the latter is effectively responsible for the West's present prosperity (and, too, many would argue, its current woes). Born out of the Enlightenment, modernity theory as propagated within the Western tradition is universalizing, totalizing, and individuating. In brief, it assumes that the rationalization of society must take a single form or social process – because, after all, reason is always and everywhere the same. The downside to this perspective has frequently been pointed out. It is reductive, and therefore the wealth of meaning which may be derived from the non-modern-Western world's diverse complexity is missed.

The link between modernism and technology is crucial for the discussion at hand. The values of Western modernism are embedded, as has been noted, in the technology this society produces. As Feenberg (2004) explains, modernity's reductivism has exposed reality to the penetration of technology, relentlessly increasing efficiency while giving humans greater power to control nature, support human organization on a mass scale, and lower the barriers presented by time and space. Despite these "plusses," it is commonplace to critique modernity on the grounds that the technologization of society appallingly objectifies human beings by incorporating them into a dystopian, machine-dominated system over which they have lost control. Without a doubt, technology may be the modern West's proverbial bargain with the devil – we increase our power over the elements of heaven and earth, but in the process we change the environment in which our souls move. We can therefore not separate the transfer of technology into non-Western, developing nations without addressing the fact that the ideological project of modernization is part and parcel of this package. Even if all the problems of material logistics inherent to development informatics were to be solved overnight, there is no guarantee that *all* those to whom the

ICTs are being offered would like to make the same reductive bargain with the devil that core, industrialized states have.

It is tempting, therefore, to explain away the intertwined failures of ICTs and development policies as outright rejections not just of technologies and policies per se, but as sinister denials of modernism at large. Of course, modernism and its associated values are under trial in their [Western] society of origin as well. There are many academics who do not yet believe that modernism is finished (Fukuyama, 1992; Habermas, 1987; Harvey, 1989; Lee, 1994), while many postmodernists – who nevertheless differ among themselves on the details of what sort of alternative paradigm should be articulated (Rosenau, 1992) – have declared modernism an exhausted metanarrative, particularly as it concerns development (Cooper & Packard, 1997; Palmer, 1990). But going off six decades of failed development, it may be asserted that the untrammeled acceptance and unrivaled spread of Western modernism (read: Westernization) is far from assured.

This places development theorists and practitioners in an intellectual bind. On the one hand, true modernists simply have no explanation for why modernism isn't spreading: it was supposed to be universal, like "reason." On the other hand, there are deep issues with postmodernists' withering critique of modernism. Postmodernists are simply hedged in by their own relativity, and unsure of what to make of things if the definition of what is reasonable, and related assumptions of social rationalism, no longer reign supreme and/or are not shared between groups. Discourse regarding development cannot but help being confused by this state of affairs – after all, is the concept of "development" even legitimate anymore? Indeed, adopting an authentic postmodernist position forces one also to accept the notion that the concept of progress has completed its evolution, paradoxically, by ceasing to exist (Shanin, 1997). Blaikie summarizes the situation excellently, explaining that,

"The realisation of the limits of discourse, and the risk of losing sight of the materiality of life and agency of nature haunt the authors of the more hostile linguistic exegesis of development texts. As the dust settles from yet another deconstruction, 'what now?' the battered modernist might be heard to mutter, and also 'so what?' Of course, the hard [postmodernist] sceptic will reply it is not their business to fill the void with yet another metanarrative – except with the metanarrative of relativity itself." (2000, p. 1034)

Unfortunately, I cannot here present an intellectual argument which definitively settles the philosophical debate between modernism and postmodernism. Indeed, I believe it is likely that the question of the spread and/or survival of Western modernism may only be answered by the forces of history. What seems appropriate to admit is that both sides are voicing a piece of the truth. The modernists are correct to say that without adopting the essentials of Western modernism, it is going to be next to impossible for developing countries to replicate exactly the occurrence of Western prosperity. Likewise, the postmodernists are right to point out that the values inherent to modernism are not universal – fine print on loan agreements notwithstanding. In fact, an empirical glance at the arc of development gives a clue that the true answer is somewhere in the middle. Where non-Western states, namely China and India, have experienced phenomenal economic growth in the Western-created and dominated world order, it has occurred alongside these nations' agreement to absorb modernist values into their productive sectors. It is notable that these nations' refused to accept much of the "one size fits all" development advice of the Western expert community, and instead took responsibility for harmonizing (with varying degrees of success, to be sure) modernist values with their own socio-cultural frameworks.

Remarkably successful processes of integration (read: China and India) have led some academics – in particular, sociologists – to theorize that there is more than one way to be "modern." The multiple modernities paradigm contends that pure modernism's uncomplicated conception of the world is flawed in its simple interpretation of empirical evidence, in addition to being of dubious normative authority; basically, it objects to the idea that modernity is a homogenizing phenomenon (Schmidt, 2006). It instead asserts that diverse cultures have taken discrete socio-historical paths because of cultural factors, especially those associated with processes of governance and religion. This is why one can observe differentiated experiences of modernity throughout the global community. The fundamental argument of those in the multiple modernities camp is therefore that non-Western forms of modernity cannot be conceptualized in accordance with Western categories and behavioral preferences. A natural extension of this concept is the idea that every civilization (Japanese, Latin American, Islamic, Judeo-Christian/Euro-American, etc.) exhibits its own, exceptional type of modernity (Huntington, 1996). Unfortunately, the vast majority of multiple modernities literature does not bother to articulate the forms this diversity will take, and when and where differences between the civilizations (or whatever social unit is preferred) are significant. Consequently, scholars such as Schmidt have questioned whether it is incorrect to speak of *multiple* moderni*ties*, and have suggested in turn that it is more correct to speak of varieties of modern*ity*; how one comes down on this point is of vast importance, because it determines the degree to which one is willing to highlight differences between discrete cultural groups – more so in the former case, less so in the latter (2006). It will suffice to say that this grey area of nuance has yet to be definitively defined. There is simply not yet enough empirical evidence to do so.

Interestingly, equivalent concepts are now being put forth in the field of economics, under the banner of "varieties of capitalism" (Hall & Soskice, 2001; Streeck & Yamamura, 2001; Yamamura & Streeck, 2003). Such economic

thought goes to great pains to privilege the differences between separate strains of capitalism, as well as explaining the strengths and weaknesses each lends to its adherents in a globalized world. However, it does not go so far as to break the universe into discrete and fundamentally opposed blocs, as does the highly controversial political "clash of civilizations" theory eluded to above. It also cannot be forgotten that there exist substantial differences within states, not simply across them (Schmidt, 2006). As Schmidt points out, for instance, Putnam (1993) argues the radically different conditions of democracy and capitalism exhibited by northern and southern Italy may be attributed to long-standing socio-cultural and institutional differences between the two regions. And Heller (1999) observes an equivalent phenomenon between the Indian state of Kerala, and other, less successful, Indian and Latin American developing states as well. It may be more accurate to compare groupings of states as opposed to civilizations; some European states' economic institutions, for example, bear a closer similarity to economic institutions in Asia than the United States (Schmidt, 2006).

Whether one prefers to think of differences as pointing to multiple modernities, or variations on a single form of modernity, the most relevant point for the discussion at hand is that academics across disciplines are moving toward a complexification of theoretical conceptions regarding modernity. There is a definite push to reconcile unique cultural (or civilization, or sub-state, etc.) values with the rather uniform exigencies of economic and political development within the context of the current globalizing, polarizing world system. Still, it is an understatement to say that these disparate ideas – which run a confusing gamut from a return to civilization-centrism to vehement neo-populism – have yet to crystallize into a viable theoretical paradigm which could present a unified challenge to the present policies of neo-liberal globalization. This sort of project is certainly beyond the scope of the present chapter, more narrowly focused on the theoretical concerns of development informatics than the theoretical needs of development at large.

As such, I suggest that ICT specialists seek to draw out of this debate an intellectual framework which allows for heterogeneity (addressing the challenge of modernist theory) while not falling prey to the negation of progress (taking into account the difficulty of postmodernist theory). This tense duality is necessary if one desires to maintain both a semblance of empirical reality and the potential for development. What does this mean for development informatics? The field must assume that the ICT experience needs to be tailored to the circumstances of the developed and the developing contexts, or even between different spheres of development. Although diversity-friendly ICTs alone will do little to pull the extreme poor out of their misery, it is possible that they could play an important role should they be incorporated into a larger vision of development, where technological "progress" was adapted to the particular sociocultural context of developing regions. This goal will be returned to later in the chapter.

Before moving forward, however, it is necessary to further examine the specific relationship between knowledge and ICT as it relates to development specifically. As Schech (2002) explains, many of those who are most optimistic about the role of technology in development are operating within the aforementioned modernist paradigm. On the opposite end of the spectrum, and far less enthusiastic about the ostensibly revolutionary potential of ICTs, are dependency and post-colonial thinkers. An examination of these various groups' backgrounds is helpful in understanding their highly discrete conclusions. Schech explains that modernizing institutions such as the World Bank rely upon a liberal conception of knowledge, viewing it as universal property of the natural order. Where Western-style development has not taken hold, the "failure" is attributed in part to a lack of access and/or adequate understanding, and application, of said knowledge. Consequently, World Bank programs such as the

Global Development Gateway seek to use the Internet 'as a tool to reduce poverty and support sustainable development' (World Bank, 2000, p. 5). This is a result of the institution's view that the best 'proactive policy' is one which 'fosters network development in emerging economies' (World Bank, 2000, p. 3). Schech is consequently able to trace a clear connection between present development efforts and the 1960s-era belief that the spread of paradigmatic Western concepts – and contingent ways of knowing – were the key to modernization. Indeed, weaving Westernism into non-Western societies was thought to be a creative act (Lerner, 1967).

But Schech also notes that the current ICT strategy of institutions like the World Bank represents a unique variation on the traditional attitude toward technology held by the original school of modernizers. It discards the concept of hierarchical communication in favor of a more decentralized of development. The "advancement" of a state government so that it has the option of relying upon up-to-date ICT as a primary conduit of information between itself and its citizen-subjects is hence no longer the primary goal for development projects. Similarly, the information transferred by the ICTs is no longer automatically assumed to be useful for those who received it. Instead, it is the ability to *access* knowledge which is considered empowering. Thus, the new goal is to use ICTs to establish this access, especially at the grassroots level. As a result, development processes are becoming more decentralized, and even cross-cultural. Of course, as Schech takes care to clarify, this movement dovetails well with the neo-liberal emphasis on the market as the "ultimate mediator." Especially in light of the multitudinous failures of Marxist-style state planning it made quite a bit of sense to try and move power away from a bureaucratic structure and into the hands of the people. Efforts representative of this philosophy include the Intermediate Technology Development Group, which was launched in Cajamarca, Peru, which has sought to sustainably provide information to individual market actors.

Yet Schech goes on to explain how the emancipatory power of such is dubious enough to call into question the conclusions of the World Bank and other, similar institutions. Under certain circumstances, the introduction of ICTs into a community only serves to exacerbate divisions between those who already have advantages and those who do not. Post-colonial and dependency theorists – in particular those at the Economic Commission for Latin America and the Caribbean (CEPAL) – argue that this is because of underlying structural inequalities in the global system. Given the exigencies of a globalized market, technological knowledge tends to "snowball" with time, allowing initially privileged states to continue developing at a faster rate than their less fortunate counterparts (James, 2000). This has led some to believe that the Internet – and the information it carries – represents only another chapter in the history of the West's efforts to intellectually colonize the Third World (Sardar, 1996). Nevertheless, Schech voices the possibility that ICT could represent a highly original way to untie truth from power. This can be seen as an improvement on the historical status quo, whereby history is written by the victors. But it does not necessarily mean that current and future progressive/radical movements will be any more able to restructure society in a more equitable fashion than were past ones, a fact which is good or bad depending on one's perspective and the situation at hand. What is certain is that non-normative ways of understanding knowledge are in danger of being drowned out by the many other manifestations of media protest.

At the end of the day, then, where is ICT's true place in the development schema? Does this technology's ability to communicate knowledge represent the new possibilities for modernization, or does it signify a new wave of Western, colonial disenfranchisement? Schech argues that both these points-of-view are limited by "a static view of knowledge and power, and a failure to grasp the creative, productive potential of new ICT in the hands of ordinary people" (p. 20). She argues this conceptualization of power and knowledge as discrete spheres is flawed. Instead, she suggests that scholars take a Foucauldian perspective, whereby knowledge is understood to be a type of power, in that it is the means by which truth is separated from falsehood, and consequently made legitimate. She acknowledges scholars' identification of this process at work in the World Bank's efforts to construct the development discourse to this end (Escobar, 1995; Ferguson, 1990). Additionally, Schech notes the way those counter-posed to the modernizers' ideology often highlight how the institution's frequently far-removed "experts" can obscure and/or miss important aspects of the issues at hand, and in turn assert the supremacy of local understanding (Mahiri, 1998). Similarly, she takes care to point out that Foucault's thinking regarding power and knowledge does not result in these concepts' "collapse into each other" (p. 21). Far from it, analysis of this construct can create a form of political opportunity. Understanding the knowledge undergirding a source of power is a means not only of better comprehending it, but possibly of subverting it (Ransom, 1997). Consequently, Schech believes that ICT's influence on knowledge has the potential to advance development, in that it allows subaltern groups the means to nurture unique ways of thinking, existing, and achieving. On this note, she points to the work of Escobar, who aptly explains that:

"As they circulate through the network, truths are transformed, reinscribed into other knowledge-power constellations, resisted, subverted, or recreated to serve other ends...by social movements, which become, themselves, the sites of important counter-discourses." (1999, p. 43).

MIRROR META-PRINCIPLE: CREATING THE CONTEXT FOR CULTURALLY SUSTAINABLE DEVELOPMENT INFORMATICS

Pulling these various strands of above information together, it would seem that the ultimate use of ICTs in development contexts would thus be the creation of "knowledge-power constellations" that reflect unique varieties of modernity. But what theoretical paradigm should development informatics specialists be using in their work in order to bring this about? After surveying the relevant literature, I believe there are several concepts already in existence which – when brought together under a single intellectual umbrella – point the way toward the achievement of this goal. Together, these make up what I call the "mirror meta-principle." I stress that I do not present the mirror meta-principle as a comprehensive successor to the universalizing and totalizing ideologies of developmentalism and neo-liberal globalization. It is rather an alternative philosophical orientation toward the historical experience and ongoing process of development activities, for use by informatics specialists. Instead of presenting a blisteringly original concept and attempting to "re-make the field" overnight, the mirror meta-principle represents an "umbrella synthesis" of intellectually significant, cutting edge ideas that appear to represent the next wave in both development studies and informatics.

Its goal is two-fold. First, it aims to articulate how specifically-designed ICT tools have the potential to be culturally sustainable *should the larger development process support this goal*. Second, it aims to serve as a starting point for subsequent development informatics theory. That being said, the primary principles of the mirror meta-principle are as follows:

- Culturally sustainable development informatics is conceptualized broadly as an ongoing process in which ICT supports steps taken toward greater economic and socio-cultural well-being. "Well-being" is here understood to mean the sum total of the goals and compromises which emerge out of continued dialogue between the developing region and the international community.

- Culturally sustainable development informatics is contingent upon said development efforts fitting closely (i.e. "mirroring") the economic and socio-cultural exigencies and traditions of developing societies. In other words, no "one size fits all" prescriptions. While there may be definite similarities across communities, states and cultures, these similarities are assumed to negate the unique differences presented by developing groups.

- These economic and socio-cultural patterns need not be in line, or need to be moved into line, with the traditional Western ideology of modernization. Indeed, development informatics efforts must be place- and culture-specific. The mirror meta-principle may thus be differentiated from previous development theories in its refusal to advise the wholesale Westernization or internationalization of developing cultures.

A mirror theoretical analysis of development informatics recognizes the field's problems essentially as technology design challenges. Its intellectual purpose would be to synchronize technology, insofar as is possible, with the particular economic and socio-cultural needs of specific developing regions, while taking into account these contexts' material-logistical constraints. While it is assumed that certain technological standards would need to be upheld in order to maintain interoperability between different regions'/communities' devices, the mirror meta-principle does not assume that there are universally applicable hardware or software "killer apps" that cover the face of the globe. The goal is to give people in development contexts the ICTs they need, not necessarily the

ICTs "we" think "they" should need. It may be that in some cases, the conceptualization of what constitutes "real" ICT has simply been too narrow to truly help development efforts move forward. Consider, for instance, the case of text-based technology in communities where there are low levels of literacy. In the long-run, one would certainly hope steps could be taken toward making these devices viable tools – perhaps their use could be tied to participation in a literacy education program for community members. But it could be unrealistic to expect text-based technology to make an immediate, good on people's lives. Perhaps development informatics theorists and practitioners should instead engineer new and/ or apply existing devices which communicate primarily through imagery images [instead of text], thereby opening the possibilities for use to large swaths of the population.

Moving development informatics toward a place- and culture-specific paradigm holds intriguing possibilities. By treating the use community as a heterogeneous living laboratory of sorts (as opposed to a homogenous market), ICTs built in accordance with the mirror meta-principle will be able to facilitate a deeper understanding of developing contexts' collective memories and communal self-representations, in addition to creating new possibilities for participative social involvement. In attempting to illustrate the connection between the mirror meta-principle and development informatics, it is helpful to discuss Lynch's consideration of "imageability," which he used as a foundation for his exploration of municipal spatial relationships, cognitive frameworks and urban structures (1960). In his text, *The Image of the City*, Lynch explained imageability as

"...that quality in a physical object which gives it a high probability of evoking a strong image in any given observer. It is that shape, color, or arrangement that facilitates the making of vividly identified, powerfully structured, highly useful mental images of the environment. It might also be called legibility." (1960, p. 9).

Lynch argues that a well formed, imageable city heightens residents' capacity to orient themselves to urban form(s), as well as their ability to navigate the municipal maze. Lynch has influenced a bevy of other theorists. Also of interest here is Nasar's *The Evaluative Image of the City* (1998), where he argues that the emotions and inferred meanings people attach to specific locations play a crucial role in defining their experience; these strong associations are most likely to come about in a memorable – imageable – situation. Building on the concepts of Lynch and Nasar, mirror meta-principle-based ICTs are meant to be imageable, in the sense that they should evoke both practically relevant and emotionally consequential associations within the context of users' lived experience. Devices built along this paradigm take steps toward restoring the meaningful and subjective components of development. The importance of these qualities has been frequently overlooked in the past, as modernist development assumptions were assumed to be value-neutral, and technology was thought to be an inanimate material instantiation (Jasanoff, 2002). Ignoring the influence of individuals' subjective perception of, and efforts to achieve meaning alongside, development and technology efforts has considerable consequences which are great of importance to informatics experts. These qualities are frequently disregarded when and where reductive "modern" models are applied, often allowing harmful power structures underlying routine practices to escape notice. Technological development efforts have thus too often helped perpetuate the political, economic, and socio-cultural woes they were attempting to solve (Jasanoff, 2002). Clearly, historical and temporal elements need to be factored into future outcomes.

While on the topics of subjectivity and meaning-making, it should be noted that the mirror meta-principle understands ICT to be a critical hermeneutic device. In their work on technology and philosophy, Cohen and Wartofsky (1986) interrogate both the nature of information, and the relationship between human reason and the processing role of contemporary technological devices. Capurro (1986; 2000) has taken this as an invitation to study the interpretive nature of the relationship between a data system and a human user. He contends that information is the form knowledge takes at the close of the modern epic, and subsequently explains that the splitting of such knowledge into a multiplicity of pieces within a data system opens up the possibilities for discrete interpretations (2000). Within this framework, people are conceptualized as inherently communal beings, as opposed to singular, isolated beings that must break through some mental enclosure in order to connect with others. Capurro (1991; 2000) explains that exploring personhood from a communal standpoint opens up possibilities for complex and diverse networks of human interaction; because information technology is embedded into these interpersonal, cultural situations, informatics may even be thought of as a type of rhetoric. These and similar arguments make possible the conclusion that humans' search for information, via technology, is an interpretive interaction between the knowledge architecture of the human searcher and that of the technology system (Ingwersen, 1992). By these lights, it is incumbent upon information technology to enable this hermeneutical search in order to successfully maximize their potential. One is hence able to see the retrieval and the exchange of data courtesy of ICTs within a development context as a hermeneutical and, at times, even existentialist exploration of the situation. Should the ICTs embedded into developing regions not fulfill their hermeneutical function – which would mean they were no longer in line with the mirror meta-principle – the technology project would ultimately prove to be unsustainable.

With this in mind, it is appropriate to consider how the mirror meta-principle influences the prac-

tical design methodology behind ICTs. A foundation for such development-friendly technology production is already being built by ICT specialists who seek to integrate the tenets of participatory design with those of community informatics. As such, it would be a transdisciplinary endeavor. Disciplines likely to find a spot on the design team include, but are not limited to: engineering, computer science, anthropology, sociology, education, cinema and media studies, graphic design, history, economics, medicine, urban planning, public policy, social welfare and religious studies. The design team should also actively solicit participation from, and actively incorporate input of communal or regional representatives from the area in which the technology is meant to be utilized. The production of ICTs should not be viewed as the end result of a linear design process but as the fruit born of an ongoing cyclical discussion between the design group and the use community. There are three main components to this recurring design process. First, the design team needs to map out the use-environment and concomitantly set up discussion sessions and/or workshops to assess the community's technology needs and constraints. Second, original ICT tools which incorporate these communal requirements need to be created and deployed. Third, after enough time has passed for reasonable assessments regarding the ICTs' viability to have been made, the design team needs to request that the community comment on, and evaluate the development informatics effort. Feedback may then be incorporated into the next cycle of development informatics work.[2]

That being said, it is important to emphasize that the progression just described can only take place in an appropriate context – one in which reality supports the participatory design process. The insights of Heeks (1999) are extremely relevant here. He points out how popular participative work has become among scholars of development. Indeed, appreciation for it is at times so great that it is at risk of being thought of as 'a "magic bullet" technique that is always relevant, always beneficial in trying to overcome the high failure rate of information systems' (p. 1). Thus, while well-meaning participatory projects are often geared toward achieving development goals, Heeks points out that they frequently prove unsustainable because they do not adequately attend to factors such as context and reality. To this end, he cites Gujit and Shah's finding (1998) that participation has sometimes been viewed as a way of using managerial and technological means to address political ends, with serious ramifications. And where development groups embrace "participation" blindly, they are in jeopardy of suffering serious consequences. These include the non-egalitarian selection of participatory group members – which inevitably obscures the true slate of communal opinions, or the gestural imposition of participation from the top-down – which can disturb otherwise helpful group dynamics already taking place "on the ground" (Heeks, 1999).

Heeks affirms that development scholars must face the many difficult realities about the participatory process, the nature of which bear summation here. First, groups and individuals must have the resources to participate in the process. They are often not – as theorists sometimes assume – a depthless font of creativity that is only waiting to be tapped. Heeks also takes seriously the finding (Dockery, 1998) that participants exhibit high levels of burnout and stress. In fact, he goes on to say, individuals must possess a number of crucial characteristics in order to make the participation process useful. Among these include a willingness to express one's opinion in public, an intention to enact decisions, and a readiness to assess accomplishments (or lack thereof) – all of which are often absent among lay persons in participatory contexts. Second, he addresses the issue of unproductive participation, wherein resources are fruitlessly consumed in the name of design democracy while a high-level decision could have produced a solution just as satisfactory but far more efficient. Even where participation does culminate in the production of an information system, it does not mean that the end results will have been improved as a result of factoring in more opinions. Third, Heeks contends that development scholars may err in their assessment that groups and individuals are motivated to participate. While it may appear that taking the opportunity to voice one's opinion is the rational choice, in some cases it actually is not. A belief that the *de facto* decision will be positive or even neutral in outcome regardless of whether or not one shares one's views, and/ or a simple lack of interest in the matter at hand – among other issues – can serve to significantly undercut both the real and perceived rewards one would hypothetically receive in exchange for the cost of participation. In this scenario, participation "forced" by well-meaning management can be resented. Fourth, Heeks considers the fact that participatory environments often lend themselves to groupthink. With Cooke (1998), he is concerned that this could at times result in non-constructive outcomes – for example, unwarranted risk-taking, or the Abilene paradox (a supposed group consensus produced by members' misunderstanding of their peers' opinions).

In an effort to sidestep these issues, Heeks (1999) elaborates three key factors which must be carefully considered before embarking upon a participatory design endeavor. First, political and cultural exigencies should be taken into account. These, far more than fine technical points, are likely to determine the direction of participative development informatics. Second, the motivation for participation should stem from a genuine aspiration to allow lay persons to assume a greater degree of ownership in technological conclusions, as well as a desire to improve the product itself. As such, it must not be driven by either a lazy wish to broaden the labor base by absorbing more individuals into the project, or by leadership's belief that having hosted a participative project will burnish their professional reputation. Third, development groups must attend to the makeup of the slate of participants. Namely, these individuals must not only be able to participate, they must desire – and have excellent reason – to do so. These persons must in turn be backed up by the resources to transform their participation into a worthwhile contribution. To close, I assert that these three criterion – appreciation for the cultural-political context, appropriate motivation, and productive participative group composition – need to be fulfilled in order for the technology design to fully and holistically "mirror" its social context. Participation is thus not recommended here as a "magic bullet," but as a synthetic *point of reference* which can be amenable in suitable development situations.

CONCLUSION: THE CHALLENGE OF DEVELOPMENT INFORMATICS

Even the short historical narrative of development efforts since the end of World War II presented herein demonstrates that both theorists and practitioners of development have yet to produce a truly sound ideology of progress (that is, of course, if one even accepts the notion of progress). The two most influential intellectual paradigms thus far, developmentalism and neo-liberal globalization, have been heavily imbued with the assumptions of Western modernism. In fact, this has proved such an enormous stumbling block that there has been a considerable push within the academic community recently either to move past with the concepts of modernity, or to substitute it with some combination of ideas regarding multiple modernities or varieties of modernity. This is quite problematic for technologists, because the philosophies which have inspired much of the ICT in question are tightly intertwined with Western notions of modernity. With the entire field of development dissolving into chaotic disagreement about its next move, it is difficult to know what kind of intellectual framework development informatics should adopt. Nevertheless, there is a growing transdisciplinary tendency to take seri-

ously the fact that discrete socio-cultural preferences and traditions make a considerable impact on development efforts, and frequently contribute to the failure of such. In light of this situation, I have suggested future development informatics be conceptualized in accordance with mirror meta-principle. The mirror meta-principle synthesizes applicable academic concepts which appear to be tied to the ability of ICTs to integrate, or "fit" well, the economic and socio-cultural frameworks of the developing sector for which they are meant. From this perspective, development informatics is a technology design challenge. Building off prior ideas regarding participatory design and community informatics, the principle indexes a transdisciplinary and use community-influenced development informatics methodology.

In conclusion, this chapter has demonstrated that it is fully within the power of development informatics experts to craft the uniquely expressive and helpful ICT devices for impoverished communities. But as anyone who has the remotest connection with development activities knows, this is a very big "if." It cannot be dismissed that long-term success in ICT undertakings is inextricably linked to the larger challenge of sustainable development. Explains McNamara,

"...many of the ICT-for-development experiments and pilot projects of recent years have not proved sustainable in the long run, because they have not been accompanied by (or failed to generate) the broader economic and social changes that would lead to sustainable demand for those ICT goods or services, especially relative to other demands on scarce resources." (2003, p. 32)

Hence, the foremost challenge facing development informatics in the future is the fact that the field itself is dependent upon the course of larger processes of social change – factors which are largely outside the control of information scientists and their colleagues. As much as we may wish for the opposite, ICTs on their own do not have the power to solve deeper economic, social, and cultural issues; indeed, they are but one tool by which sustainable development can be encouraged and poverty decreased (McNamara, 2003). In light of this difficult reality, development informatics researchers must seek to understand more accurately what kind of role ICTs play in the larger drama of development. This will be intellectually messy: it is not a research agenda where "rational" science may be divorced from the "irrational" society. And yet, if we are to move past the unworkable, universalizing development paradigms of the past, we must constantly remain abreast of the forces shaping the future – and consider what people really need from those "helping" them.

REFERENCES

Blaikie, P. (2000). Development, post-, anti-, and populist: a critical review. *Environment and Planning, 32*, 1033–1050. doi:10.1068/a3251

Brachman, J. M. (2006). High-tech terror: Al-Qaeda's use of new technology. *The Fletcher Journal of International Affairs, 30*(2), 149–164.

Brubaker, P. K. (2007). *Globalization at what price? Economic change and daily life.* Cleveland, OH: Pilgrim Press.

Capurro, R. (1986). *Hermeneutik der fachinformation.* Freiburg: Alber.

Capurro, R. (1991). Informatics and hermeneutics. In Budde, R., Floyd, C., Keil-Slawik, R., & Züllighoven, H. (Eds.), *Software Development and Reality Construction.* Secaucus, NJ: Springer-Verlag.

Capurro, R. (2000). Hermeneutics and the phenomenon of information. In Mitcham, C. (Ed.), *Metaphysics, epistemology, and technology.* New York: JAI.

Cohen, R. S., & Wartofsky, M. W. (1986). Editorial preface. In Mitcham, C., & Huning, A. (Eds.), *Philosophy and Technology II: Information Technology and Computers in Theory and Practice.* Boston: D. Redel.

Cooke, B. (1998, Nov. 3). *The social-psychological limits of participation.* Paper presented at the symposium "Participation: The New Tyranny?" Institute for Development Policy and Management, University of Manchester.

Cooper, F., & Packard, R. (Eds.). (1997). *International development and the social sciences: essays on the history and politics of knowledge.* Berkeley, CA: University of California Press.

de Santa Ana, J., Burity, J., Goudzwaard, B., Gurney, R., Hadsell, H., & Koshy, N. (2006). *Beyond idealism: a way ahead for ecumenical social ethics* (Gurney, R., Hadsell, H., & Mudge, L., Eds.). Grand Rapids, MI: William B. Eerdmans Publishing Co.

Dockery, G. (1998). Questioning participation and equity in health. Paper presented at the symposium "Participation: The New Tyranny?" Institute for Development Policy and Management, University of Manchester.

Escobar, A. (1995). *Encountering development.* Princeton, NJ: Princeton University Press.

Escobar, A. (1999). Gender, place and networks. A political ecology of cyberculture. In Harcourt, W. (Ed.), *Women@Internet. Creating New Cultures in Cyberspace* (pp. 31–54). London: Zed Books.

Feenberg, A. (2004). Modernity theory and technology studies: reflections on bridging the gap. In Misa, T. J., Brey, P., & Feenberg, A. (Eds.), *Modernity and technology* (pp. 73–104). Cambridge, MA: MIT Press.

Ferguson, J. (1990). *The anti-politics machine. 'Development, 'depoliticization, and bureaucratic power in Lesotho.* Oxford: Oxford University Press.

Foucault, M. (1980). Two lectures. In Gordon, C. (Ed.), *Power/Knowledge: Selected Interviews and Other Writings 1972-1977* (pp. 78–108). New York: Harvester Wheatsheaf.

Fredland, R. A. (2000). Technology transfer to the public sector in developing states: three phases. *The Journal of Technology Transfer, 25*, 265–275. doi:10.1023/A:1007870520985

Fukuyama, F. (1992). *The end of history and the last man*. New York: Free Press.

Gujit, I., & Shah, M. (1998). Waking up to power, conflict and process. In Gujit, I., & Shah, M. (Eds.), *The Myth of Community: Gender Issues in Participatory Development* (pp. 1–23). London: Intermediate Technology Publications.

Habermas, J. (1987). *The philosophical discourse of modernity*. Cambridge, MA: MIT Press.

Hall, P. A., & Soskice, D. (Eds.). (2001). *Varieties of capitalism: The institutional foundations of comparative advantage*. Oxford: Oxford University Press.

Harrison, L. E., & Huntington, S. P. (2000). *Culture Matters: How Values Shape Human Progress*. New York: Basic Books.

Harvey, D. (1989). *The condition of post-modernity: an enquiry into the origins of cultural change*. Oxford: Basil Blackwell.

Hasan, H., & Ditsa, G. (1999). The impact of culture on the adoption of IT: an interpretive study. *Journal of Global Information Management, 7*(1), 5–15.

Heeks, R. (1999). The tyranny of participation in information systems: Learning from development projects (Development Informatics Working Paper Series No. 4), University of Manchester. Retrieved May 24, 2009 from http://www.man.ac.uk/idpm_dp.htm#devinf_wp

Heeks, R. (2002). Information systems and developing countries: failure, success, and local improvisations. *The Information Society, 18*, 101–112. doi:10.1080/01972240290075039

Heller, P. (1999). *The labor of development: workers and the transformation of capitalism in Kerala, India*. Ithaca, NY: Cornell University Press.

Hill, C. E., Loch, K. D., Straub, D. W., & El-Sheshai, K. (1998). A qualitative assessment of Arab culture and information technology transfer. *Journal of Global Information Management, 6*(3), 29–38.

Huntington, S. P. (1996). *The clash of civilizations and the remaking of world order*. New York: Simon and Schuster.

Ingwersen, P. (1992). *Information retrieval interaction*. London: Taylor Graham.

James, J. (2000). Pro-poor modes of integration into the global economy. *Development and Change, 31*(4), 765–783. doi:10.1111/1467-7660.00176

Jasanoff, S. (2002). New modernities: reimagining science, technology and development. *Environmental Values, 11*(3), 253–276. doi:10.3197/096327102129341082

Juhasz, A. (2006). *The Bush agenda: invading the world, one economy at a time*. New York: HarperCollins.

Kamppinen, M. (1998). Technology as a cultural system: the impacts of ICT upon the primary and secondary theories of the world. *Computers & Society*, 19–21. doi:10.1145/308364.308368

Knowles, C. L. (2008). Toward a new web genre: Islamist Neorealism. *Journal of War and Culture Studies, 1*(3), 357–380. doi:10.1386/jwcs.1.3.357_1

Lee, R. M. (1994). Modernisation, post-modernism and the Third World. *Current Sociology, 42*(2), 1–63.

Lerner, D. (1967). International cooperation and communication in national development. In Lerner, D., & Schramm, W. (Eds.), *Communication and Change in the Development Countries* (pp. 103–128). Honolulu: East-West Center Press.

Lynch, K. (1960). *The image of the city.* Cambridge, MA: MIT Press.

Mabogunje, A. L. (2000). Institutional radicalization, the state, and the development process in Africa. *Proceedings of the National Academy of Sciences of the United States of America, 97*(25), 14007–14014. doi:10.1073/pnas.200298097

Mahiri, I. O. (1998). The environmental knowledge frontier: transects with experts and villagers. *Journal of International Development, 10*, 527–537. doi:10.1002/(SICI)1099-1328(199806)10:4<527::AID-JID543>3.0.CO;2-S

McNamara, K. S. (2003, December). Information and communication technologies, poverty and development: learning from experience. Background paper for the infoDev Annual Symposium, Geneva, Switzerland.

Nasar, J. (1998). *The evaluative image of the city.* Thousand Oaks, CA: Sage.

Ong, A. (2007). Neoliberalism as a mobile technology. *Transactions of the Institute of British Geographers, 32*, 3–8. doi:10.1111/j.1475-5661.2007.00234.x

Palmer, B. (1990). *Descent into discourse: the reification of language and the writing of social history.* Philadelphia, PA: Temple University Press.

Putnam, R. D. (1993). *Making democracy work: civic traditions in modern Italy.* Princeton, NJ: Princeton University Press.

Ransom, J. S. (1997). *Foucault's Discipline.* Durham, NC: Duke University Press.

REFERENCES

Rose, J. (1998). Evaluating the contribution of structuration theory to the information sciences discipline. Paper presented at the 6th European Conference on Information Systems, Aix-en-Provence, France.

Rosenau, P. M. (1992). *Post-modernism and the social sciences: insights, inroads, and intrusions.* Princeton, NJ: Princeton University Press.

Sardar, Z. (1996). Alt.civilizations.faq: cyberspace as the darker side of the West. In Sardar, Z., & Ravetz, J. R. (Eds.), *Cyberfutures: Culture and Politics on the Information Superhighway* (pp. 14–41). New York: New York University Press.

Schech, S. (2002). Wired for change: The links between ICTs and development discourses. *Journal of International Development, 14*, 13–23. doi:10.1002/jid.870

Schmidt, V. H. (2006). Multiple modernities or varieties of modernity? *Current Sociology, 54*(1), 77–97. doi:10.1177/0011392106058835

Shanin, T. (1997). The idea of progress. In Rahnema, M., & Bawtree, V. (Eds.), *The post-development reader* (pp. 65–72). London: Zed Books.

Steyn, J. (2006, October). *Community memory and ICT in a developing economy.* Paper presented at the Constructing and Sharing Memory: Community Informatics conference, Community Informatics Research Network, Prato, Italy.

Steyn, J. (2007, December). *e-Post: networking remote areas.* Paper presented at the 2007 Community Informatics Research Network conference, Prato, Italy.

Streeck, W. & Yamamura, Kozo (Eds.). (2001). *The origins of nonliberal capitalism: Germany and Japan in comparison.* Ithaca, NY: Cornell University Press.

Wallerstein, I. (2005). After developmentalism and globalization, what? *Social Forces, 83*(3), 1263–1278. doi:10.1353/sof.2005.0049

World Bank. (2000). Global development gateway project proposal draft. World Bank: Washington, DC. http://www.worldbank.org/gateway/ (accessed September 2000).

Yamamura, K., & Streeck, W. (Eds.). (2003). *The end of diversity? Prospects for German and Japanese capitalism.* Ithaca, NY: Cornell University Press.

ENDNOTES

[1] For those intrigued by the material exigencies of sustaining ICT successfully within the context of developing nations, I recommend as starting points for further research the works of R. A. Fredland (2000), R. Heeks (2002), K. S. McNamara (2003), and J. Steyn (2006; 2007).

[2] Note that a similar three-step process has been fruitfully utilized in recent years by the UCLA Center for Research in Engineering, Media and Performance in its groundbreaking cultural civic computing project, REMAPPING LA.

Chapter 6
Cultural Acceptance of ICTs:
Perceptions in Practice

Jasmine M. Harvey
University of Loughborough, UK

ABSTRACT

The emergence of new information and communication technologies (ICTs) has generated much debate both in and out of academia in relation to theories ranging from economic advancement to imperialism. In the context of the 'low-income' economies, a dominant discourse associated with ICTs persists. The discourse of development predicts that nations which have joined the global market will use ICTs to harness global knowledge that will enable them to be competitive and therefore attain development. This has led to change in policy from international to local as ICTs are embraced as the next big development tool. Recently however, there have been reports of more failures of ICTs initiatives than success as professionals in the industry complain about unsustainability of the systems. A genuine issue is that so far analysis of this discourse has tended to be economically or technically deterministic, with little attention paid to social and cultural perspectives. In order to understand how the role of norms, practices and politics of people in particular communities play in this discourse in 'low income' economies, over 1000 semi-qualitative questionnaires were analysed from five geographical locations in The Gambia. A key conclusion that has emerged from the research is that there are different attitudes towards the ICTs in the different locations, which vary from full acceptance to rejection of ICTs. Such diverse reactions are underpinned by the religion and information ecologies in which gender plays a critical part. This result challenges the ICT4D agenda, and might be applied to reports of unsustainable ICT initiatives, especially in Africa.

DOI: 10.4018/978-1-61520-799-2.ch006

INTRODUCTION

New Information and Communication Technologies (ICTs) have been accompanied by such extreme 'hypes' that debating them in 'real' terms seems less colourful. ICTs have now been firmly accepted as instruments of advancement both by governments and ruling bodies in the global North and South. However, the hype which asserts that countries in the global South— which mostly are considered low-income economies (see www.worldbank.org/data for a definition of low-income economies)—will be able to turn their economic misfortunes around, and leapfrog to 'developed' status, has led to overly-energised ICT for Development (ICT4D) policies and initiatives, thoroughly endorsed by global agencies, ranging from bi-lateral to multi-lateral agencies.

Whilst literature on how to achieve speedy 'development' in order to be significant in the global market is excellent, it is also very important to debate the impact on social and cultural values and their roles in the ICT-led development agenda. To date, debates on development in the context of new technologies have focused more on economic and technical issues rather than cultural and social issues. Furthermore, there seems to be a general assumption that the introduction of ICTs into civil society automatically embeds an ICT culture. Little consideration is given to the fact that for ICT-led development to impact on society, first there needs to be an ICT culture (such as a cyber culture from Internet use, or a cellular culture from cell phone use). In other words, it is one thing to introduce new technologies to countries of the South, but if existing local cultures form resistance to such changes, there will be an insignificant ICT culture, which will in turn constrain ICT-aided development.

Whilst for local and national governments and their sponsors, a key aim is to create new policies and re-align old ones, in order to generate access to ICTs for their peoples, there are other factors that must be included in the ICT adoption process.

Assumptions are made in the socio-cultural context. These include assumptions about how norms, beliefs, practices, and protocols play a part in the link between ICTs and the communities to which they are introduced; how these normative values help or hinder human processes in engagement with ICTs; and how much they underpin how people in a community use ICTs to support their information ecologies (that is, information and communication needs, priorities and structures), in order to create cyber and cellular cultures.

This chapter's contribution is to show how some of the assumptions made in translating policy into practice affect the way communities engage with and perceive new ICTs. In the following, I provide a brief theoretical background of the ICT4D agenda in which I highlight the economic and technical monopoly of the discourse, and then briefly describe a case study and the methodology used; and the communities that were studied, and their cyber and cell cultures (to the extent that they exist). I then discuss findings under the following headings:

- Religion as a cultural discourse. How the secularism of people's norms, practices and protocols in the different locations and communities is underpinned by the moral symbols of religion, and the role that gender plays alongside them; and,

- Locations and their information ecologies. How the secularism of the norms and practices has reinforced complex existing inequities that enabled a hierarchy of power relations, which determines the type of information and communicative structure (or information ecology) of each location, and the subsequent different priorities and information needs, and essentially, attitudes towards new ICTs, in the different locations.

In conclusion, I summarise the problem and make recommendations that add to current knowledge, and offer practical solutions for more durable ICT initiatives which might accommodate local difference.

BACKGROUND TO THE ICT-LED DEVELOPMENT AGENDA

ICT for Development (ICT4D) is on the global agenda as one of the latest ideas in a long list of development theories and approaches. Spearheaded by international agencies such as the World Bank, the International Telecommunications Union (ITU), The United Nations ICT Task Force, and the World Summit on the Information Society (WSIS), an impression is created that local, regional and national governments in the global South have seized this idea as an opportunity to achieve modernisation and development – a chance that would enable them to become part of global economic dialogue.

Suggestions that ICTs promote economic development in high income countries has inspired countries which are 'less developed' to implement ICT initiatives in order to hope to accelerate their own development. The basis of the ICT4D concept is chiefly rooted in the free flow of ideas (knowledge), goods, trade and services from the North in the form of global ICTs—defined by Appadurai (1996) as 'scapes,' and echoed by Blair (2000). The ideal is that countries in the South can take advantage of the free flow of 'scapes' in order to improve two things: firstly, the economic status of the country, and secondly, the quality of life of the people—also set out in the Millennium Development Goals (MDGs; UN 2000). Improvements will enable 'poor' nations to be competitive in the global market. In fact, some of the theories went as far as to declare that with the help of ICTs, low-income countries would avoid all their teething problems in order to achieve a 'developed' status very rapidly (Gore, 2000). Previous development concepts may have widened the gap between the global North and the South; it is no wonder that

this new concept has been seized upon by some with vigour.

Where some have expounded positively on this concept, others have logically argued that economically, low-income countries do not have adequate resources (infrastructure and skills) to successfully adopt ICTs and take advantage of the free flow of the 'scapes' (Tong, 2001, pp. 65-82; Daly 1999). In fact, the effectiveness of the 'superhighway' has been questioned by some (Ebo, 2001, pp.1-6), labelling it a 'super-hype-way'. As successful implementation of ICTs depends upon basic infrastructures which are so generally lacking in countries of the South, some fail to see how these countries can suddenly bypass the tedious stages of 'development'. In an extension of this argument, Tongia (2005) points out that

"...we live in a divided world: between rich and poor, healthy and sick, literate and ignorant, democratic and authoritarian, and between empowered and deprived. All the technologies that we developed in the past centuries and all the policies we enacted from enhancing human development have not wiped out these glaring disparities." (Tongia 2005, p 15).

In this depiction, new ICTs will neither help development nor bridge the economic or other gaps, but rather mirror and extend existing divides. These views resonate with the age-old dichotomous utopian/dystopian views in wider literature on ICTs, especially regarding the future and the Internet.

Champions of ICT4D concepts have sidestepped critiques and are widely touting them in the form of promotion of the Internet and cell phones to flesh out the positive vistas of development. Promotion is to be found in 'virtual' or electronic forms of reality, under the virtual rubrics of e-governance, e-learning, e-health, e-democracy, and e-commerce, and so on. For example, e-governance is promoted within the view that since democracy demonstrates development by encouraging liberalisation and transparency, then ICTs will assist low-income countries to emulate high-income countries by formulating methods of transparency. The World Bank, a particular advocate of this line of argument, claims that for governments in low-income countries to attain development, there must be transparency not only for the benefit of their own civil society, but also to demonstrate credibility in the global sphere (World Bank, 2005). This has pressured Southern governments to establish online political administrations, in order to publicly demonstrate their commitment to democracy; they make available electronically online policy documents, and evidence of open decision-making by means of the public provision of key government documents.

While some truly believe that the object of promoting ICTs as development tools is for the benefit of low-income countries (Sein & Harindranath, 2004; OleKambainei & Sintim-Misa, 2003), especially as it minimises censorship and threats to freedom of speech, and engages civil society in all kinds of activities including political power sharing, others believe that the real agenda for the vigorous promotion of development agenda (such as e-governance) is to permit a shift of decision-making power from national governments to the private sector multinationals, which are interested primarily in the exploitation of resources (Cline-Cole and Powell, 2004; Hall, 1999; Escobar 1994). This view echoes the post-development theory of exploitation of the South by the North for economic benefits. In spite of this brief exploration of some awareness of social and cultural implications of the spread of ICTs, the dominant debate about ICTs tools for development remains firmly based on techno-economic assumptions.

THE TECHNO-ECONOMIC MONOPOLY OF DISCOURSE

As explained, while the focus on new ICTs (in particular the Internet and the cell phone) has

been to market them as tools for socio-economic development, the promotions are almost entirely positivist in their approach. There appears to be little regard for other features, as is evident in both academic and popular literature; there is a vast volume of techno-economic publications in comparison to socio-cultural ones.

Cultural impacts of ICTs are rarely debated, especially in evidenced-based literatures. Even in recent reports of failures and unsustainable systems, discussions of and solutions for sustainable systems (personally witnessed in international workshops and seminars) tend to be rooted in the techno-economic camp, although some organisations (such as www.bridges.org) are making efforts to include other critical factors. Unfortunately, the metric to measure development is usually economics (Willis 2005, p.3). As a result, social and cultural assumptions are built into these initiatives as incidental processes, usually based on the narrow social-cultural backgrounds of the implementers themselves. The simplistic management mantra is that 'humans resist change'.

In order to present a holistic perspective, it is crucial to assess ICT4D discourse from other perspectives, in particular, how everyday beliefs and practices in a community interact and engage with the systems or initiatives. Whilst some anthropologists and some cultural experts have recently made efforts to research from human perspectives (Mercer 2006, 2004; Yan 2002), empirical studies are still scarce, especially in the context of the communities which are supposed to benefit from new ICTs influence – that is, the majority 'poor'.

CASE STUDY, METHODOLOGY, AND THE COMMUNITIES

The Gambia has been a recipient of ICT initiatives from donor conglomerates such as UNDP which first started an ICT (e-government) initiative in 1998 in order to advance The Gambia's status on the global stage. The Gambia has since collaborated with several other countries (such as India) and international agencies in order to start ICT initiatives that would help 'develop' its financial capital and peoples (ScanICT, 2007). As a result, although The Gambia is a relative newcomer to ICTs compared to countries such as Côte d'Ivoire, Ghana and Senegal, which have advanced ICT infrastructure in the Western Sub-Saharan region (Jensen 2002), it has experienced one of the fastest increases in access and usage and even diffusion (ITU, 2006; Budde, 2007). This makes The Gambia as a case study more interesting as seemingly its culture is more embracing of such changes.

The Gambia lies on Latitude 13° 28′ north of the Equator and Longitude 16° 34′ east Latitude (GreenwichMeanTime, 2009). The country borders the Atlantic Ocean on the west whilst the rest of it is engulfed by Senegal. Geographically, The Gambia is interesting because not only is it the smallest and most densely populated country in mainland Africa with a population of around 1.5 million (World Bank, 2007), but the whole country is a narrow strip of land formed around the The River Gambia. The land area, which is limited to 11,295 sq. km, is about 24-48 km wide and runs most of the length of the river (about 500 km).

Politically, The Gambia is former colonial territory of the British which gained internal self- government in 1963 and full independence with dominion status in 1965 (The Gambia Population Secretariat, 2005). There seems to be an inter-relationship between The Gambia and Senegal which was initially broken due to colonial segregation (LaViolette, 2007); most Gambians have relatives in Senegal, and vice versa. This is reflected in Gambia's political strategies (Marcel, 1998). According to the national Population Policy (The Gambia Population Secretariat, 2005), the country became a sovereign Republic within the British Commonwealth in 1970. In July 1994 the country came under military rule following a coup d'etat. After a two-year transition, presidential elections were held in 1996 and democratic civil-

ian rule was restored. Recently, The Gambia was ranked third among African countries for Good Governance (www.apnacafrica.org). Apart from the capital and its surrounding areas (Greater Banjul area), The Gambia has five other administrative regions called Divisions. These are the North Bank Division, Central River Division, Western River Division, Upper River Division and Lower River Division.

Socio-economically, The Gambian economy after Independence relied heavily on a single commodity – groundnuts, which according to Carney (1993) unevenly distributed individual economic power between genders. At present, the country ranks among the 'least developed' with a per capita Gross Domestic Product (GDP) in 2007 of US$ 0.6 billion (Worldbank.org/data, 2006). Nearly 41 per cent of cropland is under groundnut cultivation and groundnuts account for an average of 9 per cent of total exports (Gambia Population Policy, Population Secretariat, 2005). The agricultural sector accounts for the largest proportion of economically active persons with more than half of the population engaged in subsistence farming, livestock-raising and groundnut cultivation.

Socio-culturally The River Gambia divides the country into two halves; namely the North and South Banks. This division has contributed significantly towards forming The Gambia's diverse ethnic groups and their associated roles in the economy. The most dominant ethnic groups are the Mandinka, Wolof, Fula (Fulbe), Jola, Serahuli and Serer; whilst the minor groups comprise the Aku (creole), Manjanjo and Bambara. In addition, an influx of European migrants contributes to the diversity of The Gambia's population and culture. Although the various ethnic groups differ culturally and socially, their communal lives share similar structures, giving them a unifying bond. Languages of the largest ethnic groups are widely spoken in Gambia. These are the Wolof (the most popular, spoken by almost every one), Mandinka, Jola, Fula and Serahuli. These languages are broadcasted in the media, although English is the official language. Some of these groups also have identical ties with similar groups in Senegal. According to the Gambian Population Policy,

"Social and cultural norms largely influence people's perceptions of and attitudes towards population issues. Despite the cultural variations among ethnic groups, male dominance is the common norm. Gender disparities are notable in that women have little decision-making power. Due to a lack of awareness and traditional gender stereotyping, it is generally accepted by a majority of both men and women that the status of women is inferior to that of men. Early marriage is common among all ethnic groups and affects female enrolment and retention in schools, particularly in the rural area." (Gambian Population Policy, 2005, pp. 8-9).

Along the same lines, the population policy declares that there are cultural practices affecting the female population such as female genital cutting, and various post-natal rituals that aggravate the risk of maternal and child morbidity and mortality; and that frequent pregnancies, short birth intervals, and long working hours (domestic and commercial), further constrain women's schooling and self-improvement possibilities, as well undermining their health. About 50% of women were in polygamous marriages according to a 1993 census, some of these rituals being connected to religion. About 95 per cent of the population is Muslim.

ICTs AND THE GAMBIA

According to Marcel (1998), an old ICT—the radio (Radio Gambia)—has been running since 1972. It broadcasts in English and the five major languages of Gambia and still proves to be the main source of information for the majority of people in The Gambia, especially those located in the rural regions of the country. Television, however,

has a very different history compared to that of radio. Various sources (Marcel, 1998; Edie, 2000) suggest that there were no specific plans from the then government to make information available through visual means. This lack of enthusiasm for television was, according to Marcel (1998), due to the fear of the level of political awareness the television might bring to The Gambian people. However, the government which came into power in 1994, promptly set about establishing a broadcasting station. The historic lack of enthusiasm from the government meant that Gambia was one of last of the ECOWAS (Economic Community of West African States) sub-regional countries to acquire a television station, eventually in 1996 (Marcel, 1998). The Gambian national television, not quite as successful as the radio, broadcasts for a few hours per day and only in the evenings.

The fate of the fixed line telephone in retrospect appears worse than that of both the radio and television in Gambia, although many of its problems such as lack of funds to invest in the infrastructure are common to the African landscape as a whole. The telephone network in The Gambia is currently operated by the government-owned Gambia Telecommunications Company Ltd. (Gamtel) which underwent a modernisation process in 1984. Despite the effort and growth in tele-density, the fixed line telephone remains a very unsuccessful method of communication in The Gambia, in fact, in Africa as a whole (see for example Budde, 2007). The desire to obtain an effective information and communication channel resulted in a recent shift to favour ICTs such as the Internet and the cellular (mobile) phone.

Due to its contemporary status, documentation on the history of the Internet in The Gambia is very scarce. However from the little available information one can deduce that the Internet was established in 1998 in The Gambia as a United Nations Development Program (UNDP) initiative. Gambia Telecommunications (Gamtel) was the other significant stakeholder. Gamtel provided the backbone of the Internet industry by offering four commercial Internet Service Provider (ISP) services, including the international access needed to connect to international servers. Lack of growth in its usage and penetration has been attributed to inadequate basic infrastructure such as electricity and fixed-lines. In addition, inadequate technological and human resources, lack of computer skills and literacy, high costs of computers, and maintenance costs and Internet tariffs have all been held responsible for the moribund state of the Internet. According to some critics, the biggest inhibitor of all is the overwhelming lack of awareness about the very existence of the Internet (Budde, 2007, Marcel, 1998).

Compared to the Internet, cellular (mobile) networks are thriving in The Gambia in terms of access, usage and penetration; the cellular technology seeks to replace its traditional counterpart, the fixed-line telephone, as a more effective and reliable communication instrument. The first cell phone service started operation in 1996. Since the launch of Global System of Mobile (GSM) communication networks in 2001, the cell phone has been the most successful yet of the new ICTs in terms of subscribers. There are currently two cell phone networks operating in The Gambia: Gamcel, which is government owned, and Africell, which is privately owned. Together, these two networks have seen a growth of 27% penetration in 2006 with 407,800 subscribers (Budde, 2007). This puts Gambia in a positive light for an emerging ICT culture.

METHODS USED AND THE LOCATIONS STUDIED

Policy is an integral part of how ICTs are adopted, promoted, distributed and accessed in any nation or community. Marcelle (2000), for example, indicated that groups such as women were marginalised as a result of policy in the Sub-Sahara African region. We begin a thorough understanding of ICT issues in The Gambia, by assessing Gambian ICT policies: what do the policies say about Gambian level and status of ICT adoption and what agenda do the policies promote?

A content analysis was conducted with the aim of a statistical determination of the frequency of certain key words or topics in the policies. Following the content analysis, a discourse analysis was then carried out on the themes discovered in the national policies. The aim of the discourse analysis was to understand the discourse of the keywords identified in the content analysis in the policies (i.e., in relation to each other and within the policies). This meant identifying what the text is projecting and which ICT areas are covered in the policies and which areas are currently isolated. The coding framework for the discourse analysis was adapted from Rose's (2001, pp.136-138) and Foucault's (1972) framework, and was based on the policies' discursive formation: that is, the way meanings are connected together for the ICT and the socio-cultural discourse. For instance, it is necessary to ask how the keywords show the formation of certain patterns and trends? What are the contradictions, diversities and dispersions and how do they also come together to define the policy agenda? (Foucault, 1972, pp.64-70). It is critical to make clear that, whilst discursive formation is all that is required from the content of the policies, this is by no means a deep discursive analysis. In addition, there is a degree of subjectivity, as in all research methodologies. Note that the policy documents analysed here consisted of Gambian national ICT policies relevant to new ICTs that were available at the time of this study. The policies were varied and included policies from a wider and more general perspective, such as modelling national agenda to meet international benchmarks, to divisional agenda, such as access to certain sectors. The following relevant documents were analysed for content:

- Gambia's Vision 2020 (strategic plans including e-initiatives), 2003;

- The National Information and Communication Infrastructure (NICI) policy for The Gambia, 2004; and,
- The Republic of The Gambia's Education policy 2004-2015 (including two pages dedicated to ICT policy).

From the policy analysis, whilst it became evident that whilst policy enables initiatives to be targeted at some places such as schools for e-learning, civil servant offices for e-government, and the promotion of public access points for people from places where there is an impending initiative, the basic infrastructure is not yet in place. Apart from students in schools, and office workers, other communities were not properly addressed in the policies. These communities may have been left out due to several reasons, ranging from lack of basic infrastructure to technical skills. However, what it shows is that by prioritising certain locations, the policies created smaller divides. Omissions may snowball into other problems, such as leaving out the 'majority poor,' the very audience that development is supposed to be aimed at. In order to further investigate the implications of these smaller divides socio-culturally, a survey was conducted in five communities. The five communities were chosen as places that were targeted in the policy documents, and those that were not. The survey sought to understand if there are cyber and cell cultures emerging and what types, what experiences (both direct and indirect) users are associating with ICT initiatives, what types of attitudes are being associated with the introduction of the Internet and the cell phone, and whether people from the different locations are integrating new ICTs into their daily routines and lives. The survey was conducted in the following five locations and communities:

Offices – These consisted of offices in private, public (civil) and non-governmental organisation in the Greater Banjul area. Offices were chosen to study because part of the government's strategic plan is to introduce ICTs to advance and modernise

Gambia's working systems and accelerate development. Part of this plan also involved private offices introducing the Internet and sometime cell phones in order to help advance competition, whilst NGO offices are reported to be the first offices in Southern countries to introduce computers (Jensen, 2003; Nii Quaynor, 1997).

Cyber cafés – Cyber cafés were in the Greater Banjul area. They incorporated both public (Gamtel) and commercial cafés. The reason for choosing cafes is to gain responses from people who seek access to ICTs by paying. From the discourse analysis, public access emerged as another priority location; the government realises that challenges of inadequate infrastructure do not enable access to schools, some offices and the general public. Public access to the Internet has been observed by Mutula (2003) as the most popular form of access, mainly due to cost and infrastructural reasons. As a result there are increased strategies both from the government and private sectors to provide more access in the public domain.

Households – Households or compounds were in the suburbs of the Greater Banjul area. The majority of the urban population reside in this location and do not often venture into the city. Demographically inclined towards groups in the 'non-working' category, people here are often excluded from vibrant and activity-filled places. This location is not prioritised in the national policies for access to new ICTs. Targeting this location, therefore, was aimed to gain responses from people who may not necessarily be users but are nevertheless included in Gore's (2000 p.13) challenge to the telecommunications sector.

Educational institutions – These locations incorporate both public and private sector educational institutions such as schools, computer institutes and the University of the Gambia in the Greater Banjul area. There has been much effort made from the international level to introduce ICTs to this generation of pioneers of the new ICTs through schemes such as government strategies and wind-up laptops. Access to this population's

Table 1. Percentages of people who associated ICTs with certain attitudes

	ICT	Positive ranking %	Neutral ranking %	Negative ranking %	Uncertain/ not sure %
Offices	Internet	57	30	1	12
	Cell phone	65	34	0	1
Cyber cafés	Internet	74	20	1	5
	Cell phone	75	21	1	3
Households	Internet	32	29	15	24
	Cell phone	64	30	4	2
Education Institutions	Internet	73	22	2	3
	Cell phone	63	34	1	2
Markets	Internet	10	23	24	43
	Cell phone	20	53	24	3

experiences with and opinions on new ICTs proved essential to the research.

Markets – Markets are vibrant places especially in Sub-Sahara Africa. Markets in this region are the economic hubs of urban areas, where most of the local financial transactions take place. As a result, they attract a diverse range of people – people that are usually hard to pin down to a particular habitation. Also, as new ICTs have been predicted and reported to be helping local economies, responses from this location are deemed important to the overall discourse.

Over 1000 questionnaires, with at least 200 respondents from each location, were collected and analysed using SPSS. Respondents from each location were sampled randomly (using an accidental rather than a purposive sampling approach), and viewed as a representation of the peoples' views at that time. The detailed responses to the open end-ended questions also provided a qualitative additive as excerpts to the quantitative findings.

FORMATION OF CYBER AND CELLULAR CULTURES

There was evidence of cyber and cellular cultures emerging in the five locations, but the difference in advancement in the locations was very apparent in the data analysis. Both the Internet and the cell phone were used diversely, showing different information and communication priorities of each location. How willing were people to engage with particular ICTs? Different levels and types of cyber and cellular cultures were evident. Each location had a distinctive cyber and cell culture, but these were not exclusive to the location. There were overlaps due to similar user demography of the respondents in some of the locations.

In the offices, the sampled respondents consisted of 27% females and 73% males. 59% were Internet users. The largest cyber activity (apart from email) was use of the Internet to search for news of current events around the world -- 55% engaged with this activity. Attitudes toward the Internet were generally positive and it was averagely ranked as *Important* in the survey (See Table 1).

However, limitations such as lack of access to constant electricity, yearning for local content, and censoring of young people's usage (it was corrupting them), were strongly voiced. This is a typical excerpt: "So many people are getting more aware about the world because many use it to make friendship through [the Internet]. The negative side of it is that it is exploiting many children through love affairs, which I think is very bad". In the context of the cell phone, the general demography was made up of people at the higher end of the socio-economic scale. Thus 97% used the cell phone to organise their various responsibilities (from public to domestic), as they were generally the 'head' of a household. This can be described as a top-down pyramid 'vernacular' style cell culture. In summary, both cyber and cell cultures are emerging and attitudes towards ICTs were generally positive.

In the cyber cafes, users were typically young, male, mostly educated, but mostly unemployed, still studying or self-employed in jobs which they are over-qualified for. Only 16% of the respondents were females. 97% were Internet users, and 92% were cell phone users. The highest Internet activity was browsing websites, or searching for information that would enable them to access overseas opportunities. This was either done by applying for jobs or to further educational institutions abroad, or through a dating website in hope of enticing a sex tourist or a philanthropist who would help finance an eventual migration. Compared to the office users, this group engages with high level of cyber culture activities, viewing the Internet as a tool through which to improve its socio-economic situation. The cell phone represented a symbol of modernity and status— acquiring it meant that people are seen as wealthy, a vital desire for a group that is not considered as 'income earners' by its surrounding society.

Attitudes towards both ICTs in this location were very positive, as depicted in Table 1, and as Respondents 347, 294 and 374 demonstrate with these comments:

It makes easy accessibility [in order] to get in touch with someone or with institutions. It helps people to earn a living from friends or pen-pals abroad. It can also lead [people] to practice bad tricks. It brings people closer and sometimes I do have some little cash from friends.

There were concerns from the sample about the misappropriation of the Internet especially as demonstrated by a comment from Respondent 364:

It is making our communication simple. I like how [we] are planning to travel to abroad for further education ... [but] there are other websites that are destroying our Gambia women, especially girls who involve themselves in prostitution.

The general message coming from this group was a genuine belief that the Internet and cell phone were tools that would catapult them into economic wealth. There were also no statistical differences in ICT usage between genders although women were scarce in this location.

The household populations were made up of housewives, domestic helpers and carers, college dropouts, recent migrants from the villages, and self-employed small traders. There were more women in this location (49%). Only 15% of the respondents were made up of Internet users and these were usually college dropouts who used cyber cafés occasionally. As a result, cyber culture was not really active or emerging. However, out the 62% who used the cell phone, the cell culture was generally centred on giving feedback to the 'head of the household' in office locations, and keeping in touch with a diaspora. Although there were some positive attitudes towards the Internet, a large number of people here were very unsure of the Internet as it was viewed as the importer of things that are morally and socially corrupting, as depicted in Table 1. Such reactions are demonstrated by the excerpts from Respondents 426 and 430:

The system is already corrupted so it is better for me to concentrate on my Five daily prayers because I'm old and very soon I will die and leave your world with you.

It is very wrong for us to follow the way of the Tubabs [a local term for white people]. It is not

Table 2. Patterns of differences in usage of the Internet and the cell phone

Location	% of females	Statistical significance: Internet usage between genders	Statistical significance: cell phone usage between genders
Offices	27	Not significant – 0.283	Not significant – 0.123
Cyber cafés	16	Not significant – 0.205	Not significant – 1.000
Households	49	Significant – 0.003	Significant – 0.000
Educational Institutions	50	Significant – 0.035	Not significant – 1.000
Markets	52	Not significant (weak*) – 0.173	Significant – 0.005

* Denotes a weak statistical inference as only 5% of the market sample were users.
Significance measured at 5% using both Chi-square and Fisher's exact tests.

going to be possible for us to be like them, so it is better we stick to our way of life.

There was also a statistical difference between gender and Internet usage in this location (see Table 2) which shows that women here were generally reluctant to use the Internet which could be due to lack of technical skills or education, but also preconceptions.

Although the cell phone was seen as more acceptable and useful for their needs and their general information and communication structures, there were still negative perceptions associated with it as a tool which causes family breakdowns as a result of infidelity, and a tool that encourages inappropriate activities in young people. Mothers wished to protect their children especially. There was also a statistical difference between gender and cell phone usage in this location, unlike office and cybercafé locations (see Table 2, for the differences in gender usage statistics for all five locations). Whilst the lack of technical skills may have explained why women shy away from Internet use, it does not explain why the cell phone had the same results. Statistics showed that some women would not use either the Internet or the cell phone, even if they had access to them. This concurs with the general negativity voiced to the researcher on the ground during the research. There was still evident cell

culture emerging in this location, as can be deduced from the following:

[The cell phone] brings my family and other relatives very close to me because I can talk to them any time I want (respondent 516).

It makes me to have easy communication with my friends and family. Having a mobile phone, I can call and say what I want to tell the person, instead of paying [a transport] fare to go and meet the person (respondent 596).

I get calls from my people away from me and I also use [the cell phone] to call them sometimes too. The only thing I can say is that the mobile is good because I am always in touch with my people (respondent 412).

I can communicate with my friends abroad (respondent 561).

I use it to call abroad without going to the telecentres (respondent, 562).

Clearly, the information and communication structure in this location is better supported by mobile phones than the Internet.

People in the educational institutions were found to be the highest consumers of ICTs; they exploited every facility and feature that both the

Internet and the cell phone had to offer, although more people from the cybercafés associated ICTs with positive impacts. Whilst the Internet was extensively used in the search for knowledge, this was the only location at which the cell phone's standard features (such as taking pictures, texting, listening to music and playing games) were truly engaged with. As a result both ICTs are seen as tools that support information and communicative structures. Incidentally, both genders are equally represented: 50% each of the sampled population. Both cyber and cell culture were evident in this location and attitudes towards ICTs were generally positive, and similar to the offices, although usage is higher than the office location. The Internet is especially popular in this location and although there were lots of voices on the misappropriation of Internet by peers, the general tone was not to ban or remove access (as was evident in other locations), but to emphasise its advantages, then followed by expression of concern with this issue, and advice to their peers to stay away from such sites, as demonstrated by the following:

It has made educational materials easy to get when you go online. It has also changed the culture because people use it for bad reasons such as Internet theft, pornography etc (respondent, 632).

People have access to relevant educational information and communicate easily, but it also has negative impact. People sometimes use it to watch pornograph[ic] films (respondent, 774).

It makes communication easier but people should stop using the Internet to watch blue films (respondent, 647).

In the market places the traditional hardliners were most evident. Only 5% of the respondents were Internet users, hence cyber culture is non-existent. As this group was made up of a hierarchy of traders, 52% of which were women, cell culture was primarily centred on solving logistical issues

of trading. This location showed the least evidence of cyber and cell culture compared to the other locations. Only 5% use the Internet and 50% use cell phones. They also ranked ICTs as least important (Table 1). However, similar to households, statistical analysis showed that women here are not likely to use cell phones even if they had access to them, in contrast to males (Table 2).

These different levels of cyber and cellular cultures show that in places where there are ICT initiatives, there are ICT cultures emerging. Policy alone is not responsible for the different levels of ICT use. If policy alone was the responsible factor, there would have been a clear distinction between ICT initiative active areas, and initiative–inactive areas. Instead, there is graduated access, use and integration, depending on the type of gender and age that dominate any given area. For example, in areas that are made up of young people (mostly ages 16-24), there is a high level of ICT culture. The gender variable shows a different pattern:

- Where there were no or very few women, such as the cyber cafés, both cyber and cell cultures were very advanced; and attitudes towards ICTs were very positive.
- Where there was a fair degree of representation of women in a more equal occupational structure, such as offices and educational institutions, there were greater degrees of cyber and cell cultures emerging although there is a sense of a need for policing or usage limitations; attitudes towards ICTs were also generally positive.
- Where women were highly represented, and in hierarchical structures such as households and markets, there were no cyber cultures. Cell culture seemed to be emerging out of necessity, and seemed unrelated to integration into the communities. In these locations, people were either uncertain or negative about the Internet, whilst the cell phone was viewed as just another tool to perform routine tasks.

Graded perceptions of the two ICTs in the case of women could be attributed to a complex number of reasons. They include: education and technical skills, techno-confidence, and time management. Women have to juggle a number of jobs simultaneously and therefore may not have the time to integrate new ICTs into their daily routines (Rathgeber, 2000 p.23). A distinctive component of the findings (underpinning these trends) is how culture plays a significant role in the organisation of the locations or communities. As The Gambia is predominantly a Muslim nation, its general culture is shaped by codes of religious beliefs and a classical interpretation of the religious code. As a result, religion is a big player in underpinning attitudes towards new ICTs, and therefore, their acceptance or rejection by local communities depends on who inhabits the communities (i.e., if they are vulnerable and need protection, or censoring).

RELIGION'S ROLE IN SHAPING CULTURE

In The Gambia, religion appears to be a significant factor in the formation of social informative and communicative structures. Although there is no official hierarchy in Islam, the Imam or the religious elder, is usually at the top of the cultural hierarchy as the wise 'man', with the highest authority. The Imam could be the 'poorest' in his community; however, the fact that he is the Imam gives him a high cultural influence, more than (say) a rich woman who is head of an influential organisation. This type of intricate hierarchy was witnessed by the researcher during the fieldwork. For example, whilst visiting one of the cybercafés, I noticed that one of the young men was doing his best to isolate himself from his peers who were using the Internet. I asked him why, and he said: "How can I face my Imam on Friday after using the Internet". This is not to say that Imams are preaching against the Internet use -- I have no

evidence of this. It is also not to say that income and other socio-economic factors are absolutely excluded as contributing influences on structures. However, even in the presence of economic factors, it appears that religion is what guides social and cultural norms, protocols, and structures. Hierarchies are formed on the basis of faith and the power relations attached to them.

Furthermore, according to Munir (2002), the classical interpretation of certain sections of the Qu'ran legislates male authority over women, which according to Stowasser "entails the man's right to discipline his women in order to ensure female obedience both towards God and also himself" (Stowasser, 1998, p.33). Women are seen as secondary to males and females must look up to the male for moral and social guidance; males are automatically put ahead in the socio-cultural ladder. This was specifically mentioned in the Gambian population Policy (2005) and quoted in the earlier section of this chapter. It is also depicted in the exclusion of women from praying with men inside mosques, or the near exclusion of girls from education in Madrassas (Islamic religious schools). Although evidence from the offices, cybercafés and educational institutions shows that the polarisation between genders is a complex issue, these religious protocols are adhered to by women who sometimes appear to be the actual enforcers of the regulations. Wheeler (2001) points out that the whole society (not just men) becomes the executors of the strict cultural code. Using her study in Kuwait, Wheeler observes that:

"Gender boundaries are policed by eyes of the curious public and a strong sense of 'you never know who might be watching' ... Gender separation in public life is maintained by public fears of the cost of transgressing such boundaries; a cost usually assessed to a woman's, and thus a family's reputation. The social sanctions against mixed gender interactions outside of direct relatives are so active that once while I was in an Internet

café, the owner got a page on his pager. He called the number listed on his pager on his cell phone. He discovered that the page came from a woman inside the café. She had asked him to turn down the air conditioning as she was cold. She was sitting 20 feet away from the owner, yet she did not feel comfortable communicating with him face-to-face, in a public place. When I asked the owner about the curious situation, he responded emphatically, 'you know, gender issues'." (Wheeler, 2001 p.191).

Also, the older a person is, the more responsible and wiser they are deemed to be. Older males tend to have overall say in cultural guidance. Even a young male is likely to have more power in the socio-cultural structure in our locations than an older female. Although there is evidence from offices, cyber cafés and educational institutions that females are beginning to challenge these boundaries, for the majority of population these traditional inequities are still very much part and parcel of the socio-cultural structure. These are shown by the results of the research and also observed in the human-human processes in our communities. In fact, it appears that what the introduction of ICTs has done is reinforce these types of boundaries and inequities, especially in places where the cultural codes are observed more strictly, such as in households and markets. As a result, religion becomes a factor in whether people accept or reject ICTs, whether it is the more technically challenging ICT (Internet) or the less technically challenging ICT (cell phone).

RESISTANCE TO ICTs FOR RELIGIOUS REASONS

Varied reactions (positive, negative or indifference) to the introduction of ICTs into The Gambian culture can be linked to a whole host of factors, including the secularity of beliefs of the people. Some groups saw ICTs as a way to compare their level of adoption of modernity to other societies

around the world, as was found in our offices. On the other hand, others decided to use ICTs as channels to acquire knowledge that challenged local knowledge, as in the instance of young men found in educational institutions and cyber cafés. Yet one of the most powerful reactions in the findings was the use of religion to resist the impact of ICTs on norms and practices. If a choice had to be made between religion and ICTs, the latter will be abandoned.

Among older age groups and groups within which tradition is paramount, such as the market and household locations, resistance to ICTs was clearly delineated. There is no doubt that new ICTs are viewed by these groups as instruments of destruction to religion and its teachings, as was especially evident in the non-user perspectives in the survey. A more complex view depicts ICTs as a representation of the West. In effect, the import and the adoption of new ICTs are undesirable 'Western' standards which will cause the end of the "civilisation of Islamic cultures" (Anderson, 1997).

New ICTs are seen as the modern Trojan horse whereby Western powers destroy religion. In fact, the *Guardian* reporter, Robert Tait, reported in an article that the Iranian government in 2006 banned high speed Internet access in order to "stifle domestic political dissent and combat the influence of Western culture" (Tait, 2006). This action was aimed at discouraging young people from accessing materials from 'foreign' cultures -- music, films and other downloads. Although The Gambia does not widely have high speed Internet access, views which condemn Internet and cell phone access were evident in the fieldwork, especially in the less secular locations, such as households and markets. The following quotations demonstrate opposition:

Is very, very sad the way things are going, because no respect is given to the elders nowadays and also, people are turning their backs on their origin (Respondent 429).

Yes, it makes some of our sisters in bad life, meeting different men and married women playing games with their men ... please help!! (Respondent 549).

We should talk to our own children not to adapt Western culture, because is not good for our religion (Respondent, 481).

It is very bad to adopt Western culture; Islam did not take some of its ideas (Respondent, 479).

It is not good for our religion (Respondent, 472).

Apart from Islam, anything you do in this world is not good (Respondent, 447).

Because our religious leaders don't like it. The religion itself does not match with Western culture (Respondent 881).

My religion does not support [a] Western culture (Respondent 900).

It is not correct for a Muslim to take Western culture (Respondent 894).

It is not good for Islam (938).

It is not good for my religion (respondent 951).

Islam don't want that culture because Islam do not want [a] female to act like a male or otherwise (Respondent 895).

All Muslims should adopt the Islamic culture (Respondent 897).

The view of new ICTs as negative tools and the call for them to be banned were especially evident among: the women concerned about the effect of the Internet on their kids; older people who feel young people are losing their cultural morals as a result of the Internet; and some men who feel that ICTs are encouraging women's promiscuity. This

last point can have fatal results. For example, an accusation of adultery (resulting from a simple text message to a man) can incur severe punishment, including stoning, as was confirmed to me by a taxi driver whom I interviewed. As a result, engagement with ICTs for some females is too dangerous to be worth the risk.

These different reactions to new ICTs further illustrate a pattern which has emerged in different locations. Where the environment is liberal and/or male, ICTs are used as empowerment tools and where the environment is less liberal and has a large amount of women, ICTs are seen as negative influences on culture. Religion's contribution to ICT adoption is both empowering and marginalizing, according to gender and age. There was some evidence of boundaries being pushed by both women and young people. Typically, whilst both ICTs are embraced in some locations, in other locations there is a cynicism about their real value or a selectiveness about which ICT to integrate for information and communication structures (in addition to economic and educational values).

LOCATIONS AND THEIR INFORMATION ECOLOGIES

Nardi and O'Day describe information ecologies as "settings in which we individuals have an active role, a unique and valuable local perspective, and a say in what happens. For most of us, this means our workplaces, schools, homes, libraries, hospitals, community centres, churches, clubs and civic organisations. For some of us, it means a wider sphere of influence. All of us have local habitations in which we reflect on appropriate uses of technology in light of our local practices, goals, and values" (1999, p. ix).

As has been established, gender and age influence policy and the cultural discourse of access to, use of and reaction to new ICTs in the specific locations. The findings show that an accumulation of all these influences determine how ICTs are viewed in a locality as beneficial or not, that is, to what extent ICTs contribute to the daily common goals of people. In other words, the perceived importance of ICTs by a group in particular localities is shaped by these influences. The information and communication processes that occur within groups of people in a particular location constitute an information ecology of that location.

According to Nardi and O'Day "in information ecologies, the spotlight is not on technology, but on the human activities that are served by that technology" (1999 p.49). Therefore, a library's information ecology is centred on the different categories of people who might use the technologies of books, films, tapes, and librarians and computers to serve them; similarly, information ecology in a hospital's intensive care unit involves treating critically ill patients by means of the expertise of medical specialists and technologies. Applying the concept of ecology to the locations studied, it was noted that in the household population the cell phone and not the Internet is its most important technology. To serve the needs of information mobility, the household ecology is centred on the cell phone. Taking into consideration a lack of education in this environment, and concomitant lack of the extensive technological skills (for the Internet, for instance), the cell phone becomes the most appropriate technology for this location.

However, in order to understand the information ecology of a place, one has to examine the communication structures in that location. They include the systems of people, practices and values, and how ICTs are accessed, used and reacted to, in that location. In the following section, I explore the form and significance of the information ecologies in my five chosen geographical locations, structuring my discussion under these categories:

- ICT-favoured ecologies;
- ICT-centric ecologies; and
- ICT-sceptic ecologies.

ICT-FAVOURED ECOLOGIES

By ICT-favoured ecologies I mean the locations where new ICTs are viewed as not only important to development, but also to the development of the whole nation. The purpose of ICTs in these locations is seen as collective. The patterns of the information and communication structure create 'equal' access and use, to achieve development. Out of the five locations surveyed, offices and educational institutions were the locations that favoured ICTs. This can be attributed to several reasons as follows:

- The socio-economic development agenda underpinning these ecologies commit to new ICTs as appropriate tools. For example, within public sector offices, implementation of an e-government agenda in order to fit into a global ICT4D program instigated a supply of computers and Internet facilities to prop up such an agenda. Similarly, international policy agenda to encourage young people to use new ICTs as part of the ICT4D program, with the aim of producing a technologically-skilled generation is seen to aid future growth. It has pushed forward teaching and access in school and college programs.

- Policy and practices in these spaces determines that both men and women have equal access to ICTs. Although males are more represented in the overall population in both offices and educational institutions, women were fairly represented in the dominant occupational groups. This balances the location in terms of access for the different genders. However, that is not to say that the promotion of equal access translates into equal use. For example, evidence from the analysis showed that whilst females in both these locations are high users of the Internet, compared to females from other ecologies, there was still a significant difference in gender usage in favour of men.

- The relative secular nature of these locations encourages a contemporary interpretation and optimism about new ICTs.

However, there is concern that the international agenda to promote universal access to ICTs could become counter-productive and may even be an accessory to further divides. In the context of the provision of universal access to the Internet in schools, for example, Bingham, Holloway and Valentine (1999, p.39) warn that this kind of agenda could promote future social exclusion because "some children have better access to computers and the Internet than others". In The Gambia only 28% of students from educational institutions had Internet access through their educational institutions. In fact, according to Bingham, Holloway and Valentine, "this disparity is evident in terms of the differential level of hardware [which] institutions possess, the diverse ways that ICT is employed in the curriculum, and the quantity and quality of access time that children are allowed outside the structure of formal lessons" (1999, p.39). Therefore, whilst a positive agenda which enables public sector organisations, elite schools and the further education schools to have access to new ICTs, there is a divide between the connected an unconnected organisations or schools.

ICT–CENTRIC ECOLOGIES

In ICT-centric ecologies new ICTs are the focus; they are deliberately sought for specific purposes. The information and communicative structure of the people here does not only see ICT as important, but necessary to individual social, cultural and economic development. The extreme focus on ICTs makes it a technologically-centric environment. It is not very conducive to females because they display a 'fear of technology', are too pragmatic or are morally restricted. Typically,

cyber cafés were the only location which fitted these characteristics neatly. Access in cyber cafés favours males strongly, because:

- Firstly, although almost all the females in the cyber café location had similar access compared with males, and therefore were users of the Internet, cyber cafés are very masculine places where young men show off their technological abilities to their peers. Apart from being culturally restrictive as a public space, access to cafes is very intimidating. It was observed that girls are usually laughed at or teased for their incompetence, and therefore are forced to accept an inferior role. As Rathgeber (2000) suggests, women are accused of having a "fear of technology" (p.23). In this case, the fear is not only to do with the fear of lack of educational skills to operate the technology itself, but also a broader fear created by the politics of gendered structures.
- Secondly, even for those who do not have a fear of technology, Rathgeber argues that women take less interest in "new technologies out of a sense of pragmatism" (p.23). Women do not generally have the time to focus on technology as they have other things to focus on, such as caring for the family, which forces them to deal with a multitude of tasks, meet a variety of demands and play diverse roles with limited time. Women simply would not have the time to trek to cyber cafés even if the structure of the environment was inviting to women. This line of argument (p.23) also explains why women in most of the locations (even in high ICT embedded areas) engaged with less online activity compared to men on average.

The concern however, is that the intimidating environment produced by cyber cafés together with cheap access policies that enable only public access and not private access, further alienate women from ICTs, extending the gender divide.

ICT–SCEPTIC ECOLOGIES

These are locations where traditional patterns of information structures replicate themselves in the attitudes towards new ICTs. Politics within these locations and their information patterns enable ICTs to be viewed only as objects that serve a purpose – a means to an end – and, therefore, they should not be allowed to interfere with other cultural aspects of a community. Households and markets are examples of such information ecologies. In these locations, ICTs were used only for solving mobility issues or to enhance trading. People did not view ICTs as anything other than a simple tool. As a result, information and communication structures had very little dependence on new ICTs; and hence are least embedded in these locations. Several reasons can be identified:

- The non-existence of ICT-policy for these areas means that no special effort has been made to encourage access.
- There is a general cynicism about the value of ICTs, and in particular the Internet. Although the findings showed some negativity towards the cell phone as responsible for breaking up families due to 'infidelity', the cell phone was a far more favourable tool compared to the Internet, which attracted a stigma. There was general prejudice against it for corrupting young people and introducing Western values that distorted religious values. As shown by the data analysis, such attitudes are linked to levels of access. Both these locations have the least access, so ICTs were ranked as the least important.
- Interestingly, traditional attitudes were paralleled by gender status of women. In fact,

these were the only two locations (households and markets) that showed statistical difference between gender and usage of cell phones (the only embedded ICT).

Again, this demonstrates a further divide between gender and location. However, in this instance, men alone cannot be blamed as the source of the hierarchical information patterns, as similar attitudes among both genders showed that many women in these locations have accepted their traditional status as lower in the informational hierarchy than males, and they therefore adhere to, if not approve of, these patterns. In fact, in the case of the household it appeared that women as much as men were pushing this agenda and reinforcing traditional gender divides. Table 3 is a summary of ICT trends of the locations and their information ecologies.

From these findings, it is evident that a socio-cultural perspective has highlighted different attitudes associated with ICTs in the different information ecologies. This is crucial to sustainability of ICT initiatives; it gives an indication as to whether ICTs are accepted or rejected as part of the norms, protocols and practices of the locations.

In the ICT-centric ecology, the instrumental attitude towards both the Internet and the cell phone, suggests that ICT initiatives would be sustained in locations with this type of ecology in the long-term. Since the cyber café location was the only ICT-centric ecology, it explains why the cyber café system is so far the only long-term successful access point for the Internet in the African region (Sairosse & Mutula, 2004).

In the ICT-favoured ecologies, although there is a generally positive attitude towards ICTs as beneficial to their location, attitudes in these ecologies were demonstrated as the result of government promotion through policy formulated schemes and agenda. Such policy influenced offices and educational institutions. Key findings of this re-

Table 3. A summary of the locations and their information ecologies

Location	ICT embeddedness (cell phone + Internet usage) % out of 200).	Importance of ICTs overall (including older ICTs) out of 25.	ICTs perceived importance.
Offices	Efficiently embedded 126	17	Partial
Cyber cafés	Highly embedded 181	18	ICT-centric
Households	Less embedded 77	16	Sceptic
Education institutions	Efficiently embedded 169.5	17	Partial
Markets	Least embedded 55	15	Sceptic

search, therefore, suggest that, in order to sustain ICT initiatives in ICT-favoured ecologies, there should be a constant reminder and promotion of the benefits of ICTs through programmes (such as work courses or educational curriculum). This method is most likely to encourage prolonged use and positive attitudes.

In the ICT-sceptic ecologies, however, evidence showed that ICTs were only viewed as tools to aid limited communication facilities. People here did not view ICTs as tools that should be integrated into their daily lives. In fact, overall they viewed the ICTs as morally corrupting because they interfere with the norms, practices and protocols of their communities. They do not generally have positive attitudes towards them, and do not generally want to engage with them. As a result, some groups here would not use ICTs even if they have access to them, as was found in households and markets. ICT initiatives, projects or systems are not likely to be sustainable in these contexts. However, one cannot use this as a basis not to implement ICTs in these locations, as it may result in further exclusion.

A farming analogy can be used: ICT initiatives are seeds and the locations are different types of soils. Just as some seeds grow in some soils without help, a different type of soil may help the seed grow only if boosted with fertilizers, whilst in a hard soil, the seed may merely sprout or not grow at all.

CONCLUSION

Policies that target some priority areas appear to be creating a divide. Targeted areas might be based on competencies, such as technical and education skills. Complex structures in each of the communities showed that whilst some information and communication structures lend themselves to the adaptation of new ICTs, others do not. Socio-cultural factors such as gender and age are underpinned by religion, which together influence levels of authority, education and technical skills in each location. These influences shape perceptions of new ICTs and influences acceptance or rejection.

Evidence of general acceptance or rejection of ICTs, depending on the levels of faith in communities, contributes to the debate as to why the majority of ICT initiatives are unsustainable (Research ICT Africa, 2007), especially those implemented in urban communities and villages. One explanation could be that the information ecologies in these places are incompatible with sustainable ICT projects and initiatives.

Based on findings in this chapter, policy recommendations cannot be made easily in relation to complex socio-cultural factors. However, it is recommended that the ICT for Development agenda should adopt a holistic approach by seeking the expertise of a diverse range of informatics interest groups (political, economic, cultural and development), who seek to address cultural, political, economic, social and population features together. These features need to be considered in initiatives and systems at an early stage of implementation, to ensure sustainability.

REFERENCES

Anderson, J. W. (1997) Is the Internet Islam's 'Third Wave' or the 'End Of Civilization'? Globalizing politics and religion In the Muslim world. *Middle East Studies Association Bulletin.* Retrieved July 16, 2008 from http://www.press.umich.edu/jep/archive/anderson.html.

Appadurai, A. (1996). *Modernity at large: Cultural dimensions of modernity.* London, Minneapolis: University Of Minnesota Press.

Bingham, N., Valentine, G., & Holloway, S. L. (1999) Where do you want to go tomorrow? Connecting children and the Internet. *Environment and Planning D: Society and Space,* 17, pp. 655-672.

Blair, T. 'Forward' In Leer, A (2000). *Masters of the wired world: Cyberspace speaks out* (pp. viii-ix) *London:* Financial Times.

Budde, P. (2007). *Telecoms market review and statistics.* Gambia: Paul Budde Communication Pty Ltd.

Carney, J. A. (1993). Converting the wetlands, engendering the environment: The intersection of gender with agrarian change in The Gambia. *Economic Geography,* 69(4), 329–348. doi:10.2307/143593

Cline-Cole, R., & And Powell, A. (2004). ICTs, 'Virtual Colonisation' and political economy. *Review of African Political Economy,* 31(99), 5–9. doi:10.1080/0305624042000258388

Daly, J. A. (1999). *Measuring the impact of the Internet in the developing world.* Information Impact Magazine.

Ebo, B. (2001). 'Cyberglobalisation: Superhighway Or Superhypeway?' In B. Ebo (Ed) (2001), *Cyberimperialism? Global relations in the new electronic frontier* (pp.1-6). Westport, Ct: Praeger.

Escobar, A. (1994). Welcome to Cyberia: Notes on the anthropology of cyberculture. *Current Journal of Anthropology,* 35(33), 211–231. doi:10.1086/204266

Foucault, M. (1972). *The archaeology of knowledge.* London: Tavistock Publications.

Gore, A. (2000). Putting people first in the information age. In Leer, A. (Ed.), *Masters of the wired world: Cyberspace speaks out* (pp. 7–17). London: Financial Times.

Greenwichmeantime (2008) Retrieved December 08, 2008, from http://www.greenwichmeantime.co.uk/time-zone/africa/gambia/map.htm

Hall, M. (1999). Virtual Colonization. *Journal of Material Culture,* 4(1), 39–55. doi:10.1177/135918359900400103

International Telecommunications Union (ITU). (2006) Telecommunication Development Report: ICT Statistics. Retrieved at July 13, 2006 from www.itu.org/statistics.

Jensen, M. (2002) *The African Internet – A status report.* Retrieved July 13, 2007, from http://demiurge.wn.apc.org/africa/afstat.htm.

Jensen, M. (2003). The current status of information and communication technologies in Africa. In Okpaku, J. O. Sr., (Ed.), *Information and communication technologies for African development: An assessment of progress and challenges ahead* (pp. 55–78). New York: United Nations ICT Task Force.

Laviolette, A. (2007). Ceramic traditions, identities and population in Senegal and Gambia: Compared ethnography and historical reconstruction test. *Journal of African Archaeology,* 5(1), 149–150.

Marcel, L. (1998). *The Role Of The Gambian Electronic Media In The Implementation Of The Gambian Foreign Policy*. Unpublished Masters dissertation, Dept of Mass Communication, University Of Nigeria.

Marcelle, G. (2000). Getting gender into African ICT policy: A strategic view. In Rathgeber, E. M., & Adera, E. O. (Eds.), *Gender and the information revolution in Africa* (pp. 35–84). Ottawa: IDRC.

Mercer, C. (2004). Engineering Civil Society: ICT in Tanzania. *Review of African Political Economy, 31*(99), 49–64. doi:10.1080/0305624042000258414

Mercer, C. (2006). Telecentres and transformations: Modernizing Tanzania through the Internet. *African Affairs, 105*(419), 243–264. doi:10.1093/afraf/adi087

Munir, L. Z. (2002) "He is your garment and you are his...": Religious precepts, interpretations, and power relations in marital sexuality among Javanese Muslim women. *Sojourn: Journal of Social Issues in Southeast Asia, 17*.

Mutula, S. M. (2003). Cyber café industry in Africa. *Journal of Information Science, 29*(6), 489–497. doi:10.1177/0165551503296006

Nardi, B. A., & O'day, V. L. (1999). *Information ecologies: Using technology with heart*. Cambridge/Massachusetts & London: The MIT Press.

Quaynor, N. (1997). *Computer networking and accessing the Internet in Ghana: Problems and prospects* (pp. 28–40). Interlibrary Lending and Document Delivery in Developing Countries.

Rathgeber, E. M. (2000). Women, Men, And ICTs in Africa: Why gender is an issue. In E. M. Rathgeber & E. O. Adera (Eds.) (2000) *Gender and the information revolution in Africa* (pp.17-34). Ottawa: IDRC.

Research, I. C. T. Africa (2007) Success and failures of ICT projects in Africa. *Research ICT Africa*. Retrieved on November 22, 2007 from www.researchictafric.net

Rose, G. (2001). *Visual Methodologies: An introduction to the interpretation of visual materials*. Thousand Oaks, CA: Sage Publications.

Sairosse, T. M., & Mutula, S. M. (2004). Use of cyber cafes: Study of Gaborone city, Botswana. *Program-Electronic Library and Information Systems, 38*(1), 60–66. doi:10.1108/00330330410519206

Scan-ICT Report. (2007) Status of ICT, usage and exploitation in the Gambia. *Government of the Gambia and UNECA*. Retrieved July 05, 2008 from http://www.scanict-gbos.gov.gm

Sein, M. K., & Harindranath, G. (2004). Conceptualizing the ICT Artefact: Toward understanding the role of ICT in national development. *The Information Society, 20*, 15–24. doi:10.1080/01972240490269942

Stowasser, B. (1998). Gender issues and contemporary Qur'an interpretation. In Haddad, Y. Y., & Esposito, J. L. (Eds.), *New Islam, gender and social change* (pp. 30–44). New York: Oxford University Press.

Tait, R. (2006). Iran bans fast Internet to cut West's influence. *The Guardian*, October 18th, 2006. Retrieved May 25, 2008 from http://www.guardian.co.uk/technology/2006/oct/18/news.iran

The Gambia Population Secretariat (2005). Unpublished Draft Population Policy obtained from the Population Secretariat.

Tong, D. (2001). Cybercolonialism: Speeding along the superhighway or stalling on a beaten track. In Ebo, B. (Ed.), *Cyberimperialism? Global Relations In The New Electronic Frontier* (pp. 1–6). Westport, CT: Praeger.

Tongia, R., Subrahmanian, E., & Arunachalam, V. (2005). *Information and communications technology for sustainable development*. Bangalore: Allied Publishers Pvt. Ltd. Retrieved on November 02, 2008 from http://www.cstep.in/docs/ict4sd.pdf

United Nations. (UN) (2000). Millennium Development Goals (MDGs). Available Online At https://www.un.org/millenniumgoals

Wheeler, D. (2001). New technologies, old culture: A look at women, gender and the Internet in Kuwait. In Ess, C., Sudweeks, F., & Herring, S. C. (Eds.), *Culture, technology, communication: Towards an intercultural global village* (pp. 187–212). Albany, New York: Sunny Press.

Willis, K. (2005). *Theories and practices of development*. London: Routledge.

World Bank. (2005). Financing information and communication infrastructure in the Developing World: public and private roles. Draft for discussion. *Global Information and Communication Technologies Department (Gict)*. The World Bank. International Development Agencies: World Bank

World Bank. (2006) World development indicators. Retrieved on December 02, 2006 from www.worldbank.org/data

World Bank. (2007) World Development Indicators. Retrieved on October 13, 2007 from http://go.worldbank.org/k2ckm78cc0

Yan, Y. (2002). Managed globalization: State power and cultural transition in China. In P. L. Berger & S. P. Huntington (Eds.), *Many Globalizations: Cultural diversity in the contemporary world* (pp. 19-47). Oxford: Oxford University Press.

Chapter 7
A Psychological Model to Understand E–Adoption in the Context of the Digital Divide

Andrew Thatcher
University of the Witwatersrand, South Africa

Mbongi Ndabeni
Rhodes University, South Africa

ABSTRACT

The digital divide is often conceptualised as inequalities of access to technology. While access is obviously a precursor to technology use, research consistently shows that the digital divide is not explained simply by access to technology; apparent in the evidence of digital divides within communities of equitable wealth or within the same geographical location. This chapter acknowledges the interplay between psychological as well as socio-economic factors as important in the adoption of technology. Within this approach we construct a model based on the Technology Acceptance Model, the Theory of Planned Behaviour, Innovation Diffusion Theory, Hofstede's culture framework, and Social Cognitive Theory. The framework for the model is based on a combination of an extension of the Technology Acceptance Model, Innovation Diffusion Theory, and Social Cognitive Theory. The underlying theoretical assumptions are based on Social Cognitive Theory. While some aspects of these individual theories have already been applied to understanding the digital divide, this chapter develops a more comprehensive psychological model of e-adoption than currently exists in the literature.

INTRODUCTION

The existence of large disparities between individuals and societies in their access to technology is undisputed (Warschauer, 2002), although the focus has largely been on information technologies (International Telecommunications Union,

2001). Disagreement exists however, in determining the causes of such disparities. Traditionally the inequalities have been attributed to a host of socio-demographic factors (i.e. race, education, socio-economic status, language, rural communities, etc.) based primarily on socio-economic aspects as predictors of access to technology and therefore as the best indicators of the digital divide (e.g. Hoffman, Novak & Schlosser, 2000).

DOI: 10.4018/978-1-61520-799-2.ch007

However, Warschauer (2002) warns against defining the digital divide in terms of qualities such as "haves" and "have-nots". There is growing evidence that disparities in technology use continue even when the technology is available, for example the digital divide based on age factors (Venkatesh & Brown, 2001). Recent data suggest that the relatively high cost of technology in some communities is not always the only causal factor in not adopting technology (Lenhart et al., 2003). Green (2001) for example, suggests that the use of technology is socially bound, being determined by access to education and training, the perceived application within a society, and by individual ability. This situation is familiar to researchers working on psychological models of technology acceptance where it has long been recognised that simply providing people with access to technology does not guarantee that it will be adopted and used. In its extreme manifestation the failure to adopt technology has sometimes been referred to as technostress or computer anxiety (Igbaria & Parasuruman, 1989; Weil & Rosen, 1987). It must be noted that the psychological approach does not dismiss access as an unimportant variable. After all, there are few psychological e-adoption factors to consider if a person does not have access to a particular technology. Access, or the availability of technology, therefore forms the first basic pillar of the psychological model presented later in this chapter.

This chapter begins by presenting the major technology acceptance models that are based on psychological theories. Technology acceptance models arguably represent the general case for technology adoption, with the digital divide arguably representing a special case for technology adoption because of the unique social factors. Next we explore social cognitive theory, the primary psychological theory used in developing our new psychological model of e-adoption in the context of the digital divide, and how this theory relates to the technology acceptance models. We also explore Hofstede's culture framework and how

it might be applied to understanding e-adoption within a framework of technology acceptance models. The penultimate section looks at studies that have specifically used aspects of social cognitive theory and the technology acceptance models to specifically understand the digital divide. The last section presents the new psychological model that emerges from an understanding of social cognitive theory, a culture framework, and reciprocal causality. The chapter concludes with some suggestions for future research based on this model.

BACKGROUND: PSYCHOLOGICAL MODELS OF TECHNOLOGY ADOPTION

Technology Acceptance Model

One of the most widespread and empirically tested models of technology acceptance using a psychological framework is Davis' (1989) Technology Acceptance Model. The Technology Acceptance Model is loosely based on Ajzen and Fishbein's (1980) Theory of Reasoned Action although it replaces many of the attitudinal components in the Theory of Reasoned Action with only two technology-related attitudes, *perceived usefulness* of the technology and *perceived ease of use* of the technology. Davis (1989) argued that high positive ratings of these two attitudes would lead first to intentions to use a particular technology and then, if the intention levels were high, this would lead directly to the actual use (behaviour) of that technology (see Figure 1). The Technology Acceptance Model has been tested successfully on a wide variety of technologies including general information systems (Mathieson, 1991), computer applications (Karahanna, Straub & Chervany, 1999), email (Szajna, 1996), telemedicine technology (Hu, Chau, Liu Sheng & Tam, 1999), the World Wide Web (Lederer, Maupin, Sena, & Zhuang, 2000), and mobile phone applica-

Figure 1. The Technology Acceptance Model (adapted from Legris et al, 2003; p. 193)

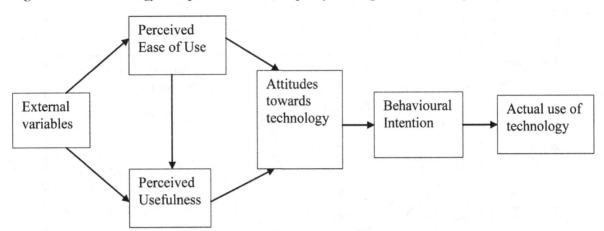

tions (Wu & Wang, 2005), amongst many other technology applications. However, on average only about 40% of the variance in behavioural intention was explained by these two attitudes (Venkatesh & Davis, 2000) in previous studies suggesting that other factors might also be at play in understanding the intention to use technology. In the original conceptualisation of the Technology Acceptance Model, Davis (1989) used a "catch all" factor called *external variables* to incorporate unexplained influences on the relationships. Typical external variables used in previous studies included past experience with the technology, gender, age, and previous education (e.g. Morris & Venkatesh, 2000; Venkatesh & Morris, 2000).

Despite the Technology Acceptance Model being one of the most widely used and replicated instruments for predicting technology use, the model has been critiqued as being too simplistic (e.g. Gefen & Straub, 1997; Hu et al, 1999; Legris, Ingham, & Collerette, 2003) in its assumption that (a) intentions will lead directly to behaviour and (b) that there are other psychological determinants that may prevent the actual adoption of the technology. In particular, within investigations of the Technology Acceptance Model other aspects of the Theory of Planned Behaviour (Ajzen, 1991), the updated version of the Theory of Reasoned Action, have been suggested as possible addi-

tional factors to consider (Mathieson, 1991; Venkatesh & Davis, 2000). In essence the Theory of Planned Behaviour proposed two further variables as important in predicting intentions, these being social influences and perceived behavioural control (Ajzen, 1991).

Venkatesh and Davis (2000) extended the original Technology Acceptance Model (i.e. TAM2, see Figure 2) to elaborate on the external variables in order to include social influences (i.e. social norms, voluntariness, and image), perceived instrumental factors (i.e. perceived relevance and perceived output quality), and the user's past experience. In particular, social norms (Karahanna et al, 1999) and past experience with the technology (Taylor & Todd, 1995) were important aspects of the Theory of Planned Behaviour included in the extension of the original Technology Acceptance Model. Past exposure to technology is particularly relevant in understanding the digital divide. This is particularly relevant to the digital divide where "divides" are typically characterised by poor access (and therefore inadequate prior exposure) to technology. Venkatesh and Davis (2000) provided empirical support for TAM2 using computer applications in four different organisations. However, TAM2 does not include perceived behavioural control, an important aspect of the Theory of Planned Behaviour, and a shortcoming that is ad-

Figure 2. Extension of the Technology Acceptance Model – TAM2 (adapted from Venkatesh and Davis, 2000; p. 188)

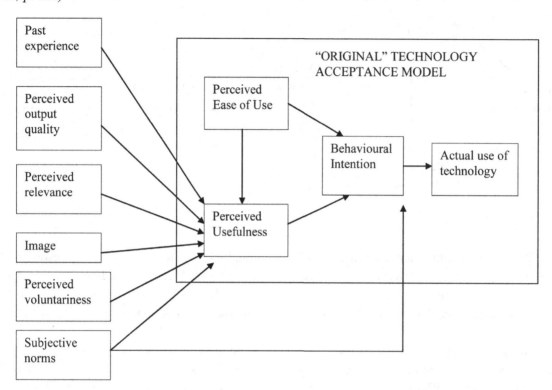

dressed when covering Social Cognitive Theory later in this chapter. One further aspect that still remains unresolved with TAM2 is the fact that technology acceptance is partly determined by how well the technology fits with the task at hand (Dishaw & Strong, 1999; Lucas & Spitler, 1999) and the capabilities of the user. For example, when integrating the Task Technology Fit model with the Technology Acceptance Model, Dishaw and Strong (1991) found that actual technology use was higher when the requirements of the task matched the capabilities of the technology.

Innovation Diffusion Theory

Some researchers (Karahanna et al. 1999; Wu & Wang, 2005) have argued that the Technology Acceptance Model is actually a subset of the Innovation Diffusion Theory. The Innovation Diffusion Theory is a decision-theoretic model (see Figure 3) based on sociological evidence, although many of its central concepts are actually psychological in nature (Rogers, 2003). According to the Innovation Diffusion Theory a person moves from first knowing about a particular innovation (knowledge stage), to forming an attitude about that innovation (persuasion stage), to making a decision whether or not to use a particular innovation (decision stage), to using an innovation (implementation stage), to finally deciding whether to continue using an innovation (confirmation stage). This decision process also has an evaluative component. Recent versions of Innovation Diffusion Theory specify five innovation attributes/predictors at the persuasion stage; relative advantage, compatibility, complexity, trialability and observability. According to Karahanna et al (1999) relative advantage is an approximate for perceived usefulness and complexity is interchangeable with perceived ease of use. Compatibility is also a close approximate of perceived relevance in TAM2 and observability is conceptually similar to perceived output quality in TAM2 (although observability is also similar to social norms from TAM2). In effect, trialability is the only attribute within Innovation Diffusion Theory that is not encompassed by the expanded TAM2. Trialability refers to the effort or risk involved in experimenting with prototypes of a system and the ability to recover from errors. When communities have poor access to technology, the ability to easily experiment with technology would be an important attribute of the technology. In integrating Innovation Diffusion Theory and TAM2, Wu and Wang (2005) introduced another variable that was overlooked in these two models, namely the perceived cost. Technology that is perceived to be too costly (either to purchase in the first place or to maintain once purchased) would struggle to be adopted. Perceived cost is included in the new model presented later in this chapter under perceived user resources (of which cost and access to finances is an obvious resource). One problem with the technology acceptance and diffusion theories covered so far is that they assume that the adoption of technology is based entirely on the features or qualities of the technology; what Green (2001) refers to as "technological determinism" (p. 2). Green (2001) proposed that it is more the social circumstances (i.e. the economic and political environment, and the existing social and physical infrastructure) that are responsible for determining technology development and use. Next we look at a psychological theory that incorporates both social and individual aspects, Social Cognitive Theory.

Social Cognitive Theory

Social Cognitive Theory proposes that personal factors, behavioural patterns, and the environment interact bi-directionally in a triadic, reciprocal, causative fashion to determine behaviour

Figure 3. The five stage model of the innovation-decision process (adapted from Rogers, 2003; p. 170)

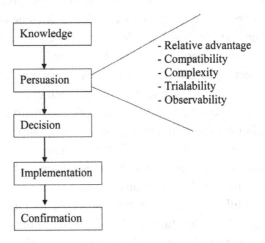

(Bandura, 1986) as demonstrated in Figure 4. Personal factors include thoughts, beliefs, perceptions, goals, affect, and intentions. In most other psychological models the personal factors are considered to have a direct, unidirectional effect on behaviour (i.e. thoughts, beliefs, and feelings affect how one behaves) whereas within Social Cognitive Theory, one's behaviour will also have an effect on the personal factors. For example, it is also evident that the effects of our actions change how we think (i.e. a negative consequence from an action will make us think twice before repeating that action). Similarly, while environmental influences shape how we think and feel, how we think and feel influences how our environment reacts to us (i.e. smiling at someone might cause them to be less defensive towards us). Finally, our behaviour alters our environment (e.g. the action of speaking one's mind influences how others will react to you) in much the same way that our environment influences our behaviour (e.g. we don't behave the same way in all contexts). Similarly, when considering the digital divide, the act of using a particular technology (e.g. the World Wide Web) changes those aspects of the environment (e.g. information) that a person can access. It is important to note that while the relationships are bidirectional this does not mean that they act simultaneously or that their influence on one another is equal (Bandura, 1986). Social Cognitive Theory is not without its criticisms. Meichenbaum (1990), for example, cautions that Social Cognitive Theory runs the risk of being seen as a collection of commonsensical tenets rather than a specific and testable theory. One such critique is the observation that reciprocal determinism is difficult to test empirically due to the complex nature of the cause-and-effect relationships. This makes it extremely difficult to propose a repeatable structural model for empirical testing.

While there have been more recent attempts to develop a structural model of Social Cognitive Theory (Bandura et al, 2001; Caprara, Regalia & Bandura, 2002), Bandura (1986) himself did not impose a structure on his original conceptualisation of the various components of Social Cognitive Theory. Broadly, Bandura (1986) recognised three general aspects of the personal factors that interact with behaviour; outcome expectations, self-efficacy, and facilitators and impediments. Self-efficacy includes (a) the ability to self-regulate behaviour and (b) the perceived proficiency in being able to execute that behaviour and is broadly similar to perceived behavioural control from the Theory of Planned Behaviour (Fishbein & Cappella, 2006). The outcome expectations are also divided into two sub-components, these being attitudes towards the behaviour and social pressures to encourage or discourage behaviour. Facilitators and impediments refer to personal,

situational, and socio-structural elements that occur within an individual. Personal factors include a host of individual characteristics including mood, emotion, personality, experience, and habits. The list of possible personal factors is potentially enormous and raises the question of which factors are most important for a particular behaviour to be enacted. Later in this chapter we focus only on those personal factors that have been proposed to have the largest influence on the digital divide in order to prevent this factor from being labelled as a "catch all" term. Situational factors refer to aspects within a given social milieu that have a direct impact on the behaviour. Situational factors include access to resources and access to learning opportunities. Finally, socio-structural elements refer to facilitator and impediment aspects of the legal, economic, and socio-political structures found in a particular society. These aspects include the legal framework and cost factors. As with the Theory of Planned Behaviour, Social Cognitive Theory predicts that these antecedent components are involved in determining proximal goals (i.e. intentions) and that these proximal goals do not automatically lead to actual behaviour. In Social Cognitive Theory the process of arriving at what one intends to do and the course of action one actually follows are separate events, moderated by a self-evaluation of possible outcomes if one actually carries out the behaviour.

At face value there is a great deal of similarity between Social Cognitive Theory and the Theory of Planned Behaviour. Both models include attitudes, social norms/pressures, and self-efficacy/perceived behavioural control. Both models have intentions/proximal goals preceding actual behaviour. However, this is where the similarity ends. Bandura's (1997) theoretical conceptualisation of self-efficacy includes not only a pro-active element (i.e. belief in one's ability to use a particular technology) but also an outcome

Figure 4. Triadic, reciprocal causation within social cognitive theory

Environmental influences

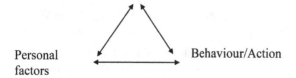

Personal factors

Behaviour/Action

expectancy element (i.e. an anticipation of what will happen if one uses the technology). Social Cognitive Theory also includes a cognitive assessment of the facilitators and impediments whereby an individual cognitively evaluates the possible motivating and de-motivating factors for using a particular technology. Further, Social Cognitive Theory introduces the need for self-evaluation aspects within the model. Self-evaluation may involve actual physical trialling (e.g. trialability) or "trialling in the mind". Bandura (1986) also proposed that vicarious learning was an important human learning element. Vicarious learning takes place when we learn from the actions of others without actually having to perform the action ourselves (e.g. early adopters who first start using new technology). Finally, within Social Cognitive Theory actual use of technology undergoes further evaluative pressure that will determine either further use (i.e. continuance intentions and behaviour) or abandonment in a similar manner to the confirmation stage in Innovation Diffusion Theory. We would argue that these evaluative aspects are important in understanding the digital divide, particularly in contexts where the technology is already available.

Within the technology acceptance literature the most commonly cited study using a Social Cognitive Theory approach is Compeau and Higgins (1995). Unfortunately, Compeau and Higgins' (1995) study was a rather incomplete test of Social Cognitive Theory, only assessing outcome expectations, self-efficacy, and behaviour. Based on Social Cognitive Theory, Compeau and Higgins (1995) hypothesised that training using a behavioural modelling technique would be more effective than traditional (non-modelled) training and that prior competencies would be positively related to self-efficacy. Compeau and Higgins (1995) found support for these aspects of Social Cognitive Theory within the context of learning to use computer software applications.

CULTURAL ASPECTS: HOFSTEDE'S CULTURE DIMENSIONS

Bandura (1986) recognised that biological attributes should also be considered as personal attributes worthy of inclusion within Social Cognitive Theory. Using the Technology Acceptance Model approach it is therefore unsurprising that studies have also uncovered cultural (Straub, 1994) and gender (Gefen & Straub, 1997) differences in the adoption of technology. Hofstede (1983) defined culture as "collective mental programming" (p. 76) emphasising a strong cognitive element to culture. Hofstede's (1980) seminal work on culture in terms of thinking and behavioural differences proposed four dimensions of cultural differentiation: 1) power distance, 2) individualism vs. collectivism, 3) uncertainty avoidance, and 4) masculinity-femininity. A fifth dimension, long-term versus short-term orientation, was added after a multinational study of students initiated in China (Hofstede, 1994). Power distance refers to the extent to which less powerful people in a group accept/expect power to be distributed unequally. This implies that inequality is inherent in the group and that less powerful people in the group acknowledge the inequality and accept that they are less powerful (Hofstede, 1994). This dimension is usually defined along a continuum from small to large power distance. The individualism versus collectivism dimension describes the way in which groups are either integrated and have strong ties between group members (i.e. collectivist) or the connections are loose (i.e. individualistic). The masculinity versus femininity dimension describes whether the group culture is more assertive and competitive (i.e. masculine) or modest and caring (i.e. feminine). The uncertainty avoidance dimension describes the extent to which a group or society is able to cope with ambiguity, especially in unstructured contexts. Cultures high on uncertainty avoidance handle the ambiguity by creating and ensuring adherence to strict laws and rules, which might also include high levels of religiosity. Finally, long term versus short-term orientation describes the differences in values within a group or society. Groups that favour perseverance and caution are considered to be associated with a long-term orientation whereas groups that favour fulfilling social obligations or "saving face" are considered to be associated with a short-term orientation (Hofstede, 1994).

Applying Hofstede's (1980) culture framework to understanding technology adoption issues has provided mixed results. In early work, Straub (1994) suggested that there would be differences in attitudes towards email and fax technology between employees in the same type of organisations in Japan and United States based on differences in the uncertainty avoidance dimension. Straub (1994) argued that email and fax were high in ambiguity (compared to face-to-face communication) and that Japanese respondents would therefore have more negative attitudes towards these technologies. Straub (1994), however, found no differences between these two "cultures" in their attitudes towards the technologies. Gefen and Straub (1997) used an interpretation of Hofstede's (1980) masculinity-femininity dimension to suggest that due to the social aspects of email, women would tend to have more favourable attitudes (perceived ease of use and perceived usefulness) than their male counterparts. However, while this was the case, this did not translate into greater email usage for women. These two studies would suggest that Hofstede's (1980) culture framework has limited contributory power for understanding e-adoption. However, more recently Veiga, Floyd and Dechant (2001) have proposed a more complete model linking four of Hofstede's (1980) dimensions to the Technology Acceptance Model. The masculinity-femininity dimension was not addressed because it "has been the most difficult to conceptualise and validate" (Veiga et al, 2001; p. 146). Veiga et al (2001) provided a set of sixteen propositions linked to technology acceptance and the four culture dimensions. There are too many propositions to present them all

here, so two propositions are provided to give the interested reader a sense: Proposition 2 posits that new information technology will be perceived as more useful in collectivist cultures if it is perceived to enhance group performance; Proposition 11 posits that new information technology will be perceived as more useful in short-term-oriented cultures if it is perceived to result in immediate work benefits. While there have been no direct, published, empirical assessments of Veiga et al's (2001) propositions there has been other support for a relationship between Hofstede's (1980) dimensions and e-adoption (e.g. Harris, Rettie & Kwan, 2005; Vishwanath, 2003), but not within the context of the digital divide.

UNIFIED THEORY OF ACCEPTANCE AND USE OF TECHNOLOGY

Venkatesh et al (2003) produced a theoretical framework that combined models derived from the majority of theories addressed in the review for this chapter (i.e. the Theory of Reasoned Action, the Theory of Planned Behaviour, the Technology Acceptance Model, the Innovation Diffusion Theory, and Social Cognitive Theory) together with the model of PC utilisation (Thompson, Higgins & Howell, 1991) that they called the Unified Theory of Acceptance and Use of Technology (UTAUT). Essentially, the model of PC utilisation included two aspects absent from the other models; job-fit (identified as a critique of TAM2) and facilitating conditions (i.e. objective factors that make a specific technology easy to use). Venkatesh et al (2003) argued that many of the concepts contained within these models were conceptually similar (see Table 1), but found moderate to poor empirical support for each of the theoretical models applied separately (i.e. predictive values ranging between $R^2=0.17$ and $R^2=0.53$). The UTAUT (see Figure 5) is comprised of four determinants (i.e. performance expectancy, effort expectancy, social influence,

Table 1. Comparison between UTAUT determinants and variables contained in other technology acceptance theories

Determinant/Variables	Theory	Empirical evidence
Perceived Expectancy		
Perceived usefulness	TPB/TAM/TAM2/TRA	Davis et al (1989)
Relative advantage	IDT	Moore & Benbasat (1991)
Job-fit	MPCU	Thompson et al (1991)
Outcome expectations	SCT	Compeau & Higgins (1995)
Perceived relevance	TAM2/TRA	
Effort Expectancy		
Perceived ease of use	TPB/TAM/TAM2/TRA	Davis et al (1989)
Complexity	IDT/MPCU	Moore & Benbasat (1991)
Social Influence		
Subjective norms	TRA/TAM2	Thompson et al (1991)
Social factors	MPCU	
Image	TRA/TAM2	
Facilitating Conditions		
Compatibility	MPCU	
Facilitating conditions	IDT	
Perceived behavioural control	TPB	Taylor & Todd (1995)

TPB= Theory of Planned Behaviour; TAM=Technology Acceptance Model; TAM2= Extended Technology Acceptance Model; TRA= Theory of Reasoned Action; MPCU= Model of PC Utilisation; SCT= Social Cognitive Theory; IDT= Innovation Diffusion Theory

and facilitating conditions) that predict intentional behaviour, which predicts actual behaviour. In addition, the model hypothesises that there are four moderating factors (i.e. gender, age, experience, and voluntariness) that influence the strength of the relationships between the determinants and behavioural intention. Venkatesh et al (2003) found good empirical support for the UTAUT in two organisational settings (i.e. predictive values of $R^2=0.69$ and $R^2=0.70$). The determinants were derived from variables contained within the different models on which the UTAUT was based as shown in Table 1. Venkatesh et al (2003) did, however, argue that self-efficacy and attitudes towards technology (in general) should not be included in their theoretical framework due to their overlap with existing components of the model. Venkatesh et al (2003) found empirical evidence for the overlap between self-efficacy and

effort expectancy and for attitudes to empirically overlap with effort and performance expectancy.

PREVIOUS PSYCHOLOGICAL RESEARCH SPECIFICALLY ADDRESSING THE DIGITAL DIVIDE

Studies applying the psychological theories discussed in previous sections specifically to understand the digital divide are rare. However, given that the digital divide is not only an issue of access, general technology acceptance/adoption theories and models should also apply to the digital divide. This is perhaps an over-simplification of the general technology acceptance models as well as the issues concerning the digital divide. The general technology acceptance models (and their derivatives) tend to focus on understanding

Figure 5. Unified Theory of Acceptance and Use of Technology – UTAUT (adapted from Venkatesh et al, 2003; p. 447)

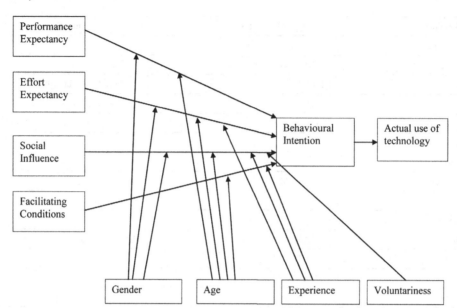

why individuals may or may not use a particular technology. Studies in the digital divide paradigm are interested in understanding why groups of people that share common characteristics (e.g. geographical location, gender, race, age, etc.) have such low technology penetration rates compared to other groups. From a psychological perspective this means trying to understand what psychological attributes are shared by the in-group but differ between groups.

Musa (2006) tackles this problem by introducing the concept of values, accessibility, and exposure to target technology into the Technology Acceptance Model. The obvious point made within the digital divide literature is that access to technology is a prerequisite for technology use (Hoffman et al, 2000), particularly (but not only) in developing world contexts. Musa (2006) argues that even when a certain technology is widely pervasive in developing world contexts (he uses the example of mobile phone accessibility in sub-Saharan Africa) the value that people attach to that technology is different compared to people

in developed countries. Musa (2006) built on Mathieson, Peacock and Chin's (2001) perceived user resources model, itself an extension of the Technology Acceptance Model. According to the perceived user resources model, perceived user resources refer to the extent to which an individual believes they have the personal and organisational resources to use the technology. Mathieson et al (2001) conceptualised the perceived user resources model in terms of four elements: user attributes such as expertise, training, educational level, and time available to learn the technology; support from others such as technical support and help desk support; system attributes such as accessibility and cost; and control-related beliefs including perceived behavioural control. Musa (2006) added three further constructs relevant to technology acceptance in developing world contexts (see Figure 6): perceived positive-impact factors, perceived negative-impact factors, and the individual's perception of the socio-economic environment.

Within Musa's (2006) extension of the Technology Acceptance Model, accessibility to tech-

Figure 6. Musa's extension of the Technology Acceptance Model (from Musa, 2006; p. 217)

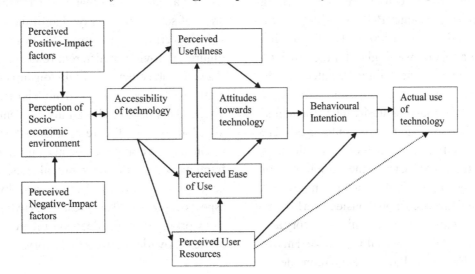

nology refers specifically to the actual physical access to technology as well as access to appropriate technological infrastructure (e.g. having a mobile phone but having no network coverage or having a personal computer but no electricity are two separate aspects). The perception of the socio-economic environment is influenced by both positive and negative factors. Positive factors include economic activity, good health systems, good governance, transport infrastructure, employment, and good education systems. Negative factors include unemployment, poverty, corruption, bribery, and minimal access to basic resources (i.e. water, food, electricity, education, and housing). Musa's (2006) model suggests a two-way interaction between the socio-economic environment and access to technology, implying that the lack of access to technology would drive the negative-impact factors while access to technology would result in the opposite outcome. In an analysis of survey data from Kenya and Nigeria, Musa (2006) found support for this extended Technology Acceptance Model in two developing world contexts.

In another assessment of the digital divide, Porter and Donthu (2006) examined how a small extension to the Technology Acceptance Model might be used to explain the digital divide in the United States (in their study the digital divide was characterised in terms of age, race, educational level, and income status with older, less educated, minority groups, with a low income status comprising the group with low Internet use). Porter and Donthu (2006) extended the Technology Acceptance Model by introducing the variable of perceived access barriers, similar to Musa's (2006) accessibility variable. However, using the demographic variables that characterised the digital divide (i.e. age, income, education, and race) as the external variables in the model, Porter and Donthu (2006) found that these aspects added no further significant explanatory variance to the model.

What Porter and Donthu (2006) did find though, was that usage behaviours were related to the purposes for which people used this technology. In other words, if people have an incentive to use the technology they were likely to overlook the perceived barriers. Using the Technology Acceptance Model framework, Venkatesh (1999) treated intrinsic motivation as an external variable preceding perceived ease of use and perceived usefulness. Venkatesh (1999) also found that user acceptance of technology was higher amongst the group that was intrinsically motivated. Working within a Theory of Planned Behaviour framework, Venkatesh and Brown (2001) also found that technology adoption was higher for those driven by social, hedonic, and utilitarian outcomes. In follow-up work looking at household technology adoption Brown and Venkatesh (2005) found that utilitarian, hedonic, and social outcomes were important predictors of technology adoption intentions thus emphasising the importance of outcome expectations in the e-adoption process.

Eastin and LaRose (2000) considered a limited set of components of Social Cognitive Theory and the digital divide. The Social Cognitive Theory aspects that Eastin and LaRose (2000) considered were outcome expectations (i.e. social, entertainment, and informational outcomes), self-efficacy, and usage behaviours, all in the context of Internet usage within the United States. Internet self-efficacy was found to be positively related to prior Internet experience, Internet usage and Internet outcome expectations. While the overall path model for these limited Social Cognitive Theory variables was supported, the inclusion of entertainment outcomes in the model was not supported, contrary to Venkatesh and Brown (2001) who found that hedonic outcomes were important in predicting personal computer use.

A NEW PSYCHOLOGICAL MODEL OF E-ADOPTION IN THE CONTEXT OF THE DIGITAL DIVIDE

Up to this point in the chapter we have addressed the background psychological theories and demonstrated how they have been related in previous studies to technology adoption in general, and technology adoption specifically in the context of the digital divide. In this section we build a theoretical psychological model based on these underlying theories. The model is necessarily incomplete as it is not possible to comprehensively note all the possible background, personal, demographic

and social interactions that may act in the diverse array of social contexts typical of the digital divide. Nevertheless, we argue that this model (see Figure 7) provides a different re-arrangement of relevant antecedents and relationships than currently exists in psychological models of the digital divide. This new model builds on Venkatesh et al's (2003) UTAUT by reorganising the variables within a more complete Social Cognitive Theory framework (including reciprocal causality as an underlying theoretical feature) and by adding aspects of perceived user resources (Musa, 2006) and working from the decision-theoretic process of the Innovation Diffusion Theory.

AWARENESS OF THE TECHNOLOGY

Knowledge that a technology exists forms the first stage in Rogers' (2003) decision-theoretic process in Innovation Diffusion Theory. Awareness of a technology is inherent in Musa's (2006) reasoning for the bi-directionality in the relationship between the perceptions of the socio-economic environment and the accessibility of technology. Musa (2006) though assumes that the relationship will act as a positive feedback loop, either making the perceptions of the socio-economic environment more negative if the technology is not accessible or more positive if the technology is accessible. There are two parts to Musa's (2006) premise that we believe are wrong. First, Musa (2006) assumes that people (particularly in developing world contexts) are aware that the technology even exists. Without the awareness of the technology it is impossible for someone to imagine that a particular technology might be their saviour from socio-economic troubles. Second, even if people are aware that a variety of technologies exist, this does not mean that people are aware of the link between a particular technology and socio-economic upliftment. Even in the information and technology literature, academics need to make cogent arguments to important

Figure 7. New psychological model of e-adoption within the context of the digital divide

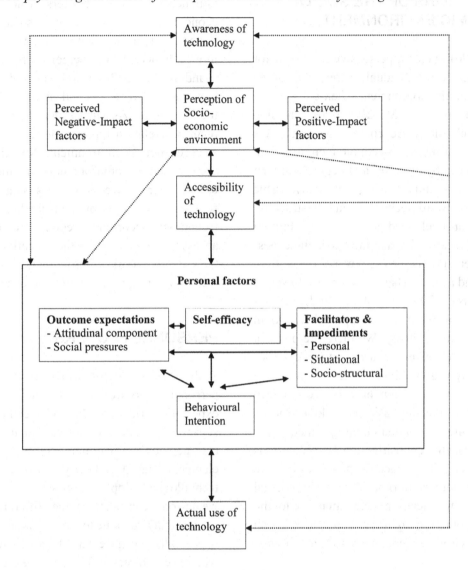

policy-makers to demonstrate the link between technology and social upliftment (e.g. Sein & Harindranath, 2004) and there are other writers who argue that the link between technology and wholesale social upliftment is over-stated (e.g. Green, 2001; Stivers, 1999). This link is therefore unlikely to be as obvious for the person living in a rural village in the Central African Republic, for example. The Innovation Diffusion Theory recognises that knowing about a particular technology is also the first stage of technology adoption (Rogers, 2003). This particular aspect of awareness

is especially important for economic strategists, policy-makers, and governments to understand as it acknowledges that technology education strategies are pivotal in technology adoption. The logical starting point in the model is therefore these two aspects of awareness: (1) awareness that a technology exists, and (2) awareness that the specific technology may have some positive impact on socio-economic upliftment.

PERCEPTIONS OF THE SOCIO-ECONOMIC ENVIRONMENT

Musa (2006) makes a persuasive argument for the importance of individuals' perceptions of the socio-economic environment when considering the digital divide. In Musa's (2006) extension of the Technology Acceptance Model, one's perceptions of the socio-economic environment are influenced by positive- and negative-impact factors. Positive-impact factors include favourable perceptions towards technological infrastructure, employment levels, and education and training systems. Negative-impact factors include pessimistic perceptions such as poverty, corruption, bribery, and access to basic resources. However, Unlike Musa's (2006) model, our model follows the reciprocal determinism approach found in Social Cognitive Theory. We therefore propose feedback mechanisms with the awareness concept. Highly negative-impact perceptions of the socio-economic environment will force people to concentrate on meeting basic, physiological needs (i.e. sourcing and/or maintaining water, food, and shelter). Highly positive-impact perceptions will leave cognitive space for people to explore new technological territory. For technological strategists this means paying attention to the socio-economic environment in order to establish a social environment conducive to technological adoption.

ACCESSIBILITY OF TECHNOLOGY

As Porter and Donthu (2006) and Musa (2006) correctly highlight, the issue of technology adoption cannot be considered unless people actually have access to the target technology. This component of the model only considers whether the target technology is actually available or not. Porter and Donthu (2006) emphasised perceived access barriers as part of this component of the model. In Porter and Donthu's (2006) conceptualisa-tion, perceived access barriers (which were only economic) are very similar to the socio-structural impediments and facilitators found in Social Cognitive Theory and the perceived user resources found in Musa's (2006) model and therefore are hypothesised to be personal situational factors in the new model. As Musa (2006) notes, there is a reciprocal relationship with the perceptions of the socio-economic environment. Negative-impact socio-economic environments are more likely to be barriers to access whereas positive-impact socio-economic environments facilitate access to technology. According to reciprocal determinism, access to technology has the potential to change the socio-economic environment, but only if the technology is appropriately adopted and used.

PERSONAL FACTORS

Within Social Cognitive Theory a number of personal factors are considered, notably outcome expectations (i.e. attitudes and social pressures), self-efficacy, and facilitators and impediments (i.e. personal, situational, and socio-structural elements). Based on the psychological models of technological adoption reviewed in this chapter, we introduce aspects of the different existing models that add value to the new model focusing specifically on those aspects which we believe will have a direct influence on explaining the digital divide.

Outcome Expectations

Outcome expectations comprise a general attitudi-nal component and a social pressures component. The **b** to attitudes that one holds towards technol-ogy in general (i.e. a general disposition towards the value of technology in society in general and in one's life specifically). The reciprocal relation-ships (especially considering general attitudes towards technology) with technology awareness and with how technology can assist with changing perceptions of the socio-economic environment are rather obvious. A low regard for the importance of technology (i.e. unfavourable attitudes towards technology) would have a negative impact on awareness of technology and would drive down the need to access technology (and vice versa). Drawing from UTAUT the "attitudes" towards the specific technology would consist of perceived performance expectancy and perceived effort expectancy. Technologies that are perceived to lead to social upliftment and that require minimal effort will be favoured over technologies that have purely hedonistic outcomes or are difficult to use. Drawing from TAM2, perceived relevance and perceived output quality are incorporated as aspects of perceived performance expectancy. There have also been a range of other perceptions that could also be considered as extensions of Technology Acceptance Model. However, their added value in explaining the digital divide would need to be explored empirically. These variables include perceived reliability of the technology (Liao & Wong, 2004), perceived security of the technology (McCloskey, 2003), and perceived convenience of the technology (Yoon & Kim, 2007), amongst others. Given that the digital divide is characterised by poor access to technology we would argue that perceived trialability of the technology as proposed within Innovation Diffusion Theory (Rogers, 2003) is also an important attitudinal component within the digital divide context. It is expected that technologies that are perceived to be easy to "try out" will be more readily adopted compared to technologies that discourage experimentation.

The social pressures component in Social Cognitive Theory is equivalent to the social norms aspect of Theory of Planned Behaviour and TAM2 and to social influences in UTAUT. Social pressures refer to the influences that significant others exert in order to encourage or discourage the use (misuse or disuse) of the target technology. Reciprocal relationships are evident between social pressures and attitudes as attitudes are clearly informed by the social interaction and attitudes clearly inform which social referents one chooses to listen to. Reciprocal relationships also exist between social pressures and perceptions of the socio-economic environment as well as determining which technology is available within a particular social context. Significant others include peers, managers, society leaders, opinion leaders, and pressure groups. The influence of the media, advertising, and other social networking processes should also not be discounted as important social pressures, depending on the social context of the technology. The influence of social pressures acts in two ways. First, social pressures act by providing an environment that either encourages or discourages the use of the technology. Second, if the technology is used then social pressures act by determining how the technology is used (i.e. whether only certain functionality is adopted or whether experimentation with new functionality is tolerated). As should already be evident, culture forms an important part of the social pressures component. While Veiga et al's (2001) sixteen propositions linking four of Hofstede's (1980) five dimensions to technology acceptance have yet to be empirically assessed, there is promising evidence to suggest that the propositions hold some value (e.g. Gefen & Straub, 1997; Harris et al, 2005; Straub, 1994; Vishwanath, 2003). Given the proliferation of online social networking tools in recent years, we believe that Hofstede's (1980) masculinity-femininity dimension may require further examination, despite the fact that Gefen and Straub (1997) found no relationship with actual technology use. It is also likely that certain cultures place more emphasis on social pressures (i.e. the collectivism-individualistic dimension), which may have an impact on technology adoption. We have also noted several criticisms levelled at Hofstede's (1980) dimensions. Hofstede's (1980) culture framework is not the only conceptualisation of culture, but is certainly the most widely applied. While new approaches to understanding culture and technology may also fit neatly within the social pressures component, Hofstede's (1980) framework is currently the dominant approach. In contexts where technology adoption is low, the influence of significant others will be particularly important, acting to encourage initial adoption and emphasising the potential value to community members.

Self-Efficacy

Despite Venkatesh et al's (2003) reservations about including self-efficacy as a separate variable, Eastin and LaRose (2000) demonstrated empirically that self-efficacy is important in understanding the digital divide. One aspect of self-efficacy that Eastin and LaRose (2000) did not include was past exposure and past experience with the target technology and with related technology. We propose that these aspects should be included as important components of self-efficacy beliefs within the context of the digital divide. We believe that self-efficacy measures should be developed based on Bandura's (1997) recommendations for the development of self-efficacy measures that assess both aspects of self-efficacy: the pro-active and the outcome expectancy elements (Bandura 1986; 1997). Self-efficacy plays a central role within Social Cognitive Theory models and would be expected to have reciprocal relationships with the other components of the model. Self-efficacy and attitudes have an obvious reciprocal relationship (e.g. high self-efficacy beliefs would have a positive impact on one's attitudes towards a target technology and in return, positive attitudes tend to make one more confident to experiment with technology).

Facilitators and Impediments

According to Bandura (1986) there are three different types of facilitators and impediments: personal, situational, and socio-structural facilitators and impediments. Personal impediments and facilitators refer primarily to demographic aspects

of the individual which play a role in determining whether or not that individual is able to use the target technology or not. The list of possible personal factors is potentially endless. Here we focus on those factors that emerge from studies relevant to the digital divide. Arising from the demographic research, important personal factors to consider within the digital divide are female groups, minority groups, low educational attainment groups, and low socio-economic status groups. One important personal factor that we have not yet considered in this chapter is the literacy level of the user, especially within developing world contexts (Thatcher & Ndabeni, 2005). Many information and communication technologies require a basic level of literacy in order to use the technology. A low level of literacy may therefore be an important impediment to adopting that technology. However, one must also bear the reciprocal relationships in mind. If there is sufficient incentive from the socio-economic environment then this barrier may actually be re-interpreted by the individual as a facilitator. As we demonstrated in our earlier work (Thatcher & Ndabeni, 2005), technology may actually be perceived as an enabler for literacy development, not as a barrier. Other personal factors may also be important in understanding the digital divide. Porter and Donthu (2006) suggest another possible personal facilitating factor, intrinsic motivation. If the technology encourages intrinsic motivating factors then the personal facilitating factors will be enhanced and the person would be more likely to attempt to adopt the technology. Personal factors would also have important reciprocal relationships with self-efficacy.

Perceived resources (Mathieson et al, 2001; Musa, 2006) would most easily match with situational facilitators and impediments. Situational facilitators and impediments are aspects of the particular social context and refer specifically to technological infrastructure and technical support. Examples of situational factors include access to training, past experience with the technology, and education opportunities. Other important situational factors within the digital divide context are access to technical support (e.g. training manuals and technical personnel), access to electricity, and access to supporting technologies (e.g. access to software if the technology is a personal computer). Situational factors would interact in a reciprocal relationship with perceptions of the socio-economic environment and with self-efficacy beliefs. The socio-structural facilitators and impediments refer to legal, economic, and socio-political aspects that either impede or facilitate technology adoption. Musa's (2006) conceptualisation of perceived user resources model included economic aspects (i.e. cost factors that serve as facilitators or impediments) within the digital divide context. Given the social upliftment benefits inherent in bridging the digital divide, economic factors (such as the cost of technology) are obviously important aspects of the model. It is also important to consider other factors such as legal restrictions to technology use (e.g. legislation that prevents access to certain information websites) or the political will to introduce a new technology (for example, legal and political barriers to encouraging a free media may impact on whether digital television is adopted). The socio-structural factors will have obvious reciprocal relationships with perceptions of the socio-economic environment and with social pressures. It must be remembered that we are dealing with the perceptions and not necessarily the physical reality. This means that the same environmental conditions might be perceived as insurmountable obstacles for one individual (or community) and as challenges that can be overcome by another individual (or community).

USAGE INTENTIONS AND COGNITIVE APPRAISAL

The majority of psychological models that we have considered (Technology Acceptance Model, Theory of Planned Behaviour, Social Cognitive

Theory) have placed usage intentions as an antecedent factor to actual technology usage. Bandura (1986) is quite clear in drawing a distinction between the intention and the actual action. One of the reasons for drawing this distinction within Social Cognitive Theory is for the cognitive appraisal (and re-appraisal) of the action. A similar process is suggested by Innovation Diffusion Theory whereby an initial adoption or rejection may subsequently be re-evaluated leading to continued adoption, late adoption, discontinuance, or continued rejection (Rogers, 2003). In technology terms this means that once the intention to use a target technology is raised then people are likely to experiment with using the technology. This might occur as an actual behavioural action (i.e. usage), as vicarious learning (i.e. watching others use the technology), or purely as a cognitive exercise (i.e. "trialling in the mind"). Based on the reciprocal nature of the model, the results of the intention and cognitive appraisal deliberations will be influenced (and will influence) directly by the personal factors and the environment. What is important to remember is that the intention does not automatically translate into the continued use of the technology.

USAGE BEHAVIOURS AND CONTINUANCE INTENTIONS

The obvious intended outcome in addressing the digital divide would be actual technology usage behaviour. We would encourage a more nuanced view of usage behaviours. Technology usage is not a simple dichotomy (i.e. use or non-use) but should also incorporate aspects such as the quantity of the usage, the extent of the usage, and the quality of the usage (e.g. does it actually bring about the social upliftment effects). These aspects have an important impact on whether a person will continue to use the technology. If, for example, the social upliftment effects are not realised, then a person may stop using the technology. This aspect reflects the importance of feedback loops within the model.

•

FUTURE TRENDS

In order to facilitate future studies that may wish to evaluate this new model we have suggested scales for how each variable might be measured (see Table 2). Many of the measures are taken from Venkatesh et al's (2003) UTAUT, which were themselves derived from various other concepts found in various theoretical approaches (e.g. Innovation Diffusion Theory, Model of PC Utilisation, Technology Acceptance Model, and TAM2). There are some instances where suitable measures do not yet exist (e.g. awareness of the

technology and socio-structural facilitators and impediments) and in most instances, the measures would have to be adapted slightly to match the specific technology under investigation and elaborated on to capture the nuances expressed in this model's description. These measures are therefore provided as suggestions, not as theoretically and empirically validated measurement instruments.

We are quite aware that the new psychological model of e-adoption in the context of the digital divide has not been empirically assessed as an entire model. The model has been derived from empirically tested models (e.g. Bandura et al, 2001; Eastin and LaRose, 2000; Mathieson et al, 2001; Musa, 2006; Straub, 1994; Venkatesh & Davis, 2000; Venkatesh et al, 2003), but some aspects of the model have not been empirically

Table 2. Summary table of variables and possible measures in the new psychological model

Variables	Theory	Measure
Awareness of the technology	IDT	No measure available
Simple measure of awareness that technology exists and that it will lead to social upliftment		
Perceptions of the Socio-economic environment	PUR	From Musa (2006)
Includes perceptions of:		
Positive- and negative-impact		
Accessibility of Technology	PUR	No measure available
Simple measure of accessible or not		
Personal Factors		
A. Outcome Expectations Affective component *-Performance expectancy* *-Effort expectancy* *-Trialability* Social Pressures *-Social pressure* *-Culture*	UTAUT UTAUT IDT UTAUT/IDT Hofstede	From Venkatesh et al (2003) From Venkatesh et al (2003) From Moore & Benbasat (1991) From Venkatesh et al (2003) From Veiga et al (2001)
B. Self-Efficacy	SCT	From Eastin & LaRose (2000)
C. Facilitators & Impediments Personal Situational Socio-structural	SCT UTAUT SCT	Demographic characteristics From Venkatesh et al (2003) No measure available
D. Usage Intentions	SCT/UTAUT	From Venkatesh et al (2003)
E. Usage Behaviours	SCT/UTAUT	From Venkatesh et al (2003)

PUR= Perceived User Resources model; UTAUT= Unified Theory of the Acceptance and Use of Technology; SCT= Social Cognitive Theory; IDT= Innovation Diffusion Theory assessed (e.g. Veiga et al, 2001) or are new to existing models (i.e. awareness of technology). The model is presented as an advancement to existing models, providing an overall theoretical structure taken primarily from Social Cognitive Theory in order to demonstrate the interplay between personal factors, the environment, and the technology. Empirical research is required to validate or refute the model (and even particular aspects of the model such as the centrality of self-efficacy beliefs). We would be interested to explore which social referents are the most important in determining the digital divide in different contexts. Given the reciprocal causality nature of the relationships we would argue that longitudinal, experimental research would be required to uncover the exact nature of the relationships. We strongly suspect that cross-sectional, self-report studies may not be sufficient to uncover the reciprocity inherent in the model. In reciprocal relationships time is also a variable in the model as all the relationships cannot occur at the same time. The obvious choice of research design to explore the nature of these relationships would be a longitudinal design. Longitudinal designs would also be better for establishing the causality within the model, already a difficult task given the anticipated reciprocity of the relationships. Within technology acceptance research Compeau, Higgins and Huff (1999) have conducted a longitudinal study using variables from Social Cognitive Theory to confirm a causative model, suggesting that an extension to the digital divide context is feasible. We have also suggested that the model is incomplete. There are a wide range of attitudes, particularly from the technology acceptance model paradigm that we have not included in this new model. Instead, we have attempted to focus on those aspects that would be specifically related to understanding the digital divide. We openly acknowledge that this approach means that other variables that we have not considered may also prove to be important

determinants in explaining the digital divide from a psychological perspective.

CONCLUSION

In this chapter we have moulded together two different psychological theories of behaviour (notably Social Cognitive Theory and Hofstede's cultural framework) with a number of technology acceptance models (specifically the perceived user resources model, the UTAUT, the Technology Acceptance Model, TAM2 and the Innovation Diffusion Theory) in order to develop a new psychological model of e-adoption. The model attempts to focus on components that are particularly pertinent to the digital divide (e.g. technology awareness, technology availability, socio-economic issues, self-efficacy, literacy levels, and the specific facilitators and impediments unique to many digital divide contexts) and therefore we have chosen aspects from the various models that we believe would best help researchers to understand when and how the digital divide might be most prevalent. It is our contention, following Social Cognitive Theory, that the best way to understand the digital divide is to understand the interplay between the potential users, the specific technology, and the environment in which the interactions occur.

REFERENCES

Ajzen, I. (1991). The theory of planned behavior. *Organizational Behavior and Human Decision Processes*, *50*(2), 179–211. doi:10.1016/0749-5978(91)90020-T

Ajzen, I., & Fishbein, M. (1980). *Understanding attitudes and predicting social behavior*. Englewood Cliffs, NJ: Prentice-Hall.

Bandura, A. (1986). *Social foundations of thought and action. A social cognitive theory*. Englewood Cliffs, NJ: Prentice-Hall.

Bandura, A. (1997). *Self-efficacy: The exercise of control*. New York: WH Freeman & Company.

Bandura, A., Caprara, G. V., Barbaranelli, C., Pastorelli, C., & Regalia, C. (2001). Sociocognitive self-regulatory mechanisms governing transgressive behaviour. *Journal of Personality and Social Psychology, 80*(1), 125–135. doi:10.1037/0022-3514.80.1.125

Brown, S. A., & Venkatesh, V. (2005). Model of adoption of technology in households: a baseline model test and extension incorporating household life cycle. *Management Information Systems Quarterly, 29*(3), 399–426.

Caprara, G. V., Regalia, C., & Bandura, A. (2002). Longitudinal impact of perceived self-regulatory efficacy on violent conduct. *European Psychologist, 7*(1), 63–69. doi:10.1027//1016-9040.7.1.63

Compeau, D., Higgins, C. A., & Huff, S. (1999). Social Cognitive Theory and individual reactions to computing technology: a longitudinal study. *Management Information Systems Quarterly, 23*(2), 145–158. doi:10.2307/249749

Compeau, D. R., & Higgins, C. A. (1995). Application of Social Cognitive Theory to training for computer skills. *Information Systems Research, 6*(2), 118–143. doi:10.1287/isre.6.2.118

Davis, F. D. (1989). Perceived usefulness, perceived ease of use, and user acceptance of information technology. *Management Information Systems Quarterly, 13*(3), 319–340. doi:10.2307/249008

Dishaw, M. T., & Strong, D. M. (1999). Extending the technology acceptance model with task-technology fit constructs. *Information & Management, 36*(1), 9–21. doi:10.1016/S0378-7206(98)00101-3

Eastin, M. S., & LaRose, R. (2000). Internet self-efficacy and the psychology of the digital divide. *Journal of Computer-Mediated Communication, 6*(1). Retrieved October 2009 from http://jcmc.indiana.edu/vol6/issue1/eastin.html

Fishbein, M., & Cappella, J. N. (2006). The role of theory in developing effective health communications. *The Journal of Communication, 56*(Supp. 1), S1–S17. doi:10.1111/j.1460-2466.2006.00280.x

Gefen, D., & Straub, D. W. (1997). Gender differences in the perception and use of e-mail: an extension to the technology acceptance model. *Management Information Systems Quarterly, 21*(4), 389–400. doi:10.2307/249720

Green, L. (2001). *Communication, Technology and Society*. London: Sage Publications.

Harris, P., Rettie, R., & Kwan, C. C. (2005). Adoption and use of m-commerce: a cross cultural comparison of Hong Kong and the United Kingdom. *Journal of Electronic Commerce Research, 6*(3), 210–224.

Hoffman, D. L., Novak, T. P., & Schlosser, A. E. (2000). The evolution of the digital divide: how gaps in Internet access may impact electronic commerce. *Journal of Computer-Mediated Communication, 5*(3). Retrieved October 2009 from http://jcmc.indiana.edu/vol5/issue3/hoffman.html

Hofstede, G. (1980). *Culture's Consequences: International Differences in Work-Related Values*. London: Sage Publications.

Hofstede, G. (1983). The cultural relativity of organizational practices and theories. *Journal of International Business Studies, 14*(2), 75–89. doi:10.1057/palgrave.jibs.8490867

Hofstede, G. (1994). The business of international business is culture. *International Business Review, 3*(1), 1–14. doi:10.1016/0969-5931(94)90011-6

Hu, P. J., Chau, P. Y. K., Liu Sheng, O. R., & Tam, K. Y. (1999). Examining the technology acceptance model using physician acceptance of telemedicine technology. *Journal of Management Information Systems, 16*(2), 91–112.

Igbaria, M., & Parasuraman, S. (1989). A path analytic study of individual characteristics, computer anxiety and attitudes toward microcomputers. *Journal of Management, 15*(3), 373–388. doi:10.1177/014920638901500302

International Telecommunications Union. (2001). *Digital divide. Overview.* Retrieved October 2009 from http://www.itu.int/ITU-D/digitaldivide

Karahanna, E., Straub, D. W., & Chervany, N. L. (1999). Information technology adoption across time: a cross-sectional comparison of pre-adoption and post-adoption beliefs. *Management Information Systems Quarterly, 23*(2), 183–213. doi:10.2307/249751

Lederer, A. L., Maupin, D. J., Sena, M. P., & Zhuang, Y. (2000). The technology acceptance model and the World Wide Web. *Decision Support Systems, 29*(3), 269–282. doi:10.1016/S0167-9236(00)00076-2

Legris, P., Ingham, J., & Collerette, P. (2003). Why do people use information technology? A critical review of the technology acceptance model. *Information & Management, 40*(3), 191–204. doi:10.1016/S0378-7206(01)00143-4

Lenhart, A., Horrigan, J., Rainie, L., Allen, K., Boyce, A., Madden, M., et al. (2003). The ever-shifting internet population: a new look at internet access and the digital divide. The Pew internet and American life project. Retrieved October 2009 from http://www.pewinternet.org/Reports/2003/The-EverShifting-Internet-Population-A-new-look-at-Internet-access-and-the-digital-divide.aspx

Liao, Z., & Wong, W. (2004). Key success factors of smartcard-based electronic payment: an empirical analysis. In *Proceedings of The Eighth Pacific-Asia Conference on Information Systems 2004 (PACIS 2004)*, Shanghai, China, 8-11 July, 2004 (pp. 2065-2071).

Lucas, H. C., & Spitler, V. K. (1999). Technology use and performance: a field study of broker workstations. *Decision Sciences, 30*(2), 291–311. doi:10.1111/j.1540-5915.1999.tb01611.x

Mathieson, K. (1991). Predicting User Intentions: Comparing the Technology Acceptance Model with the Theory of Planned Behavior. *Information Systems Research, 2*(3), 173–191. doi:10.1287/isre.2.3.173

Mathieson, K., Peacock, E., & Chin, W. W. (2001). Extending the technology acceptance model: the influence of perceived user resources. *The Data Base for Advances in Information Systems, 32*(3), 86–112.

McCloskey, D. (2003). Evaluating electronic commerce acceptance with the technology acceptance model. *Journal of Computer Information Systems, 44*(2), 49–57.

Meichenbaum, D. (1990). Review: paying homage: providing challenges. *Psychological Inquiry, 1*(1), 96–100. doi:10.1207/s15327965pli0101_25

Moore, G. C., & Benbasat, I. (1991). Development of an instrument to measure the perceptions of adopting an information technology innovation. *Information Systems Research, 2*(3), 193–222. doi:10.1287/isre.2.3.192

Morris, M. G., & Venkatesh, V. (2000). Age differences in technology adoption decisions: implications for a changing workforce. *Personnel Psychology, 53*(2), 375–403. doi:10.1111/j.1744-6570.2000.tb00206.x

Musa, P. F. (2006). Making a case for modifying the technology acceptance model to account for limited accessibility in developing countries. *Information Technology for Development, 12*(3), 213–224. doi:10.1002/itdj.20043

Porter, C. E., & Donthu, N. (2006). Using the technology acceptance model to explain how attitudes determine Internet usage: The role of perceived access barriers and demographics. *Journal of Business Research, 59*(9), 999–1007. doi:10.1016/j.jbusres.2006.06.003

Rogers, E. M. (2003). *The diffusion of innovations* (5th ed.). New York: Free Press.

Sein, M. K., & Harindranath, G. (2004). Conceptualising the ICT artifact: towards understanding the role of ICT in national development. *The Information Society, 20*(1), 15–24. doi:10.1080/01972240490269942

Stivers, R. (1999). *Technology as magic. The triumph of the irrational*. New York: Continuum Publishing.

Straub, D. W. (1994). The effect of culture on IT diffusion: email and fax in Japan and the U.S. *Information Systems Research, 5*(1), 23–27. doi:10.1287/isre.5.1.23

Szajna, B. (1996). Empirical evaluation of the revised technology acceptance model. *Management Science, 42*(1), 85–92. doi:10.1287/mnsc.42.1.85

Taylor, S., & Todd, P. (1995). Understanding information technology usage: a test of competing models. *Information Systems Research, 6*(2), 144–176. doi:10.1287/isre.6.2.144

Thatcher, A., & Ndabeni, M. (2005). HCI accessibility guidelines and illiteracy: developing a model of illiteracy and engagement with technology. *Ergonomics SA, 17*(1), 13–24.

Thompson, R. L., Higgins, C. A., & Howell, J. M. (1991). Personal computing: toward a conceptual model of utilization. *Management Information Systems Quarterly, 15*(1), 124–143. doi:10.2307/249443

Veiga, J. F., Floyd, S., & Dechant, K. (2001). Towards modelling the effects of national culture on IT implementation and acceptance. *Journal of Information Technology, 16*(3), 145–158. doi:10.1080/02683960110063654

Venkatesh, V. (1999). Creation of favorable user perceptions: exploring the role of intrinsic motivation. *Management Information Systems Quarterly, 23*(2), 239–260. doi:10.2307/249753

Venkatesh, V., & Brown, S. A. (2001). A longitudinal investigation of personal computers in homes: adoption determinants and emerging challenges. *Management Information Systems Quarterly, 25*(1), 71–102. doi:10.2307/3250959

Venkatesh, V., & Davis, F. D. (2000). A theoretical extension of the technology acceptance model: four longitudinal field studies. *Management Science, 46*(2), 186–204. doi:10.1287/mnsc.46.2.186.11926

Venkatesh, V., & Morris, M. G. (2000). Why don't men ever stop to ask for directions? Gender, social influence, and their role in technology acceptance and usage behavior. *Management Information Systems Quarterly, 24*(1), 115–139. doi:10.2307/3250981

Venkatesh, V., Morris, M. G., Davis, G. B., & Davis, F. D. (2003). User acceptance of information technology: toward a unified view. *Management Information Systems Quarterly, 27*(3), 424–478.

Vishwanath, A. (2003). Comparing online information effects. *Communication Research, 30*(6), 579–598. doi:10.1177/0093650203257838

Warschauer, M. (2002). Reconceptualizing the digital divide. *First Monday, 7*(7). Retrieved October 2009 from http://firstmonday.org/htbin/cgi-wrap/bin/ojs/index.php/fm/article/view/967/888

Weil, M. M., & Rosen, L. D. (1998). *TechnoStress: Coping With Technology @work, @home, @play.* New York: John Wiley & Sons.

Wu, J., & Wang, S. (2005). What drives mobile commerce? An empirical evaluation of the revised technology acceptance model. *Information & Management, 42*(5), 719–729. doi:10.1016/j.im.2004.07.001

Yoon, C., & Kim, S. (2007). Convenience and TAM in a ubiquitous computing environment: the case of wireless LAN. *Electronic Commerce Research and Applications, 6*(1), 102–112. doi:10.1016/j.elerap.2006.06.009

Section 2
Social Inclusion and Bottom–Up

Chapter 8
What Does it Mean to Bridge the Divide?
Learning from Spontaneous Practices towards ICTs

Suely Fragoso
Universidade do Vale do Rio do Sinos (Unisinos), Brazil

Denise Cogo
Universidade do Vale do Rio do Sinos (Unisinos), Brazil

Liliane Dutra Brignol
Universidade do Vale do Rio do Sinos (Unisinos) & Centro Universitario Franciscano (Unifra), Brazil

ABSTRACT

This chapter discusses the success and failure of initiatives which provide access to Information and Communication Technologies (ICTs) as a means of promoting social inclusion. We believe that there is often a disparity between the supposed and the true needs and desires of the minority groups at the receiving end of digital divide initiatives. Observation of practices towards ICTs which are spontaneously developed by a minority group indicate that important achievements are being overlooked by formal evaluations of digital divide projects and policies. The observed practices are organized into six categories and a change of paradigm is proposed for further actions.

INTRODUCTION

By definition, the intention of digital inclusion initiatives is to 'bring to the network' minority groups which face enormous difficulties in acquiring and using ICTs. Whether target groups wish to be included or whether they understand how to be included, remains questionable. Those who design digital and social inclusion projects and policies simply assume that all groups want 'to be included' in the same way.

Often there is a disparity between the supposed and the true needs and desires of minority groups. The cultural values and beliefs inherent in the configuration of the technologies themselves are frequently alien to the target public

DOI: 10.4018/978-1-61520-799-2.ch008

of the initiatives. This creates fertile ground for unexpected forms of appropriation of ICTs, reported in previous literature as deviant modes. Supposedly undesirable attitudes towards ICTs are often interpreted as an incapacity on the part of the target populations. This chapter proposes that, in many cases, the difference between the way the minorities appropriate and use ICTs and the initial expectations of the groups which provide them with access is misunderstood. The achievement of broad objectives, such as the increase of technical literacy, general knowledge and critical capacity, remains unnoticed, leading to negative interpretations of fruitful outcomes.

A revision of attitudes of previous policies and initiatives is a necessary first step in addressing the issue.

BACKGROUND

A considerable part of the literature about the digital divide presents results and discusses outcomes of existing initiatives. Many such texts propose methods to increase the success of future actions. Some examples from different parts of the world include: the examination of a community-based ICT project in New Zealand by Crump & McIlroy (2003); Menou, Poepsel & Stoll's review of the situation of community tele-centers in Latin America (2004); and Kumar's considerations of the diffusion and use of tele-centers in rural India (2006).

Other authors propose new ways as a guide for future initiatives. Examples are the comparison of the availability and use of ICTs in Californian high schools by Warschauer, Knobel & Stone (2004); and Bieber, McFall, Rice & Gurstein's proposal of a framework to help the design of community-based initiatives (2007).

A third approach questions whether it is possible to bridge the digital divide at all. This point of view focuses on the correlation between social inequality and technological exclusion by address-

ing the centrality of ICTs in contemporary life, but showing that it is not caused by ICTs. Thus actions to bridge the digital divide are topical remedies at best. "ICTs will not close the loopholes where investments in the education, labor and health sectors have gone awry" (West, 2006, Examining Information and Communication Technologies section, para. 9).

Those living in less dramatic conditions are not always able to take full advantage of the potential benefits of ICTs. For example, in recent years the Brazilian government, private entrepreneurs and NGOs have made considerable progress towards the dissemination of public internet access points, which doubled in number in 2007 (Bechara, 2008, p.47). The percentage of users accessing the internet in public points (49%) have surpassed those using home connections (40%) (CGI, 2008, p. 149). These positive results are challenged by Brazilian literacy indicators: in 2007, 7% of the Brazilian population were considered illiterate and more than 65% were sub-literate, that is, not able to understand and interpret longer written texts (Instituto Paulo Montenegro, 2007, p. 9). Further demographics of internet use in Brazil suggest that users of public access points are mostly young and with higher levels of education (CGI, 2008, p. 142). Many of these will be home internet users also. Because they have low speed home access or out-of-date equipment, they use public points to have better quality connections or to avoid the high cost of domestic connections, as has been reported by Barros (2008, p.8) and Lacerda (2008, p. 219-220, 246). Economic constraints are particularly important in countries where the price of hardware and software is higher and the average income is frequently lower (Gopal & Sanders, 2000).

Availability, reliability and capacity of the telecommunication infra-structure, as well as the different forms of charging for internet access, vary considerably around the world. Poor connections, outdated telephone networks, instability and interruptions in the electricity supply, significantly affect the experience of many internet users even in the richest regions of Latin America (Fragoso, 2004). The importance of these disparities is highlighted by the recognition that the type of connection used to access the internet has a stronger impact on the amount of time spent online than other digital divide demographics, such as education, race or gender (Davidson & Cotten, 2003). Comparisons of the online activities of broadband[1] and dial-up US internet users indicate a correlation between higher speed access, more frequent access and involvement with a larger scope of online activities (Horrigan, 2008).

Having said that not using ICTs or not keeping up with the last technological developments is not always optional, it is important to recognize that at times it is. Some people have no interest or prefer to maintain the equipment and type of connection they already have. The majority of the literature on the digital divide, however, does not recognize the legitimacy of the option to remain offline and approaches the existence of late technology adopters, drop-outs (ex-internet users) or non-users (herein defined as those who have the means to access the internet but choose not to do so) as a problem to be overcome (as, for example, Mossberger, Tolbert & Stansbury, 2003 and van Dijk, 2005). More than a third (69%) of the users surveyed by Horrigan (2007) were not fully positive about ICTs[2]. Nearly all (92%) UK adults surveyed by Selwyn, Gorard and Furlong (2005) had means of using a computer and the internet, but more than half (59%) reported having rarely done so or not at all in the previous 12 months. Personal interviews performed as part of the same study indicated that non-users did not access the internet due to a combination of choice, interest and disposition, while, despite the empowering and transforming discourse surrounding internet use, most "people who were using the internet on a broad and frequent basis were generally building upon and extending previously developed interests" (Selwyn, Gorard & Furlong, 2005, p.13). Observation of a community–based

project in a lower socio–economic urban area in New Zealand, led Crump and McIlroy (2003) to the conclusion that the belief that all want to participate in ICTs is flawed:

Not all 'have-nots' necessarily wanted to be 'haves' and neither did they view engagement in ICTs as a positive force that would transform the quality of their life . . . This group believes they are able to do their jobs, communicate, and when asked if they felt 'left out' of the world evolving around them, three quarters answered 'No'. (Analysis and Conclusion section, para. 2).

These findings invite reconsideration of the underlying assumption of most studies and initiatives that social inclusion has become inextricably linked to ICTs adoption (as, for example, in Hilbert, 2001 and Warschauer, 2004). The assumption of an information or knowledge economy (Drucker, 1992; Castells, 1999) is strong:

Knowledge and information are becoming the focus of activity, penetrating and dominating capital, natural resources and the workforce. [Thus] degrees of development will be determined by the capacity to manage and take advantage of technologies that support the processing of information and the generation of knowledge (Hilbert, 2001, p 7).

The idea that individuals and nations which do not fully and effectively use ICTs will be 'left behind' quickly progresses from the need to provide means of access to the necessity of imposing on the less aware. Transforming disinterest into participation, and offline people into ICT mandatory users, allows for no option but to join.

Recognition of this paradoxical 'imposition' invites the discussion of the hidden motivations and possible negative consequences of digital initiatives. Kvasny & Keil (2006) warn against the naturalization of the idea of inferiority implicit in the presupposition that minorities and poor countries need to 'reach' the developed nations or otherwise they will 'lag behind' the technological elites. At the individual level, Warschauer (2002) agrees that "lack of access (however defined) to computers and the Internet harms life chances" (Rethinking the Digital Divide section, para. 5), but remembers, with Henry Jenkins, that "the rhetoric of the digital divide holds open this division between civilized tool-users and uncivilized non-users. As well meaning as it is as a policy initiative, it can be marginalizing and patronizing in its own terms" (Jenkins in Young, 2001, para. 3). What is at stake is the unifying and linear vision of modernity and development behind the notions and differentiations amongst poor countries, developing countries and developed countries. Martin-Barbero (1995), for example, proposes that the concept of a single *modernity* is replaced by a plural idea of *modernities*, as the possibility of 'being modern' in Latin America, for example, requires, prior to anything else, breaking up with the unitary view of the European modernization project. His proposition that Latin America's heterogeneity requires a decentralized and plural conception of modernity can be coherently generalized to encompass the multiplicity and diversity of the world *in toto*.

There are authors who question the pertinence of digital divide initiatives on other grounds. For some, bridging initiatives are unnecessary because market forces are already closing the gap, exactly as has happened with previous communications technologies such as radio or television (Compaine, 2001). For others, the notion of the digital divide is little more than a marketing campaign for Internet service providers (Gurstein, 2003) which induces consumption of a myriad of communication devices and products.

Across their breadth and depth, computer networks link with existing capitalism to massively broaden the effective reach of the marketplace. Indeed, the internet comprises nothing less than the central production and control apparatus of *an increasingly supra-national market system (Schiller, 2000, p xiv).*

Encompassing the media industry as well as the education system, ICTs are considered a new powerful alienating factor (Postman, 1990; Chomsky, Mitchell & Schoeffel, 2002).

Another line of argument derives from the perception that projects designed to use ICTs as a means to promote the social inclusion of those truly at the bottom of the global social and economic hierarchy often create benefit for three already privileged actors: information capital, governments of developing countries, and the 'development industry' (that is, the large and powerful set of institutions involved in economic and humanitarian projects dedicated to change society through planned intervention). "Given their strength, it is likely that these groups are capable of capturing most of the advantages new ICTs can offer marginalized peoples." (Luyt, 2004, Conclusion, last paragraph).

The above considerations could be roughly summarized as four approaches to the question of the digital divide. The first consists of taking the experience of previous discussions and initiatives to ameliorate some following actions. The second includes proposals to adopt new points of departure in order to design new strategies. The third line of argument questions whether it is possible to bridge the digital divide at all, and argues that resources should be diverted to more realistic goals. The fourth addresses the very relevance of the digital divide discourse and actions. Important assumptions behind these approaches tend to remain little recognized or discussed. The next section of this chapter shines light on such hidden assumptions.

Hidden Assumptions and Spontaneous Practices

An important set of premises underpins the four approaches to the question of the digital divide.

The first part of this section of the chapter attempts to unveil these assumptions, using as illustrations cases previously considered unsuccessful or deviant by the existing literature on the subject. The second part of this section discusses spontaneous modes of gaining access to and appropriating ICTs found from field observations. Following DeCertau (1994), we choose to call these practices 'tactics', as we understand that "these 'ways of operating' constitute the innumerable practices by means of which users re-appropriate the space organized by techniques of socio-cultural production" (p. xiv). The aggregation of the various tactics towards ICTs we nominate 'micro-politics', as molecular infiltrations that work in favour of, but can present an obstacle to, policies on a grand scale (Deleuze and Guatari, 1987, p. 204).

The intention is to facilitate a comparison between the 'failures' reported by literature described in part 1, and the outcomes of the spontaneous practices observed, which are reported here in part 2. There are misunderstandings between the ways that minorities appropriate and use ICTs, and the initial expectations of the groups which provided them with access in the first place. As a result, the achievement of broad objectives, such as an increase of technical literacy, general knowledge and critical capacity, can be overlooked, leading to negative interpretations of quite fruitful projects and policies.

Deviant, Inappropriate or Misinterpreted?

Designers of digital and social inclusion projects and policy-makers assume that everyone wants 'to be included' the same way, but this is not necessarily true. We believe that mismatches between the supposed and the true needs and beliefs of the minority groups are fertile ground for unexpected forms of appropriation of ICTs. The generalized assumption that computers at home are more appropriate than in public places, for example, is based on arguments from the likes of DiMaggio,

Hargittai, Celeste & Schaffer (2004), for whom domestic access means greater autonomy and allows for more time online. On the other hand, it has been observed that access in a public place facilitates peer learning of technical skills and helps forming and solidifying social ties within the community served by the public access point (Crump & McIlroy, 2003; Kvarni e Keil, 2006; Lacerda, 2008; Barros, 2008). These different findings probably relate to variations in the cultural beliefs of target groups as much as of researchers, project managers and policy makers. Deeper still than these lie the cultural assumptions inbuilt in the design of digital technologies, that have frequently been recognized to relate to a white, male, Anglo-Saxon community within which computers and the internet were developed (Straton, 1997; McIlveny, 1999; Streeter, 1999).

The low-income group of US women observed in a longitudinal study by Eubanks (2007) were optimistic about the impact ICTs could have on their lives, but very critical of the metaphor of technologies as a bridge across the digital divide. Far from information-poor or technologically naïve, these women had plenty of previous experiences with technology, but mostly of the negative type: they had been subject to technologically-mediated surveillance at work, unfairly treated with arguments based on the infallibility of computer systems, and lived in technologically-degraded environments. For Eubanks, the distributive model and the deficit orientation that frame most digital divide interventions "*obscure* the kinds of day-to-day interactions [which] low-income women have with technology" and underestimate their resources "to interact with, design and produce 'popular technologies,' rather than being passive recipients of elite-produced technology tools" (Eubanks, 2007, para. 2). Milheim notes that "[o]ne of the biggest challenges surrounding the Divide is the lack of relevant content on the Internet for individuals in marginalized groups", what "can become discouraging to those individuals seeking information which they can identify with, and prohibit those in marginalized groups from being motivated to use the computer and Internet" (p.10). Moreover, there is the issue of the *quality* of the content available on-line, which raises doubts about the virtues of internet access in general (Cordes & Miller, 2000), but is even more intense in cultures that differ from the Western values that are predominant online (Albirini, 2006).

It is practically consensual that technologies provided in digital inclusion initiatives must be used for studying and acquiring computer skills that mean better qualification for the job market. Many authors report dismaying results in this area, which they attribute to a lack of disposition on the part of the target populations (for example, Williams, Sligo & Wallace, 2004, p. 9 and Lengyel et al., 2006). The most frequent uses amongst recipients of digital initiatives appear to be the same throughout the world: entertainment and socializing. Despite these activities being popular with the internet population as well, in the context of inclusion initiatives they tend to be seen as inadequate, and are attributed to certain minority groups. For some authors, people with higher levels of education and income use information, work, business and shopping applications, while entertainment, instant messengers and chat rooms are typical of the less educated and of those with lower income (van Dijk, 2005; Neves & Gomes, 2008, p.11). Similar differences in internet use are attributed to race and gender (van Dijk, 2005, pp.111-113). Kvasny & Keil (2006) reproduce the testimony of an instructor of a digital divide initiative in Atlanta, USA, for whom;

problems occur mostly for the black males. Some of them don't even try. They don't want to do any work. I try to introduce them to applications like Word, Excel, and PowerPoint, but they would rather download music and play games (p. 31).

Children's preference for playing games and drawing with paint systems caused parents to have ambivalent feelings about the *Hole-in-the-Wall*

experiment in India. This preponderant use, which Warschauer attributes to the 'minimal invasive' model of education that inspired the project (2004, p. 2), is remarkably comparable to the equipment which the same author describes as having been provided to the street children who comprised the target of the initiative:

*An outdoor five-station computer kiosk was set up in one of the poorest slums of New Delhi. Though the computers themselves were inside a booth, the monitors protruded through the holes in the walls, as did **specially designed joysticks and buttons that substituted for the computer mouse. Keyboards were not provided.** The computers were connected to the internet through dial-up access (p. 1, added emphasis).*

Use of Social Network Sites has also been condemned by reinforcing social exclusion and taking time that should be dedicated to 'better' uses (Bredarioli, 2008, p. 8). Despite its incredible popularity in Brazil[3], access to the SNS *Orkut* has been forbidden in many Brazilian schools and universities for several years. More recently, *Orkut, Twitter* and *MSN Messenger* have been included in a list of sites which "contain material related to sex, drugs, pornography, pedophilia, violence and weaponry" compiled by São Paulo City Council. As a result, access to *Orkut* has been blocked in all schools and tele-centers in São Paulo (São Paulo, 2008).

Economic factors are not sufficient to explain digital inequalities, but acquisitive power remains an important element of social exclusion. The scale of its relevance at times is beyond the comprehension of the policy makers and project managers. Kvasny & Keil report how residents of the LaGrange area did not consider that the internet access provided was free, as had been announced. "To get the 'free' system, one must already have or be willing to pay for basic cable TV at a cost of $8.70 per month" (2006, p.28), a prohibitive cost for some residents. City managers failed to see the connection between this cost and the low adherence to the project, and argued that "under the existing franchise every home has to be served with cable if the customer requests it." (p. 29); "what we've found is just hesitancy, a lack of understanding, a lack of appreciating what it potentially means, and breaking through that" (p.25). Similarly, the fees for internet access services charged in the kiosks of the SARI4 project in rural areas of India were prohibitive for people with lower economic status. The majority of SARI kiosk users observed by Kumar (2006) were from higher casts, more educated and had higher income levels than the overall population of the area.

Provision of free access to ICTs can also be a source of frustration as people struggle to maintain the equipment (Warschauer, 2002), fear future loss of their access (Kvasny & Keil, 2006), or develop a desire for acquiring means of access (that is the model which underlines the design of ICTs). An intention to buy computers on the part of subjects who have been targets of digital inclusion initiatives have been reported by many authors (for example, Williams, Sligo & Wallace, 2004; Kvasny & Keil, 2006; Lengyel et al., 2006). It often leads to the acquisition of second hand equipment, followed by the discovery of a new level of needs for peripherals, software, and internet access. This escalation of necessities equates the internet to "...a kind of mind destruction", in the words of a member of the black community targeted by a project. "The White man is ... programming my family to want this stuff. The Black man can't afford to give his family all of this stuff. So technology becomes a nightmare for us." (Kvasny & Keil, 2006, p. 32-33).

Mismatches between the beliefs of policymakers and target populations can be identified in the suspicion expressed by some LaGrange citizens, that the two-way nature of the internet would allow the government to spy on them. Despite the fact that internet surveillance is a real problem, project administrators did not considered

that element seriously: "[Some people] didn't want it because they thought we were spying on them. I mean that sounds funny, but they really do think that you are spying on them . . . they don't trust us" (Kvasny & Keil, 2006, p. 28).

The above examples point to important mismatches between the ways in which target populations understand ICTs to be suited for their own needs, and the expectations of those who invest effort and money in digital divide initiatives, leading to disappointment and frustration for both parties.

A comparison of such 'failures' and the spontaneous tactics to gain access and appropriate ICTs is misunderstood. Lack of sufficient comprehension of the ways in which the communities understand ICTs causes significant achievements to be overlooked by formal evaluations.

We identified a coherent set of inventive ways of gaining access and appropriating ICTs amongst the daily practices of various Latin American migrants[5] which were not at the receiving end of any specific digital divide initiative. Empirical observations took place in the context of a set of longitudinal studies of international immigrants and media, developed by the *Research Group on Media, Culture and Citizenshi*[6], Unisinos, Brazil. More than 200 migrants were observed between 2004 and 2008 in two metropolitan areas: Porto Alegre (Brazil) and Barcelona (Spain)[7]. Field work included life histories and focus groups in Greater Porto Alegre and in-depth interviews in Porto Alegre and Barcelona, from which testimonies are reproduced below.

That the digital divide did not figure as the primary concern of this set of studies does not weaken the points discussed above. Although the profile of the observed population and the specific location in which field observations took place are likely to have influenced the findings, neither profile nor location need to be considered central for our present argument. It is possible that observation of other social groups, migrant or not, in other locations, could have revealed a different set of practices. However, what is important for the argument presented here is the very *existence* of those tactics. It is therefore possible to postulate their ubiquity as part of the large and widely spread set of modes of "making do" (De Certeau, 1994) which are tactical in character. On the other hand, the profile of the social group effectively observed is likely to have increased the incidence and perhaps the intensity of everyday practices, an active position towards the improvement of their own situation being characteristic of migrants generally (Orozco, 2004; Portes, 1997; Solé & Parella, 2005).

It is important that the observed appropriations took place independently of initiatives or policies for digital inclusion (such as the development of free or subsidized tele-centers or the provision of equipment in public or private spaces), as independence from the rules and regulations of digital divide actions can have contributed to the spontaneity of inventive adoption.

Spontaneous Tactics towards ICTs

The Latin-American migrants we observed and interviewed are aware of the centrality of ICTs in contemporary life and the majority of them have a positive attitude towards them. The various tactics towards ICTs which we have encountered in their testimonies can be categorized as follows: (a) access; (b) literacy and education; (c) occupation and profession; (d) social networks; (e) information gathering, and (f) avoidance.

Access

The majority of the Latin-American migrants living in the Barcelona and Porto Alegre metropolitan regions try to find a way to access to the internet at home or in public places. To this end, they share and borrow equipment from friends and families and use computers available at workplaces, universities, public libraries, commercial and subsidized public access points.

Migration can change the conditions of access for better or for worse. Claudio, who was a domestic internet user in Buenos Aires (Argentina), now has to resort to a public point located far from his residence in Porto Alegre. His motivation to keep using the internet comes from his wife and daughter:

Internet is a problem here, first because of our home location: we have no bus for the internet and have to walk fifteen blocks. We do this walk on Sunday because my daughter likes to chat with friends in Buenos Aires and I, as I am around the city centre, I have a look at the internet at some point or another (Claudio, 57 years old, from Argentina).

The number of public internet access points is greater in Barcelona and they are very popular amongst migrants, who are the majority of users and often also managers and owners. Called 'locutórios', they often associate internet access with telephone services, remittances, and small shops. The presence of ethnic signs testifies to their function as reference points for migrant communities. These conveniences do not equate the experience of those accessing the internet in public points to that of home users. Prices are relatively low, but can be a restriction for those with a lower income. Time is another limiting factor, as most interviewed migrants worked longer hours and had difficulty to find time to go to the locutórios. A third restriction comes from the presence of others, which constrains the use of voice devices.

I haven't had home access to the internet for around four years ... Thus, I have to resort to going to the Pakistanis.[8] This has limited my usage a lot. I used to connect every night. (Hilário, 55 years old, from Argentina).

One solution to the limitations imposed by commercial public points is to use the equipment available at workplaces. This does not overcome time restrictions:

I use the internet everyday and read the newspapers from Bolivia, from EEUU. I love it, from Japan, it is fine, the people or the things that happen ... I like to browse, I am always looking for what is up. I don't have Internet at home, but I use it at work. I have it all day long. Because I work with tourists I have to see the reservations ... And I always use the internet, one hour per day more or less (Francisco, 45, from Bolivia, our emphasis).

Having had internet access before, it is frustrating to loose it. Carla, a 26-year-old Peruvian, could access the internet both at home and at her workplace, but after an equipment failure at home and a job dismissal, she now resorts to her mother's home computer to keep in contact with relatives and friends still living in Peru. Borrowing equipment time from relatives, friends or housemates is a common practice amongst migrants. Many users access the internet in different settings:

On the internet I use e-mail, the chat, or to download programs ... that I need to use and, well, it depends, if I have to look for some specific information and what else, the University page. I use here and I use in the University. I don't have my own [computer] but use from a flat-mate. And I also go to the public point. We take advantage ... if there is one here or two blocks that has offers like ... I don't know ... 5 hours or ... or 8 hours 5 Euros, this kind of stuff (Jina, 25, Argentina).

Absence or precarious conditions of internet access in the country of origin is often a problem. Telecommunications infrastructure is very widespread in Latin America (Fragoso & Maldonado, 2009). Three migrants living in Porto Alegre, for example, emphasize the difficulties of their families in finding internet access in Cuba. The

internet experiences of these three Cuban migrants have many points in common, but differences. Comparing their personal experiences can help understanding the diversity of opportunities which minority groups encounter, and the various tactics that they develop towards ICTs. The first of these Cuban migrants is trying to regularize his situation in Brazil as a refugee and, in the meantime, occasionally works as a carpenter. Now, he uses the internet to exchange e-mails with his family in Cuba. Having to resort to paid public internet points, he emphasizes the problem of access prices:

As I don't have at home, it is there, in the cyber, the more time, more you have to pay. At times I don't have money. Then I go more for e-mail, for friendship, when there is a party, when they dance salsa⁹, when something is to arrive (Fernando, 43).

The two other Cubans whom we interviewed have home internet access. One is a 41-year-old woman, graduate student, and married to a Brazilian, who remembers being introduced to the internet by a local vicar while still in Cuba, 12 years ago. The other Cuban home user is a dance teacher, specialized in salsa, whose internet experience is intense and diversified.

Music, computer, these things, I live for them, they are my life ... I live for that, when I come home, I take shelter in the computer. I get news from Cuba, talking to other friends who live away from Cuba, in Spain, in the US, Germany, so, I live for that, for music, dance, that is what I like ... Sites, sites for chat, I even have one open there, Yahoo Messenger, they have rooms for Cubans ... So, this people, the majority of these Cubans, they are away from Cuba, they are homesick, they are going through the same situation I am. Then we talk, play some music on the site and remember. My mother, my brother, my sister-in-law, my nephews, in Havana ... aunts, cousins ... in Havana and Santiago de Cuba (Alberto, 35).

Literacy and Education

In relation to the acquisition of technological literacy (b), we witnessed a predominance of self-motivation and self-teaching, yet there are those who look for formal training courses. It was in a paid training course that Nuria, for example, used a computer for the first time. Having access only during classes, she reported difficulties handling the computer and the internet, but was enthusiastic about the experience:

I was in the informatics course in [name of school], I was loving it ... I learned to put the CD file, I learned, learned many things. My dream is to complete this course ... I was searching for horoscopes and that type of stuff on the internet. And I had to stop, because I could not afford it ... It has been a while, some 10 months I think (Nuria, 36 years old, from Uruguay).

Shared equipment, or the companionship of internet users, can be a source of enthusiasm and motivation. Help from friends and family can be decisive for the beginners who are not certain about what can be done with ICTs or how to do it. Juana, 75, is leader of an association of Ecuadorian migrants in Porto Alegre, and counts on her daughter's help with the internet for the necessary research and for managing the Association's mailing list. The president of an association of Peruvian migrants also in Porto Alegre, Cesar is a Bachelor in Psychology and has dial-up home internet access. He was very resistant to ICTs at first, but was persuaded by his wife and son, and now is enthusiastic about reading online news, which he also prints and shares with others during community events.

Marta lives in Porto Alegre and does not have a home computer or go online by herself. Her two daughters, however, use computers at the university and regularly print the e-mails they receive from family in Bolivia for their mother to read. This experience of vicarious internet ac-

cess made Marta aware of internet's possibilities. She talks about the desire to include ICTs in her daily routine:

As soon as I finish paying for the construction material I bought in 18 payments, then I am going to buy. It is not a luxury, it is necessity ... What I need most and want most is computer, internet, I really need, I miss it very much. My daughters need it for university research and for me it is my dream purchase, I could talk to the people there, because telephone I don't have, had twice, and both times I cut it. It is too much, too expensive, only pre-paid mobiles, if that much (Marta, 43, Bolivia).

Help from family, friends and others can be decisive in the first days of internet use. One of the instructors working in a public point in Porto Alegre undertook a formal course to learn advanced computer skills, but emphasizes the importance of the initial support he was given:

I never saw the internet in Paraguay. Really, I never saw a computer in Paraguay. I just came to know computers in 2000, in the Catholic University's library, because they told me that one could use the internet for free and I wanted to know and I wanted to have an e-mail, so I went there. But I did not use the internet to read the news. That is, I only used the e-mail and that was it, nothing more. Then I was kind of ... digitally excluded. And then it was only [Brazilian printed] newspapers, newspapers, newspapers ... Yes, I looked for it. I remember that the librarian had to teach me because I did not know anything. I didn't even know how to hold the mouse, I remember once that my father sent me some photos, that was 2000, 2001, he sent me some photos by e-mail. It has been years since I last saw my father ... And now, for example, that I work in the field, with computer networks, now I left the [printed] newspaper and read everything all over the internet. Now it is all the time. That is, news, national, international, books, news about the things I work with. All internet now (Konrad, 28, Paraguay).

Occupation and Profession

Several migrants referred to the importance of ICTs for their professional lives and occupations (c). Many acknowledge the importance of technological literacy as a qualification for the job market, but investments in paid courses can be insufficient to compensate existing access restrictions. The availability of computers and access to the internet, on the other hand, can be decisive for career success. Konrad, who was previously quoted in regard to the importance of informal help in the acquisition of basic computer literacy, became a professional in the field.

Cultural activities are common amongst Latin-American migrants, several of whom are in creative fields, as musicians, dancers, craft workers, moviemakers. Many of them develop their artistic skills as hobbies, but our sample also included some professionals. Computer literacy means better chances in the job market for most people, but for these artists, internet access is also a means to acquire visibility, expand their resources and manage their careers. Carmen, Chilean, 40 years old, says that buying a computer was the essential move that enabled her to produce press releases for her salsa band and deliver them to the traditional media, which has since then been reporting on their activities.

Social Networks

Online interaction proved important for territorially dispersed individuals for maintaining their social networks (d). ICTs allow for a mode of 'connected presence' in which distance from family and friends is ameliorated through the use of synchronous and asynchronous online communication tools. Fernando, living in Brazil for 29 years, uses the internet to keep in touch with friends and family and also to know the news from

Chile. Besides their frequent use of telephone, e-mail and instant messengers, he and his parents also visit each other once a year.

All my generation from University in Chile is more or less the same age, and our children are around the same age too, then we exchange information… My children and their children communicate too. It is very interesting, we weave a net of friendships (Fernando, 48, Chile).

Being mostly owned and heavily used by migrants, Barcelona's public internet points function as both online and offline meeting places, bridging migrants and their countries of origin in the sense of Peñaranda Cólera's 'transnational social spaces' (2005). As an example of an online bridge, a 28 years old female Peruvian migrant interviewed in Barcelona remembers the creation of their 'family site':

Before I went everyday to the internet, everyday I called, at times twice, now I call only on Sundays because it is the day in which nearly everyone is at home and I connect to the internet twice a week because, of course, when I open the chat all come in, and don't allow me to do what I have to do. Then I tell myself not to open because between my sister, my cousins, we have in my home, my family, created a page. And now we talk through that, and so, and we all come in and we stay hours and I have to go (Susana, 28, Peru).

Information Gathering

Public access points, personal social networks and the internet are three important sources of information (e), often appropriated in combination with other media. Locutórios provide access to other migrants and to alternative media, as Fabian, 33, from Argentina, who does not use the internet much, but is often at the internet access points in Barcelona socializing and reading the free press.

Rafael, a 29-year-old migrant, comes from the Uruguay countryside and his family does not have access to ICTs. He uses the internet to access media from his country of origin, as newspapers from Montevideo are available in Porto Alegre, where he now lives, but at high prices. He is also subscriber to Hierba Mate, an electronic news bulletin dedicated to Uruguayan migrants distributed by e-mail. The internet is certainly not used in isolation in this search for proximity and for information. Most migrants report using several means of contact and sources of news, amongst which the telephone is often emphasized for its capacity to provide 'emotionally richer' contacts. For some migrants, their family and friends at home are the most reliable source of news.

Peru is in permanent war with Ecuador since I was born, I think, even before, for sure, because of some lands to the North. Ecuador says it is theirs, Peru says it is theirs, it is constant war. My cousin was in this war six years ago, he was imprisoned there, suffered horrendously, was tortured, he came back a rag of a human being. You don't see this in the newspapers ever, and it is constant, it is like that. Things that don't, no they don't appear here, when they appear is like, OK, The Shining Path. Then it calls attention and appears, but you don't see what is really happening. The problem in Toledo, at Fujimori's time, it was high stress that did not appear here, but there, my brother used to tell, you see, my brother now was saying: "Look, civil war is coming, because the situation here is chaotic" (Carla).

Parallel to the search for news from their country of origin, migrants use the internet to gather information about their host destinations. This was frequently mentioned by those interviewed in Barcelona, who report having searched the internet to know more about the city where they intended to go. Combined with the low consumption of local media while living in Barcelona and with the frequent communication and search for news of

their countries of origin, this suggests a pattern of 'connected displacement' in which migrants use ICTs to connect with the place where they are not physically located, be it their homeland or their intended destinations.

The www.cubasi.cu, there is the www.elnuevo. com, a newspaper. At times I access the Granma[10], which is the official one from the Cuban government, the main news of Cuba, and then some sites from Cuba. Some sites say good things, other say bad things. Then, there are forums as well, there are sites with forums from Cuba, there are radio stations. I hear the radio stations from Cuba through the internet, the television from Cuba, then I know what is going on in Cuba. I like that, to know (Alberto).

Some interviewed migrants were skilled internet users. These are often the ones who use the internet for work, information and shopping, take part in *fora* and, in some cases, maintain their own personal sites or blogs.

We were used for example to see the newspaper and the news and we... read and have to read it. So this new technology, they are promoting it a lot now, but it is still in a state that just the very technological people know it. But soon it will be massive, and then one can make their own newspaper. That means, if I want I can read the Editorial from El Mundo, news from Cataluña from La Vanguardia, from El País... economy, from Marca[11] sports ... So I can have all this information, with information from Peru, all in one place. That I am talking about, I am also educating myself, because it is a matter of habit. Everyone is used to browse different web pages and see all things, and see it from one place (Manuel, 28, Peru).

Avoidance

Others find it hard to include digital technologies in their daily lives, characterizing a position of avoidance (f). Difficulties to handle technological tools and to understand the logic of online communication are complicated by those who find it hard to deal with content in English.

Computer is a hassle for me, because I did not know even how to type. Today I use it as a typewriter, to write, it is practical, and to exchange emails with someone, but beyond that I don't know anything, I don't no how to handle it (Teresa, 50, Uruguay).

Many are positive about the need to overcome their difficulties one way or another:

I find my ways as I can so it takes long to access, to program, thus ... I was going to study to know faster ... My world would open up a lot. I will have to study, even at 55 (Jaime, 55, Uruguay).

Some prefer not to use computers or the internet, for different reasons. Mario is not keen of media in general:

Not a lot of internet, also not mobile phone. So I don't like the dependency ... Although technology can be very good, and makes many things easier, but, it does not differ from, from you being dependent upon it. There are people who stay 24, 12 hours behind a computer, or behind a radio, or behind a television ... Not if I say to you, I said to my friends, that here, nothing interests me. Absolutely nothing, nothing of nothing, of media, nothing (Mario, 38, Chile).

There are cases of preference for media other than ICTs. Sandra, a 33 years old Argentinean living in Barcelona, prefers television and radio to the internet due to her difficulties in handling computers. Mariana, on the other hand, does not lack technological literacy or access to an internet connection, but still prefers other forms of communication:

I had informatics in the University, then I fiddled a little more with my friend, but it does not catch my attention. I know it is very important, but ... I prefer direct contact, with the human being. Understand, I am very front-to-front, face-to-face, which is my way (Mariana, 34, Peru).

POSITIVE OUTCOMES OF INVENTIVE APPROPRIATIONS

Several ways in which the migrants we interviewed appropriate the internet can be incompatible with what is usually considered 'good use' of ICTs. Their many and varied positive outcomes, on the other hand, are directly related to the broad objectives of policies and actions to bridge the digital divide: migrants have conquered or increased their technical literacy, general knowledge and civic engagement; have accessed information relevant to their lives; improved their professional qualifications, boosted their personal careers. Social ties were formed, developed and reinforced, families and friends kept in contact and valuable information was shared through social networks, as well as using institutionalized and alternative media. Social interaction was also one of the most frequent and strong motivations for the acquisition of technological literacy and means of access. Peer help was mentioned more often as a decisive factor in learning to use computers, more than formal training, with many migrants referring to the importance of the initial help they got from relatives, friends, workmates, school and university colleagues and also from people with whom they had no previous relations. Vicarious use has proven to have positive effects directly or as a motivation for the acquisition of literacy and the desire for better conditions of access. Beyond the provision of internet access for those without a domestic connection, public points function as gathering places, identity references and sources of information. Previous authors have reported on the use of such places as gathering points for Brazilian youngsters (Lacerda, 2008; Barros, 2008) and we have verified that, in the case of migrants in Barcelona, they also function as identity references (as testified by the presence of ethnic signs) as well as meeting places.

In all cases, access and appropriation are conditioned by socioeconomic factors, local characteristics and opportunities, individual life and migration histories and also by the availability of ICTs for migrants' families and friends. Individual practices and habits are conditioned by time, cost and distance from the point of access, as much as by the routines and uses of their social networks. We believe that changing the focus from what people *should* be doing with the technology, to the tactics the observed migrants developed to gain access and the spontaneous modes of ICT appropriation allowed us a broader perception of the variety of ways in which technology can be incorporated into someone's life for their own benefit. So far, many designers, policy-makers and researchers have focused on how digital inclusion initiatives should or could be designed and implemented. The positive outcomes of the spontaneous tactics towards ICTs we observed indicate that the desires, motivations and ways in which the target communities appropriate ICTs must be a departure point for the design of digital inclusion actions and policies. This idea meshes with the proposals of what we have called, at the beginning of this chapter, the 'third generation' of digital divide actions, often identified by the denomination 'community informatics', which emphasizes the importance of local social actors (Gurstein, 2000; Williams, Sligo & Wallace, 2004). The present proposition advances that paradigm by stating that it is not enough to ensure that the target communities share control and ownership of the initiative (Gaved and Anderson, 2006, p. 6). Full appreciation of the positive values of the various ways in which communities understand and appropriate ICTs requires open-mindedness about how they modify – even subvert – the original offers.

The diversity of contexts that condition access to ICTs as well as the variety of interests and goals that motivate their appropriation call for recognition of the need for flexible and variable policies and actions, capable of catering for the complexity inherent to the real people and the receiving end of digital inclusion initiatives. The starting point is the adoption of a non-patronizing attitude, that is, trust that the targeted minorities will use technology exactly as any other social group: with failures and successes.

CONCLUSION

The centrality of ICTs in contemporary life suggests that the provision of access to computers and the internet can help promote social inclusion. As a result, several initiatives to 'bridge the digital divide' have been initiated in the last decades. These soon progressed from the mere provision of equipment to the recognition that it was important to take into consideration not only economic, but also educational, ethnic, gender, age, linguistic and geographical disadvantages. More recently, the importance of local actors for the success of initiatives and policies to grant access and advance the use of ICTs has also been recognized. We took this approach to a new depth by trying to unveil hidden premises which led to unbalanced understandings of the outcomes of digital divide actions and policies.

Examples of results of digital divide initiatives reported as unsuccessful by literature on the subject were outlined in an attempt to understand which modes of ICT appropriation tend to be considered inappropriate or deviant. Examples of spontaneous practices towards ICTs by migrants who were not at the receiving end of digital divide initiatives were presented for comparison. These originated from a set of studies which took place between 2004 and 2008 in the metropolitan areas of Porto Alegre (Brazil) and Barcelona (Spain). Central to our argument is the existence of the inventive ways of gaining access and appropriating ICTs described by the interviewed migrants. We believe that the profile of the observed group favoured the incidence of the reported tactics, as migrants are characteristically pro-active and self-motivated.

The spontaneous tactics developed by the observed migrant population to appropriate ICTs related to (a) access; (b) literacy and education; (c) occupation and profession; (d) social networks; (e) information gathering and (f) avoidance. The general picture points towards achievements of uppermost importance. The most common goals of digital divide actions and policies are amongst the outcomes reported by the subjects interviewed: they gained technical literacy, improved their qualifications for the job market, boosted their careers, acquired more information, kept contact with family and friends, established new social relations. The variety of ways leading to these results indicates that modifications, even subversions, of the original offers, are not necessarily undesirable.

We believe that many digital divide actions and policies are reported as 'failures' due to a misinterpretation of unexpected responses. Full appreciation of the positive importance of the various ways that communities use ICTs requires more open-minded interpretations. The most important source of information and decisions for initiatives to 'bridge the digital divide' are the communities themselves. A non-patronizing attitude is a necessary first step for promoting autonomy and bridging not only the digital, but the social gap. The question is not so much whether target groups are capable of using ICTs as wisely as any other social group, but if policy-makers, designers and scholars are prepared to believe in their ability to do so.

ACKNOWLEDGMENT

This chapter presents partial results of research sponsored by CNPq (Conselho Nacional de Desenvolvimento Científico e Tecnológico) and CAPES (Coordenação de Aperfeiçoamento de Pessoal de Nível Superior), Brazil.

REFERENCES

Adital (Agência de Informação Frei Tito sobre a América Latina). (2008). *Notícias da América Latina e Caribe*. Retrieved January 1st, 2009, from http://www.adital.com.br

Albirini, A. *(2006). Cultural perceptions: The missing element in the implementation of ICT in developing countries*. International Journal of Education and Development using ICT, 2*(1)*. RetrievedDecember21, 2008, fromhttp://ijedict. dec.uwi.edu/index.php

Barros, C. (2008). Games e redes sociais em lan houses populares: um olhar antropológico sobre usos coletivos e sociabilidade no "clube local". *III Simpósio Internacional de Administração e Marketing V Congresso de Administração da ESPM*. São Paulo.

Bechara, M. (2008). Banda larga: Os espaços públicos de acesso à internet. In CGI.br (Comitê Gestor da Internet no Brasil). *Pesquisa sobre o uso das tecnologias da informação e da comunicação 2007 (*pp. 47-50). São Paulo.

Bieber, M., McFall, B., Rice, R. E., & Gurstein, M. (2007). Towards systems design for supporting enabling communities. *Journal of Community Informatics, 3*(1). Retrieved December 22, 2008, from http://ci-journal.net/index.php/ciej/article/view/281/31

Bredarioli, C. M. M. (2008). Comunicação em rede e novos agentes socializadores: recepção e práticas culturais no consumo de Internet em lan-houses. In *Intercom – Sociedade Brasileira de Estudos Interdisciplinares da Comunicação XXXI Congresso Brasileiro de Ciências da Comunicação*, Natal, RN. Retrieved December 23, 2008, from www.intercom.org.br

Castells, M. (1999). *A Sociedade em Rede - a era da informação: economia, sociedade e cultura.* São Paulo: Paz e Terra.

Castells, M. & Tubella, I. (Dir.). (2007). *La transición de la sociedad red.* Generalit de Catalunya: Editorial UOC/Ariel.

CGI.br. (Comitê Gestor da Internet no Brasil). *Pesquisa sobre o uso das tecnologias da informação e da comunicação 2007.* (2008). São Paulo.

Chen, S., & Ravallion, M. (2008). The Developing World Is Poorer Than We Thought, But No Less Successful in the Fight against Poverty. *World Bank Policy Research Working Paper,* 4703. Retrieved December 12, from http://econ.worldbank.org

Chomsky, N., Mitchell, P. R., & Schoeffel, J. (2002). *Understanding Power: The Indispensable Chomsky.* New York: The New Press.

Cogo, D. & Brignol, L.D. (2009). Latinoamericanos en el sur de Brasil: recepción mediática y ciudadanía de las migraciones internacionales. *Comunicación y Sociedad.* Guadalajara, 11, Nueva Época, January-June 2009, 135-162.

Cogo, D., Gutiérrez, M., & Huertas, A. (Eds.). (2008). *Migraciones transnacionales y medios de comunicación: relatos desde Barcelona e Porto Alegre.* Madrid: Los Libros de la Catarata.

Compaine, B. M. (2001). *The Digital Divide: Facing a Crisis or Creating a Myth?* MIT Press.

ComScore. *Comscore Brasil Report,* (2007). Retrieved January 25, 2008, from http://www.comscore.com/metrix

Cordes, C., & Miller, E. (2000). Fool's Gold: A Critical Look at Computers in Childhood. In *Alliance for Childhood 2000.* Retrieved December 24, 2008, from http://www.allianceforchildhood.org/projects/computers/computers_reports.htm

Crump, B., & McIlroy, A. (2003). The digital divide: Why the "don't–want–tos" won't compute: Lessons from a New Zealand ICT Project. *First Monday, 8*(12). Retrieved December 12, 2008, from http://firstmonday.org/issues/issue8_12/crump/index.html

Davidson, E., & Cotten, S. R. (2003). Connection discrepancies: Unmasking further layers of the digital divide. *First Monday,* 8(3). Retrieved September 18, 2008, from http://firstmonday.org/issues/issue8_3/davison/index.html

DeCerteau, M. (1994). *A Invenção do Cotidiano: Artes do fazer.* São Paulo: Vozes.

Deleuze, G., & Guatari, F. (1987). *A thousand plateaus: capitalism and schizophrenia.* Minneapolis: University of Minnesota Press.

DiMaggio, P., Hargittai, E., Celeste, C., & Shafer, S. (2004). Digital Inequality: From Unequal Access to Differentiated Use. In K. Neckerman. (Ed.), *Social Inequality* (pp. 355-400). New York: Russell Sage Foundation. Retrieved December 26, 2008, from http://www.webuse.org/papers?id=digitalinequality

Drucker, P. F. (1992). *The Age of Discontinuity: Guidelines to Our Changing Society.* Transaction Publishers.

Eubanks, V. E. (2007). Trapped in the Digital Divide: The Distributive Paradigm in Community Informatics. *The Journal of Community Informatics, 3*(2). Retrieved September 19, 2008 from http://www.ci-journal.net/

FCC. (2008). FCC Consumer Facts: getting broadband. Retrieved from http://www.fcc.gov/cgb/consumerfacts/highspeedinternet.html

Fragoso, S. (2004). As Múltiplas Faces da Exclusão Digital. *Ícone, 6*(7), 110-122.

Fragoso, S., & Maldonado, A. E. (2009). (forthcoming). *A Internet na América Latina.* Porto Alegre, Sulina. *Unisinos.*

Gopal, R. D., & Sanders, G. L. (2000). Global software piracy: you can't get blood out of a turnip. *Communications of the ACM, 43*(9), 82–89. doi:10.1145/348941.349002

Gurstein, M. (2000). *Community Informatics: Enabling Communities with Information and Communications Technologies.* Hershey, PA: Idea Group.

Gurstein, M. (2003). Effective use: A community informatics strategy beyond the digital divide. *First Monday, 8*(12). Retrieved from http://firstmonday.org/issues/issue8_12/gurstein/index.html.

Hargittai, E. (2002). Second-Level Digital Divide: Differences in People's Online Skills. *First Monday, 7*(4). Retrieved December 26, 2008, from http://firstmonday.org/issues/issue7_4/hargittai

Hilbert, M. R. (2001). *Latin America on Its Path Into the Digital Age: Where are We?* United Nations Publications.

Horrigan, J. B. (2008). Home Broadband Adoption 2008. *Pew Internet & American Life Project.* Retrieved December 28, from http://www.pewinternet.org/

IBICT. Estatítiscas. (2008). *Inclusão Digital.* Retrieved December 29, 2008, from http://inclusao.ibict.br

Instituto Paulo Montenegro. (2007). *Indicador de Alfabetismo Funcional INAF / Brasil 2007.* Retrieved February 29, 2009, from http://www.ipm.org.br/

ITU Internet Reports - Birth of Broadband Executive Summary. (2003). Retrieved from http://www.itu.int/osg/spu/publications/sales/birthofbroadband/exec_summary.html

Kumar, R. (2006). Social Impact and Diffusion of Telecenter Use: A Study from the Sustainable Access in Rural India Project. *The Journal of Community Informatics, 2*(3). Retrieved December 21, 2008 from http://www.ci-journal.net/

Kvasny, L., & Keil, M. (2006). The Challenges of Redressing the Digital Divide: A Tale of Two U.S. Cities. *Information Systems Journal, 16*(1), 23–53. doi:10.1111/j.1365-2575.2006.00207.x

Lacerda, J. S. (2008). *Ambiências Comunicacionais e Vivências Midiáticas Digitais.* Unpublished doctoral thesis presented to the PostGraduate Programme in Communications of the Universidade do Vale do Rio do Sinos, Unisinos, as partial fullfilment of the requirements for the degree of Doctor in Communications.

Lengyel, G., Eranusz, E., Füleki, D., Lörincz, L., & Siklós, V. (2006). The Cserénfa experiment – on the attempt to deploy computers and Internet in a small Hungarian village. *The Journal of Community Informatics, 2*(3). Retrieved December 21, 2008 from http://www.ci-journal.net/.

Luyt, B. (2004). Who benefits from the digital divide? *First Monday, 9*(8). Retrieved December 24, 2008 from http://firstmonday.org/issues/issue9_8/luyt/index.html

Martín Barbero, J. (1995). Modernidad, posmodernidad, modernidades: discursos sobre la crisis y la diferencia. *Intercom - Revista Brasileira de Comunicação, 23*(2).

McIlvenny, P. (1999). Avatars R Us? Discourses of Community and Embodiment in Intercultural Cyberspace. *Journal of Intercultural Communication, 1*(2). Retrieved 24 December, 2008 from http://www.immi.se/

Menou, M. J., Poepsel, K. D., & Stoll, K. (2004). Latin American Community Telecenters: "It's a long way to TICperary". *The Journal of Community Informatics, 1*(1), 39-57. Retrieved September 18, 2008 from http://www.ci-journal.net

Mossberger, K., Tolbert, C. J., & Stansbury, M. (2003). *Virtual Inequality: Beyond the Digital Divide*. Washington, DC: Georgetown University Press.

NBTF. (2006).*National Broadband Task Force Report - The National Dream: networking the nation for broadband access*. Retrieved December 20, 2008 from http://www.collectionscanada.gc.ca/.

Neves, B. C., & Gomes, H. F. (2008). A convergência dos aspectos de inclusão digital: experiência nos domínios de uma universidade. *Encontros Bibli: Revista Eletrônica de Biblioteconomia e Ciência da Informação, 13*(26). Retrieved December 23, from http://www.periodicos.ufsc.br/

NTIA. *Falling through the net: a survey of the 'have nots' in rural and urban America*. (1995). National Telecommunications & Information Administration, U.S. Department of Commerce. Retrieved June 3, 2008, from http://www.ntia.doc.gov

NTIA. *Falling Through the Net II: New Data on the Digital Divide*. (1998). National Telecommunications & Information Administration, U.S. Department of Commerce. Retrieved June 3, 2008, from http://www.ntia.doc.gov

NTIA. *Falling through the net: defining the digital divide - a report on the telecommunications and information technology gap in America*. (1999). National Telecommunications & Information Administration, U.S. Department of Commerce. Retrieved June 3, 2008, from http://www.ntia. doc.gov

NTIA. *Falling through the net: toward digital inclusion – a report on American's access to technology tools,* October. (2000). National Telecommunications & Information Administration, Economic and Statistics Administration. Retrieved June 3, 2008, from http://www.ntia.doc.gov

Orozco, M. (2004). Remesas económicas y migración – cuestiones y perspectivas sobre el desarrollo. *Vanguardia Dossier: Los hispanos en Estados Unidos*. Barcelona, *13*, 75-81.

Peñaranda Cólera, M. C. (2008). Tecnologías que acercan distancias? Sobre los "claroscuros" del estudío de las tecnologías en los procesos migratorios transnacionales. In Santamaría, E. (Ed.), *Retos epistemológicos de las migraciones transnacionales* (pp. 133–164). Barcelona: Anthropos.

Portes, A. (1997). Globalization from below: the rise of transnational communities. *Transnational Communities Programme Working paper series*, WPTC-98-01. Retrieved May, 12, 2009, from http://www.transcomm.ox.ac.uk/working%20 papers/portes.pdf

Postman, N. (1990). *Informing ourselves to death*. Speech at the German Informatics Society (Gesellschaft für Informatik). In Stuttgart, October 11, 1990. Retrieved January 1, 2009, from http://world.std.com/~jimf/informing.html

São Paulo. (2008). *Decreto nº 49.914, de 14 de agosto de 2008*. Diário Oficial da Cidade de São Paulo.

Schiller, D. (2000). *Digital Capitalism: Networking the Global Market System*. MIT Press.

Selwyn, N., Gorard, S., & Furlong, J. (2005). Whose Internet is it Anyway? Exploring Adults' (Non)Use of the Internet in Everyday Life. *European Journal of Communication, 20*(1), 5–26. doi:10.1177/0267323105049631

Solé, C., & Parella, S. (2005). *Negocios étnicos: Los comercios de los inmigrantes no comunitarios en Cataluña*. Barcelona: Fundación CIDOB.

Straton, J. (1997). Cyberspace and the globalization of culture. In Porter, D. (Ed.), *Internet Culture* (pp. 253–276). Routledge.

Streeter, T. (1999). "That deep romantic chasm": libertarianism, neoliberalism, and the computer culture. In Calabrese, A., & Burgelman, J. C. (Eds.), *Communication, Citizenship, and Social Policy: Re-Thinking the Limits of the Welfare State* (pp. 49–64). Rowman & Littlefield.

Van Dijk, J. A. G. M. (2005). *The Deepening Divide: Inequality in the Information Society*. Thousand Oaks, CA: SAGE Publications.

Warschauer, M. (2002). Reconceptualizing the Digital Divide. *First Monday, 7*(7). Retrieved September 18, 2008, from http://firstmonday.org/issues/issue7_7/warschauer/index.html

Warschauer, M. (2004). *Technology and Social Inclusion: Rethinking the Digital Divide*. MIT Press.

Warschauer, M., Knobel, M., & Stone, L. (2004). Technology and Equity in Schooling: Deconstructing the Digital Divide. *Educational Policy, 18*(4), 562–588. doi:10.1177/0895904804266469

West, A. R. (2006). Related Dangers: The issue of Development and Security for Marginalized Groups in South Africa. *The Journal of Community Informatics, 2*(3). Retrieved December 21, from http://www.ci-journal.net/

Williams, J., Sligo, F., & Wallace, C. (2004). What a difference it makes? The internet in the Everyday lives of new user families. In *Anzca04: making a difference annual conference of the Australian and New Zealand Communication Association*. University of Sydney. Retrieved September 18, 2008, from http://conferences.arts.usyd.edu.au/

Young, J. R. (2001). Does 'Digital Divide' Rhetoric Do More Harm Than Good? *The Chronicle of Higher Education - Information Technology*. Retrieved December 20, 2008 from http://chronicle.com/free/v48/i11/11a05101.htm

ENDNOTES

[1] Definitions of what consists a broadband connection are far from consensual. The ITU (International Telecommunications Union) Standardization Sector defines broadband transmission those faster than 1.5 (ITU, 2003). In the US, transmissions at 200kbps or higher are considered broadband (FCC, 2008) while in Canada the minimum rate has been set at 1.5MBps (NBTF, 2006).

[2] The ten proposed types and the proportion of users per type are: Omnivores (8%), the most active participants in the information society; Connectors (7%) participate actively in online life; Lackluster Veterans (8%) are frequent users but not thrilled with ICT-enabled connectivity; Productivity Enhancers (9%) have strongly positive views about technology; Mobile Centrics (10%) are highly attached to their mobile phones but rarely use the internet; Connected but Hassled (9%) have invested in a lot of technology, but find the connectivity a hassle; Inexperienced Experimenters (8%) make occasional use of technology but could do more if they had access; Light but Satisfied (15%) have the basics of information technology, use it infrequently and do not consider ICTs an important part of their lives; Indifferents (11%) have either cell phones or online access, use ICTs only intermittently and find connectivity annoying and Off the Net (15%) have neither mobile phones nor internet connection and are content with old media. (Horrigan, 2007).

[3] More than 12 million unique users were reported to have accessed Orkut in Brasil in December 2007. This corresponds to more than 68% of the total number of internet users in the country (ComScore, 2007).

[4] The Sustainable Access in Rural India (SARI) project was implemented in Tamil Nadu, India, starting 2001.

[5] Our choice of the word 'migrants' instead of 'immigrants' intends to emphasise the multiple dimensions of transit and mobility of contemporary migratory movements, which comprise a variety of destinations and temporalities. It goes beyond the classic idea of movements from a place of origin to a place of destination and encompasses

temporary as well as permanent changes of location.

6 http://www.midiaculturaecidadania.word-press.com/

7 The authors are grateful to their colleagues from Unisinos and Universidad Autónoma de Barcelona, who competently participate in the collection of data presented here. General results can be found for example in Cogo, Gutiérrez & Huertas (eds., 2008) and Cogo & Brignol, (2009).

8 Several internet public places in Barcelona are owned by migrants from Pakistan.

9 Salsa is a Latin-American style of music and dance.

10 *Granma International Digital*, at http://www.granma.cu

11 Respectively at http://www.elmundo.es, http://www.lavanguardia.es, http://www.elpais.com and http://www.marca.com

Chapter 9

A New Development Opportunity Confronts Old Paradigms:
Exploring the Multiplicity Theory to Combat the Global Digital Divide

Peter A. Kwaku Kyem
Central Connecticut State University, USA

ABSTRACT

There is a considerable debate about how the technological gap between rich and poor countries of the world can be bridged or eliminated. Technological optimists argue that Information and Communication Technology (ICT) can bring accelerated development to poor countries. Others question the viability of relying on ICT for development in low income countries. The ensuing debate has masked the digital divide problem and prevented a true discussion of how ICT can be deployed for the benefit of low income countries. On the otherhand, confronted with the persistent failures of one-size-fits-all economic development models, low income countries can no longer treat modernization as the pivot towards which all ICT-related development efforts must gravitate. There is a need to drop the singular vision of development which is premised on the experiences of Western developed nations and rather restore local actors and their cultures into the actual roles they play in development processes that occur within localities. Accordingly, this chapter reviews the perspectives that currently shape the ICT for development discourse and offers the multiplicity theory to bridge the gap in development theory and promote a development strategy which incorporates activities of both local and global actors in the development of localities.

INTRODUCTION

The influential relationship between technology and society dates back to the beginning of human history. Every stage of human development

is linked with some technology that supplies the tools which humans use to construct the social order (Ihde, 1990; Burke, 1985). Whether it was the crude tools of the stone age, the agricultural machinery of the green revolution or the factories of industrialization, the prevailing technology has often determined the type of most profitable

DOI: 10.4018/978-1-61520-799-2.ch009

work people do, the popular gadgets people use, and the institutions that come to be established (Mitchell, 2003, Mumford, 1934). The problem is that technological opportunities are not evenly distributed among individuals, nations and regions of the world. The pattern of access to technology shows a significant separation between rich and poor nations. The concentration of resources and technological innovations in rich countries and the lack of such opportunities in low income countries create a technological dualism which results in imbalances in access to technology, wealth and power (Singer, 1970). The unevenness of access to technology is a microcosm of the inequality that exists between two worlds - the so called Developed and Underdeveloped, the First and the Third, the Poor and Rich, High and Low-income countries or the Global North and Global South. The gap in technological adoption often threatens to deepen the existing disparities between the rich and poor nations. Accordingly, the role that technology plays in the development of nations fuels an endless debate. A similar disagreement is currently ranging over the technological gap which has resulted from the digital revolution. It is this discourse and its implications for bridging the global digital divide that form the subject matter of discussion in this chapter.

There is widespread agreement on the potential impacts of the digital divide between rich and poor countries, but despite the consensus on problem identification among scholars, strategies for bridging the divide are mainly disjointed (Kole, 2002; Schech, 2002). Proponents of the modernization and dependency theories that dominate the debate on ICT and development disagree on how the digital divide can be narrowed (Ojo, 2004). As ICT's are increasingly recognized as important factors in economic development (UNDP, 1998; World Bank, 1998; Heeks and Jagun, 2007), and as world leaders strive to identify strategies for promoting ICT-led growth in low-income countries, it becomes imperative to examine the discourse which strongly informs the case for bridging the

technological gap. This chapter examines whether the main theories that currently drive the ICT4development debate can generate policy guidelines that will stimulate ICT-led development in low-income countries. Specific questions that will be addressed in the chapter include the following:

a. To what extent do explanations offered by the modernization and dependency theories validate the potentials of ICT to facilitate or impede economic development in the low-income countries of the world?

b. Can ICT be deployed to correct decades of stagnant economic growth in poor countries and empower them to leapfrog several stages of their development into technological opportunities?

c. Can the poor countries of the world ignore the transformative power and the development potentials of ICT and follow an exclusionary development path to economic development in a globalized society?

In answering the above questions, the chapter relies on published literature to explain the digital divide concept. Thereafter, global attempts to monitor the divide and track progress in efforts being made to close the technological gap are discussed. This is followed by a critical review of the main arguments in the ICT4development discourse. The analysis focuses on contradictory claims about the role ICT may play in the development of low-income countries. The extent to which the digital divide debate directly echoes assumptions of the Modernization and Dependency theories on development are then examined. The chapter concludes with a discussion of the multiplicity theory which argues against the subject-object assumptions of the dominant theories and promotes a development strategy which incorporates the values of people in both rich and poor countries.

BACKGROUND OF THE DIGITAL DIVIDE DEBATE

Opinions vary as to the exact definition of the digital divide but generally, the technological gap between rich and poor countries is viewed as the difference between individuals, households, companies, countries or regions regarding the access to, and usage of ICT, for socio-economic development (Souter, 2004). The International Telecommunication Union (ITU) offers this explanation of the digital divide on its website:

The term digital divide came into use in the mid 1990s addressing the troubling disparities in terms of access to information technology. Originally coined with respect to computer access, the advent of technology has seen the term evolve in reference to Internet access, broadband access, and more recently, access to the full spectrum of information and communication technologies. (ITU, 2008a http://www.itu.int/newsroom/features/ict_africa.html)

Known generally as the gap between nations whose citizens have access to, and use a variety of ICT, and those nations whose citizens have limited or no access to the technologies, the global digital divide represents the area of overlap between the economic and social aspects of the global information society (Sciadas, 2005a). The divide between the technology "haves" and the technology "have-nots" is often portrayed as a technological access problem which can be addressed with the provision of computing and communication technologies and internet connectivity. On the contrary, the differential extent to which rich and poor countries benefit from technological adoption and usage is not a mere technological access problem but the product of broader dynamics of social stratification and economic development that shape not just access to ICT, but also, the distribution of global economic opportunities between the rich and poor.

The processes that created and still sustain the digital divide are not new. The phenomenon is a product of the same processes that created the developed as well as underdeveloped countries of the world today (James, 2007; Murdock, 2002). The technological gap is therefore a symptom of a deeper and more important divides of income, development, and literacy which separates the rich and poor countries of the world. As a product of the global economic divide, the digital inequality reflects the socio-economic divisions in the world (Dzidonu, 2001).

MONITORING THE GLOBAL DIGITAL DIVIDE

Several indices have been developed to measure the digital divide in terms of the availability, affordability and utilization of ICT among different social groups. Currently, there are at least six different ways of measuring the divide. The most recent of these measures include the Digital Opportunity Index (DOI) and the ICT Opportunity Index which were designed to monitor the digital divide and to evaluate progress towards implementation of the outcomes of two recent World Summits on the Information Society (ITU, 2006b).

THE DIGITAL OPPORTUNITY INDEX

The DOI, which was first published in February 2007, is a composite index comprising of eleven indicators that are grouped into three clusters to measure Digital Opportunity, ICT Infrastructure and ICT Utilization and Usage (ITU/UNCTAD, 2007). The DOI report for 2007 revealed that global access to ICT continues to grow and the gap separating rich and poor countries is shrinking in most technologies, particularly mobile telephony. The report disclosed that disparities in access to ICT were evolving and the digital divide was taking on new forms in regards to

Table 1. Digital opportunity worldwide: 2004-2006

REGIONS	Average Digital Opportunity By Region, 2006	Gains in Overall Digital Opportunity By Region 2004-2006
Europe	0.58	0.07
Americas	0.45	0.06
Asia	0.40	0.04
Africa	0.22	0.04
World	0.40	0.05

Source: (ITU/UNCTAD, 2007 p. 41

differences in the speed and quality of access to ICT. DOI scores were also found to be sharply differentiated. As shown in Table 1, the average DOI scores for Europe and the Americas were higher than the world average. The DOI score for Asia was equal to the world average while Africa had an average DOI score of only 0.22. The report concluded that the availability and affordability of broadband internet connection in low-income countries remain a major cause for concern in the efforts to close the digital divide.

ICT OPPORTUNITY INDEX

Unlike the DOI, the ICT Opportunity Index was designed to track progress in global efforts to bridge the digital divide. The index measures ICT opportunities in economies based on the degree of infodensity and info-use within a given period (ITU, 2006b). Infodensity represents the productive capabilities and the capacity of an economy measured in terms of ICT labor stocks and ICT capital. Info-use refers to an economy's ICT consumption or use. The Opportunity Index for 2007 revealed that the highest ICT penetration levels are in mobile cellular subscription (ITU, 2007). As a region, Africa's mobile phone market for the five year period between 2001 and 2006 was the fastest growing. The report found internet user penetration rates to be relatively small for low-income countries. There was an average of 4% internet penetration in 2005 for low-income countries compared to 30% and over 55% rates for upper and high-income countries. The differences in ICT opportunities was most striking in terms of broadband subscribers where high-income countries had an average of 17% against penetration levels of between 4% and 0.1% for low-income countries (ITU, 2006b).

DYNAMICS OF THE DIGITAL DIVIDE

If there is any notable conclusion to be drawn from the above reports on the global digital divide, it is the overwhelming importance of wireless networks, especially the mobile phone, in bridging the digital divide in low-income countries. As a result of this development, the recent increases in mobile phone subscription in Africa and other developing regions have formed the basis of bold predictions about the closing of the technological gap (Fink and Kenny, 2002; ITU, 2006b). However, other authors are more cautions in extrapolating the recent positive trends in mobile phone subscription into future developments in the global digital divide (Martin, 2003). This is partly because the positive development in access to ICT is based on sheer increases in the number of mobile phone subscriptions that provide little or no clues about how ICT is used. Advances in ICT (e.g., internet) and effective uses of the technology entail complex tasks that require cumulative sets of advanced education and sophisticated digital skills that only a handful of the people in low-income countries possess (James, 2006; Mason and Hacker, 2003). On the other hand, mobile phone usage does not require formal education and training that other ICT such as computers or the internet require of users. This makes mobile telephony accessible to a great number of rural as well as urban dwellers in low-income countries (Kyem and LeMaire, 2006). Accessibility to mobile phones in low-income countries is further enhanced by factors such as the low up-front expenditure that is required to set up a business, flexible pricing plans (compared to fixed lines), and the ease of sharing mobile handsets among rural folks (Vodafone 2005).

It is therefore not surprising that the poorest regions of the world are experiencing the most rapid increases in mobile phone subscriptions. Other forms of communication (e.g., postal systems, roads and fixed-line phones) are either non-existent or far removed from the majority of people in these regions. For example, it takes the average Ghanaian living in any of the major cities of the country about half an hour to reach a post office to mail a letter (Frempong et. al., 2005). On the other hand, the mobile phone provides a point of contact for text, voice and video communications and therefore enables users to actively participate in the social and economic systems in their countries (Vodafone 2005). In low-income countries, mobile phones are primarily substitutes and not complements to fixed phone lines and other forms of telecommunication (Sciadas, 2005b). In addition, while capital for development is lacking in these countries, Direct Foreign Investment (DFI) is readily available as a vital source of investment in wireless telecommunication networks in low-income countries (Kyem and LeMaire, 2006; Vodafone, 2005).

Another reason why the recent trends in mobile phone subscriptions cannot be extrapolated into the future of the digital divide has to do with low broadband penetration in the poor countries. Despite experiencing the highest level of mobile phone subscription of any region in the world since 2002, broadband internet connection is not available in several low-income countries and even when the connection is available, the majority of the people cannot afford it (ITU, 2006b). The lack of broadband connection is a great set back to efforts being made to increase digital opportunities in low-income countries. The broadband is not only a platform for other ICT applications, but also, as a transmission medium, the broadband offers high speed but low cost transfer of text, video and

audio data (Kyem and LeMaire, 2006). Predictions about the closing of the global digital divide based on the recent explosion in mobile phone subscription in poor countries are therefore premature. The predictions offer few or no explanation for the consistently skewed distribution of other ICT and the economic development opportunities that follow their applications.

For low-income countries at the receiving end of the imbalance in digital opportunities, the digital divide is not a lack of access to information technology. Rather, the threat posed by the digital inequality is playing out to be an economic development problem (Dzidonu, 2001). The metaphor of a digital divide is therefore a simplification of the complex phenomenon of inequality between rich and poor countries and among social groups (van Dijk, 2005). There is little evidence to support the notion that the digital gap can be closed by the provision of ICT alone. In fact access to ICT brings no automatic benefit to development. As Castells (1996) has pointed out, the overproduction and access to television and radio that preceded ICT did little to overcome information inequality among the rich and poor. As such, there is little reason to believe the mere presence of internet connectivity and ICT devices will bridge the technological gap. The digital divide concept therefore provides a poor roadmap for understanding the true links between ICT and economic development. The concept overemphasizes importance of the physical presence of computers and connectivity to the exclusion of other more important divides of income, literacy, political power, and cultural divides that shape the influence of ICT on development (Warschauer, 2002; Wilson, in Chen & Wellman, 2003).

Furthermore, the term "divide" implies a simple split between the haves and have-nots and the connected and disconnected but ICT adoption is not a two-fold split as suggested by the digital divide concept. Rather, the adoption and use of ICT fall along a continuum (Cisler, 2000). There are disparities in the frequency of ICT usage (e.g., daily users, occasional users, and those who use it sparingly), age of the users, types of services (e.g., e-mail, Web, mobile phone, text messaging) and the devices employed (e.g., PC, cell phones, WebTV) (Vehovar et. al., 2006). Those people who are experienced and familiar with technology benefit more from using the ICT devices. Similarly, those that have had exposure to a variety of ICT use the devices in a more sophisticated manner, and for more types of information retrieval than those people that are unfamiliar with technology in general (Robinson et. al., 1997). Accordingly, the digital divide encompasses among other things, a technical dimension (soft-ware, hardware, quality of connectivity), a skill dimension (ability to use different features and services), and the evolving patterns of social usage (texting, telephony, e-mails etc.,) (Hargittai, 2002).

There is also a domestic variant of the global digital divide within both the rich and poor countries which manifests itself in regards to access to ICT between individuals and groups in urban and rural areas and the suburbs and inner cities of large urban centers. Like its global counterpart, the domestic digital divide is a reflection of existing economic inequities among individuals and groups within countries (Gillwald, 2005). Furthermore, the digital divide metaphor creates the false impression that the technological gap between rich and poor countries is a static condition. On the contrary, access to ICT devices and internet connectivity does not guarantee full and optimum services over a long period of time without further inputs and outlays. ICT adoption involves periodic expenditure and changes in connections to ICT devices all of which exert significant influences on the nature of applications. Warschauer (2003) and DiMaggio and Hargittai (2001) have consequently argued that there is no binary divide and no single overriding factor for determining the digital divide. Rather, there are degrees of technological inequality that are woven into complex sociopolitical systems and processes that shape the world's socio-economic order.

LEVELS OF TECHNOLOGICAL INEQUALITY

A great deal of variation in the digital divide exists among high, middle and low-income countries. Several reasons may account for this. They include the large economic development gap between the countries and lack of data on economic transactions in low-income countries. A study commissioned by OECD in 2003 revealed that the digital inequality between high-income and low-income countries is in part due to differences in the production and diffusion of ICT within their economies. The report explained that wealthy countries have large and established service and manufacturing sectors that make intensive use of ICT while the economies of low-income countries are dominated by raw material production and subsistence agriculture where ICT adds much less value to the production processes. The society in most low income countries is also oriented towards communal economic activities that do not involve calculated arrangements of capitalist accounting. Avgerou (1998) has explained that in systems like those in low income countries, reciprocative and redistributive rationality such as mutual responsibility and common welfare of members of the community prevail over the freedom of enterprise to accumulate capital. As a result, ICT can add much less value to the economic production processes that occur in those countries, at least, during the initial stages of ICT adoption. Furthermore, the domestic markets of low income countries include large numbers of people with significantly low disposable income such that response to opportunities offered by ICT may be recorded more in social than direct economic uses of the technology (OECD, 2003). In addition, ICT investment is generally much higher in low-income countries where almost all ICT equipment is imported. The fundamental differences in the economies of rich and poor nations make ICT investment in low-income countries more expensive, more difficult to implement or less cost-effective thereby limiting both ICT impact on productivity and the ability of local ICT-investing firms to gain competitive advantage (OECD, 2003). The situation is however different in the transition (or middle income) economies in central and eastern Europe or countries in Asia and Latin America with established manufacturing sectors – or very large countries, such as India and China, whose population sizes give them substantial domestic markets and skilled workforces that are required to make effective use of ICT (OECD, 2003). The domestic market of transitional economies such as Brazil, China or India, includes both substantial populations with significant disposable income and large numbers of people such that the response to opportunities offered by ICT in middle-income economies is closer to those of high-income countries (OECD, 2003). The technological gap between the high-income and middle income countries is therefore very small and may not take long to close.

It is important to mention that the presence of factors that inhibit ICT adoption and usage in low-income countries does not suggest that ICT investment will not happen, or that benefits in productivity and economic growth will not arise (OECD, 2003). The hindrances do not alter the fundamental relationship between improvements in micro- and macro-economic performance, nor reduce the important impact of ICT in bringing positive changes to the business environment. Rather, the OECD study found that, investments in ICT and resulting benefits take longer to materialize in low-income countries (OECD, 2003). Thus, for the potentials of ICT to be translated into digital opportunities in low-income countries, the current paradigm which guides development policy must change and assumptions that underlie development programs must be discarded. However, these can only be accomplished if the people, rather than the market, become the focus of development practice.

THE NEED TO BRIDGE THE DIGITAL DIVIDE

The exclusion of the majority of the world's population from benefits of the digital revolution has become one of the most serious political and economic problems facing world leaders today. However, despite the dangers posed by the divide, bridging the technological gap between rich and poor countries will not come easily and may take some time to be realized. This is partly because technological advances are often accompanied by different levels of access, intensity of usage and applications among different social groups and individuals (Norris, 2001; Werle, 2005). During the adoption of a new technology, the gap between those that are able to innovate and those that are unable to do so widens with time. Under such conditions, attempts to bridge the technological gap often turn into futile exercises in technological catch-up (Govindan, 2005). When the poor and less educated try to draw level, the skilled and affluent groups in society develop and use new and advanced models or find new uses for the existing technology. For example, while mobile phone users in many low-income countries today are just beginning to use 2.5G model of digital wireless services, their counterparts in technologically advanced countries (e.g., USA, Korea and Sweden) are already experiencing sharp increases in the use of 3G and even 4G models, and a decline in 2G handset subscription. As a result, some form of a technological gap is expected between rich and poor nations. The key questions for policy makers are; (1) the extent to which the technological imbalance matters in terms of its human welfare implications and equity in development among individuals, social groups and nations (2) the degree to which the digital divide is likely to deepen or diminish over time, and (3) the development and implementation of policies that can bridge the divide to reduce the technological inequality among individuals and groups.

HOW THE DIGITAL DIVIDE AFFECTS POOR NATIONS

What makes the bridging of the global digital divide very urgent today is the extent to which the divide affects other aspects of human development in the poor countries despite the promised benefits of globalization, integrated markets and information technology (Govindan, 2005). Information flow is a vital link in the chain of economic development process comprising of production, distribution and marketing of goods and services. Through timely delivery of information required for production, marketing and consumption, information handling technologies such as ICT play critical enabling roles in the economic development of nations (Beninger 1986). For example, in the context of economic development in a low-income country, a mobile phone is not simply a connection between people, but also, a tool which can be used to shorten time delays in disseminating price information between trading centers. With international trade and global events being conducted with ICT, excluded countries will most likely lose out in their abilities to actively participate in international trade and international organizations where ICT is effectively embedded in all activities. Marker and others (2002) have argued that the poor are not just poor because they lack basic resources but, they are so and continue to be poor because they lack access information about income-earning opportunities, information about market prices for the goods they produce and the institutions that shape their lives. Without access to ICT, the poor has limited opportunities to learn skills that are essential in today's job market or even learning about their rights and entitlements to government services (Hall, 1998). The poor in non-ICT adopting countries therefore stands to benefit from improved information flows through society which may improve the effectiveness of government, their access to markets, education, health and other institutions that affect their welfare (Marker et. al., 2002).

There is therefore a real danger that the inequity in ICT access and usage could widen the already existing disparities in income, health, education and other socio-economic indicators between rich and poor households and countries (Smillie, 1999). The potential and likely consequences of the digital divide therefore engender a need to understand the phenomena and work to reduce the imbalances in ICT access and usage (Kauffman and Techatassanasoontorn, 2005). The need for action on the global digital divide was confirmed by leaders from G8 nations when they declared during their 2000 summit meeting that "global digital equality is a prerequisite to achieving and sustaining global development" (G8 Information Center, 2000:5). Others contend that eliminating the differences between information rich and poor countries is critical to the removal of other inequalities in development between the Global North and South (Kuttan and Peters, 2003:105). International organizations (e.g., World Bank, International Monetary Fund, United Nations etc.,), community activists and policy makers among others, have also recognized the digital divide as a significant social problem that must be addressed (World Bank, 1998; UNDP, 2005). Consequently, the digital inequality has been the principal driving force behind two world summits held at Geneva in 2003 and in Tunis in 2005 to craft strategies for monitoring the global digital divide (ITU, 2008b).

WHY THE DIGITAL DIVIDE IS A CONCERN FOR WEALTHY NATIONS

There are also moral and economic arguments as to why the rich countries should be concerned about the global digital inequality. Some have argued that the rich countries of the world cannot disown all interests in global poverty and inequality because the rich has a hand in the underdevelopment of the poor (Milanovic, 2005). Saachs (2005:231) has also argued that the rich and poor countries of the world have become interconnected and interdependent such that "extreme poverty in poor countries now threatens the unity and security of the rich countries in the world". Saachs explain that poor and desperate youth elsewhere in the world remain fertile recruiting grounds for terrorist organizations such as Al-Qaida that target the wealthy nations. As well, the economic collapse and attendant failures of poor countries abroad (e.g., Iraq, Somalia and Afghanistan) always pose significant security problems for the rich nations and in the case of Somali pirates, the world as a whole. It would therefore seem that, in the very near future, the question will not be whether the rich will help the poor to develop, but whether the rich can afford not to help the poor to progress (Saachs, 2005).

However, it seems more likely that it is on the basis of economic self interest that the rich countries may be compelled to intervene and become actively involved in the efforts to close the development gap and thereby help narrow or eliminate the digital divide. Recent trends in ICT dissemination and adoption reveal that the digitally excluded countries have become especially attractive targets for foreign investments in ICT (ITU, 2008a; Prahalad and Hart, 2002). The millions of people in the underdeveloped world who are entering the market economy for the first time (via subscriptions to ICT networks) provide a real source of market promise for multinational network companies. Major network companies including Vodafone and Motorola have not only taken over national telecommunication industries in developing countries in Africa, the Middle East and Asia, but also, the network companies are selling low-cost mobile handsets in low-income countries throughout the world (BBC, 2009). The attraction here seem to be the opportunity to produce and sell ICT products on a large scale at a low profit margin and still make huge profits. The economic opportunities and promise of huge profits attract not only investment but also jobs to low-income countries. The concentration of

investments and the outsourcing of jobs to the low-income countries deprive citizens of the advanced economies of good paying jobs and taxes for development and must therefore have a bearing on the question of whether developed countries will respond positively to the challenge of reducing the digital divide (James, 2007).

In some countries, closing the domestic version of the digital divide assumes more prominence over the global divide. This is because heightened inequalities in technological adoption within a country can lead to protests and internal political discontent. It can also serve as a rallying point for mobilizing opposition against the government (Milanovic, 2005). There is also the concern that unequal adoption of ICT within a country may favor the relatively affluent minority, such that the internal divide may grow even as the gap between countries shrinks (ibid). The potentially damaging impacts aside, failure to address inequities in the ability to access, own, and use ICT (be it at the local or global level) can lead to deeply entrenched imbalances in human welfare between historically privileged and disenfranchised groups. This disparity can have devastating impacts on other existing gaps in income, education and even democracy. This is because information is a gatekeeper to a whole range of resources that serve to facilitate democratic and participatory decision making and the empowerment of marginalized groups in society (Kole, 1998).Unequal access to information and the mechanisms for delivering it may therefore prevent several people in poor countries from actively engaging in public debates. The ITU has consequently equated the lack of access to basic communication and information services to a denial of the benefits of the Universal Declaration of Human Rights to the majority poor people in the world (ITU quoted in Smillie, 1999).

For the reasons above and possibly others not mentioned, closing the digital divide has become a contested area of scholarly research but much of the studies focus on the supply and acquisition of ICT (Martin, 2003). While a difference in the proportion of subscribers and users in different regions may reveal a digital divide, a real change in digital inequality occurs only if the ICT are deployed to facilitate socio-economic development. Unfortunately this aspect of the investigation into the global divide problem has been ignored. There is little reliable evidence on actual movements towards the closing of the divide. For example, the body of research on causes of the digital inequality disproportionally focuses on economic wealth and regime types as explanatory variables. Rarely are variations in national telecommunications policy decisions considered. As well, several explanatory variables have been used in the investigations but very little of the observed variation in ICT access and usage between countries and among social groups have been analyzed. Many indices that have been created to measure the digital divide also focus mainly on existing patterns of internet access and speculative aspects of network readiness that provide little insight into cultural and policy aspects of ICT adoption and actual usage between rich and poor countries (Persaud, 2001). The controversy about the global digital divide concept offers an insight into the larger theoretical debate which is the subject matter of discussion in the remaining of the chapter.

ISSUES, CONTROVERSIES AND PROBLEMS

On the one hand, the adoption and use of a technology that has a great potential to carry the economies of low-income countries more deeply than before into the global information economy is problematic and probably risky to the future development of the low-income countries. The past development experiences of these countries and their continued underdog statuses in the global exchange of goods and services make it difficult to defend programs that encourage their profound assimilation into global capitalism.

Yet, on the other, there is a good chance that with ICT, low-income countries are on the threshold of securing a breakthrough in economic growth which has eluded them for several years (Castells, 2000; UNDP, 1998). Herein lies the paradox in the ICT-led development proposition for low-income countries. In spite of this, the digital divide problem presents a challenge to scholars and world leaders to search for a solution to the dilemma. Nobody knows exactly what the future of the global digital divide will be, but there is little doubt that the decisions we make about the digital inequality presently, based on theories that drive the debate, will influence the future of the technological gap between rich and poor countries (Mitchell, 2003; McAnany, 1983). In the sections which follow, we will assess the main theories that drive the digital divide debate.

A review of literature on the digital divide reveals that two theories currently dominate the discourse about the role ICT can play in the economic development of low-income countries. These are the Modernization and Dependency theories of development. Scholars from both schools of thought are discussing the digital divide but a fundamental problem of the discourse is that definitions of the problem are different and as such strategies recommended for dealing with it offer diverse policy recommendations. The global digital divide has both managerial and policy implications (Mitchell, 2003) and as such a thorough understanding of the perspectives that drive and sustain the debate is important. This will not only help with scholarly research about the problem but also, the experience will be useful in the search for strategies that might have a good chance of bridging the technological gap.

MODERNIZATION THEORY PERSPECTIVES

The modernization theory emerged from Neo-classical perspectives on economic development and as such supports an optimistic viewpoint in the digital divide debate. In explaining the gap between rich and poor countries, modernization theorists examine the processes of development and offer a composite portrait of two worlds namely "modern" and "traditional" societies (Roberts and Hite, 2007). Proponents of the theory view the economic development of nations as as unilinear and evolutionary processes of economic growth that transforms traditional (underdeveloped countries) into modern (developed nations) (Huntington, 1971). The main thrust of the modernization theory is the belief that progress in underdeveloped countries depends upon their capacities to absorb and replicate technological innovations already available in wealthy nations (Schramm, 1979). Consequently, the central problem of economic development in the low-income countries is believed to revolve around 'bridging the gap' through an imitation process by which traditional societies (at a lower stage of the economic development ladder) attempt to catch up to modern societies (Lerner, 1958; Schramm, 1979).

According to Chambers (1980), because of the grotesquely unequal leverage between scientific knowledge (which drives modern development) and indigenous local knowledge of rural people, scholars who subscribe to the Modernization theory find it difficult to accept that there is a parallel system of knowledge or rationality to their own which is complimentary, valid or at times even superior within the localities where development takes place. Development practitioners therefore fail to recognize the clash of rationalities when they strive to emulate the progress that technology has enabled in developed countries in the context of the developing countries (Avgerou, 2000). Thus, alternative ways of perceiving the value of technological innovation are poorly understood. At the same time, the adoption of science-based innovations by local groups has been stifled by the incompatibility between the modernization rationality for development and the local systems of reasoning. The tension between the two epis-

temologies has plagued many economic development projects developing countries.

Although some current supporters of the modernization theory take exemptions to some generalizations embedded in earlier explanations of underdevelopment, the main assumption that "societies will ultimately modernize to liberal democracies" still pervade in their writings (Roberts and Hite, 2007). To close the global digital inequality therefore, modern day supporters of the modernization theory argue that developing countries must adopt the advanced innovations and ICT techniques that wealthy nations have used, or are currently using in their development (UNCTAD, 2008). This way, it is argued, low-income countries will prevent errors that the wealthy nations made during their development and skip several stages of technological progress to attain development earlier than they would normally do (UNDP, 1998). Supporters of the theory also argue that ICT can bring accelerated development to low-income countries through the leapfrogging potentials of the technology (Heeks, 1999; UNCTAD, 2006; UNDP, 1998).

The technological optimists caution that it will be a mistake for poor countries to ignore development opportunities that ICT offer for their development. They urge critics and observers alike to recognize and embrace the transformative power of ICT. They contend that ICT is not just another technology but one which belongs to a special category of technological innovations (including the printing press, electricity and steam engine) that usually bring changes to transform both the domestic life of people and the way businesses and life in general are conducted and organized around the world (Jovanovic and Rousseau, 2005). Explaining further, supporters of the theory contend that ICT is a product of two distinct technologies that were crucial in past attempts at economic development (Dicken, 2007). These are (a) communication technologies – concerned with transmitting information, and (b) computer technology – concerned with the processing of information. ICT has broken the link and hence made it necessary to treat transportation and communication as intimately related technologies (Dicken, 2007:78). For example, mobile phones can become effective time and space control systems for entrepreneurs in low-income countries and thereby enable businesses to create new paths to efficiency, savings and profit making.

Supporters of the theory explain that the piggybacking of new ICT on old infrastructure occur more in the wealthier nations because the right of way has already been established in those places. They however contend that wireless networks has the potential to transform this pattern because a mobile phone is not tied to specific locations and neither does it rely on permanent electricity supply and a land line. The technological optimists argue that, unlike previous agents of economic development (e.g., factories and industry) whose influence were limited to urban enclaves in low-income countries, beneficial impacts of ICT reach anywhere without an expensive landline infrastructure and with little capital outlay (Sciadas, 2005b; Vodafone, 2005). With mobile phones, geographical enclaves in the poor countries once separated by distance and time, develop new virtual relationships that are uninhibited by conventional notions of distance and transportation (IFPRI, 2006). The implications of these cross-community and national contacts for the development of rural communities in low-income countries can be quite immense.

Responding to a criticism that the most pressing issue about development in low-income countries is not the introduction and use of ICT but solutions to basic problems such as the lack of clean drinking water, shelter and health care, the technological optimists explain ICT adoption per se, may not feed or clothe the people directly, but it can empower them to attain those materials. In the long run, they argue, ICT will contribute to the production of clean water, enough food, good hospitals and informed citizenry if it is effectively integrated into productive ventures. Proposals for bridging the digital divide and for economic development in poor countries should not be viewed as mutually exclusive. Rather, the two work to reinforce each other. Economic development is intertwined with the growth in access and use of ICT whilst efficient uses of ICT lead to greater wealth and economic development.

DEPENDENCY THEORY PERSPECTIVES

Proponents of Dependency theory and World systems analyses have assembled a body of literature to show that the international market system which connects both rich and poor countries in an unequal exchange of goods and services is the main cause of underdevelopment in low-income countries. The unequal interdependent relationship allows rich nations that are endowed with superior technological and commercial abilities to exploit the poor countries and extract part of their locally produced surplus to develop and expand their economies. Dependency theorists explain that that the terms of trade between advanced (core) countries and developing (peripheral) countries evolve to the disadvantage of the poor countries and as such they become relatively more impoverished (Dos Santos, 1970; Pritchett 1997). Similarly, scholars of the world-system school of thought believe that market forces within a "world-system" created by capitalist development generate profound inequalities between the developed "core," the developing "semi-periphery," and the undeveloped "periphery". A country's chances of developing within the system therefore depend on the nature of relationship it has within the world system (Wallerstein 1974; Van Rossem 1996). When it comes to the question of how a dependency situation can be fixed, the dependency school of thought offers two solutions. The first of this proposition is exemplified by the writings of scholars such as Gundar Frank (1972), Paul Baran, Dos Santos (1970) and Samir

Amin (1976) who argue that underdevelopment is not a phase but a permanent condition which underdeveloped countries can only reverse by evading the entire capitalist system. The other solution (represented by authors like Cardoso, Gerefi (1989) and Evans (1979) envision a possibility for some associated, but still dependent development to occur in peripheral countries. This can happen by way of cheap exports and the adoption of sets of policies known generally as "import substitution" by which domestic industries are developed and protected as a way of creating a comparative advantage in products to reduce the dependency on global capitalism.

Unlike adherents of modernization theory, current supporters of the dependency theory hold a pessimistic view about the adoption of ICT for economic development in low-income countries. They contend that that the global digital divide will be likely to grow over time as ICT become pervasive around the globe (Boafo, 1991; Chacko, 2005). Some recount the economic stagnation and collapse that low-income countries experienced under projects and development programs (e.g., structural adjustment) initiated by the same international organizations (e.g., World Bank and International Monetary Fund) that are currently spearheading ICT adoption in the poor countries (Boafo-Arthur, 2003; Wilson, 2000). They point to past failures in similar revolutions in agriculture and industry in the low-income countries and predict the same fate for ICT unless drastic changes occur in the relations between the rich and poor countries. With increases in the subscription of ICT devices, the ICT sector has gradually become the economic engine as well as the enabler of social, educational and medical progress in low-income countries. But in spite of the huge investment returns, the profits from investment in ICT have accrued mainly to foreign network companies that have taken over the telecommunications industry in low-income countries (Ojo, 2004). Nokia which made over 40% of all mobile phones sold in 2007 is reported to have earned a profit margin of $8.4

billion that year alone (Corbett, 2008). Even the recent increases in ICT subscription in low-income regions of the world has been propelled mainly by supply-side factors such as favorable regulatory reforms, huge profits, technological innovation and an almost insatiable ICT market waiting to be explored in low-income countries (James, 2005). The technological pessimists therefore warn that disappointment and failure can happen with a dependency on information technology that is not locally produced and cannot be locally supported and maintained (Boafo, 1991; James, 2005).

There is therefore a growing voice in the development field which raises serious concerns and doubts about globalization and the intended impacts of ICT usage amongst the poor. Stiglitz (2003) for example has argued that the diminishing of spatial barriers under globalization gives transnational capital a brand new energy to exploit low-income countries. He explains that under globalization and a push from ICT, the poor countries are exposed to intense exploitation from foreign companies. At the same time, the countries are progressively losing their abilities to capture and redirect surpluses from external trade through fiscal or monetary interventionist mechanisms that many of them had used in the past to protect local industries and also earn foreign exchange for development. Many followers of the dependency school of thought therefore question the feasibility of low-income countries relying on ICT to usher them into economic development.

A REVIEW OF THE MAIN ARGUMENTS IN THE DIGITAL DIVIDE DEBATE

It is clear from the above discussion that the two theories that currently dominate the ICT4development debate are in disagreement over the roles external market agents and internal non-market actors play in the development and underdevelopment processes in low-income countries. However, both theories share some common shortcomings. While proponents of both theories agree that economic development in low-income countries result from strategic interactive processes that occur between local and global actors, they both ignore the role which local actors play in the interactive process and consider development to be a passive process that is driven solely by lead market and global actors (Escobar, 2001). For example, in explaining the development and underdevelopment processes, both theories overemphasize factors at either the local or global levels. Neither of the theories addresses the combined impacts of the local and global factors on development processes that occur in localities (Kole, 2002). Whilst the Modernization theory considers beneficiaries of the development interaction to be passive objects that need to emulate wealthy nations, Dependency theorists believe people in the localities are not subjects of the process but objects who respond to orders from external agents (Berger, 2002). In addition, the modernization theory ignores complexities entailed in the processes of change and pays little attention to the consequences of economic, political and cultural processes that occur within the localities. The perspective according to which the poor are just receptacles of ideas and traditional cultures are backward and antithetical to progress provides justification for development practitioners to ignore local knowledge in all development interventions. We know however that culture is a unique institution which strongly determines whether a development policy intervention will succeed or fail (Mitchell, 2003). Culture is also one of the most effective social institutions that is capable of influencing the adoption and use, or a rejection of ICT. Traditions of the people dictate initial uses of technology and can also exert a lasting influence on successful integration of technology into businesses and other productive ventures in the locality. A successful ICT adoption would require full recognition of the historical conditions and rules of practice that shape behavior and work arrangements in

particular societies (Coco and Short, 2004). This is because humans do not experience the world passively but rather, they actively construct their own realities through the ways they learn to understand or describe them in their cultures (Weick, 1995). As a result, the construction of meaningful actions (such as decisions to adopt and use ICT) occurs in culturally and historically conditioned ways within specific cultures. It is therefore crucial that we rise above the ethnocentric conceptions in development policy and focus equal attention on how both local and global actors intervene in the development process.

It is equally difficult to defend the claim that external factors alone account for the lack of development in low-income countries. On the contrary, several factors influence the economic development process in low-income countries. The first of these interventions results from the action of non-market actors (individuals, communities and public officials in the localities) that may facilitate or raise barriers to entry into local ICT-led businesses. Local actors are not passive elements of the development process as Dependency theorists would want us to believe, but rather active participants in any local development practice. It is individuals in the low-income countries who make the choices to own or forgo mobile phones and ICT devices. Consequently, the actors are important constituents in development and underdevelopment processes that occur in localities. Leaders of the poor countries also intervene in local ICT adoption and use policy making and choices to promote or resist ICT adoption, select specific network companies over others, or plan for integration of the technology into local productive ventures. In some low-income countries today, ICT has become favorable targets for executive control so that public officials can manipulate information in support of unpopular programs and governments. In some cases, ICT companies and network services are targeted as sources of unrestrained income for national budget deficits (Kyem and LeMaire, 2006). There are also cases where public officials are openly accused of corrupt practices regarding the sale of state-controlled telecommunication companies to foreign network companies (Ghana News Agency, 2008). These interventions by citizens and leaders of low-income countries have significant impacts on the adoption of ICT and in their integration into productive economic ventures in the respective countries.

It is important to also mention that a self reliance approach to the resolution of the digital inequality problem as contained in explanations offered by some supporters of the Dependency theory entail an unrealistic and undesirable isolation of the poor countries from the rest of the world. In a world that is increasingly becoming interdependent, no country or community can function completely autonomously and no country (whether rich or poor) can be completely self-sufficient in all aspects of life. Neither is the development of any country determined exclusively by external or internal factors but by both domestic and external events. Even if the self-reliance approach to development were approved and adopted, several of the countries in Africa, Asia, Latin America and the Caribbean that are currently struggling to join the information society will simply be too weak economically to operate autonomously (Friberg and Hettne, 1985). Also true is the fact that most low-income countries today are poorly equipped to undertake integrated research about the roles ICT that can play, and the impacts which the technology might have on different sectors of the economy (OECD, 2003). For these reasons, an exclusionary self-reliant development policy will be counterproductive because it imposes artificial and self-damaging constrictions on the development potentials that ICT may bring to the poor countries.

The two theories also fail to incorporate recent important changes in development practice into their analyses. With globalization and the growing interdependence of regions, nations and communities, the traditional demarcation of the world into core and periphery or developed and underdeveloped regions can no longer be preserved. This is partly because processes that lead to digital inequality and uneven accumulation of wealth appear to be unfolding in accordance with a social order and not along the lines of core and peripheral development regions (Robinson, 2002). Robinson therefore urges a rethink of development under ICT not as a national event in which what develops is a nation but in terms of social groups that occupy contradictory locations in a transnational development. Thus, the digital divide between rich and poor countries remains important for its theoretical and practical implications for development. The main question is whether the digital divide is static or whether the technological gap between rich and poor countries can be offset by development opportunities that may result from the adoption and use of ICT. The recent development experience of some Asian countries (e.g., South Korea, Malaysia and Singapore) reveal that the rich-poor divide is not static but fluid and evolving.

SOLUTIONS AND RECOMMENDATIONS

The tremendous attention which the Modernization and Dependency theories focus on the impacts that global networks exert on local actors is understandable given the size, wealth, power and reach of global production and distribution networks. However, by failing to consider the local institutional context explicitly, the two theories tacitly portray local and regional actors as passive elements, rather than active objects of the development process (Gibson-Graham, 1996). Even though local actors in low-income countries constantly engage powerful agents of modernization, their livelihoods are not dictated by market economic relations alone (Gibson-Graham, 2003). The majority of economic relations and exchange that occur within the communities take place outside formal markets. In some cases, activities such as the unofficial currency exchange, hoarding of cash and other activities that take place in the informal economy undermine official fiscal and monetary policies. In spite of the challenges that the informal sector poses to the development of the formal economy, the sector persists in poor countries because it offers the best safeguard assurance and economic stability for local actors. Thus, contrary to views expressed in the dominant theories, local contextual factors play a significant role in determining the outcome of any agency-driven development program.

The highlighting of local contextual factors in this instance does not in any way imply that the local is fixed, permanent or unconnected. The fact is that localities in Africa, Asia and Latin America have co-existed with the global for such a long period of time that we seem to have accepted the inevitable hybridization that has resulted from the interaction. However, the continuous engagement with global networks has not made the local less local nor more global, only differently so (Escobar, 2001). Due to the discourse of exclusion which the dominant theories advocate, the proponents are not able to fully appreciate how global production and distribution systems are embedded territorially in particular localities, or how local and regional economies and power structures engage global actors in a development intervention (Gibson-Graham, 2003). Consequently the localities continue to be subjected to economic development policies (i.e., structural adjustment) that focus solely on activities of the global networks. This is notwithstanding of the fact that the localities have experienced little or no progress under such policies. It is therefore important that we strive to discover how local actors "practice the local within the global" (Friedman, 1997:276) or how people in the communities construct localities even as they participate in translocal networks (Escobar, 2001:147). Accordingly, we need to consider the ICT4development challenge not only from the

perspective of global actors, but also, from the local outlook as well.

THE MULTIPLICITY THEORY AND ICT FOR DEVELOPMENT

Confronted with persistent failures of the one-size-fits-all models of development, low-income countries can no longer treat modernity as the pivot towards which all development-related activities must gravitate. We need to move away from the singular vision of development which is premised on the experiences of wealthy nations and recognize that capitalist development exists side-by-side with non-market systems throughout communities in the developing world (Gibson-Graham, 1996). In this regard, Chang (2007) has called for a radical shift in economic development thinking. The famous economist argues that the imposition of neoliberal development policies on developing countries of modern time is likely to condemn them to stagnation over the long term. Accordingly, the author has argued for a rejection of the neoliberal policies that have dominated economic development in poor countries and reliance instead on creative and developmentalist policies that closely resemble strategies the developed countries adopted when they themselves were trying to industrialize (Chang, 2007).

Thus, if ICT deployment is going to exert meaningful impacts on the economy of the low-income countries and improve the wellbeing of the people, then development agencies and experts must stop viewing people in the poor as passive and acted upon objects, and rather think of them as active agents of change who simultaneously engage in market and non-market activities to cultivate their own non-capitalist forms of engagement and livelihoods (Escobar, 2004; Murphy, 2008). In addition, if we are going to make meaningful impacts on development policy debates and offer realistic strategies for improving livelihoods of people in low-income countries, it is necessary for scholars, practitioners and policymakers to see people in communities as complex groups of actors who simultaneously engage in market and non-market activities to produce their own means of livelihood. In fact, the application of any prescriptive theory or strategy that is intended to close the technological gap will fail unless such an approach responds to the cultural, economic and political realities that shape and define societies where the policies may be applied. According to Dirlik (2000:39), the survival of local cultures will be ensured when the symmetry between local and the global is reintroduced into theories of economic development and rendered into policy recommendations and strategies for action.

The primary development challenge today therefore is a demand of development practitioners and scholars alike to reposition local actors and their culture in the actual roles they play in development processes that occur within localities (Gibson-Graham, 2003; Escobar, 2001; Murphy, 2008). Strategies for bridging the digital divide must recognize and respond to the socio-cultural systems and institutions in which the digital divide persists (Mitchell, 2003). It is important that we reject the assumptions of theories that currently shape the digital divide debate so we can begin fresh efforts to address the self-determined needs of people in the poor countries (Sein and Harindranath, 2004, 2007; Kole, 2002). Accordingly, an alternative perspective on the ICT4Development discourse which acknowledges local actors and their cultures and also recognizes the diverse ways that local actors engage global networks becomes necessary. We need a development paradigm which treats the interaction between local actors and agents of global networks as a true multiplicity where trajectories are manifold and can lead to many development models (Graham-Gibson 1996). In this regard, I join scholars such as Kole (2002), Servaes and Malikhao (2002), Gibson-Graham (2005) and Schech (2002) in suggesting an alternative development paradigm which questions the dominant role of global actors

and neglects all other realities (including local resistance and co-operatives) in the continuous encounter that occurs between local and global actors. The new development paradigm, which is called the multiplicity theory or critical theory, addresses mainly non-economic factors (e.g., local context, cultural tradition and self-empowerment) in the ICT4development debate. The paradigm places basic needs of people at the center of the development process (Kole, 1998; Servaes, 2002; Friberg & Hettne, 1985). It views the people as actors who actively attempt to influence structural relations from the bottom-up while the structural relations and other processes on the global level also influence individuals and groups within the communities from the top down (Berger, 2002). The multiplicity paradigm considers technology to be a product of dynamic social, political, economic and cultural processes (Berger, 2002; Kole, 2002). Technology is a cultural product which embodies societal norms and values including political interests. Within the localities, a technology such as ICT offers dual capabilities to challenge top-down controlling processes as well as tools for bottom-up empowerment possibilities to meet local needs. In this regard, ICT and the development of localities co-evolve through the dialectic tension between the bottom-up and top-down processes that characterize the global-local interactions. In the end, a multiplicity theory which re-instates the local in its natural role in the development discourse may well offer the timely end to "the false division that has separated the rest from the West" (Gibson-Graham, 2005:21).

DESIRABLE QUALITIES OF THE MULTIPLICITY THEORY

There has been no technology for development that is so easily accessible, easy to own and use and yet very adaptable to the traditional socio-economic practices of people in poor countries. However for the development potentials of ICT to be fully realized in the low-income countries, policies intended to use ICT for development must necessarily adopt an integrated approach which focus on the traditions and culture of the people and the activities of global actors. The growth dividend for ICT is far greater in low-income countries than the high-income countries. This is because ICT such as the mobile phone supplants the information-gathering role of fixed-line systems (Kyem and LeMaire, 2006). Furthermore, notwithstanding its Western origins, ICT offers opportunities for development in low-income countries that are fundamentally unique and unmatched by technologies that preceded it. Wireless networks expand interactivity between rural and urban areas and thereby provide essential tools for spreading economic benefits to many people who had in the past been excluded from any means of economic advancement. For example, mobile phones open up entirely new means of communication in remote locations in poor countries. The networks integrate rural sectors into national economies and also open up rural and urban sectors of the economy to entirely new economic opportunities. Perhaps the most important attributes of ICT that makes it the ideal tool for economic development in low-income countries are the flexibility and mobility of the tools. The supple qualities of many ICT tools allow for diverse social and economic applications that are unimpeded by language, location and nationality. ICT tools are exceptionally flexible in the manner they incorporate social structures, languages and local modes of organization and production. The versatility of ICT tools (e.g. computers and mobile phones) in regards to the incorporation of cultures testifies to the need to tailor technological adoption to the belief systems and cultural practices of people in the adopting communities. Effective and sustained ICT adoption in the poor countries will therefore require that we look beyond the expectations about pre-established uses of the technology and rather focus on the adaptable qualities of the technology

to create applications that are consistent with the traditions and culture of the people.

In low-income countries, the potential gains from computers and other forms of ICT are likely to depend on fundamental issues (related to the day-to-day activities of the people) than just well planned development models and business practices. In fact, there appear to be differences in the productivity gains from ICT even among the developed countries. According to Varian (2006), European economies did not enjoy the same productivity growth as the United States in the past decade. The difference, according to the author, lies in the organizational differences between the two regions that manifests in the effectiveness with which IT is used. It is therefore possible that acknowledgement of the role of local cultures in development intervention may release more non-capitalist imaginaries into the ICT4development discourse to bring about innovation. Focusing on localities will also provide legitimacy to development policy decisions and economic development projects. The recognition of local actors in the multiplicity theory will allow for the defense of local cultures from their marginalization by dominant cultures so the people will become effective political and life forces in their own development (Dirlik, 2000:39). In addition, knowledge about the locality and identity can help produce different meanings of the local informal economy also help identify power relations within the locality that can enhance our understanding of the global-local interactions within the community.

The multiplicity paradigm offers several advantages over theories that drive the discourse about ICT for development in low-income countries. Unlike the dominant theories that emphasize either the local or global actors, the multiplicity perspective injects local knowledge into the discourse. By introducing local actors into the ICT for development debate, the multiplicity theory brings back contextualized and situated notions of human practice that are consistent with the traditions and culture of the people. Generally, development projects fail to produce expected positive changes in the lives of the target population when the programs ignore local knowledge and also fail to consider traditional practices of the intended beneficiaries. Warschauer reveals some of the empirical evidence of failures in contemporary conceptualizations of the digital divide in a case study involving a national information technology adoption program in Egypt (Warschauer, 2003). In a 3-year longitudinal study of an IT adoption project, the author found ample evidence of how a program that was intended to introduce ICT into Egyptian schools failed to make a meaningful impact on ICT adoption and usage amongst the people. According to the author, the ICT project failed because the technology was thrust upon a dysfunctional social system that undermined the best possible uses of the technology. The author explained that the development agency did not take into account the different ways in which information was shared within the culture and the institutional environment. Another unsuccessful attempt at bridging the digital divide that has been widely reported in the literature occurred in Atlanta, Georgia, USA. After monitoring an outreach program involving the establishment of 14 community technology centers operated by the DeKalb County School System in Atlanta, Georgia, for some time, O'Neil and Baker (2003) found little evidence of success in closing the technological gap. The authors reported that successful efforts at ICT adoption must be tied to a combination of local and external factors including an environment that is suitable for change, the participation and active involvement of key stakeholders and the ability of important local and external change agents to draw upon their resources to leverage a digital divide policy initiative. Other important factors include an understanding how such projects unfold within the locality, the obstacles to implementation, and how organizational settings in the community function. The authors explained that an understanding of the culture and traditions within a locality helps to prepare ICT specialists to

easily identify and tackle inequities in information technology opportunities. The research by O'Neil and Bake underscores the need for a participatory development approach to the implementation of ICT programs in localities. The above examples of unsuccessful attempts to bridge the digital divide (one each from a low and high-income country) offer practical examples of the liabilities of technology-centered approaches to ICT adoption. The failures in both cases could have been avoided if the intended beneficiaries were actively involved in the planning and implementation of the projects. It is possible that the integration of local actors into the economic development process will create new structures of local power and expertise that can be used to strengthen and empower institutions that are at the forefront of ICT adoption.

In fact, when the focus of ICT adoption has been shifted from the market on to the traditions and actual needs of people within localities, success has been attained. The problem is that except in a few cases such as the Grameen Telecom in Bangladesh, evidence concerning the direct influence of technological adoption on poverty is rarely available (Bayes et al., 1999). Yet one cannot ignore the few stories that get published following widespread successes in project implementation. For example, in early March 2009, the BBC reported on the unveiling of several initiatives that had been designed to turn mobile handsets into mobile banking schemes in low-income countries (BBC, 2009). The initiatives included the South African mobile operator MTN's plan to launch a mobile banking service for its customers in 21 nations and a plan by the Mi-Pay and Isys companies to expand mobile banking into 22 nations in Africa and the Middle East. Other initiatives included a deal struck between Monitise and E-Fulusi Africa to set up mobile banking systems in East Africa and Standard Chartered and Citibank's mobile banking service called Zap that they hoped to take to more than 100m Africans. These initiatives build on the huge success of mobile banking such as the

M-Pesa system in Kenya and Grameen Telecom and banking schemes in Bangladesh.

The problem with these and similar successful ICT-related development programs in the poor countries is not that they do not work. Unquestionably, each of the mobile banking schemes benefits a large number of people (the M-Pesa and Grameen Telecom initiatives reaches millions of villagers in Africa and Bangladesh respectively). Such mobile banking schemes also introduce many of the people who have had no prior involvement with the formal economic sector to be brought into the formal economy – a move that enhances economic development within the country. The problem is rather that, economic development projects like these that are built purely on the traditional and everyday practices of people in the localities are not popular in national development plans and have not therefore been widely advertized and applied. Yet, the failures of mainstream economic policies have become too common and it is time to turn a new direction in development practice. The focus of ICT adoption policy should therefore be on replicating existing successful development models that are rooted in the socio-cultural practices of people in the low-income countries. Efforts should also be made to discover new institutional forms and uses of ICT that are appropriate to the people rather than projects that are based on the experiences of people in the rich countries.

Recent events in development practice also present evidence that augurs well for the success of the multiplicity theory. The first of these relates to increased recognition among development theorists and practitioners that there is not a universal development model which fits all societies (Servaes, 2002; Gibson-Graham, 1996). Consensus is emerging around the belief that different approaches must be adopted to deal with development problems that occur within specific localities. This is partly a recognition of the fact that localities and their non-capitalist traditions are not completely defined by global capitalism (Gibson-Graham 2003) but rather, cultures

throughout the developing world have their own unique stories to tell. Attention has also been directed lately, to the content of the development concept itself. Development has been redefined in human terms with the basic needs of people placed at the center of the development process (Sen, 1992, 1997a). Development is viewed as a process that is intended to improve the lives of individuals and groups in society (Sen, 1997b). As a result, emphasis is increasingly being placed on a multiplicity of approaches that best fits local institutions and the basic needs of the people (Kole, 2002). This approach echoes Paul Freire's suggestion that development succeeds best if the target communities actively participate in their own development (Freire, 1972). To facilitate community involvement in the development process therefore, the multiplicity paradigm emphasizes participatory decision-making, dialogue and the need for negotiating skills and partnerships in charting the economic development process. The participatory strategy has the potential to strengthen autonomy in the communities and at the same time decrease the people's dependence on wealthy and powerful partners (Berger, 2002). Self-reliance in this context does not imply economic self-sufficiency but a belief which strengthens endogenous development and autonomy (Servaes, 1989:53). Ultimately, the multiplicity theory will bridge the gap in development strategy and contribute towards a reconstituted vision of development which incorporates the values and expectations of people in both rich and poor countries.

CONCLUSION

The debate about the digital divide is not new. Even though the imbalance in technological adoption poses a great challenge for development in poor countries, if it is well handled, the technological gap can present a historic opportunity for those lagging behind to transform the technological divide into technological opportunities to enhance their development. The main question is whether low-income countries looking to adopt ICT can rely on development policies modeled on the dominant economic theories to correct decades of stagnant economic growth. Can the countries apply these theories to ICT adoption and jump over several stages of their development into a stage where they fully enjoy technological opportunities? Opinions vary about the right answer to this question but it is clear that the ongoing debate between technological optimists and pessimists has offered no tangible answer to the development problem in low-income countries to date.

Explanations that the modernization and dependency theories offer for ICT-led development in low-income countries are stuck in history. Assumptions that underlie the two theories have not been reviewed even though conditions in the world that the theories were developed originally to explain, have changed in many fronts. In fact, strict adherence to development programs derived from modernization theory perspectives by institutions such as the International Monetary Fund and the World Bank have failed to close the poverty gap which partly produced the digital divide between the rich and poor countries. Neither has the adoption of stringent socialist policies borrowed from neo-Marxist perspectives produced any long-lasting improvements in the lives of the world's poor. Meanwhile, there have been visible efforts to redefine the concept of development, the rigid boundaries between core and peripheral developed regions are now more dynamic than before and new a tool (ICT) with development potentials never before experienced by low-income countries have emerged to offer new opportunities for development.

Furthermore, with proper planning, some current developments under globalization can, in the long run, help to reduce the poverty gap which sustains the digital divide between rich and poor nations. The outsourcing of jobs from rich to poor countries and the relocation of skilled men and women from low-income into the wealthy coun-

tries could provide necessary skills, wealth and the motivation needed to initiate economic progress in low-income countries. Already, remittances from natives abroad exceed what some low-income countries (including the Philippines, Ghana, Zimbabwe) receive in annual grants and development assistance from the wealthy countries. We may also take consolation from the fact that the movements against slavery, colonialism, racism and apartheid systems (all of which were endemic to the poor countries) looked hopeless from the start but ultimately "the human will triumphed and what seemed impossible was transformed into the inevitable" (Saachs, 2005:364). In the same way, the bridging of the technological gap will occur even though under current conditions, it might take some time for such a feat to be attained on a global scale.

It must be kept in perspective that technical solutions, including those offered by ICT, can become valuable tools for economic development in low-income countries. However, technical solutions to the complex socio-political and cultural problems of development should never be pursued as ends in themselves. In the same vein, simplistic assumptions about the wonders that ICT can create for the development of the world's poor must be questioned, but this should not lead us to dismiss the transformative power of ICT and the risks to low-income countries if the global digital inequality persists or deepens. In many ways, the digital divide debate masks the economic development problem facing low-income countries. It also prevents a true discussion of the ICT role in the economic development of the poor countries. Meanwhile, as the digital inequality debate rages on, the global digital divide deepens in many fronts and citizens of many low-income countries rush to join the digital revolution without any proper national plans to channel such subscriptions into economic productive ventures. The time is therefore ripe for us to move beyond the entrenched positions of the modernization and dependency theories to pave the way for answers guided by a new perspective on development that bridges the gap in development strategy. The multiplicity theory presents a good opportunity for us to combine the shared values and aspirations of people from both rich and poor countries to create a new vision for the emerging global information society.

ACKNOWLEDGMENT

I would like to express my gratitude to the Connecticut State University (CSU) System for its support in funding the research for this paper through the University Research Grant Program. The University Research Grant is a competitive annual program which offers funds that enhance the ability of faculty within the CSU system to be productive and innovative in their fields of expertise.

REFERENCES

G8 Information Center. (2000). *Okinawa Charter on Global Information Society*. Retrieved September 6, 2006 from www.g8.utoronto.ca/summit/2000okinawa/gis.htm

Amin, S. (1976). *Unequal development: an essay on the Social Formation of Peripheral Capitalism*. Sussex: Harvester Press.

Avgerou, C. (1998). How can IT enable economic growth in developing countries? *Information Technology for Development, 8*(1), 15. doi:10.1080/02681102.1998.9525288

Avgerou, C. 2000: Recognising Alternative Rationalities in the Deployment of Information Systems, *Electronic Journal on Information Systems in Developing Countries* 23(3) 7, 1–17.

Bayes, A., von Braun, J., & Akhter, R. (1999). *Village Pay Phones and Poverty Reduction: Insights from a Grameen Bank initiative in Bangladesh. Discussion papers on Development Policy No. 8. Center for Development Research*. Bonn: ZEF.

BBC. (2009). Deals drive mobile money services. Technology news of Monday, 16 March 2009. Retrieved on April 25, 2009 from http://news.bbc.co.uk/2/hi/technology/7945878.stm

Beninger, J. (1986). *The Control Revolution: Technological and Economic Origins of the Information Society*. Cambridge, MA: Harvard University Press.

Berger, G. (2005). *Modernization and Africa's emerging engagement with the Information Society*. Paper presented at *AfroGEEKS: Global Blackness and the Digital Public Sphere*. University of California, Santa Barbara. May 19-25.

Boafo, K. S. T. (1991). Communication Technology and Dependent Development in Sub-Saharan Africa. In Sussman, G., & Lent, J. A. (Eds.), *Transnational Communications: Wiring the Third World* (pp. 103–124). Thousand Oaks, CA: Sage.

Boafo-Arthur, K. (2003). Tackling Africa's Developmental Dilemmas; Is globalization the answer? *Journal of Third World Studies*. Retrieved July 29, 2008 from http://findarticles.com/p/articles/mi_qa3821/is_200304/ai_n9173427

Burke, J. (1985). *The day the universe changed*. Boston: Little, Brown and Company.

Cardoso, F. H. (1972). Dependency and Development in Latin America. *New Left Review, 74,* 83–95.

Castells, M. (1996). *The rise of the network society*. Malden, MA: Blackwell.

Castells, M. (2000). Materials for an exploratory theory of the network society. *The British Journal of Sociology, 51*(1), 5–24. doi:10.1080/000713100358408

Chacko, J. G. (2005). Paradise lost? Reinstating the human *development* agenda in ICT policies and strategies. *Information Technology for Development, 11*(1), 97–99. doi:10.1002/itdj.20005

Chambers, R. (1980). The small farmer is professional. *Ceres*, (March-April): 19–23.

Chang, H.-J. (2007). *Bad Samaritans: Rich Nations, Poor Policies, and the Threat to the Developing World*. London: Random House.

Chen, W., & Wellman, B. (2003). *Charting and bridging digital divides: Comparing socioeconomic, gender, life stage and rural-urban internet access and use in eight countries*. AMD Global Consumer Advisory Board. Retrieved on September 12, 2005 from http://www.amd.com/us-en/assets/content type/

Cisler, S. (2000). Subtract the digital divide. *San Jose Mercury.* Retrieved May 15, 2005 from http://www0.mercurycenter.com/svtech/news/indepth/docs/soap011600.htm

Coco, A., & Short, P. (2004). History and habit in the mobilization of ICT resources. *The Information Society, 20*, 39–51. doi:10.1080/01972240490269997

Dicken, P. (2007). *Global Shift: mapping the changing contours of the World Economy*. New York: Guilford Press.

DiMaggio, P. J., & Hargittai, E. (2001), *From the Digital Divide to Digital Inequality': Studying Internet Use as Penetration Increases*, Working Paper 15. Princeton: Princeton University Center for Arts and Cultural Policy Studies.

Dirlik, A. (2000). Place-based imagination: Globalism and the politics of place. In Dirlik, A. (Ed.), *Places and politics in the age of globalization*. New York: Rowman and Littlefield.

Dos Santos, T. (1970). The Structure of Dependency. *The American Economic Review, 60*(21).

Dzidonu, C. K. (2001). *The Socio-Economic Development Implications of the Digital Divide within the Context of African Countries*. Paper presented at the Joint African Finance and Economic Planning Ministers Meeting of the ECA, Algiers, Algeria, 8-10 May 2001.

Escobar, A. (2001). Culture sits in places: reflections on globalism and subaltern strategies of localization. *Political Geography, 20*, 139–174. doi:10.1016/S0962-6298(00)00064-0

Evans, P. (1979). *Dependency development: the Alliance of Multinationals, State and Local Capital in Brazil*. Princeton, NJ: Princeton Univ. Press.

Fink, C., & Kenny, C. (2002). *Whither the Digital Divide? Mimeo*. Washington, DC: World Bank.

Frank, A. G. (1972). *Lumpen bourgeoisie: Lumpen development: Dependence, Class and Politics in Latin America* (M. D. Berdecio, Trans.). New York: Monthly Review Press. (Original published 1970).

Freire, P. (1970). The adult literacy process as cultural action for freedom. *Harvard Educational Review, 40*, 205–212.

Friberg, M., & Hettne, B. (1985) The Greening of the World. Towards a Non-Deterministic Model of Global Processes. In Hodder & Stoughton (Eds.), *Development as Social Transformation. Reflections on the Global Problematic* (pp. 204-270). Sevenoaks: The United Nations University.

Friedman, J. (1997). Simplifying complexity. In Olwig, K. F., & Hastrup, K. (Eds.), *Siting culture* (pp. 268–291). London: Routledge.

Gerefi, G. (1983). *Rethinking Development Theory: Insights from East Asia and Latin America*. Princeton, NJ: Princeton Univ. Press.

Ghana News Agency (2008, July 25). ISODEC urges Parliament to pull brake on GT sale.

Gibson-Graham, J. K. (1996). *The End of Capitalism as We Knew It? A Feminist Critique of Political Economy*. Blackwell.

Gibson-Graham, J. K. (2003). An ethics of the local. *Rethinking Marxism, 15*(1), 49–74. doi:10.1080/0893569032000063583

Gibson-Graham, J. K. (2005). Surplus possibilities: Post development and Community Economies. *Singapore Journal of Tropical Geography, 26*(1), 4–26. doi:10.1111/j.0129-7619.2005.00198.x

Govindan, P. (2005). The Digital Divide and Increasing Returns: Contradictions of Informational Capitalism. *The Information Society, 21*, 41–51. doi:10.1080/01972240590895900

Hall, P. (1998). *Cities in Civilization: Culture, Innovation and Urban Order*. London: Weidenfield and Nicholson.

Hammond, A. L., Kramer, W. J., Katz, R. S., Tran, J. T., & Walker, C. (2007). *The Next 4 Billion: Market Size and Business Strategy at the Base of the Pyramid*. Washington, DC: World Resource Institute & International Finance Corporation.

Hargittai, E. (2002). Second-level digital divide: differences in people's online skills, *First Monday, 7*(4). Retrieved May 6, 2008 from http://firstmonday.org/issues/issue7_4

Heeks, R. (1999). Information and Communication Technologies, Poverty and Development. *Development Informatics*. Working Paper Series, Number 5. Manchester, UK: Institute for Development Policy and Management. Retrieved October 6, 2005 from: http://www.undp.org/info21/

Heeks, R. B., & Jagun, A. (2007). Mobile Phones and Development: The Future in New Hands? *ID21 Insights Special Issue*, no.69. Retrieved May 6, 2008 from http://www.id21.org/insights/insights69/insights69.pdf

Howard, P. N. (2007). Testing the Leap-frog hypothesis: the impact of existing infrastructure and telecommunications policy on the global digital divide. *Information Communication and Society, 10*(2), 133–157. doi:10.1080/13691180701307354

Hudson, H. E. (2001). *The potential of ICT for development: Opportunities and Obstacles*. Background paper for the World Employment Report 2001. Retrieved April 6, 2006 from http://www.bib.ulb.ac.be/cdrom/wer_lawitie/back/hud_toc.htm

Huntington, S. (2007). The Change to Change: Modernization, Development and Political Order in Changing Societies. In Roberts, T. R., & Hite, A. B. (Eds.), *The Globalization and Development Reader; perspectives on Development and Global Change*. Malden, MA: Blackwell Publishers.

IFPRI. (2006). *Information and Communication Technologies for Development and Poverty Reduction: The Potential of Telecommunications* (Torero, M., & von Braun, J., Eds.). Washington, DC: Johns Hopkins University Press and IFPRI.

Ihde, D. (1990). *Technology and the lifeworld*. Bloomington, IN: Indiana University Press.

International Tel ecommunication Union (ITU) (2007). *Measuring the Information Society*. ITU, Geneva. February 2007. Retrieved December 5, 2008 from http://www.itu.int/ITU-D/ict/publications/ict-oi/2007/index.html

International Telecommunication Union (ITU). (2008a). *ICT in Africa: Digital Divide to Digital Opportunity*. ITU, Geneva. Retrieved on December 5, 2008 from http://www.itu.int/newsroom/features/ict_africa.html

International Telecommunication Union (ITU). (2008b). *Report on the World Summit on the Information Society Stocktaking: World Conference on the Information Society Geneva 2003 - Tunis 2007*. Place des Nations 1211 Geneva 20, Switzerland. Retrieved March 20, 2009 from http://www.itu.int/wsis/stocktaking/docs/2008/WSIS-Stocktaking2008-e.pdf

International Telecommunications Union (ITU). (2006a). World Telecommunication/ICT Development Report 2006: Measuring ICT for social and economic development. Retrieved December 5, 2008 from http://www.itu.int/ITU-D/ict/publications/wtdr_06/index.html

International Telecommunications Union (ITU). (2006b). Trends in the Information Society, ITU, Geneva. Executive Summary, Retrieved December 20, 2008 from http://www.itu.int/dms_pub/itu-s/opb/pol/S-POL-WSIS.RPT-2006-R1-SUM-PDF-E.pdf

ITU/UNCTAD. (2007). *World Information Society Report: Beyond WSIS*. Combined Reports for UN Summit held in Geneva December 2003 and Tunis in November 2005. ITU/UNCTAD, Geneva. Retrieved December 5, 2008 from www.itu.int/wisr and on the UNCTAD website at www.unctad.org/wisr

James, J. (2005). The global digital divide in the Internet: Developed countries constructs and Third World realities. *Journal of Information Science, 31*(2), 114–123. doi:10.1177/0165551505050788

James, J. (2006). Bridging the source of the digital divide. In *Digital Opportunity Forum, Background Papers and Presentations* (Seoul, Republic of Korea). Retrieved September 5, 2008 from http://www.dof.or.kr/htm/2/ann_001.asp

James, J. (2007). From origins to implications: key aspects in the debate over the digital divide. *Journal of Information Technology, 22*(3), 284–296. doi:10.1057/palgrave.jit.2000097

Johnson, J. (1996). *The information highway from hell: a worst-case scenario.* Paper presented at the Association for Computing Machinery's 1995 Conference on Computer-Human Interaction, 1996. Retrieved March 20, 2000 from Gopher://gopher. etext.org/h0/CPSR/nii/hell

Jovanovic, B., & Rousseau, P. (2005). General Purpose Technologies. NBER Working Paper Series, No. W11093. Retrieved August 2, 2007 from http://.com/abstract=657607

Kauffman, R., & Techatassanasoontorn, A. A. (2005). International Diffusion of Digital Mobile Technology: A Coupled-Hazard State-Based Approach. *Information Technology Management, 6*(2-3), 253–292. doi:10.1007/s10799-005-5882-3

Kole, E. S. (1998). Myths and Realities in Internet Discourse: Using Computer Networks for Data Collection and the Beijing World Conference on Women. *The Gazette. The International Journal for Communication Studies, 60*(4), 343–360.

Kole, E. S. (2002). An Alternative Conceptualization of ICT and Development, position statement for the conference. *Global E-Quality. Rethinking ICT in Africa, Asia and Latin America*. Organized by the International Institute of Infonomics and the A3 Network, 24-27 March 2002, Maastricht, the Netherlands. Retrieved October 5 2008 from: http://www.infonomics.nl/globalequality/ideas/kole.htm

Kuttan, A., & Peters, L. (2003). *From digital divide to digital opportunity*. Lanham, MD: Scarecrow Press.

Kyem, P. A. K., & Kyem, O. (2006). Africa's Participation in the Revolution in Information and Communications Technology: an Opportunity for Economic Development or Deprivation. In K. Konadu-Agyemang & K. Panford (Eds.), *Africa's Development in the Twenty First Century: Pertinent Socio-Economic and Development Issues* (pp. 358-390). Ashgate: UK.

Kyem, P. A. K., & LeMaire, P. K. (2006). Transforming Recent Gains in the Digital Divide into Digital Opportunities: Africa and the Boom in Mobile Phone Subscription. *Electronic Journal of Information Systems in Developing Countries, 28*. Retrieved December 5, 2008 from http://www.ejisdc.org/ojs2/index.php/ejisdc/article/view/343

Lerner, D. (1958). *The Passing of Traditional Society: Modernizing the Middle East*. New York: Free Press.

Marker, P., McNamara, K., & Wallace, L. (2002). *The significance of information and communication technologies for reducing poverty*. Department of International Development UK, London. Retrieved April 25, 2009 from http://www.dfid.gov.uk/Pubs/files/ictpoverty.pdf

Martin, S. (2003). Is the Digital Divide Really Closing? A critique of inequality measurement in a nation online. *Information Technology and Society*, *1*(4), 1–13. doi:10.1080/0268396031000077413

Mason, S., & Hacker, K. (2003). Applying Communication Theory to Digital Divide Research, *Information. Technology and Society*, *1*(5), 40–55.

Mayur, R., & Daviss, B. (1998). *The Technology of Hope: Tools to Empower the World's Poorest Peoples. The Futurist*. January-February.

McAnany, E. (1983). From Modernization and Diffusion to Dependency and Beyond: Theory and Practice in Communication for Social Change in the 1980s. *Development Communications in the Third World, Proceedings of a Midwest Symposium*. University of Illinois.

Milanovic, B. (2005). *Worlds Apart: Measuring International and Global Inequality*. Princeton, NJ: Princeton University Press.

Mitchell, M. M. 2003. Possible, Probable and Preferable Futures of the Digital Divide. *Informing Science InSITE - Where Parallels Intersect*. Retrieved May 8, 2007 from http://www.informingscience.org/proceedings/IS2003Proceedings/docs/083Mitch.pdf

Mumford, L. (1934). *Technics and civilization*. New York: Harcourt, Brace and Company.

Murdock, G. (2002). Review Article: Debating Digital Divides. *European Journal of Communication*, 17, 385. Retrieved December 7, 2008 from http://ejc.sagepub.com/cgi/content/abstract/17/3/385

Murphy, J. T. (2008). Economic Geographies of the Global South: Missed Opportunities and promoting intersections with development studies. *Geography Compass*, *2*(3), 851–873. doi:10.1111/j.1749-8198.2008.00119.x

Norris, P. (2001). *Digital Divide: Civic Engagement, Information Poverty, and the Internet Worldwide*. Cambridge: Cambridge University Press.

O'Neil, D. V., & Baker, P. M. A. (2003). The role of institutional motivations in technological adoption: Implementation of DeKalb County's Family Technology Resource Centers. *The Information Society*, *19*(4), 305–314. doi:10.1080/01972240309485

OECD. (2003). *ICT and Economic Growth: Evidence from OECD Countries, Industries and Firms*. Paris, France. Retrieved October 2009 from http://www.labs-associados.org/docs/OCDE_TIC.PDF

Ojo, T. (2004). Old paradigm and Information & Communication Technologies for Development Agenda in Africa: Modernization as Context. *Journal of Information Technology Impact, 4*(3), 139-150. Retrieved May 7, 2009 from http://www.allacademic.com/meta/p14108_index.html.

Persaud, A. (2001). The knowledge gap. *Foreign Affairs (Council on Foreign Relations)*, *80*(2), 107–117.

Pritchett, L. (1997). Divergence, Big Time. *The Journal of Economic Perspectives*, *11*(3), 3–17.

Roberts, T. R., & Hite, A. B. (Eds.). (2007). *The Globalization and Development Reader; perspectives on Development and Global Change*. Malden, MA: Blackwell Publishers.

Robinson, J. P., Barth, K., & Kohut, A. (1997). Social Impact Research – Personal Computers, Mass Media, and Use of Time. *Social Science Computer Review*, *15*(1), 65–82. doi:10.1177/089443939701500107

Sachs, J. D. (2005). *The end of poverty: economic possibilities for our time*. New York: Penguin Press.

Schech, S. (2002). Wired for change: the links between ICT and development discourses. *Journal of International Development, 14*(1), 13–23. doi:10.1002/jid.870

Schramm, W. (1979). *Mass Media and National Development*. Paris: UNESCO.

Schuurman, F. (1993). Development Theory in the 1990s, introduction. In Schuurman, F. (Ed.), *Beyond the Impasse. New Directions in Development Theory*. London, New Jersey: Zed Books.

Sciadas, G. (2005a). Infostates across Countries and Over Time: Conceptualization, Modeling, and Measurements of the Digital Divide: View from Practice. *Information Technology for Development, 11*(3), 299–304. doi:10.1002/itdj.20018

Sciadas, G. (Ed.). (2005b). *From digital divide to digital opportunities; measuring infostates for development*. Montreal, Quebec: Claude-Yves Charron. Retrieved May 20, 2009 from http://www.itu.int/ITU-D/ict/publications/dd/material/index_ict_opp.pdf

Sein, M. K., & Harindranath, G. (2004). Conceptualising the ICT artefact: Towards understanding the role of ICT in national development. *The Information Society, 20*, 15–24. doi:10.1080/01972240490269942

Sen, A. (1992). *Inequality Reexamined*. Oxford: Oxford University Press.

Sen, A. (1997a). *Development and Thinking at the Beginning of the 21ˢᵗ Century. STICERD – Development Economics Papers 02. Suntory and Toyota International Centres for Economics and Related Disciplines*. LSE.

Sen, A. (1997b). *What's the Point of a Development Strategy. STICERD – Development Economics Papers 03. Suntory and Toyota International Centres for Economics and Related Disciplines*. LSE.

Servaes, J. (1989). *One World, Multiple Cultures. A new paradigm on Communication for Development*. Leuven: Acco.

Servaes, J. (Ed.). (2002). *Approaches to Development Communication, Part 1 Development Theory*. Paris: UNESCO.

Servaes, J., & Malikhao, P. (2002). Development communication approaches in international perspective. In Servaes, J. (Ed.), *Approaches to development communication*. Paris: UNESCO.

Singer, H. (1970). Dualism Revisited: A new approach to problems of the dual society. *The Journal of Development Studies, 7*(1), 60–75. doi:10.1080/00220387008421348

Smillie, I. (1999). Narrowing the digital divide: Notes on a global Netscape. Retrieved December 28, 2008 from http://www.unites.org/html/resource/smillie/smillie0.htm

Souter, D. (2004). ICT and Economic Growth in Developing Countries, Part I. *The DAC Journal, 5*(4).

Stiglitz, J. E. (2003). *Globalization and Its Discontents*. New York: W.W. Norton.

Sunkel, O. (1972, April). "Big Business" and "Oependencia.". *Foreign Affairs (Council on Foreign Relations)*, 517–531.

UNDP. (1998). Information and Communication Technologies for Development. UNDP, New York. Retrieved June 20, 2005 from http://www.undp.org/info21/

UNDP. (2005) *UN Millennium Project: Investing in Development: A practical Plan to Achieve the Millennium Development, Goals. Overview*. Washington, D.C. UNDP. Retrieved June 20, 2008 from http://www.unmillenniumproject.org/reports/index_overview.htm van Dijk, Jan (2005). Pitfalls of a Metaphor. Retrieved November 10, 2008 from http://www.gw.utwente.nl/vandijk/research/digital_divide/Digital_Divide_overigen/a_framework_for_digital_divide.doc/

United Nations Conference on Trade and Development (UNCTAD), (2006). *The Digital Divide Report: ICT Development Indices.* United Nations, New York and Geneva. Retrieved June 20, 2008 from http://www.unctad.org/en/docs/sdteecb20061_en.pdf

United Nations Conference on Trade and Development (UNCTAD) (2008). *Information Economy Report; Science and Technology for Development; the new paradigm for ICT.* UNITED NATIONS New York and Geneva. Retrieved June 28, 2008 from: http://www.unctad.org/en/docs/sdteecb20071_en.pdf

Van Rossem, R. (1996). The world-system paradigm as general theory of development: A cross-national test. *American Sociological Review, 61,* 508–527. doi:10.2307/2096362

Varian, H. (2006, January 12). American Companies Show an Edge in Putting Information Technology to Work. *New York Times.* Retrieved August 10, 2007 from http://www.topics.mytimes.com/top/reference/timestopics/people/v/hal_r_varian/index.html/?offset¼10& Vehovar, V., Sicherl, P., H¨using, T., & Dolnicar, V. (2006). Methodological Challenges of Digital Divide Measurements. *The Information Society,* 22, 279–290.

Vodafone, (2005). Africa: Impact of Mobile Phones: Moving the debate forward. *Mobile Phone Paper Series* No. 3. Retrieved July 2, 2008 from http://www.vodafone.com/etc/medialib/attachments/cr_downloads.Par.78351.File.tmp/GPP_SIM_paper_3.pdf

Waisbord, S. (2001). *Family Tree of Theories, Methods and Strategies in Development Communication.* Prepared for The Rockefeller Foundation, May 2001. Retrieved on July 2nd 2008 from: http://www.comminit.com/pdf/familytree.pdf

Wallerstein, I. (1974). *The Modern World System.* Academic Press.

Wallerstein, I. (1979). *The Capitalist World Economy.* Cambridge: Cambridge University Press.

Warschauer, M. (2002). Reconceptualizing the Digital Divide. *First Monday, 7*(7). Retrieved July 7, 2008 from http://131.193.153.231/www/issues/issue7_7/warschauer/index.html

Warschauer, M. (2003). Dissecting the "Digital Divide": A Case Study in Egypt. *The Information Society, 19*(4), 297–304. doi:10.1080/01972240309490

Waverman, L., Meschi, M., & Fuss, M. (2005). The Impact of Telecoms on Economic Growth in Developing Countries. *The Vodafone Policy Paper Series, 3,* 10-23. Retrieved July 2, 2008 from http://www.vodafone.com/etc/medialib/attachments/cr_downloads.Par.78351.File.tmp/GPP_SIM_paper_3.pdf

Weick, K. (1995). *Sense making in organizations.* Thousand Oaks, CA: Sage.

Werle, R. (2005). *The Dynamics of the digital divide.* Retrieved June 15,2008 from http://www.mpi-fg-koeln.mpg.de/people/we/Links/Digital%20Divide%20Dynamics.pdf

Wilhelm, A. G. (2000). *Democracy in the Digital Age: Challenges to Political Life in Cyberspace.* New York: Routledge.

World Bank. (1998). *World Development Report.* World Bank, Washington, DC. Retrieved September 6, 2006 from www.g8.utoronto.ca/summit/2000okinawa/gis.htm

Chapter 10
Social Capital and Third Places through the Internet:
Lessons from a Disadvantaged Swedish Community

Duncan Timms
University of Stirling, Scotland

Sara Ferlander
Södertörn University, Sweden

ABSTRACT

Although Sweden is generally considered to be at the forefront of the ICT revolution and to have high levels of social capital – interpersonal trust and participation – there remain areas and populations which are relatively disadvantaged. In this chapter we examine a number of efforts which have attempted to make use of ICT to enhance social capital in a Stockholm suburb which has been stigmatised in the press and which contains relatively high proportions of immigrants, single parents and the unemployed, all groups which are relatively excluded. An initial effort, based on the installation of a local community network, largely failed. A second effort, based on a locally-run Internet Café was more successful, with the café operating as a Third Place, both online and offline, bridging many of the divisions characterising the community. Despite its success in encouraging participation, trust and community identity, the IT-Café could not be sustained following the end of project funding and a change in personnel. The factors accompanying the success and failure of the Swedish undertakings provide lessons for other efforts to use ICTs in attempts to enhance social inclusion and community.

INTRODUCTION

Social capital, defined in terms of the density and nature of social participation, the degree of trust and the sense of community identity, has become a pivotal concept in both social theory and social policy (see for example Bourdieu, 1985; Coleman, 1988; Putnam, 1993, 2000; Field, 2003; Halpern, 2005). An important facilitator of social capital in local communities has been the existence of 'third places', informal public meeting spaces, apart from work and home, which provide the setting

DOI: 10.4018/978-1-61520-799-2.ch010

for informal public life. According to Oldenburg (1989, p.16):

The third place is a generic designation for a great variety of public spaces that host the regular, voluntary, informal, and happily anticipated gatherings of individuals beyond the realms of home and work.

In a celebration of the "great good places at the heart of our communities", Oldenburg (2001, p.2) writes about the contribution of third places to informal collective effort:

Essential to informal collective effort is the habit of association, and essential to informal association are places where people may gather freely and frequently and with relative ease.

Effective third places provide arenas for the creation of both bonding and bridging forms of social capital (Putnam, 2000), providing opportunities for people to bond with others similar to themselves, while at the same time facilitating the development of bridging relationships with others who are different. Bonding relationships, sometimes associated with kinship ties, give rise to strong feelings of identity and are often multi-stranded. Bridging relationships are more likely to be single-stranded; Granovetter (1973, 1982) refers to such ties as being "weak", but as implying the existence of "thin impersonal trust with strangers" Both forms of relationship are likely to be sparse in communities which combine diversity with disadvantage and their relative absence is associated with other indicators of low social capital such as a lack of trust and low community identity.

Developments in Western urban society, including developments in communications technologies, the segregation of workplace and home, changes in the nature and allocation of roles between the genders and the generations and the economics of leisure, have led to a perceived decline in the number of physical locations which can serve as third places, especially in suburban areas. Public houses, coffee bars, community centres, corner shops and other sites which served as third places up to and including the middle decades of the twentieth century, find themselves under increasing pressure to meet commercial and other targets, which limit their potential to offer public places where people can drop in and meet with others on an informal basis.

The decline in the number of third places reduces the opportunity for social encounters outside home and work and leads to an impoverishment of social capital.

Without casual regular encounters it is very difficult for all the other steps in community building to take place: discussion, organisation, action. (Advomatic, 2008)

In this view third places are a casualty of the "balkanisation" of society. The impact is likely to be especially deleterious to social capital in communities marked by heterogeneity and scarce resources, reducing the chances of strangers meeting each other in non-threatening situations and threatening both bonding and bridging relationships.

THE INTERNET, THIRD PLACES AND SOCIAL CAPITAL

The question posed by the Internet and other forms of social computing, which emphasise interactivity rather than passivity, is whether they can provide a new virtual space for informal social participation which can fulfil the roles previously played by physical third places. Dystopians suggest that rather than socialising in public, families have withdrawn to the privacy of their homes, passively watching television or sitting in front of a computer screen at the expense of engaging in "real" relationships. Supporters of the role of social computing in social inclusion believe that the facility of connecting with people and organisations free from the constraints of space and time heralds a new foundation for social capital, providing new arenas for developing the ties, shared trust and common identity which provide the foundation of social cohesion (e.g. Katz and Rice, 2002, chap.14). According to Wellman (1996, p.352):

Computer-supported social networks sustain strong, intermediate, and weak ties that provide information and social support in both specialized and broadly based relationships... Computer-mediated communication accelerates the ways in which people operate at the centers of partial, personal communities, switching rapidly and frequently between groups of ties.

From this perspective, chat rooms and other social networking sites provide online third places in which people can drop-in and socialise in ways which are analogous to those characteristic of physical third places. In his work on "virtual communities", Rheingold (2000) suggests that contacts made online can provide the basis for enduring relationships in both virtual and real worlds. A long-running series of studies in Blacksburg Electronic Village in Virginia (Kavanaugh et al., 2000, 2005) indicate a strong and reciprocal relationship between community involvement offline and use of the Internet for communication with a variety of formal and informal groups.

The potential benefits of interactive ICT may be especially pronounced in culturally diverse communities which lack physical locations where people from divergent groups can gather together in a non-threatening environment. A European Commission Worksop on ICT, Social Capital and Cultural Diversity comments:

In the context of cultural diversity, social computing could act as an enabler for social inclusion in many ways. When IEM [Immigrants and Ethnic Minorities] arrive in host countries,

they are faced with various challenges, varying from finding housing, establishing careers and searching for social support, at a point when they have just changed their social networks. Social computing applications provide new forms of social networking and knowledge sharing. Their potential in building and transforming social networks across space and time enable users to expand their social networks and the resources that emerge from these networks, hence their potential to raise social capital. They also allow a great deal of free expression and interaction amongst users, irrespective of their background. This might be an effective way of enabling and supporting social and economic integration. (Cachia et al., 2007: p.2)

Empirical studies suggest that there is a complex interplay between ICT and other forms of social interaction. Use of the Internet tends to complement other forms of communication, rather than supplanting them, and ICT can serve as either a positive or negative influence on social capital, depending on the way and context in which it is used (for an extended analysis see Pigg and Crank, 2004). In communities which already possess high social capital, the Internet provides a further arena for third place activity. It is less clear what the effect will be in less-advantaged communities characterised by cultural diversity, a general lack of trust and a poor sense of community identity. Research reported here, which concentrates on two projects which were introduced in a deliberate effort to employ ICT to overcome perceived low social capital in a marginalised Swedish community, helps to address the issue.

THE SWEDISH CONTEXT

Sweden is often cited as being at the vanguard of the Information Society. Most Swedish households have access to the Internet at home and more than three-quarters (79%) of Swedes used the Internet in 2004 (Statistics Sweden, 2004). The extent of use makes the position of those who do not use the Internet all the more disadvantaged. Castells (2001, p. 277) has pointed to the danger of digital exclusion in circumstances where most people are connected:

In a global economy, and in a network society where most things that matter are dependent on these Internet-based networks, to be switched off is to be sentenced to marginality...

Despite the widespread diffusion of ICT in Sweden across geographical divisions, educational and income levels, gender and age groups, there remain considerable variations in both access and usage, with those occupying more vulnerable social and economic positions or living in marginalised communities being at a heightened risk of exclusion (ITPS, 2003; Statistics Sweden, 2004; Ferlander & Timms, 2006). The Nordicom Internet Barometer for 2002 records that 88 per cent of those aged 25-44 years had access to a PC at a home, compared with only 34 per cent of those aged 65-79 years. Daily use of the Internet varied between 43 per cent among those aged 25-44 years and 8 per cent among those aged over 65 years. Similar distinctions are found by educational and workforce category and by household size. Ten per cent of those classified as "pensioners" made use of the Internet on an "average" day compared with 26 per cent of those classified as unemployed and 57 per cent of those classified as being in higher service occupations. Eleven per cent of those with an elementary level of education (less than nine years) made use of the Internet on a daily basis, compared with 35 per cent of those who had completed upper secondary education and 49 per cent of those with a three-year university qualification. No data exists on variations in access and usage among ethnic groups, but it may be assumed that the differences between Swedish-born and lower status migrant groups will be of a similar order of

magnitude to those generated by the other socio-demographic factors.

THE CASE STUDIES

The research reported here is located in a multi-cultural suburban area of Stockholm, Skarpnäck, about ten kilometres from the city centre. The area was developed in the mid-1980s, with houses arranged in apartment blocks around central car-free courts and has a population of around 8600. In comparison with the rest of Stockholm, the area contains relatively many people belonging to disadvantaged categories, such as single parents, households with low levels of income and residents with a foreign background – categories generally considered to be at higher risk of both social and digital exclusion. In 1998, 28 per cent of the residents had a foreign background (foreign citizens born abroad or in Sweden or foreign-born Swedish citizens), compared with a figure of 18 per cent in Stockholm as a whole, and a similar proportion of all households with children were headed by single parents. In 1999, the median income was 178,000 SEK (cf. 205,200 SEK in the rest of Stockholm) (USK, 2000; Ferlander, 2003). There is a high degree of mobility, with many residents being newcomers.

The majority of houses are rented from public housing companies. The area has been stigmatised in the media, where it has been described as having 'high levels of social problems and criminality'. An article in the main Stockholm newspaper Dagens Nyheter (Bengtsson, 1999 p.3) was almost apocalyptic:

Skarpnäck was to be the new suburb where one had learnt from mistakes from older suburban areas. However, ... Skarpnäck is the vision that crashed. The social problems are immense and people are fleeing the area. Still, Skarpnäck is probably only at the beginning of its descent ... Today criminality is also a big problem. Of all suburbs Skarpnäck had the highest number of reported crimes per inhabitant in 1996-1997... Nowhere else is the gap between Swedes and foreign citizens as big as it is in Skarpnäck.

According to data from the Swedish Research and Statistics Office (Ivarsson, 1997), many residents share the negative perception of the area held by outsiders, expressing dissatisfaction with safety and order, complaining about features like graffiti, vandalism, theft, burglary and violence and bemoaning the lack of local facilities. Surveys of residents conducted in 1999 found a low level of social capital in the area (Ferlander, 2003; Ferlander and Timms, 2007). Respondents reported little local participation or informal support, had few contacts outside the area, exhibited high levels of distrust, perceived considerable tension between ethnic groups and generations, and expressed significantly lower levels of local identity than found in other areas of Stockholm.

Skarpnäck was the site of two projects specifically designed to utilise ICT in an attempt to enhance social capital: a Local Net and a publicly-funded IT-Café.

LOCAL NETS AND IT-CAFÉS

The two ICT initiatives examined are both examples of what Loader et al (2000, p.81) have termed community informatics:

Community Informatics is an approach which offers the opportunity to connect cyber-space to community-place: to investigate how ICTs can be geographically embedded and developed by community groups themselves to support networks of people ...

Local Nets, or Community Networks (Schuler, 1996), are computer networks located in geographically based communities and characterised by a focus on local issues. Their basic goal can

be described as the provision of a third place online, which can enhance social capital offline (Blanchard, 2004; Davies, 2004). Digital inclusion and community building are typically stated as explicit goals (Ferlander, 2003). In a wide-ranging review of the community networking movement, Schuler (1996) concludes that Local Nets can serve a variety of important roles in enhancing local social capital, strengthening organizations, providing local information and developing civic bonds. When successful, Local Nets can operate as (virtual) third places,

having a playful, convivial atmosphere, where conversation is [a] main activity. They are accessible and accommodating to different people, feel like a 'home away from home', where there are neither guests nor hosts, simply regular users who share the space and engage with one another as and when they choose. (Schuler, 1996)

The biggest differences between Local Nets and IT-Cafés lie in the way they provide access and the scope of the content they make available.. Both aim to make access as easy and inexpensive as possible, but, whereas Local Nets characteristically provide private access in subscribers' homes, IT-Cafés provide access in an informal public setting, combining IT provision with informal social space.

IT-Cafés take a variety of forms (see Liff and Laegran, 2003), ranging from purely commercial undertakings, in which Internet access is an adjunct to a regular café, to centres run by local authorities or voluntary agencies. These latter are frequently presented as means to overcome problems of digital exclusion and to contribute to community development. A variety of names has been used to describe such centres, for example grass-roots Telecentres, telecottages, local access centres, infocentres or community technology centres. An overview of grass-roots telecentres is provided in the web pages of telecentre.org (Telecentre 2009). All local access centres offer access to the Internet and other forms of ICT, but differ in their specific orientation and mode of operation. IT-Cafés emphasise the combination of ICT provision with an informal physical setting in which people are encouraged to relate offline as well as online. This distinguishes them from other access centres, such as those often found in libraries or schools, in which the emphasis is on training and informal face-to-face interaction may actively be discouraged.

Local Nets have as their core local pages, providing information and contacts relating to the local area; they may be organised as Intranets, with restricted access to sites outside the confines of the local community. IT-Cafés, on the other hand, provide computer and Internet access which may have few or no geographical constraints. In contrast to Local Nets, where the sharing of space is virtual rather than physical, IT-Cafés exist in a geographically-defined location and participation includes face-to-face interaction.

Both Local Nets and IT-Cafés have been presented as means of tackling low social capital in disadvantaged communities, but the volume of research on their impact remains sparse. The need for more robust empirical research on local computer initiatives has been noted by several writers (e.g. Loader & Keeble, 2004; Ferlander & Timms, 2006; Gaved et al., 2006). The relationship between Local Nets and patterns of informal association has been widely discussed, but subject to relatively little empirical research (Prell, 2003). Even less academic attention has been paid to IT-Cafés (Wakeford, 2003).

This chapter aims to examine how a Local Net and a public IT-Café in a disadvantaged area of Stockholm have influenced social capital as indexed by informal and formal association, trust, social cohesion and local identity, and the extent to which they have provided new locations for the development of third places. The projects took place sequentially, but differences in their impact suggest a number of lessons for other efforts to use ICTs in the process of community building.

Field research took place between 1998 and 2003 and included a number of questionnaire surveys, focus groups and a series of interviews (for details of the research procedures see Ferlander, 2003).

THE LOCAL NET

Skarpnet, owned by the main housing company in Skarpnäck, was one of the first local nets to be established in Sweden and its launch in August 1998 was the object of considerable attention in the media, with positive reports on TV, radio and in some newspapers. Tenants interviewed at the inception of the project were enthusiastic about the potential benefits for social cohesion in Skarpnäck and for its effect on the reputation of the area (Ferlander, 2003).

The promotional literature accompanying the launch of the service stated that the overall goal of Skarpnet was to increase social inclusion, especially that of disadvantaged groups, such as immigrants, the unemployed and single-parent families. The language used is redolent of the desire to use the local net as a way of developing a third place online which would lead to greater social cohesion offline. As expressed by the Skarpnet manager (a senior officer at the housing company):

In Skarpnäck, there are many neighbours who meet on the stairs without talking to each other. The aim with the project is to get people engaged with one another, getting to know each other as a way of creating integration. (Personal interview)[1]

Skarpnet had ambitious and explicit goals relating to the enhancement of social capital in Skarpnäck. The Project aimed to improve the reputation of the area, making it more attractive to potential residents and promoting local pride, encouraging those already in the area to stay. It was planned that Skarpnet would provide access to useful information about the community and the services which were available. The interactive facilities of the Net were to be exploited in a variety of ways, for example by offering booking services and chat-lines with local politicians. Other services that the Project Manager planned to provide included distance education programmes, a web journal and an online newspaper.

THE INAUGURATION AND DEMISE OF SKARPNET

Skarpnet went online in August 1998. Day-to-day responsibility for Skarpnet rested with a single enthusiast, a manager in the housing company. Several organisations and funding bodies, including the city council, initially expressed interest in Skarpnet, but failed to provide any funding.

It was recognised that the creation of a successful Local Net required the participation of all groups in the area. The need to involve residents in the running of Skarpnet was recognised by the Manager:

As a housing company we should definitely not run a Local Net. It is not our role in society. It may be too much directed towards the interest of the housing company. It should be in the residents' interest. (Personal interview)

To help meet the goal of community involvement a representative 'reference group' was established. The reference group was scheduled to hold regular meetings. Among those represented in the group were the local council, the local community centre, the police, various voluntary associations, including the sports club, the 'crime prevention' group and the tenants' association, and three tenants (including one who was visually disabled). The meetings turned out to be not as regular as had been hoped. Two volunteer enthusiasts living in the area were appointed as 'ambassadors' to help create an interest in ICT, provide assistance to novice users and recruit new members to Skarpnet. The goal was to appoint an

ambassador in each apartment block, but in the event only two were appointed.

In the first stage of the project 234 households were offered a free home connection to the local network by the housing company. These households were chosen as test areas or pilots. In the event only one-fifth of these (46 households) took up the offer and were connected to the Local Net. For households which did not possess a computer with Internet capabilities, around half at the time of the Project's launch, the alternative was offered of renting a low cost Net Computer (NC). The network infrastructure was provided by a 2 Mbps Telia cable, which already existed in the area.

The Project aimed to make access to Skarpnet as cheap as possible. Despite this, financial constraints meant that charges had to be imposed: the price for surfing on Skarpnet was initially fixed at 395 SEK (c. £35) per month, with an additional price of 20 öre per minute online. It was soon realised that these prices were too high, but reductions were late in coming.

The aim was connect all tenants of the housing company, 1200 households in the area, and then to extend the Local Net to the remaining 3,400 households in Skarpnäck. The company tried to persuade the other housing agencies to join the Project. At first, there was considerable interest, but the interest cooled with time and the other agencies eventually signed a networking contract with a different operator offering ADSL broadband, a technology that came later and was cheaper.

Access to Skarpnet was controlled through passwords. Postings were monitored, enabling the Manager to keep track of people's pattern of usage and the content of their messages. A number of rules were laid down, including prohibitions on postings judged to be racist or pornographic. In addition, and more controversially, given the number of foreign-born migrants and other ethnic minorities in the area, users had to write in Swedish.

By the end of 1999, 16 months after its inception, only one-sixth of those eligible, about 200 households, had signed up to the Local Net. Usage statistics are not available, but interview data suggest that few people made more than occasional visits to the site and little of the promised content was made available. Few local agencies supplied up-to-date information and the promised interactive facilities were largely dormant. According to one interviewee (Magnus, 58):

I don't visit Skarpnet very often ... There's nothing there... You can't even get into the ICA [the main local food store].

One of the ambassadors (Anders, 48) noted that, to be successful, Skarpnet

has to include more content. It cannot only include fault reports to the housing company. It has to be something attractive so that people feel involved in it. For example on the Internet you can go to AltaVista and search for a word and get 3000 or 30000 hits ... and spend hours online, but not on Skarpnet. It's like being in a small flat, you walk round it pretty fast.

Far from the vibrant social space described by Schuler (1996) - an online third place, where people drop in to enjoy "a playful, convivial atmosphere, where conversation is [a] main activity" - Skarpnet remained a barren and formal space. Thomas (31) was pessimistic about its future:

I want to meet people [on the Net], but there is nobody there. How many actually visit the local site? I think the most important thing to do is to advertise it more, [along the lines of]: 'Everyone who has a computer should visit the site, where you can chat, exchange ideas and adverts!' Then there would be some life, but a site without content is utterly worthless, especially since not even half the residents are connected. The risk is that it will die if not put up properly.

The initial enthusiasm and general optimism expressed by the residents of Skarpnäck about

the Local Net proved to be misplaced. Problems arose in terms of finance and management and in relation to the technology. It had been intended to help finance the Project through commercial adverts, but no companies paid for advertisements, which made it even more difficult to involve others or to attract new users.

In addition to the lack of partners and financial difficulties, several technological problems affected Skarpnet. The Internet provider was not able to maintain the promised standards, resulting in irritation among users, especially novices. The booking system for the laundry rooms did not work properly, most of the other forms of booking never materialised and the promised NCs were delayed. Near the end of the Project, in order to include as many users as possible, the restriction on access to the Local Net, which required a specific password, was lifted and the Intranet-based Local Net was replaced by more general Internet access, with the Local Net being available to all free of charge. By then, however, it was too late. According to the Manager, speaking with hindsight in 2000:

Today we should never have started with an internal Intranet, but that was the only possible solution at the time. Today when there is a fixed cost and one can surf as much as one likes, the idea falls totally. When you work with the Internet there is no need of an Intranet and you can include anyone regardless of what system they use. (Personal interview)

As result of the slow take-up and the other problems, it was decided to close Skarpnet at the end of 1999. Although Skarpnet itself disappeared as a separate project, the interest and enthusiasm it had aroused resulted in a further development. Phoenix-like, an IT-Café, supported by the local council, emerged from the remnants of the Local Net.

THE IT-CAFÉ

The IT-Café was officially opened in April 2000, following a campaign by local residents, including several who had been involved in Skarpnet, complaining about the lack of local meeting-places and services. The Café was opened and sponsored by a combination of the local council, the two main housing associations in Skarpnäck and an Internet provider. It was located in the local community centre, the Culture House, situated on the main avenue which runs through the centre of Skarpnäck, within easy walking distance of the underground station connecting the suburb with the city centre.

The Culture House contained a number of other facilities, including a library, cinema, play area and meeting rooms. In a survey of Stockholm residents' views of public services, conducted in 1997, the Culture House emerged as one of the most highly regarded community facilities in Skarpnäck (Ivarsson, 1997). The full-time staff of the Café consisted of a single person, the Café-Manager, a network technician who lived in the area, had been one of the users of Skarpnet, and had a background in community work. The Café was open daily from Monday to Friday and on one evening a week. Visitors to the Café were offered access to computers and the Internet, with, if needed, IT-support and help from the manager. The Café also offered several computer courses for its visitors, including ones specially designed for elderly users and another for Spanish speakers. The Café was easily accessible by wheel chair users and had a well-used coffee area, where visitors were encouraged to chat and hold meetings.

The IT-Café offered subsidised access to computers and to the Internet. The prices were relatively low: 10 SEK (£ 0.80) for half an hour, 20 SEK (£ 1.60) for an hour and 100 SEK (£8) for a monthly membership card, which gave unlimited access during the opening hours of the Café (with a maximum of one hour if the Café was full). The equipment available to all users consisted of 13 computers, two printers (one colour and one black and white), a scanner, a fax, a digital camera and a computer projector. All the computers had Internet access and were loaded with basic productivity tools.

THE IT-CAFÉ AS A THIRD PLACE

The stated aims of the IT-Café were similar to those of Skarpnet. Both digital and social inclusion were stated as goals and the Café aimed to provide a welcoming environment, combining ICT training with the encouragement of social contacts, especially among migrants and across generations. As stated on the home page, the intention was:

To increase knowledge about the new media and to create a place where people, old and young and from different nationalities, can meet and in that way increase communication between people in the area. (Home page, accessed 2000)

The Café made a determined effort to attract groups that might otherwise be excluded from the Information Society, such as elderly people and people with a foreign background. An 81-year old interviewee explained:

The Café approached us pensioners because we are a group that doesn't work and who need to learn about computers. There was great interest from the whole of Skarpnäck and beyond. I took part in two courses and learnt a lot.

The Café appears to have been especially successful in attracting pensioners. More than a quarter, 28 per cent, of the Café users who replied to a survey of visitors, were aged over 65 years and older, compared to none among the users of Skarpnet and 11 per cent in the population of Skarpnäck as a whole. Visitors to the Café included significant numbers of single parents and the unemployed. A wide variety of mother languages was represented including Danish, Estonian, Finnish, Indonesian, Italian, Norwegian, Persian, Polish, Romany, Russian, Serbo-Croat, Turkish and Urdu. A Spanish-speaking group met weekly in the Café.

Eva (48) commented on the diversity of Café visitors: "Every time I have been here it has been very mixed." Katitzi (26) described ways in which the Café operated as an archetypal third place, encouraging bridging relationships across groups:

I have got in touch with many people in the Café. If you sit here you naturally talk to other people – different people: immigrants, Swedes, youngsters... If you make a joke everyone laughs... It's a kind of meeting-place for everyone. Not just a youth club or something only for the mentally ill. This is something for everyone.

Jurgita (47) noted that

People socialise in the Café. I've seen that. And my children have met other children here.

Greta (81) stressed ways in which the Café helped to break down barriers between the generations:

Today the girl next to me has helped me. We became friends. They are so 'sweet', these young people!

Observing cross-group interactions, the Café Manager noted

I feel quite touched when I see a youngster helping an elderly person or when an immigrant asks straight out in the room about the spelling of a word. These things happen here in the IT-Café, and I definitely think that the Café integrates people in Skarpnäck.

The Café was instrumental in developing both bridging and bonding relationships and provided a third place combining online and offline interaction. When asked whether visits to the Café had led to any new relationships, bridging differences, more than two-fifths of visitors stated that they had developed friendly contacts with people different from themselves in terms of age or nationality (43 per cent), 38 per cent reported new relationships across the gender divide and 18 per cent said they had made friends with people with different interests to themselves. Similar proportions mentioned that they had made bonding contacts with people they had not met before, but who were similar to themselves in terms of age (47 per cent), interests (38 per cent), nationality (18 per cent) or gender (18 per cent).

Several users commented that the experience of working alongside others in the Café had increased their general level of trust and confidence in others in Skarpnäck. Birgitta (59) addressed the issue specifically:

You get a feeling that people who come here are pretty decent... It is not the same feeling when you go down in the underground in the city. Then another feeling appears. When you come in here, without thinking about it, you take it for granted that the people are pretty decent. This may increase general trust in the area.

Many users explicitly appreciated the combination of face-to-face meetings and access to the Internet which the Café provided. Some specifically contrasted the social setting provided in the Café with the experience of going online at home. Margareta (68), a pensioner living on her own, was explicit:

I don't want the Internet at home because then I would be stuck at home. And I don't want that. It's so easy to come here and it is also so nice.

Similar sentiments were expressed by a younger visitor (Lucia, 22):

If you just sit in front of the computer at home, you may have difficulties in face-to-face contacts and become isolated.

Birgitta (59) noted:

It may well be that people who come here are a bit lonelier than the average ... I sometimes come here for that reason, since I work on my own I spend a lot of time at home on my own writing. Then I may as well go to the Café to print etc. and at the same time meet some people. I think the IT-Café can replace something for lonely people who find it difficult to get in contact with other people. Here you can get out and get contacts on the Internet via the computer. When you come here you don't feel totally lonely. There are other people here in the Café as well as people to chat with on the Internet.

Visitors made contact both online and offline. Immigrants used the Web to read papers from their homelands and to email friends and relatives. Lucia (22) noted that "Thanks to email I can keep in touch with my family in Italy". Jurgitta (47) found people online (in the USA) who shared her interest in pit-bull terriers. Julio (24) and Ricardo (22) used the Internet to chat with girls "from all over the world" as well as maintaining contact with girlfriends elsewhere in Sweden. Maria (31), a single parent, used the web to contact others in a similar position:

Through reading all the emails it was easy to find someone I felt a little bit extra for. I got in touch with a couple of mothers who had had similar experiences as me. They replied and I kept in regular contact with one of them. Being able to find someone like that is fantastic!

Katitzi pointed out

You can talk about everything between heaven and earth with people on the Internet... I think the

Internet leads to the creation of different interest groups and if you join those kinds of groups, for example about music or other things, you can find people with similar interests. And perhaps meet with them face-to-face.

Considerable pride was expressed in the fact that Skarpnäck was the home of a local IT facility. Katitzi observed:

I think it was a super idea. Skarpnäck needs an IT-Café instead of cutting every-thing important here. A computer is something everyone needs just now....It just struck me: I hope they don't close this place too! Then it would really be so bloody dead here! ... I think Skarpnäck becomes more attractive. It's a cool thing! When I heard there was something new I thought 'WOW – they have come up with a great idea!' First, everyone likes computers in some way. If you haven't tried them you will do it anyway since it is there all the time. Second, it simply attracts people. It really does! It looks good for Skarpnäck's appearance. If you compare with Kärrtorp and Björkhagen [neighbouring suburbs], there is nothing. As such, people come from the whole of the Green Line [the underground line connecting Skarpnäck with the city centre], so, of course, it looks good.

THE IMPACT OF THE LOCAL NET AND THE IT-CAFÉ ON SOCIAL CAPITAL

In view of the limited take up of Skarpnet, it is not surprising that it appears to have had little if any impact on social capital in the area. Even among the few people who registered for the service there is no indication of their having developed more contacts in the area, being more trusting of people in general or of public officials, or believing they had much in common with their neighbours. The only positive result was in terms of the use of the Local Net as a way of exploring the Internet, echoing the concern expressed by Doheny-Farina (1996) that Local Nets might come to resemble a "dying mid-town shopping centre".

The IT-Café was much more successful as a tool for enhancing social capital, certainly as far as its visitors were concerned. In contrast to non-visitors, Café visitors had more friends, were more trusting of others in general and public officials in particular, were less likely to perceive tensions between ethnic groups or the generations and had a much more positive image of Skarpnäck (Ferlander and Timms, 2006). The Café succeeded in developing bonding links between groups of similar individuals and bridging links across divisions, both within Skarpnäck itself and across the wider society. In each case the contacts were both online and offline.

The IT-Café is a close fit to Oldenburg's description of third places: spaces where people meet together, without deep commitment, in a friendly, semi-structured and non-frightening environment. The informality of the Café was a major factor in its success, distinguishing it from other public access points, such as those provided in libraries and schools, which are more likely to stress bureaucratic procedures, may be perceived as intimidating and have an instrumental orientation.

The literature on community development (e.g. Gilchrist, 2004) stresses the role which open and welcoming third places such as the IT-Café can play in fostering social relations among otherwise divergent groups, providing places "where people meet each other regularly, exchange pleasantries and eventually begin to form low-intensity but potentially helpful relationships" (p. 94). Effective third places provide the basis for the development of the

well-connected community ... based on flexible, self-reliant networks that contain, or have links to, a 'sufficient diversity' of skills, knowledge, interests and resources for the formation of any number of possible groups and collective initiatives. (Gilchrist, 2004, p. 94)

In communities characterised by heterogeneity and social divisions, such as Skarpnäck, third places are spaces where social capital can be maximised. They provide a neutral space where people from different backgrounds can meet, in the process exploring both the things which bond them together and those which bridge differences. The IT-Café facilitated such ties both online and offline.

REASONS FOR SUCCESS AND FAILURE

According to Rao (2001), successful community networking initiatives must be integrative, participatory and sustainable, build upon local knowledge bases, serve educational functions and support local decision-making in a context of global networking. Unfortunately Skarpnet failed to meet any of these criteria. The design of the Project included the development of a local steering group but this did not materialise and the management of Skarpnet was left in the hands of a single housing officer. The insistence on Swedish as the language for postings deterred many residents from non-Swedish backgrounds. The failure of the local authority and commercial organisations to provide financial support meant that the Project rapidly became a non-sustainable charge on the housing company. As users noted, little local information was provided and the facility to take part in online discussion forums was largely still-born. The site effectively failed as a social space. Similarly, nothing seems to have come from the plans to use the Local Net for the provision of educational materials. Only a year or so after its inauguration Skarpnet, had become little more than a gateway to the Internet. Good intentions and public enthusiasm were not able to compensate for the lack of involvement and lack of content which eventuated in the demise of Skarpnet.

The failure of Skarpnet to act as a site for local community participation is in sharp contrast to the success of the local net in "Netville", a middle-class suburb of Toronto, described by Hampton and Wellman (2002, 2003). In Netville take-up was extensive and the local net led to an increase in social participation and civic involvement. Similar findings are reported for Blacksburg Electronic Village (Kavanaugh, Cohill & Patterson, 2000). In contrast to Skarpnäck, both Netville and Blacksburg were characterised by high social capital before the installation of the community network, adding to the hypothesis that the successful use of a local net to enhance local participation may demand that social capital is high before the introduction of the technology. Where users are relatively isolated, untrusting and uninvolved, the provision of a local net, by itself, may not be sufficient to enhance social capital. Indeed it may actually be deleterious, exaggerating differences between those who are confident users and those who for one reason or another find themselves excluded.

The IT-Café in Skarpnäck satisfied all the criteria for the success of community networking initiatives outlined by Rao and added to these the combination of online and face-to-face interaction in a friendly and supportive environment. It functioned both as a physical third place and as a facilitator of online participation. The role of the Manager and the location of the Café in a well-used Community Centre were pivotal to success. As Berry, Harris and Jones pointed out in 2002 (p.1), describing the development of successful IT access centres:

Access centres function best as part of wider generic community resources that attract local people for a range of activities. ...Where they are part of generic community resources, access centres fulfil fundamental social roles that contribute to government objectives on community cohesion, social capital, and community capacity building. They reach parts that other agencies cannot reach,

and seen in this context they justify public funding. Such funding would need to reflect recognition of their role as community sector resources rather than as centres of formal learning.

The Café Manager served an important brokerage role. By specifically targeting groups of the population who were otherwise at risk of both digital and social exclusion – for example, pensioners and members of minority language groups – he was able to extend the appeal of the Café. Through a stress on informality and peer-assistance he was able to ensure that the Café operated as an archetypal third place at the heart of the community. People were able to drop in, use the Internet and chat, both online and offline. Even if they were not involved in immediate face-to-face interaction - though they often were – the fact that they could share the environment provided a basis for the development of mutual respect and trust. In the process they developed both bonding and bridging social capital. Immigrants were able to bond with others in their country of origin and to use the Internet to get up-to-date information and views about their homeland. At the same time, they were also able to develop bridging links with other members of the Skarpnäck community whom they met in the Café and to use the Internet to access other resources. Pensioners chatted with each other, online and offline, but also related to young people. Unemployed people used the Net to search for jobs, but also discovered other interests they shared. Single parents used the Web to share experiences and to make contact with others in similar circumstances, some within Skarpnäck, others elsewhere. The IT- Café operated as a third place in both physical space and, to a lesser extent, in cyberspace. It offered an informal public space where people from differing backgrounds met together in a safe and supportive context and jointly explored the opportunities offered online. It typified the communal place "which people use for specific purposes, but where they will also encounter on an equal basis people with different needs and lifestyles" (Gilchrist, 2004, p.93. Emphasis in original). Those who used the IT-Café were more trusting, had more friends and had a heightened sense of community identity than non-users. The development of bridging and bonding ties both offline and online across and among the diverse ethnic and generational groups who used the Café was a significant contribution to social capital.

THE PROBLEM OF SUSTAINABILITY: AFTER THE IT-CAFÉ

Despite the apparent success of the IT-Café as a popular third place, its survival was not guaranteed. In common with many similar projects, it was dependent on the commitment of its Manager and the availability of public funds. Neither of these proved sustainable.

It has long been characteristic of community development projects that they operate on relatively short-term financial and managerial arrangements. The IT-Café was no exception, with funding generally being provided on a year-by-year basis. Obtaining funds depended, to a large extent, on the ability of the Manager to negotiate support from local politicians. These negotiations became increasingly difficult as the years progressed and funding was constantly under threat. The "project mentality" meant that an increasing amount of effort had to be devoted to securing next year's funding, rather than expanding the services available. In the light of this, it was not surprising that the Manager decided to leave the Café in 2004, some four years after its opening and two years after the field study reported previously. Commenting on a community IT centre in south-west England, Liff and Steward (2001, p.341) note that the networking required to ensure support from funding bodies

was often sustained at high personal cost to the individuals concerned in terms of hours of work and/or low levels of pay and yet can be shown to be vital to the centre's successful operation.

Following the resignation of the original Manager, a new Manager, from outside the area and with a background in teaching and audio-visual production, rather than community work, was appointed to run the Café. A number of changes were instituted in the operation of the Café. These involved closer integration with the other activities taking place in the Culture House and a concentration on audio-visual activities. The new centre, renamed as the Mediaroom ('Medierummet'), was open on a more restricted basis than the old Café – three afternoons a week rather than daily. Its website invited residents in Skarpnäck to 'Come and make films, surf, study or why not email local politicians?'

Usage statistics are not available, but it appears that there was a considerable change in the nature of the visitors to the centre, with pensioners largely dropping out and being replaced by children and young people, mainly interested in playing games and generally 'hanging-out'. There is little evidence of any concerted attempt to widen the clientèle of the Centre, perhaps trying to re-engage the pensioner and foreign-born users who had been attracted to the IT-Café in its earlier guise. Resources were not forthcoming to enable the centre to update its equipment or to introduce new training programmes. In these circumstances, it is little surprise that the Mediaroom lost its local authority support. Financial aid was withdrawn in 2008 and at the end of November that year the Mediaroom was closed. The web page for the facility contains a simple announcement that it is closed and refers visitors to local libraries and to unspecified Internet Cafés elsewhere in Stockholm.

CONCLUSION: LESSONS FROM SKARPNÄCK

Despite the enthusiasm and good intentions of its proponents, the Local Net in Skarpnäck was essentially still-born. Its failure to attract local users and local content meant that it failed to provide an online third place and it had little or no effect on social capital. The technology adopted, designed to be user-friendly, failed to deliver and users found it difficult to get support. Insufficient attention was paid to attracting relevant local material and Skarpnet effectively became a portal to the worldwide web rather than a facility to be used by and for the local community. Few people bothered to log into the system, further reducing its attractiveness. The policy of insisting that all messages be in Swedish disenfranchised many residents in what is a multi-ethnic community. Paradoxically, what had been intended as a vehicle for enhancing a feeling of commonality and community identity had the effect of emphasising differences. The centralization of management and the lack of community involvement in the running of the local net contributed to the belief that it was a creature of the housing association, rather than something which belonged to the community. Good intentions, high expectations and the provision of ICT are not sufficient in and of themselves to guarantee their use for community building. If it is to help in the enhancement of social capital, a local net must be rooted in the community, cheap and easy to use by everyone, present relevant information and services, and encourage local participation.

The IT-Café addressed many of the weaknesses which plagued the earlier initiative. It used standard technology and had assistance on hand for those who were unfamiliar with its use. Training was available, designed to meet varying needs, and peer-support was encouraged. For four years, between 2000 and 2004, the Café provided a third place in the centre of the community. As a physical meeting place, it offered a neutral and supportive environment in which a variety of different groups, who otherwise had little contact with each other, came together, practised new skills and developed new relationships. Membership was socially inclusive and the Café was conveniently located and accessible. Users included a regular core, the atmosphere was friendly and support was available enabling people to develop their skills. The Manager acted as the facilitator of both online and offline interaction and succeeded in appealing to a wide cross-section of the community, spanning age, gender and ethnic divisions. Stress was placed on the use of ICT to connect with others and users reported a variety of ways in which they had developed bonding relationships with people sharing similar backgrounds or interests both within the local area and on a world-wide basis. Bridging relationships, crossing ethnic, generational and political divides were also developed..Within the group of users new friendships came into being between Swedish-born and foreign residents and between pensioners and youngsters. The Web was used to seek out information relating to job opportunities, health issues and a range of cultural matters. The Café provided a fertile ground for the development of enhanced social capital and those who used it reported significantly higher levels of participation and trust than non-users.

The apparent success of the IT-Café as a tool for enhancing social capital was not sufficient for it to make the transition from project to core-funding status or to raise other sources of support which would guarantee its continuation. To be sustainable, local facilities need to be firmly embedded in their community, attract support across political divides and have a financially-viable budget. The transition from IT-Café to Mediaroom weakened these supports. Rather than being perceived as a third place for the whole community, the Centre came to be seen as an expensive facility for groups of people, mainly youngsters, who could be catered for in other ways. In an era of public economies the demise of the Centre became all but inevitable. In his editorial introduction to a special issue of the Journal of Community Informatics devoted to the topic of sustainability Gurstein (2005, p.3) points out that

the challenge is to make the uses of ICTs in communities so transparent in their implementation and so compelling in their application that the issue of sustainability in effect disappears.

To attract public funding ICT initiatives must be seen as providing a general community service.

However, if the facility is seen as only providing a service to specific individual users, then the model of sustainability must necessarily be one of identifying individual revenue sources (fees for service) and immediately puts the facility into the context of market driven mechanisms. (Gurstein, 2001, p. 279)

Whether based on ICT or other forms of communication, interventions designed to enhance social capital must be owned by the communities involved and have secure funding. Although the IT-Café was well-regarded by the residents of Skarpnäck it was not able to sustain support across political parties. A commercial model, relying on user fees and financial contributions from businesses was not considered feasible or desirable. Instead reliance was placed on obtaining a succession of short-term grants from local government agencies. This approach imposes a heavy burden on project managers, diverting attention from service provision to the chase for finance. It seems inevitable that the chase will eventually fail. To be self-sustaining local centres need to mobilise a variety of resources, utilising the time and energy of local volunteers and attracting financial contributions from users as well as service providers. These contributions are difficult to mobilise in disenfranchised communities and require an additional set of brokerage activities on the part of managers.

The evidence from Skarpnäck is that ICT can be an effective tool in community building, but the provision of access by itself is not sufficient. In communities which already possess high levels of social capital, local nets can provide a valuable local facility, providing an online third place which encourages participation and facilitates social action both within and out-with the local community. In communities with a lower level of social capital, in which a sense of local community is weak, more is required. The provision of a physical location, where people can meet together on "neutral" ground in a friendly and supportive environment, is likely to be particularly important in areas where divisions and mistrust are high and people have low confidence in their abilities. What is on offer, online and offline, must be seen to be relevant and responsive to local concerns. To be successful in community-building, ICT initiatives need to be rooted in the community, able to mobilise financial and other forms of support and be perceived as being significant local assets. Successful community ICT initiatives have a reciprocal relationship with social capital (Simpson, 2005). They need to address bonding and bridging relationships within and out-with the local area and to provide third places in which members can come together. ICT provides a useful set of tools for community building, but it is the way in which they are used and the social context in which they are embedded which are of prime importance.

REFERENCES

Advomatic (2004). The Internet as Third Place. Retrieved July 3, 2009, from http://www.advomatic.com/thirdplace

Bengtsson, J. (1999). Skarpnäck – Visionen som kraschade. Dagens Nyheter 991103.

Berry, J., Harris, K., & Jones, S. (2002). The future of community-based UK online centres: Discussion paper to Dfes. Retrieved July 3, 2009 from http://www.local-level.org.uk/uploads/Future%20of%20community%20based%20centres.pdf

Blanchard, A. (2004). The Effects of Dispersed Virtual Communities on Face-to-Face Social Capital . In Huysman, M., & Wulf, V. (Eds.), *Social Capital and Information Technology*. Cambridge: The MIT Press.

Bourdieu, P. (1985). The forms of capital . In Richardson, J. G. (Ed.), *Handbook of Theory and Research for the Sociology of Education*. New York: Greenwood Press.

Cachia, R., Kluzer, S., Cabrera, M., Centeno, C., & Punie, Y. (2007). ICT, Social Capital and Cultural Diversity: Report on a Joint IPTS-DG INFOSO Workshop held in Istanbul (Turkey), 25 April 2007. Retrieved July 3, 2009 from http://www.kennisland.nl/binaries/documenten/rapporten/e-inclusion-eur23047en.pdf

Castells, M. (2001). *The Internet Galaxy*. Oxford: Oxford University Press.

Coleman, J. (1988). Social capital in the creation of human capital. *American Journal of Sociology*, *94*(Supplement), S95–S120. doi:10.1086/228943

Davies, W. (2004). Proxicommunication - ICT and the Local Public Realm. iSociety report. London: The Work Foundation. Retrieved July 3, 2009, from http://www.theworkfoundation.com/research/isociety/proxi_main.jsp

Doheny-Farina, S. (1996). *The Wired Neighborhood*. New Haven: Yale University Press.

Ferlander, S. (2003). The Internet, Social Capital and Local Community. Doctoral Dissertation. Stirling: University of Stirling. Retrieved July 3, 2009 from http://www.crdlt.stir.ac.uk/publications.htm

Ferlander, S., & Timms, D. (2006). Bridging the Dual Digital Divide: A Local Net and an IT-Café in Sweden. *Information Communication and Society*, *9*(2), 137–159. doi:10.1080/13691180600630732

Ferlander, S., & Timms, D. (2007). Social Capital and Community Building through the Internet: a Swedish Case Study in a Disadvantaged Suburban Area. Sociological Research Online, 12(5). Retrieved July 3, 2009 from http://www.socresonline.org.uk/12/5/8.html

Field, J. (2003). *Social Capital*. London: Routledge.

Gaved, M., & Anderson, B. (2006). The Impact of Local ICT Initiatives on Social Capital and Quality of Life. Chimera Working Paper 2006-6, Colchester: University of Essex.

Gilchrist, A. (2004). *The Well-Connected Community: A networking approach to community development*. Bristol: Policy Press.

Granovetter, M. S. (1973). The Strength of Weak Ties. *American Journal of Sociology*, *78*, 1360–1380. doi:10.1086/225469

Granovetter, M. S. (1982). The Strength of Weak Ties: A network theory revisited . In Marsden, P., & Lin, N. (Eds.), *Social Structure and Network Analysis*. Beverly Hills, CA: Sage.

Gurstein, M. (2001). Community Informatics, Community Networks and Strategies for Flexible Networking . In Keeble, L., & Loader, B. (Eds.), *Community Informatics: Shaping Computer-mediated Social Relations*. London: Routledge.

Gurstein, M. (2005). Editorial: Sustainability of Community ICTs and its Future. Journal of Community Informatics, 1(2). Retrieved July 3, 2009 from http://ci-journal.net/index.php/ciej/artcile/view/230/186

Halpern, D. (2005). *Social Capital*. Cambridge: Polity Press.

Hampton, K. (2003). Grieving for a Lost Network: Collective action in a wired suburb. The Information Society, 19(5), 1-13. Retrieved July 3, 2009 from http://www.mysocialnetwork.net/downloads/mobilization-final.pdf

Hampton, K., & Wellman, B. (2003). Neighboring in Netville: How the Internet supports Community and Social Capital in a Wired Suburb. City and Community, 2, 277-311. Retrieved July 3, 2009 from http://www.chass.utoronto.ca/~wellman/publications/.../neighboring/ neighboring_netville.pdf

ITPS, Swedish Institute for Growth Policy Studies. (2003). *A Learning ICT Policy for Growth and Welfare, ITPS's final report on its assignment of evaluating the Swedish ICT policy.* Stockholm: Elanders Gotab.

Ivarsson, J.-I. (1990). Medborgarinflytande i Stockholm. Levnadsförhållanden och medborgaraktiviteter i sex stadsdelar. [Stockholm: USK.]. *Utredningsrapport, 1990,* 4.

Ivarsson, J.-I. (1993). Stadsdelsnämndsförsöken i Stockholm – invånarnas reaktioner och synpunkter. [Stockholm: USK.]. *Utredningsrapport, 1993,* 3.

Ivarsson, J.-I. (1997). Så tycker brukarna om servicen i stadsdelen. [Stockholm: USK.]. *Utredningsrapport, 1997,* 3.

Ivarsson, J.-I. (2000). Servicen i stadsdelen 1999 – så tycker brukarna, jen ämförelse med 1996. [Stockholm: USK.]. *Utredningsrapport, 2000,* 1.

July 3, 2009, from http://www.isoc.org/oti/articles/0201/rao2.html

Katz, J. E., & Rice, R. E. (2002). *Social Consequences of Internet Use.* Cambridge, MA: The MIT Press.

Kavanaugh, A., Carroll, J. M., Rosson, M. B., Zin, T. T., & Reese, D. D. (2005). Community Networks: Where Offline Communities Meet Online. Journal of Computer-Mediated Communication, 10(4). Retrieved July 3, 2009, from http://jcmc.indiana.edu/ vol10/issue4/kavanaugh.html

Kavanaugh, A., Cohill, A., & Patterson, S. (2000). The use and impact of the Blacksburg Electronic Village . In Cohill, A., & Kavanaugh, A. (Eds.), *Community Networks: Lessons from Blacksburg.* Norwood, MA: Artech House.

Liff, S., Fred, S., & Watts, P. (1998). Cybercafés and Telecottages: Increasing public access to computers and the Internet. Survey report, Virtual Society? Programme, Economic and Social Research Council, United Kingdom. Retrieved July 3, 2009 from http://virtualsociety.sbs.ox.ac.uk/ text/reports/access.htm

Liff, S., & Laegran, A. S. (2003). Cybercafés: Debating the Meaning and Significance of Internet Access in a Café Environment. *New Media & Society, 5,* 307–312. doi:10.1177/14614448030053001

Liff, S., & Steward, F. (2001). Communities and community e-gateways: Networking for social inclusion . In Keeble, L., & Loader, B. D. (Eds.), *Community Informatics: Shaping Computer-Mediated Social Relations.* London: Routledge.

Loader, B. D., Hague, B. N., & Eagle, D. (2000). Embedding the 'Net: community development in the age of information . In Gurstein, M. (Ed.), *Community Informatics: Enabling Communities with Information and Communications Technologies.* Hershey, PA: Idea Group.

Loader, B. D., & Keeble, L. (2004). A Literature Review of Community Informatics Initiatives. York: Joseph Rowntree Foundation. Retrieved July 3, 2009, from http://www.jrf.org.uk/publications/ literature-review-community-informatics-initiatives

NORDICOM. (Nordiskt Informationscenter för Medie- och Kommunikationsforskning) (2002). Internetbarometern 2002. Retrieved July 3, 2009, from http://www.nordicom.gu.se/mt/filer/Inetbar%202002-3.pdf

Oldenburg, R. (1989). *The Great Good Place* (3rd ed.). New York: Paragon House.

Oldenburg, R. (2001). *Celebrating the Third Place: Inspiring Stories about the "Great Good Places" at the Heart of Our Communities*. New York: Marlowe & Company.

Pigg, K. E., & Crank, L. D. (2004) Building Community Social Capital: The Potential and Promise of Information and Communication Technologies. Journal of Community Informatics, 1(1). Retrieved July 3, 2009, from http://ci-journal.net/index.php/ciej/article/view/184/132

Prell, C. (2003). Community Networking and Social Capital: Early investigations. Journal of Computer-Mediated Communication, 8(3). Retrieved July 3, 2009, from http://jcmc.indiana.edu/vol8/issue3/prell.html

Putnam, R. D. (1993). *Making Democracy Work: Civic traditions in modern Italy*. Princeton, NJ: Princeton University Press.

Putnam, R. D. (1995). Tuning in, Tuning out: The strange disappearance of social capital in America. *Political Science and Politics, 28*, 664–683. doi:10.2307/420517

Putnam, R. D. (2000). *Bowling Alone: The collapse and revival of American community*. New York: Simon Schuster.

Rao, M. (2001). *Local Community Networks: The Human Face of the Internet Economy*. Retrieved.

Rheingold, H. (2000). *The Virtual Community: Homesteading on the Electronic Frontier* (Revised ed.). Cambridge, MA: The Harvard University Press.

Schuler, D. (1996). *New Community Networks: Wired for change*. New York: Addison-Wesley.

Simpson, L. (2005). Community Informatics and Sustainability: Why Social Capital Matters. Journal of Community Informatics, 1(2). Retrieved July 3, 2009, from http://ci-journal.net/index.php/ciej/articles/view/184/132

Statistics Sweden. (2004). Use of Computers and the Internet by Private Persons in 2004. Stockholm: Statistiska centralbyrån.

Telecentre.org. (2009). From the Ground Up: The Evolution of the Telecentre Movement. Retrieved July 3, 2009, from http://ebook.telecentre.org/

USK. (2008). Statistics by time. Retrieved July 3, 2009, from http://www.usk.stockholm.se/internet/omrfakta/tabellappl.asp?omrade=0&appl=Tidserier&resultat=Andel&sprak=eng

Wakeford, N. (2003). The Embedding of Local Culture in Global Communication: Independent Internet Cafés in London. *New Media & Society, 5*, 379–399. doi:10.1177/14614448030053005

Wellman, B. (1986). Are Personal Communities Local? A Dumpterian Reconsideration. *Social Networks, 18*(3), 347–354.

ENDNOTE

[1]   All interviews were conducted by Sara Ferlander. The majority were in Swedish. Translations are by the researchers. All names of interviewees and other informants have been changed. All those quoted have given permission.

Chapter 11
An Analysis of the Research and Impact of ICT in Education in Developing Country Contexts

Nitika Tolani-Brown
American Institutes for Research, USA

Meredith McCormac
American Institutes for Research, USA

Roy Zimmermann
American Institutes for Research, USA

ABSTRACT

Rigorous evaluations on the impact of information and communication technologies (ICTs) on learning outcomes in developing countries is sparse and often lacks the methodological quality necessary to guide policymakers towards sound, evidence-based practices. This desk study reviews research undertaken to date on the impact of ICTs on learning outcomes in developing countries. First, a series of in-depth, structured interviews with a range of stakeholders, including policymakers and academicians, researchers, users and developers of ICTs, was conducted, followed by a global literature review of published and unpublished evaluations on the educational impacts of ICTs. This study found that while qualitative studies often highlight the benefits of ICTs for learners and other stakeholders, there is little rigorous research to support a causal linkage between student learning outcomes and ICTs in the developing world. This study concludes that decision makers in developing countries are guided not by evidence or data but by intuition and other influences when choosing to invest in technology in an effort to upgrade the quality of instruction in their schools. Finally, recommendations for future evaluations are offered while considering important lessons learned from extant research.

INTRODUCTION

Globalization and rapid technological change have made knowledge a critical determinant of competitiveness in the world economy. Within less-developed countries in particular, it is becoming increasingly important for local leaders and national policymakers to use innovative information and communication technologies (ICTs) to

DOI: 10.4018/978-1-61520-799-2.ch011

develop a more sophisticated labor force, manage administrative information systems and contribute to national strategies to reduce poverty and other social issues (Pringle & Subramanian, 2004). ICT is an umbrella term that includes all technologies that manipulate and transmit information, such as radios, cellular phones, and computer hardware and software, in addition to the services and applications associated with them, such as video conferencing or distance learning (European Commission, 2001). Within the education sector, the importance of ICT lies in its potential to increase access to knowledge and services and to improve the quality of instruction for marginalized or traditionally underserved populations.

ICTs are often anecdotally associated with improvements in quality of classroom instruction, provision of innovative instructional opportunities for teachers and students, and improvements to capacity at the administrative or policy level (H. Tahar, personal communication, September 9, 2008; R. Karmacharya, personal communication, August 28, 2008). There is a sense of positive impact among practitioners, but upon closer inspection there is an absence of rigorous research to support this "positive feeling" (Trucano, 2005; Wagner et al., 2004; Wagner et al., 2005). Further, governments in developing countries (i.e. Ministries of Education) sometimes find themselves in "situations where there is pressure to acquire and adopt new technologies because of the claims of what these technologies could do to aid and leapfrog their development" (Hooker, 2008, p. 3). The hope among these practitioners is that by merely updating materials and resources, an upgraded quality of instruction will result. However, these decisions are made without a comprehensive evidence base that is grounded in rigorous evaluation methodologies. It is therefore an impossible task to estimate "the potential and reach of ICTs" and to understand the contexts in which they succeed or fail (Hooker, 2008, p. 3). In the absence of experiments in particular, such as randomized controlled trials (RCTs), it is easy

to persist in the notion that ICTs are "a magic bullet that will provide the answer to long standing educational challenges" (Derbyshire, 2003, p. 42; see also Bakia, 2001). Further, there is the danger that "technologies introduced into environments characterized by social and economic inequality tend to reinforce and even exacerbate" those inequalities, highlighting the need for incontrovertible evidence on the impacts of ICTs on student learning outcomes if accurate and reliable decisions are expected from policymakers and practitioners (Derbyshire, 2003, p. 42; see also Wagner et al., 2004; Wagner et al., 2005).

The purpose of this chapter is to examine what conclusive research has been conducted to determine the impact that ICT in education has had on student learning in developing country contexts. The current evidence base assessing the impacts of ICTs on student learning outcomes in developing countries consists primarily of qualitative studies. Very few true experiments, where participants are randomly assigned to receive an intervention, have been conducted in this arena, leaving unanswered important questions regarding the educational benefits of ICT interventions on beneficiaries. Extensive descriptive information on and evaluations of projects incorporating ICTs in educational settings in advanced economies (and even some developing countries) does exist. However, the context for studies in North America and Europe is very different from the social, economic and cultural realities often found within communities in developing countries. For example, the goals of and resources available to implementers in less-developed countries may differ significantly from goals and resources available to implementers in developed countries. In addition, the challenges associated with implementation of ICT interventions, such as physical infrastructure and telecommunication, will differ widely across and even within countries, especially when comparing developed and developing countries (Derbyshire, 2003; D. Silvernail, personal communication, August 25, 2008). In order to develop and refine

Figure 1.

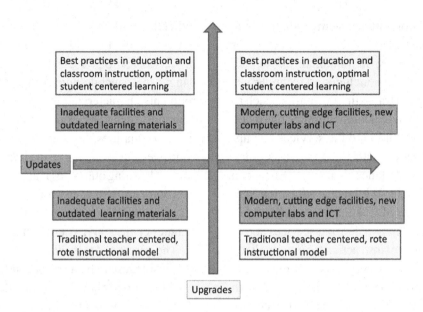

targeted educational programming, as well as broader social and educational policies, questions on the differential effects of using ICTs across subgroups (e.g. boys versus girls, special needs students versus mainstreamed students, or interventions using ICTs versus interventions that do not use ICTs) and the factors that enhance or mitigate the success of ICT interventions need to be answered. This review is a first step to consolidating the existing knowledge on the impacts of educational interventions with ICTs on student learning outcomes in developing countries.

Updating vs. Upgrading

The interviews and literature review conducted for this chapter reveal an interesting tension between updating and upgrading student learning through ICT integration. Figure 1 below suggests a framework that illustrates the outcomes of updating versus upgrading. Updates are easier to quantify, observe and implement and are therefore often placed at the top of spending priority lists. Examples of updates include new computers or other ICT equipment, new software or other programs

to replace existing resources. Other examples of updates include replacing hard copy encyclopedias with digital encyclopedias such Microsoft's Encarta or access to Wikipedia, or substituting a chalk board with higher tech presentation tools such as PowerPoint. These sorts of updates are generally considered intervention outputs.

Upgrades are a different sort of intervention and provide a more qualitative change to classroom instruction and learning. Upgrades include changes to pedagogy, such as moving from a teacher-focused delivery of instruction to a child or learner-centered model of teaching and learning, encouraging children to research, build media literacy, and construct their own meaning and understanding of knowledge.

The top right quadrant in the graphic illustrates where updates and upgrades happen together to maximize the potential of new materials with optimal models of learning. In this domain, students might use computers and the internet to discover new information, analyze and compare it to construct their own meaning and understanding of knowledge. Another example might be the use of PowerPoint as an updated mechanism for fostering peer based learning and reporting. Students might be encouraged to use PowerPoint to organize and present knowledge to one another, small groups or their entire class to solicit feedback, make revisions and share again helping them to better understand concepts and content. Multimedia and simulations might also be incorporated to address multiple learning modalities and make difficult concepts more accessible to learners therefore upgrading the quality of learning through updated ICT.

A danger exists when updating is confused or used synonymously with upgrading; when a stakeholder believes that by merely providing new/updated ICTs that the result will be an upgrade or improvement in the quality of instruction and student learning. What makes this confusion even more perplexing is that there are readily available, widely accepted toolkits and blueprints for effective integration of ICT in education designed specifically for developing country contexts. Resources such as infoDev/World Bank's ICT in Education Toolkit, GESCI's Low cost Computing Devices Analysis Toolkit and UNESCO's ICT in Education reports are provided free of charge on their web sites. However even a cursory examination of these resources reveals the complexity, challenges and costs associated with a best practice approach. Considerations must be given to a host of issues that immediately amplify both the costs and the human level of effort that will be required to effectively integrate ICT in education. Issues around professional development and training, hardware and software maintenance and replacement plans, identifying and securing content and software on a regular and continual basis, are just a small sample of issues that these toolkits highlight as essential but often go unaddressed in actual implementation.

Necessity of Monitoring and Evaluation

The primary impetus behind this desk study is to address the fact that many ICT-based reforms are approved based on a myriad of motivations (e.g. political incentives, funding, community demands, intuition, good intentions, etc.) rather than research or science. This study will demonstrate that many ICT efforts, while well intentioned, have been launched with limited amounts of empirical research to support programmatic choices. In this chapter, student learning outcomes are defined in terms of the knowledge, skills, and abilities that students have attained as a result of their involvement in a particular set of educational experiences. Multiple examples of student learning outcomes exist, from the more commonly studied achievement scores, to critical thinking and communication skills, to "technological awareness," (i.e. advanced computing and Internet skills) an important outcome when examining the effects of ICT interventions on students. For example, advocates for the integration of ICTs into educational programming suggest that ICTs can enhance student outcomes, such as attitudes towards school, achievement in key subjects, acquisition of skills such as proficiency with computing technology and the Internet, and preparation for entry into the 21st century workforce (F. Barrera, personal communication, August 25, 2008). Further, advocates of ICT integration also argue that the introduction of ICTs in the classroom can benefit teachers by improving their technology skills and awareness of innovative pedagogical approaches that are more active and student-centered than non-ICT modes of teaching. Finally, advocates argue that impacts may extend beyond the classroom and school walls to local community members who are given increased access to adult education and literacy programs through usage of ICTs (Wagner et al., 2005). However, these assertions are made in the absence of rigorous experimental evidence. Implementers and policymakers need to know more about the combinations of factors that enhance or mitigate the effects of ICTs on students in educational settings if they are to make decisions based on evidence rather than intuition.

Monitoring and evaluation (M&E) of educational programs incorporating ICTs is thus an important and highly complex issue. Setting M&E goals can facilitate successful program implementation by forcing practitioners to clearly and precisely define the scope of their programs and their expectations for impact (e.g. Wagner et al., 2005). M&E also highlights accountability, which is attractive to donors and policymakers and other key stakeholders (Wagner et al., 2005). Without rigorous evaluation, it is an almost impossible task to reach reliable and justifiable conclusions about the impacts of an intervention on key stakeholders and assess whether there is a need to adjust programming implementation and process (Wagner et al., 2005). A common problem with in programs with ICT interventions is that M&E studies track indicators and milestones and can indicate whether projects have achieved their outcomes, but few outcomes evaluations actually track impact (B. Spielvogel, personal communication, September 16, 2008).

Unfortunately, much of the existing research demonstrating the impacts of interventions employing ICTs with students and adults are from advanced economies. Studies conducted in developed countries have demonstrated that the relationship between ICTs and student outcomes is a relatively complex one. Clear consensus has not emerged on the direction or the magnitude of ICTs' effects on students, due in part to the design of program evaluations. Moreover, conclusive evidence on factors that mediate or moderate the relationship between ICTs and educational outcomes has not been demonstrated. Taking the availability of computers and student achievement as an example, Fuchs and Woessman (2004) found a negative relationship between computer availability in the home and achievement scores for students in the U.S., while several other large-scale studies also conducted within the United States found a positive relationship between computer availability in homes and test scores (e.g. Blackmore et al., 2005; National Center for

Educational Statistics, 2001). Such conflicting results within the developed world point to the need for rigorous research in both advanced and developing countries as many important questions on the impact of ICTs on student learning outcomes remain unanswered.

Descriptive, or qualitative, approaches provide the foundation for higher-level, advanced statistical analyses and more complex evaluation designs that are needed to assess whether an ICT indeed causes a particular learning or other education-related outcome. It is this association that is of most interest to program implementers and policymakers. Causation can only be assessed through carefully controlled experiments, wherein the effects of an independent variable (or multiple independent variables) are measured on a dependent variable, or outcome. The hallmark of an experiment is that confounding factors that could also affect the relationship between the independent variables of interest and the outcome are controlled for; in other words, the independent variable is the only factor that varies systematically. Conclusions are most readily drawn when supporting evidence is available from series of rigorous and carefully controlled experiments. Such experiments, however, are difficult to conduct given their costs in developing country contexts where resources are scarce—highlighting one of the many challenges to rigorous M&E efforts related to ICTs and education in developing countries.

Most evaluations (e.g. Kozma et al., 2004; Light et al., 2008; Linden et al., 2003; 2008) of ICTs in developing countries rely on correlational designs to test whether variables are associated with each other and utilize a qualitative or case study approach. Such an approach provides a detailed look into why and how ICTs may be used within educational settings to boost learning outcomes, but not whether their usage leads to desired outcomes over time. Moreover, there exists an ongoing discussion on how to define and measure impact in this field, creating a substantial barrier to conducting rigorous research and developing comparable evaluation designs. Challenges also exist at the program implementation level. Competition for scarce funding often detracts from the importance of measuring impact for policymakers and practitioners. M&E is often trivialized or given short shrift either due to the complexity of M&E tasks or a preferred focus on program activities. There may also, for example, be ethical concerns in the provision of an important resource, such as an intervention employing ICTs that increases access to educational programming, to one group of learners while denying the same resource to an equivalent disadvantaged group.

METHODOLOGY AND STRUCTURE OF REPORT

This study is unique in its focus on studies conducted within developing countries to better understand benefits and challenges to implementation in those contexts. In this study, both qualitative and more rigorous experimental techniques are discussed. The findings presented in this chapter are based on two sets of activities:

Literature Review

The literature for this report was identified through several mechanisms, including web-based searches of educational and other special interest databases, a call for papers[1] and recommendations resulting from in-depth qualitative interviews conducted with experts in the field including practitioners, developers and users of ICTs. Extant literature on the impacts of interventions employing ICTs can be divided into five groups: (1) empirical and qualitative research on ICT interventions in the US and other advanced economies (e.g. Angrist & Lavy, 2002; Cox & Marshall, 2007); (2) empirical and qualitative research on ICT interventions in developing countries; (3) theoretical reviews on the importance and utility of ICT in the education sector (e.g. Hepp et al.,

2004); (4) studies examining the cost effectiveness of ICT interventions (e.g. Bakia, 2001; Potashnik & Adkins, 1996; Wolff, 1999); and (5) policy-level reviews or "educational technology master plans, that provide a vision for the use of technology in education and institute programs that support this vision" (Commonwealth of Learning, date unknown; Kozma et al., 2004; Light & Manson, 2007; Powell, 2006) conducted by Ministries of Education in developing countries. The focus of this chapter is solely on extant evaluations of ICTs on student learning outcomes within developing countries.

Qualitative Interviews

In preparation for this review, AIR also contacted 40 experts in this field, including researchers, academicians, policy makers and practitioners, working both within the United States and Europe and in developing countries such as India, Nepal, Zambia and Afghanistan. This is a unique component not found in traditional desk studies. The goal of this effort was to request unpublished reports on the educational impacts of ICT in the developing world and to obtain a more detailed first-hand account of the challenges associated with developing, implementing and evaluating ICT interventions in developing countries. These in-depth, qualitative interviews were conducted with 25 experts.

In the remainder of this chapter, we present and discuss existing literature on the impacts of educational interventions with ICT components on student learning outcomes in developing countries. We divide the research into two categories: experimental evaluations and qualitative evaluations that use a case study approach. Following this discussion, we identify the challenges that exist to conducting evaluations of these types of interventions in the developing world. This chapter concludes with a review of the lessons learned from investment and activities witnessed during the past decade, including successes and failures, related to ICT use in education, and recommendations on how these lessons can inform policy dialogues and intervention development within the education sector in future years, focusing on the areas we believe are most salient for practitioners and policymakers.

EXPERIMENTAL EVALUATIONS ASSESSING IMPACT

Few experimental evaluations have been conducted on the impact of ICTs on student outcomes in the developing world.[2] Advocates frequently propose ICTs in the classroom, but often do so with little rigorous evidence to support their claims (F. Barrera, personal communication, August 25, 2008). Additionally, very few randomized controlled trials (RCTs) have been conducted and as a result, important questions remain unanswered, such as whether differential effects across subgroups exist, whether certain ICT interventions are more successful than others, and what factors mitigate and enhance the success of ICT interventions.

Studies employing rigorous methodologies, such as RCTs, allow researchers to generalize study findings beyond the study participants, an important design consideration when funding for evaluation is limited. By conducting experiments, researchers can attempt to construct cause-and-effect relationships and subsequently determine what types of interventions "work" and what do not. But even with the careful control of variables, causal relationships can be difficult to establish within complex social phenomena (Mertons, 2005). Ethical concerns can also surface when applying a "treatment" to one group but not to another, especially when the "treatment" is a possibly beneficial intervention for children in the developing world where resources are scarce. In this section, we review a series of experiments conducted by Linden and his colleagues (2003; 2008) estimating the effects of computer assisted learning on student achievement in India. Second,

we discuss an evaluation of the World Links Initiative, designed to establish global, educational on-line communities for secondary school students and teachers (Kozma et al., 2004). We conclude with a review of an evaluation of the Jordan Education Initiative, a set of educational reforms designed to improve the quality of education in Jordan through ICTs (Light et al., 2008).

Computer Assisted Learning in India

Our review uncovered two experimental evaluations (Linden, Bannerjee, & Duflo, 2003; He, Linden, & MacLeod, 2007) demonstrating positive impacts of computer assisted learning (CAL) in India on student achievement outcomes. Linden et al. (2003) evaluates a policy established by the government of Gujarat in 2000 that delivered four computers to each of 100 municipal primary schools in Vadodara. Pratham, a local non-governmental organization, used these computers to implement a CAL program which enabled students to spend two hours of shared computer time to play educational games that reinforce mathematic competencies ranging from first grade to the third grade. The authors utilized a randomized experimental evaluation that applied verbal and mathematics pre-tests, mid-tests, and post-tests over the course of a year to control and treatment groups of students. The results of these assessments showed statistically significant positive impacts (.47 standard deviations on average) on student achievement in mathematics.

The second set of studies (He et al, 2007) demonstrated similar outcomes. Using a randomized design, the authors assessed the outcomes of several modes of implementation of an Indian English curriculum, including a new implementation strategy for teaching English to pupils in grades 1 – 5 wherein students used a "PicTalk" machine (similar to the "Leap Frog" machine in the United States). The authors utilized a research design that allowed for evaluation of the program in a variety of locations (both rural and urban) and for implementation of the program by external players and the localities' own teachers and teaching assistants. This allowed the authors to assess the effects of the new curriculum, while also investigating the differing methods for delivering the curriculum.

The authors assessed 5,317 students in 97 schools using baseline test scores, follow-up test scores, attendance data, and demographic data. The results of the assessment showed that while the interventions were equally effective on average (.3 standard deviations), students benefitted differentially from individual technologies. For example, higher-performing students benefitted more from self-paced "PicTalk-only" interventions, but lower-performing students benefitted more from interventions that included teacher participation. This research demonstrates the benefits of conducting randomized evaluations as they can illuminate differential effects of ICTs on subgroups and form the basis for relevant and needs-based interventions.

While these studies point to the positive impacts ICTs can have on student achievement, Linden (2008) notes that this pattern occurs when ICTs change pedagogical methods, or when updates to resources happen alongside upgrades to instruction. Thus it may not be the ICT solution *itself*, but rather its impact on pedagogy that improves learner outcomes. Linden further cautioned that these experiments "do not consider variation in the way that the individual programs interact with existing resources in the classroom" (2008, p. 3). In other words, these studies do not control for other important factors in the classroom, such as teacher-student relationships, peer collaboration, and infrastructure, which may interact with ICTs and alter its relationship with learning outcomes.

Using a pair of randomized evaluations that assessed baseline test score, follow-up test scores, and demographic data, Linden's most recent study investigates the outcomes of another computer assisted learning program in Gujurat, India on

student achievement (Linden, 2008). Linden questions the "accepted knowledge" of many ICT advocates that the use of computers creates an opportunity to improve productivity in the classroom, or that updating resources automatically results in upgrading pedagogy. Such advocates claim that computers can provide a dynamic learning environment that can be tailored to the individual student's needs (Anderson, Boyle, & Reiser, 1985; Scholfield, Eurich-Fulcer, & Britt, 1994). As basic literacy and numeracy rates for students in India lag behind those of other nations, many educators view ICTs as a means of improving these indicators. To address this idea, Linden takes into account *existing* resources within classrooms by evaluating the use of computers as both a substitute and a complement to regular teaching methods. The ICT solution in this case was intended to reinforce the normal curriculum. The program allowed students one hour of independent daily computer practice with software that reinforced the days' math curriculum. Linden found that when implemented as a substitute or update (in-school program that substitutes for traditional classroom teaching), the ICT solution proved unproductive by actually lowering student test scores by .57 standard deviations. But when implemented as a complement or upgrade (out-of-school independent program) to traditional teaching in the classroom, the ICT solution had a significant effect on student learning, increasing students' tests scores by .28 standard deviations.

These studies suggest that it may not always be the ICT solution itself that leads to improvements in student achievement, but rather how the new solution is applied and how it interacts with existing resources that determine its success (Linden, 2008). These findings suggest the need to apply a broader lens to ICT interventions that focus not only on the utility of the ICT solution itself, but also on how well the solutions work relative to the specific learning environment.

The Digital Divide

Kozma, McGhee, Quellmalz, and Zalles (2004) evaluated the World Links program, a World Bank Economic Development Institute initiative that conducted a pilot program to establish global, educational on-line communities for secondary school students and teachers to expand distance learning opportunities and build broad support for economic and social development. Program activities included providing Internet connectivity for 1000 secondary schools in 26 developing countries, training and educational content, regional and global partnerships with public, private, and non-governmental organizations, telecommunications policy advice for the education sector, and monitoring and evaluation support (Kozma et al, 2004).

The evaluation of the World Links program utilized a quasi-experimental design and focused on a broad range of outcomes, including both immediate and long-term impacts on students and teachers. To test the effects of this program, Kozma et al. (2004) created surveys to collect data on the services provided by the program and distributed them to students, teachers, technology coordinators, and administrators. Performance assessments were also given to students to assess the impact of the program on student learning. Results of the surveys found that a majority of students *perceived* that the program had significant effects on their knowledge of and skills in using technology, communication and reasoning skills, and attitudes toward school and future employment. Self-reports, including in this case students' perceptions about their knowledge, skills, and abilities, can be unreliable tools of measurement. To account for this weakness, Kozma et al strove for triangulation of sources when cases of data collection consisted of self-reports. Student assessments also pointed to increased ICT skills, critical reasoning and communication skills and higher performance on academic knowledge tests for students who participated in the program, as

compared to the controls groups who did not participate. These findings suggest that ICTs (updates), when applied with intensive teacher training programs and innovative, student centered pedagogic techniques (upgrades), can bring about significant changes in educational outcomes within developing country contexts.

The Jordan Education Initiative

The Jordan Education Initiative (JEI) was launched at the Extraordinary Meeting of the World Economic Forum at the Dead Sea in Jordan in 2003. The program has four main objectives: (1) improving the delivery of education to Jordan's citizens through public-private partnerships; (2) unleashing the innovation of teachers and students through the effective use of ICT; (3) building the capacity of the local information technology industry; and (4) creating a model of reform that can be used by other countries. Light, Method, Rockman, Cressman, and Daly (2008) authored an evaluation of the JEI program. While the scope of both the JEI program and the evaluation itself is quite broad, the report uncovered valuable conclusions on the impact of ICTs and other mitigating factors, such as pedagogic techniques, on learning outcomes in students.

The evaluation utilized both quantitative and qualitative approaches to data collection. The combined efforts included surveys of teachers, principals, and 10th grade students in 20 schools, interviews with 61 school-based educators and 28 JEI stakeholders, focus groups with 36 students, visits to 14 schools and observations in 184 classrooms, interviews with relevant Ministry of Education officials, and reviews of JEI site survey data and project documentation (Light et al, 2008, p. 8). The findings indicate that the outcomes of the JEI program do not fully align with the original vision. Specifically, the vision of improved student-centered learning and its resulting positive student outcomes have not been fully realized through the program. As other studies in this report suggest, this is due in large part to teachers' perceptions of and approach towards implementing ICTs. Light et al. (2008) indicate that most teachers in the JEI program perceived ICT as a tool solely to support student memorization and practice (an update), rather than as a tool for more active, innovative approaches to learning (an upgrade). While the authors were careful to recognize teachers who did use ICT with a student-centered approach, the overall outcomes indicate that the majority of teachers did not utilize ICT in this way.

Conclusion

This section has highlighted several experimental evaluations examining the impacts of ICTs on learning outcomes in students in a range of developing country contexts, including India, Jordan, and others. While drawn from a limited pool, these studies represent a diverse set of approaches and methodological rigor. While the studies demonstrate mixed findings (i.e. both positive and negative effects on student learning outcomes), they also consistently point to the need for more focused and rigorous monitoring throughout the life of an intervention and comprehensive impact evaluation at the conclusion of the intervention. For example, Light et al. (2008) indicate that an additional weakness in the evaluation of the JEI program was a lack of internal capacity for M&E and formative research techniques to continually measure the impacts of the ICT interventions. This is a serious and pervasive challenge facing researchers and will continue to be addressed throughout this study.

QUALITATIVE EVALUATIONS ASSESSING IMPACT

Quantitative data helps analysts and policy makers understand progress towards achieving targets or pre-defined objectives (Powell, 2006). However, quantitative data does not explain *why* difficulties were experienced in achieving a particular target or exploring the context in which learning takes place (Powell, 2006). Qualitative analysis can provide data that is policy-relevant and informative. Moreover, qualitative analysis provides richer descriptive data and enables a rich, in-depth exploration of complex phenomena in a way that quantitative data cannot.

As discussed earlier, our literature review uncovered a limited pool of evaluations utilizing quantitative and mixed-methods techniques to assess the impacts of ICT interventions on students' educational outcomes in developing countries. Excluded were evaluations that examined the impacts of ICTs on teacher outcomes (e.g. Burns, 2006a; Burns, 2006b), education information management systems (including communication between networks of schools) and policy-level reviews on the "state of ICT" within countries. The number of purely qualitative evaluations, or case studies, available for review was even smaller, but included a short-term field study of a radio program designed to increase access to primary education for children in Zambia (Hollow, 2006); an evaluation of promising models of ICT integration in rural and remote areas of Mongolia (Strigel, Ariunaa & Enkhjargal, 2007); a policy-level evaluation of the conditions under which Open Educational Resources (OER), digitized materials offered freely and openly for educators, students and self-learners to use and reuse for teaching, learning and research education, improve dissemination of knowledge in sub-Saharan Africa (Mulder, 2008); and a field study exploring the role of ICT in the lives of low-literate youth in Ethiopia and Malawi (Geldof, 2008), among others. In this section, we present and discuss three qualitative evaluations of educational interventions implementing ICTs; these studies were selected because they represent a diverse set of approaches and methodological rigor within the qualitative arena. First, we discuss an evaluation of a project that integrated handheld technologies in science and mathematics enrichment courses in Thailand; second, we discuss a unique comparative evaluation of computer-based education programs in Chile and Costa Rica; finally, we discuss an evaluation of a pilot implementation of One Laptop Per Child's initiative in Ethiopia.

A Comparative Approach: Computer-Based Education in Chile and Costa Rica

In 1998, a team of researchers from Chile and Costa Rica conducted a qualitative study on the impact of introducing technology into their educational systems at the program, school, and classroom levels (Alvarez et al., 1998). This study provided the research team with a valuable opportunity to investigate in depth the impacts of computer-based education programs on schools in two developing, middle-income countries. Within Chile, the *Enlaces* program was selected. *Enlaces* was first implemented as a pilot project in 1993 as one component of a larger reform effort called the Primary Education Improvement Project (i.e. MECE) to improve the quality of primary and secondary education in Chile. *Enlaces* created a telecommunications and computer network among 100 Chilean primary schools and educational institutions to promote a variety of outcomes including "cooperative learning, higher level thinking, data management and communications skills" (Alvarez et al., 1998, p. 2). During the pilot stage of the program, *Enlaces* surpassed its original targets and integrated computers into approximately 180 schools at the primary and secondary levels (Alvarez et al., 1998). Due to the success of the pilot program, the Chilean Ministry of Education eventually scaled up the *Enlaces* program nationally, providing immediate funding for all secondary schools and half of all primary schools.[3]

In Costa Rica, the *Costa Rican Computers in Education* program was selected for evaluation by the Alvarez research team. Begun in 1988, the goal of the program was also to improve the quality of education and to increase children's ac-

cess to technology in rural and poor urban areas. This program was designed to impact outcomes such as the provision of innovative learning opportunities, student creativity, student cognitive skills and collaborative learning among students.

The qualitative study by Alverez et al. on the two programs used a case study approach at three levels of analysis – country, school and classroom and consisted of a detailed historical review of each country's technology program, semi-structured interviews with teachers, principals, and computer technology coordinators, and structured observations in classrooms where computer-based technology was used and comparison classrooms where such technology was not used. Eleven schools (6 in Chile and 5 in Costa Rica) that self-reported successful integration of technology programs were included in the sample to better understand how these programs changed student and teacher behaviors. Sample schools were all public or privately subsidized, served middle- to low-income communities, and had at least two years of experience using technology.

A breadth of outcomes was assessed in this comparative evaluation. The research team was quick to note, however, that "whereas this study provides insight into each country's experience with education technology, a much larger prospective study based on a random sample of schools would be needed to provide generalizable, systematic evidence concerning outcomes" (Alvarez et al., 1998, p. 2). While this study did not directly address student learning, it focused more on behavioral and attitudinal shifts that may have occurred as a result of introduction of computers in the classroom. These are, according to the authors, "good predictors of student learning" and "merit the continued attention of policymakers and specialists" (Alvarez et al., 1998, p. 29). Results from the evaluation indicated that students did collaborate more while using computers; moreover, students were less fearful and exhibited greater autonomy than in the traditional, non-technology based classrooms where non-ICT modes of teaching were still employed. Students in the former displayed a relaxed enthusiasm for learning not observed in the latter. Further, interviews with teachers suggested that students were also better behaved after the introduction of technology into classroom teaching and learning activities and were more motivated to come to school. Finally, some of the teachers and principals interviewed by the research team believed that the introduction of technology into classroom activities enhanced students' thinking skills, even for those students with learning disabilities, increased students' abilities to be more active and involved in the learning process, and improved the "level of sophistication and creativity in some student-developed work" (Alvarez et al., 1998, p. 30). The final report presented by the research team was able to provide individualized examples illustrating these results, context not available to studies relying on purely quantitative techniques.

While these results seem promising for advocates of computer-based educational programs, the results drawn from this evaluation must be interpreted with caution for several reasons. First, the sampling technique employed by the research team was biased. The research team asked educational supervisors to identify which schools met certain criteria, including those that were most successful in implementing computer-based educational programs. From the pool of schools identified by the computer technology trainers, the research team selected the sample schools for this evaluation. Such a sampling technique does not guarantee that the participating schools are representative of the diverse conditions and experiences for students attending Chilean and Costa Rican schools. As Alvarez et al. (1998), noted, these results were "drawn from small, non random sample of schools selected based on their [perceived] success with technology programs"—useful for "obtaining insights into successful implementation strategies," but not representative of Chilean or Costa Rican schools overall (1998). Further, by excluding schools that are not successful in implementing

computer-based educational programs, the risk of underestimating the challenges associated with implementation is heightened. Finally, this evaluation was conducted in the late 1990s. Since then, technologies have been adapted and refined in dramatic and innovative ways, country contexts—economic, social and political—have evolved significantly and even students themselves may have changed due to broader cultural shifts. Each of these schisms impacts the effects of an educational intervention—especially one that involves ICTs—on beneficiaries and highlights the need for ongoing evaluation to ensure continuing relevance of these interventions for beneficiaries.

Handheld Technologies in Science and Mathematics: A Thai Case Study

In 2000, an evaluation sponsored by the Thai Institute for the Promotion of Teaching Science and Technology (IPST) was conducted to explore the uses and impacts of handheld technologies in science and mathematics enrichment programs (Waitayangkoon, 2004 as cited in Wagner et al., 2005). The program targeted upper secondary students in seven schools, providing these students with handheld tools (updates) and teachers with professional development and curriculum materials (upgrades) on how to integrate handheld devices into classroom activities.

While the description of data collection and analysis techniques in this study is quite limited, the author did note that M&E activities, such as school and classroom observations, collection and review of teacher and student portfolios, and interviews with school principals, were conducted in order to assess the impacts of this program on secondary students' achievement and teachers' attitudes and behaviors. The project involved using low-cost technologies such as calculators, probes, and sensors to assess the design patterns of sticky rice baskets for maintaining appropriate temperature and humidity of steamed sticky rice.

Results from school and classroom observations point to a "high number of award winning student science projects," which were attributed to the "effective use of technologies, handhelds in particular" (Waitayangkoon, 2004 as cited in Wagner et al., 2005). School director reports and classroom observations also suggested that learning activities using handheld devices encouraged students to work collaboratively, bring a new level of enthusiasm and curiosity towards learning, a willingness to explore new concepts, in addition to gaining a "deeper understanding of Thai heritage and [enhanced] higher-order thinking skills" (Waitayangkoon, 2004 as cited in Wagner et al., 2005).

While the findings seem relatively small and their reliability tenuous at best (due in part to an absence of information on the data collection and analysis techniques employed in this evaluation), the implications of such a study lie in the fact that schools with limited access to ICTs, including the infrastructure and connectivity necessary to support and maintain such solutions, can effectively integrate handheld technology into secondary-level science and mathematics curricula with support from school leadership and "a collaborative network among stakeholders" (Waitayangkoon, 2004 as cited in Wagner et al., 2005). However, the importance of documenting methodology cannot be overstated. Such documentation provides other researchers the ability to verify, replicate or extend extant research to further the knowledge base on a given topic, especially important in a burgeoning field such as ICT in education (McCaston, 2005).

One Laptop per Child Initiative in Ethiopia: Piloting the XO Laptop

In recent years, prices of hardware have decreased significantly leading to an increase in low-cost computing devices in both developed and developing countries. The One Laptop per Child (OLPC) initiative was launched at the 2005 convening of the World Summit on the Information Society (WSIS) as a viable solution to meeting the Millennium Development Goals that seek to provide boys and girls with equal access to primary education. A hallmark of OLPC is the XO Laptop, or $100 Laptop as it is known informally. The primary goal of this initiative is to increase children's access to inexpensive computing technology. In her detailed commentary on and historical account of 1:1 learning approaches (wherein every teacher and student are provided with a portable laptop, notebook, or tablet PC for continuous use both in school and home) in the educational systems of developing countries, Hooker (2008) states that the emergence of low-cost digital devices represents an important trend in educational technology in conjunction with wireless communication capabilities.

For these reasons, the OLPC initiative and others, such as Intel's Classmate PC, Eduvisions's Tablet Computer, the Handheld Personal Digital Assistant, and MP3 players such as the Apple iPod, are viewed to be key tools to increasing access to education for the disadvantaged populations in developing world (Hooker, 2008). However, there is a dearth of "hard replicable evidence" on the educational impacts of these laptop innovations and the benefits to using such devices within educational settings (Hooker, 2008, p. 4).

A pilot test using a case study approach was conducted by GTZ (2008) in order to assess the impact of low-cost computing devices—specifically the OLPC XO-laptop—on disadvantaged children in the developing world. Eduvision's *Melepo* software was added to the laptops' existing software so that Ethiopian textbooks could be transmitted to students' laptops in a digital and interactive format. These textbooks were used as a launching pad for additional content that could catalyze teacher-student interaction and student collaboration, thereby updating the materials and potentially upgrading classroom instruction. The pilot test also sought to assess the educational and technical suitability of the *Melepo* software for use on XO laptops in the Ethiopian classrooms (Haertel, 2008; Hollow, 2008).

Twelve second, seventh and eighth grade teachers from two primary schools were provided with five three-hour training sessions on basic computer applications, such as reading, typing, and browsing (GTZ, 2008; Haertel, 2008). Two supplementary training sessions were then provided to teachers on how to plan classroom activities using these computing devices. During these sessions, teachers were not given a previously constructed plan, but were encouraged to develop their own strategies and activities based on their competence and comfort level with the computer applications discussed during the training. This is consistent with the OLPC model which advocates end-user centered approaches. In total, 120 students participated in the evaluation.

GTZ (2008) conducted a formative evaluation over a six week period.[4] In addition to process, the evaluation focused on students' learning behaviors, such as whether they were on task when working with the computers. According to Hollow (2008), every lesson that took place with the XO laptop during the two month trial was monitored by trained observers who completed these structured observation forms. The primary objective was to assess teacher and student behavior and impact on class environment. Students were also given a descriptive test to assess the intuitiveness of the *Melepo* software. Finally, teacher and student focus group discussions, teacher questionnaires, and headmaster interviews were administered to gain a deeper understanding of the benefits and challenges associated with implementing this intervention and the suitability of the technology for participating students and teachers.

The first phase of student observations suggested that students were successful in learning how to open the intended applications. The observations did not demonstrate whether primary students understood concepts such as how to name, save or open a file; however, several children interviewed in this study stated that this program increased their motivation to study. According to Hollow (2008), older students seemed to benefit

from the current version of the *Melepo* software but the reasons behind this conclusion are not immediately clear. Teachers requested an additional training session on intermediate computer applications, such as painting and writing, and repeatedly told the research team that the trainings "diffused a lot of their initial fear and their intrinsic resistance to introducing technology into their classes" (Hollow, 2008, p. 4). This finding suggests that with small investments in professional development, teachers are able to learn basic manipulations of computing applications and have let go of any resistance to integrating technology within their classrooms.

This pilot suffered from several challenges, demonstrative of the weaknesses of qualitative field research in general. First, faulty hardware resulted in students having to share computers. Although exact numbers were not made available, this suggests that the effectiveness of the 1:1 approach in a classroom setting could not be fully tested. In addition, the design of the evaluation was descriptive in nature and the sample size was quite small. Specifically, the final database of classroom observations included only two classes (ratings by two teachers), and 26 documented hours of observations. Finally, the evaluation took place over a period of several months, a short period of time from which to extrapolate conclusions. This suggests that conclusions drawn from this pilot should be interpreted with caution and offer limited ability to generalize.

Conclusion

This section has highlighted several well-known case studies examining the impacts of ICTs on learning outcomes in students in a range of developing country contexts, including Ethiopia, Chile, Costa Rica and Thailand. The results of these studies are mixed, pointing to both positive and negative effects on student learning outcomes, but without quantitative verification of these results, it is difficult to ascertain the significance of these findings. Case studies alone do not provide a rigorous enough base from which to draw policy-relevant or programmatic conclusions. Studies employing both quantitative and qualitative techniques will likely offer the most comprehensive assessment of impact given that researchers can use statistical techniques to identify specific factors that enhance or dilute an intervention's effectiveness and also explore, through interviews and observations, why and how these factors operate.

CHALLENGES FACING EVALUATION OF ICT FOR EDUCATION IN DEVELOPING COUNTRY CONTEXTS

Educational interventions that seek to integrate ICTs into the classroom or other learning environments will face a different set of challenges in developing country contexts compared to interventions taking place in developed countries, such as economic (including infrastructural), cultural, and social factors that impact on how an intervention program is implemented and the differing resultant outcomes (Horton & Mackay, 1999). Reliable and high quality evaluations to assess if and when ICT solutions work in educational settings is of the utmost importance given competition for scarce resources that occurs within most developing countries. Further, best practices in evaluation techniques and areas for future research should be generated from the evidence we know to be valid and reliable, in order to avoid making costly programmatic or investment mistakes. In order to do so, several challenges must be resolved.

Challenge: Absence of Standardized Evaluation Framework for Educational Interventions using ICTs

As reviewed in this chapter, a comprehensive and rigorous body of evidence of the educational impacts of ICT interventions in developing countries does not yet exist and is needed to better understand if and how particular interventions will prove effective, and to guide local and national decision making and spending of scarce donor resources. Program evaluation is an essential component to the implementation of effective educational interventions, especially those that employ innovative technologies. Creating a standardized evaluation framework that is flexible enough to allow for the multitude of resource constraints, as well as other economic and socio-cultural factors often found in developing countries, is a necessary precursor to establishing a cohesive body of evidence demonstrating the impacts of ICTs. Also important to consider are contextual factors, such as the commitment of leaders and organizational resources that can also impact the effectiveness of an intervention or may be themselves impacted by an intervention. Creating such a framework has proven to be a formidable challenge as there is no one size fits all approach that is equally effective across a diverse range of schools. However, UNESCO Institute for Statistics (2006) has made substantive strides towards this goal, generating a working list of the most commonly used indicators on ICT use in formal education.[5]

Developing evaluation standards can begin with tackling the primary challenge facing implementers and researchers in developing countries, which is to design an evaluation strategy that is appropriate for the intervention and addresses a program's potential for being scaled up or replicated in other settings. Typically, the size and complexity of an evaluation should be based upon the "pre-existing amount of evidence that is predictive of the project's effect" (Wynn, Dutta & Nelson, 2005, p. 17). Resources funneled towards evaluation activities also should be proportional to the resources invested in project activities (Wynn, et al., 2005). For example, large-scale programs that practitioners and policymakers hope to scale up or replicate nationally should be subject to a comprehensive and rigorous impact evaluation such as a RCT to ensure that the findings are generalizable to different cultural, social and economic groups. This is especially crucial in the burgeoning field of ICT in education where policymakers are increasingly called upon to make evidence-based decisions often in the absence of valid data on the educational impacts of ICT.

Challenge: Limited Local Capacity for Evaluation

Researchers and evaluators in developed countries have extensive experience in empirical—both quantitative and qualitative—techniques and evaluation design. Often, local researchers within developing countries need to be trained in modern data collection methodologies, monitoring and analysis. Training should be provided to local researchers on multidisciplinary or mixed methods approaches, wherein quantitative and qualitative data are collected to assess process and impact. For example, rapid measurement techniques that "secure the quick snapshot data that are needed to gain at least a basic sense of trends and real-world impact" are also an important tool for evaluators in developing country contexts where resources needed to do more comprehensive and time-consuming evaluations may not exist (Wynn et al., 2005, p. 35). Local expertise, "seldom harnessed by local organizations to meet local needs," is an essential and valuable resource that should be tapped in evaluation efforts (Horton & Mackay, 1999, p. 5).

Education officials also need technical assistance on how to create and maintain basic statistical systems (i.e. Educational Management Information Systems [EMIS]) and budgetary tracking systems (Kusik & Rist, 2004). Hiring external evaluators from developed nations increases the cost of such activities and potentially decreases the likelihood that the results will be fed back into program design locally. These challenges are sometimes compounded by "brain drain" in some countries (i.e. sub-Saharan Africa or conflict/post-conflict environments), or the emigration of

well-qualified students and educators out of the region (Kusek & Rist, 2004).

Standards that challenge funders to expand and enhance the type of support provided to local researchers have been developed in the domain of public health (see Wynn et al., 2005). These standards can be adapted and applied to the field of ICT in education. For example, external funders can work towards the goal of increasing local capacities for M&E by:

- Serving as a resource for local researchers focusing on ICT in education vis-à-vis provision of training on modern evaluation methodologies and issues;
- Encouraging partnerships between researchers and local projects;
- Advocating for and funding impact evaluations utilizing an experimental design and random assignment that help establish "best practices" evaluation models;
- Developing an open access clearinghouse for evaluations of ICT in education in developing and developed countries, including literature on evaluation methodologies and issues; and
- Encouraging further standardization of reporting of evaluation findings and of indicators (Wynn et al., 2005).

Challenge: Limited Funding and Resource Constraints for M&E

Most projects in the education sector have specific monies set aside for M&E activities. M&E plans often must be connected with and driven by funding streams and other administrative aspects of projects. However, additional monies often need to be allocated in order to conduct a comprehensive impact evaluation which is very difficult when resources are scarce to begin with and existing funds for M&E are diverted to program activities (B. Spielvogel, personal communication, September 16, 2008). Some researchers have suggested that grants for evaluation activities would be more attractive to government administrators than would loans for this purpose (Duflo, 2003; Wynn et al., 2005). Wynn et al. (2005) also suggest that "matching grants, or outright grants, from international funding organizations could be a way to encourage both nongovernmental organizations and government programs to undertake evaluations" (p. 19).

The costs of conducting comprehensive M&E activities can be significant, serving as a deterrent for research teams in developing countries who may lack the necessary funding or other resources. Some research suggests that between 10-20% of funds should go towards M&E (World Bank, 2004 cited in Kusek & Rist, 2004). However, the costs for a randomized or quasi-experimental impact evaluation range from $50,000 to $1 million, depending on the complexity and scope of the project, with the typical evaluation costing several hundred thousand dollars (World Bank, 2004 cited in Kusek & Rist, 2004). Further, impact evaluations can take one to five years to complete, depending on the amount of time it takes the long-term systemic effects to emerge. These challenges often create "real-world" restraints on the feasibility of randomized or quasi-experimental evaluations, causing practitioners to repeat qualitative case study models (J. Price, personal communication, September 5, 2008). While additional investment in evaluating educational interventions is clearly needed, scarce resources and limited local capacities for rigorous evaluation suggest that it is especially important for evaluators to conduct necessary and timely assessments that provide reliable and valid results which can be used to inform practice and policy.

Challenge: Lack of Demand and Ownership of Evaluations

The most basic requirement for developing a results-based M&E system, either project-based or within an overall government-sponsored framework, and for a culture of M&E to truly take root, is the commitment and enthusiasm of project stakeholders and funders. For example, Schacter (2000) found that "the key constraint to successful M&E capacity development in sub-Saharan Africa is lack of demand. Lack of demand is rooted in the absence of a strong evaluation culture, which stems from the absence of performance orientation in the public sector" (Schacter, 2000, p. 15; see also Hollow, 2008; Kusek & Rist, 2004). Relatedly, "weak political will and institutional capacity" may make long-term strategic economic, investment and policy planning challenging, and difficulties in inter-ministerial cooperation (including alignment of priorities and coordination of strategic agendas) may also exist (Schacter, 2000, p. 15).

Challenge: Confusing Updating with Upgrading

Given the dearth of evidence that correlates ICT with improved student learning, why then are so many developing countries headed down this path? Clearly, the research shows that many stakeholders and decision-makers in developing countries are driven by their intuition, that by modernizing learning environments with computers and other ICTs they believe they will be improving the learning and teaching that occurs in classrooms. Social and political pressures may also influence where scarce resources are allocated, hoping to realize the biggest and quickest impact towards reaching goals of improved student learning. However, by simply updating materials, infrastructure and resources, schools and education systems are not likely to accomplish the desired upgrades to classroom instruction and student learning.

LESSONS LEARNED AND FUTURE TRENDS

This chapter has reviewed extant experimental and qualitative evaluations on the impacts of ICTs on learning outcomes within developing countries. The pool of evidence is limited and as illustrated above, various limitations exist with the data and with the conclusions that may be drawn. First, extant evaluations using qualitative methodologies often rely on self-reported data, without validation or triangulation across multiple sources. This can lead to an *inflation, or positive bias, of the effectiveness of ICTs in educational settings*. Bias is a very real issue in most of the M&E activities conducted for educational programs with an ICT component. According to Trucano (2005; personal communication, August 27, 2008), these biases are often introduced at the M&E design stage, and include a lack of relevant and appropriate control groups, biases on the part of "independent evaluators" who may be invested in demonstrating positive effects, and biases on the part of those evaluated who may wish to demonstrate they have used the investments in ICTs well and wisely. Many ICT projects are evaluated using the funds of the project sponsors themselves, thus creating potential conflicts of interest. Additionally, when project proponents are involved in the evaluation work (especially as funders) the ideal objective nature of assessment is brought into question.

Several resources exist detailing the elements of a rigorous, comprehensive and well-designed evaluative strategy (e.g. Ripsey et al., 2004; Trucano, 2005; Wagner et al., 2005) and suggest a second lesson learned - that *evaluation can and should inform each phase of a project*. In order to establish the scope and intended objectives of a project and finalize its design, future evaluations of ICTs in the educational sector should include *a formative evaluation during the intervention's developmental phase*. An important aspect of formative evaluation is the collection of baseline data which helps to control for pre-existing conditions that may vary across locations or time points and that can significantly affect the impacts of an intervention on its beneficiaries. Relatedly, *process evaluations are a necessary component to comprehensive program evaluation* that should

occur on an ongoing basis throughout the life of the project. A process evaluation provides implementers and researchers with continuous (real-time) feedback on how the project has been implemented—and whether the program is faithful to its original design and intended scope—and any improvements or adaptations that are necessary to activities. Next, an *impact evaluation to assess the overall effects of the intervention on beneficiaries* and whether intended goals were achieved is also crucial to understanding if and why an educational intervention is effective and relevant. Finally, *wide dissemination of findings to relevant stakeholders* is also critical after a project has finished ensuring its accountability to donors and the sustainability of effects for beneficiaries.

A third lesson learned is that project *M&E activities should also include cost benefit and effectiveness analyses*, although this is seldom done in practice. In the course of this desk study, we uncovered three cost analyses that have been conducted in recent years (i.e. Bakia, 2001; Potashnik & Douglas, 1996; and Wolff, 1999). Funding allocated towards interventions with an ICT component could be used towards other non-ICT interventions. Even in settings where ICTs are demonstrated to lead to positive learning outcomes, there may be less costly interventions that could result in similar impacts on learners, perhaps providing an upgrade to instruction and learning without necessarily providing any update to materials. Similarly, funding for training and capacity building on the use of ICT interventions should be carefully and intentionally used (A. Johnson, personal communication, September 9, 2008). In developing countries where competition for scarce resources is often high, cost effectiveness and cost-benefit analyses are of great value. While RCTs can also point to the benefits of receiving an intervention (compared to receiving an alternative intervention or none at all) as this review has shown, very few RCTs have been conducted in this field. Further, monetary trade-offs such as these are rarely considered in extant evaluations examining the impacts of ICTs on learners.

Fourth, this study also found that *ICTs and their evaluations must be context-sensitive*. A uniform approach to implementation and evaluation cannot be universally applied. For each intervention, researchers must consider national-level educational goals and the fit of ICT solutions within this policy framework. For example, many countries are currently developing a national framework to guide their investment in ICTs within the educational sector. The benchmarks against which outcomes are measured should be contextualized within these frameworks such that evaluations are measuring the effectiveness of ICTs for learners and not simply for developers of ICTs. Relatedly, evaluations should consider the level and commitment of leadership for the ICT intervention, issues of infrastructure and connectivity, human resource and technical capacities, funding, and stakeholder perceptions of ICTs in the educational sector (Garrell, Isaacs, & Trucano, 2007).

A fifth lesson gleaned from our review of extant evaluations on the educational impacts of ICT in developing countries is that the *impact of ICT is also dependent upon exogenous factors*, such as teacher training and support, classroom management techniques, and support from school leadership. Successful school integration depends heavily on effective and integrated leadership at the school, regional and national levels; support systems across sectors (including professional development, infrastructure maintenance, etc.); and curricular content that is relevant to needs and interests of teachers and students.

Finally, an important lesson learned is that it is equally important to know about *the "failures" of ICT use in education*. Important data can be gleaned from these stories to inform planning and roll out of ICT interventions in other countries within developing regions in the future. Further, documenting what does not work provides policymakers with the opportunities to form evidence-based decisions and informs donors and practitioners on benefits to ICT interventions and challenges to implementation.

Suggestions for Future Evaluations

The design of future evaluations should capitalize on the lessons we have learned from evaluations of ICTs over the past few decades. Several suggestions are noted below:

Assess Impacts Longitudinally

Generally the uptake of ICTs in schools is a long process. It can take years for teachers to fully appropriate the technology and even longer to be able to effectively integrate ICT into their teaching routines. Therefore studies should look at the impact on students over a period of years. Additionally, researchers should look for differential rates of impact across subgroups. For example, socio- economic, gender, ethnic/minority status, language minority status, locality (urban or rural). This will assist in both the design of future interventions and in mid-term adjustments.

Be Comprehensive in Scope

Trucano (2005) found that the quantitative monitoring or impact data that has been collected in these evaluations focuses primarily on infrastructure (i.e. "the presence and functionality of ICT-related hardware and software") as that is the most straightforward and easiest to collect (p. 13). However, ICT interventions are often implemented in combination with other components of curricular reform or other interventions which may also impact learning outcomes. Using quantitative techniques such as surveys and qualitative techniques such as classroom observations and focus group discussions can help inform researchers and practitioners on the array of possible effects and explanations for observed effects.

Employ Mixed Methodologies

In recent years, a mixed-methods approach has become a popular alternative to selecting a purely quantitative or purely qualitative design (Day, Sammons & Gu, 2008). There is a reciprocal synergy between quantitative and qualitative approaches—for example, one may find compelling descriptions in qualitative interviews with stakeholders that can be further explored on a larger scale with survey or assessment data. On the other hand, one may want to delve into interesting patterns or trends found in survey or assessment data with in-depth interviews with relevant stakeholders. Qualitative research involves extensive time and commitment (labor intensive process) and is ultimately an approach that relies exclusively on descriptive techniques, which are very subjective. Quantitative evaluation techniques and statistical analysis, however, offer an important counter or verification to the trends observed in qualitative data collection, but do not often provide rich answers to the how and why of phenomena (e.g. Pryor & Ampiah, 2003). Evaluation designs that are dependent upon one perspective—either quantitative or qualitative—often "illuminate some part of the field... while ignoring the rest... and that... [t]he danger for any field of social science or educational research lies in its potential corruption (or worse, trivialization) by a single paradigmatic view" (Shulman, 1986, p. 4).

Explore Innovative Research Questions

Future research should extend beyond the descriptive to inform development of effective and relevant interventions that truly capitalize upon the strengths of ICTs in educational settings for learners. Indeed, the studies reviewed earlier in this chapter as well as others have pointed to several questions including the differential impacts of ICTs across school subjects, gender, and students with special needs or disabilities (e.g. Wagner & Daswani, 2006). Experts such as Trucano (2005) have suggested other research questions to pursue, such as the conditions under which technologies become a hindrance to classroom learning, the impacts of technologies on teaching and learning styles and whether the exposure to and use of ICTs affects future educational and employment outcomes for learners.

CONCLUSION

The role of and potential for ICTs in the education sector is not an issue separate from educational reform efforts, but rather inextricably intertwined. ICTs are important tools to meet Millennium Development Goals of access to and quality improvements of educational programming for all children. This chapter has reviewed relevant literature that investigates the impacts of ICT interventions on student learning outcomes and has highlighted the challenges that hinder rigorous evaluation of such interventions. Evaluation is a crucial process to assess how and when to use ICTs to achieve desired outcomes and to what degree perception and reality align. However, the number of reliable and methodologically rigorous studies that have been conducted on the impacts of ICTs in educational settings within developing countries is small. From this small pool, our review suggests that the impacts of ICTs on learner outcomes vary, whether positive, negative, or no impact at all. The *perception* of ICT impacts however among stakeholders is mostly positive and whether ICTs can meet these expectations is dependent upon how such solutions are implemented.

ACKNOWLEDGMENT

This work was supported by a Leader Award through USAID's EQUIP1 funding mechanism. The authors would also like to thank Mike Trucano, Senior ICT and Education Specialist with The World Bank, for his thoughtful review and constructive criticisms of an earlier version of this chapter. Finally, we also wish to thank the many individuals who agreed to be interviewed for this study and contributed their time; their feedback proved invaluable during the course of this desk review.

REFERENCES

Alverez, M. I., Roman, F., Dobles, M. C., Umana, J., Zuniga, M., Garcia, J., et al. (1998). Computers in schools: A qualitative study of Chile and Costa Rica. *Education and Technology Series: Special Issue.* Washington: The World Bank. Retrieved September 30, 3008, from http://www-wds.worldbank.org/external/default/WDSContentServer/WDSP/IB/2000/02/24/000094946_99031910575711/Rendered/PDF/multi_page.pdf

Anderson, J., Boyle, C., & Reiser, B. J. (1985). Intelligent Tutoring Systems. *Science, 228*(4698), 456–462. doi:10.1126/science.228.4698.456

Angrist, J., & Lavy, V. (2002). New evidence on classroom computers and pupil learning. *The Economic Journal, 112,* 735–765. doi:10.1111/1468-0297.00068

Bakia, M. (2001). *The costs of computers in classrooms: Data from developing countries.* Washington, DC: The Consortium for School Networking. Retrieved June 18, 2008, from http://classroomtco.cosn.org/cic.pdf

Blackmore, J., Hardcastle, L., Bamblett, E., & Owens, J. (2003). *Effective use of information and communication technology (ICT) to enhance learning for disadvantaged school students.* Centre for Education and Change; Institute of Disability Studies, Deakin University and Institute of Koorie Education. Retrieved August 3, 2008, from http://www.dest.gov.au/sectors/school_education/publications_resources/profiles/effective_use_technology_enhance_learning.htm

Burns, M. (2006a). *Using ICT for teacher professional development in Namibia.* Infodev Working Paper No. 1. Retrieved October 7, 2008, from http://www.infodev.org/en/Publication.499.html

Burns, M. (2006b). *Improving teaching quality in Guinea with interactive radio instruction.* Infodev Working Paper No. 2. Retrieved November 12, 2008, from http://www.infodev.org/en/Publication.500.html

Commonwealth of Learning. (n.d.). *An international scan of the use of ICT in education.* Washington, DC. *Commonwealth of Learning.*

Day, C., Sammons, P., & Gu, Q. (2008). Combining qualitative and quantitative methodologies in research on teachers' lives, work, and effectiveness: From integration to synergy. *Educational Researcher, 37*(6), 330–342. doi:10.3102/0013189X08324091

Derbyshire, H. (2003). *Gender issues in the use of computers in education in Africa.* London: Department for International Development (Imfundo).

European Commission (2001, December 14). *Subject: information and communication technologies in development: The role of ICTs in EC development policy.* Communication from the Commission to the Council and the European Parliament. Brussels, 770, 3.

Fuchs, T., & Woessman, L. (2004). Computers and student learning: Bivariate and multivariate evidence on the availability and use of computers at home and at school. CESifo Working Paper Series (no. 1321). Munich, Germany: CESIfo.

Geldof, M. (2008). *The interaction between low-literate youth and ICT in Ethiopia and Malawi: Fieldwork report.* Retrieved November 1, 2008, from http://www.gg.rhul.ac.uk/ict4d/workingpapers/GeldofNGOs.pdf

Haertel, H. (2008). *Low-cost devices in educational systems: The use of the "XO-Laptop" in the Ethiopian Educational System. Deutsche Gesellschaft fuer Technische Zusammenarbeit.* GTZ.

He, F., Linden, L. L., & MacLeod, M. (2007). *Teaching what teachers don't know: an assessment of the Pratham English language program.* Columbia University Department of Economics. Retrieved July 28, 2008, from http://www.columbia.edu/~ll2240/PicTalk_Working_Paper_2007-03-26.pdf

Hepp, P., Hinostroza, E., Laval, E., & Rehbein, L. (2004). *Technology in schools: Education, ICT and the knowledge society.* Washington: The World Bank.

Hinostroza, J. E., Guzmán, A., & Isaacs, S. (2002). Innovative uses of ICT in Chilean schools. *Journal of Computer Assisted Learning, 18*(4), 459–469. doi:10.1046/j.0266-4909.2002.00257.doc.x

Hollow, D. (2006). *The Lifeline Radio in Zambia: Findings and recommendations.* Working paper series. ICT4D Collective. Retrieved September 10, 2008, from www.gg.rhul.ac.uk/ict4d/HollowFreeplay.doc

Hollow, D. (2008). *Low-cost laptops for education in Ethiopia: Summary of Addis Ababa implementation report.* Internal report, ICT4D Collective. Retrieved December 2, 2008, from http://www.gg.rhul.ac.uk/ict4d/workingpapers/Hollowlaptops.pdf

Hooker, M. (2008). 1:1 Technologies/computing in the developing world: Challenging the digital divide. Working paper. Global e-Schools and Communities Initiative (GeSCI).

Horton, D., & Mackay, R. (1999). Evaluation in developing countries: An introduction. *Knowledge. Technology & Policy, 11*(4), 5–12.doi:10.1007/s12130-999-1001-9

Kozma, R., McGhee, R., Quellmalz, E., & Zalles, D. (2004). Closing the digital divide: Evaluation of the World Links Program. *International Journal of Educational Development, 24*(4), 361–381. doi:10.1016/j.ijedudev.2003.11.014

Kusek, J. Z., & Rist, R. C. (2004). *Ten steps to a results-based monitoring and evaluation system: A handbook for development practitioners.* Washington, DC: The World Bank.

Light, D. Method, F., Rockman, C., Cressman, G.M., & Daly, J. (2008). *Synthesis report: Overview and recommendations to the Jordan Education Initiative.* Washington, DC: Education Development Center, Inc.

Light, D., & Manson, M. (2007). *An educational revolution to support change in the classroom: Colombia and the educational challenges of the twenty-first century.* Washington, DC: Education Development Center, Inc, Center for Children and Technology.

Linden, L., Banerjee, A., & Duflo, E. (2003). *Computer-Assisted Learning: Evidence from a Randomized Experiment.* Poverty Action Lab Paper No. 5. Cambridge, MA: Poverty Action Lab. Retrieved October 4, 2008, from http://www.povertyactionlab.org/papers/5_Duflo_Computer-Assisted_Learning.pdf

Linden, L. L. (2008). *Complement or substitute? The effect of technology on student achievement in India.* Infodev Working Paper No. 17. Retrieved November 11, 2008, from http://www.infodev.org/en/Publication.505.html

Maclay, C., Kirkman, G., & Hawkins, R. (2005). *Global networked readiness for education: Preliminary findings from a pilot project to evaluate the impact of computers and the Internet on learning in eleven developing countries.* Washington, DC: The World Bank. Retrieved July 13, 2008, from http://siteresources.worldbank.org/EDUCATION/Resources/ 278200-1126210664195/1636971-1126210694253/Global_Network_Readiness.pdf

McCaston, M. K. (2005). *Documenting our methods and major findings*. CARE Newsletter. Retrieved August 10, 2008, from http://pqdl. care.org/Practice/Documenting%20Methods%20 and%20Findings.pdf

Mertons, D. (2005). *Research and evaluation in education and psychology: Integrating diversity with quantitative, qualitative, and mixed methods*. Thousand Oaks, CA: Sage Publications, Inc.

Mitra, S., Dangwal, R., Chatterjee, S., Jha, S., Bisht, R. S., & Kapur, P. (2005). Acquisition of computing literacy on shared public computers: Children and the "hole in the wall". *Australasian Journal of Educational Technology, 21*(3), 407–426.

Mulder, J. (2008). *Knowledge dissemination in Sub-Saharan Africa: What role for Open Educational Resources (OER)?* Master's thesis, International School for Humanities and Social Sciences, University of Amsterdam. Retrieved October 4, 2008, from http://www.gg.rhul.ac.uk/ ict4d/workingpapers/mulderOER.pdf

National Center for Educational Statistics (NCES). (2001). *The nation's report card: Mathematics 2000*. Washington, D.C.: National Center for Educational Statistics.

Potashnik, M. and Douglas Adkins (1996). Cost Analysis of Information Technology Projects in Education: Experiences from Developing Countries. *Education and Technology Series, 1*(3). Washington, DC: The World Bank.

Powell, M. (2006). *Rethinking education management information systems: Lessons from and options for less-developed countries*. Infodev Working Paper No. 6. Retrieved November 8, 2008, from http://www.infodev.org/en/Publication.504.html

Pringle, I., & Subramanian, S. (Eds.). (2004). *Profiles and experiences in ICT innovation for poverty reduction*. Paris: UNESCO.

Pryor, J., & Ampiah, J. G. (2003). *Understandings of education in an African village – the impact of ICTs. Report on DFID Research Project Ed2000-88*. London: DFID. Retrieved December 2, 2008, from http://www.dfid.gov.uk/Pubs/files/ understandedafricaedpaper52.pdf

Scholfield, J., Eurich-Fulcer, R., & Britt, C. (1994). Teachers, computer tutors, and teaching: The artificially intelligent tutor as an agent for classroom change. *American Educational Research Journal, 31*(3), 579–607.

Shulman, L. S. (1986). Those who understand: Knowledge growth in teaching. *Educational Researcher, 15*(2), 4–14.

Strigel, C., Ariunaa, L., & Enkhjargal, S. (2007). *Where desert meets technology: Findings from ICT in education initiatives in rural schools in Mongolia*. Washington, DC: RTI International.

Tinio, V. L. (2003). *ICT in education*. Bangkok: UNDP-Asia Pacific Development Information Programme (APDIP). Retrieved September 1, 2008, from http://www.apdip.net/publications/ iespprimers/eprimer-edu.pdf

Trucano, M. (2005). *Knowledge maps: ICT in education*. Washington, DC: infoDev / World Bank. Retrieved November 22, 2008, from http:// www.infodev.org/en/Publication.8.html

UNESCO Institute of Statistics. (2006). *ICTs and education indicators: Suggested core indicators based on meta-analysis of selected International School Surveys*. Montreal: UNESCO Institute of Statistics. Retrieved October 15, 2008, from http:// www.itu.int/ITU-D/ict/partnership/material/ICT_ Education_Paper_Nov_2006.pdf

Wagner, D. A., & Daswani, C. J. (2006). *Bridges to the Future Initiative: Project update and research report*. Philadelphia, PA: International Literacy Institute, University of Pennsylvania.

Wagner, D. A., & Day, B. James, T., Kozma, R.B., Miller, J. & Unwin, T. (2005). *Monitoring and evaluation of ICT in education projects: A handbook for developing countries*. Washington, DC: infoDev/World Bank. Retrieved July 24, 2008, from http://www.infodev.org/en/Publication.9.html

Wagner, D. A., Day, B., & Sun, J. (2004). *Information technologies and education for the poor in Africa (ITEPA): Recommendations for a pro-poor ICT4D non-formal education policy. Technical Report*. Philadelphia, PA: International Literacy Institute, University of Pennsylvania.

Waitayangkoon, P. (2004). *Thai project on the uses of low-cost technology in science and mathematics*. Paper presented at the International Conference on Educational Technology, Singapore.

Wolff, L. (1999). Costa Rica: Are computers in school effective? *TechKnowLogia*. Retrieved December 2, 2008, from http://www.techknowlogia.com/TKL_active_pages2/CurrentArticles/main.asp?IssueNumber=2&FileType=PDF&ArticleID=42

World Bank. (2004). *Monitoring and evaluation: Some tools, methods and approaches*. Washington, DC: The World Bank.

Wynn, B. O., Dutta, A., & Nelson, M. I. (2005). *Challenges in program evaluation of health interventions in developing countries*. Santa Monica, CA: RAND.

ENDNOTES

[1] AIR announced a Call for Input at the convening of the World Summit on the Information Society (WSIS) in May of 2008 in Geneva, Switzerland. The announcement invited policymakers, academicians, researchers and practitioners in the field of ICT to submit reliable and rigorous research undertaken to

date on the deployment of ICTs to support education goals around the world with an emphasis on the developing world. Further, these studies were to contribute towards discussions of ICTs' impact, efficacy, return on investment, and total cost of ownership. A project website was developed: www.ictimpact.org for this purpose.

[2] This literature review uncovered several experimental evaluations that investigate the impacts of ICTs on learning outcomes. As mentioned earlier, given this chapter's focus on developing country contexts, evaluations that focused on advanced economies were excluded (e.g. Angrist & Lavy, 2002; Cox & Marshall, 2007). Other studies, such as the Mitra et al (2005) evaluation of children engaging in unsupervised group learning with computers, were innovative yet only tangentially related to our focus on student learning outcomes. Additionally, Maclay et al.'s evaluation (2005) of the Global Networked Readiness for Education project presents valuable findings on possible measurements of ICT success, but its broad scope precludes detailed attention in our study. While also not within the scope of this chapter, of importance are Potashnik and Adkins' (1996) cost-benefit analysis of ICT projects in education and Tinio's (2003) outline of uses and challenges in ICT in education interventions. Such articles are illustrative of the range of methodologies used to measure the impacts of ICTs on learners.

[3] In 2000, an independent follow-up evaluation of the Enlaces program was conducted to better understand the use of ICT in Chilean schools (Hinostroza, Guzman & Isaacs, 2002). A case study approach was again utilized. Seven Chilean schools were selected. The focus of the analysis centered on identifying good practices for teachers, as well as measuring impacts on students and

the types of teaching and learning activities that were conducted in the classroom. The authors found no significant impacts on student achievement as defined by the national curriculum (measured by pass rates on national achievement tests) but study results did point to increases in skill transfer (i.e. developing "cross-curricular abilities") and opportunities to practice ICT-related skills (Hinostroza et al., 2002).

4   An expanded evaluation to be conducted by Eduvision in collaboration with the Engineering Capacity Building Programme (ECBP), with a planned rollout of 40,000 – 50,000 XO-laptops and extended formative and summative assessment, is anticipated in the near future (Hartel, 2008; Hollow, 2008; Hooker, 2008). According to GTZ (2008), this second evaluation will seek to compare students participating in the pilot program with those students not participating on several outcomes – changes in drop-out rates, improvements in achievement (measured by changes in standardized test results) and successful transition to secondary school.

5   In 2004, The Partnership on Measuring ICT for Development, an international, multi-stakeholder initiative was launched with two goals: to achieve a common, core set of international indicators that can be enhanced and expanded over time and to enhance the technical capacities of statistical offices in developing countries. In 2007, the working list of indicators was endorsed by the UN Statistical Commission and the Partnership's Task Group on Capacity-Building (TGCB) was formed to begin capacity building work at the international, national and regional levels.

Section 3
ICT4D and Economic Improvement

Chapter 12
Networking for Development:
Cornerstone for Efficiency and Impact of ICT for Development Projects

Fabio Nascimbeni
MENON Network, Belgium & Universidad Oberta de Catalunya, Spain

ABSTRACT

The chapter is about the importance of networking activities in building successful and sustainable international development cooperation (IDC) experiences. The reasoning starts from the consideration that, while society is going through a deep change process and is moving towards a network model (the so-called network society), international development cooperation still seems to adopt models and practices that were conceived for an industrial society. A brief review of the most common critics to IDC shows that increasing the level of networking and knowledge-sharing could contribute to effectively tackling the main inadequacies and challenges that IDC is facing. In turn, this would also help networking for development studies to find their place both in academic and in non-academic research and to be taken in greater account by policy makers. The concept of "networking for development", introduced in the central part of the chapter, is analyzed from different angles: first by defining the actors that should be involved and the mechanisms that should be put in place, second by reasoning on the added value of networking and on the ways to demonstrate its potential impact on IDC, and finally by mapping the relevance of the issue in a some donors' strategy.

INTRODUCTION: A GROWING NETWORKED SOCIETY

The concept of network, in all its facets, fully embodies the capacity to describe our present world as well as our perception of it. In both

developed and growing economies, we more and more use transport networks, rely on energy networks, communicate through ICT networks, collaborate in social networks, work in enterprises networks, and so on. Concepts such as "network society", "information society" and "knowledge society", are currently used by sociology, economics and other disciplines as a way to describe and

DOI: 10.4018/978-1-61520-799-2.ch012

understand our world and its dynamics built on connections, nodes, and communication fluxes; in a word, networks.

Among the vast literature that describes the raise of importance of networks in all spheres of our societies, we will refer to three fundamental authors, giving three different but convergent views on the raise of importance of networks in our societies: Manuel Castells, Jochai Benkler and Catherine Distler.

Manuel Castells, considered by many as the father of the concept of network society, claims that the new central role that information and knowledge have in all human activities with respect to the era priori to what he calls the "information revolution", are defining the emergence of the "information society" and, in terms of economic systems, of the "networked information economy." In four conferences given by Castells in Milan, Rome, New York and Boston, whose text are collected in the Italian "La città delle Reti" (Castells, 2004), the author presents his view on this "network societal paradigm". He does so by focusing on three areas: education, enterprise, and urban planning. In these fields, the accent of policies and practices is moving from the actors (institutions and individuals) to the relations among the actors, and on the networking dynamics among them. Castells notes the importance of the inner multistakeholder nature of modern networks: not only networks are built among similar actors (networked enterprises, networked civil society, etc), but among actors of different nature (Castells, 2001), this adding complexity and presenting new challenges to social studies.

Yochai Benkler, one of the most relevant observers of economic networks in post-modern society, gives another important contribution to understand the "networks-driven" change that is taking place in society. In his "The wealth of networks", Benkler claims that not only networks are substituting most of the basic structures of the industrial society, but also that the presence of these networks is changing the very inner nature

of human activities, impacting on concepts like property, time and space. He concludes that if we put the accent on a multiple number of relations taking place at the same time and no more on an actor or on a bilateral relation, the whole value system is affected and needs to be analyzed through different lenses (Benkler, 2006).

Catherine Distler, in her work with Albert Bressand focusing on social networks, claims that the focus of modern societies has moved, with strong differences depending on geographical and economical contexts, from the individual to a technology-mediated relationship between individuals and between the individual and the world. This is true "in relationships among people, like on the Internet; or relationships among companies, like on an electronic data interchange network; or relationships among nations, like when central banks use clearing and settlement networks. Most of what is called information technology today has already outgrown the name and is now relationship technology." (Distler and Bressad, 1995).

What the three authors agree upon is that virtually every sphere of human activity, especially in developed countries but more and more in developing ones also, is today working through and relying on networks: economy - how could a multinational company live without international networking, or how could an SME survive without local networking?; finance - how would a working day at the London stock exchange look without the support of ICT networks?; entertainment and leisure - would it be the same without Youtube?; daily communication - how would your life be without email?; social movements - without the internet the strongest campaign against McDonald's would not have been fought; and to a lesser extent policy and citizens participation are based on technological, social and relational networks much more than ever.

When looking at this change process from a society based on individual actors who interact mainly bilaterally on a punctual basis to a model based on a multiplicity of actors who continuously interact in a multilateral facet, one important aspect to be taken into account is the speed of change. Not only change towards network-based models is happening, but also it is happening much faster than ever before. A global survey conducted by the Institute for Development Studies reports that development researchers from all over the world perceive that global economic, physical, political and social phenomena follow some kind of Moore's law, meaning that their speed of change doubles every 18 months (Haddad, 2006). Finally, it is important to mention that the adoption of networking and relational models proceeds at different paces in different areas of the world and in different spheres of human activity. For example, business is rapidly and smoothly adopting network-based practices, while sectors like education and public administration are much more resistant and slow to adopt networking models. On the other hand, a "slow-adoption" sector such as education in a country such as Finland seems to be much more network-based than a "fast-adoption" one like business practices in a country such as Haiti.

THE PROBLEM OF INTERNATIONAL DEVELOPMENT COOPERATION: AN UNCHANGING MECHANISM IN A CHANGING WORLD

International Development Cooperation (IDC) can be defined as the set of actions (policies, programmes, projects, etc.) put in place by the so-called "developed countries" and by existing multilateral organizations (such as the United Nations, the World Bank or the International Monetary Fund) in order to improve the economic and social situation of the so-called "developing countries". A vast literature on IDC exists[1], out of which we will just extract some considerations about the actors and the main dynamics and the problems that affect the IDC process, with the aim of showing to which extent the adoption of more

focused networking practices could contribute to solve these problems.

The actors populating the IDC arena are many and of extremely different natures. A very incomplete list of the main development actors would begin, at least in terms of size and political influence, with the World Bank and its regional development banks, one each for Africa, Latin America, Asia, and the Caribbean. Other key actors in the IDC community are the major bilateral government agencies such as USAID, the German Federal Ministry of Economic Cooperation and Development, and the Japanese International Cooperation Agency (JICA). The European Union has a specific Development office (EuropeAid) and a specific fund, the European Development Fund; the United Nations have a range of aid organizations: the United Nations Development Programme (UNDP), the Food and Agriculture Organization (FAO), the World Food Programme (WFP), the International Fund for Agricultural Development (IFAD), the United Nations International Children Emergency Fund (UNICEF), and the United Nations Educational, Social, and Cultural Organization (UNESCO). In the non-governmental sector, a full spectrum of NGOs, research actors, think tanks, consultancies, academic programs, technical support and training organizations are part of the IDC community. Even this incomplete list adequately shows that development stakeholders do belong to all sectors of society, obviously bringing different visions, value-sets, practices and expectations into the collaboration and networking process.

In terms of general dynamics, the 2007 OECD Development Cooperation Report offers an idea of the "state of health" of IDC. In terms of funding (the "how much" question), in the last ten years Official Development Assistance (ODA) has been on the rise in most of the countries where it is most needed, meaning the least developed countries and the lower middle-income countries. Both donors and recipient countries have made considerable efforts to improve the quality and effectiveness of ODA - for example in the way aid is delivered and managed in the health and basic education sectors. Nevertheless, in 2006, the total ODA provided by the members of the international DAC (Development Aid Committee) fell to USD 104.4 billion, 4.5% lower than in 2005, this being the first fall since 1997 (OECD, 2007), and the attention to ODA for the next years, also due to the global financial crisis, will most probably keep on decreasing.

In terms of efficiency and effectiveness (the "how" question), looking at the many actors involved as well as at the many programmes and projects in place, the sensation is that a lot of initiative exists and do have an impact, but do not seem to work in an articulated nor synergetic way, neither at local nor at international level. It is for example common, at the local level, that more than one development action exists targeting the same community with the same objective, without a real coordination among them, maybe because they belong to different frameworks, or, at the international level, that two or more donors run programs with the same objectives and the same target regions without keeping constant contact. It somehow seems as if the IDC community is not able to "work in a networked way" by, for example, not taking full advantage of the possibilities provided by ICT. Some important decisions such as the 2005 Paris Declaration on Aid Effectiveness and the agreement of the UN Millennium Development Goals do show some strategic convergence among donors countries and agencies, but the way to reach a real transparent cooperation practice able to improve the effectiveness and impact of IDC still seems to be a long off. The Paris Declaration on Aid Effectiveness, for example, states that the following conditions shall be the cornerstones of Development Aid: ownership, alignment, harmonization, results, mutual accountability. Although these are fundamental aspects that should drive future IDC, the impression is that what the Declaration pushes for are more efficient IDC practices under the usual paradigm, and not a new way of thinking by the IDC.

The paradox is that, while in the past decades the social and economic dynamics of both developed and – to a lesser extent - developing countries have been changing as rapidly as never before relying more and more on information, knowledge and networking, IDC has not been following this process at the same pace of change.

One way to understand the effective capacity of IDC to adapt to the changes described above in terms of network society is to analyse the most common critique levelled against the IDC and to search for "change evidences" along these critical lines. This analysis should be able to demonstrate that adopting a network and relational based model can contribute to solve those problems. As a general introduction, one could say that the common perception of IDC by non IDC professionals is a rather negative one: the most common general critique being that the effort put in by donor countries is not enough or at least not enough with respect to the ambitious objectives set at international level[2], that the aid is too much linked to the donors' economic and political interest, that most of IDC programmes and projects are weakened by unprofessionalism and corruption, and so on. An analysis of the most critical literature on IDC (Amin, 2001; Black, 2004; Reinert, 2004) shows that the "problems" of IDC are of three natures: ideological, when the object of the critics is the very concept of development aid and its starting assumptions; political, when the objective of the critics is the way priorities are decided and funding is assigned, and technical, when the objective of the critics is the way IDC programmes are managed in terms of actors involved, processes and dynamics.

The critics of the first kind touch upon the very concept of development aid, and claim that the whole "development circus", meaning the vast group of development professionals, does nothing more than pushing a dominant western development model in a non-scientific and antidemocratic way. These critics, grounded on data that show how the number of poor people in the world has proportionally increased since the very creation of the development concept (Black 2004), are normally put forward by NGOs or activist groups. In our opinion, most of the times we are dealing with a communication problem, which prevents serious development actors to show their results and to change this negative perception, and at the same time with an accountability problem, which protects governments and development decision-makers form being monitored and punctually judged. Moving towards a "networked development cooperation" model would help in both these directions, since it would facilitate open flow of information both by governments (that could be obliged to provide that by the network itself) and by development actors, therefore increasing accountability and correct communication of the results of IDC and in the last instance improving the perception of IDC by non-professionals.

The critics of the political kind mainly emphasise the agenda-making process of development cooperation: common claims are that most of IDC policies and funding decisions are driven by the economic and political agenda of the donors, and that the agenda of multilateral organisation is self-referential and self-oriented. The typical case is the correspondence between the money lent by the World Bank to a specific country and the liberalization (westernization) policies that this country must put in place in the sector where this money would be used. Furthermore, it is undeniable that some kind of competition among donors is present (event if the situation is improving, mainly thanks to the OECD Office for Development Aid articulation work) and that the IDC policy community has not been able to put the general issue of development cooperation at the top of the policy agendas of donor's countries. Also in this case, adopting a network based approach in the process of defining the agenda, even if it might not solve the problem, would contribute to transparency and openness.

The critics of the third kind, concerning technical matters, emphasises the way IDC actions are planned, managed, evaluated, disseminated, and sustained. The main recognised problems in this sense are the "atomisation" of projects, with the deriving overlapping and redundancy, the lack of continuity and sustainability of development actions, and the frequent adoption of actions based on a "technology transfer" paradigm, typical of the North-South cooperation schemes. In terms of evaluation of IDC actions, the focus is normally put on the results and not on the impact of the project, with cultural differences and adaptation needs not taken enough into account or at least not in a long-term perspective. Most of the times, reading collections of development cooperation projects is like walking through a cemetery: sustainable and alive actions are rare exceptions, repetition seems to be the norm, evaluation based on data and long term needs is a mirage. Adopting a scheme based on networking can improve this situation, helping to avoid redundancy and duplication and facilitating the involvement of the actors that might guarantee that projects do not get lost when the funding ends.

Having considered the three critical dimensions (ideological, political and technical) of IDC, it appears that devoting more attention and resources to the networking dimension of development cooperation could contribute to solve some of the problems which put in danger the impact and functioning of aid policies and projects. Of course, networking is not a panacea to solving all these problems. To significantly improve the situation it would be necessary to introduce networking mechanism in a gradual and context-sensible way, accompanying the process with a continuous and sound monitoring of the effects of these dynamics on ICD practices. It must also be noted, especially when we discuss problems of ideological or political nature, that introducing networking practices would have to be done very carefully, since the "power of networking" could, as well as improve the situation of IDC, worsen some aspects of it.

As any powerful tool, networking and knowledge sharing could in fact be used, for example, by rival factions to more quickly spread propaganda and coordinate counter-attacks, verbal or otherwise, against one another.

A POSSIBLE SOLUTION: FOSTERING NETWORKING IN DEVELOPMENT COOPERATION

An analysis of the critical views on IDC seems to bring to the conclusion that networking, if properly embedded into mainstreaming development cooperation policies and practices, could refresh the IDC panorama, contributing to move towards a knowledge-based model that would fit the network society scenario presented at the beginning of the chapter.

Similar considerations can be extracted from the positions by Castells, Benkler and Distler presented at the beginning of the chapter. First, the rise of importance of non proprietary processes: *"non-proprietary strategies have always been more important in information production than they were in the production of steel or automobiles, even when the economics of communication weighed in favor of industrial models"* (Benkler, 2006, p. 16); second, the importance of the individuals as knowledge creators: *"what characterizes the networked information economy is that decentralized individual action plays a much greater role than it did, or could have, in the industrial information economy"* (Benkler, 2006, p. 15); third, the importance of ICT-mediated relations as ways to reach a higher transparency, accountability and openness of the whole IDC process, therefore improving the efficiency and effectiveness of ICT and network-based cooperation processes (Distler and Bressad, 1995).

Four Factors to Consider for Networking

We will now briefly present factors that show how the role of networking as a fundamental component of IDC is gaining ground among the professionals of IDC.

A first interesting conceptualization that seems to be in line with the change towards network-based development cooperation described above is the "human development paradigm" put forward by Nobel Prize Amartya Sen and somewhat adopted by the UNDP. The strength of the concept stands in the fact that it grounds human development on the basis of the degrees of freedom (functionings) of a specific target individual and not only on the satisfaction of basic needs/human rights. This means that the opportunities that an individual has are the ones that can bring her/him to a better life and to other opportunities that derive from these. This paradigm goes somehow in the direction of assigning more importance to the networking aspects of development, since networking, as all activities based on information and knowledge, is about "empowering people", a step forward with respect to – of course not a substitute of – basic needs, for instance "feeding people". To describe Sen's theory from a network perspective, we could say that the sum of the degrees of freedoms of a quantity of individuals in a network is higher than the sum of these degrees when those individuals do not constitute a network. This is because knowledge, as the good normally exchanged though human networks, is a non-exclusive good that can be transferred from one individual to another without having to maintain the same total quantity; knowledge, when channeled into a social network, tends to expand in an exponential way.

The second concept is that of partnership for development, which represent an important advance with respect to plain bilateral donation schemes towards a scheme that puts more emphasis on concepts such as communication, involvement of all stakeholders and trust. As the World Bank states: "[*we should*] *treat partnerships as an organic process, in which trust is built over time, in which steps are taken to weave a "fabric of sustainability"; and consider how mutual accountability may be built*" (Maxwell and Conway, 2000 p viii). Examples of IDC schemes based on this concept are, for example, "local development enterprises" where the shareholders are at the same level as the development professionals, the local governments and the local development actors. This approach of IDC visionaries seems to be gaining ground in practice and should be further pursued. Gilchrist (2004) provides a detailed description of the importance of networking practices at community level, showing that the more the members of a community are allowed to build networks among themselves, the more the community is able to face change and problems.

A third concept has to do with a "paradigm shift" by some national agencies in charge of development cooperation towards a network-based model which puts knowledge and information at the centre of the development process. This paradigm, born out of the Scandinavian IDC tradition, is gaining ground especially in Europe. For example, in February 2008 public and private actors met in Gijon, Asturias, to discuss a new model for the Spanish DC strategy, under the slogan "Cooperation 2.0". Reading from the conclusions of the event, "The reticulation of cooperation is the answer to its evolutive adaptation to the environment of the Web Society. These are gradual processes that arise bottom-up, whether within an organisation or within huge international systems of cooperation. In such processes structures and dynamics of the cooperation evolve, fostering horizontal relationships, collaboration, and access to shared resources as well as to knowledge management" (Notes of the author, Cooperation 2.0 Conference, Gijon 2008). During the Gijon conference, it was stated that the so-called "empowering networks models" are probably those that offer the best possibilities for working in development cooperation since they foster the strengthening of nodes, their collaborative capacity as well as their operational autonomy. It was also recognized that for a network to be successful an adequate design and a confident management with appropriate levels of leadership is key, and that the skills related to the management of networks are just starting to being developed. The emergence of the Web 2.0 and of a number of ICT tools aimed at facilitating participation and collaboration offers interesting opportunities for reticulating development cooperation work, which deserve to be included as much as possible in IDC initiatives. As it was stated during the Conference: "We should start thinking of the networks of tomorrow, because there are already here today".

A fourth important development has to do with the rise of importance of the concept of south-south cooperation. This modality of cooperation, which deals with development cooperation schemes between and among developing countries, started in the 70s as a way to push "south-south solidarity" for collectively influencing the international political and economic order and to show different possible development models (Schumacher, 1973). It is now gaining a new momentum, mainly thanks to the rapid development of economies like Brazil, India and South-Africa. Probably due to the cultural proximity among donors and receivers, or because of the fact that the scheme started quite recently, the model adopted in south-south development cooperation schemes, as for example the relation between Brazil and Angola, seems to be more attentive to innovation and knowledge, and to be based on a mutual benefits scheme in terms of economic growth and poverty reduction. The data on the actual scale of South-South development cooperation are still fragmentary. However one example may give an idea of the phenomenon reach. Over the last ten years developing countries have been increasingly investing in each others' economies, reaching a total of USD 47 billion in 2003 (OECD, 2007).

Finally, it is worth mentioning that the United Nations Development Program created a Special Unit for South-South Cooperation (SU-SSC), with the aim to create a platform to strengthen sustained intra-South business collaboration and technology exchanges - once again a conformation of the rise of the concept of networking and knowledge exchange in IDC policy.

The Concept of Networking for Development

The four trends presented above embody a strong networking dimension, and go in the direction of both considering knowledge as a fundamental component of the IDC process and of equipping IDC professionals with networking tools aimed at facilitating the flowing and the exchange of the explicit and tacit knowledge produced by IDC actions. Here we will try to systematize these inputs around the concept of "networking for development", which represents a proposal to fully integrate the potential of knowledge-based networking activities in IDC practice and policy.

First, it is important to define what we mean with development networks. A general definition of network is provided by Tania Boerzel, who claims that networks include private and public organizations and individuals with common interests, which commit in exchange processes to pursue a common aim, acknowledging that cooperation is the best way to achieve this aim (Boerzel, 1998). In line with this definition, the International Development Research Centre (IDRC) defines networks as social arrangements of organizations and/or individuals linked together around a common theme or purpose, working jointly but allowing members to maintain their autonomy as participants. In this definition, networks promote knowledge sharing, facilitate communication, and foster a culture of innovation and change. Finally, we can move closer to our target by using the words of Ricardo Wilson-Grau, who defines networks in development settings as groups of autonomous organizations (and perhaps individuals) in two or more countries or continents who share a purpose and voluntarily contribute knowledge, experience, staff time, finances and other resources to achieve common goals. (Wilson-Grau, 2006).

With reference to the four concepts introduced above, a first consideration is that they seem to be built around the importance of knowledge in IDC settings. If we want to substantially improve the way development cooperation works as well as the way it is perceived by society, we need to move towards a paradigm that puts knowledge at the centre as a key asset produced by IDC. In other words, in a knowledge-based paradigm of development cooperation (able to follow the development of the knowledge society) knowledge is to be considered as essential resources for both personal and social development; or in Labelle's words: "empowerment through information" (Labelle, 2003). The key driver for this to happen is to understand that knowledge has an inner value for both the target participants and for the professionals of any IDC action. The value of the introduction of networking seems directly proportional to the value that the knowledge produced, shared and documented has for all the participants in the development programme.

As a second point, the relation between information and knowledge in development settings must be made clear. Producing high quantity of information and data without clear mechanisms and strategies to store, update, share, spread it can be counterproductive and create a feeling of overloading, especially when dealing with individuals that are not prepared nor "educated" to deal with such an amount of information, typically the case in the context of development cooperation actions. In order to fully uncap the potential of the "knowledge revolution", we need to invest on the networking dimension of IDC. Networks capable of facilitating information flowing and appropriation should be built and maintained and finally, transformation of information into knowledge. The idea is that information is transformed into knowledge through a sharing and networking process that should aim at generating a sense of ownership among all the actors who take part in the development process.

These two conditions are fundamental if we want to speak of "networking for development". In broad terms, networking for development can be defined as the application of networking methods as primary tools of IDC, with the aim of putting knowledge at the centre of the IDC process. It is about building *development networks*, which shall then be in charge of running projects and development activities. The novelty with respect to the present situation, where development projects are sometimes run by networks of actors, stands in the fact that development networks must be built *before* the definition of the projects, and not as ancillary elements to development actions, making sure that the knowledge sharing element is present throughout the whole cooperation action and represent the sustainability and transferability guarantee of the whole process. Development networks are multistakeholder aggregations including donors, receivers and intermediaries as well as other involved actors, open to new members, in charge of defining their own priorities and of monitoring and evaluating the impact of development actions they are concerned with. These networks shall be the drivers, the monitors, and finally the owners of all the development cooperation process, and should be based on concepts such as trust, ownership of results, and continuous involvement of users. The model is strongly based and relying on ICT-based technological and human networks which give priority to knowledge management, canalisation of social capital in and through the internet and implementation of multilateral actions with the participation of policy actors, civil society, companies, universities and other agents.

At this point a specification is needed. Networking in IDC settings refers to four broad categories:

- Networking among donors and IDC agencies. This refers to fostering contacts and dialogue among the actors that draw the agendas of IDC and that decide the priorities of specific IDC programs. With respect to the existing dialogue schemes made of meetings and agreements, the model introduces a continuous flow of information and a number of validation and sense-making actions.

- Networking and knowledge sharing among IDC professionals. This refers to fostering knowledge sharing among the professional of IDC on a global scale, regardless of the institution they belong. Some efforts in this sense exist, such as the Development Gateway network, the Global Knowledge Partnership or the World Bank's InfoDev Program, and should be strengthened and enlarged both horizontally, meaning fostering cross-fertilization among them, and vertically, meaning involving all stakeholders from the top (policy makers) to the bottom (professionals on the ground) of the IDC value chain.

- Program-related networking. This means including a strong networking component at the level of the many existing development programs, which can be of global or local nature, and which normally suffer from the problems described above, typically the atomization and the lack of sustainability of their actions and results. Adding a sound networking component able to involve all possible stakeholders from the very conception of these programs would contribute solving these problems.

- Project-related networking. Normally of local nature, this refers to the importance of including the creation, improvement, enlargement or strengthening of networks of local actors in virtually all IDC projects. This is happening more and more but most of the time in an informal and not recognized way, bearing the risk that at the end of the funding period of a project the network that had been created disappears. The aim should not be that these networks should survive forever, but rather that they should openly adapt and be ready to work on other IDC projects as active aggregations of stakeholders.

In all these cases, networking for development is, above all, about applying serious network science analysis to all the phases of a development process, from the agenda definition, to the planning and budgeting, to the programs and projects definition, implementation, evaluation and sustainability building.

The Added Value of Networking

In order for this concept to be broadly accepted at all the levels of the IDC process, a problem to be overcome is the natural volatility of networking activity and the perception of communication activities as ancillary to hardcore development actions. One could ask: why investing in networking while we lack bread?. This perception exists not only among decision makers, who more and more are accepting the idea that investing in networking activities has a return, but also among the grassroots actors, who tend to prefer actions that concentrate on tangible outcomes.

Furthermore, making sure that all actors perceive networking activities as valuable is fundamental in order for the networks themselves to flourish and to grow. In fact, most of the network studies literature (for example Bala and Goyal, 2000, or Jackson and Wolinsky, 1996) assume that agents (in our case stakeholders) make a discrete decision on whether or not to connect to other agents and how much to invest in pursuing and maintaining a specific link, and this depends on the value that those agents assign to being part of the specific network.

The justification of networking activities in IDC starts from the fact that in present societies the focus of the value in any productive chain, this being valid for business as well as for development cooperation, does no longer depend either on labor or in capital, but in the collaboration an exchange process among individuals that produce knowledge, goods and services (Benkler, 2006). The concepts of reciprocity and exchange, which are at the very basis of the most ancient modality of social regulation that was there before the State and the Market and that has been relegated to a marginal role in industrial society, seem to be acquiring again a fundamental value in social innovation and dynamics. In other words, value creation is deeply embedded in extended social relations.

As said before, due to the fact that knowledge is a non-exclusive good, knowledge networks are in principle capable of multiplying the knowledge of the individual agents by facilitating information sharing and dialogue. Marvin Minsky describes collective intelligence as a complex function of many little parts, each mindless by itself, which, when they join, create intelligence (Minsky, 1986). In this light, working as a network benefits each and every node, since by joining it gets access to the network knowledge.

The added value of networking in IDC activities can be expanded in three directions.

- First, networking is a way to overcome mere market logics, where market is intended in its broader sense. IDC actions respond in fact to a logic quite similar to the one of commercial markets, since they derive from open or tacit negotiations and do work in a limited resources scheme. Networks facilitate exchanges (market model of social reproduction), redistribution (non-monetary model of social reproduction) and reciprocity (non monetary collaboration-based exchange). In this last mechanism the focus is on the actors rather than on the relations, since they are the ones who drive the process, not the market or an external authority.

- Second, networking is a way to better predict peers' moves based on open sharing of knowledge. This is particularly important in IDC settings in view of avoiding projects failures due to cultural differences and to different understandings of a specific IDC action logic, objectives and expected impact. In this line, a normally neglected value of networking stands in what is called the "long tail of networking": if through networking one can do better what he could do alone, he can also get access to new ideas and activities. Although this is not the reason why he is in the network, it does represent an added value.

- Third, networking is a way to facilitate both cooperation among all involved actors, therefore increasing the efficiency of the system, and transparent competition among different stakeholders. Both donors and aid recipients in fact share the same objectives and risk to run overlapping actions and to compete for the same resources when complete information is lacking.

Apart from these dimensions of value, probably the most important long-term added value of networking activities has to do with its capacity to increase the social capital of a group a stakeholders, intended as the sum of the relations that grants access to a set of resources (in our case both knowledge and IDC resources).

James Coleman, father of the definition of social capital, claims that authority, trust and norms contribute to the creation of social capital (Coleman, 1998). In the frame of development networks, the individual member optimizes its choices following its preferences, and by doing so he impacts on the social capital of the network, seen both as an individual and as a common resource: thanks to the networking activity, he increases his common and shared value offered by the actions that individual members carry on for their own interest. Coleman identifies three factors having an impact on the growth of social capital that are valid also in development cooperation settings: the density of the relations in the network, the stability and durability of the relations, the ideological orientation and the dependency among actors. In the words of Putnam, these are the relational assets (Putnam, 2000) that add value to networks: values like reciprocity, trust, communication and cooperation are valuable both for the individual and for the community.

A last important contribution to understand the value of networks comes from Robert Axelrod. In his The Evolution of Cooperation, the author demonstrates that, given that market reciprocity cannot explain a number of high-value experiences (such as the distributed supercomputer Seti@home[3] in the field of science) that are based on pure collaboration principles, the capacity of constructing relations built on trust and reciprocity is the basis for grounding cooperation practices that are durable and valuable. He distinguishes between asset, positional and generative value. Asset value stands in the talent and resources of the network members, positional value stands in the awareness of the network and in its potential access to assets, while generative value stands for the ability and willingness to engage in trust building and collaboration activities (Axelrod, 1984). In development settings, generative value seems to be the most important, since it deals with deepening the relations level and with increasing the level of inclusion and connectivity of the network members.

It must be noted that networks are not adding value simply because they exist, but rather they multiply the positive value of their members and of the activities that are run through them. It can be demonstrated that networks of good will and motivated people working in development settings can increase the impact of IDC; but this does not mean that the logic should be to "build network" in a blind way. In a number of cases and conditions, fostering networking in a problematic area can result in a worse situation. For example, it can happen that a development network set up by well-intended development agents transforms a new resource for local actors (the local "big men") and affects negatively the whole IDC process. To solve these potential problems, it is important that the networks that are fostered consider a number of conditions, such as the presence of multiple stakeholders' categories.

The Importance of the Multistakeholder Approach

A fundamental concept to deal with when working on networking in development settings is that of multistakeholder partnership. This concept has become, in the last years, an extremely politically correct condition of most development projects. The reason behind this is that, in order to maximize the impacts of a development operation, a strong and continuous collaboration among all the actors involved in the project shall benefit the operation. The justification stands in the fact that each stakeholder category brings its own vision to the project and therefore impact on the operation with its own peculiarities and following its mission. Briefly, the government can assign priority to an action, civil society can provide users' needs and feedback, academia can contribute with research input and analysis, the private sector can provide technical solutions and contribute to sustainable take-up and sponsoring. Virtually all major donors do agree with the importance of implementing multistakeholder partnerships and some of them consider the concept as a flagship of their policies. Nevertheless, few documented cases of success can be found, if success means the involvement of stakeholders that have made a real impact on the whole process, beyond the obvious benefits of informing the actors of what is happening.

Reading from the conclusions of the Report "Multistakeholder Partnerships and Digital Tech-nology for Development in Latin America and the Caribbean" by the Omar Dengo Foundation, which reviews three multistakeholder partnership cases from Latin America, *"multistakeholder partnerships need to have an objective shared by the parties; they must be kept from searching in different directions"* (Omar Dengo Foundation, 2007, p. 31). Some success factors of MSP seem to be the acknowledgment of mutual need and complementarity, transparency, clarity of roles, interests, expectations, equality in decision making processes, independence and trust, mutual benefit, flexibility, openness to review and renegotiate agreements, will for understanding. As said before, it goes without saying that these factors are fundamental for the networking for development concept.

Still, multistakeholder networking, even in the cases where some examples are documented and reported, is normally limited to the "project" level, normally not going beyond that, while the ND concept advocates for applying this approaches to all the levels of IDC.

ICT AND NETWORKING FOR DEVELOPMENT: DONORS STRATEGIES AND RESEARCH DEBATES

ICT for Development

Similarly to Networking for Development, ICT for Development (ICT4D) puts information and communication processes at the centre of the development processes, and therefore encompasses a strong networking nature both in terms of information networks (connecting computers to facilitate communication and information sharing among development actors and users) and in terms of social and human networks. For understanding the nature of ICT4D and the problem of the digital divide and entering into the debate around those concepts, it is important to move from the concept of technology for development to the concept of networking for development.

Information and Communication Technologies (ICT) encompasses the vast group of media that allow users to produce, process, document, distribute, share and access information, including digital media such as PCs, the internet, email, databases, mobile phones and analogue media such as telephone, radio and TV. ICT for development is about fostering the use of ICT in development settings and actions. The justification of the use of ICT in development actions stands in the fact that information and knowledge can improve the possibility of choices (functionings, in Sen's terminology) of human beings and therefore their human development.

In historical terms, the concept of Information and Communication Technologies for Development was born within the framework of a UN–driven elaboration of an international agenda, which has seen its peak in the organization of the World Summit on Information Society (2003-2005) and in the subsequent creation of the Global Alliance for ICT and Development (GAID) in 2005[4]. In terms of research, from the beginning of the 90s a number of reports, case studies, and discussion papers on ICT4D started to be produced by academia, civil society and research units of donor institutions, with the effect to "push" a number of international organizations to invest in the issue. A very recent work by Tim Unwin presents the issue of ICT4D in all its facets (Unwin, 2009).

Networking for development (ND) and ICT for development (ICT4D) are somehow similar strategies to include knowledge sharing at the centre of IDC, but some differentiations must be made. ICT4D brings forward the use of Information and Communication Technologies in development actions (both in on the ground projects and among development professionals), while ND introduces ICT as a tool to improve networking, focusing rather on social, cultural and institutional communication among stakeholders. What the two concepts have in common is that both present a strategy to improve IDC, both in terms of projects development and in terms of efficiency and transparency of IDC processes. Where they differ is that while introducing ICT does not per se affect the principles of IDC, the effect of introducing a sound networking component changes the very basis of a development action. On the other hand, ICT by nature supports networking and knowledge sharing/building and is therefore a key component of any ND policy and practice. As Giarchi (2001) has pointed out, networking refers to a formal, systemic form of organization and communication and is "something more" – or at least something different - than a mere aggregation of actors using ICT for communicating and collaborating (Giarchi refers to these informal aggregations as "social circles"). In our definition of development networks, although taking into account Giarchi's conceptualisation, we do take into account both the formal and the informal dimensions of networking. For example, a development network can be created among actors that have a formal agreement to cooperate for a certain time around a contract, but it is composed also of the many informal contacts and links that each of these actors have and that are related to the project.

Borrowing a metaphor by Manuel Acevedo, if the classic IDC mantra was "don't give a fish to the poor, give a rod and teach them how to fish" and the ICT4D mantra is "give them a rod and some ICT, in order for the fisherman to be able to get information on fish market prices in different ports, on weather forecast, on all existing fishes species in the area, or on where to buy a better rod", the networking for development mantra should be "give them a rod and ICT, and help them building a community of fishermen in order to exchange experiences and information, solve common problems together, help each other, be stronger in their requests to the government, etc..".

Networking and ICT for Development: Some Donors' Perspectives

As said before, most of the major donors are beginning to include networking and knowledge sharing as key component of their development cooperation strategies. For example, the World Bank claims to be a "Knowledge Bank" and has created a set of units and programs devoted to networking, ICT and knowledge-sharing for development, practically all sectors and regions, such as:

- the Development Gateway, "a development issues Web portal, for users to gain access to information, resources, and tools and to contribute their knowledge and experience";
- the Global Knowledge Partnership, "an evolving informal partnership of public, private, and not–for–profit organizations in both developing and industrial countries. Its members are committed to sharing information, experiences, and resources to promote broad access to — and effective use of — knowledge and information as tools of sustainable development";
- the World Links for Development, "providing Internet connectivity and training for teachers, teacher trainers and students in developing countries in the use of technology in secondary education";
- the Global Development Learning Network, "linking decision-makers around the globe, through telecommunications systems, as participants in global learning activities"
- the InfoDev, "a global grant program to promote innovative projects on the use of information and communication technologies for economic and social development"
- the Indigenous Knowledge, "providing users with quick access to syntheses of country–specific cases of indigenous/traditional practices, in–country sources of knowledge, and Bank–supported projects related to IK issues"
- the B–SPAN, "an Internet–based broadcasting station that presents World Bank seminars, workshops, and conferences on a variety of sustainable development and poverty reduction issues".

From the list above, it clearly appears that knowledge-sharing and networking are seen as central assets for development in virtually all fields of action of the bank, confirming once more the transversal nature of networking for development.

Other development organizations have also been investing in networking, mostly under the ICT for development slogan, as part of their operations and programs. Two examples deserve attention: the Canadian International Development Agency, in its "Strategy on Knowledge for Development through Information and Communication Technologies", claims that "information and knowledge are among the resources fundamental to the development process. Access to information and knowledge, other than strengthening civil society, contributes to poverty reduction by allowing individuals and communities to expand their choices". Similarly, the Asian Development Bank has declared that: "ICT has become a powerful tool in the fight against world poverty, providing developing countries with an unprecedented opportunity to meet vital development goals, such as poverty reduction, basic health care, and education, far more effectively than before. The countries that succeed in bridging the digital divide by harnessing the potential of ICT can look forward to enhancing economic growth, and improving human welfare and good governance practices".

The Debate Around ICT, Knowledge, and Networking for Development

As stated above, although the importance of ICT, knowledge and networking in development settings is being more and more accepted by

257

the mainstream discourse and adopted by most donors as a key element in their policies and programs, some critical voices exist and must be reported, which refer both to the introduction of ICT in development settings and – either directly or indirectly – to the increased presence of communication, knowledge-based and networking activities in development settings.

A first critical view refers to the relevance and effective impact of ICT, knowledge and networking for development. A number of observers have been claiming that the positive impact of networking and communication activities on poverty as well as on other areas is not statistically proved, an argument similar to the 1987 claim by economist Robert Solow that the effect of the "computer revolution" was not visible in the US productivity statistics.[5] These observers claim that the "productivity paradox" - that is the absence of evidence of a direct impact of ICT in economic growth – applies also to development cooperation policies and actions. In line with this reasoning, Brendan Luyt observes that the promotion of ICT and networking for development are policy issues which tend to benefit four major groups: the "information capitalists", the developing countries governments, the development "industry" and the global civil society. He also notes that "the fact that the gap between ICT access in the developed and developing countries is now on the agenda at international conferences and summits around the world does not necessarily reflect the intrinsic importance of that gap to world affairs. What it does reflect is a particular convergence of interests and their ability to collectively set the political agenda in such a way that the digital divide is now seen as a serious and important social problem" (Luyt, 2004).

A second critical view concerns the side effects of ICT and networking for development, and can be summarized in the view of Bernardo Sorj. The Brazilian author claims that "*the introduction of ICT increases social exclusion and inequality*" and that "*the richest sectors of society are the*

first to have access to new products, they have the benefits of a decisive competitive advantage when they master using them. At the same time, those who are excluded face new, or greater, disadvantages" (Sorj, 2004, p. 3). If on one hand it is true that each social innovation can open new divides, on the other hand the situation seems to be more positive when we refer to knowledge-based innovations, due to the non-exclusive economic nature of knowledge. In general terms, this means that barriers to social sharing of knowledge do exist, especially but not only in and with respect to developing countries, but it seems to be easier to overcome with respect to material barriers.

In line with this reasoning and moving back to the institutional side of the picture, it is possible to read the UNDP's three levels of utility of ICT (UNDP, 2001) as critical elements of ICT and networking for development. Concerning knowledge, UNDP claims that ICT can bring down barriers and allow equitable access to education and information for all. Nevertheless, many researches, such as the HELIOS Report, 2006 in the education field, show that the ones that benefit the most from ICT use are the ones that need it the less, or in other words that ICT improves the access (to education, for example) of the ones that already have access, and does not allow massive access of excluded groups. Concerning participation, UNDP claims that through ICT remote communities can participate in collective actions; on the contrary it could be claimed that even when they participate they do so by respecting the linguistic and cultural rules of the ones who set up the participation system. Concerning economic opportunity, UNDP claims that ICT improves the capacities of excluded groups to access new markets and to be better equipped for competition; on the contrary data show that the gap between the rich and the poor at world and at local level is generally increasing.

The balanced truth is that, as with any powerful means, ICT and networking can be used to close or to widen divides: what is important is the consideration that policy makers and development practitioners have of these tools. The view that information and communication activities per se can solve most of the development problems is false, but so is the view that they by nature widen divides. More and more, a balanced attitude is beginning to appear in many policy documents. This attitude considers ICT and networking as a fundamental support for development policies, extremely useful only if applied in the frame of well-planned actions.

NETWORKING DIVIDE, RESEARCH AND APPLICATION PERSPECTIVES

To conclude the chapter, we will propose a move in three steps: from the well-known concept of digital divide to the paradigmatic divide, and finally to the networking divide. The aim is to spell out the importance of the networking dimension as a divide to be bridged both in terms of IDC practice and policy.

The concept of "digital divide" refers to the divide, typical of the information society, between the persons or communities that can benefit from the use of ICT and the ones that cannot. Many definitions have been given, moving from the original ones focusing on infrastructure connectivity (following the adagio "to be or not to be connected"), to the most recent focusing on ICT use, claiming that being connected without motivation or training to use ICT in a meaningful way is useless or even dangerous. If we look at the digital divide through the Sen's human development lens, we can define it as the difference between the communities and individuals that can take advantage of the possibilities provided by ICT and the ones that cannot. Unanimity seems to exists on the fact that the digital divide depends and at the same time influences other divides, such as the economic, social, educational divides, and that it is a dynamic and changing problem, difficult to measure and to address. To use the words of the Okinawa Charter, "the challenge of bridging the international information and knowledge divide cannot be underestimated. We recognize the priority being given to this by many developing countries. Indeed, those developing countries which fail to keep up with the accelerating pace of IT innovation may not have the opportunity to participate fully in the information society and economy. This is particularly so where the existing gaps in terms of basic economic and social infrastructures, such as electricity, telecommunications and education, deter the diffusion of IT" (Okinawa Charter, 2000, p. 4). The digital divide shall not be considered as a stand-alone phenomenon, but rather as a multifaceted (and sometimes controversial) issue. As O'Hara and Stevens describe it in their work, where the multidimensional nature of the phenomenon is well analyzed: "the more important the services that ICT provides, and the more central its role in the lives of citizens, the more important it is in a just society that people get sufficient access to ICT to play their part in the democratic organisation of their society, to be able to achieve their reasonable preferences and pursue their conception of the good, and to avoid their voices being drown out by the richer and more powerful" (O'Hara and Stevens, 2006 p. 283).

Moving one step further with respect to the digital divide, an interesting concept is the one of paradigmatic divide, described as the divide between the different "development paradigms", or visions, that exist and guide development policies (Pimienta, 2003). For example, the typical development paradigm of many ICT4D policies, especially in the 80s and 90s but in some case still today, is that the urgent thing to do is to connect anybody anywhere, in the belief that once connectivity is there, services and applications – but also capacity to use ICT – will follow. This vision, mainly driven by the private sector interests, has proved to be far from working, and has been heavily criticized by the promoters of a completely different paradigm, proper of civil society movements, which focuses on appropriate use of ICT, knowledge sharing dynamics, social appropriation of technology, and more attention to the human side of the picture. The distance between these two visions represents a paradigmatic divide that has affected many ICT4D policies in the last years.

Building on the different paradigms of development can help us to identify, along with the concept of networking for development, another important divide linked to the digital divide, not often mentioned but seriously affecting many development dynamics. We may call it *networking divide*. This divide can be defined as the difference of opportunity between the actors that are included into healthy and working development networks and actors that are not. Being part of a network, especially in developing countries, can provide opportunities in terms of participation in development actions and in terms of further developing the skills and capacities acquired through specific development works. This divide has somehow to do with the structural absence of a networking culture among development actors, and can result in paradoxical situations in which, in a same community, two or more development aid project are active but do not share knowledge nor cooperate, and sometimes even compete.

As with any divide, the networking divide can be bridged but in a different way than simply wiring communities. This has to do with promoting a networking culture among actors that for a number of reason are not part of any healthy and active network, as well as with building trust between the networks gatekeepers and members. Even if applying the networking for development concept would need some "system changes" that are obviously not easy to happen, some possible steps can be identified. As seen before, the first step has to do with convincing the actors in charge of defining development policies of the value of networking, in terms of present and future opportunities and in terms of direct and indirect effects. Normally the best way to do so is through pilot actions that are able to show the effect of networking on

people's lives, but some capacity building on the importance of networking (both towards recipients and donors) would also be important.

As with any new concept, networking for development should be the object of research and pilot actions. In terms of research, putting the accent on communication and networking opens up a rather unexplored area of international development studies, that is the application of network theories and concepts to development actions. More than establishing new research lines in this direction, it would be interesting to embed this dimension in some running research actions in the field of IDC. Consider an example out from development research teams which are struggling to fight against the problems presented in this paper. A very interesting case is the reflection that the Brighton Institute for Development Studies carried out in 2006 by organising 45 Roundtables around the world to discuss the state and problems of development research. These gatherings reflected on many development-related issues and the results of this reflection (Haddad, 2006) seem to confirm that most researchers in the field share the concerns on IDC described in this paper. Strangely enough, the networking dimension of IDC, although appearing underneath many of the discussions, seems not to have had a relevant place in this debate, showing once more that, even in the cases when it is considered, it is perceived as an instrumental dimension to other development issues and not as a key leverage for development per se.

REFERENCES

Amin, S. (2001). *Il capitalismo del nuovo millennio*. Milano, Italy: Punto Rosso.

Asian Development Bank website (n.d.). Retrieved January 2009 from http://www.adb.org

Axelrod, R. (1984). *The Evolution of Cooperation*. New York: Basic Books.

Bala, V., & Goyal, S. (2000). *A Strategic Analysis of Network Reliability*. Oxford, UK: Review of Oxford Economic Design.

Benkler, Y. (2006). *The Wealth of Networks: how social production transforms markets and freedom*. New Heaven, UK: Tale University Press.

Black, M. (2002). *La cooperazione allo sviluppo internazionale*. Roma, Italy: Carocci.

Boerzel, T. (1998). Le reti di attori pubblici e privati nella regolazione europea. In *Stato e Mercato, n. 3*. Bologna, Italy: Il Mulino.

Canadian International Development Agency website (n.d.). Retrieved January 2009 from www.acdi-cida.gc.ca

Castells, M. (2001). *The Internet Galaxy: reflections on the Internet*. Oxford, UK: Blackwell.

Castells, M. (2004). *La città delle reti*. Venezia, Italy: Marsilio Editori.

Coleman, J. (1988). *Social Capital in the Creation of Human Capital*. Chicago: American Journal of Sociology, University of Chicago Press.

Distler, C., & Bressand, A. (1995). *Le planete relationelle*. Paris: Flammarion.

Giarchi, G. G. (2001). Caught in the nets: a critical examination of the use of the concept of networks in community development studies. *Community Development Journal, 16*, 63–71. doi:10.1093/cdj/36.1.63

Gilchrist, A. (2004). *The well-connected community: a networking approach to community development*. London: The Policy Press.

Haddad, L. (2006). *Reinventing Development Research: listening To the IDS40 Roundtables*, Conference background paper for IDS40 Conference. Brighton, UK: Institute for Development Studies, University of Sussex.

Jackson, M.O. & Wolinsky, A. (1996) *A Strategic Model of Social and Economic Networks*. Oxford, UK: Journal of Economic Theory.

Japanese Ministry of Foreign Affairs. (2000) *Okinawa Charter on Global Information Society*. Retrieved January 2009 from www.mofa.go.jp

Kingsbury, D. (2004). *International Development: Issues and Challenges*. New York: Palgrave Macmillan.

Labelle, R. (2005). *ICT Policy Formulation and E-Strategy Development: A Comprehensive Guidebook*. Elsevier: UNDP-APDIP.

Lora, E. (2004). *A Decade of Development Thinking*. Washington, DC: Inter-American Development Bank.

Luyt, B. (2004). Who benefits from the digital divide. *First Monday*. Retrieved January 2009 from www.firstmonday.org

Maxwell, S., & Conway, T. (2000). *Perspectives on partnership*. Washington, DC: World Bank.

Michel, L. (2006). *Compendium on development cooperation strategies*. Brussels, Belgium: European Commission.

Minsky, M. (1986). *The society of mind*. New York: Simon & Schuster.

O'Hara, K., & Stevens, D. (2006). *Inequality. Com: Power, Poverty and the Digital Divide*. New York: OneWorld Publications.

OECD. (2008). *2007). Development Cooperation Report*. Paris, France: OECD.

Omar Dengo Foundation. (2007). *Multistakeholder Partnerships and Digital Technology for Development in Latin America and the Caribbean*. San Jose, Costa Rica: Ediciones innova.

Pimienta, D. (2005). *Measuring Linguistic Diversity on the Internet*. Paris, France: UNESCO.

Putnam, R. (2000). *Bowling Alone: The Collapse and Revival of American Community*. New York: Simon & Schuster.

Reinert, E. S. (2004). *Globalisation, Economic Development and Inequality*. Northampton, UK: Edward Elgar Publishing.

Schumacher, E. F. (1973). *Small is Beautiful. Economics as people mattered*. New York: Simon and Schuster.

Sen, A. (1992). *Inequality Reexamined*. Oxford: Oxford University Press.

Sen, A. (1999). *Development as Freedom*. New York: Anchor Books.

Sen, A. (2002). *Rationality and Freedom*. Harvard: Harvard Belknap Press.

Sorj, B. (2005). *Civil Societies North-South Relations: NGOs and Dependency*. Sao Paulo, Brazil: Edelstein Center for Social Research.

United Nation, Millennium Development Goals. (n.d.). Retrieved January 2009 from www.un.org/millenniumgoals

Unwin, T. (Ed.). (2009). *ICT4D*. Cambridge: Cambridge University Press.

Wilson-Grau, R. (2006). *Complexity and Evaluation in International Networks*. Toronto, Canada: International Development Research Centre.

ENDNOTES

[1] See for example Black, 2002, Lora et al., 2004, Michel, 2006, Sen, 1999, Kingsbury et al., 2008.

[2] To make an example, in 2002 Italy has committed to devote 0,5% of its GDP to development aid, but the assigned figure for 2008 is 0,2% and the revision for 2009 is 0,1%.

[3] SETI@home is a scientific experiment that uses Internet-connected computers in the Search for Extraterrestrial Intelligence (SETI). You can participate by running a free program that downloads and analyzes radio telescope data. See http://setiathome.berkeley.edu.

[4] Other important initiatives in this respect are the UN ICT Task Force, the G8 Meetings of Okinawa, Genoa, Kananakis, and the Davos World Economic Forum meetings.

[5] For a detailed description of the productivity paradox debate see Dedrick et al., 2003.

Chapter 13
Information Communication Technology and its Impact on Rural Community Economic Development

Kenneth Pigg
University of Missouri, USA

ABSTRACT

Much rhetoric has been expended by researchers and advocates alike regarding the transformational effects of information communication technology (ICT) on economic and social conditions. Most such rhetoric posits very positive outcomes from the impending changes, economic development being just one of several. This research reports the findings of a three-year effort to determine whether such claims are actually being experienced in rural areas where access is often restricted because of public and private policies. The research findings highlight the importance of social conditions on the capacity of rural communities to effectively harness the potential of ICT for beneficial purposes.

INTRODUCTION

Rhetorical enthusiasm aside, the adoption and diffusion of information and communications technology (ICT) via broadband communications—internet, wireless and satellite—in rural areas of the United States has been remarkably swift. Beginning in the early 1990s with the Clinton Administration's "Information Superhighway" initiative and relying for the most part on private sector investments, nearly all rural residents were able to get access to these services by 2006-07.

For example, recent data released by the Federal Communications Commission for 2007 shows that there is at least one broadband provider in ninety-eight per cent of the zip codes in the U.S. (FCC, 2007). That does not mean that everyone in those areas is actually connected or using these services, but that they are available at market rates.

This lack of accurate data is unfortunate because the general consensus among economists and other observers is that information technology is at the core of future development trajectories in the U.S. and globally. For example, Henton and associates (1997) argue that this technology and its uses is one of four elements representing

DOI: 10.4018/978-1-61520-799-2.ch013

the characteristics of the future that communities must address. Don Tapscott (1996) discusses this impact on the business sector at length (as well as in education). Echoing these and other related changes, Mitchell (1995) argues that:

...the most crucial task before us is not one of putting in place the digital plumbing of broadband communications links and associated electronic appliances (which we will certainly get anyway), nor even of producing electronically deliverable 'content,' but rather one of imagining and creating digitally mediated environments for the kinds of lives that we will want to lead and the sorts of communities that we will want to have. ...It matters because the emerging civic structures and spatial arrangements of the digital era will profoundly affect our access to economic opportunities and public services, the character and content of public discourse, the forms of cultural activity, the enaction of power, and the experiences that give shape and texture to our daily routines. (1995: 5)

As might be imagined, the actual nature of the diffusion and utilization of ICT in rural areas presents a very uneven picture (Bell, et al, 2004). Despite reliance of policy makers on the private sector for service provision and infrastructure development, many rural communities have taken it upon themselves to develop their own infrastructure out of fear they were going to be left out when the private sector made its infrastructure investment decisions (Pigg and Crank, 2005). At best, many rural areas suspected that private investment that would provide broadband ICT services would be delayed until very late in the process. Especially for those communities that already operated their own utilities, this investment decision was straightforward and different systems—fiber optic, copper, wireless, etc.—were all considered for adoption and implementation with communities choosing those that appeared to best meet their needs. In this study we are primarily interested in the adoption and deployment of

broadband services that support internet access. As noted by Bell and associates (2004), the nature of internet service provision in rural areas is quite diffuse with few large private providers serving this market. Further, it is substantiated by our study that many rural internet users indicate they only have one provider available to them and, even in 2003, many of these services did not provide access to broadband (80% of those using the internet were still using dial-up services in 2003).

In this study we were able to determine that these investment decisions were made in some rural communities even before the Clinton initiative was announced. Sometimes rural communities were able to leverage private sector plans for infrastructure investments into implementation of service delivery to their communities that might have otherwise been bypassed. The general attitude for rural community leaders was that, for economic development purposes, remaining competitive in the global economy meant having access to ICT for business and residential use. Repeatedly, when community leaders were asked in this study to identify reasons for their decisions to invest in ICT infrastructure, they responded that this technology was central to commercial interests and, as a rural area, they did not want to be left out of consideration for any type of possible development activity. Beyond that, local development strategies were remarkably unchanged from those documented widely in the literature; industrial attraction still dominated the thinking of rural leaders in this study.

BACKGROUND

ICT Effects: Where are Rural Areas?

There continues to be little information available that speaks directly to rural areas and the effects of ICT infrastructure development and utilization. Some of the available research relies on the ongoing Pew Internet and American Life surveys for information on rural users (e.g., Bell, et al, 2004) and other analyses rely on data from the FCC (e.g., Lehr, et al, 2006). The Federal Communications Commission (FCC) reports the numbers of providers by zip code, but providers only have to report one account in order to have residents in this zip code designated as having access to broadband; the actual number of users or accounts is not reported. The National Agricultural Statistics Service conducts a biennial survey of farms that includes several questions on internet and computer use, but their approach uses an area sample that does not provide for aggregation at any level lower than that of the state (e.g., NASS, 2007). The National Telecommunications Cooperative Association conducted its own survey in 2003 and determined that virtually all of their 200+ member organizations (the majority of whom likely serve mostly rural and small town residents) were offering internet service via broadband infrastructure but only a small portion of their clientele subscribed to this service (NTCA, 2003).

The "demand" factor for rural America may cause some delay in service provision. Without adequate, demonstrated demand for broadband services, the private sector is unlikely to extend services to new areas (Civille, et al, 2001). The difficulty in extending services at a reasonable cost is a well-known factor in the decision making of private carriers to rural users, especially in the more remote areas. At the same time, the NTCA study (2003) and that of Bell and associates (2004) would suggest that rural clients are less educated and have lower incomes, factors related to lower use rates among the general population. If so, the larger proportion of rural residents fitting such categories may explain the slower "uptake" of services now available and the slow growth of private sector providers. In addition, rural users tend to be attracted to different applications or reasons for being online than the general population (Bell, et al, 2004). The Pew survey data indicate, again confirmed by our research, that email is

still the "killer application" for rural users, likely related to their more remote locations. There may be a greater distrust of this communication form at present as Bell and associates (2004) found that rural users are less likely to make purchases online, conduct their financial affairs online or make travel reservations.

Notwithstanding these reports, there is not very much known about rural areas and their uses of broadband, especially in a community development context. As it can be seen from the above references, most research now available deals with individual or household users. There is a very limited amount of information available about business use, especially in rural areas. Most studies related to economic development activities use national data sets with little regard for rural distinctions. For example, in a study of home-based businesses Phillips (2002) ignores rural altogether. In another study related to human capital needs the Small Business Administration noted that the shortage of qualified information technology workers was a real obstacle to entrepreneurial activity and this would be particularly acute in rural areas (J. Popkin & Co., 1999), a situation echoed by Van Wart and associates (2000).

Community Economic Development

Community economic development (CED) is not focused on growth for growth's sake, but on the changes necessary to increase the capacity to produce sustainable economic systems (Shaffer, et al, 2006). It involves more than the typical land, labor, physical and financial assets of communities. Community economic development also addresses community culture, social capital, decision-making and leadership capacity. It involves the way in which the community deals with innovation and related technology and change. Successful communities may not grow in size, but their economies may change in ways that make them more sustainable over time and will likely exhibit the kind of broad perspectives that recognize attitudes and values as important as factors of production (Henton, et al, 1997).

Within this context, information and communications technology may play a very important role. Such computer-based technology is being integrated into systems of production at ever increasing rates. Beyond that, these technologies increase productivity by also decreasing transaction costs, especially in regional clustering strategies for economic development and in helping firms deal with global marketplaces (Pigg and Bradshaw, 2003; Shaffer, et al, 2006). Unfortunately, one of the findings of this study is that communities—and many rural businesses—do not understand the capacity of broadband ICT to improve productivity and profitability (Pigg, 2005). While there are a few examples identified in this research where rural businesses have profitably engaged ICT capacity, the vast majority uses it primarily for email and file transfer, with some limited use as a base for transaction management. Pigg (2005) has attributed this to a lack of appreciation for the functional dimensions of ICT—content management, appropriation, interaction and scalability. For this and, perhaps, other reasons (e.g, lack of appropriate resources), rural communities in this study generally fail to take full advantage of the capacity of ICT to support fundamental development changes in local economies.[1]

Community economic development strategies have used a number of approaches, often at the same time. In fact, some would argue that the only way for rural communities to be successful is to do more than one thing with regard to their strategy. Focusing efforts only on industrial attraction or tourism, while neglecting other possible avenues for development (such as entrepreneurship or existing business development) represents a strategy too narrow to engender much confidence of success.

RESEARCH DESIGN AND IMPLEMENTATION

Purpose of Research

The purpose of this research was to determine the relationship between ICT deployment and rural community economic development. Rather than take a technological deterministic approach a selective sample was developed of rural communities that had deployed broadband technology for the purposes of CED. In other words, this deployment was (supposedly) a central part of their strategy for CED.

A number of broad macro studies (e.g., Lehr, 2006) have been completed that reported on the impact of this technology on the economy, but few have directly addressed rural places and concerns. Further, even some of these studies have noted that, when rural issues are considered or when the actual mechanisms that influence the relationship between the technology and the economic development results are considered, smaller scale case study approaches would be very helpful (Lehr, 2006). This study anticipated some of these concerns and should help answer some of these questions.

Research Design

Using a comparative case study approach, this research identified twenty-three rural communities that met certain criteria. These criteria included:

1. Located at least 70 miles from an international airport;[2]
2. Population of 10,000 or fewer;[3]
3. An explicit link between broadband deployment and local economic development strategy; and,
4. Having deployed broadband for at least five years prior to this investigation.

This last criterion assumes that there is likely some time lag between deployment and its effects (Lehr, 2006). In addition, an effort was made to limit the locations in each state to no more than two. This was done in order to minimize the effects of specific state policies at encouraging the spread of broadband services such as has occurred in Kentucky, North Carolina, Iowa, Missouri, Texas and a few other states.[4]

Cases were identified using several means. Published lists of communities deploying this technology were screened to find suitable locations. Online searches were conducted using key words such as "community network" to find locations. In addition, the researcher's personal professional network of people working in this field was consulted to identify potential sites. In each case, of the ability of each case to meet the other criteria for selection was checked using telephone screening interviews and online resources.

Secondary data on economic performance was assembled to determine how each site chosen had performed in the past decade, a period that covered the deployment of this technology. As it would be expected, the early time point selected was 1990 for most all data used with the latest time point being 2005 for some data and 2003 for other data (depending on the source). Selected indicators were used in the final data analysis as both dependent and independent variables.

Data on the process and effects of broadband deployment was assembled from key informant interviews conducted with selected community leaders in each community. In most cases the number of interviewees numbered eight to ten people and included a variety of perspectives on local activities and decision-making. Both positional and reputational criteria were used to select key informants (see below). These interviews were generally conducted over a period of five days on site with a few follow-up phone interviews to capture information from people not available in the personal visit.

In addition to these interviews, secondary sources were used to verify and elaborate on interview data. Most of these communities maintain extensive web sites about their communities that often contained useful information about local activities. Most useful were those sites that provided links to local media such as newspaper archives that were searched for additional information as appropriate.

Once data files were completed a coding procedure was developed and tested against several of the pre-test interview results. The coding was organized around the primary independent variables, the components of the Entrepreneurial Social Infrastructure (ESI) (Flora, et al, 1997b) framework. This coding protocol was developed to reflect the various elements in the framework being tested in this research. For example, in the ESI framework one of the central elements is "mobilization of resources" addressing the community's ability to access and organize internal (to the community) and external resources, both human and financial. There were four types of resources considered based on the original work: public, private, institutional and fundraising in reference to both internal and external sources.[5] If the combined data sources provided reliable evidence of successful access to either human or financial resources in each of these eight possible categories, a score of "1" was entered. There was a total possible score of 14 for this element. Similar procedures were used for each of the elements of the two frameworks. In some instances, only the presence or absence of a specific indicator was used. For example, whether or not the community served as the county seat was coded either "1" or "0" and used as a proxy for being a central place. In other cases, a numerical score was used to designate the summation of several indicators such as the indication that several specific strategies were being used in the pursuit of economic development objectives. In this case, the higher the score, the more strategies were being employed (without regard for the relative success of any particular strategy).[6]

As indicated above, communities for study were selected by combining information from various secondary and primary sources. The final study sample includes twenty-three sites as noted in the Appendix. An original list that contained as many as forty possible sites was screened to identify 25-28 sites that likely met study criteria when the sample was first chosen.

Data Collection Procedures

A semi-structured survey was developed and pre-tested.[7] The final survey consisted of a series of questions that addressed topics such as: local economic development strategy, the process of broadband infrastructure deployment, partnerships developed during the process, relative success of development strategy, the role of broadband in this strategy, future directions, indicators related to the Entrepreneurial Social Infrastructure, special factors that may have affected development activities, and other specific activities or efforts that may have been identified during each interview. Interviews were conducted with community leaders who were in roles related to broadband deployment, economic development, local government, media representatives, library directors, healthcare system administrators, school system officials, local business people and anyone else identified by local informants in an abbreviated "snowball" process. This sort of key informant strategy is widely used in community research and case study research (Krannich and Humphrey, 1986). Each interview was either recorded or was subject to extensive note taking; each interview was subsequently entered into a word processing file for future reference.

Entrepreneurial Social Infrastructure

The model used here has been described in previous research by Flora and Flora (1993) who de-veloped the Entrepreneurial Social Infrastructure (ESI) as a framework of components, structure, and process indicators that encourage collective action to achieve tangible goals in which social capital is a necessary, but not a complete prerequisite. Flora (1998) discusses the relationship between collective action within the community and the social infrastructure arguing that communities that engage in collective action to better the community are "entrepreneurial." Flora and Flora (1993) had found that those communities with a recent locally generated economic development project were more likely to possess the presence of the ESI main components (see Figure 1). The following components encompass the ESI framework: *legitimacy of alternatives*, the *mobilization of diverse resources*, and the *presence of network qualities* (Flora, 1998: 490-493).

In order to empirically test the components of ESI, Flora et al. (1997b) used a sample of key informant surveys of non-metropolitan towns. They found that communities with successful economic development projects are best carried out when the community possesses the presence of the following (examples of structural indicators):

- *A newspaper that initiated the flow of information about local issues.* This provided a way that controversial issues could be exposed and discussed by the community in an unbiased fashion in which the diversity of opinions of the community could be included. (Legitimacy of Alternatives)

  Financial institutions which play a financial role to community projects by providingcommercial loans at a low-interest; Grants, donations, foundations or other contributions of service on a financial committee (Resource Mobilization)

- *Larger number of horizontal/vertical linkages within and outside the community* (Network Qualities)

Figure 1. The entrepreneurial social infrastructure model (Flora 1998: 491)

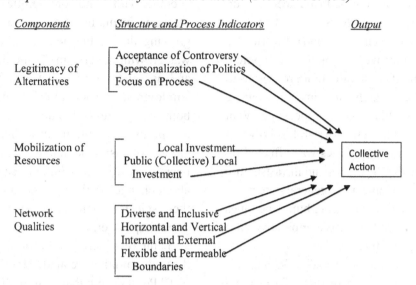

According to Flora (1998), the presence of ESI indicators are first dependent upon the presence of social capital, the broadness of community participation in local projects, and the ability to create and participate in local community economic development projects. These factors will significantly enhance the likelihood of a greater amount of Entrepreneurial Social Infrastructure (ESI). The ESI framework was used to study the relationship between ICT infrastructure and social organization regarding the achievement of economic development outcomes in rural communities that have deployed ICTs expressly for achieving local economic development. Our study was carried out like Flora et al.'s (1997a) study of Riverview. The operationalization of the components of ESI in our study of rural communities is discussed below.

RESEARCH FINDINGS

Community Economic Development

The communities studied in this research appear to be pretty typical for rural communities in the United States with certain exceptions (see Table 1). Their population in the 2000 Census was about 7,000 people with some of the communities being smaller than this and one being about 18,000 people. Median household income in 2000 was below the national average for rural counties in the U.S. ($32,022) showing that these were not exceptionally wealthy communities that deployed broadband technology. Not quite one-third of the population (2,986 people) was employed on average and the unemployment rate in 2000 was below the national average at 4.6 per cent (compared to 6.1%) although the range of unemployment was rather large (.9% to 18.6%). All of these communities had some information, communication technology businesses and an average of nearly 250 people employed in such businesses, an average higher than the average for all U.S. counties (160 persons employed). It cannot be determined how many of these may were employed in broadband-related firms. When compared to county figures for all U.S. rural counties, one can see these case study communities are likely to be found in typically smaller, less wealthy places with smaller work-forces and small, but not insignificant numbers of ICT workers and businesses. Some of these other places likely have broadband access as do those selected for this study. Some of them may even have deployed their broadband infrastructure in an effort to improve economic development prospects. Without substantial more resources to be invested in the research effort, investigating the complete scope of this impact is impossible. What can be determined from this research is how this selected group of communities was affected by their decision to deploy broadband infrastructure for economic development. No general statements for all rural places can be made, but some clues may become evident from this comparative case study that can guide future efforts.

When the direction of a decade of changes is examined (see Table 2) a picture of relatively healthy, viable communities is evident. These communities all were growing in population and income with a mean population change of nearly seven thousand people and an average household income change of forty-two per cent. Employment grew an average of nine per cent although at least one community experienced a loss of employment of over fourteen per cent. Another measure of economic change is the change in income inequality as measured by the Gini coefficient; this figure increased by a small amount, just two per cent on

average, with some communities showing a decrease in inequality. So, even as incomes were growing during the decade, income inequality was growing a very small amount. As Isserman and associates (2007) have shown, growth in employment and declining income inequality are both strongly related to the development of rural prosperity. In addition, these data show that the number of businesses and workers in ICT-related businesses were growing. Given what we know about changes in the rural economy in the U.S., these selected communities seem to be in pretty good shape overall.

Is the relatively good economic condition of these communities related to their deployment of ICT? Perhaps, but that is more difficult to determine. This study did not find much evidence that deployment of broadband led to increased business/industry use, especially for the kinds of uses that would be considered productivity increasing. While isolated, specific examples were identified in most of the counties, to say that widespread utilization was occurring would be inaccurate. Further, as indicated in Figures 2 and 3, there does not appear to be any relationship evident between employment growth, 1990-2000 or change in income inequality (as measured by the Gini coef-

Table 1. Descriptive Statistics for Case Study Communities, 2000

	Case Study Communities			All US Rural Counties
	Minimum	Maximum	Mean	Mean
Median Household Income	20,268	40,167	29,922.95	32,022
Population	1,817	17,994	6,929.05	23,800
Employment	868	7,891	2,986.67	10,352
High School Enrollment	272	1,751	803.48	n/a
ICT Workers	10	1,278	248.10	160
ICT Businesses	1	55	15.57	9
Unemployment Rate	.9	18.6	4.64%	6.10%

Note: Data suppressed for 706 counties for ICT related measures.
Data Source: US Bureau of Census, 2000 and Bureau of Labor Statistics, 2003

Table 2. Change in Economic Status, 1990-2000

	Minimum	Maximum	Mean
Population change	1816.00	17993.00	6928.0476
Per cent change in ICT workers	4.00	572.00	138.1905
Per cent population change	18.16	179.93	69.2805
Per cent income change	18.75	77.70	42.2448
Per cent employment change	-14.25	63.70	9.1407
Per cent change in ICT businesses	1.00	31.00	9.0952
Per cent change in Gini coefficient	-11.11	13.33	2.1662

ficient), 1990-2000 and income growth for the same period. Therefore, it is difficult to claim that broadband access is directly tied to economic improvements such as increased employment. This is especially true because, in nearly every community studied, the economic development "strategy" was no different than that regarding any other type of infrastructure improvement: "build it and they will come." There were several communities where the strategy had been extended beyond an industrial attraction strategy to include a "new business development/technology-diffusion" strategy. However, these were so early in their implementation that it would be hard to say that any substantive economic improvement in these secondary data could be identified.[8]

Further, as it regards actual business use, there were only a few businesses in a few communities that were making innovative uses of ICT and most of these had developed their applications "on their own" without much assistance from local development actors.

So, if this economic status cannot be explained by or attributed to the presence of broadband in the community, what might explain it?

Figure 2. Scatterplot: Per Cent Income Growth × Per Cent Employment Change

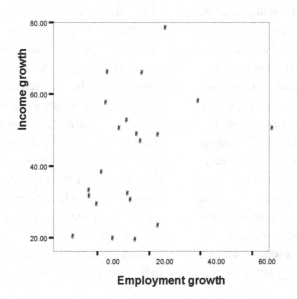

Figure 3. Scatterplot: Percent Income Growth × Percent Gini Coefficient

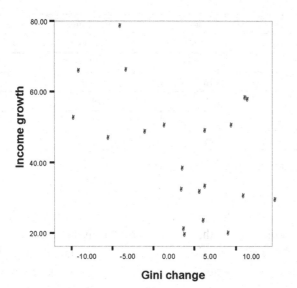

A Development Model Identified

The research tested the ESI model as identified above in recognition that a technological determinism was not appropriate nor was a model based only on macro or economic factors. The research was organized to provide information useful for determining whether this model was valid. Measures were developed for the primary conceptual indicators in the model and, along with some standard macro indicators from the literature on economic development at local levels for rural communities, tests were conducted to determine which indicators best fit the analytical model.

The primary variables included in the analysis are shown in Table 3. The ESI scores were developed using the methodology described above and were used as independent variables. The mean score for ESI was 15.8 with a minimum score of eleven and a maximum score of twenty-one.

The other variables were calculated using data from the U.S. Census Bureau comparing 1990 and 2000 data sources to produce indicators of change. The two variables representing change in the ICT economic sector, change in the number

of ICT workers and ICT businesses, should represent the direct impact of the deployment of ICT and broadband in these communities as a direct effect. As noted in Table 2, there is considerable variation in this effect across the study communities. The indicators of "development" in the broader sense, change in population, change in household income levels and change in employment, are rather traditional measures found in much of the literature on this topic. The inclusion of the Gini coefficient indicator is an attempt to determine whether the economic effects of broadband deployment are isolated or more widespread in the community. As Isserman and associates (2007) have shown, increasing rural community prosperity is strongly associated with decreasing income inequality. These macro indicators were used as independent variables as well, except for the change in income variable that used as the dependent variable to represent "development." As noted in Table 3, there are only isolated instances where correlations are significant between any of these indicators. One of these is to be expected: the close association between the change in ICT workers and the change in ICT businesses.

Table 3. Partial Correlations for Analytic Variables

Variable	Per cent population change	Per cent change in # ICT workers	Per cent income change	Per cent change in employment	Per cent change in ICT businesses	Per cent change in Gini coefficient	ESI Score
Per cent population change	1.000						
Per cent change in # ICT workers	.249	1.000					
Per cent income change	-.115	.120	1.000				
Per cent change in employment	-.238	-.090	.364	1.000			
Per cent change in ICT businesses	.244	.905**	-.203	-.030	1.000		
Per cent change in Gini coefficient	.448*	.070	-.075	.028	.068	1.000	
ESI Score	.040	.067	.416	-.006	.139	.024	1.000

*. Correlation is significant at the 0.05 level (2-tailed).

**. Correlation is significant at the 0.01 level (2-tailed).

The second is also not unusual: the modest association between change in income and change in employment. Other such variables representing the trends in the local community economies could have been shown here, but the trends identified are similar.

For the rural/non-metro U.S. as a whole, median family income grew forty-three per cent from 1990 to 2000 as compared to the 42.2 per cent growth in this sample. So, this small sample of ICT enabled counties has not experienced any greater growth in income than all non-metro counties, again bringing into question the effect of broadband deployments.

A linear regression analysis was explored to determine the effects of various indicators on "economic development" as measured, in this case, as household income change. Other indicators might have been used such as overall population change or employment change, but this indicator seems fundamental to the development outcomes most people are concerned about. Unless employment growth is linked to income growth, it is hardly to be considered "develop-

ment." Unless population growth is similarly linked to income growth, most observers would agree that development has not occurred. Linear regression analysis explored several combinations of variables including income growth, employment growth and population growth as dependent variables, always trying to test the effects of the theoretical models introduced in this study. The use of employment growth and population growth did not produce results with very large amounts of variance explained. However, when income growth was used as the dependent variable, about forty per cent of the variance in this indicator was explained by growth in employment, change in the Gini coefficient, county seat status (likely associated with a central role in local economies), presence of a diverse strategy for community economic development, and the total score on the ESI index (See Table 4). Running this model with only the most significant variables produces an adjusted R-square of .404 and this model is statistically significant. With this result, the ESI model is a significant predictor variable along with the change in income inequality. Perhaps, because

Table 4. Linear Regression Model of Rural Community Economic Development and Entrepreneurial Social Infrastructure

Variable	Beta (standardized)	Adjusted R-square	Significance
Per Change in Household Income: Dependent			
Per Cent Change in Employment, 1990-2000	.414		.530
Per Change in Gini coefficient Score, 1990-2000	-.421		.031**
County Seat (Yes/No)	.316		.117
Presence of a diverse economic development strategy? (1-5)	-.256		.228
ESI Score	.366		.089*
Total		.404	.022**

* Sig. at 0.05 level
** Sig. at 0.01 level

the ESI framework addresses a broader variety of elements or because of the theoretical power of the concept and its measurement, it provides a more robust model.

While not a statistically significant contributor in this model, the employment change variable has a substantial effect on the results of the model, increasing the adjusted R-square from .234 to .404. It may be an artifact of the data itself since this indicator is not highly correlated with the per cent income change over time (Pearson's correlation of .364).

The negative signs on the Gini coefficient change indicator and the diverse economic development strategy indicator are interesting to consider. The first appears quite logical and satisfactory in that community economic development efforts are often aimed at developing better wages for the work force and the efforts of these communities appears to be linked to this process successfully. This finding confirms that of Isserman and his associates (2007) in recent work showing the importance of declining income inequality on rural prosperity at the county level. One of the factors at play here may be the increased access to information provided by ICT deployment across

a broad spectrum of households and commercial enterprises that may contribute to increased economic opportunity and a general "flattening" of the income distribution in the community. The second result seems counter-intuitive as most rural development observers argue for "doing more than just one thing," and having several approaches to community economic development. However, this result suggests that having multiple approaches so severely taxes local resources as to make one or more of these strategies, if not all, ineffective and efforts are better spent on a more focused, targeted, strategic approach. The presence of the county seat indicator suggests some linkage to central place theory and the continuing focus on dominant places within a region as the most successful economic development sites.

CONCLUSION

Is There an ICT Effect?

There does not seem to be a direct effect on community economic development from ICT deployment for the cases studied as all had deployed

ICT as part of their CED strategy; however, the measures of the economic development status of these cases are generally not that much different than that of other rural locations. Further, there was little evidence of actual application of this deployment for CED purposes. While residential adoption was evident in growing numbers of subscribers to internet service reported, business and community use was minimal. As noted above, electronic mail use was still the killer application 5-10 years after broadband deployment, even when the system is community owned. A few businesses had developed online catalogs and transaction support for taking orders and making shipments. Some businesses were using file attachments on their email messages to exchange business related files and many businesses had their own websites for marketing purposes. This limited use shows little understanding of the broader functional capability of the Internet to accomplish a variety of objectives related to CED (Pigg, 2005).[9]

The use of the Internet for businesses that do not or cannot depend on local consumers alone to make a good profit is especially important. While located in rural areas, some business ventures may depend on a regional or national clientele for success. For example, a specialty auto parts business for antique vehicles cannot make a decent profit by depending on a clientele in a rural community of only several thousand people and will, instead, have to develop markets nationally. Analysis by Quaddus and Achjari (2005) suggest business adoption is not so much a factor of overcoming internal or external obstacles, as it is being able to actually determine the real benefits of Internet adoption to an enterprise. In rural areas where there are few other examples to learn from, a concrete demonstration of benefits may be very difficult. Along with these benefits is the necessity of building a recurring revenue stream to support the continuous need for technological change and system upgrades as noted by some of the case study informants.

Further, there is little evidence of a "community" effect of Internet use. There is very little understanding of how to build community using ICT. For example, one of the case study locations was represented online by over twenty different locally maintained websites, but there was no "community" site and no apparent recognition of a community information infrastructure that was using ICT to achieve civic objectives, including CED. When multiple community sites exist, some redundancy could be used to interconnect these and make sure non-conflicting information is present. Communities also need to make sure that inconsistent "branding" for their community is avoided, a real problem for achieving CED success.

Using ICT to achieve civic objectives is also not apparent in this study. Community leaders (and residents) do not view the Internet as a source of local civic/community information. For example, very few local newspapers (if a community had one) featured an online version of the paper and those that do have difficulty building financial support for this version. The dependence of news media on advertising for revenues may be an obstacle here, especially when ownership is not local. If local businesses see little return for online advertising they are unlikely to support an electronic version of the newspaper. Further, local governments in rural communities are not adopting e-government services at a rapid rate.

Implications for Practice

There are tremendous opportunities in ICT applications for the extension of work being done in public and private arenas. Building an understanding of the capacity of ICT to transform social and economic systems at the community and regional levels is the central challenge in this opportunity. Demonstration projects that focus on the benefits to economic and civic life is fundamental to long-term success. Traditionally, one might think of achieving this success through training activity.

Most users at present are figuring out how to do things on their own. They draw upon their own skills and knowledge to develop an understanding of network hardware and applications. They also draw upon local "experts" who may spend a great deal of time working in this field either as an economic venture or as a pastime (Stewart, 2007). However, this learning curve can be very steep if you can only spend a couple hours a week learning something new about technology use. Learning to use this technology is a function of imagination and training, so training itself needs to be of a different sort with plenty of opportunities provided to stretch one's imagination (Nnadi and Gurstein, 2007). Such training is likely expensive and may only be feasible in institutional settings such as schools.

Interestingly, some of the institutions most typically seen as key to community deployment of ICT—schools, libraries, health care facilities—seem woefully unprepared to undertake this role. Libraries often see themselves in this role, but have few resources to use to make any training they currently provide very helpful in the general sense. It tends to be very introductory for users as a matter of practical consideration. Health care facilities are generally only beginning to make broad use of ICT in rural settings as their resources are constrained. Schools are, perhaps, better positioned for such a role, but many do not see "community education" as within their scope of responsibility. They are often doing a remarkable job of introducing ICT to their own students in imaginative ways. For example, in several of the case study sites local schools had mobilized enough resources to have a technology education program in place that was very diverse including having their own radio and television stations (with students to staff production), computer graphics labs and animation courses, and some work in entrepreneurship so that graduates might think about setting up a related business in the community in which they reside. Community-based training systems were largely non-existent in these

rural communities except for a few "technology incubators" for new business development where training was largely on a one-to-one basis.

One of the most glaring needs is for a "model" community resource—I hesitate to call it a web site as I think that may be too restrictive—that demonstrates how to use ICT to build community and to build capacity for community and economic development across the community's members. Such a resource would be civic in its orientation and demonstrate the resources available and provide examples of the kinds of applications that could be employed for building community capacity—collective rather than individual. During the course of this research many individual, limited examples were found that, if organized in one location for general electronic access, might be very useful. Ideally, however, community groups would organize such a project on their own tailoring the model to meet local needs and their own vision of where they wish to go as a community.

In the design of community development programs to build community capacity for development beyond ICT training, the ESI framework offers some useful guidance. Strengthening the appreciation for diversity and capacity for conflict management is but one challenge presented by this framework. Assisting with the mobilization of resources, both internal and external, is another primary challenge. Finally, building and strengthening the political and economic networks that can support local efforts is an ongoing challenge. It should also be recognized that many rural communities are conservative and protective of the status quo. Change is disliked and to be avoided if at all possible (Norris, 2001; Procter, 2005). So, using ICT in new ways is a challenge to the status quo as is anything else that is "new" and may be strongly resisted. Building on the ideas contained in Henton, et al (1997) and encouraging the involvement of civic entrepreneurs may be an appropriate community development strategy in such settings.

Implications for Policy

In the U.S. for the past eight years a policy based on increasing competition has been followed with rather limited intervention by federal (and state) governments. Less success can be documented for rural areas with low population density even though this policy appears to have generated significant infrastructure investment and improved access in metropolitan and suburban areas (with high population density). From a competitive standpoint, such differentiation makes sense as the costs of infrastructure deployment are more difficult to recapture in a reasonable amount of time. It is, perhaps, indicative of the difficulties faced in such a policy regime that many local entities have taken initiative to supplement this competitive strategy with interventions designed to increase access and build user capacity through public investment (Picot and Wernick, 2007). As indicated in this study, many key informants expressed frustration with the private sector's lack of attention to their rural communities resulting in local investment decisions to construct their own infrastructure. In many cases, this decision was facilitated by the presence of a locally owned or municipal utility that could undertake such a venture (NTCA, 2003). Clearly, such efforts can expand access and there appears to be little reason to establish obstacles to such local investment in places where the private sector has little incentive to invest. Combining some aspects of public good policy with this competitive basis would support such local initiatives more aggressively.

FUTURE RESEARCH NEEDS

As Firth and Mellor (2005) have pointed out, there is little documented impact of broadband deployment in the literature in education, healthcare, social relations, or economic prosperity. The processes involved in all these areas are complex and it is unlikely that one factor alone will have much effect when it is changed. In the economic field these authors note that, while the greatest number of jobs created is usually by small and medium sized enterprises (SME), it is these ventures that are the slowest, generally, to adopt ICT changes in their activities. This is largely because they do not have the expertise or the resources to acquire them without some substantial demonstration of benefit to be gained.

On the other hand, large scale studies by Lehr, et al (2006) and others would indicate there is some impact to be demonstrated on the economy as a whole. There is demonstrated growth in jobs, particularly those related to the "knowledge industry" as was true in the sites in this study, as well as in changes in income levels. However, for community economic development in rural areas, this link is likely more complex and involves the availability of human capital to work in related jobs, educational programs to prepare such workers, and support for entrepreneurial and small business development efforts. Research to demonstrate these linkages, as well as others not anticipated here, would support community efforts to redirect their resources in ways more conducive to leveraging this technology for positive development outcomes. Further, despite the lack of evidence cited by Firth and Mellor (2005), this study has found a limited number of SMEs that were fully engaged in the use of ICT in their business, often in innovative ways. These were mostly retail enterprises where entry costs are relatively cheaper than in manufacturing enterprises, but further documentation of the obstacles faced and the resources necessary to overcome them would be productive of important changes that would assist rural places.

As noted by Strover and associates (2004) in their assessment of the Texas Infrastructure Fund's efforts to increase public access, "... building community is a necessary precursor to building a successful community network" (p. 482). The research reported here extends this notion to include the efforts necessary to build community so as to leverage the investments made in deployment of the infrastructure, since building a "community network" takes even more effort. The fact that quite a few of the locations studied in this research had deployed broadband over ten years ago would indicate how important it is to know what to do with the infrastructure once it is in place. Recently, I have become aware of a growing number of rural communities that have deployed broadband in the form of wireless technology and it would be interesting to compare the developmental experience of those places with the rural communities in this study that have nearly all relied on wireline technology for deploying broadband. It may be that local loop unbundling (LLU) of the ICT infrastructure can overcome impediments in employing the technology for achieving economic and social outcomes (Picot and Wernick, 2007). Such efforts should be more fully investigated to see if, in fact, this LLU process can effect broadband adoption in rural places (Distaso, et al, 2006). In conjunction with such research, a comparison of demand side and supply side policy comparisons should be undertaken to determine whether local initiatives such as those studied here might be a key to greater deployment of ICT for rural communities (Picot and Mellor, 2007).

Despite this research and the calls for more recognition of the importance of the community building process in relation to achieving economic and social objectives, this field suffers from too little research investment in understanding the elements of this process and its outcomes. This research does not fully address the question of the impact of ICT deployment since it does not include a group of control communities, but it does demonstrate in a very preliminary manner that the technology by itself cannot achieve success in community economic development. The research was limited by available resources to finding communities where the technology had been deployed ostensibly for the purpose of development and determining what development objectives had been achieved. The findings

underscore the importance of factors other than technology in achieving development objectives. The resources necessary to draw a sample from the population of all rural communities and do a better comparative study might produce different results than those in this study or such a study may only confirm what this study has found. The point is that this is a research area that is lacking in access to adequate resources and faces a number of data problems regarding measures of infrastructure access and availability due to policies implemented by federal and state agencies.

ACKNOWLEDGMENT

This research was conducted with financial support from the USDA/CSREES, National Research Initiative under Project No. Project No. 2003-35401-13769 and institutional support from the University of Missouri.

REFERENCES

Bell, P., Ready, P., & Rainie, L. (2004). *Rural Areas and the Internet*. Washington, D.C.: Pew Internet and American Life Project.

Civille, R., Gurstein, M., & Pigg, K. E. (2001). *Access to What? First Mile Issues for Rural Broadband. Report prepared for the Computer Science and Telecommunications Board, Broadband Last Mile Technology Project*. Washington, D.C.: National Research Council.

Distaso, W., Lupi, P., & Manenti, F. M. (2006). Platform competition and broadband uptake: Theory and empirical evidence from the European Union. *Information Economics and Policy, 18*(1), 87–106. doi:10.1016/j.infoecopol.2005.07.002

Federal Communications Commission (FCC). (2007). *Local Telephone Competition and Broadband Deployment*. Washington, D.C.: United States Department of Commerce. Retrieved October 2009 from http://www.fcc.gov/wcb/iatd/comp.html

Firth, L., & Mellor, D. (2005). Broadband: benefits and problems. *Telecommunications Policy, 29*(2), 223–236. doi:10.1016/j.telpol.2004.11.004

Flora, C. B., & Flora, J. L. (1993). Entrepreneurial Social Infrastructure: A Necessary Ingredient. *The Annals of the American Academy of Social and Political Sciences, 529,* 48–58. doi:10.1177/0002716293529001005

Flora, C. B., Hales, B., Petrzelka, P., Trca-Black, S., & Zacharakis-Jutz, J. (1997a). *Social Reconnaissance: Field Research by a Student Team to Inform a Participatory Community Development Project.* Paper presented at the Annual Meeting of the Community Development Society, Athens, GA, July 27-30.

Flora, C. B., Sharp, J., Flora, C. B., & Newlon, B. (1997b). Entrepreneurial Social Infrastructure and Locally-Initiated Economic Development. *The Sociological Quarterly, 38*(4), 623–645. doi:10.1111/j.1533-8525.1997.tb00757.x

Flora, J. L. (1998). Social Capital and Communities of Place. *Rural Sociology, 63*(4), 481–506.

Gillett, S., Lehr, W. H., Osario, C., & Sirbu, M. A. (2006). *Measuring the Economic Impact of Broadband Deployment*. Washington, D.C., U.S. Dept. of Commerce/EDA: 53.

Henton, D., Melville, J., & Walesh, K. (1997). *Grassroots Leaders for a New Economy: How Civic Entrepreneurs are Building Prosperous Communities.* San Francisco: Jossey-Bass.

Isserman, A. M., Feser, E., & Warren, D. (2007). Why Some Rural Communities Prosper While Others Do Not. Report prepared for the Office of the Under Secretary for Rural Development, USDA. Urbana-Champaign: University of Illinois. Retrieved November 2007 from http://www.ace.uiuc.edu/Reap/IssermanFeserWarren_070523_RuralProsperity.pdf

J. Popkin & Company. (1999). *Labor shortages, needs and related issues in small and large businesses*. Report prepared for the Office of Advocacy of the U.S. Small Business Administration. Washington, D.C. December. Retrieved Octonber 2009 from www.sba.gov/advo/research/#wages

Krannich, R. D., & Humphrey, C. R. (1986). Using Key Informant Data in Comparative Community Research: An Empirical Assessment. *Sociological Methods & Research, 14*(4), 473–493. doi:10.1177/0049124186014004006

LaRose, R., Gregg, J. L., Strover, S., Straubhaar, J., & Carperter, S. (2007). Closing the rural broadband gap: Promoting adoption of the Internet in rural America. *Telecommunications Policy, 31*(6-7), 359–373. doi:10.1016/j.telpol.2007.04.004

Lehr, W. Osorio, C.A., Gillett, S. & Sirbu, M.A. (2006). *Measuring Broadband's Economic Impact*. Cambridge, MA: MIT, Engineering Systems Division, ESD-WP-2006-02. http://esd.mit.edu/WPS/esd-wp-2006-02.pdf Last accessed October 2009.

Mitchell, W. J. (1995). *City of Bits: Space, Place and the Infobahn*. Cambridge, MA: MIT Press.

National Agriculture Statistics Service. (2007). *Farm Computer Usage and Ownership*. Washington, DC: USDA, NASS.

National Telecommunciations Cooperative Assocation (NTCA). (2003). *NTCA 2003 Internet/Broadband Availability Survey Report*. Washington, DC. NTCA. Retrieved October 2009 from http://www.ntca.org/content_documents/2003broadband.pdf

Nnadi, N., & Gurstein, M. (2007). Towards Supporting Community Information Seeking and Use. *Journal of Community Informatics, 3*(1). Retrieved October 2009 from http://ci-journal.net/index.php/ciej/article/view/325

Norris, K. (2001). *Dakota: A Spiritual Geography*. New York: Houghton-Mifflin Co.

Picot, A., & Wernick, C. (2007). The role of governments in broadband access. *Telecommunications Policy, 31*(10/11), 660–674. doi:10.1016/j.telpol.2007.08.002

Pigg, K. E. (2005). Community Informatics and Community Development. *Community Development: Journal of the Community Development Society, 36*(1), 1–8. doi:10.1080/15575330509489867

Pigg, K. E., & Bradshaw, T. K. (2003). Catalytic Community Development: A Theory of Practice for Changing Rural Society. In Brown, D. L., & Swanson, L. (Eds.), *Challenges for Rural America in the 21ˢᵗ Century. State College*. PA: State University Press.

Pigg, K. E., & Crank, L. D. (2005). Do Information Communication Technologies Promote Rural Economic Development. *Community Development: Journal of the Community Development Society, 36*(1), 65–76. doi:10.1080/15575330509489872

Procter, D. (2005). *Civic Communion: The Rhetoric of Community Building*. Manhattan, KS: Kansas State University Press.

Quaddus, M., & Achjari, D. (2005). A model for electronic commerce success. *Telecommunications Policy, 29*(2-3), 127–152. doi:10.1016/j.telpol.2004.11.009

Shaffer, R., Deller, S., & Marcouiller, D. (2006). Rethinking Community Economic Development. *Economic Development Quarterly, 20*(1), 59–74. doi:10.1177/0891242405283106

Stewart, J. (2007). Local Experts in the Domestication of Information and Communication Technologies. *Information Communication and Society, 10*(4), 547–569. doi:10.1080/13691180701560093

Strover, S., Chapman, G., & Waters, J. (2004). Beyond community networking and CTCs: access, development and public policy. *Telecommunications Policy, 28*(7/8), 465–485. doi:10.1016/j.telpol.2004.05.008

Tapscott, D. (1996). *The Digital Economy: Promise and Peril in the Age of Networked Intelligence*. New York: McGraw-Hill.

Van Wart, M., Rahm, D., & Sanders, S. (2000). Economic Development and Public Enterprise: The Case of Rural Iowa's Telecommunications Utilities. *Economic Development Quarterly, 14*(2), 131–145. doi:10.1177/089124240001400201

ENDNOTES

[1] Later in this report, we will discuss some of the exceptions to this statement.

[2] This criterion is generally considered a key for economic developers as the emphasis on just-in-time manufacturing procedures and a global economy means locations are definitely important.

[3] One location is larger than this as initial data was incorrect.

[4] Broadband is a term that has many definitions. To the FCC, broadband means at least 200 Kbytes of service available to users. To many observers, this definition is out of date and inaccurate given its adoption in the 1990s. A broad definition was accepted for this research as some services were deployed as early as the late 1980s and some as recently as 2002. The sample of cases includes wireless and wired, copper and optical fiber as

well as coaxial. Each of these infrastructures delivers a different level of service, but each has been determined to meet the definition specified by the FCC criteria. In this study, it does not appear that the level of service provided has any special effect.

[5]   Fundraising was considered to be only relevant to internal resources given the definitions used in the original source (i.e., Flora, et al, 1997).

[6]   The complete instrument and codebook are available in the final project report to the sponsor.

[7]   The information from these pre-test sites was not used in the final study as some information was not available from these initial interviews.

[8]   The recently published study by Gillett, et al (2006) appears to contradict this conclusion, but the data problems associated with the Gillett et al study—which used zip code units of analysis-- make their findings somewhat suspect, especially for rural areas.

[9]   Residential adoption does not represent the same kind of challenge as business adoption. Residential use is likely the function of a different set of factors than is business use (LaRose, et al, 2007).

APPENDIX

List of Case Study Communities

1. Adel, Georgia
2. Sandersville, Georgia
3. Swainsboro, Georgia
4. Montpelier, Idaho
5. Salem, Illinois
6. Williamsport, Indiana
7. Centerville, Iowa
8. Colby, Kansas
9. Columbus, Kansas
10. Glasgow, Kentucky
11. Lebanon, Missouri
12. Taos, New Mexico
13. Oneonta, New York
14. Sparta, North Carolina
15. Legrande, Oregon
16. Bloomsburg, Pennsylvania
17. Tullahoma, Tennessee
18. Hamilton, Texas
19. Kilgore, Texas
20. Abingdon, Virginia
21. Broadway, Virginia
22. Forks, Washington
23. Fennimore, Wisconsin

Chapter 14
International ICT Spillover

Saeed Moshiri
University of Saskatchewan, Canada

Somaieh Nikpoor
University of Ottawa, Canada

ABSTRACT

Recent developments in information and communication technology (ICT) have affected all economic activities across the world. Although there is ample evidence for the direct impact of ICT on productivity, the spillover effect of ICT has so far not been sufficiently investigated, especially in the international context. This chapter discusses ICT and its spillover effects on labor productivity using an empirical growth model and panel data for 69 countries over the period 1992-2006. The results show that ICT and its spillover have positive impacts on productivity worldwide, but the effects are much stronger in developed countries than those in the less developed countries.

INTRODUCTION

For the past two decades, the ICT investment has been steadily increasing in many countries across the world. The global investment in ICT on average has increased from about 3 percent of GDP to about 8 percent for the period 1992-2006 (figure 1). In the same period, the labour productivity and total factor productivity have increased noticeably, particularly in the developed and some developing countries. Despite the earlier skepticism, the direct contribution of ICT

DOI: 10.4018/978-1-61520-799-2.ch014

investment on the recent productivity rise is now widely recognized in the literature (Jorgenson, 2001 & 2005; Oliner and Sichel, 2000 & 2002; Pilat and Van Ark, 2002; Stiroh, 2002; Stiroh and Jorgenson, 2000; Gordon, 2000).

The direct or capital deepening, effect of ICT on productivity is observed by the fact that the rapid technological progress in ICT capital has led to lower quality-adjusted prices and increasing output. However, ICT is a general purpose technology and its effect on productivity goes beyond the capital deepening effect (Lipsey *et al*, 2005). ICT is a form of knowledge and network capital that can improve overall productivity across dif-

Figure 1. World ICT Spending by its Components (1992-2006) – percent of GDP

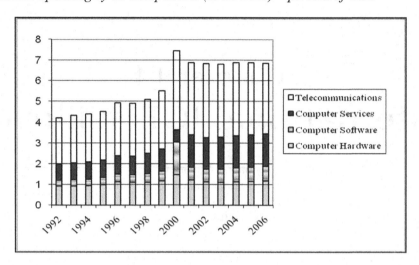

ferent sectors in the economy by its effects on organization, management, and human capital. ICT as knowledge capital is a non-rival good; the use of ICT products, such as software by one person does not need to detract its use by others. ICT also disrespects geographical distance, i.e. its products such as internet can be transmitted at a negligible cost (Quah, 2001). As network capital, ICT has a characteristic which implies that with more firms adopting it, the more the benefit that would accrue to existing ICT user firms without the latter bearing extra costs. Lee U Wen and Der Weil (2003), Arvantis (2005), Bartel and Shaw (2007) and Moshiri *et al* (2008) using firm-level data in different countries show that there is a positive and significant effect of ICT spillover on firms' productivity.

The idea of ICT spillover can be generalized to the international level. ICT tackles some of the main barriers to economic growth in less developed countries (LDCs), namely the lack of knowledge and information, scarce human capital, inefficient resource management and governance. ICT can help improve the standard of living in the LDCs not only by allowing them to produce ICT goods and services, but also by providing easy access to information and knowledge along with facilitating the use of other technologies. The investment in

ICT would also bring about higher educational attainment, better training, more skilled labour and, in general, higher level of human capital (Tallon and Kraemer, 1999, Mansell, 2000, and Wolf, 2003).

ICT distribution in the world is still polar. Not only the technology frontier and research and development in ICT remain merely in the developed world, but also ICT use is largely limited to the developed and some developing countries (OECD outlook, 2004.) As Figure 2 shows, the average ICT spending per GDP in North America is twice as much as that in Middle East.

Table 1 also shows a large disparity in ICT stocks between developed and less developed nations. Although the ICT distribution across the globe has become less unequal since 1993, a gap still remains large. For instance, for every 100 people having access to ICT in developed countries, there are only 4 to 6 persons that can use different forms of ICT in low income countries. This numbers in low-mid income countries are in the range of 11 to 30 people and in up-mid income countries 32 to 47 persons.

Although a large body of literature exists at the individual country or the regional level about ICT effect on the economy, little is known about the ICT effects at the international level. Most

Figure 2. ICT Spending by Regions, 2006- (percent of GDP

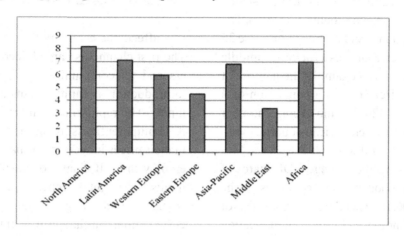

studies have focused on OECD countries or, in the case of developing nations, on individual countries or individual regions. This chapter has two objectives. First, it examines the direct productivity effects of ICT across the globe to shed some light on the differences between developed and less developed counties. Second, it investigates the spillover effect of ICT in these two groups of countries. More specifically, we seek answers to the following questions: (1) do developed and less-developed countries benefit from the ICT investment to the same extent? And (2) are there any ICT spillover effects among countries? To address these questions, we use a panel of data consisting of 14 years of observations for 69 countries. Our rather large data set allows us to capture the possible varying effects of ICT between different development blocks.

The next section reviews sample data. The model will be discussed in section 3 followed by the estimation results in sections 4 and 5. Section 6 concludes the chapter.

DATA

Investment in ICT has increased worldwide in recent decades. In 1995 the share of ICT spending in OECD countries was 8 percent of GDP, but it increased to 10 percent in 2001. In 2002 the trade in ICT goods was more than 14 percent of the world's trade (OECD Outlook, 2004). Table 1 displays data on ICT capital and its use. The huge gap in ICT investment between developed-developing countries is evident. The number of personal computers and The internet users per 1000

Table 1. World ICT infrastructure*

	Personal computers		Internet users		Telephone mainlines		Mobile phones	
	1993	2006	1993	2006	1993	2006	1993	2006
High income	1	1	1	1	1	1	1	1
Upper middle income	0.17	0.32	0.1	0.47	0.26	0.42	0.11	0.53
Lower middle income	0.06	0.11	0	0.20	0.15	0.27	0.03	0.29
Low income	0.02	0.05	0	0.06	0.02	0.04	0	0.06

* The numbers are the ratios with respect to the high income countries.
Sources: WITSA and author's calculation

people is more than 20 times as high in high-income countries as in low-income countries in 2006. The numbers of telephones and mobile phones are 25 times as high in rich countries as in lower- middle income countries. As an example, the number of Internet users in Ireland with a population of 4 million in 2003 is 324, but the average number of internet users in seven African countries with a population of 147 million is 297.

Figure 1 presents the average GDP shares of ICT-spending components in 69 countries for the period 1993-2006. ICT spending, which consists of information technology (IT) and communication technology (CT) expenditures, has increased from 4.2 percent of GDP in 1993 to about 8 percent in 2000 before decreasing to 7 percent in 2003. The hardware spending share of GDP has risen from 1 to 2 percent during the period. Software spending accounted for 0.2 percent of GDP in 1993 and 0.8 percent in 2006. Spending on computer services has increased from 0.8 to 1.3 percent of GDP during the same period. Spending on Telecommunication, which is the largest component of ICT spending, has increased by 1 percentage point for the post 14 years.

Figure 3 displays the relationship between the average ICT-spending ratio over 1993-2006 and GDP per capita in 2006 in 69 countries. It shows a positive correlation between ICT spending and the level of development measured by the GDP per capita. It also clearly shows significant disparities between developed and developing countries. Low and middle income countries are located in the left block, whereas the high income countries in the opposite block. This simple correlation may not fully capture the relationship between ICT investment and productivity growth, since it does not take into account the effects of other variables, such as human capital and investment rate, on growth. Therefore, we will estimate the relationship between ICT investment and economic performance using regression analysis, where we can control for the effects of other variables, in the section 4.

THEORETICAL FRAMEWORK

ICT affects the economy through two channels. The first channel is capital deepening. Computers and telecommunication devices contribute to production as capital inputs along with other inputs. The rapid improvement in the quality of ICT equipment and software and the sharp decline in their prices induce profit-maximizing firms to employ more ICT and to substitute it for other inputs. The capital deepening effect of ICT will change output along the aggregate production curve similar to a change in other inputs and therefore is subject to the diminishing returns of inputs. The second channel is spillover: ICT raises productivity through changes in organization, labour structure, and human resource management. The spillover impact will shift the aggregate production curve upward. To examine the impact of ICT on productivity, we use the following Cobb-Douglas aggregate production function:

$$Y = C^{a_c} . K^{a_k} . H^{a_h} . (AL)^{a_l} \tag{1}$$

Where Y is aggregate value added, C is ICT capital, K is physical (non-ICT) capital, H is human capital and AL is a labor augmenting technology. The a_i's are the input shares which add up to 1 under the assumption of constant returns to scale. Using a neoclassical growth model framework, we can write the evolution of different stocks of capitals as follows:

$$\frac{dc(t)}{dt} = s_c \cdot y(t) - (g + n + \delta) \cdot c(t)$$
$$\frac{dk(t)}{dt} = s_k \cdot y(t) - (g + n + \delta) \cdot k(t) \tag{2}$$
$$\frac{dh(t)}{dt} = s_h \cdot y(t) - (g + n + \delta) \cdot h(t)$$

where y is the level of output per effective labor, $y = Y\!\!\Big/\!\!_{AL}$, c, k, and h are the respective stocks

Figure 3: ICT spending and GDP per capita in 69 countries

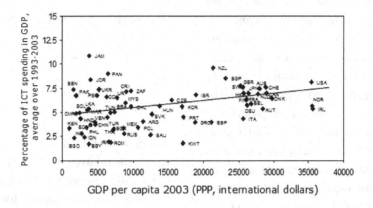

of different capital per unit of effective labor. The s-coefficients are the saving rates in each type of capital and δ is the rate of depreciation. Labor force and technology are assumed to grow at exogenous rates of n and a, respectively. In the long run, per effective labour capitals (c, k, and h) will be constant. Therefore, solving equation 2 for the steady state values of the capital stocks and inserting the results into the aggregate production function (1) result in the following equation for the steady state level of labour productivity.

$$Ln\frac{Y}{L} = a_{\circ} + \frac{a_c}{1-\beta}\cdot LnS_c + \frac{a_k}{1-\beta}\cdot LnS_k + \frac{a_h}{1-\beta}\cdot LnS_h - \frac{a_c+a_k+a_h}{1-\beta}\cdot LnZ$$

(3)

where, $a_{\circ} = \ln A + g\cdot t, \beta = a_c + a_k + a_h$ and $Z=g+n+\delta$. The depreciation rates δ are assumed to be the same for all types of capital. The steady state level of output per worker is positively related to the rates of saving in each type of capital. If data are available on the rates of saving (investment) in each type of capital, equation (3) can be estimated for a cross section of countries.

Equation (3) is based on the assumption that all countries are in their steady states. However, convergence to steady state is known to be slow and, therefore, the equation should be modified to reflect the adjustment process to the steady state.

We can model the dynamic process of convergence as follows:

$$\frac{d\ln y_t}{dt} = \lambda(\ln y * - \ln y_{\circ})$$

where y* is the steady-state level of output per effective labour, and λ is the adjustment rate to the steady-state condition. The adjustment process can be written as

$$\ln y_t = (1 - e^{-\lambda t})\ln y * + e^{-\lambda t}\ln y$$

or

$$\ln y_t - \ln y_0 = (1 - e^{-\lambda t})\ln y * - (1 - e^{-\lambda t})\ln y_0$$

Substituting for y* from (3), the following equation can be derived:

$$\ln\frac{Y(t)}{L(t)} - \ln\frac{Y(0)}{L(0)} = \theta.\ln A(0) + g.t + \theta.\frac{a_c}{1-\beta}.\ln s_c + \theta.\frac{a_k}{1-\beta}\ln s_k + \theta.\frac{a_h}{1-\beta}\ln s_h$$
$$-\theta.\frac{a_c+a_h+a_k}{1-\beta}\ln Z - \theta.\ln\frac{Y(0)}{L(0)}$$

(4)

where Y(0) and L(0) are output and labor in the initial period and where $\theta=(1-e^{-\lambda t})$ with $\lambda=\beta(g+n+\delta)$ that measures the speed of convergence (Mankiw, Romer and Weil, 1992). We can estimate equation (4) for a cross section of countries. This equation predicts that countries which have lower output per effective labor will grow faster until a higher steady state output per effective labor is reached.

In this model, ICT investment triggered by technology advances affects economic growth. In equation (4), the direct contributions of inputs to production growth are captured by the coefficients, but the indirect effect of inputs on production growth will be accumulated in the residual term. To isolate the indirect spillover effect, we need to construct a measure of international spillover. We apply the same measure of international trade used by Coe and Helpman's (1995) and Coe, Helpman, and Hoffmaisten (1997) for R&D spillover. The ICT spillover is measured by the following equation.

$$ICTF_i = \sum_j Im_{ig} / Im_i).ICTD_j \quad (5)$$

where $ICTD_j$ is domestic ICT investment in country j, Im_{ij} is the import by country i from country j, Im_i is country i's total imports, the ratio Im_{ij} / Im_i is bilateral import share which is used as a weight to country j's domestic ICT investment. Therefore, ICT spillover into country j is measured as ICT investment in country j's trading partners, weighted by bilateral import shares. Adding the spillover effect to equation (4), the equation for economic growth will take the following form:

$$\ln y_t - \ln y_0 = \theta.\ln A_0 + g.t + \theta.\frac{a_c}{1-\beta}.Lns_c + \theta.\frac{a_k}{1-\beta}Lns_k$$
$$+\theta.\frac{a_h}{1-\beta}Lns_h - \theta.\frac{a_c + a_h + a_k}{1-\beta}\ln Z - \theta.\ln y_0 + \varphi\ln ICTF_t$$
$$(6)$$

Labor productivity growth in a country is affected by not only ICT investment in that country, but also ICT investment in trading partners.

ESTIMATION RESULTS

We rewrite equation 6 as follows.

$$G_y = \theta.\ln A(0) + g.t + \varphi_c.\ln s_c + \varphi_k.\ln s_k + \varphi_h.\ln s_h + \varphi_4.\ln Z + \varphi_5.$$
$$\ln ICTF + \varphi_6.\ln y_0 \quad \varphi_i = \theta(\frac{a_i}{1-\beta}), i = c, k, h, \quad \varphi_4 = \sum_{i=c,k,h} \varphi_i$$
$$(7)$$

where, G_y is the change in real GDP per labor in each year relative to the real GDP in 1993. s_k is the saving rate which is measured by the ratio of gross domestic capital formation to GDP. s_c is the ratio of ICT spending to GDP as a proxy for investment rate in ICT. s_h is the investment rate in human capital which is measured by the ratio of secondary pupils to population. ICTF is the spillover variable that is equal to a country's bilateral import share weighted-average of domestic ICT investment of trading partners. Z is equal to $n+g+\delta$, where δ is the depreciation rate, n is population growth rate, and g is the average output per capita growth rate for the period 1993-2003. Δ is assumed 3 percent. g is 2 percent for OECD countries and 1 percent for non-OECD countries. y0 is GDP per labor in 1993.

We estimate equation 7 using panel data from 69 countries for the period 1993-2006. Data on GDP, gross domestic capital formation, labor force, population, price index and total import are obtained from World Development Indicators (WDI). Information about ICT spending is obtained from World Information Technology and Services Alliance (WITSA, 2002, 2004, and 2006). Data on secondary pupils and bilateral imports are from Euro Monitor's Global Market Information Database. The 69 countries in the sample are divided into OECD countries and non-OECD countries[1]. To avoid the spurious regression problem, we test the variables for unit root. The results of ADF-Fisher and PP-Fisher tests for unit root in panel data in Table 2 indicate that the variables do not have unit root, and, therefore, can be used as shown in equation 7.

Table2. The Panel Unit Root Tests

Test	G_y	s_k	s_c	ICTF	s_h	Z
ADF-Fisher Chi-Square	151.19	162.39	106.35	253.69	203.02	171.99
PP-Fisher Chi-Square	200.23	155.42	128.07	236.17	246.72	147.03

Before estimating equation 7, we use the F-test to test the hypothesis of the constant terms being equal. The results, which are shown in lower parts of Table 3 and Table 4, reject the hypothesis of same intercepts for all countries. We then apply the Hausman test that tests the orthogonally of the random effects and the regressors. Under the hypothesis of no correlation, both fixed effect and random effect are consistent but fixed effect is inefficient. Under the alternative hypothesis, fixed effect is consistent but random effect is not. The results of the Hausman test, which are shown in lower parts of Table 3 and Table 4, indicate that the fixed effect model should be used.

Table 3 shows the estimation results of the model presented by equation 7 for a sample of 69

Table 3. The Fixed Effects Estimation Results

	World (1) (2)		OECD (3) (4)		Non-OECD (5) (6)	
S_k	0.13** (0.018)	0.178*** (0.02)	0.318*** (0.053)	0.494*** (0.01)	0.093*** (0.018)	0.094*** (0.019)
LICTF	0.042* (0.016)	0.02 (0.015)	0.116** (0.032)	0.055* (0.026)	0.007 (0.011)	0.014 (0.009)
S_c	0.074*** (0.012)		0.16*** (0.031)		0.033* (0.012)	
S_{c1}		-0.005 (0.009)		-0.016 (0.015)		0.009 (0.01)
S_{c2}		0.089*** (0.009)		0.176*** (0.013)		0.023** (0.011)
S_h	0.012 (0.013)	0.016 (0.01)	0.029 (0.017)	0.039* (0.013)	-0.003 (0.017)	-0.004 (0.018)
z	-0.032*** (0.006)	-0.018* (0.006)	0.004 (0.008)	0.009 (0.007)	-0.082*** (0.011)	-0.077*** (0.012)
Y_0	0.642*** (0.077)	0.651*** (0.083)	-5.4+E11 (4.9E+12)	-2.6E+12 (3.9E+12)	0.662*** (0.073)	0.67*** (0.076)
R^2	0.68	0.72	0.47	0.63	0.81	0.82
F-Test	4.37	14.048	6.439	14.041	17.98	18.541
Hausman-Test	84.02	103.7	24.046	202.423	67.04	87.104

Note: Standard errors are in parentheses. * = significant at 5 per cent. ** = significant at 10 per cent. *** = significant at 1 per cent. The Hausman statistic with Chi-do distribution and k-1 degree of freedom is significant at 5, 10 and 1 per cent. Dependent variable is the change in the real GDP per labour from the year 1993 to 2003. s_k investment rate in physical capital, s_c investment rate in ICT capital, s_{c1} investment rate in hardware, software, office equipment and internal spending, s_{c2} investment rate in communication, s_h investment rate in human capital, LICTF is ICT spillovers, Z is $n+g+\delta$, y0 output per labor in initial period.

Table 4. Estimation Results with a New Measure of ICT Spillover

	World	Non-OECD
S_k	0.122*** [0.019]	0.09*** [0.019]
LITFOECD	0.078*** [0.016]	0.042* [0.015]
S_c	0.062*** [0.012]	0.027** [0.012]
S_h	0.01 [0.012]	-0.007 [0.017]
Z	-0.03*** [0.006]	-0.079*** [0.011]
Y_0	0.644*** [0.077]	0.665*** [0.073]
R^2	0.68	0.82
F-Test	11.418	20.509
Hausman-Test	97.39	66.556

Note: Standard errors are in parentheses. * = significant at 5 per cent. ** = significant at 10 per cent. *** = significant at 1 per cent. The Hasman statistic with Chi-do distribution and k-1 degree of freedom is significant at 5, 10 and 1 per cent. Dependent variable is the change in the real GDP per labour from the year 1993 to 2003. investment rate in physical capital, investment rate in ICT capital, investment rate in hardware, software, office equipment and internal spending, investment rate in communication, investment rate in human capital, LICTF is ICT spillovers, ITFOECD is ICT spillover from OECD countries, Z is , output per labor in initial period.

countries combined as well as for separate samples of 26 OECD countries and 44 non-OECD countries for the period 1993-2006. Column (1) presents the estimation results for equation (7) using the full sample size. They confirm that both physical capital and ICT affect productivity growth. The results also show that ICT spillover has positive and statistically significant impact on economic growth for 69 countries. Our results do not confirm the convergence hypothesis. This is understandable, as convergence takes a long time and it would not be captured during the rather short period covered in our study. Positive coefficient for initial output per labor indicates that high income countries, which have higher initial output per worker, could reap more benefits

from ICT investment during 1990s and, as a result, they were able to experience higher growth rates than low income countries.

ALTERNATIVE ESTIMATIONS

For further investigation we make some changes to our regression estimation. First, we estimate equation 7 for two groups of countries: OECD and non-OECD. Second, we divide ICT spending into IT (information technology) and CT (communication technology). And third, we create a new spillover variable using only OECD countries as trading partners. To compare the ICT effect on productivity growth between the OECD countries and non-OECD countries, we run two separate regressions for each group. The results are presented in columns (3) and (5) of Table 3. ICT has positive effect on productivity in OECD and in non OECD countries, but the effect in the former is five times as much as that in the latter. Moreover, the spillover has positive and statistically significant impact on economic growth in the OECD countries, but not in the non-OECD countries. Economic growth in OECD countries is boosted by the ICT investment in their trading partners, which are mostly the OECD countries. Human capital has also a significant impact on economic growth in OECD countries but not in non OECD countries.

ICT investment can be divided into two IT and CT investments. IT investment, denoted by s_{c1}, is the sum of hardware, software, office equipment, and internal spending, and CT investment, denoted by s_{c2}, is the communication spending. Since investment in IT is much higher than investment in CT, we examine their effects individually to find out which of these technologies is primarily responsible for the ICT effects on growth. The estimation results are presented in columns 2, 4 and 6 for the total sample, OECD and non OECD countries, respectively. Investment in information technology (IT) has a positive and significant impact on economic growth in all three groups, but investment in communication technology (CT) does not. The effect of investment in information technology on economic growth in OECD countries is on average nine times as much as that in non-OECD countries.

Finally, we specify the spillover variable assuming that the OECD countries are the only trading partners for both OECD and non OECD countries. Columns 2 and 3 of Table 4 present the estimation results of equation 7 with the new measure of ICT spillover. The results show that ICT spillover effect becomes significant for non-OECD countries when OECD countries are chosen as the trading partners. This implies that trading with OECD frontier countries will improve the technological transfer and economic growth.

CONCLUSION

In this chapter, we investigate the impact of ICT and its spillover on productivity growth among developed and less developed countries using a panel data set of 69 countries. The results of our growth model indicate that on average one percent rise in the ICT investment rate will lead to 0.07 percent increase in economic growth worldwide. The effect of ICT investment on economic growth is, however, found to vary among the countries. One percent increase in ICT investment rate in the OECD countries will increase productivity growth by as much as 0.16 percent and only by 0.03 percent in the non-OECD countries.

The ICT spillover measured by a bilateral trade index effects is also found to have significant impact on output per worker growth across countries. On average, one percent increases in spillover will lead to an increase in productivity by 0.04 percent. The impact of ICT spillover is also much larger in the OECD countries than the non-OECD countries. The ICT spillover is not a significant factor for a change in productivity growth in non-OECD countries. However, the

ICT spillover effect becomes significant when we limit the trading partners to only OECD countries in measuring the ICT spillover. This finding suggests that the new technology spillover flows from developed countries to less developed countries.

We also disaggregate the ICT investment into the communication technology (CT) investment and the information technology (IT) investment. The IT investment shows a positive and significant effect on economic growth in the total sample, as well as separately for OECD and non OECD countries. The effect is larger for the OECD countries (0.176) than for the non-OECD countries (0.023). The effect of CT is not found to be significant for any of the three groupings. Our results of positive and significant effects of ICT investment on productivity are consistent with Kraemer and Dedrick (2000). However, our findings of positive and significant relationship between the ICT investment and economic growth do not support the finding by Pohjola (2002) that there is no significant relationship between ICT investment and economic growth. Nor do our findings support the claim that developing countries can reap more benefits from ICT investment than the developed countries (Mansell, 2000). The lower impact of ICT on economic growth in non-OECD countries may be arising from the facts that the level of ICT investment in those countries is very low, and that developing countries lack physical and social infrastructures necessary to obtain full benefits of ICT investment.

The less developed countries (LDCs) have a great opportunity to improve their productivity and standard of living by investing in information and communication technology. The use of ICT, such as the internet, would make the markets more competitive, transparent, and efficient. It would induce not only investment in human capital but also organizational changes that reduce inefficiencies. Access to and use of ICT, especially high speed internet, may also attract more FDI from developed countries and reinforce research and scientific activities. Evidence suggests that although multinational companies tend to cluster in certain areas to reduce their transportation and communication costs in host countries, they may explore new areas if the distance barrier is removed (Ko, 2007). The use of ICT among the landlocked countries, the majority of which are among the least developed countries, is particularly important. Higher transportation and communication costs in these countries are one of the major barriers that impede FDI inflow from multinational companies (Faye *et al*, 2004). ICT may reduce the distance barrier facing the landlocked countries.

There is no universal pattern and investment strategy for less developed countries to expand their ICT sector and reap its benefits. ICT is a general technology with broad applications in hardware, software, and services. Although some developing countries, mostly in East Asia, have already invested in hardware production, but there is only a limited prospect in this line of development as the lion share of the hardware production still remains in the industrialized world. However, production of software, and more importantly, the use of both hardware and software can be done in a relatively short time span in many LDCs. For instance, the LDCs can enact policies that endorse development and upgrading of indigenous software with applications in health, education, and business in public and private sectors. While these activities create new jobs, they also create new incentives to learn ICT and facilitate access to other technologies. Countries like China, India, Iran, and Turkey are among developing countries that have been successfully developing their localized software to meet their needs. Unfortunately, the limited market size in some LDCs may hinder investment in indigenous ICT products. This market size limitation may be overcome to a large extent by developing software with regional, rather than national, characteristics.

In expanding the ICT sector in LDCs, it is important not to overestimate its short run effects on growth and to recognize the difference between availability of ICT and its use and the importance of necessary investment in information infrastructure.

ICT is a general purpose technology that its effects on economic growth follow a nonlinear pattern: The initial destructive effect will be followed by an upward trend and leveling off at the end (Lipsey *et al*, 2005). Therefore, the initial negative impact of ICT on some economic activities, and particularly reducing employment in some sectors, should not be viewed as an overall trend of the technology.

Although the availability and access to technology is necessary, it is by no means a sufficient condition for reaping its benefits. If people do not have an incentive to use new technology, its sole availability will not have much positive effect on the economy. Thus, the policy should not just be restricted to promoting investment in physical ICT capital and infrastructure whether is hardware or software, it should also facilitate and encourage the use of ICT and its various applications. For instance, policies aiming at training and education at schools and workplaces would help spread the use of new technology across the economy. Similarly, developing localized software may facilitate and speed up the diffusion of the new technology across the borders.

Finally, the existence of complementary factors is vital to the development of ICT. These include hard and soft infrastructure. Hard infrastructure such as computers, broadband internet lines, and communication devices need to be imported by government, private sector, or by the help of international organizations. But soft infrastructure, like education, health, and efficient government policies can be produced within the borders. Policies that increase literacy rate and improve people's health are necessary for diffusion of any technology. The LDCs, however, should review their education systems so as pupils are given the right tools to be able to compete in today's world. This may sound an ambitious policy for many LDCs that suffer from low literacy rates. However, the goals of educating people to have basic skills such as logic and problem solving can be embedded in the basic literacy programs. Moreover, the political structure and governance that recognize property rights and foster competition and transparency would be essential in creating incentives to use new technology. As Baily and Lawrence (2001) note, the main reason for the US being frontier in technological advancement, including ICT, is the fact that the US has a highly competitive environment in which businesses constantly seek out new technologies to improve their productivity.

Based on evidence of a weak correlation between ICT and economic growth in LDCs, some researchers like Kenny (2002) suggest that policy makers need to be more cautious in allocating resources to ICT. Investment in ICT in the form of importing computer, communication, and network equipment does not, according to this argument, lead to a fast and easy transformation of LCDs. However, although investment in ICT will not be able to solve all socio-economical problems of LDCs in a very short time, the costs of failing to join the digital world are enormous. The LDCs have to prepare to deal with a new world of business environment and the failure to do so will exacerbate the existing gap between the developed and less developed countries, especially in the areas of human capital, productivity, and technology transfer.

ACKNOWLEDGMENT

The authors would like to thank Jesse Vorst, John Serieux, Ardeshir Sepehri, and the referees for their thoughtful comments on the earlier draft of this paper.

REFERENCES

Arvanitis, S. (2005). Computerization, Workplace Organization, Skilled Labour and Firm Productivitiy: Evidence for the Swiss Business Sector. *Economics of Innovation and New Technology*, *14*(4), 225–249. doi:10.1080/1043859042000226257

Baily, M. N., & Lawrence, R. Z. (2001). Do We Have a New E-conomy? *American Economic Review. Papers and Proceedings*, *91*, 308–312.

Bartel, A., Ichniowski, C., & Kathryn, S. (2007). How Does Information Technology Affect Productivity? Plant-level Comparisons of Product Innovation, Process Improvement and Worker Skills. *The Quarterly Journal of Economics*, *122*(4), 1721–1758. doi:10.1162/qjec.2007.122.4.1721

Brynjolfsson, E., & Hitt, L. M. (2002). Computing Productivity: Firm-Level Evidence. *The Review of Economics and Statistics*, *85*(4), 793–808. doi:10.1162/003465303772815736

Coe, D. T., & Helpman, E. (1995). International R&D Spillovers. *European Economic Review*, *39*, 859–887. doi:10.1016/0014-2921(94)00100-E

Coe, D. T., Helpman, H., & Hoffmaister, A. W. (1997). North-South R&D Spillovers. *The Economic Journal*, *107*, 134–149. doi:10.1111/1468-0297.00146

Cogburn, D. L., & Adeya, C. N. (2001). Prospects for the Digital Economy in South Africa: Technology, Policy, People, and Strategies. *WIDER Discussion Paper* No. 2001/77. Helsinki: UNU/WIDER.

Faye, M., & John, L., Mcarthur, Jeffrey W., Sachs D., & Snow, T. (2004). The Challenges Facing Landlocked Developing Countries. *Journal of Human Development*, *5*(1). doi:10.1080/14649880310001660201

Gordon, R. (2000). Does The New Economy Measure Up to The Great Inventions of The Past? *NBER Working Paper*, 7833.

Jorgenson, D. W. (2001). IT and The US Economy. *The American Economic Review*, *91*, 1–32. doi:10.1257/aer.91.1.1

Kenny, C. (2002). The Internet and Economic Growth in Least Developed Countries, A Case of Managing Expectations? Discussion Paper No. 2002/75, United Nation University.

Ko, K. W. (2007). Internet Externalities and Location of Foreign Direct Investment: A Comparison between Developed and Developing Countries. *Information Economics and Policy Journal*, *19*, 1–23. doi:10.1016/j.infoecopol.2006.08.001

Kraemer, K., & Dedrick, J. (1999). *Information Technology and Productivity: Results and Policy Implication of Cross Country Studies*. Prepared for the UNU/WIDER Study on IT and Economic Development, Working Paper No. PAC-144, 2-99.

Kraemer, K., Dedrick, J., & Shih, E. (2000). *Determinants of IT Investment at Country Level. CRITO*. Graduate School of Management, University of California.

Leeuwen, G. V., & Vander Weil, H. P. (2003). Spillover Effects of ICT. *CBP Report* 2003/3.

Lipsey, R. G. Carlaw, K. I., & Bekar, C. (2005). *Economic Transformations: General Purpose Technologies and Long-run Economic Growth*. Oxford, UK: Oxford University Press.

Mankiw, N. G., Romer, D., & Weil, D. N. (1992). A Contribution to the Empirics of Economic Growth. *Journal of Economics*, *107*(2), 407–437.

Mansell, R. (2000). Information and communication technologies for development: Assessing the potential and the risks. *Telecommunications Policy*, *23*, 35–50. doi:10.1016/S0308-5961(98)00074-3

Moshiri, S. (2010). *Information Technology and Changing the Workplace; Firm Level Evidence*. St. Thomas More College, University of Saskatchewan.

OECD (2004). *ICT and Economic Growth in Developing Countries*. Development and Co-Operate Directorate, Development Assistant Committee Network on Poverty Reduction, 10-Dec.

Oliner, S. D., & Sichel, D. E. (2000). The Resurgence of Growth in The Late 1990s: Is The Story? *The Journal of Economic Perspectives*, *14*, 3–22. doi:10.1257/jep.14.4.3

Oliner, S. D., & Sichel, D. E. (2002). IT and Productivity: Where Are We Now and Where Are We Going? *Economic Review (Federal Reserve Bank of Atlanta)*, *87*(3), 15–44.

OECD Outlook (2004). ICT and Economic Growth in Developing Countries.

Pilat, L., & Ark, V. (2002). Production and Use of ICT: A Sectoral Perspective on Productivity Growth in OECD Area. *OECD Economic Studies*, 35.

Pohjola, M. (1998). Information Technology and Economic Development: An Introduction to the Research Issue, UNU/WIDER Working Paper, No:153.

Pohjola, M. (2002). New Economy in Growth and Development, Presented in UNU/WIDER Conference on New Economy in Development, 10-11 May, Helsinki.

Quah, D. (2001). The Weightless Economy in Economic Development. In Pohjola, M. (Ed.), *Information Technology Productivity, and Economic Growth*. Oxford: Oxford University Press.

Stiroh, K. J. (2002). ICT Spillovers Driving The New Economy? Federal Reserve Bank of New York. *Review of Income, Wealth Series*, *48*(1).

Stiroh, K. J., & Jorgenson, D. (2000a). Raising the Speed Limit: U. S. Economic Growth in the Information Age. *BPEA*, *1*, 125–211.

Tallon, P. P., & Kraemer, K. L. (1999). IT and Economic Development: Ireland's Coming of With Lessons for Developing Countries. In *Proceedings of Hawaii International Conference on System Science*, Jan, 5-8.

Van Leeuwen, G., & Vander Weil, H. (2003). Spillover Effects of ICT, *CPB Report*, 2003/3.

Wolf, S. (2001). *Determinants and Impact of ICT Use for African SMEs: Implications for Rural South Africa*. Paper prepared for TIPS Forum.

ENDNOTE

[1] The real ICT spending is calculated using CPI. Total imports for Singapore are obtained from Euromonitor as it was not available in WDI. The 2003 values for total imports for nine countries are extrapolated using their respective trends.

APPENDIX

SAMPLE COUNTRIES AND DATA SOURCES

A.   Sample Countries
1.   High Income:
   a.   Canada, Denmark, Finland, France, Germany, Greece, Hong Kong, Ireland, Israel, Italy, Japan, Korea Rep., Kuwait, Netherlands, Newzealand, Norway, Portugal, Singapore, Spain, Sweden, Switzerland, UK, US
2.   Mid Income:
   a.   Argentina, Bolivia, Brazil, Bulgaria, Chili, China, Colombia, Costa Rica, Czech Rep., Ecuador, Egypt, Honduras, Hungry, Indonesia, Iran, Jamaica, Jordan, Malaysia, Mexico, Morocco, Panama, Peru, Philippines, Romania, Poland, Russia, South Africa, Saudi Arabia, Slovak Rep., Sri Lanka, Thailand, Tunisia, Turkey, Ukraine, Uruguay, Venezuela,
3.   Low Income:
   a.   Bangladesh, Cameroon, India, Kenya, Pakistan, Senegal, Zimbabwe
B.   Data Sources
1.   GDP per capita: World Development Indicator
2.   Investment Ratio: World Development Indicator
3.   ICT investment: WITSA (2004, 2006)
4.   Population growth: World Development Indicator
5.   Bilateral Trade: Direction of Trade, IMF
6.   The ratio of secondary pupils to population: World Development Indicator

Chapter 15
Understanding the Policy Implications of ICT for Development

Matthew Clarke
Deakin University, Australia

ABSTRACT

Information and communication technologies are thought by some to offer a new solution to world poverty. It is argued that information and communication technologies (ICT) allow poor countries to 'leap-frog' traditional stages of development and become immediately engaged with the 'new economy'. Such an optimistic view requires appropriate government policies to facilitate this shift. Interventions required would include improving access levels and quality of telecommunication and electricity infrastructure, improved quality of education and numbers of those accessing education, and providing both direct and indirect support to encourage local firms to become engaged with the global economy. Ironically, these policies are consistent with current orthodox development policies currently pursued within the 'traditional' economy. This chapter therefore considers what exactly is new about ICT in terms of its potential impact on the poor.

INTRODUCTION

This chapter questions whether there is anything 'new' regarding the policy prescriptions required to enhance the lives of the poor through information and communication technologies (ICTs). The world economy continues to evolve and in recent years has been most markedly shaped by the convergence of two long-run broad trends:

DOI: 10.4018/978-1-61520-799-2.ch015

globalization and advances in information and communication technology (ICT) (see Solow, 1987; Pohjola, 2002a; Sheehan et al., 1995; OECD, 1996a, 1996b; World Bank, 1999). The result of this convergence is a 'new' economy, in which knowledge takes prominence over traditional productivity inputs (land, labour and capital) in driving economic growth (Drucker, 1993). Within this new economy, ICTs have assumed a dominant role and are thought by some to offer a new approach to development and improving the life of the poor. It is argued that ICT allows poor countries to 'leap-frog' traditional stages of development and become immediately engaged with the 'new economy' and take advantage of emerging opportunities to achieve economic growth and raise material standards of living. But are the policies required to take advantage of this new environment substantially different to mainstream policies required to achieve development within the 'traditional' economy?

Over the past five decades (and increasingly so over the past two decades) the conflation of the rise in the relatively free flow of trade and capital between most countries and acceleration of advances in ICT and the subsequent increase in the knowledge intensity of the production process has resulted in a 'new' economy. Knowledge now characterizes this new economy and provides the competitive advantage for firms and countries seeking to increase economic growth and social well-being (Mansell, 2002; Mansell et al., 1999; World Bank, 1999). The central tenet of this new economy is the significance of knowledge to the global economic process. The codification of knowledge allows it to be quickly and cheaply delivered to where it is needed, be transformed as required and be made effective in machines and other production and service delivery processes. This codification has enhanced the impact of ICT as a means of production. Knowledge has been so incorporated into the world economy that it has caused structural and qualitative changes in how the global economy operates. Within this economic reality, such knowledge-intensive development has been termed as e-development (Clarke, 2006).

The truly revolutionary aspect of this new economy is that knowledge has become un-bundled from its physical carrier (Quah, 2001). The consequence of this is that it is now possible to separate the economics of knowledge from the economics of physical objects. Where the means of the production traditionally have had a physical presence (it was possible to handle land, labour or capital), this is no longer the case with the new

economy. As knowledge becomes the central means of production, its physical manifestation is no longer important. As a result, as economies grow within this new economy, an increasing percentage of a nation's income will have little or no physical presence.

This sits in contrast to the past in which poor countries and wealthy countries were largely divided by an 'object gap'. Economic development required ownership of or access to resources (natural raw materials, labour) and physical capital (engines, factories, roads). However, within the new economy, constraint to economic development is less concerned with access to 'objects' per se and more related to access to knowledge. The 'digital gap' means a lack of an educated workforce, but also a lack of suitable investment in appropriate ICT that is integrated into the economy. Presently, poor countries that experience this digital gap, lack the ideas or knowledge that are used in industrial countries to generate economic value (Warschauer, 2003). It is important to note that these two 'gaps' are not mutually exclusive and poor countries generally suffer both. However, as the new economy becomes more dominant, the relative importance of the objects gap to achieving economic development will lesson in favour of minimizing the digital gap (though this view is contested – Wilson and Heeks, 2000). Within the new economy, the burden of the object gap and its constraint to development are not as of great importance than in the traditional economy (Mansell et al., 1999; Mansell 2001). Opportunities therefore now exist within the new economy for developing countries to experience accelerated growth by taking advantage of what might be termed 'e-development', which is development based on maximizing the opportunities provided by investment in and use of ICT.

It is possible to imagine a spectrum of possible outcomes that may result from the shift to the new economy brought about by the conflation of globalisation and the ICT revolution. However, highlighting two extreme views might assist in better identifying the implications for developing countries of the new economy on potential economic development (Clarke 2006). The first extreme view, as discussed above, is that the new economy will allow developing countries to bridge the current inequality between them and developed countries by dent of replacing the importance resources with knowledge. The alternative view is that new economy will exacerbate existing inequality because the replacement of the objects gap with the digital gap will be just as insidious for developing countries to close and perhaps even easier for already wealthy and ICT-investing developed countries to expand leaving developing countries languishing further behind developed countries without hope of catching-up.

Interestingly, both these extreme scenarios lead to the same policy imperative: developing countries must participate in the new economy: if for no other reason than not to be left behind. There is no guarantee that investing in ICT enhances economic development – the uneven productivity returns between nations demonstrate this – however, it is not a realistic policy position for developing countries to not seek to fully realize the potential of the new economy. This requires these countries to seek to reduce the existing differential of new economy engagement that presently exists between poor and wealthy countries.

It is therefore necessary that new policies be considered in light of this evolution to a new economy. This chapter is interested in government policies that facilitate a shift from policies that support traditional development to policies that support e-development within developing countries. This involves developing and implementing policies at both the micro and macro levels to ensure the opportunities prevalent in this new environment are maximized. Interventions required would include improving access levels and quality of telecommunication and electricity infrastructure, improved quality of education and numbers of those accessing education, and provid-

ing both direct and indirect support to encourage local firms to become engaged with the global economy. Significant investment, particularly in human capital but also other physical infrastructure, in order to maximize growth opportunities within the new economy is therefore required. Ironically, these policies are consistent with current orthodox development policies currently pursued within the traditional economy.

The direct and immediate impact of this on the poor's material standard of living is not as obvious or great as that of the resource gap. Therefore, it is appropriate to question what priority should be given to overcoming this digital gap vis-à-vis the resource gap. Specifically, how does digital poverty compare to more conventional forms of poverty in developing countries – lack of access to nutrition, basic healthcare, safe drinking water, and to education? Economics is concerned with the allocation of scarce resources. Should developing countries divert scarce resources from traditional sectors in order to close the digital gap? This chapter argues that the similar nature of policies required to reduce both the resource gap and the digital gap provide an opportunity to simultaneously achieve reductions in both these gaps. Given the potential that ICT promises in terms of improving the lives of the poor, this complimentarily in policy and necessary investments is indeed a favorable occurrence.

This chapter is set out as follows: this first section has introduced the chapter. The second section briefly notes the unique characteristics of the core industries of the new economy, before the third section considers both pessimistic and optimistic views associated with the potential of ICT to positively impact upon poverty in developing countries. The policy implications of the new economy are discussed in the fourth section before these new policies are contrasted with more traditional development policies in the fifth section. The chapter is concluded in the final section.

THE NEW ECONOMY

Consideration of the new economy must be cognizant that the core industries of this new economy have certain characteristics that make them quite distinct from industries within the traditional economy (see Clarke, 2003). Therefore, governments must be prepared to interact with these new industries in different ways than industries associated with the traditional economy.

Innovation-Intensive Competition

Protection of intellectual property is a central component in a successful suite of government policies addressing the new economy. With knowledge as a key factor of production, economic activity in the new economy has two phases: innovation and imitation. Such are the short production cycles common in the new economy, that firms have limited time to recoup their investment before their market distinction is lost to imitators. Firms participating in the innovation phase often acquire a dominant market position. During this phase the profit margins are protected by imperfect competition due to inherent technological entry barriers. Over time these technological entry barriers break down as intra- and inter-industry spillovers making it possible for imitating firms to profitably enter the market and successively reduce the sustainable profit margins. Thus, substantial profit margins occur only in the innovation stage. Investment must therefore be protected by the enforcement of intellectual property rights.

TECHNOLOGICAL SCALE ECONOMIES AND PRODUCT VERSIONS

Value in the new economy is weightless and knowledge has no physical embodiment. While marginal costs of production are low (if not negligible or nil) because of the very high economies of scale associated with knowledge-based goods, there are substantial 'first-copy' costs. This characteristic shows up in increased price-cost margins, widening the gap between market equilibrium and social efficiency. While this may be less than optimal in the traditional economy, Governments must accept this within the new economy.

Network Externalities

Where value is normally a (partial) function of scarcity, the opposite is true of knowledge-based goods. Within these goods, value is created through networking and more people using them. Information goods and services are more valuable the higher the number of consumers using them. Through these network effects, the information economy is thus characterized by strong demand-side economies of scale. A consequence of this is highly concentrated industries, which in turn has strong implications for market structures. While government policies may be encouraging or 'pushing' firms and individuals to use information and communication technologies, they must also be simultaneously aware that doing so may result in network effects whereby an incumbent firm, as soon as it has accumulated a critical mass of consumers, can expand its market share without being more efficient than its competitors. Governments must therefore be able (and willing) to enforce anti-competitive measures in such circumstances.

Monopoly

Notwithstanding potential negative externalities associated with network effects discussed above, the new economy naturally is inclined to monopolies being short-lived and therefore reducing harm to consumers. While knowledge intensive goods form natural monopolies, rapid technological advancements ensure that firms replace one another as market leaders. So whilst there exists a tendency for single firms to dominate high-tech industries, these firms are unable to sustain their monopoly position over time.

DEVELOPMENT OPPORTUNITIES RESULTING FROM ICT

Improving the lives of the poor is a complex undertaking (see for instance Sachs 2005, Stiglitz 2007 and Easterly 2002 for diverging views of its success and failure). Using the most common World Bank measure of poverty, over one billion of the world's population live in poverty and exist on less than US$1 a day (and nearly 3 billion live on less than US$2 a day). More than one billion people around the globe do not have access to safe water, 115 million children do not attend primary school and 10 million children die each year of preventable illness (World Bank, 2008). Over the past fifty years various approaches to improving the lives of the poor have been proposed at the international level – though it is important to note that these approaches to development have had at their core the primacy of economic growth, which itself is based on the assumption that involvement in the cash economy is an uncritical 'good'. The vitality of subsistence economies has been largely ignored. However, for those living in poverty, the reality is harsh and inhumane: life is characterized by ill health, limited access to clean water and hygienic sanitation, poor quality housing, hunger, illiteracy and premature death (Kingsbury et al., 2008).

As noted, emphasis in these mainstream approaches has been given to the achievement of economic growth. Early approaches to macro development emphasized large national infrastructural programs, monetarisation of the local economy, support of import substitution industries, and trade (see Rostow, 1960). This *modernization* approach was critiqued on the grounds that it failed to deliver the economic expansion it promised, with many countries continuing to languish in terms of national income (see Gunder Frank,

1967). Despite these criticisms, achievement of economic growth remained the orthodox position at the macro level. However during the last thirty years, the prescription to achieve this has moved away from the *modernization* approach to a *neo-liberal* or *Washington Consensus* approach in which the market place was given primacy to determine the allocation of scarce resources (see Bhargava, 2006). This meant reducing regulation, liberalizing markets, selling state-owned enterprises and becoming more export-orientated (see Dollar and Kraay, 2004). As with the preceding 'modernization' approach, this approach has also recently been criticized for failing to meet the needs of the poorest members of the community (De Paula and Dymski, 2005). The recent global financial crisis will undoubtedly bring this approach under even closer review (see Naude, 2009).

Alternative approaches to development that do not prioritize the achievement of economic growth include human development approach first conceived by Sen (1985). This approach emphasizes the process of expanding people's choices and capabilities by empowering them to have a long and healthy life, have access to knowledge, have a decent standard of living, and play an active life in their communities. Another alternative is an ecologically sustainable approach to development (see Daly, 1996) in which it is recognised that achieving economic growth to reduce poverty has associated costs to well-being. Proposed policies include production self-sufficiency, increased efficiency to reduce the resource intensity of economic activity, natural capital investment and the preservation of critical ecosystems, support for import-replacement industries, eventual transition to a steady-state economy, and ecological tax reform (see Lawn and Clarke, 2008).

However, the recent international meetings of the world's leading economies (i.e., G20 in London in April 2009) suggest though that the orthodox *Washington Consensus* approach will remain dominant in the foreseeable future. Therefore, as the Washington Consensus remains the dominant approach which informs international and national policies aimed at improving the lives of the poor, it is reasonable therefore to contrast the policy recommendations made within this framework to enhance to development against more recent policy recommendations made in relation to ICT and development specifically. The primary purpose of this chapter is to note the striking similarities between the traditional policy recommendations and the ICT-focused policy recommendations.

The common factor to all these international efforts has been a real commitment to improve the lives of the poor. In 2000, leaders of nearly 200 countries committed the international community to improve the lives of the poor by 2015 through the achievement of the Millennium Development Goals (MDGs) at the United Nations Millennium Summit. The importance of the MDGs lies in the fact that for the first time, the international community actually set itself both targets and timelines for improving the lives of the poor. Such consensus had never before been reached. The MDGs are a set of eight internationally agreed goals to improve the well-being of the poor in developing countries. The MDGs are designed to address many of the multidimensional aspects of poverty and include: (1) eradicating extreme income poverty and hunger; (2) achieving universal primary education; (3) promoting gender equality; (4) reducing child mortality; (5) improving maternal health; (6) combating HIV/AIDS, malaria and other diseases; (7) ensuring environmental sustainability; and (8) developing a global partnership for development. It is interest to note that the use or uptake of ICT itself is not a Goal within the Millennium Declaration. This may be explained by the fact that the MDGs emanated from a number of international conferences during the 1990s, some of which drew on pre-existing goals and targets dating back to aspirations espoused by the international community before World War II. With such a pre-history, it

is therefore not surprising that explicit reference to ICT is not made. The use of ICT though may enhance the achievement of the MDGs.

Some strong progress towards the achievement of the MDGs has been made globally. Until recently, the world as a whole was on track to achieve the first MDG of reducing by half the proportion of people living in poverty. This was due to remarkable progress made by the world's two largest developing economies: China and India. But global averages also mask inequities, with many African states, parts of Asia-Pacific and Latin America failing to achievement modest (or any) progress towards these goals achievement (Feeny and Clarke, 2009). However, many recent gains in poverty reduction and falls in malnutrition have been wiped out by the food price crisis and increases in oil prices in 2008 and the global financial crisis in 2009. All of which threatens further progress towards the goals with tens of millions of people expected to fall back into poverty (see Naude 2009).

Responsibility for MDG achievement lies with both developed and developing countries. Developed countries have obligations to increase the level and quality of their foreign assistance, provide greater access to their domestic markets and reduce the debt burden of their development partners. At the same time, responsibility for achieving the MDGs rests largely with the governments of developing countries and requires a strengthening of their own commitment to poverty reduction.

As mentioned, the exact role that ICT will play in improving the lives of the poor in progressing towards these Goals is not explicit itself within the Millennium Declaration. It is though up to developing countries and their donors to determine the most effective manner in which ICT can be used[1]. The ability of ICT to assist in achieving these development goals and improving the lives of the poor more widely falls into two main camps: pessimistic and optimistic. Pessimists hold little hope in ICT positively impacting on the lives of the poor, while optimists see ICT as an opportunity to make significant gains on these goals.

Pessimism

The visible changes associated with the rise of the 'new' economy are quite obvious. It is difficult to escape the now all-pervading computer, internet and mobile phone. Surprising though, whilst the ICT revolution is widely visible in the new economy – its impact on productivity and economic growth is surprisingly difficult to detect. Whilst evidence from the United States suggests that ICT investment is associated with some economic growth, it is difficult to find correlation between ICT investment and economic growth. This has been coined a productivity paradox, because while it is not possible to dismiss the important and increasing role that ICT plays in the global economy, it is difficult to assign a precise measure the role of ICT has had on productivity, income or welfare (Mansell, 2001).

Solow's (1987) oft-quoted quip "you can see the computer age everywhere but in the productivity statistics" remains true over two decades later. The correlation between technology investment and economic growth exists for the United States but is weak for other developed countries (Pohjola, 2001a). It is estimated that the contribution of investment in ICT in the United States to output (in the non-farm sectors) increased in the last decade of the last century, whilst the contribution to output of non-ICT capital actually declined in importance to the previous two decades (Javala and Pohjola, 2001). Benefits accruing to ICT investment in Europe for this same period were around half these levels. However, there was also disparity within Europe, with the UK, Sweden and the Netherlands outperforming Italy, Greece and Spain (Pohjola, 2001b).

So whilst the productivity benefits are an unknown quantity, the ability to engage with the new economy is also difficult for developing countries. Entering the ICT manufacturing sector is almost impossible for many developing countries that do not already have a strong history of related manufacturing (Joseph, 2001; Arora and Athreye, 2001). Not only is significant capital and specialized staff required, many smaller countries cannot compete with the domestic markets of China and India, which themselves are negotiating with multinationals for production of technology transfer in return for market access. While the digital gap is supposedly more amenable to being closed than the traditional resource gap, so far this is yet to transpire, with no developing country presently having large-scale access to ICT technology. It is arguable that digital inequality exceeds resource inequality (Kenny, 2002; Kapur, 2002; Muller, 2002).

At the local level, the success of ICT bridging non-economic divides, such as social exclusion, is also viewed pessimistically by some. Work by Chigona and Mbhele (2008) in South Africa suggests that the use of the Internet does not automatically reduce social exclusion and the benefits of increased Internet connection are hoarded by a few. Governments cannot expect provision alone to rectify this disadvantage. Other policies are also required if ICT is to improve inclusivity within developing countries -- see Warschauer (2003) for similar analysis in Egypt.

Optimism

Opportunities for developing countries emanating from the rise of the new economy have also been presented in very optimistic terms (see Mansell, 2001, 2002; Mansell et al., 1999; Drucker, 1993; Kransberg, 1985; Neef, 1998; World Bank, 1999; Tapscott, 1996). Castells (2001) summarises this optimism clearly: 'my starting point, and I am not alone in this assumption, is that, at the end of the twentieth century, we lived through one of these rare intervals in history. An interval characterized by the transformation of our "material culture" by the works of a new technological paradigm organised around information technologies' (p.

28). According to Drucker knowledge has become the "basic economic resource" (1993, p. 7) and therefore the resource gap is no longer of great determination in a country's development future.

The central tenet within this optimistic literature is the significance of knowledge to the global economic process in the new economy. As knowledge can now be quickly and cheaply delivered to where it is needed, be transformed as required and be made effective in machines and other production and service delivery processes, future economic development will be driven by access to knowledge above all other resources (also see Quah, 2001). This degree of incorporation of knowledge into global economic activity is so significant, that it has caused structural and qualitative changes in how the world economy operates.

While the evidence of the impact of informational technologies on economic growth outside of the experience of the United States is weak (as discussed above), there are five plausible arguments however why this 'productivity paradox' does not exist (Clarke 2006):

There is no paradox – a long-term characteristic of information and communication technology has been declining prices over time. This drop in cost has generated sizable pecuniary externalities through the substitution of computer services for other inputs in production. Therefore, there is no paradox as there is no evidence for non-pecuniary externalities generating productivity growth.

Fallacy of measurement – As discussed, the new economy differs dramatically from the traditional economy in that it has become weightless of dematerialized as knowledge becomes the central resource and driver of activity. An increasing fraction of GDP now resides in knowledge products. Such knowledge products include all goods and services that can be expressed in digital form and include computer software, telecommunications, financial services, electronic databases and Internet delivery of goods and services. Productivity statistics were not designed to capture the benefits

that these knowledge products deliver, such as improved product quality, variety, timeliness, and customization. While the well-being of consumers increases with enhanced levels of product quality and customer service, this does not transfer to the national accounts. An incorrect yardstick is therefore being used to assess the impact of ICT. It is inappropriate to use national accounts or productivity statistics to measure these improvements.

Need for supporting infrastructure – investment in ICT requires complimentary investment in supporting organizational infrastructure to obtain maximum returns. It is necessary to have mature stocks of physical infrastructure, human capital and government policies to amplify the effects of investments in ICT, yet it is precisely these resources that developing countries, by definition, lack. Within this environment economic returns from ICT investments will be limited. This contrasts to developed countries that have existing infrastructure around which new information and communication technologies is built, i.e., telecommunications infrastructure.

Impact Delay – a critical characteristic of informational communication is that a critical mass of investment must first be reached before the productivity benefits are apparent. A productivity delay is likely as the impact between investment and enhanced output can take some time as existing capital is re-organised (or scrapped or re-engineered) to take advantage of the new technology. Likewise, it can take time for human practices (including management and production practices) to also shift to fully realize the benefits of new technological investments.

Oversized Expectations – investment in information and communication technologies is still relatively small compared to total capital investment in most economies – around five percent. It is quite possible therefore that even large improvements resulting from these investment are overwhelmed (or lost) or will not be obvious in national accounts within the total economy. Moreover, expectation of the impact of information and communication growth may also be too large for its relatively modest contribution to overall capital investment. More realistic expectations of gains in productivity might therefore be required before proper analysis of its impact can be assessed.

Finally, any future productivity payoffs of investment in information and communication technology will be largely dependent upon other factors, including business models, market access, a competitive environment, human capital and government policies. It is precisely these factors that currently constrain development in poorer countries operating under the guise of the traditional economy.

If these explanations are reasonable, there may then be reason to be optimistic about the role ICT can play in improving the lives of the poor. Therefore, a major opportunity for improving the lives of the poor in developing countries exists if this optimistic picture of the new economy is accurate (Mansell, 2002). Indeed, a new approach to e-development now exists requiring developing countries to consider a new set of development policies (Clarke 2006). It is no longer sufficient for developing countries to pursue past policy recommendations or development plans. Rather they must re-imagine their entire approach to development, including how developed in defined (Xue and Sheehan, 2002; Heeks, 2002).

POLICY IMPLICATIONS OF ICT

Accepting the optimistic view that a new economy exists and that e-development can occur because the resources gap that constrained previous economic growth is less relevant, has certain policy implications. These policies are predicated on the view that knowledge is the new driver of productivity and growth and that the digital gap can be overcome (in a short-time) by any nation willing to invest sufficiently in information and communication technologies. Further, not only is it not possible (within this optimistic standpoint)

for developing countries to achieve rapid development, it is now possible for these same countries to entirely bypass certain traditional phases of development in the conventional, long-lasting and belt tightening process of structural change from an agrarian to an industrial and, ultimately, to knowledge-based service economies (Wong, 2002). 'With communications costs plummeting, transferring knowledge is cheaper than ever. Given these advances, the stage appears to be set for a rapid narrowing of knowledge gaps and a surge in economic growth and human well-being' (World Bank, 1999, p. 2). The limitations of natural resources are no longer considered a constraint to development within this optimistic view. Rather, poor countries are now able to focus on implementing new policies to facilitate their participation in the new economy that will reward their population in terms of increased wealth and prosperity.

E-Development Policies

Governments in developing countries have the primary role in formulating and implementing public policies that in turn shape development strategies. While certain aspects of globalization have limited the influence which domestic governments have in all realms of economic activities in their own countries, they still retain sovereignty over local laws and policy settings. While it is overly simplistic to lay responsibility for a nation's development solely on the government (business and civil society are also central as other external factors, including international trade regulations), domestic governments do have an important role in defining and establishing an enabling environment in which e-development occurs. Domestic governments set the parameters and structures that encourage economic and non-economic activities in which subsequent development occurs.

Appropriate public policies must be adopted that support an enabling environment in developing countries that align with the opportunities available in the new economy and ensure that progress within this new world setting is achieved. The following policy settings would, if implemented, support the achievement of e-development within the new economy.

Capital Investment

Advantages that are available for developing countries require substantial investment in capital across a range of spheres. Governments must be prepared to directly invest or provide incentives for private investment in these areas. Investment in both physical and human capital is a key factor in economic development in both developed and developing countries. Securing maximum benefits from investment in information and communication technology requires countries to develop a mature stock of infrastructure and human capital that supports, enhances and amplifies the effects of ICT (Kapur, 2002).

Telecommunication infrastructure is central to the operations of a new economy. However, unlike in the traditional economy, telecommunications infrastructure within the new economy differs in its primary purpose. Rather than being necessary largely for the transmission of voice, this infrastructure within the new economy is central to the transmission of data via the Internet and other associated ICT (Kapur, 2002; Mansell, 2002). 'Expanding telecommunications holds the promise to improve every developing country's capacity to absorb knowledge' (World Bank, 1999, p. 10). But, existing telecommunications infrastructure within developing countries is quite low. In least developed countries, there is less than one telephone line per 100 people compared with 54 lines per 100 people in the United States. Personal computer ownership in least developed countries is only 1.25 per 100 people compared to 80 computers per 100 people in the United States. The low rate of computer access and access to telephone lines combines to result in a low internet usage rate in least developed countries of

1.4 users per 100 people compared to 73 users per 100 users in the United Sates (World Bank, 2008). Investment in telecommunication infrastructure is therefore necessary in developing countries to ensure access to the new economy.

Access to telecommunication infrastructure presupposes access to a regular and reliable supply of electrical power. Even when telecommunications have been digitialised (see for example Djibouti, Mauritania, Maldives and Qatar – World Bank 1999), electricity infrastructure is still a basic necessity in order for the supporting hardware (mobile phones, computers, Blackberrys) to be used or batteries recharged. The 'lack of generally available and reliable electricity supply, especially in the villages of lower income countries, is also a major problem in establishing network connectivity' (Mansell, 2002, p. 318). Over two billion people do not have access to electricity, including all those living in rural communities in developing countries - especially within Africa (IEA, 2002). Investment in electrical infrastructure - regardless of the source of power (i.e. solar, wind, or its delivery mechanism - i.e., local, grid) is expensive particularly for those living in rural environments. Rural populations are also associated with relatively lower usage and lower capacity to pay for their electricity use (regardless of how low that is), thus resulting in relative low returns to investment. However, priority must be given to its provision, despite these high costs, due to its central role in economic productivity.

Full participation in the new economy requires more than just functional literacy. Governments must therefore prioritize education in planning for the new economy. While private benefits of education are demonstrably high in the new economy - in parts of Africa, basic computer trained locals can earn up to 15 times that of average per capita income (Kenny, 2002) – there are substantial public benefits that reinforce the provision of education as a public good. While commercial firms will invest in information and communication to benefit from 'rent' or profit associated with these investments, they are not in the position to provide basic education to potential workforce as the opportunity for opportunistic 'free-riding' by other firms is too high. Therefore, as in developed countries, governments must remain responsible for the provision of primary and secondary education. Indeed, investment in human capabilities is as important, if not more important, than investment in ICT as this also addresses other skills (behavioural and interpersonal) required for the successful adoption of new technologies (Mansell, 2002; Mansell et al., 1999). While general investment in primary and secondary education is necessary, governments must – at least in the initial stages of their investment in information and communication technologies – also assist in the training of specialized ICT professionals (Kapur, 2002). Governments will also be required to assist with the gap between those directly benefiting from higher wages available in the new economy compared to wages in the traditional economy. Income differentials in developing (and developed) countries are increasing between those with and without appropriate skills and it is likely that this differential will widen, as approximately one-third of adults in developing countries are illiterate (World Bank, 2008).

Governments will also have to address cultural aspects associated with investment in information and communication technology. For even those literate in their local language, a significant barrier to active engagement with the new economy is English language skills. Whilst the importance of local languages has recently been recognized by some, English language remains the dominant language on the Internet. The large majority of those who do use the Internet from across a range of non-English speaking countries also consider themselves fluent in English. Whereas those that report low levels of English proficiency also report low levels of Internet usage. Governments must therefore prioritise English language education within the primary, secondary and tertiary sectors

notwithstanding criticisms that this may jeopardize local languages or culture (Kapur, 2002).

Mainstreaming ICT

Governments must also take responsibility for themselves using and promoting information and communication technologies. The experiences of countries in the EU have proven that governments often lead the commercial sector in ICT adoption and 'force' them to follow suit (Joseph, 2002; Pohjola, 2002b). It is unlikely that many developing country governments could replicate in its entirety the EU's 'Promotion and Use' policy, various aspects of this approach which aimed to introduce all citizens, businesses and administrations into the digital age and create a digitally literate community might be possible. It would be necessary to ensure that the whole process is socially inclusive, builds consumer trust, and strengthens social cohesion. Donors could also provide support for the implementation of this type of integration-policy. It is necessary that developing country governments pursue this type of policy as the existing digital gap between wealthy and poor countries is already expanding due to such initiatives as in this EU. National governments therefore have a responsibility to promote the use of informational and communication technologies (Wong, 2001). To achieve this, governments could lower certain taxes, tariffs and other trade barriers on computer imports, encourage competition in telecommunications, become sophisticated users of ICT themselves, and promote the use of the Internet in schools, libraries and other public institutions (Stenbacka, 2001). Support is required to assist developing country governments to make information and communication technologies affordable in developing countries. This may involve direct aid support, subsidies or transfer of technologies by the commercial sector. Governments, the private sector and other third-parties (including donors and multilateral organisations) must work together to bridge the digital gap before its expanse is too wide to overcome. This largely revolves around increasing the affordability of information and communication technologies (Pohjola, 2002b; Niitamo, 2000).

Legal Support

Moreover, governments must also support the commercial sector (and investors) in enforcing intellectual property regimes (Joseph, 2002). Wealth creation in the new economy depends upon weightless ideas more so than on physical resources. The protection of intellectual property rights is therefore paramount in order to encourage investment in the new economy. While governments have traditionally been assessed by their ability to uphold and enforce the rule of law – itself wedded to the protection of resources -- the focus in the new economy will widen to include the protection of knowledge (Drucker, 1999; Mansell, 2002). Investment in information and communication technologies will require stringent enforcement of intellectual property tights though this is perhaps unlikely in various developing countries.

The importance of established (western) legal and regulatory structures can be underestimated within developing countries in influencing investment decisions by international firms. The new economy requires a range of financial and legal institutions, investments and forms of control to operate optimally. Attracting the necessary investment requires insulating investors from excessive risk (but not absolving them of all risk). Investment with the new economy is characterized by its diverse nature and the evolving pattern of control by different investor groups at different times. While traditional stock markets are still important in raising capital via 'initial public offerings', venture capital is more common within the new economy (Mayer, 2002). Governments in developing countries must again be supportive

and accommodating of this diverse range of financial arrangements and not constrain different types of ownership at the infancy stage of firms' development. This may also involve new policies addressing competition within a new economy. Traditional competition policies have assumed a largely static view of competition that may not suit the dynamic features of competition in the high-technology network industries (Kapur, 2002; Stenbacka, 2001). The new economy is fast moving and companies employ different strategies than those found in the more traditional or static sectors of the economy. Therefore policy makers must be more attuned to these strategies (Stenbacka, 2001; Kapur, 2002).

IMPLEMENTING OLD AND NEW POLICIES

With nearly three billion of the world's population living (surviving) on less than US$2 per day, there is a real urgency for the need to improve the lives of the poor. The lives of these poor are characterized by constant hunger, premature death (often from preventable illnesses), poor shelter, no access to clean water or health sanitation, illiteracy and limited or no health care. The new economy offers opportunities for developing countries to improve the lives of the poor, but the new economy requires enormous investment and the lag-effect may take some time before benefits are realized. Moreover, investment in the new economy consequently means an opportunity cost in terms of investment in traditional development strategies. For the immediate future of developing countries achieving knowledge-intensive e-development is important, but so too is achieving traditional development. The policies that are required to support e-development also support traditional development. It is therefore possible for a government to simultaneously focus on infrastructure, education and a functioning marketplace maximizes the

Table 1. Policies Associated with Improving Lives of the Poor

Policy	E-Development	Traditional Development
Investment in telecommunication infrastructure	Yes	Yes
Investment in electricity infrastructure	Yes	Yes
Investment in education (including English)	Yes	Yes
Government use and promotion of ICT	Yes	Less relevant
Improve domestic demand for ICT	Yes	No
Increase diffusion and access of ICT and the Internet	Yes	Less relevant
Encourage software development by local firms	Yes	No
Encourage adaptation and imitation by local firms	Yes	No
Encourage use of ICT by local exporting firms	Yes	Yes
Strengthen intellectual property rights	Yes	Yes
Strengthen financial and legal sectors	Yes	Yes
Revise competition policies	Yes	Less relevant

Source: adapted from Clarke, 2003, 2006

potential benefits from both. Perhaps then, e-development and traditional development should not be seen as mutually exclusive within the new economy but rather be seen as complimentary.

Developing countries do not yet have the supporting infrastructure required to maximize the benefits that e-development can offer. Further, the productivity paradox that is evident in most developed countries' experience of ICT investment suggests that the pay-off from this investment does suffer significant lags. The reality of the new economy for developing countries most likely lies somewhere between the pessimistic and optimistic scenarios outlined above. The greater danger for developing countries is that they do not invest in information and communication technologies and find themselves behind developed countries, this time on the low side of the digital gap rather than the resources gap. Governments must therefore seek to achieve both e-development and traditional development simultaneously, at least in the short term. As will be discussed, the policies required to achieve this do not significantly differ from one another (see Table 1).

Balancing Old and New Policy Tensions

The policies discussed above to enhance outcomes and disseminate the benefits of the new economy to a country's population are not new to those interested in improving the lives of the poor. The majority of these policies, if fully implemented, could also have a significant positive impact on the well-being of the poor even if the new economy did not exist. Governments therefore face less an opportunity cost in terms of investment and priorities than might otherwise be thought. The possibilities of achieving development in either the new economy or the traditional economy are therefore not mutually exclusive.

While the full potential of the new economy is yet to be fully understood in terms of its impact on the lives of the poor, it is clear that investment of information and communication technologies will be insufficient to ensure sustained economic development. Developing country governments must create an enabling environment that will support the achievement of progress that investment in engagement with the new economy will make possible (though not inevitable). Policy makers must also guard against a 'technology fundamentalism', in which the idea that investment in information and communication technologies becomes the only need of developing countries, and is given priority over all other competing development needs.

Developing country governments face a tension as they engage with the new economy. On one side, they must not abandon current strategies and policies targeted at alleviating the poverty felt by the most poor. However, they must sufficiently invest in the new economy so that the digital gap does not widen to a point where its can no longer be traversed or overcome. Governments in developing countries must put in place certain policies that create an enabling environment that will encourage investment participation and development within this new economy. However, they must not rely entirely on the possibility of knowledge-intensive e-development to deliver them from poverty. They must not stop their present development strategies or retreat from principles of equity to encourage investment in information and communication technologies. As always, designing public policies is a balancing act between competing needs. The rise of the new economy has changed the environment, but the balancing act remains.

Of great importance in this new environment is the relative ignorance which policy makers (and observers and participants) have about the potential impact on the poor of the new economy. There is no certainty how engagement with the new economy will improve or worsen the lives of the poor in the short, medium and longer term. Nor is there certainty around which policy prescriptions will optimize the benefits of the new economy. For example, public policy makers must determine whether the focus of internet access should be ensuring business access at the cost of equitable social access, without prior knowledge as to the likely outcome. Similarly with education, there is no existing knowledge as to whether public poli-

cies should prioritize universal primary education, or specialist university training for the few.

CONCLUSION

Those who have faith in technology to deliver untold benefits believe that the new economy provides an opportunity for faster path of poverty for hundreds of millions of people living in countries that are constrained by natural resources gaps. Such a path requires a link between investment in information and communication technologies and improved economic productivity. Whilst a number of industrial countries, including the United States, seem to have benefited from this investment, dramatic improvements in ICT-led productivity increases in developing countries is unlikely in the immediate term. Developing countries, by definition, do not have access to the capital required to invest in the necessary infrastructure and human capital required to benefits from the potential gains available. While new economy optimists argue that the digital gap can be leap-frogged by developing countries, this does not take into account the actions and efforts of countries currently benefiting from their ascendancy within the new economy to maintain this position. This existing digital divide may be worsened as governments (and firms) in developed countries try to protect themselves and their new on-line market share and advantage (Dewan and Riggens 2005). The majority of developing countries have either not yet made this investment or received any obvious productivity gains from the investment which they have made. Full benefits of participation in the new economy require significant on-going investment in traditional infrastructure, investment that is unlikely to provide any immediate return or dividends for investors (see for example Courtright, 2007 on the importance of non-economic returns of telecommunications).

However, even in the face of this pessimistic outlook, it is not reasonable for developing countries to ignore the changing global economy and not engage with the new economy. Even if investment in information and communication technologies does not offer developing countries a short-cut to prosperity, development policy that excludes investment or participation in the new economy will worsen the digital divide and impoverish these nations in the future (Warscahuer 2003). The success of the new economy 'first-comers' may not be replicated, at least not to the same extent, because the 'latecomers' may not achieve the same rate of return. If so, the case for investing in the new economy needs to be made on a more pragmatic and piece-meal basis. E-development and traditional development must therefore occur side by side for the near future.

Countries cannot ignore the need to invest in investment and communication technologies. The global economy has changed (and continues to do so) and the gap between rich and poor continues to widen and leave behind those already incredibly poor. Irrespective of whether the gap is material- or knowledge-based, those who are poor will remain so as long as these gaps exist.

Technology is of course not the sole solution to poverty. It has however become an increasingly important parameter of the new economic space in which the issue of poverty must be addressed. The new economy provides new opportunities for countries to develop, as their object gap becomes less important than it was in the past. However, the new economy also provides new dangers as the widening of the digital gap can occur quickly and will reduce the capacity of poor countries to develop. Governments, as always, must balance competing needs in an environment characterized by ignorance. It is quite possible that development within the new economy will mirror the slow and frustrating progress achieved through traditional development strategies. However, to maximize this progress, governments must establish a new enabling environment that supports investment in information and communication technologies and participation in the new economy.

It can be said that the more things change, the more they stay the same. Investment in infrastructure, physical capital and education remain the keys to improving the lives of the poor. This is, of course, an old policy prescription in the economics of development. What is new is the view that the knowledge content of these investments should be high. The dissemination of knowledge that is so closely interwoven into all modern economic processes is so widespread that no single country can ignore any longer the needs to invest in these technologies of it wants to improve the standard of living of its citizens.

Optimists must remain cognizant that their assertions are yet to be properly tested. Whilst investment in information and communication technologies and the new economy will present some opportunities, most developing countries lack the requisite physical and human capital to immediately exploit these opportunities. Governments of developing countries must therefore balance the tensions between meeting existing demands for improving the lives of the poor with investing in and participating in the new economy, to ensure that being left on the wrong side of the digital gap does not exacerbate their future levels of poverty.

It is foolish to claim that development in the new economy has replaced development in the traditional economy as the new hope for the world's impoverished people. It is likewise foolish to ignore its potential. It is possible though to simultaneously implement complimentary policies that aid and abet the achievement of both development in the new economy and traditional development. Perhaps then, e-development and traditional development are not mutually exclusive. Whether it is in the new economy or traditional economy, investment in infrastructure, physical capital and education remain the key to improving the lives of the poor.

REFERENCES

Arora, A., & Athreye, S. (2001). The Software Industry and India's Economic Development, *WIDER Discussion Paper No. 20*. Helsinki: WIDER/UNU.

Castells, M. (2001). *The Rise of the Network Society*. Oxford: Blackwell.

Chigona, W., & Mbhele, F. (2008). Does the internet contribute towards eliminating social exclusion? *South African Computer Journal, 41*, 75–85.

Clarke, M. (2003). *E-development? Development and the New Economy. UNU/WIDER Policy Brief No. 7*. Helsinki: WIDER.

Clarke, M. (2006). Are the Development Policy Implications of the New Economy, New? All that is Old is New Again for E-development. *Journal of International Development, 18*, 639–648. doi:10.1002/jid.1254

Courtright, C. (2004). Which lessons are learned? Best practices and World Bank Rural Telecommunications Policy. *The Information Society, 20*(5), 345–356. doi:10.1080/01972240490507983

Daly, H. (1996). *Beyond Growth*. Boston: Beacon Press.

De Paula, S., & Dymski, G. (2005). *Reimagining Growth*. London: Zed Books.

Dewan, S., & Riggins, F. (2005). The Digital Divide: Current and Future Research Directions. *Journal of the Association for Information Systems, 6*(12), 298–337.

Dollar, D., & Kraay, A. (2004). Trade, Growth, and Poverty. *The Economic Journal, 114*(493), F22–F49. doi:10.1111/j.0013-0133.2004.00186.x

Drucker, P. (1993). *Post-capitalist Society*. Oxford: Butterworth-Heinemann.

Easterly, W. (20020, *The Illusive Quest for Growth*. Cambridge, MA: MIT Press.

Feeny, S., & Clarke, M. (2009). *The Millennium Development Goals and Beyond: International Assistance to the Asia-Pacific*. London: Palgrave-MacMillian. doi:10.1057/9780230234161

Gunder Frank, A. (1967). *Capitalism and Underdevelopment in Latin America*. New York: Monthly Review.

Heeks, R. (2002). I-development, not e-development. *Journal of International Development, 14*(1), 1–11. doi:10.1002/jid.861

International Energy Agency (IEA). (2002). *World Energy Investment Outlook*. Paris: IEA.

Javala, J., & Pohjola, M. (2001). Economic Growth in the New Economy. *Information Economics and Policy, 14*(2), 189–210. doi:10.1016/S0167-6245(01)00066-X

Joseph, K. (2001). IT Boom, the Economy and Labour. *Labour and Development, 7*(2), 1–36.

Kapur, S. (2002). Developing Countries in the New economy: The Role of Demand-side Initiatives. *WIDER Discussion Paper 75*. Helsinki: WIDER/UNU.

Kenny, C. (2002). Information and Communications Technologies for Direct Poverty Relief: Costs and Benefits. *Development Policy Review, 20*(2), 141–157. doi:10.1111/1467-7679.00162

Kingsbury, D., McKay, J., Hunt, J., McGillivray, M., & Clarke, M. (2008). *International Development*. London: Palgrave-MacMillian.

Kranzberg, M. (1985). The Information Age: Evolution or revolution? In Guile, B. (Ed.), *Information Technologies and Societal Transformation*. Washington, DC: National Academy of Engineering.

Lawn, P., & Clarke, M. (2008). *Sustainable Welfare in the Asia-Pacific: Studies Using the Genuine Progress Indicator*. London: Edward Elgar.

Mansell, R. (2001). Digital Opportunities and the Missing Link for Developing Countries. *Oxford Review of Economic Policy*, *17*(2), 282–295. doi:10.1093/oxrep/17.2.282

Mansell, R. (2002). Constructing the Knowledge Base for Knowledge-driven Development. *Journal of Knowledge Management*, *6*(4), 317–329. doi:10.1108/13673270210440839

Mansell, R., Steinmueller, W., & Montalvo, U. (1999). Opportunities for Knowledge-based Development: Capabilities, Infrastructure, Investment and Policy. *Science & Public Policy*, *26*(2), 91–100. doi:10.3152/147154399781782572

Mayer, C. (2002). Financing the New economy: Financial Institutions and Corporate Governance. *Information Economics and Policy*, *14*(2), 311–326. doi:10.1016/S0167-6245(01)00072-5

Muller, P. (2002). Internet Use in Transition Economies. *WIDER Discussion Paper No. 95*. Helsinki: WIDER/UNU.

Naudé, W. (2009). The Financial Crisis of 2008 and the Developing Countries. *Discussion Paper No. 2009/01*. World Institute for Development Economics Research, UNU, Helsinki.

Neef, D. (Ed.). (1998). *The Knowledge Economy*. Oxford: Butterworth-Heinemann.

Niitamo, V. (2000). *IT, Economic Growth and Development*. Presented at UN ECOSOC 2000 Preparatory Process. New York: 5 May.

Organization for Economic Cooperation and Development (OECD). (1996a). *Technology, Productivity and Job Creation*. Paris: OECD.

Organization for Economic Cooperation and Development (OECD). (1996b). *Employment and Growth in the Knowledge-Based Economy*. Paris: OECD.

Pohjola, M. (Ed.). (2001). *Information Technology, Productivity and Economic Growth*. Oxford: Oxford University Press.

Pohjola, M. (2001b). Information Technology and Economic Development: A Cross-Country Analysis. In Pohjola, M. (Ed.), *Information Technology, Productivity and Economic Growth*. Oxford: Oxford University Press.

Pohjola, M. (2002a). The New economy: Facts, Impacts and Policies. *Information Economics and Policy*, *14*(2), 133–144. doi:10.1016/S0167-6245(01)00063-4

Pohjola, M. (2002b). New Economy in Growth and Development. *WIDER Discussion Paper No. 67*. Helsinki: WIDER/UNU.

Quah, D. (2001). The Weightless Economy in Economic Development. In Pohjola, M. (Ed.), *Information Technology, Productivity and Economic Growth*. Oxford: Oxford University Press.

Rostow, W. (1960). *The Stages of Economic Growth*. London: Cambridge University Press.

Sachs, J. (2005). *The End of Poverty*. London: Penguin.

Sen, A. (1985). *Commodities and Capabilities*. Amsterdam: North Holland.

Sheehan, P., Pappas, N., Tikhomirova, G., & Sinclair, P. (1995). *Australia and the Knowledge Economy: An Assessment of Enhanced Economic Growth through Science and Technology*. Melbourne: Centre for Strategic Economic Studies, Victoria University.

Solow, R. (1987). We'd better watch out. *New York Times Book Review*. New York: 12 July.

Stenbacka, R. (2001). Microeconomic Policies in the New Economy. *WIDER Discussion Paper No. 73*. Helsinki: WIDER/UNU.

Stiglitz, J. (2007). *Making Globalization Work*. New York: Norten.

Tapscott, D. (1996). *Digital Economy: Promises and Peril in the Age of Networked Intelligence*. London: McGraw-Hill.

Warscahuer, M. (2003). Dissecting the "Digital Divide": A Case Study in Egypt. *The Information Society, 19*, 297–304. doi:10.1080/01972240309490

Wilson, G., & Heeks, R. (2000). Technology, Poverty and Development. In Allen, T., & Thomas, A. (Eds.), *Poverty and Development into the 21st Century*. Oxford: Oxford University Press.

Wong, P.-K. (2001). The Contribution of Information Technology to the Rapid Economic Growth of Singapore. In Pohjola, M. (Ed.), *Information Technology, Productivity and Economic Growth*. Oxford: Oxford University Press.

Wong, P.-K. (2002). ICT Production and Diffusion in Asia: Digital Dividends or Digital Divides? *Information Economics and Policy, 14*(2), 167–188. doi:10.1016/S0167-6245(01)00065-8

World Bank. (1999). *World Development Report: Knowledge for Development*. New York: Oxford University Press.

World Bank. (2003). *World Development Indicators*. New York: World Bank.

Xue, L., & Sheehan, P. (2002). China's Development Strategy. In Grewal, B. (Eds.), *China's Future in the Knowledge Economy: Engaging the New World*. Beijing: Tsinghua University Press.

ENDNOTE

[1]   It is not proposed that this chapter survey the success of otherwise of ICTs in achieving the MDGs. While a worthy exercise it falls outside the scope of this research.

Compilation of References

Abraham, R. (2007). Mobile Phones and Economic Development: Evidence from the Fishing Industry in India. *Information Technologies and International Development*, *4*(1), 5–17. doi:10.1162/itid.2007.4.1.5

Accascina, G. (2000). Information technology and poverty alleviation, in SD Dimensions, Food and Agricultural Organisation of the United Nations (FAO), Rome. Retrieved September 2009 from www.fao.org/sd/CDdirect/CDre0055h.htm.

Ackoff, R. (1969). Systems, organizations, and interdisciplinary research. In Emery, F. (Ed.), *Systems thinking* (pp. 330–347). Middlesex, England: Penguin Books.

Adital (Agência de Informação Frei Tito sobre a América Latina). (2008). *Notícias da América Latina e Caribe*. Retrieved January 1st, 2009, from http://www.adital.com.br

Adria, M., Bakardjieva, M., Poitras Pratt, Y., & Mitchell, D. (2006). *The Constructive Role of Researchers in the Social Shaping of Technology in Communities*. Paper presented at 3rd Prato International Community Informatics Conference. Retrieved December 2006 from http://www.ccnr.net/?q=node/123

Advomatic (2004). The Internet as Third Place. Retrieved July 3, 2009, from http://www.advomatic.com/thirdplace

Ajzen, I. (1991). The theory of planned behavior. *Organizational Behavior and Human Decision Processes*, *50*(2), 179–211. doi:10.1016/0749-5978(91)90020-T

Ajzen, I., & Fishbein, M. (1980). *Understanding attitudes and predicting social behavior*. Englewood Cliffs, NJ: Prentice-Hall.

Alampay, E.A. (2006). Beyond access to ICTs: Measuring capabilities in the information society. *International Journal of Education and Development using Information and Communication Technology, 2*(3), 4-22.

Alampay, E.A. (2006). Beyond access to ICTs: Measuring capabilities in the information society. *International Journal of Education and Development using Information and Communication Technology (IJEDICT) 2*(2), 4-22.

Albirini, A. *(2006). Cultural perceptions: The missing element in the implementation of ICT in developing countries*. International Journal of Education and Development using ICT, 2*(1). Retrieved December 21, 2008, from* http://ijedict.dec.uwi.edu/index.php

Alfaro Moreno, R. (2006). *Otra brújula: Innovaciones en comunicación y desarrollo*. Lima, Peru: Calandria.

Alverez, M. I., Roman, F., Dobles, M. C., Umana, J., Zuniga, M., Garcia, J., et al. (1998). Computers in schools: A qualitative study of Chile and Costa Rica. *Education and Technology Series: Special Issue*. Washington: The World Bank. Retrieved September 30, 3008, from http://www-wds.worldbank.org/external/default/WDSContentServer/WDSP/IB/2000/02/24/000094946_99031910575711/Rendered/PDF/multi_page.pdf

Amin, S. (1976). *Unequal development: an essay on the Social Formation of Peripheral Capitalism*. Sussex: Harvester Press.

Amin, S. (2001). *Il capitalismo del nuovo millennio*. Milano, Italy: Punto Rosso.

Anand, S., & Sen, A. (1994). *Sustainable human development: concepts and priorities*. New York: United Nations Development Programme.

Anderson, J., Boyle, C., & Reiser, B. J. (1985). Intelligent Tutoring Systems. *Science, 228*(4698), 456–462. doi:10.1126/science.228.4698.456

Anderson, J. W. (1997) Is the Internet Islam's 'Third Wave' or the 'End Of Civilization'? Globalizing politics and religion In the Muslim world. *Middle East Studies Association Bulletin.* Retrieved July 16, 2008 from http://www.press.umich.edu/jep/archive/anderson.html.

Andrew, T., & Petkov, D. (2003). The need for a systems thinking approach to the planning of rural telecommunications infrastructure. *Telecommunications Policy, 27*(1-2), 75–93. doi:10.1016/S0308-5961(02)00095-2

Angrist, J., & Lavy, V. (2002). New evidence on classroom computers and pupil learning. *The Economic Journal, 112*, 735–765.doi:10.1111/1468-0297.00068

Appadurai, A. (1996). *Modernity at large: Cultural dimensions of modernity.* London, Minneapolis: University Of Minnesota Press.

Ariely, D. (2008). *Predictably irrational. The hidden forces that shape our decisions*. London: Harper.

Arora, A., & Athreye, S. (2001). The Software Industry and India's Economic Development, *WIDER Discussion Paper No. 20*. Helsinki: WIDER/UNU.

Arvanitis, S. (2005). Computerization, Workplace Organization, Skilled Labour and Firm Productivitiy: Evidence for the Swiss Business Sector. *Economics of Innovation and New Technology, 14*(4), 225–249. doi:10.1080/1043859042000226257

Asian Development Bank website (n.d.). Retrieved January 2009 from http://www.adb.org

Assumpção, R. O. (2001). *Além da inclusão digital: O projeto sampa.org*. Unpublished masters dissertation. University of São Paulo, São Paulo, SP. Retrieved December 22, 2008, from http://referencias.onid.org.br/media/arquivos/dissertacao_Rodrigo.pdf

Avgerou, C. (2008). Information Systems in Developing Countries: a critical research review. *Journal of Information Technology, 23*, 133–146. doi:10.1057/palgrave.jit.2000136

Avgerou, C. (1998). How can IT enable economic growth in developing countries? *Information Technology for Development, 8*(1), 15. doi:10.1080/02681102.1998.9525288

Avgerou, C. 2000: Recognising Alternative Rationalities in the Deployment of Information Systems, *Electronic Journal on Information Systems in Developing Countries 23*(3) 7, 1–17.

Axelrod, R. (1984). *The Evolution of Cooperation*. New York: Basic Books.

Baily, M. N., & Lawrence, R. Z. (2001). Do We Have a New E-conomy? *American Economic Review. Papers and Proceedings, 91*, 308–312.

Bakia, M. (2001). *The costs of computers in classrooms: Data from developing countries*. Washington, DC: The Consortium for School Networking. Retrieved June 18, 2008, from http://classroomtco.cosn.org/cic.pdf

Bala, V., & Goyal, S. (2000). *A Strategic Analysis of Network Reliability*. Oxford, UK: Review of Oxford Economic Design.

Bandura, A. (1986). *Social foundations of thought and action. A social cognitive theory*. Englewood Cliffs, NJ: Prentice-Hall.

Bandura, A. (1997). *Self-efficacy: The exercise of control*. New York: WH Freeman & Company.

Bandura, A., Caprara, G. V., Barbaranelli, C., Pastorelli, C., & Regalia, C. (2001). Sociocognitive self-regulatory mechanisms governing transgressive behaviour. *Journal of Personality and Social Psychology, 80*(1), 125–135. doi:10.1037/0022-3514.80.1.125

Bar, F., Cohen, S., Cowhey, P., DeLong, B., Kleeman, M., & Zysman, J. (2000). Access and innovation policy for the third-generation internet. *Telecommunications Policy, 24*, 489–518. doi:10.1016/S0308-5961(00)00047-1

Barros, C. (2008). Games e redes sociais em lan houses populares: um olhar antropológico sobre usos coletivos e sociabilidade no "clube local". *III Simpósio Internacional de Administração e Marketing V Congresso de Administração da ESPM*. São Paulo.

Barroso, M. (2007, 25-27 October). *Waves in the forest - Radio communication and livelihoods in Brazilian Amazonia*. Paper presented during the World Congress on Communication for Development. Rome.

Bartel, A., Ichniowski, C., & Kathryn, S. (2007). How Does Information Technology Affect Productivity? Plant-level Comparisons of Product Innovation, Process Improvement and Worker Skills. *The Quarterly Journal of Economics*, *122*(4), 1721–1758. doi:10.1162/qjec.2007.122.4.1721

Barzilai-Nahon, K. (2006, November-December). Gaps and bits: Conceptualizing measurements for digital divides. *The Information Society*, *22*(5), 269–278. doi:10.1080/01972240600903953

Bayes, A., von Braun, J., & Akhter, R. (1999). *Village Pay Phones and Poverty Reduction: Insights from a Grameen Bank initiative in Bangladesh. Discussion papers on Development Policy No. 8. Center for Development Research*. Bonn: ZEF.

BBC. (2009). Deals drive mobile money services. Technology news of Monday, 16 March 2009. Retrieved on April 25, 2009 from http://news.bbc.co.uk/2/hi/technology/7945878.stm

Beardsley, S., von Morgenstern, B., Enriquez, L., & Kipping, C. (2002). Telecommunications sector reform - A prerequisite for network readiness. In Kirkman, G., Sachs, J., Schwab, K., & Cornellius, P. (Eds.), *The Global Information Technology Report 2001-2002: Readiness for the networked world* (pp. 118–136). Oxford, UK: Oxford University Press.

Bechara, M. (2008). Banda larga: Os espaços públicos de acesso à internet. In CGI.br (Comitê Gestor da Internet no Brasil). *Pesquisa sobre o uso das tecnologias da informação e da comunicação 2007 (*pp. 47-50). São Paulo.

Bell, P., Ready, P., & Rainie, L. (2004). *Rural Areas and the Internet*. Washington, D.C.: Pew Internet and American Life Project.

Bengtsson, J. (1999). Skarpnäck – Visionen som kraschade. Dagens Nyheter 991103.

Beninger, J. (1986). *The Control Revolution: Technological and Economic Origins of the Information Society*. Cambridge, MA: Harvard University Press.

Benkler, Y. (2006). *The Wealth of Networks: how social production transforms markets and freedom*. New Heaven, UK: Tale University Press.

Bennetts, P., Wood-Harper, A., & Mills, S. (2000, April). A holistic approach to the management of information systems development: A review using soft systems approach and multiple viewpoints. *Systemic Practice and Action Research*, *13*(2), 189–205. doi:10.1023/A:1009594604515

Berger, G. (2005). *Modernization and Africa's emerging engagement with the Information Society*. Paper presented at *AfroGEEKS: Global Blackness and the Digital Public Sphere*. University of California, Santa Barbara. May 19-25.

Bernard, A. (2004). Philippe Dreyfus, in TechnoScience. net. Retrieved September 2009 from http://www.technoscience.net/?onglet=glossaire&definition=7447.

Berry, J., Harris, K., & Jones, S. (2002). The future of community-based UK online centres: Discussion paper to Dfes. Retrieved July 3, 2009 from http://www.local-level.org.uk/uploads/Future%20of%20community%20based%20centres.pdf

Besson, É. (2008). *France Numeric 2012: Plan de développement de l'économie numérique*. Paris, Secrétariat D'État Chrgé de la Prospective, de L'Évaluation des Politiques Publiques et du Développement de L'Économie Numérique, Républic Française. Retrieved November 29, 2008, from http://francenumerique2012.fr/html/france_2012.html

Bieber, M., McFall, B., Rice, R. E., & Gurstein, M. (2007). Towards systems design for supporting enabling communities. *Journal of Community Informatics, 3*(1). Retrieved December 22, 2008, from http://ci-journal.net/index.php/ciej/article/view/281/31

Biggs, P., Kelly, T., Lee, S-H., Lozanova, Y., Nemoto, T., Sund, C., Hamdi, M., & Minges, M. (2007). ITU/UNCTAD 2007 World Information Society Report: Beyond WSIS.

Bingham, N., Valentine, G., & Holloway, S. L. (1999) Where do you want to go tomorrow? Connecting children and the Internet. *Environment and Planning D: Society and Space,* 17, pp. 655-672.

Black, M. (2002). *La cooperazione allo sviluppo internazionale.* Roma, Italy: Carocci.

Blackmore, J., Hardcastle, L., Bamblett, E., & Owens, J. (2003). *Effective use of information and communication technology (ICT) to enhance learning for disadvantaged school students.* Centre for Education and Change; Institute of Disability Studies, Deakin University and Institute of Koorie Education. Retrieved August 3, 2008, from http://www.dest.gov.au/sectors/school_education/publications_resources/profiles/effective_use_technology_enhance_learning.htm

Blaikie, P. (2000). Development, post-, anti-, and populist: a critical review. *Environment and Planning, 32,* 1033–1050. doi:10.1068/a3251

Blair, T. 'Forward' In Leer, A (2000). *Masters of the wired world: Cyberspace speaks out* (pp. viii-ix) *London*: Financial Times.

Blanchard, A. (2004). The Effects of Dispersed Virtual Communities on Face-to-Face Social Capital. In Huysman, M., & Wulf, V. (Eds.), *Social Capital and Information Technology.* Cambridge: The MIT Press.

Boafo, K. S. T. (1991). Communication Technology and Dependent Development in Sub-Saharan Africa. In Sussman, G., & Lent, J. A. (Eds.), *Transnational Communications: Wiring the Third World* (pp. 103–124). Thousand Oaks, CA: Sage.

Boafo-Arthur, K. (2003). Tackling Africa's Developmental Dilemmas; Is globalization the answer? *Journal of Third World Studies.* Retrieved July 29, 2008 from http://findarticles.com/p/articles/mi_qa3821/is_200304/ai_n9173427

Boerzel, T. (1998). Le reti di attori pubblici e privati nella regolazione europea. In *Stato e Mercato, n. 3.* Bologna, Italy: Il Mulino.

Bohman, J. (2005). *2009 from http//:plato.stanford.edu./entires/critical-theory.* Critical Theory. In Stanford Enyclopedia of Philosophy. Retrieved October.

Bond, P. (2006). *Looting Africa. The economics of exploitation.* London: Zed Books.

Bourdieu, P. (1985). The forms of capital. In Richardson, J. G. (Ed.), *Handbook of Theory and Research for the Sociology of Education.* New York: Greenwood Press.

Boyle, M., Kay, J., & Pond, B. (2001). Monitoring in support of policy: An adaptive ecosystem approach. In Munn, T. (Ed.), *Encyclopedia of Global Environmental Change* (*Vol. 4*, pp. 116–137). London: John Wiley and Sons.

Brachman, J. M. (2006). High-tech terror: Al-Qaeda's use of new technology. *The Fletcher Journal of International Affairs, 30*(2), 149–164.

Bredarioli, C. M. M. (2008). Comunicação em rede e novos agentes socializadores: recepção e práticas culturais no consumo de Internet em lan-houses. In *Intercom – Sociedade Brasileira de Estudos Interdisciplinares da Comunicação XXXI Congresso Brasileiro de Ciências da Comunicação,* Natal, RN. Retrieved December 23, 2008, from www.intercom.org.br

Bridges.org. (2001). Spanning the Digital Divide: Understanding and Tackling the Issues. Retrieved October 6, 2008 from http://www.bridges.org/publications/65

Broad, R., & Cavanagh, J., (2006). The hijacking of the development debate. How Friedman and Sachs got it wrong. *World Policy Institute,* 21-30.

Brooks, T. (Ed.). (2008). *The global justice reader.* London: Blackwell Publishing.

Brown, W. (in press). *Leveraging Information and Communications Technologies for Development of the Bottom of the Pyramid ICT Market in South Africa.*

Brown, S. A., & Venkatesh, V. (2005). Model of adoption of technology in households: a baseline model test and extension incorporating household life cycle. *Management Information Systems Quarterly, 29*(3), 399–426.

Brubaker, P. K. (2007). *Globalization at what price? Economic change and daily life*. Cleveland, OH: Pilgrim Press.

Bryden, J. (1994). Towards sustainable rural communities: From theory to action. In Bryden, J. (Ed.), *Towards sustainable rural communities: The Guelph Seminar Series* (pp. 211–233). Guelph, Canada: University of Guelph School of Rural Planning and Development.

Brynjolfsson, E., & Hitt, L. M. (2002). Computing Productivity: Firm-Level Evidence. *The Review of Economics and Statistics, 85*(4), 793–808. doi:10.1162/003465303772815736

Budde, P. (2007). *Telecoms market review and statistics*. Gambia: Paul Budde Communication Pty Ltd.

Bunge, M. (1998). *Social science under debate*. Toronto: University of Toronto Press.

Burke, J. (1985). *The day the universe changed*. Boston: Little, Brown and Company.

Burns, M. (2006a). *Using ICT for teacher professional development in Namibia*. Infodev Working Paper No. 1. Retrieved October 7, 2008, from http://www.infodev.org/en/Publication.499.html

Burns, M. (2006b). *Improving teaching quality in Guinea with interactive radio instruction*. Infodev Working Paper No. 2. Retrieved November 12, 2008, from http://www.infodev.org/en/Publication.500.html

Burrell, J., & Toyama, K. (2009). What Constitutes Good ICTD Research? *Information Technologies and International Development, 5*(3), 82–94.

Butcher, G., & Yaron, G. (2006). *Scoping study: Monitoring and evaluation of research communication*. Prepared for the Research Communication M&E Steering Group, London. Retrieved December 5, 2008 from http://www.healthlink.org.uk/PDFs/scoping.pdf

Byrne, A. (2007, November). Working towards evidence-based process: Evaluation that matters. *Mazi, 13*. Retrieved December 5, 2008 from http://www.communicationfor-socialchange.org/mazi.php?id=13

Cachia, R., Kluzer, S., Cabrera, M., Centeno, C., & Punie, Y. (2007). ICT, Social Capital and Cultural Diversity: Report on a Joint IPTS-DG INFOSO Workshop held in Istanbul (Turkey), 25 April 2007. Retrieved July 3, 2009 from http://www.kennisland.nl/binaries/documenten/rapporten/e-inclusion-eur23047en.pdf

Caldeira, F. (2005). *Exclusão social: uma aventura histórica pela busca de um conceito*. Paper presented in 4th Geography Week, FCT/Unesp, Presidente Prudente, SP.

Camacho, K., Villalobos, V., & Shrader, E. (2000). Building an ICT Evaluation Framework: IDRC Workshop Proceedings. El Tirol, Costa Rica. Retrieved February 9, 2005 from http://www.bellanet.org/leap/docs/Building_an_ICT_Evaluation_Framework.doc?OutsideInServer=no

Canadian International Development Agency website (n.d.). Retrieved January 2009 from www.acdi-cida.gc.ca

Caprara, G. V., Regalia, C., & Bandura, A. (2002). Longitudinal impact of perceived self-regulatory efficacy on violent conduct. *European Psychologist, 7*(1), 63–69. doi:10.1027//1016-9040.7.1.63

Capurro, R. (1986). *Hermeneutik der fachinformation*. Freiburg: Alber.

Capurro, R. (1991). Informatics and hermeneutics. In Budde, R., Floyd, C., Keil-Slawik, R., & Züllighoven, H. (Eds.), *Software Development and Reality Construction*. Secaucus, NJ: Springer-Verlag.

Capurro, R. (2000). Hermeneutics and the phenomenon of information. In Mitcham, C. (Ed.), *Metaphysics, epistemology, and technology*. New York: JAI.

Cardoso, F. H. (1972). Dependency and Development in Latin America. *New Left Review, 74*, 83–95.

Carney, J. A. (1993). Converting the wetlands, engendering the environment: The intersection of gender with agrarian change in The Gambia. *Economic Geography, 69*(4), 329–348. doi:10.2307/143593

Carney, D., Drinkwater, T., Rusinow, K., Neefjes, S., Wanmali, S., & Singh, N. (1999, February). *Livelihoods approaches compared. A brief comparison of the livelihoods approaches of the UK Department for International Development (DFID), CARE, Oxfam and the United Nations Development Program (UNDP)*. FAO E-Conference and forum on Operationalizing Participatory Ways of Applying a Sustainable Livelihoods Approach. Rome: FAO.

Carpentier, N., & Servaes, J. (Eds.). (2004). *Deconstructing WSIS: Towards a Sustainable Agenda for the Future Information Society*. Bristol, UK: Intellect Books.

Carroll, T. (2009). 'Social Development' as Neoliberal Trojan Horse: The World Bank and the Kecamatan Development Program in Indonesia. *Development and Change, 40*(3), 447–466. doi:10.1111/j.1467-7660.2009.01561.x

Castel, R. (1998). *As metamorfoses da questão social: uma crônica do salário*. (I.D. Poleti, Trans.). Petrópolis: Vozes. (Original work published 1995).

Castells, M. (2001). *The Internet Galaxy: reflections on the Internet*. Oxford, UK: Blackwell.

Castells, M. (Ed.). (2004). *The network society*. Northampton, MA: Edward Elgar.

Castells, M. (1999). *A Sociedade em Rede - a era da informação: economia, sociedade e cultura*. São Paulo: Paz e Terra.

Castells, M. (1996). *The rise of the network society*. Malden, MA: Blackwell.

Castells, M. (2000). Materials for an exploratory theory of the network society. *The British Journal of Sociology, 51*(1), 5–24. doi:10.1080/000713100358408

Castells, M. (2004). *La città delle reti*. Venezia, Italy: Marsilio Editori.

Castells, M. (2001). *The Rise of the Network Society*. Oxford: Blackwell.

Castells, M. (2004a). Informationalism, networks, and the network society: a theoretical blueprint. In Castells, M. (Ed.), *The network society: A cross-cultural perspective* (pp. 3–45).

Castells, M. & Tubella, I. (Dir.). (2007). *La transición de la sociedad red*. Generalit de Catalunya: Editorial UOC/Ariel.

Cazeloto, E. (2008). *Inclusão digital. Uma visão crítica*. São Paulo: Senac.

CGI.br. (Comitê Gestor da Internet no Brasil). *Pesquisa sobre o uso das tecnologias da informação e da comunicação 2007*. (2008). São Paulo.

Chacko, J. G. (2005). Paradise lost? Reinstating the human *development* agenda in ICT policies and strategies. *Information Technology for Development, 11*(1), 97–99. doi:10.1002/itdj.20005

Chambers, R. (1997). *Whose reality counts? Putting the first last*. London: IT Publications.

Chambers, R. (2005). *Ideas for development*. London: Earthscan.

Chambers, R. (1980). The small farmer is professional. *Ceres*, (March-April): 19–23.

Chang, H.-J. (2007). *Bad Samaritans: Rich Nations, Poor Policies, and the Threat to the Developing World*. London: Random House.

Chapman, J. (2004). *System failure: Why governments must learn to think differently*. London: Demos.

Chapman, R., Slaymaker, T., & Young, J. (2005). *Livelihood approaches to communication and information in support of rural poverty elimination and food security* [ODI]. London, Rome: DFID and FAO.

Chen, S., & Ravallion, M. (2008). The Developing World Is Poorer Than We Thought, But No Less Successful in the Fight against Poverty. *World Bank Policy Research Working Paper, 4703*. Retrieved December 12, from http://econ.worldbank.org

Chen, W., & Wellman, B. (2003). *Charting and bridging digital divides: Comparing socio-economic, gender, life stage and rural-urban internet access and use in eight countries.* AMD Global Consumer Advisory Board. Retrieved on September 12, 2005 from http://www.amd.com/us-en/assets/content type/

Chigona, W., & Mbhele, F. (2008). Does the internet contribute towards eliminating social exclusion? *South African Computer Journal, 41*, 75–85.

Chomsky, N., Mitchell, P. R., & Schoeffel, J. (2002). *Understanding Power: The Indispensable Chomsky.* New York: The New Press.

Cisler, S. (2000). Subtract the digital divide. *San Jose Mercury.* Retrieved May 15, 2005 from http://www0.mercurycenter.com/svtech/news/indepth/docs/soap011600.htm

Civille, R., Gurstein, M., & Pigg, K. E. (2001). *Access to What? First Mile Issues for Rural Broadband. Report prepared for the Computer Science and Telecommunications Board, Broadband Last Mile Technology Project.* Washington, D.C.: National Research Council.

Clarke, M. (2003). *E-development? Development and the New Economy. UNU/WIDER Policy Brief No. 7.* Helsinki: WIDER.

Clarke, M. (2006). Are the Development Policy Implications of the New Economy, New? All that is Old is New Again for E-development. *Journal of International Development, 18*, 639–648. doi:10.1002/jid.1254

Cline-Cole, R., & And Powell, A. (2004). ICTs, 'Virtual Colonisation' and political economy. *Review of African Political Economy, 31*(99), 5–9. doi:10.1080/0305624042000258388

Coco, A., & Short, P. (2004). History and habit in the mobilization of ICT resources. *The Information Society, 20*, 39–51. doi:10.1080/01972240490269997

Coe, D. T., & Helpman, E. (1995). International R&D Spillovers. *European Economic Review, 39*, 859–887. doi:10.1016/0014-2921(94)00100-E

Coe, D. T., Helpman, H., & Hoffmaister, A. W. (1997). North-South R&D Spillovers. *The Economic Journal, 107*, 134–149. doi:10.1111/1468-0297.00146

Cogburn, D. L., & Adeya, C. N. (2001). Prospects for the Digital Economy in South Africa: Technology, Policy, People, and Strategies. *WIDER Discussion Paper* No. 2001/77. Helsinki: UNU/WIDER.

Cogo, D., Gutiérrez, M., & Huertas, A. (Eds.). (2008). *Migraciones transnacionales y medios de comunicación: relatos desde Barcelona e Porto Alegre.* Madrid: Los Libros de la Catarata.

Cogo, D. & Brignol, L.D. (2009). Latinoamericanos en el sur de Brasil: recepción mediática y ciudadanía de las migraciones internacionales. *Comunicación y Sociedad.* Guadalajara, 11, Nueva Época, January-June 2009, 135-162.

Cohen, R. S., & Wartofsky, M. W. (1986). Editorial preface. In Mitcham, C., & Huning, A. (Eds.), *Philosophy and Technology II: Information Technology and Computers in Theory and Practice.* Boston: D. Redel.

Coleman, J. (1988). *Social Capital in the Creation of Human Capital.* Chicago: American Journal of Sociology, University of Chicago Press.

Colle, R. D. (2008). Threads of Development Communication. In Servaes, J. (Ed.), *Communication for Development and Social Change.* New Delhi: UNESCO & Sage.

Commonwealth of Learning. (n.d.). *An international scan of the use of ICT in education.* Washington, DC. *Commonwealth of Learning.*

Compaine, B. M. (2001). *The Digital Divide: Facing a Crisis or Creating a Myth?* MIT Press.

Compeau, D., Higgins, C. A., & Huff, S. (1999). Social Cognitive Theory and individual reactions to computing technology: a longitudinal study. *Management Information Systems Quarterly, 23*(2), 145–158. doi:10.2307/249749

Compeau, D. R., & Higgins, C. A. (1995). Application of Social Cognitive Theory to training for computer skills. *Information Systems Research, 6*(2), 118–143. doi:10.1287/isre.6.2.118

ComScore. *Comscore Brasil Report*, (2007). Retrieved January 25, 2008, from http://www.comscore.com/metrix

Cooke, B., & Kothari, U. (1998). *Participation: The new tyranny?* London: Zed Books.

Cooper, F., & Packard, R. (Eds.). (1997). *International development and the social sciences: essays on the history and politics of knowledge*. Berkeley, CA: University of California Press.

Cordes, C., & Miller, E. (2000). Fool's Gold: A Critical Look at Computers in Childhood. In *Alliance for Childhood 2000*. Retrieved December 24, 2008, from http://www.allianceforchildhood.org/projects/computers/computers_reports.htm

Cornwall, A. (2002). Making spaces, changing places: Situating participation in development. *IDS Working Paper, vol. 170*. Sussex, UK: Institute for Development Studies.

Courtright, C. (2004). Which lessons are learned? Best practices and World Bank Rural Telecommunications Policy. *The Information Society, 20*(5), 345–356. doi:10.1080/01972240490507983

Coward, C. (2009). Second Recess, RSS feed, 11 March. Retrieved September 2009 from http://chriscoward.wordpress.com/2009/03/11/ict4d-ictd-or-what/.

Crump, B., & McIlroy, A. (2003). The digital divide: Why the "don't–want–tos" won't compute: Lessons from a New Zealand ICT Project. *First Monday, 8*(12). Retrieved December 12, 2008, from http://firstmonday.org/issues/issue8_12/crump/index.html

da Costa, A. B. (1998). *Exclusões sociais*. Lisbon: Gradiva.

Dacey, A. (2008). *The secular conscience. Why beliefs belong in public life*. New York: Promethus Books.

D'Agostino, F. (1985). Ontology and explanation in historical Linguistics. *Philosophy of the Social Sciences, 15*, 147–165. doi:10.1177/004839318501500202

Daly, J. A. (1999). *Measuring the impact of the Internet in the developing world*. Information Impact Magazine.

Daly, H. (1996). *Beyond Growth*. Boston: Beacon Press.

Damasio, A. R. (1994). *Descartes'error. Emotion, reason and the human brain*. New York: Avon Books.

Damasio, A. R. (2004). *Looking for Spinoza. Joy, sorrow and the feeling brain*. London: Vintage.

Dart, J., & Davies, R. (2003). A dialogical, story-based evaluation tool: The most significant change technique. *The American Journal of Evaluation, 24*(2), 137–155.

Dart, J. (2006). *Key questions for evaluation*. In Evaluation in Practice Website. Retrieved October 9, 2008 from http://www.evaluationinpractice.wordpress.com/2008/01/questionschoices.pdf

Darwin, C. (1968 / 1859). *The origin of species*. Harmondsworth, Middlesex: Penguin.

Davenport, T., & Prusak, L. (1997). *Information ecology: Mastering the information knowledge environment*. New York, Oxford: Oxford University Press.

Davidson, E., & Cotten, S. R. (2003). Connection discrepancies: Unmasking further layers of the digital divide. *First Monday, 8*(3). Retrieved September 18, 2008, from http://firstmonday.org/issues/issue8_3/davison/index.html

Davies, W. (2004). Proxicommunication - ICT and the Local Public Realm. iSociety report. London: The Work Foundation. Retrieved July 3, 2009, from http://www.theworkfoundation.com/ research/isociety/proxi_main.jsp

Davis, F. D. (1989). Perceived usefulness, perceived ease of use, and user acceptance of information technology. *Management Information Systems Quarterly, 13*(3), 319–340. doi:10.2307/249008

Day, C., Sammons, P., & Gu, Q. (2008). Combining qualitative and quantitative methodologies in research on teachers' lives, work, and effectiveness: From integration to synergy. *Educational Researcher, 37*(6), 330–342. doi:10.3102/0013189X08324091

De Haan, A. (2001). Social exclusion: enriching the understanding of deprivation. In World development report 2001 forum on inclusion, justice and poverty reduction. Retrieved October 2008 from http://www.sussex.ac.uk/cspt/documents/issue2-2.pdf

de Miranda, A. (2005, November) *Technological determinism and ideology: questioning the 'Information Society' and the 'digital divide'*. Paper presented in 'The Future of Research in the Information Society' event, parallel to the World Summit on Information Society, Tunis, Nov 16-18, 2005. Retrieved November 29, 2008, from http://www.ces.uc.pt/bss/documentos/2006_11_13_alvaro_de_miranda.pdf

de Moor, A. (2009). Moving Community Informatics research forward. *Journal of Community Informatics, 5*(1). Retrieved September 2009 from http://ci-journal.net/index.php/ciej/article/viewArticle/546/434

De Paula, S., & Dymski, G. (2005). *Reimagining Growth*. London: Zed Books.

de Santa Ana, J., Burity, J., Goudzwaard, B., Gurney, R., Hadsell, H., & Koshy, N. (2006). *Beyond idealism: a way ahead for ecumenical social ethics* (Gurney, R., Hadsell, H., & Mudge, L., Eds.). Grand Rapids, MI: William B. Eerdmans Publishing Co.

De Soto, H. (1989). *The other path: the economic answer to terrorism*. New York: Basic Books.

DeCerteau, M. (1994). *A Invenção do Cotidiano: Artes do fazer*. São Paulo: Vozes.

Deleuze, G., & Guatari, F. (1987). *A thousand plateaus: capitalism and schizophrenia*. Minneapolis: University of Minnesota Press.

Demo, P. (1998). *Charme da exclusão social*. Campinas: Autores Associados.

Derbyshire, H. (2003). *Gender issues in the use of computers in education in Africa*. London: Department for International Development (Imfundo).

DeRenzi, B. (2008). Thoughts on Challenges in ICTD for Young Researchers. University of Washington. Retrieved October 2009 from www.cs.washington.edu/homes/bderenzi/.../derenzi_yrictd09.pdf

Development Informatics Research Group, Council for Scientific and Industrial Research. (2009). Knowledge generation for an efficient and competitive built environment. Retrieved September 2009 from http:www.csir.co.za/Built-environment/Planning_support_system/devinfo.html

Dewan, S., & Riggins, F. (2005). The Digital Divide: Current and Future Research Directions. *Journal of the Association for Information Systems, 6*(12), 298–337.

Diamond, J. (1987). The Worst mistake in the history of the human race. *Discover*, 64–66.

Diamond, J. (2005). *Collapse. How societies choose to fail or survive*. London: Penguin.

Dicken, P. (2007). *Global Shift: mapping the changing contours of the World Economy*. New York: Guilford Press.

DiMaggio, P. J., & Hargittai, E. (2001), *From the Digital Divide to Digital Inequality': Studying Internet Use as Penetration Increases*, Working Paper 15. Princeton: Princeton University Center for Arts and Cultural Policy Studies.

DiMaggio, P., Hargittai, E., Celeste, C., & Shafer, S. (2004). Digital Inequality: From Unequal Access to Differentiated Use. In K. Neckerman. (Ed.), *Social Inequality* (pp. 355-400). New York: Russell Sage Foundation. Retrieved December 26, 2008, from http://www.webuse.org/papers?id= digitalinequality

Dirlik, A. (2000). Place-based imagination: Globalism and the politics of place. In Dirlik, A. (Ed.), *Places and politics in the age of globalization*. New York: Rowman and Littlefield.

Dishaw, M. T., & Strong, D. M. (1999). Extending the technology acceptance model with task-technology fit constructs. *Information & Management, 36*(1), 9–21. doi:10.1016/S0378-7206(98)00101-3

Distaso, W., Lupi, P., & Manenti, F. M. (2006). Platform competition and broadband uptake: Theory and empirical evidence from the European Union. *Information Economics and Policy, 18*(1), 87–106. doi:10.1016/j.infoecopol.2005.07.002

Distler, C., & Bressand, A. (1995). *Le planete relationelle.* Paris: Flammarion.

Dockery, G. (1998). Questioning participation and equity in health. Paper presented at the symposium "Participation: The New Tyranny?" Institute for Development Policy and Management, University of Manchester.

Doheny-Farina, S. (1996). *The Wired Neighborhood.* New Haven: Yale University Press.

Dollar, D., & Kraay, A. (2004). Trade, Growth, and Poverty. *The Economic Journal, 114*(493), F22–F49. doi:10.1111/j.0013-0133.2004.00186.x

Dos Santos, T. (1970). The Structure of Dependency. *The American Economic Review, 60*(21).

Dosa, M. (Ed.). (1997). *Across all borders; international information flows and applications; collected papers.* London: Scarecrow Press.

Drucker, P. F. (1992). *The Age of Discontinuity: Guidelines to Our Changing Society.* Transaction Publishers.

Drucker, P. (1993). *Post-capitalist Society.* Oxford: Butterworth-Heinemann.

Dzidonu, C. K. (2001). *The Socio-Economic Development Implications of the Digital Divide within the Context of African Countries.* Paper presented at the Joint African Finance and Economic Planning Ministers Meeting of the ECA, Algiers, Algeria, 8-10 May 2001.

Earl, S., Carden, F., & Smutylo, T. (2003). *Outcome mapping.* Ottawa: IDRC.

Easterly, W. (2006). *The white man's burden. Why the west's efforts to aid the rest have done so much ill and so little good.* Oxford: Oxford Univ Press.

Easterly, W. (20020, *The Illusive Quest for Growth.* Cambridge, MA: MIT Press.

Eastin, M. S., & LaRose, R. (2000). Internet self-efficacy and the psychology of the digital divide. *Journal of Computer-Mediated Communication, 6*(1). Retrieved October 2009 from http://jcmc.indiana.edu/vol6/issue1/eastin.html

Ebo, B. (2001). 'Cyberglobalisation: Superhighway Or Superhypeway?' In B. Ebo (Ed) (2001), *Cyberimperialism? Global relations in the new electronic frontier* (pp.1-6). Westport, Ct: Praeger.

Edwards, M., (2008). Philanthrocapitalism: after the goldrush. *OpenDemocracy* 20-03-2008.

Ehrlich, P. J. (2000). *Human natures. Genes, cultures and the human prospect.* New York: Penguin.

Elder, L. (2009). Elder Musings, Monday, April 13, 2009. Retrieved September 2009 from http://eldermusings.blogs pot.com/2009/04/words-words-more-words-and-acronyms.html

Escobar, A. (1995). *Encountering development: The making and unmaking of the Third World.* Princeton, NJ: Princeton University Press.

Escobar, A. (1994). Welcome to Cyberia: Notes on the anthropology of cyberculture. *Current Journal of Anthropology, 35*(33), 211–231. doi:10.1086/204266

Escobar, A. (2001). Culture sits in places: reflections on globalism and subaltern strategies of localization. *Political Geography, 20*, 139–174. doi:10.1016/S0962-6298(00)00064-0

Escobar, A. (1999). Gender, place and networks. A political ecology of cyberculture. In Harcourt, W. (Ed.), *Women@Internet. Creating New Cultures in Cyberspace* (pp. 31–54). London: Zed Books.

Eubanks, V. E. (2007). Trapped in the Digital Divide: The Distributive Paradigm in Community Informatics. *The Journal of Community Informatics, 3*(2). Retrieved September 19, 2008 from http://www.ci-journal.net/

European Commission (2001, December 14). *Subject: information and communication technologies in development: The role of ICTs in EC development policy.* Communication from the Commission to the Council and the European Parliament. Brussels, 770, 3.

European Journal of Development Research. (2009). Retrieved September 2009 from http://www.plagrave-journals.com/ejdr/about.html

Evans, P. (1979). *Dependency development: the Alliance of Multinationals, State and Local Capital in Brazil.* Princeton, NJ: Princeton Univ. Press.

FAO. (1994). *Communication: A key to human development.* Rome: Communication for Development Service, FAO.

FAO. ODI, & DFID. (2002). A Livelihoods Approach to Information and Communication: A proposal. Retrieved February 9, 2007 from http://www.livelihoods.org/info/linksevents_sub/linksevents_FAO_ICTs.html

Faye, M., & John, L., Mcarthur, Jeffrey W., Sachs D., & Snow, T. (2004). The Challenges Facing Landlocked Developing Countries. *Journal of Human Development, 5*(1). doi:10.1080/14649880310001660201

FCC. (2008). FCC Consumer Facts: getting broadband. Retrieved from http://www.fcc.gov/cgb/consumerfacts/highspeedinternet.html

Feather, F. (2004). *The information society; a study of continuity and change.* London: Facet.

Federal Communications Commission (FCC). (2007). *Local Telephone Competition and Broadband Deployment.* Washington, D.C.: United States Department of Commerce. Retrieved October 2009 from http://www.fcc.gov/wcb/iatd/comp.html

Feenberg, A. (2004). Modernity theory and technology studies: reflections on bridging the gap. In Misa, T. J., Brey, P., & Feenberg, A. (Eds.), *Modernity and technology* (pp. 73–104). Cambridge, MA: MIT Press.

Feeny, S., & Clarke, M. (2009). *The Millennium Development Goals and Beyond: International Assistance to the Asia-Pacific.* London: Palgrave-MacMillian. doi:10.1057/9780230234161

Ferguson, N. (2009). *The ascent of money. A financial history of the world.* London: Penguin Books.

Ferguson, J. (1990). *The anti-politics machine. 'Development,' depoliticization, and bureaucratic power in Lesotho.* Oxford: Oxford University Press.

Ferlander, S., & Timms, D. (2006). Bridging the Dual Digital Divide: A Local Net and an IT-Café in Sweden. *Information Communication and Society, 9*(2), 137–159. doi:10.1080/13691180600630732

Ferlander, S. (2003). The Internet, Social Capital and Local Community. Doctoral Dissertation. Stirling: University of Stirling. Retrieved July 3, 2009 from http://www.crdlt.stir.ac.uk/publi-cations.htm

Ferlander, S., & Timms, D. (2007). Social Capital and Community Building through the Internet: a Swedish Case Study in a Disadvantaged Suburban Area. Sociological Research Online, 12(5). Retrieved July 3, 2009 from http://www.socresonline.org.uk/12/5/8.html

Field, J. (2003). *Social Capital.* London: Routledge.

Figueroa, M., Kincaid, L., Rani, M., & Lewis, G. (2002). *Communication for social change: An integrated model for measuring the process and its outcomes.* New York: The Rockefeller Foundation.

Fink, C., & Kenny, C. (2003). W(h)ither the Digital Divide? *Info, 5*(6), 15–24. doi:10.1108/14636690310507180

Fink, C., & Kenny, C. (2002). *Whither the Digital Divide? Mimeo.* Washington, DC: World Bank.

Firth, L., & Mellor, D. (2005). Broadband: benefits and problems. *Telecommunications Policy, 29*(2), 223–236. doi:10.1016/j.telpol.2004.11.004

Fishbein, M., & Cappella, J. N. (2006). The role of theory in developing effective health communications. *The Journal of Communication, 56*(Supp. 1), S1–S17. doi:10.1111/j.1460-2466.2006.00280.x

Flora, C. B., & Flora, J. L. (1993). Entrepreneurial Social Infrastructure: A Necessary Ingredient. *The Annals of the American Academy of Social and Political Sciences, 529*, 48–58. doi:10.1177/0002716293529001005

Flora, C. B., Sharp, J., Flora, C. B., & Newlon, B. (1997b). Entrepreneurial Social Infrastructure and Locally-Initiated Economic Development. *The Sociological Quarterly, 38*(4), 623–645. doi:10.1111/j.1533-8525.1997.tb00757.x

Flora, J. L. (1998). Social Capital and Communities of Place. *Rural Sociology, 63*(4), 481–506.

Flora, C. B., Hales, B., Petrzelka, P., Trca-Black, S., & Zacharakis-Jutz, J. (1997a). *Social Reconnaissance: Field Research by a Student Team to Inform a Participatory Community Development Project.* Paper presented at the Annual Meeting of the Community Development Society, Athens, GA, July 27-30.

Foley, P., Codagnone, C., & Osimo, D. (2008). *An analysis of international digital strategies: Why develop a digital inclusion strategy and what should be the focus?* Research report. Tech4i2/Department for Communities and Local Government, London, UK Crown. Retrieved November 29, 2008, from http://www.communities.gov.uk/documents/communities/pdf/1000425.pdf.

Foucault, M. (1972). *The archaeology of knowledge.* London: Tavistock Publications.

Foucault, M. (1980). Two lectures. In Gordon, C. (Ed.), *Power/Knowledge: Selected Interviews and Other Writings 1972-1977* (pp. 78–108). New York: Harvester Wheatsheaf.

Fragoso, S., & Maldonado, A. E. (2009). (forthcoming). *A Internet na América Latina.* Porto Alegre, Sulina. *Unisinos.*

Fragoso, S. (2004). As Múltiplas Faces da Exclusão Digital. *Ícone, 6*(7), 110-122.

Frank, A. G. (1972). *Lumpen bourgeoisie: Lumpen development: Dependence, Class and Politics in Latin America* (M. D. Berdecio, Trans.). New York: Monthly Review Press. (Original published 1970).

Fredland, R. A. (2000). Technology transfer to the public sector in developing states: three phases. *The Journal of Technology Transfer, 25*, 265–275. doi:10.1023/A:1007870520985

Freire, P. (1970). The adult literacy process as cultural action for freedom. *Harvard Educational Review, 40*, 205–212.

Friberg, M., & Hettne, B. (1985) The Greening of the World. Towards a Non-Deterministic Model of Global Processes. In Hodder & Stoughton (Eds.), *Development as Social Transformation. Reflections on the Global Problematic* (pp. 204-270). Sevenoaks: The United Nations University.

Friedman, T. L. (2004). *The world is flat: a brief history of the twenty-first century.* New York: Farrar, Straus and Giroux.

Friedman, J. (1997). Simplifying complexity. In Olwig, K. F., & Hastrup, K. (Eds.), *Siting culture* (pp. 268–291). London: Routledge.

Fuchs, T., & Woessman, L. (2004). Computers and student learning: Bivariate and multivariate evidence on the availability and use of computers at home and at school. CESifo Working Paper Series (no. 1321). Munich, Germany: CESIfo.

Fukuyama, F. (1992). *The end of history and the last man.* New York: Free Press.

G8 Information Center. (2000). *Okinawa Charter on Global Information Society.* Retrieved September 6, 2006 from www.g8.utoronto.ca/summit/2000okinawa/gis.htm

Gates, B. (2008). How to fix capitalism. *Time, 172*(6), 24–29.

Gaved, M., & Anderson, B. (2006). The Impact of Local ICT Initiatives on Social Capital and Quality of Life. Chimera Working Paper 2006-6, Colchester: University of Essex.

Gefen, D., & Straub, D. W. (1997). Gender differences in the perception and use of e-mail: an extension to the technology acceptance model. *Management Information Systems Quarterly, 21*(4), 389–400. doi:10.2307/249720

Geldof, M. (2008). *The interaction between low-literate youth and ICT in Ethiopia and Malawi: Fieldwork report.* Retrieved November 1, 2008, from http://www.gg.rhul.ac.uk/ict4d/workingpapers/GeldofNGOs.pdf

Gerefi, G. (1983). *Rethinking Development Theory: Insights from East Asia and Latin America.* Princeton, NJ: Princeton Univ. Press.

Ghana News Agency (2008, July 25). ISODEC urges Parliament to pull brake on GT sale.

Giarchi, G. G. (2001). Caught in the nets: a critical examination of the use of the concept of networks in community development studies. *Community Development Journal, 16*, 63–71. doi:10.1093/cdj/36.1.63

Gibson-Graham, J. K. (1996). *The End of Capitalism as We Knew It? A Feminist Critique of Political Economy.* Blackwell.

Gibson-Graham, J. K. (2003). An ethics of the local. *Rethinking Marxism, 15*(1), 49–74. doi:10.1080/0893569032000063583

Gibson-Graham, J. K. (2005). Surplus possibilities: Post development and Community Economies. *Singapore Journal of Tropical Geography, 26*(1), 4–26. doi:10.1111/j.0129-7619.2005.00198.x

Giddens, A. (1991). *Modernity and self-identity; self and society in the late modern age.* Stanford: University Press.

Giddens, A. (1984). *The Constitution of Society.* Los Angeles: Univ California Press.

Gilchrist, A. (2004). *The well-connected community: a networking approach to community development.* London: The Policy Press.

Gillett, S., Lehr, W. H., Osario, C., & Sirbu, M. A. (2006). *Measuring the Economic Impact of Broadband Deployment.* Washington, D.C., U.S. Dept. of Commerce/EDA: 53.

Gilling, J., Jones, S., & Duncan, A. (2001). Sector approaches, sustainable livelihoods and rural poverty reduction. *Development Policy Review, 19*(4), 303–319. doi:10.1111/1467-7679.00136

Glasbergen, P. (1996). Learning to manage the environment. In W. Lafferty & J. Meadowcraft (Eds.), *Democracy and environment: Problems and prospects.* (pp. 175-193). Chettenham: Edward Elgan.

Godin, B. (2008). The information economy: the history of a concept through its measurement, 1949–2005. *History and Technology, 24*(3), 255–287. doi:10.1080/07341510801900334

Gopal, R. D., & Sanders, G. L. (2000). Global software piracy: you can't get blood out of a turnip. *Communications of the ACM, 43*(9), 82–89. doi:10.1145/348941.349002

Gordon, R. (2000). Does The New Economy Measure Up to The Great Inventions of The Past? *NBER Working Paper, 7833.*

Gore, A. (2000). Putting people first in the information age. In Leer, A. (Ed.), *Masters of the wired world: Cyberspace speaks out* (pp. 7–17). London: Financial Times.

Gould, S. J. (1996). *The mismeasure of man.* New York: WW Norton.

Gould, S. J. (2006). The richness of life. (P. McGarr & S. Rose, eds.) S. London: Vintage Books.

Govindan, P. (2005). The Digital Divide and Increasing Returns: Contradictions of Informational Capitalism. *The Information Society, 21*, 41–51. doi:10.1080/01972240590895900

Grameen Bank. (n.d.). Retrieved September 2009 from http://www.grameen-info.org/

Grameenphone (n.d.). Retrieved September 2009 from http://www.grameenphone.com/

Granovetter, M. S. (1973). The Strength of Weak Ties. *American Journal of Sociology, 78*, 1360–1380. doi:10.1086/225469

Granovetter, M. S. (1982). The Strength of Weak Ties: A network theory revisited. In Marsden, P., & Lin, N. (Eds.), *Social Structure and Network Analysis.* Beverly Hills, CA: Sage.

Grayling, A. C. (2003). *What is good? The search for the best way to live*. London: Phoenix.

Grayling, A. C. (2006). *The heart of things. Applying phisolophy to the 21st century*. London: Phoenix.

Green, L. (2001). *Communication, Technology and Society*. London: Sage Publications.

Greenwichmeantime (2008) Retrieved December 08, 2008, from http://www.greenwichmeantime.co.uk/time-zone/africa/gambia/map.htm

Grossberg, A., Struwig, J., & Tlabela, K. (1999). Contextualising the global information revolution in a development arena: A case study. *Communicare, 18*(2), 81–103.

Grunfeld, H. (2007). Framework for evaluating contributions of ICT to capabilities, empowerment and sustainability in disadvantaged communities. Paper presented at the *CPRsouth2 Conference*. IDRC. Chennai, India, Dec. 15-17.

GSM World for Uganda. (n.d.). Retrieved September 2009 from http://www.gsm.org/cgi-bin/ni_map.pl?cc=ug&net=mt

Guba, E. (1990). *The paradigm dialogue*. Newbury Park, CA: Sage Publications.

Guijt, I., & Sidersky, P. (1996, December). Agreeing on indicators. *ILEIA Newsletter, 12*(3), 9–11.

Gujit, I., & Shah, M. (1998). Waking up to power, conflict and process. In Gujit, I., & Shah, M. (Eds.), *The Myth of Community: Gender Issues in Participatory Development* (pp. 1–23). London: Intermediate Technology Publications.

Gunder Frank, A. (1967). *Capitalism and Underdevelopment in Latin America*. New York: Monthly Review.

Gurstein, M. (2000). *Community Informatics: Enabling Communities with Information and Communications Technologies*. Hershey, PA: Idea Group.

Gurstein, M. (2003). Effective use: A community informatics strategy beyond the digital divide. *First Monday, 8*(12). Retrieved from http://firstmonday.org/issues/issue8_12/gurstein/index.html.

Gurstein, M. (2001). Community Informatics, Community Networks and Strategies for Flexible Networking. In Keeble, L., & Loader, B. (Eds.), *Community Informatics: Shaping Computer-mediated Social Relations*. London: Routledge.

Gurstein, M. (2005). Editorial: Sustainability of Community ICTs and its Future. Journal of Community Informatics, 1(2). Retrieved July 3, 2009 from http://ci-journal.net/index.php/ ciej/artcile/view/230/186

Habermas, J. (1987). *The philosophical discourse of modernity*. Cambridge, MA: MIT Press.

Haddad, L. (2006). *Reinventing Development Research: listening To the IDS40 Roundtables*, Conference background paper for IDS40 Conference. Brighton, UK: Institute for Development Studies, University of Sussex.

Haertel, H. (2008). *Low-cost devices in educational systems: The use of the "XO-Laptop" in the Ethiopian Educational System. Deutsche Gesellschaft fuer Technische Zusammenarbeit*. GTZ.

Haidt, J. (2006). *The happiness hypothesis. Putting ancient wisdom and philosophy to the test of modern science*. London: Arrow Books.

Hall, P. A., & Soskice, D. (Eds.). (2001). *Varieties of capitalism: The institutional foundations of comparative advantage*. Oxford: Oxford University Press.

Hall, M. (1999). Virtual Colonization. *Journal of Material Culture, 4*(1), 39–55. doi:10.1177/135918359900400103

Hall, P. (1998). *Cities in Civilization: Culture, Innovation and Urban Order*. London: Weidenfield and Nicholson.

Halpern, D. (2005). *Social Capital*. Cambridge: Polity Press.

Hammond, A. L., Kramer, W. J., Katz, R. S., Tran, J. T., & Walker, C. (2007). *The Next 4 Billion: Market Size and Business Strategy at the Base of the Pyramid*. Washington, DC: World Resource Institute & International Finance Corporation.

Hampton, K. (2003). Grieving for a Lost Network: Collective action in a wired suburb. *The Information Society,* 19(5), 1-13. Retrieved July 3, 2009 from http://www.mysocialnetwork.net/downloads/mobilization-final.pdf

Hampton, K., & Wellman, B. (2003). Neighboring in Netville: How the Internet supports Community and Social Capital in a Wired Suburb. *City and Community,* 2, 277-311. Retrieved July 3, 2009 from http://www.chass.utoronto.ca/~wellman/publications/.../neighboring/neighboring_netville.pdf

Hargittai, E. (2002). Second-Level Digital Divide: Differences in People's Online Skills. *First Monday,* 7(4). Retrieved December 26, 2008, from http://firstmonday.org/issues/issue7_4/hargittai

Harris, P., Rettie, R., & Kwan, C. C. (2005). Adoption and use of m-commerce: a cross cultural comparison of Hong Kong and the United Kingdom. *Journal of Electronic Commerce Research,* 6(3), 210–224.

Harrison, L. E., & Huntington, S. P. (2000). *Culture Matters: How Values Shape Human Progress.* New York: Basic Books.

Harvey, D. (1989). *The condition of post-modernity: an enquiry into the origins of cultural change.* Oxford: Basil Blackwell.

Hasan, H., & Ditsa, G. (1999). The impact of culture on the adoption of IT: an interpretive study. *Journal of Global Information Management,* 7(1), 5–15.

He, F., Linden, L. L., & MacLeod, M. (2007). *Teaching what teachers don't know: an assessment of the Pratham English language program.* Columbia University Department of Economics. Retrieved July 28, 2008, from http://www.columbia.edu/~ll2240/PicTalk_Working_Paper_2007-03-26.pdf

Heeks, R. (2006). Theorizing ICT4D Research. *Information Technologies and International Development,* 3(3), 1–4. doi:10.1162/itid.2007.3.3.1

Heeks, R. (Ed.). (1999). *Reinventing government in the information age. International practice in IT-enabled public sector reform.* London: Routledge. doi:10.4324/9780203204962

Heeks, R. (2002). I-development not e-development: Special issue on ICTs and development. *Journal of International Development,* 14(1), 1–11. doi:10.1002/jid.861

Heeks, R. (2007a). Theorizing ICT4D research. *Information Technologies and International Development,* 3(3), 1–4. doi:10.1162/itid.2007.3.3.1

Heeks, R. (2002). Information systems and developing countries: failure, success, and local improvisations. *The Information Society,* 18, 101–112. doi:10.1080/01972240290075039

Heeks, R. (1999). Information and Communication Technologies, Poverty and Development. *Development Informatics.* Working Paper Series, Number 5. Manchester, UK: Institute for Development Policy and Management. Retrieved October 6, 2005 from: http://www.undp.org/info21/

Heeks, R. (1999). The tyranny of participation in information systems: Learning from development projects (Development Informatics Working Paper Series No. 4), University of Manchester. Retrieved May 24, 2009 from http://www.man.ac.uk/idpm_dp.htm#devinf_wp

Heeks, R. (2007b). *Impact assessment of ICT4D projects: A partial review of frameworks.* Unpublished paper prepared for the Investigating the Social & Economic Impact of Public Access to Information & Communication Technologies (IPAI) project.

Heeks, R. (2008). ICT4D 2.0: The next phase of applying ICT for international development. *IEEE Computer,* 26-33.

Heeks, R. B., & Jagun, A. (2007). Mobile Phones and Development: The Future in New Hands? *ID21 Insights Special Issue,* no.69. Retrieved May 6, 2008 from http://www.id21.org/insights/insights69/insights69.pdf

Heller, P. (1999). *The labor of development: workers and the transformation of capitalism in Kerala, India.* Ithaca, NY: Cornell University Press.

Henton, D., Melville, J., & Walesh, K. (1997). *Grassroots Leaders for a New Economy: How Civic Entrepreneurs are Building Prosperous Communities.* San Francisco: Jossey-Bass.

Hepp, P., Hinostroza, E., Laval, E., & Rehbein, L. (2004). *Technology in schools: Education, ICT and the knowledge society*. Washington: The World Bank.

Hilbert, M. R. (2001). *Latin America on Its Path Into the Digital Age: Where are We?* United Nations Publications.

Hill, C. E., Loch, K. D., Straub, D. W., & El-Sheshai, K. (1998). A qualitative assessment of Arab culture and information technology transfer. *Journal of Global Information Management, 6*(3), 29–38.

Hillier, J. (2000). Going round the back? Complex networks and informal action in local planning processes. *Enivornment and Planning A, 32*, 33–54. doi:10.1068/a321

Hinostroza, J. E., Guzmán, A., & Isaacs, S. (2002). Innovative uses of ICT in Chilean schools. *Journal of Computer Assisted Learning, 18*(4), 459–469. doi:10.1046/j.0266-4909.2002.00257.doc.x

Hoffman, D. L., Novak, T. P., & Schlosser, A. E. (2000). The evolution of the digital divide: how gaps in Internet access may impact electronic commerce. *Journal of Computer-Mediated Communication, 5*(3). Retrieved October 2009 from http://jcmc.indiana.edu/vol5/issue3/hoffman.html

Hofstede, G. (1980). *Culture's Consequences: International Differences in Work-Related Values*. London: Sage Publications.

Hofstede, G. (1983). The cultural relativity of organizational practices and theories. *Journal of International Business Studies, 14*(2), 75–89. doi:10.1057/palgrave.jibs.8490867

Hofstede, G. (1994). The business of international business is culture. *International Business Review, 3*(1), 1–14. doi:10.1016/0969-5931(94)90011-6

Hollow, D. (2006). *The Lifeline Radio in Zambia: Findings and recommendations*. Working paper series. ICT4D Collective. Retrieved September 10, 2008, from www.gg.rhul.ac.uk/ict4d/HollowFreeplay.doc

Hollow, D. (2008). *Low-cost laptops for education in Ethiopia: Summary of Addis Ababa implementation report*. Internal report, ICT4D Collective. Retrieved December 2, 2008, from http://www.gg.rhul.ac.uk/ict4d/workingpapers/Hollowlaptops.pdf

Hongladarom, S. (2003). Exploring the philosophical terrain of the digital divide. *ACM CRPIT '03: Selected papers from conference on Computers and philosophy* (Vol. 37, pp. 85-89).

Honneth, A. (2007). *Disrespect: The Normative Foundations of Critical Theory*. Polity Press.

Hooker, M. (2008). 1:1 Technologies/computing in the developing world: Challenging the digital divide. Working paper. Global e-Schools and Communities Initiative (GeSCI).

Horrigan, J. B. (2008). Home Broadband Adoption 2008. *Pew Internet & American Life Project*. Retrieved December 28, from http://www.pewinternet.org/

Horton, D., & Mackay, R. (1999). Evaluation in developing countries: An introduction. *Knowledge. Technology & Policy, 11*(4), 5–12. doi:10.1007/s12130-999-1001-9

Howard, P. N. (2007). Testing the Leap-frog hypothesis: the impact of existing infrastructure and telecommunications policy on the global digital divide. *Information Communication and Society, 10*(2), 133–157. doi:10.1080/13691180701307354

Hu, P. J., Chau, P. Y. K., Liu Sheng, O. R., & Tam, K. Y. (1999). Examining the technology acceptance model using physician acceptance of telemedicine technology. *Journal of Management Information Systems, 16*(2), 91–112.

Hudson, H. E. (2001). *The potential of ICT for development: Opportunities and Obstacles*. Background paper for the World Employment Report 2001. Retrieved April 6, 2006 from http://www.bib.ulb.ac.be/cdrom/wer_lawitie/back/hud_toc.htm

Huntington, S. P. (1996). *The clash of civilizations and the remaking of world order*. New York: Simon and Schuster.

Huntington, S. (2007). The Change to Change: Modernization, Development and Political Order in Changing Societies. In Roberts, T. R., & Hite, A. B. (Eds.), *The Globalization and Development Reader; perspectives on Development and Global Change*. Malden, MA: Blackwell Publishers.

Ianni, O. (1992). *A sociedade global*. Rio de Janeiro: Civilização Brasileira. IT for Change. (2007, January). *Development in the Information Society: exploring a social policy framework*. Workshop Report, Bangalore. Retrived May 17, 2009, from http://www.itforchange. net/media/wksp_reports/workshop_report_development_in_the_information_society_2007.pdf

IBICT. Estatítiscas. (2008). *Inclusão Digital*. Retrieved December 29, 2008, from http://inclusao.ibict.br

Igbaria, M., & Parasuraman, S. (1989). A path analytic study of individual characteristics, computer anxiety and attitudes toward microcomputers. *Journal of Management, 15*(3), 373–388. doi:10.1177/014920638901500302

Ihde, D. (1990). *Technology and the lifeworld*. Bloomington, IN: Indiana University Press.

Information Technologies Group. (n.d.). *Readiness for the networked world: A guide for developing countries*. Cambridge, MA: Center for International Development. *Harvard University.*

Ingwersen, P. (1992). *Information retrieval interaction*. London: Taylor Graham.

Instituto Paulo Montenegro. (2007). *Indicador de Alfabetismo Funcional INAF / Brasil 2007*. Retrieved February 29, 2009, from http://www.ipm.org.br/

International Energy Agency (IEA). (2002). *World Energy Investment Outlook*. Paris: IEA.

International Tel ecommunication Union (ITU) (2007). *Measuring the Information Society*. ITU, Geneva. February 2007. Retrieved December 5, 2008 from http://www.itu.int/ITU-D/ict/publications/ict-oi/2007/index.html

International Telecommunication Union United Nations Conference on Trade and Development. World Summit on the Information Society, *Geneva 2003, Tunis2005.*

International Telecommunications Union (ITU). (2006). Telecommunication Development Report: ICT Statistics. Retrieved July 2006 from http://www.itu.org/statistics

International Telecommunications Union. (2001). *Digital divide. Overview*. Retrieved October 2009 from http://www.itu.int/ITU-D/digitaldivide

International Telecommunication Union (ITU). (2008a). *ICT in Africa: Digital Divide to Digital Opportunity*. ITU, Geneva. Retrieved on December 5, 2008 from http://www.itu.int/newsroom/features/ict_africa.html

International Telecommunication Union (ITU). (2008b). *Report on the World Summit on the Information Society Stocktaking: World Conference on the Information Society Geneva 2003 - Tunis 2007*. Place des Nations 1211 Geneva 20, Switzerland. Retrieved March 20, 2009 from http://www.itu.int/wsis/stocktaking/docs/2008/WSIS-Stocktaking2008-e.pdf

International Telecommunications Union (ITU). (2006a). World Telecommunication/ICT Development Report 2006: Measuring ICT for social and economic development. Retrieved December 5, 2008 from http://www.itu.int/ITU-D/ict/publications/wtdr_06/index.html

International Telecommunications Union (ITU). (2006b). Trends in the Information Society, ITU, Geneva. Executive Summary, Retrieved December 20, 2008 from http://www.itu.int/dms_pub/itu-s/opb/pol/S-POL-WSIS.RPT-2006-R1-SUM-PDF-E.pdf

Isserman, A. M., Feser, E., & Warren, D. (2007). Why Some Rural Communities Prosper While Others Do Not. Report prepared for the Office of the Under Secretary for Rural Development, USDA. Urbana-Champaign: University of Illinois. Retrieved November 2007 from http://www.ace.uiuc.edu/Reap/IssermanFeserWarren_070523_RuralProsperity.pdf

ITPS, Swedish Institute for Growth Policy Studies. (2003). *A Learning ICT Policy for Growth and Welfare, ITPS's final report on its assignment of evaluating the Swedish ICT policy.* Stockholm: Elanders Gotab.

ITU Internet Reports - Birth of Broadband Executive Summary. (2003). Retrieved from http://www.itu.int/osg/spu/publications/sales/birthofbroadband/exec_summary.html

ITU/UNCTAD. (2007). *World Information Society Report: Beyond WSIS.* Combined Reports for UN Summit held in Geneva December 2003 and Tunis in November 2005. ITU/UNCTAD, Geneva. Retrieved December 5, 2008 from www.itu.int/wisr and on the UNCTAD website at www.unctad.org/wisr

Ivarsson, J.-I. (1990). Medborgarinflytande i Stockholm. Levnadsförhållanden och medborgaraktiviteter i sex stadsdelar. [Stockholm: USK.]. *Utredningsrapport, 1990,* 4.

Ivarsson, J.-I. (1993). Stadsdelsnämndsförsöken i Stockholm – invånarnas reaktioner och synpunkter. [Stockholm: USK.]. *Utredningsrapport, 1993,* 3.

Ivarsson, J.-I. (1997). Så tycker brukarna om servicen i stadsdelen. [Stockholm: USK.]. *Utredningsrapport, 1997,* 3.

Ivarsson, J.-I. (2000). Servicen i stadsdelen 1999 – så tycker brukarna, jen ämförelse med 1996. [Stockholm: USK.]. *Utredningsrapport, 2000,* 1.

J. Popkin & Company. (1999). *Labor shortages, needs and related issues in small and large businesses.* Report prepared for the Office of Advocacy of the U.S. Small Business Administration. Washington, D.C. December. Retrieved Octonber 2009 from www.sba.gov/advo/research/#wages

Jackson, M.O. & Wolinsky, A. (1996) *A Strategic Model of Social and Economic Networks.* Oxford, UK: Journal of Economic Theory.

James, J. (2000). Pro-poor modes of integration into the global economy. *Development and Change, 31*(4), 765–783. doi:10.1111/1467-7660.00176

James, J. (2005). The global digital divide in the Internet: Developed countries constructs and Third World realities. *Journal of Information Science, 31*(2), 114–123. doi:10.1177/0165551505050788

James, J. (2007). From origins to implications: key aspects in the debate over the digital divide. *Journal of Information Technology, 22*(3), 284–296. doi:10.1057/palgrave.jit.2000097

James, J. (2006). Bridging the source of the digital divide. In *Digital Opportunity Forum, Background Papers and Presentations* (Seoul, Republic of Korea). Retrieved September 5, 2008 from http://www.dof.or.kr/htm/2/ann_001.asp

Janneck, M. (2009). Recontextualising Technology in Appropriation Processes. In Whitworth, B., & De Moor, A. (Eds.), *Handbook of Research on Socio-Technical Design and Social Networking Systems* (pp. 153–166). Hershey, PA: IGI.

Japanese Ministry of Foreign Affairs. (2000) *Okinawa Charter on Global Information Society.* Retrieved January 2009 from www.mofa.go.jp

Jasanoff, S. (2002). New modernities: reimagining science, technology and development. *Environmental Values, 11*(3), 253–276. doi:10.3197/096327102129341082

Javala, J., & Pohjola, M. (2001). Economic Growth in the New Economy. *Information Economics and Policy, 14*(2), 189–210. doi:10.1016/S0167-6245(01)00066-X

Jennett, P., Yeo, M., Pauls, M., & Graham, J. (2003). Organizational readiness for telemedicine: Implications for success and failure. *Journal of Telehealth and Telecare, 9*(Suppl. 2), S2: 27-39.

Jensen, R. (2007). The Digital Provide: Information (Technology), Market Performance, and Welfare in the South Indian Fisheries Sector. *The Quarterly Journal of Economics, 122*(3). doi:10.1162/qjec.122.3.879

Jensen, M. (2003). The current status of information and communication technologies in Africa. In Okpaku, J. O. Sr., (Ed.), *Information and communication technologies for African development: An assessment of progress and challenges ahead* (pp. 55–78). New York: United Nations ICT Task Force.

Jensen, M. (2002) *The African Internet – A status report.* Retrieved July 13, 2007, from http://demiurge.wn.apc. org/africa/afstat.htm.

Jiggins, J., & Röling, N. (2000). Adaptive management: Potential and limitations for ecological governance. *International Journal of Agricultural Resources. Governance and Ecology*, *1*(1), 28–43.

Jiggins, J., & Röling, N. (1997). Action research in natural resource management: Marginal in the first paradigm, core in the second. In C. Albadalejo & F. Casabianca (Eds.), *Pour une méthodologie de la recherche action.* (pp. 151-169). Versailles: INRA/SAD.

Johanson, G. (2008). Flicking the Switch: social networks and the role of Information and Communications Technologies in social cohesion among Chinese and Italians in Melbourne, Australia. In *Proceedings, The Role of New Technologies in Global Societies: Theoretical Reflections, Practical Concerns, and Its Implications for China, Conference at the Department of Applied Social Sciences.* The Hong Kong Polytechnic University, HKSAR, China, 30th-31st July 2008.

Johnson, J. (1996). *The information highway from hell: a worst-case scenario.* Paper presented at the Association for Computing Machinery's 1995 Conference on Computer-Human Interaction, 1996. Retrieved March 20, 2000 from Gopher://gopher. etext.org/h0/CPSR/nii/hell

Jorgenson, D. W. (2001). IT and The US Economy. *The American Economic Review*, *91*, 1–32. doi:10.1257/aer.91.1.1

Joseph, K. (2001). IT Boom, the Economy and Labour. *Labour and Development*, *7*(2), 1–36.

Jovanovic, B., & Rousseau, P. (2005). General Purpose Technologies. NBER Working Paper Series, No. W11093. Retrieved August 2, 2007 from http://.com/abstract=657607

Jubert, A. (1999). Developing an infrastructure for communities of practice. In B. McKenna, (Ed.), *Proceedings of the 19th International Online Meeting* (pp. 165-168). Hinksey Hill, U.K.: Learned Information.

Juhasz, A. (2006). *The Bush agenda: invading the world, one economy at a time.* New York: HarperCollins.

July 3, 2009, from http://www.isoc.org/oti/articles/0201/rao2.html

Kamppinen, M. (1998). Technology as a cultural system: the impacts of ICT upon the primary and secondary theories of the world. *Computers & Society*, 19–21. doi:10.1145/308364.308368

Kane, L. (2008). The World Bank, community development and education for social justice. *Community Development Journal*, *43*(2), 194–209. doi:10.1093/cdj/bsl043

Kanji, N., & Greenwood, L. (2001). *Participatory approaches to research and development in IIED: Learning from experience.* London: IIED.

Kapur, S. (2002). Developing Countries in the New economy: The Role of Demand-side Initiatives. *WIDER Discussion Paper 75.* Helsinki: WIDER/UNU.

Karahanna, E., Straub, D. W., & Chervany, N. L. (1999). Information technology adoption across time: a cross-sectional comparison of pre-adoption and post-adoption beliefs. *Management Information Systems Quarterly*, *23*(2), 183–213. doi:10.2307/249751

Katz, J. E., & Rice, R. E. (2002). *Social Consequences of Internet Use.* Cambridge, MA: The MIT Press.

Kauffman, R., & Techatassanasoontorn, A. A. (2005). International Diffusion of Digital Mobile Technology: A Coupled-Hazard State-Based Approach. *Information Technology Management*, *6*(2-3), 253–292. doi:10.1007/s10799-005-5882-3

Kavanaugh, A., Cohill, A., & Patterson, S. (2000). The use and impact of the Blacksburg Electronic Village. In Cohill, A., & Kavanaugh, A. (Eds.), *Community Networks: Lessons from Blacksburg*. Norwood, MA: Artech House.

Kavanaugh, A., Carroll, J. M., Rosson, M. B., Zin, T. T., & Reese, D. D. (2005). Community Networks: Where Offline Communities Meet Online. Journal of Computer-Mediated Communication, 10(4). Retrieved July 3, 2009, from http://jcmc.indiana.edu/ vol10/issue4/kavanaugh.html

Kay, J. (2008). An introduction to systems thinking. In Waltner-Toews, D., Kay, J., & Lister, N.-M. (Eds.), *The ecosystem approach: Complexity, uncertainty and managing for sustainability*. New York, Chichester: Columbia University Press.

Keeble, L. (2007). Community Informatics: building civil society in the Information Age? In Clay, C. J., Madden, M., & Potts, L. (Eds.), *People and places: an introduction towards understanding community*. New York: Palgrave Macmillan.

Kenny, C. (2002). Information and Communications Technologies for Direct Poverty Relief: Costs and Benefits. *Development Policy Review*, 20(2), 141–157. doi:10.1111/1467-7679.00162

Kenny, C. (2002). The Internet and Economic Growth in Least Developed Countries, A Case of Managing Expectations? Discussion Paper No. 2002/75, United Nation University.

King, K. (2005). Knowledge-based Aid: A New Way of Networking or a New North-South Divide? In Stone, D., & Maxwell, S. (Eds.), *Global Knowledge networks and International Development; Bridges across Boundaries*. Oxford: Routledge. doi:10.4324/9780203340387_chapter_5

Kingsbury, D. (2004). *International Development: Issues and Challenges*. New York: Palgrave Macmillan.

Kingsbury, D., McKay, J., Hunt, J., McGillivray, M., & Clarke, M. (2008). *International Development*. London: Palgrave-MacMillian.

Kirkman, G., Osorio, C., & Sachs, J. (2002). The networked readiness index: Measuring the preparedness of nations for the networked world. In Kirkman, G., Sachs, J., Schwab, K., & Cornellius, P. (Eds.), *The Global Information Technology Report 2001-2002: Readiness for the networked world* (pp. 10–29). Oxford, UK: Oxford University Press.

Knowles, C. L. (2008). Toward a new web genre: Islamist Neorealism. *Journal of War and Culture Studies*, 1(3), 357–380. doi:10.1386/jwcs.1.3.357_1

Ko, K. W. (2007). Internet Externalities and Location of Foreign Direct Investment: A Comparison between Developed and Developing Countries. *Information Economics and Policy Journal*, 19, 1–23. doi:10.1016/j.infoecopol.2006.08.001

Kok, D. (2005). SAP invests in South African Technology Research Skills. Retrieved September 2009 from http://www.sap.com/southafrica/about/press/press.epx?pressid=4914

Kole, E. S. (1998). Myths and Realities in Internet Discourse: Using Computer Networks for Data Collection and the Beijing World Conference on Women. *The Gazette. The International Journal for Communication Studies*, 60(4), 343–360.

Kole, E. S. (2002). An Alternative Conceptualization of ICT and Development, position statement for the conference. *Global E-Quality. Rethinking ICT in Africa, Asia and Latin America*. Organized by the International Institute of Infonomics and the A3 Network, 24-27 March 2002, Maastricht, the Netherlands. Retrieved October 5 2008 from: http://www.infonomics.nl/globalequality/ideas/kole.htm

Kozma, R., McGhee, R., Quellmalz, E., & Zalles, D. (2004). Closing the digital divide: Evaluation of the World Links Program. *International Journal of Educational Development*, 24(4), 361–381. doi:10.1016/j.ijedudev.2003.11.014

Kraemer, K., Dedrick, J., & Shih, E. (2000). *Determinants of IT Investment at Country Level. CRITO*. Graduate School of Management, University of California.

Kraemer, K., & Dedrick, J. (1999). *Information Technology and Productivity: Results and Policy Implication of Cross Country Studies*. Prepared for the UNU/WIDER Study on IT and Economic Development, Working Paper No. PAC-144, 2-99.

Krannich, R. D., & Humphrey, C. R. (1986). Using Key Informant Data in Comparative Community Research: An Empirical Assessment. *Sociological Methods & Research, 14*(4), 473–493. doi:10.1177/0049124186014004006

Kranzberg, M. (1985). The Information Age: Evolution or revolution? In Guile, B. (Ed.), *Information Technologies and Societal Transformation*. Washington, DC: National Academy of Engineering.

Kuhn, T. S. (1990). *A estrutura das revoluções científicas* (Boeira, B. V., & Boeira, N., Trans.). São Paulo: Perspectiva. (Original work published 1962)

Kumar, R. (2006). Social Impact and Diffusion of Telecenter Use: A Study from the Sustainable Access in Rural India Project. *The Journal of Community Informatics, 2*(3). Retrieved December 21, 2008 from http://www.ci-journal.net/

Kusek, J. Z., & Rist, R. C. (2004). *Ten steps to a results-based monitoring and evaluation system: A handbook for development practitioners*. Washington, DC: The World Bank.

Kuttan, A., & Peters, L. (2003). *From digital divide to digital opportunity*. Lanham, MD: Scarecrow Press.

Kvasny, L., & Keil, M. (2006). The Challenges of Redressing the Digital Divide: A Tale of Two U.S. Cities. *Information Systems Journal, 16*(1), 23–53. doi:10.1111/j.1365-2575.2006.00207.x

Kyem, P. A. K., & Kyem, O. (2006). Africa's Participation in the Revolution in Information and Communications Technology: an Opportunity for Economic Development or Deprivation. In K. Konadu- Agyemang & K. Panford (Eds.), *Africa's Development in the Twenty First Century: Pertinent Socio-Economic and Development Issues* (pp. 358-390). Ashgate: UK.

Kyem, P. A. K., & LeMaire, P. K. (2006). Transforming Recent Gains in the Digital Divide into Digital Opportunities: Africa and the Boom in Mobile Phone Subscription. *Electronic Journal of Information Systems in Developing Countries, 28*. Retrieved December 5, 2008 from http://www.ejisdc.org/ojs2/index.php/ejisdc/article/view/343

Labelle, R. (2005). *ICT Policy Formulation and E-Strategy Development: A Comprehensive Guidebook*. Elsevier: UNDP-APDIP.

Lacerda, J. S. (2008). *Ambiências Comunicacionais e Vivências Midiáticas Digitais*. Unpublished doctoral thesis presented to the PostGraduate Programme in Communications of the Universidade do Vale do Rio do Sinos, Unisinos, as partial fullfilment of the requirements for the degree of Doctor in Communications.

LaRose, R., Gregg, J. L., Strover, S., Straubhaar, J., & Carperter, S. (2007). Closing the rural broadband gap: Promoting adoption of the Internet in rural America. *Telecommunications Policy, 31*(6-7), 359–373. doi:10.1016/j.telpol.2007.04.004

Latouche, S. (2007). De-growth: an electoral stake? *The International Journal Of Inclusive Democracy, 3*,1. Retrieved September 2009 from http://www.inclusivedemocracy.org/journal/vol3/vol3_no1_Latouche_degrowth.htm

Laviolette, A. (2007). Ceramic traditions, identities and population in Senegal and Gambia: Compared ethnography and historical reconstruction test. *Journal of African Archaeology, 5*(1), 149–150.

Law, P. L., Fortunati, L., & Yang, S. (Eds.). (2006). *New technologies in global societies*. Singapore: World Scientific. doi:10.1142/9789812773555

Lawn, P., & Clarke, M. (2008). *Sustainable Welfare in the Asia-Pacific: Studies Using the Genuine Progress Indicator*. London: Edward Elgar.

Leal, G. F. (2004). *A noção de exclusão social em debate: aplicabilidade e implicações para a intervenção prática*. Paper presented at the 14th Brazilian Association of Population Studies (ABEP) meeting, Caxambu, MG. Retrieved November 29, 2008, from http://www.abep.nepo.unicamp.br/site_eventos_abep/PDF/ABEP2004_42.pdf

Lederer, A. L., Maupin, D. J., Sena, M. P., & Zhuang, Y. (2000). The technology acceptance model and the World Wide Web. *Decision Support Systems*, *29*(3), 269–282. doi:10.1016/S0167-9236(00)00076-2

Lee, K. (1993). *Compass and gyroscope: Integrating science and politics for the environment.* Washington, D.C.: Island Press.

Lee, M. (2001). A refusal to define HRD. *Human Resource Development International*, *4*(3), 327–341. doi:10.1080/13678860110059348

Lee, R. M. (1994). Modernisation, post-modernism and the Third World. *Current Sociology*, *42*(2), 1–63.

Lee, K. (1995). Deliberately seeking sustainability in the Columbia River Basin. In Gunderson, L., Holling, C., & Light, S. (Eds.), *Barriers and bridges to the renewal of ecosystems and institutions* (pp. 214–238). New York: Columbia Press.

Lee, K. (1998, September 16-19.). *Appraising adaptive management.* Adaptive Collaborative Management of Protected Areas: Advancing the Potential. Cornell University, Center for International Forestry Research.

Leeuwen, G. V., & Vander Weil, H. P. (2003). Spillover Effects of ICT. *CBP Report* 2003/3.

Legris, P., Ingham, J., & Collerette, P. (2003). Why do people use information technology? A critical review of the technology acceptance model. *Information & Management*, *40*(3), 191–204. doi:10.1016/S0378-7206(01)00143-4

Lehr, W. Osorio, C.A., Gillett, S. & Sirbu, M.A. (2006). *Measuring Broadband's Economic Impact.* Cambridge, MA: MIT, Engineering Systems Division, ESD-WP-2006-02. http://esd.mit.edu/WPS/esd-wp-2006-02.pdf Last accessed October 2009.

Lengyel, G., Eranusz, E., Füleki, D., Lőrincz, L., & Siklós, V. (2006). The Cserénfa experiment – on the attempt to deploy computers and Internet in a small Hungarian village. *The Journal of Community Informatics, 2*(3). Retrieved December 21, 2008 from http://www.ci-journal.net/.

Lenhart, A., Horrigan, J., Rainie, L., Allen, K., Boyce, A., Madden, M., et al. (2003). The ever-shifting internet population: a new look at internet access and the digital divide. The Pew internet and American life project. Retrieved October 2009 from http://www.pewinternet.org/Reports/2003/The-EverShifting-Internet-Population-A-new-look-at-Internet-access-and-the-digital-divide.aspx

Lerner, D. (1958). *The Passing of Traditional Society: Modernizing the Middle East.* New York: Free Press.

Lerner, D. (1967). International cooperation and communication in national development. In Lerner, D., & Schramm, W. (Eds.), *Communication and Change in the Development Countries* (pp. 103–128). Honolulu: East-West Center Press.

Liao, Z., & Wong, W. (2004). Key success factors of smartcard-based electronic payment: an empirical analysis. In *Proceedings of The Eighth Pacific-Asia Conference on Information Systems 2004 (PACIS 2004)*, Shanghai, China, 8-11 July, 2004 (pp. 2065-2071).

Liff, S., & Laegran, A. S. (2003). Cybercafés: Debating the Meaning and Significance of Internet Access in a Café Environment. *New Media & Society, 5*, 307–312. doi:10.1177/14614448030053001

Liff, S., & Steward, F. (2001). Communities and community e-gateways: Networking for social inclusion. In Keeble, L., & Loader, B. D. (Eds.), *Community Informatics: Shaping Computer-Mediated Social Relations*. London: Routledge.

Liff, S., Fred, S., & Watts, P. (1998). Cybercafés and Telecottages: Increasing public access to computers and the Internet. Survey report, Virtual Society? Programme, Economic and Social Research Council, United Kingdom. Retrieved July 3, 2009 from http://virtualsociety.sbs.ox.ac.uk/ text/reports/access.htm

Light, D., & Manson, M. (2007). *An educational revolution to support change in the classroom: Colombia and the educational challenges of the twenty-first century.* Washington, DC: Education Development Center, Inc, Center for Children and Technology.

Light, D. Method, F., Rockman, C., Cressman, G.M., & Daly, J. (2008). *Synthesis report: Overview and recommendations to the Jordan Education Initiative.* Washington, DC: Education Development Center, Inc.

Lincoln, Y. (1990). The making of a constructivist. A remembrance of transformations past. In Guba, E. (Ed.), *The paradigm dialogue* (pp. 67–87). Newbury Park: Sage Publications.

Linden, L. L. (2008). *Complement or substitute? The effect of technology on student achievement in India.* Infodev Working Paper No. 17. Retrieved November 11, 2008, from http://www.infodev.org/en/Publication.505.html

Linden, L., Banerjee, A., & Duflo, E. (2003). *Computer-Assisted Learning: Evidence from a Randomized Experiment.* Poverty Action Lab Paper No. 5. Cambridge, MA: Poverty Action Lab. Retrieved October 4, 2008, from http://www.povertyactionlab.org/papers/5_Duflo_Computer-Assisted_Learning.pdf

Lipsey, R. G. Carlaw, K. I., & Bekar, C. (2005). *Economic Transformations: General Purpose Technologies and Long-run Economic Growth.* Oxford, UK: Oxford University Press.

Lizardo, O. (2008). *Beyond the Antinomies of Structure: Recovering the Insights of Methodological Structuralism.* Paper presented at the annual meeting of the American Sociological Association Annual Meeting, Sheraton Boston and the Boston Marriott Copley Place, Boston, MA, Jul 31, 2008. Retrieved September 2009 from http://www.allacademic.com/meta/p239582_index.html

Loader, B. D., Hague, B. N., & Eagle, D. (2000). Embedding the 'Net: community development in the age of information. In Gurstein, M. (Ed.), *Community Informatics: Enabling Communities with Information and Communications Technologies.* Hershey, PA: Idea Group.

Loader, B. D., & Keeble, L. (2004). A Literature Review of Community Informatics Initiatives. York: Joseph Rowntree Foundation. Retrieved July 3, 2009, from http://www.jrf.org.uk/publications/ literature-review-community-informatics-initiatives

Lora, E. (2004). *A Decade of Development Thinking.* Washington, DC: Inter-American Development Bank.

Lucas, H. C., & Spitler, V. K. (1999). Technology use and performance: a field study of broker workstations. *Decision Sciences, 30*(2), 291–311. doi:10.1111/j.1540-5915.1999.tb01611.x

Luyt, B. (2004). Who benefits from the digital divide? *First Monday, 9*(8). Retrieved December 24, 2008 from http://firstmonday.org/issues/issue9_8/luyt/index.html

Lynch, K. (1960). *The image of the city.* Cambridge, MA: MIT Press.

Mabogunje, A. L. (2000). Institutional radicalization, the state, and the development process in Africa. *Proceedings of the National Academy of Sciences of the United States of America, 97*(25), 14007–14014. doi:10.1073/pnas.200298097

Maclay, C., Kirkman, G., & Hawkins, R. (2005). *Global networked readiness for education: Preliminary findings from a pilot project to evaluate the impact of computers and the Internet on learning in eleven developing countries.* Washington, DC: The World Bank. Retrieved July 13, 2008, from http://siteresources.worldbank.org/EDUCATION/Resources/278200-1126210664195/1636971-1126210694253/Global_Network_Readiness.pdf

Mahiri, I. O. (1998). The environmental knowledge frontier: transects with experts and villagers. *Journal of International Development, 10,* 527–537. doi:10.1002/(SICI)1099-1328(199806)10:4<527::AID-JID543>3.0.CO;2-S

Mankiw, N. G., Romer, D., & Weil, D. N. (1992). A Contribution to the Empirics of Economic Growth. *Journal of Economics, 107*(2), 407–437.

Mansell, R. (2000). Information and communication technologies for development: Assessing the potential and the risks. *Telecommunications Policy, 23,* 35–50. doi:10.1016/S0308-5961(98)00074-3

Mansell, R. (2001). Digital Opportunities and the Missing Link for Developing Countries. *Oxford Review of Economic Policy, 17*(2), 282–295. doi:10.1093/oxrep/17.2.282

Mansell, R. (2002). Constructing the Knowledge Base for Knowledge-driven Development. *Journal of Knowledge Management*, 6(4), 317–329. doi:10.1108/13673270210440839

Mansell, R., Steinmueller, W., & Montalvo, U. (1999). Opportunities for Knowledge-based Development: Capabilities, Infrastructure, Investment and Policy. *Science & Public Policy*, 26(2), 91–100. doi:10.3152/147154399781782572

Mansell, R., & Wehn, U. (1998). *Knowledge societies: Information technology for sustainable development.* Oxford: Published for and on behalf of the United Nations by Oxford University Press.

Marcel, L. (1998). *The Role Of The Gambian Electronic Media In The Implementation Of The Gambian Foreign Policy.* Unpublished Masters dissertation, Dept of Mass Communication, University Of Nigeria.

Marcelle, G. (2000). Getting gender into African ICT policy: A strategic view. In Rathgeber, E. M., & Adera, E. O. (Eds.), *Gender and the information revolution in Africa* (pp. 35–84). Ottawa: IDRC.

Marker, P., McNamara, K., & Wallace, L. (2002). *The significance of information and communication technologies for reducing poverty.* Department of International Development UK, London. Retrieved April 25, 2009 from http://www.dfid.gov.uk/Pubs/files/ictpoverty.pdf

Martin, S. (2003). Is the Digital Divide Really Closing? A critique of inequality measurement in a nation online. *Information Technology and Society*, 1(4), 1–13. doi:10.1080/0268396031000077413

Martín Barbero, J. (1995). Modernidad, posmodernidad, modernidades: discursos sobre la crisis y la diferencia. *Intercom - Revista Brasileira de Comunicação, 23*(2).

Mason, S., & Hacker, K. (2003). Applying Communication Theory to Digital Divide Research, *Information. Technology and Society*, 1(5), 40–55.

Masuda, J. (1981). *The Information Society as Post-Industrial Society.* Washington: World Future Society.

Mathieson, K. (1991). Predicting User Intentions: Comparing the Technology Acceptance Model with the Theory of Planned Behavior. *Information Systems Research*, 2(3), 173–191. doi:10.1287/isre.2.3.173

Mathieson, K., Peacock, E., & Chin, W. W. (2001). Extending the technology acceptance model: the influence of perceived user resources. *The Data Base for Advances in Information Systems*, 32(3), 86–112.

Mattelart, A. (2002). *História da sociedade da informação* (Campanário, N. N., Trans.). São Paulo: Loyola. (Original work published 2001)

Maturana, H. R., & Varela, F. J. (1980). *Autopoiesis and cognition.* Dordrecht, Holland: D Reidel.

Max-Neef, M. A. (1982). *From the outside looking in. Experiences in 'barefoot economics.* London: Zed Books.

Maxwell, S., & Conway, T. (2000). *Perspectives on partnership.* Washington, DC: World Bank.

Mayer, C. (2002). Financing the New economy: Financial Institutions and Corporate Governance. *Information Economics and Policy*, 14(2), 311–326. doi:10.1016/S0167-6245(01)00072-5

Mayur, R., & Daviss, B. (1998). *The Technology of Hope: Tools to Empower the World's Poorest Peoples. The Futurist.* January-February.

Mbeki, M., Vale, P. (2009). Community is the new state. *Mail & Guardian*, 27.

McAlpine, P., & Birnie, A. (2006). Establishing sustainability indicators as an evolving process: Experience from the Island of Guernsey. *Sustainable Development*, 14(2), 81–92. doi:10.1002/sd.301

McAnany, E. (1983). From Modernization and Diffusion to Dependency and Beyond: Theory and Practice in Communication for Social Change in the 1980s. *Development Communications in the Third World, Proceedings of a Midwest Symposium.* University of Illinois.

McCaston, M. K. (2005). *Documenting our methods and major findings*. CARE Newsletter. Retrieved August 10, 2008, from http://pqdl.care.org/Practice/Documenting%20Methods%20and%20Findings.pdf

McCloskey, D. (2003). Evaluating electronic commerce acceptance with the technology acceptance model. *Journal of Computer Information Systems, 44*(2), 49–57.

McConnaughey, J. W., & Lader, W. (1998). Falling through the Net II. New Data on the Digital Divide. NTIA Report. Retrieved October 2008 from http://www.ntia.doc.gov/ntiahome/net2/falling.html

McGowan, P. J., Cornelissen, S., & Nel, P. (Eds.). (2006). *Power, wealth and global equity. An international relations textbook for Africa*. Cape Town: UCT Press.

McIlvenny, P. (1999). Avatars R Us? Discourses of Community and Embodiment in Intercultural Cyberspace. *Journal of Intercultural Communication, 1*(2). Retrieved 24 December, 2008 from http://www.immi.se/

McIver, W. (2003). Community Informatics for the Information Society. In Girard, B., & Siochru, S. O. (Eds.), *Communicating in the Information Society*. Geneva: United Nations Research Institute for Social Development.

McLuhan, M. (1965). *Understanding media: The extensions of man*. New York: McGraw-Hill Book Company.

McLuhan, M., & Fiore, Q. (1967). *The medium is the massage*. New York, London, Toronto: Bantam Books.

McNamara, K. S. (2000). *'Why be Wired? The Importance of Access to Information and Communication Technologies'. TechKnowLogia, March/April 2000*. Knowledge Enterprise, Inc.

McNamara, K. S. (2003, December). Information and communication technologies, poverty and development: learning from experience. Background paper for the infoDev Annual Symposium, Geneva, Switzerland.

Meichenbaum, D. (1990). Review: paying homage: providing challenges. *Psychological Inquiry, 1*(1), 96–100. doi:10.1207/s15327965pli0101_25

Melucci, A. (2001). *A invenção do presente: movimentos sociais na sociedade complexa.* (M.C.A. Bomfim, Trans.) Petrópolis: Vozes. (Original work published 1982).

Menou, M. (2008, April). *ImperialICTism: the highest stage of capitalism?* Keynote address [La Habana, Cuba, Foro Sociedad del Conocimiento: nuevos espacios para su construcción.]. *Info,* ▪▪▪, 2008.

Menou, M., & Taylor, R. (2006, November-December). A "Grand Challenge": Measuring information societies. *The Information Society, 22*(5), 261–267. doi:10.1080/01972240600903904

Menou, M. J., Poepsel, K. D., & Stoll, K. (2004). Latin American Community Telecenters: "It's a long way to TICperary". *The Journal of Community Informatics, 1*(1), 39-57. Retrieved September 18, 2008 from http://www.ci-journal.net

Mercer, C. (2004). Engineering Civil Society: ICT in Tanzania. *Review of African Political Economy, 31*(99), 49–64. doi:10.1080/0305624042000258414

Mercer, C. (2006). Telecentres and transformations: Modernizing Tanzania through the Internet. *African Affairs, 105*(419), 243–264. doi:10.1093/afraf/adi087

Meredith, M. (2006). *The state of Africa. A history of fifty years of independence.* Johannesburg: Jonathan Ball.

Mertons, D. (2005). *Research and evaluation in education and psychology: Integrating diversity with quantitative, qualitative, and mixed methods*. Thousand Oaks, CA: Sage Publications, Inc.

Michel, L. (2006). *Compendium on development cooperation strategies.* Brussels, Belgium: European Commission.

Milanovic, B. (2005). *Worlds Apart: Measuring International and Global Inequality*. Princeton, NJ: Princeton University Press.

Minges, M. (2002). *Counting the Net: Internet Access Indicators*. Geneva: ITU.

Minsky, M. (1986). *The society of mind*. New York: Simon & Schuster.

Mitchell, W. J. (1995). *City of Bits: Space, Place and the Infobahn*. Cambridge, MA: MIT Press.

Mitchell, M. M. 2003. Possible, Probable and Preferable Futures of the Digital Divide. *Informing Science InSITE - Where Parallels Intersect.* Retrieved May 8, 2007 from http://www.informingscience.org/proceedings/IS2003Proceedings/docs/083Mitch.pdf

Mitra, S., Dangwal, R., Chatterjee, S., Jha, S., Bisht, R. S., & Kapur, P. (2005). Acquisition of computing literacy on shared public computers: Children and the "hole in the wall". *Australasian Journal of Educational Technology, 21*(3), 407–426.

Moore, S. K., & Gardner, A. (2007, June). Megacities by the numbers. *IEEE Spectrum*, •••, 16–17. doi:10.1109/MSPEC.2007.295503

Moore, G. C., & Benbasat, I. (1991). Development of an instrument to measure the perceptions of adopting an information technology innovation. *Information Systems Research, 2*(3), 193–222. doi:10.1287/isre.2.3.192

Moore, D. (Ed.). (2007). *The World Bank development, poverty, hegemony*. Scottsville: University of Kwazulu-Natal Press.

Morris, M. G., & Venkatesh, V. (2000). Age differences in technology adoption decisions: implications for a changing workforce. *Personnel Psychology, 53*(2), 375–403. doi:10.1111/j.1744-6570.2000.tb00206.x

Moshiri, S. (2010). *Information Technology and Changing the Workplace; Firm Level Evidence*. St. Thomas More College, University of Saskatchewan.

Mossberger, K., Tolbert, C. J., & Stansbury, M. (2003). *Virtual Inequality: Beyond the Digital Divide*. Washington, DC: Georgetown University Press.

Mosse, D. (1993). *Authority, gender and knowledge: Theoretical reflections on the practice of participatory rural appraisal. Network Paper (Vol. 44)*. London: ODI.

Moyo, D. (2009). *Dead Aid. Why aid is not working and how there is another way for Africa*. London: Allen Lane.

Mulder, J. (2008). *Knowledge dissemination in Sub-Saharan Africa: What role for Open Educational Resources (OER)?* Master's thesis, International School for Humanities and Social Sciences, University of Amsterdam. Retrieved October 4, 2008, from http://www.gg.rhul.ac.uk/ict4d/workingpapers/mulderOER.pdf

Muller, P. (2002). Internet Use in Transition Economies. *WIDER Discussion Paper No. 95*. Helsinki: WIDER/UNU.

Mumford, L. (1934). *Technics and civilization*. New York: Harcourt, Brace and Company.

Munir, L. Z. (2002) "He is your garment and you are his...": Religious precepts, interpretations, and power relations in marital sexuality among Javanese Muslim women. *Sojourn: Journal of Social Issues in Southeast Asia, 17.*

Murdock, G. (2002). Review Article: Debating Digital Divides. *European Journal of Communication, 17*, 385. Retrieved December 7, 2008 from http://ejc.sagepub.com/cgi/content/abstract/17/3/385

Murphy, J. T. (2008). Economic Geographies of the Global South: Missed Opportunities and promoting intersections with development studies. *Geography Compass, 2*(3), 851–873. doi:10.1111/j.1749-8198.2008.00119.x

Musa, P. F. (2006). Making a case for modifying the technology acceptance model to account for limited accessibility in developing countries. *Information Technology for Development, 12*(3), 213–224. doi:10.1002/itdj.20043

Mutula, S. M. (2003). Cyber café industry in Africa. *Journal of Information Science, 29*(6), 489–497. doi:10.1177/0165551503296006

Myers, M. (2004). *Evaluation methodologies for information and communication for development (ICD) programmes*. London: DFID.

Narayan, D., Chambers, R., Shah, M. K., & Petesch, P. (2000). Crying Out for Change. *Voices of the Poor: Vol. 2. World Bank*. Oxford: University Press.

Narayan, D., Patel, R., Schafft, K., Rademacher, A., & Koch-Schulte, S. (1999). Can Anyone Hear Us? *Voices of the Poor*: *Vol. 1. World Bank*. Oxford: University Press.

Narayan, D., & Petesch, P. (2002). From Many Lands. *Voices of the Poor*: *Vol. 3. World Bank*. Oxford: University Press.

Nardi, B. A., & O'day, V. L. (1999). *Information ecologies: Using technology with heart*. Cambridge/Massachusetts & London: The MIT Press.

Nasar, J. (1998). *The evaluative image of the city*. Thousand Oaks, CA: Sage.

National Agriculture Statistics Service. (2007). *Farm Computer Usage and Ownership*. Washington, DC: USDA, NASS.

National Center for Educational Statistics (NCES). (2001). *The nation's report card: Mathematics 2000*. Washington, D.C.: National Center for Educational Statistics.

National Research Council. (1998). *Internet counts: Measuring the impacts of the internet*. Retrieved February 9, 2005 from www.bsos.umd.edu/cidcm/wilson/xnasrep2.htm

National Social Inclusion Programme of the UK. (n.d.). Retrieved March 2008 from http://www.socialinclusion.org.uk/

National Telecommunciations Cooperative Assocation (NTCA). (2003). *NTCA 2003 Internet/Broadband Availability Survey Report*. Washington, DC. NTCA. Retrieved October 2009 from http://www.ntca.org/content_documents/2003broadband.pdf

National Telecommunications and Information Administration (NTIA). (1995). *Falling through the Net: a survey of the 'have-nots' in rural and urban America*. Washington, DC, U.S. Department of Commerce. Retrieved December 23, 2008, from http://www.ntia.doc.gov/ntiahome/fallingthru.html

National Telecommunications and Information Administration (NTIA). (1999). *Falling through the Net: defining the digital divide*, Washington, DC, U.S. Department of Commerce. Retrieved December 23, 2008, from http://www.ntia.doc.gov/ntiahome/fttn99/contents.html

National Telecommunications and Information Administration (NTIA). (2000). *Falling through the Net: toward digital inclusion*, Washington, DC, U.S. Department of Commerce. Retrieved December 23, 2008, from http://www.ntia.doc.gov/ntiahome/fttn00/contents00.html

Naudé, W. (2009). The Financial Crisis of 2008 and the Developing Countries. *Discussion Paper No. 2009/01*. World Institute for Development Economics Research, UNU, Helsinki.

NBTF. (2006). *National Broadband Task Force Report - The National Dream: networking the nation for broadband access*. Retrieved December 20, 2008 from http://www.collectionscanada.gc.ca/.

Neef, D. (Ed.). (1998). *The Knowledge Economy*. Oxford: Butterworth-Heinemann.

Negroponte, N. (1995). *Being digital*. New York: Routledge.

Neves, B. C., & Gomes, H. F. (2008). A convergência dos aspectos de inclusão digital: experiência nos domínios de uma universidade. *Encontros Bibli: Revista Eletrônica de Biblioteconomia e Ciência da Informação, 13*(26). Retrieved December 23, from http://www.periodicos.ufsc.br/

Nguyen, T. T. (2008). *Seeking Thachsanh's Rice Bowl: an Exploration of Knowledge, ICTs and Sustainable Economic Development in Vietnam*. Unpublished Doctor of Philosophy dissertation. Melbourne, Australia: Faculty of Information Technology, Monash University.

Niitamo, V. (2000). *IT, Economic Growth and Development*. Presented at UN ECOSOC 2000 Preparatory Process. New York: 5 May.

Nnadi, N., & Gurstein, M. (2007). Towards Supporting Community Information Seeking and Use. *Journal of Community Informatics, 3*(1). Retrieved October 2009 from http://ci-journal.net/index.php/ciej/article/view/325

Nora, S., & Minc, A. (1978). *A informatização da sociedade* (de Vasconcelos, P., Trans.). Lisbon: Sociedade Astória.

NORDICOM. (Nordiskt Informationscenter för Medie-och Kommunicationsforskning) (2002). Internetbarometern 2002. Retrieved July 3, 2009, from http://www.nordicom.gu.se/mt/filer/Inetbar%202002-3.pdf

Norris, P. (2003). *Digital divide. Civic engagement, information poverty, and the internet worldwide*. Cambridge: Cambridge University Press.

Norris, P. (2001). *Digital Divide: Civic Engagement, Information Poverty, and the Internet Worldwide*. Cambridge: Cambridge University Press.

Norris, K. (2001). *Dakota: A Spiritual Geography*. New York: Houghton-Mifflin Co.

Notley, T., & Foth, M. (2008). *Extending Australia's digital divide policy: an examination of the value of social inclusion and social capital policy frameworks*. Retrieved October 2008 from http://eprints.qut.edu.au/

NTIA. (1995). Falling Through the Net: A Survey of the 'Haves' and 'Have Nots' in Rural and Urban America. Retrieved October 2008 from http://www.ntia.doc.gov/ntiahome/fallingthru.html

NTIA. *Falling through the net: defining the digital divide - a report on the telecommunications and information technology gap in America*. (1999). National Telecommunications & Information Administration, U.S. Department of Commerce. Retrieved June 3, 2008, from http://www.ntia.doc.gov

NTIA. *Falling through the net: toward digital inclusion – a report on American's access to technology tools,* October. (2000). National Telecommunications & Information Administration, Economic and Statistics Administration. Retrieved June 3, 2008, from http://www.ntia.doc.gov

NTIA. *Falling Through the Net II: New Data on the Digital Divide*. (1998). National Telecommunications & Information Administration, U.S. Department of Commerce. Retrieved June 3, 2008, from http://www.ntia.doc.gov

O'Donnell, d., & Henriksen, L.B. (2002). Philosophical foundations for a critical evaluation of the social impact of ICT. *Journal of Information Technology, 17*(2), 88–99.

O'Hara, K., & Stevens, D. (2006). *Inequality.Com: Power, Poverty and the Digital Divide*. New York: OneWorld Publications.

OECD (2004). *ICT and Economic Growth in Developing Countries*. Development and Co-Operate Directorate, Development Assistant Committee Network on Poverty Reduction, 10-Dec.

OECD. (2008). *2007). Development Cooperation Report*. Paris, France: OECD.

OECD. (2003). *ICT and Economic Growth: Evidence from OECD Countries, Industries and Firms*. Paris, France. Retrieved October 2009 from http://www.labs-associados.org/docs/OCDE_TIC.PDF

Ojo, T. (2004). Old paradigm and Information & Communication Technologies for Development Agenda in Africa: Modernization as Context. *Journal of Information Technology Impact, 4*(3), 139-150. Retrieved May 7, 2009 from http://www.allacademic.com/meta/p14108_index.html.

Oldenburg, R. (1989/1997). *The Great Good Place*. New York: Paragon House.

Oldenburg, R. (2001). *Celebrating the Third Place: Inspiring Stories about the "Great Good Places" at the Heart of Our Communities*. New York: Marlowe and Company.

Oliner, S. D., & Sichel, D. E. (2000). The Resurgence of Growth in The Late 1990s: Is The Story? *The Journal of Economic Perspectives, 14,* 3–22. doi:10.1257/jep.14.4.3

Oliner, S. D., & Sichel, D. E. (2002). IT and Productivity: Where Are We Now and Where Are We Going? *Economic Review (Federal Reserve Bank of Atlanta), 87*(3), 15–44.

Omar Dengo Foundation. (2007). *Multistakeholder Partnerships and Digital Technology for Development in Latin America and the Caribbean*. San Jose, Costa Rica: Edicciones innova.

O'Neil, D. V., & Baker, P. M. A. (2003). The role of institutional motivations in technological adoption: Implementation of DeKalb County's Family Technology Resource Centers. *The Information Society, 19*(4), 305–314. doi:10.1080/01972240309485

Ong, A. (2007). Neoliberalism as a mobile technology. *Transactions of the Institute of British Geographers, 32*, 3–8. doi:10.1111/j.1475-5661.2007.00234.x

Ongley, E. D. (1996). Control of water pollution from agriculture - FAO irrigation and drainage paper 55. FAO (Food and Agriculture Organization of the United Nations). Retrieved September 2009 from http://www.fao.org/docrep/W2598e/w2598e00.htm

Onis, Z., & Senses, F. (2005). Rethinking the Emerging Post-Washington Consensus. *Development and Change, 36*(2), 263–290. doi:10.1111/j.0012-155X.2005.00411.x

Organization for Economic Cooperation and Development (OECD). (1996a). *Technology, Productivity and Job Creation*. Paris: OECD.

Organization for Economic Cooperation and Development (OECD). (1996b). *Employment and Growth in the Knowledge-Based Economy*. Paris: OECD.

Orozco, M. (2004). Remesas económicas y migración – cuestiones y perspectivas sobre el desarollo. *Vanguardia Dossier: Los hispanos en Estados Unidos*. Barcelona, *13*, 75-81.

Pacey, A. (1999). *Meaning in technology*. Cambridge, MA: The MIT Press.

Palmer, B. (1990). *Descent into discourse: the reification of language and the writing of social history*. Philadelphia, PA: Temple University Press.

Parkinson, S. (2005). *Telecentres, access and development: Experience and lessons from Uganda and South Africa*. Warwickshire, UK; Kampala; Ottawa: ITDG, Fountain Publishing, IDRC.

Parkinson, S., & Ramírez, R. (2006). Using a sustainable livelihoods approach to assessing the impact of ICTs in development. *Journal of Community Informatics, 2*(3). Retrieved October 7, 2008 from http://ci-journal.net/index.php/ciej/issue/view/15

Parks, W. with Felder-Gray, D., Hunt, J., & Byrne, A. (2005). *Who measures change? An introduction to participatory monitoring and evaluation of communication for social change*. New Jersey, USA: Communication for Social Change Consortium.

Partnership on measuring ICT for development. (2005). *Core ICT Indicators*. Beirut, Lebanon: United Nations - ESCWA.

Pasquali, A. (2003). A brief descriptive glossary of communication and information (aimed at providing clarification and improving mutual understanding). In Girard, B., & Siochru, S. O. (Eds.), *Communicating in the Information Society*. Geneva: United Nations Research Institute for Social Development.

Patton, M. (2008). *Utilization-focused evaluation, 4*th. Thousand Oaks, CA: Sage Publications.

Peñaranda Cólera, M. C. (2008). Tecnologías que acercan distancias? Sobre los "claroscuros" del estudio de las tecnologías en los procesos migratorios transnacionales. In Santamaría, E. (Ed.), *Retos epistemológicos de las migraciones transnacionales* (pp. 133–164). Barcelona: Anthropos.

Pereira, P. A. (2007). *Necessidades humanas. Subsídios à crítica dos mínimos sociais*. São Paulo: Cortez. (Original work published 2000)

Persaud, A. (2001). The knowledge gap. *Foreign Affairs (Council on Foreign Relations), 80*(2), 107–117.

Phahlamohlaka, J., Braun, M., Romijn, H., & Roode, D. (Eds.). (2008). *Community-driven projects: reflections on a success story. A case study of science education and information technology in South Africa*. Pretoria: Van Schaik Publishers.

Phelps, E. S. (1997). *Rewarding Work. How to Restore Participation and Self-Support to Free Enterprise*. Cambridge, Massachusetts: Harvard Univ Press.

Picot, A., & Wernick, C. (2007). The role of governments in broadband access. *Telecommunications Policy*, *31*(10/11), 660–674. doi:10.1016/j.telpol.2007.08.002

Pigg, K. E., & Crank, L. D. (2005). Do Information Communication Technologies Promote Rural Economic Development. *Community Development: Journal of the Community Development Society*, *36*(1), 65–76. doi:10.1080/15575330509489872

Pigg, K. E., & Bradshaw, T. K. (2003). Catalytic Community Development: A Theory of Practice for Changing Rural Society. In Brown, D. L., & Swanson, L. (Eds.), *Challenges for Rural America in the 21ˢᵗ Century. State College*. PA: State University Press.

Pigg, K. E., & Crank, L. D. (2004) Building Community Social Capital: The Potential and Promise of Information and Communication Technologies. Journal of Community Informatics, 1(1). Retrieved July 3, 2009, from http://ci-journal.net/index.php/ciej/article/view/184/132

Pilat, L., & Ark, V. (2002). Production and Use of ICT: A Sectoral Perspective on Productivity Growth in OECD Area. *OECD Economic Studies*, 35.

Pimienta, D. (2005). *Measuring Linguistic Diversity on the Internet*. Paris, France: UNESCO.

Pisón, J. M. (1998). *Políticas de bienestar. Un estudio sobre los derechos sociales*. Madrid: Universidad de la Rioja.

Pitula, K., & Radhakrishnan, T. (2007). A Framework and Process for Designing Inclusive Technology. In *International Conference on Software Engineering Advances (ICSEA 2007)*. Retrieved October 2009 from http://ieeexplore.ieee.org/stamp/stamp.jsp?tp=&arnumber=4299944&isnumber=4299877

Pochmann, M. (2002). *e-Trabalho*. São Paulo: Publisher Brasil.

Pohjola, M. (Ed.). (2001). *Information Technology, Productivity and Economic Growth*. Oxford: Oxford University Press.

Pohjola, M. (2002a). The New economy: Facts, Impacts and Policies. *Information Economics and Policy*, *14*(2), 133–144. doi:10.1016/S0167-6245(01)00063-4

Pohjola, M. (2001b). Information Technology and Economic Development: A Cross-Country Analysis. In Pohjola, M. (Ed.), *Information Technology, Productivity and Economic Growth*. Oxford: Oxford University Press.

Pohjola, M. (1998). Information Technology and Economic Development: An Introduction to the Research Issue, UNU/WIDER Working Paper, No:153.

Pohjola, M. (2002). New Economy in Growth and Development, Presented in UNU/WIDER Conference on New Economy in Development, 10-11 May, Helsinki.

Pohjola, M. (2002b). New Economy in Growth and Development. *WIDER Discussion Paper No. 67*. Helsinki: WIDER/UNU.

Polikanov, D., & Abramova, I. (2003). Africa and ICT: a chance for breakthrough? *Information, Communication & Society, 6*(1), 42:56.

Porter, C. E., & Donthu, N. (2006). Using the technology acceptance model to explain how attitudes determine Internet usage: The role of perceived access barriers and demographics. *Journal of Business Research*, *59*(9), 999–1007. doi:10.1016/j.jbusres.2006.06.003

Portes, A. (1997). Globalization from below: the rise of transnational communities. *Transnational Communities Programme Working paper series*, WPTC-98-01. Retrieved May, 12, 2009, from http://www.transcomm.ox.ac.uk/working%20papers/portes.pdf

Postman, N. (1993). *Technopoly. The surrender of culture to technology*. New York: Vintage Books. (Original work published 1992)

Postman, N. (1990). *Informing ourselves to death*. Speech at the German Informatics Society (Gesellschaft für Informatik). In Stuttgart, October 11, 1990. Retrieved January 1, 2009, from http://world.std.com/~jimf/informing.html

Potashnik, M. and Douglas Adkins (1996). Cost Analysis of Information Technology Projects in Education: Experiences from Developing Countries. *Education and Technology Series, 1*(3). Washington, DC: The World Bank.

Powell, M. (2006). *Rethinking education management information systems: Lessons from and options for less-developed countries.* Infodev Working Paper No. 6. Retrieved November 8, 2008, from http://www.infodev. org/en/Publication.504.html

Prell, C. (2003). Community Networking and Social Capital: Early investigations. Journal of Computer-Mediated Communication, 8(3). Retrieved July 3, 2009, from http:// jcmc.indiana.edu/vol8/issue3/prell.html

Pretty, J. (1994). Alternative systems of inquiry for a sustainable agriculture. *IDS Bulletin, 25*(2), 37–48. doi:10.1111/j.1759-5436.1994.mp25002004.x

Pringle, I., & Subramanian, S. (Eds.). (2004). *Profiles and experiences in ICT innovation for poverty reduction.* Paris: UNESCO.

Pritchett, L. (1997). Divergence, Big Time. *The Journal of Economic Perspectives, 11*(3), 3–17.

Procter, D. (2005). *Civic Communion: The Rhetoric of Community Building.* Manhattan, KS: Kansas State University Press.

Pryor, J., & Ampiah, J. G. (2003). *Understandings of education in an African village – the impact of ICTs. Report on DFID Research Project Ed2000-88.* London: DFID. Retrieved December 2, 2008, from http://www. dfid.gov.uk/Pubs/files/understandedafricaedpaper52.pdf

Putnam, R. D. (1993). *Making Democracy Work: Civic traditions in modern Italy.* Princeton, NJ: Princeton University Press.

Putnam, R. D. (1995). Tuning in, Tuning out: The strange disappearance of social capital in America. *Political Science and Politics, 28,* 664–683. doi:10.2307/420517

Putnam, R. (2000). *Bowling Alone: The Collapse and Revival of American Community.* New York: Simon & Schuster.

Qiang, C. Z.-W., & Pitt, A. (2003). *Contribution of Information and Communication Technologies to Growth.* Washington: The World Bank. doi:10.1596/0-8213-5722-0

Quaddus, M., & Achjari, D. (2005). A model for electronic commerce success. *Telecommunications Policy, 29*(2-3), 127–152. doi:10.1016/j.telpol.2004.11.009

Quaghebeur, K., & Masschelin, J. (2003, 27-28 February). *Participation making a difference? Critical analysis of the participatory claims of change, reversal and empowerment.* Paper presented at the workshop on Participation: From tyranny to transformation? Exploring new approaches to participation in development. University of Manchester.

Quah, D. (2001). The Weightless Economy in Economic Development. In Pohjola, M. (Ed.), *Information Technology Productivity, and Economic Growth.* Oxford: Oxford University Press.

Quarry, W., & Ramírez, R. (2009). *Communication for another development: Listening before telling.* London: Zed Books.

Quaynor, N. (1997). *Computer networking and accessing the Internet in Ghana: Problems and prospects* (pp. 28–40). Interlibrary Lending and Document Delivery in Developing Countries.

Ramamritham, K., & Bahuman, A. (2005). Developmental Informatics: Potential and Challenges. *Media Asia, 32*(3), 165–167.

Ramdas, K. N. (2008). Philanthrocapitalism in denial. *OpenDemocracy.* Retrieved October 2008 from http:// www.opendemocracy.net/article/globalization/philanthrocapitalism_in_denial

Ramírez, R. (2001). Understanding the approaches for accommodating multiple stakeholders' interests. *International Journal of Agricultural Resources. Governance and Ecology, 1*(3/4), 264–285.

Ramírez, R. (2003). Bridging disciplines: The natural resource management kaleidoscope for understanding ICTs. *The Journal of Development Communication*, *14*(1), 51–64.

Ramírez, R. (2007, March-April). Appreciating the contribution of broadband ICT with rural and remote communities: Steppingstones towards an alternative paradigm. *The Information Society*, *23*(2), 85–94. doi:10.1080/01972240701224044

Ramírez, R., & Lee, R. (2008). Service delivery systems for natural stakeholders: Targeting information and communication functions and policy considerations. *Agronomía Colombiana*, *XXV*(2), 357–366.

Ramírez, R., & Richardson, D. (2005). Measuring the impact of telecommunication services on rural and remote communities. *Telecommunications Policy*, *29*, 297–319. doi:10.1016/j.telpol.2004.05.015

Ramírez, R. 2008. A 'meditation' on meaningful participation and engagement. *The Journal of Community Informatics 4*(3). Retrieved 1 June 2009 from http://ci-journal.net/index.php/ciej/article/view/390/424

Ramírez, R., Murray, D., Kora, G., & Richardson, D. (2000). *Evaluation Report: Rural Resources Partnership for Oxford County Library and HRDC*. Guelph, Canada: University of Guelph.

Ransom, J. S. (1997). *Foucault's Discipline*. Durham, NC: Duke University Press.

Rao, M. (2001). *Local Community Networks: The Human Face of the Internet Economy*. Retrieved.

Rathgeber, E. M. (2000). Women, Men, And ICTs in Africa: Why gender is an issue. In E. M. Rathgeber & E. O. Adera (Eds.) (2000) *Gender and the information revolution in Africa* (pp.17-34). Ottawa: IDRC.

Reed, M., Fraser, E., & Dougill, A. (2006). An adaptive learning process for developing and applying sustainability indicators with local communities. *Ecological Economics*, *59*(4), 406–418. doi:10.1016/j.ecolecon.2005.11.008

Reinert, E. S. (2004). *Globalisation, Economic Development and Inequality*. Northampton, UK: Edward Elgar Publishing.

Renfrew, C., & Bahn, P. (2004). *Archaeology: theories, methods and practice*. London: Thames and Hudson.

Research, I. C. T. Africa (2007) Success and failures of ICT projects in Africa. *Research ICT Africa*. Retrieved on November 22, 2007 from www.researchictafric.net

Retrieved October 2008 from http://www.opendemocracy.net/article/globalization/visions_reflections/philanthro-capitalism_after_the_goldrush

Rheingold, H. (2000). *The Virtual Community: Homesteading on the Electronic Frontier* (Revised ed.). Cambridge, MA: The Harvard University Press.

Richardson, D., & Paisley, L. (1998). *The first mile of connectivity: Advancing rural telecommunications through a communication for development approach*. Rome: FAO.

Richardson, D., Ramírez, R., Aitkin, H., & Kora, G. (2002). Sustaining ICTs for rural development. *INASP Newsletter*, *20*, 5.

Roberts, T. R., & Hite, A. B. (Eds.). (2007). *The Globalization and Development Reader; perspectives on Development and Global Change*. Malden, MA: Blackwell Publishers.

Robinson, J. P., Barth, K., & Kohut, A. (1997). Social Impact Research – Personal Computers, Mass Media, and Use of Time. *Social Science Computer Review*, *15*(1), 65–82. doi:10.1177/089443939701500107

Rodino-Colocino, M. (2006). Laboring under the digital divide. *New Media Society, 8 (487)*. Sage Publications, London, Thousand Oaks; CA and New Delhi. Retrieved November 29, 2008, from http://nms.sagepub.com/cgi/content/abstract/8/3/487

Roduner, D., & Schläppi, W. (2008). Logical framework approach and outcome mapping: A constructive attempt of synthesis. *Rural Development News*, *2*, 9–19.

Rogers, P. (2008). Using programme theory to evaluate complicated and complex aspects of interventions. *Evaluation, 14*(1), 29–48. doi:10.1177/1356389007084674

Rogers, E. M. (2003). *The diffusion of innovations* (5th ed.). New York: Free Press.

Röling, N. (2003). From causes to reasons: The human dimension of agricultural sustainability. *International Journal of Agricultural Sustainability, 1*(1), 73–88. doi:10.3763/ijas.2003.0108

Röling, N., & Jiggins, J. (1998, September 16-19, 1998). *The soft side of land: An incomplete exploration of the implications of seeing ecological sustainability as emerging from human learning and inter-action.* Paper presented at the Symposium on Adaptive Collaborative Management of Protected Areas. Cornell University and CIFOR.

Room, G. (1995). Poverty and social exclusion: the new European agenda for policy and social research. In Room, G. (Ed.), *Beyond the Threshold: The Measurement and Analysis of Social Exclusion* (pp. 1–9). Bristol: The Policy Press.

Rosanvallon, P. (1998). *A nova questão social* (Bath, S., Trans.). Brasília: Instituto Teotônio Vilela. (Original work published 1995)

Rose, S. (2005). *Lifelines. Life beyond the gene.* London: Vintage.

Rose, G. (2001). *Visual Methodologies: An introduction to the interpretation of visual materials.* Thousand Oaks, CA: Sage Publications.

Rose, J. (1998). Evaluating the contribution of structuration theory to the information sciences discipline. Paper presented at the 6th European Conference on Information Systems, Aix-en-Provence, France.

Rosenau, P. M. (1992). *Post-modernism and the social sciences: insights, inroads, and intrusions.* Princeton, NJ: Princeton University Press.

Rostow, W. (1960). *The Stages of Economic Growth.* London: Cambridge University Press.

Rousseau, J. (1984). *A discourse on inequality.* London: Penguin. (Original work published 1754)

Sachs, J. (2005). *The end of poverty. How we can make it in our lifetime.* London: Penguin Books.

Sachs, J. (2008). *Common wealth. Economics for a crowded planet.* London: Penguin Books.

Sachs, J. D. (2005). *The end of poverty: economic possibilities for our time.* New York: Penguin Press.

Sairosse, T. M., & Mutula, S. M. (2004). Use of cyber cafes: Study of Gaborone city, Botswana. *Program-Electronic Library and Information Systems, 38*(1), 60–66. doi:10.1108/00330330410519206

São Paulo. (2008). *Decreto nº 49.914, de 14 de agosto de 2008.* Diário Oficial da Cidade de São Paulo.

Sardar, Z. (1996). Alt.civilizations.faq: cyberspace as the darker side of the West. In Sardar, Z., & Ravetz, J. R. (Eds.), *Cyberfutures: Culture and Politics on the Information Superhighway* (pp. 14–41). New York: New York University Press.

Saul, J. R. (2009). *The collapse of globalism and the reinvention of the world.* London: Atlantic Books. (Original work published 2005)

Scan-ICT Report. (2007) Status of ICT, usage and exploitation in the Gambia. *Government of the Gambia and UNECA.* Retrieved July 05, 2008 from http://www.scanict-gbos.gov.gm

Schech, S. (2002). Wired for change: The links between ICTs and development discourses. *Journal of International Development, 14*, 13–23. doi:10.1002/jid.870

Schiller, D. (2000). *Digital Capitalism: Networking the Global Market System.* MIT Press.

Schmidt, V. H. (2006). Multiple modernities or varieties of modernity? *Current Sociology, 54*(1), 77–97. doi:10.1177/0011392106058835

Scholfield, J., Eurich-Fulcer, R., & Britt, C. (1994). Teachers, computer tutors, and teaching: The artificially intelligent tutor as an agent for classroom change. *American Educational Research Journal, 31*(3), 579–607.

School of Informatics, University of Edinburgh. (2002). What does Informatics mean? Retrieved September 2009 from http://www.dai.ed.ac.uk/homes/cam/informatics.shtml.

Schramm, W. (1979). *Mass Media and National Development*. Paris: UNESCO.

Schuler, D. (1996). *New Community Networks: Wired for change*. New York: Addison-Wesley.

Schumacher, E. F. (1973). *Small is Beautiful. Economics as people mattered*. New York: Simon and Schuster.

Schuurman, F. (1993). Development Theory in the 1990s, introduction. In Schuurman, F. (Ed.), *Beyond the Impasse. New Directions in Development Theory*. London, New Jersey: Zed Books.

Sciadas, G. (2005a). Infostates across Countries and Over Time: Conceptualization, Modeling, and Measurements of the Digital Divide: View from Practice. *Information Technology for Development, 11*(3), 299–304. doi:10.1002/itdj.20018

Sciadas, G. (Ed.). (2005b). *From digital divide to digital opportunities; measuring infostates for development*. Montreal, Quebec: Claude-Yves Charron. Retrieved May 20, 2009 from http://www.itu.int/ITU-D/ict/publications/dd/material/index_ict_opp.pdf

Scoones, I. (1998). Sustainable rural livelihoods: A framework for analysis. *IDS Working Paper, vol. 72*. Brighton, UK: IDS.

Sein, M. K., & Harindranath, G. (2004). Conceptualizing the ICT Artefact: Toward understanding the role of ICT in national development. *The Information Society, 20*, 15–24. doi:10.1080/01972240490269942

Sein, M. K., & Harindranath, G. (2004). Conceptualising the ICT artifact: towards understanding the role of ICT in national development. *The Information Society, 20*(1), 15–24. doi:10.1080/01972240490269942

Selener, D. (1997). *Participatory action research and social change*. Quito, Ecuador: Global Action Publications.

Selwyn, N., Gorard, S., & Furlong, J. (2005). Whose Internet is it Anyway? Exploring Adults' (Non)Use of the Internet in Everyday Life. *European Journal of Communication, 20*(1), 5–26. doi:10.1177/0267323105049631

Sen, A. (2001). *Development as freedom*. Oxford: University Press.

Sen, A. (2006). *Identity and violence: the illusion of destiny*. New York: W.W. Norton.

Sen, A. (2005). Human Rights and Capabilities. *Journal of Human Development, 6*(2), 151–166. doi:10.1080/14649880500120491

Sen, A. (1992). *Inequality Reexamined*. Oxford: Oxford University Press.

Sen, A. (1997a). *Development and Thinking at the Beginning of the 21ˢᵗ Century. STICERD – Development Economics Papers 02. Suntory and Toyota International Centres for Economics and Related Disciplines*. LSE.

Sen, A. (1997b). *What's the Point of a Development Strategy. STICERD – Development Economics Papers 03. Suntory and Toyota International Centres for Economics and Related Disciplines*. LSE.

Sen, A. (1999). *Development as Freedom*. New York: Anchor Books.

Sen, A. (1985). *Commodities and Capabilities*. Amsterdam: North Holland.

Sen, A. (2002). *Rationality and Freedom*. Harvard: Harvard Belknap Press.

Sengupta, A. (2000). Realizing the Right to Development. [Blackwell Publishers.]. *Institute of Social Studies, 31*, 553–578.

Servaes, J. (Ed.). (2002). *Approaches to Development Communication, Part 1 Development Theory*. Paris: UNESCO.

Servaes, J., & Malikhao, P. (2002). Development communication approaches in international perspective. In Servaes, J. (Ed.), *Approaches to development communication*. Paris: UNESCO.

Servaes, J. (1989). *One World, Multiple Cultures. A new paradigm on Communication for Development*. Leuven: Acco.

Servon, L. J. (2002). *Bridging the digital divide: Technology, community, and public policy*. Oxford: Blackwell Publishing. doi:10.1002/9780470773529

Shaffer, R., Deller, S., & Marcouiller, D. (2006). Rethinking Community Economic Development. *Economic Development Quarterly*, *20*(1), 59–74. doi:10.1177/0891242405283106

Shanin, T. (1997). The idea of progress. In Rahnema, M., & Bawtree, V. (Eds.), *The post-development reader* (pp. 65–72). London: Zed Books.

Sheehan, P., Pappas, N., Tikhomirova, G., & Sinclair, P. (1995). *Australia and the Knowledge Economy: An Assessment of Enhanced Economic Growth through Science and Technology*. Melbourne: Centre for Strategic Economic Studies, Victoria University.

Shulha, L. M., & Cousins, J. B. (1997). Evalution use: theory, research, and practice since 1986. *Evaluation Practice*, *18*(3), 195–208. doi:10.1016/S0886-1633(97)90027-1

Shulman, L. S. (1986). Those who understand: Knowledge growth in teaching. *Educational Researcher*, *15*(2), 4–14.

Simpson, L. (2005). Community Informatics and Sustainability: Why Social Capital Matters. Journal of Community Informatics, 1(2). Retrieved July 3, 2009, from http://ci-journal.net/ index.php/ciej/articles/view/184/132

Singer, P. (1972). Famine, affluence, and morality. *Philosophy & Public Affairs*, *1*(3), 229–243.

Singer, H. (1970). Dualism Revisited: A new approach to problems of the dual society. *The Journal of Development Studies*, *7*(1), 60–75. doi:10.1080/00220387008421348

Smillie, I. (1999). Narrowing the digital divide: Notes on a global Netscape. Retrieved December 28, 2008 from http://www.unites.org/html/resource/smillie/smillie0.htm

Smith, A. (2003). *The wealth of nations* (Classic, B., Ed.). Kruger, AB. (Original work published 1776)

Snowden, D. (2005). *Multi-ontology sense making: A new simplicity in decision making*. Singapore: The Cynefin Centre.

Snyman, M., & Snyman, M. M. M. (2003). Getting information to disadvantaged rural communities: the centre approach. *South African Journal of Library and Information Science*, *69*(2), 95–107.

Social Inclusion Board, Government of South Australia. (n.d.). Retrieved March 2008 from http://www.socialinclusion.sa.gov.au/

Solé, C., & Parella, S. (2005). *Negocios étnicos: Los comercios de los inmigrantes no comunitarios en Cataluña*. Barcelona: Fundación CIDOB.

Solow, R. (1987). We'd better watch out. *New York Times Book Review*. New York: 12 July.

Sorj, B. (2005). *Civil Societies North-South Relations: NGOs and Dependency*. Sao Paulo, Brazil: Edelstein Center for Social Research.

Souter, D. (2004). ICT and Economic Growth in Developing Countries, Part I. *The DAC Journal*, *5*(4).

Spirakis, P., Manolopoulos, C., & Efstathiadou, R. (2008, May). *The socioeconomic aspects of digital divide*. Proceedings of the Bridging the digital divide in rural communities: practical solutions and policies Conference. Athens, Greece.

Srinivasan, R. (2006). Where information society and community voice intersect. *The Information Society*, *22*, 355–365. doi:10.1080/01972240600904324

Statistics Sweden. (2004). Use of Computers and the Internet by Private Persons in 2004. Stockholm: Statistiska centralbyrån.

Stenbacka, R. (2001). Microeconomic Policies in the New Economy. *WIDER Discussion Paper No. 73*. Helsinki: WIDER/UNU.

Stewart, J. (2007). Local Experts in the Domestication of Information and Communication Technologies. *Information Communication and Society, 10*(4), 547–569. doi:10.1080/13691180701560093

Steyn, J. (2006, October). *Community memory and ICT in a developing economy.* Paper presented at the Constructing and Sharing Memory: Community Informatics conference, Community Informatics Research Network, Prato, Italy.

Steyn, J. (2007, December). *e-Post: networking remote areas.* Paper presented at the 2007 Community Informatics Research Network conference, Prato, Italy.

Steyn, J. (2008). Book series, in IDIA International Development Informatics Association. Retrieved September 2009 from http://www.developmentinformatics.org/projects/book/index.html.

Steyn, J. (2009). ePost: Networking Remote Areas. In L. Stillman, G. Johanson, & R. French (Eds.), *Communities in Action: Papers in Community Informatics* (pp. 60-67). Cambridge Scholars Publishing.

Stiglitz, J. E. (2002). *Globalization and its discontents.* London: Penguin.

Stiglitz, J. E. (2006). *Making globalization work.* London: Penguin Books.

Stiglitz, J. E. (2003). *Globalization and Its Discontents.* New York: W.W. Norton.

Stiglitz, J. (2007). *Making Globalization Work.* New York: Norten.

Stillman, L., Johanson, G., & French, R. (Eds.). (2009). *Communities in Action: Papers in Community Informatics.* Cambridge Scholars Publishing.

Stiroh, K. J., & Jorgenson, D. (2000a). Raising the Speed Limit: U. S. Economic Growth in the Information Age. *BPEA, 1*, 125–211.

Stiroh, K. J. (2002). ICT Spillovers Driving The New Economy? Federal Reserve Bank of New York. *Review of Income, Wealth Series, 48*(1).

Stivers, R. (1999). *Technology as magic. The triumph of the irrational.* New York: Continuum Publishing.

Stoecker, R. (2005). *Research Methods for Community Change: A Project-based Approach.* Thousand Oaks: Sage.

Stoll, K., Menou, M., Camacho, K., & Khellady, Y. (2002). *Learning about ICTs' role in development: A framework towards a participatory, transparent and continuous process.* Ottawa: IDRC.

Stowasser, B. (1998). Gender issues and contemporary Qur'an interpretation. In Haddad, Y. Y., & Esposito, J. L. (Eds.), *New Islam, gender and social change* (pp. 30–44). New York: Oxford University Press.

Straton, J. (1997). Cyberspace and the globalization of culture. In Porter, D. (Ed.), *Internet Culture* (pp. 253–276). Routledge.

Straub, D. W. (1994). The effect of culture on IT diffusion: email and fax in Japan and the U.S. *Information Systems Research, 5*(1), 23–27. doi:10.1287/isre.5.1.23

Streeck, W. & Yamamura, Kozo (Eds.). (2001). *The origins of nonliberal capitalism: Germany and Japan in comparison.* Ithaca, NY: Cornell University Press.

Streeter, T. (1999). "That deep romantic chasm": libertarianism, neoliberalism, and the computer culture. In Calabrese, A., & Burgelman, J. C. (Eds.), *Communication, Citizenship, and Social Policy: Re-Thinking the Limits of the Welfare State* (pp. 49–64). Rowman & Littlefield.

Strigel, C., Ariunaa, L., & Enkhjargal, S. (2007). *Where desert meets technology: Findings from ICT in education initiatives in rural schools in Mongolia.* Washington, DC: RTI International.

Strover, S., Chapman, G., & Waters, J. (2004). Beyond community networking and CTCs: access, development and public policy. *Telecommunications Policy, 28*(7/8), 465–485. doi:10.1016/j.telpol.2004.05.008

Sunkel, O. (1972, April). "Big Business" and "Oependencia.". *Foreign Affairs (Council on Foreign Relations)*, 517–531.

Sweeney, S. (2007). Globalization, Multiple Threats and the Weakness of International Institutions: a Community-centred Response. In Clay, C. J., Madden, M., & Potts, L. (Eds.), *People and Places: an Introduction towards Understanding Community*. New York: Palgrave Macmillan.

Szajna, B. (1996). Empirical evaluation of the revised technology acceptance model. *Management Science, 42*(1), 85–92. doi:10.1287/mnsc.42.1.85

Tait, R. (2006). Iran bans fast Internet to cut West's influence. *The Guardian*, October 18th, 2006. Retrieved May 25, 2008 from http://www.guardian.co.uk/technology/2006/oct/18/news.iran

Tallon, P. P., & Kraemer, K. L. (1999). IT and Economic Development: Ireland's Coming of With Lessons for Developing Countries. In *Proceedings of Hawaii International Conference on System Science*, Jan, 5-8.

Tapscott, D. (1996). *The Digital Economy: Promise and Peril in the Age of Networked Intelligence*. New York: McGraw-Hill.

Taylor, S., & Todd, P. (1995). Understanding information technology usage: a test of competing models. *Information Systems Research, 6*(2), 144–176. doi:10.1287/isre.6.2.144

Telecentre.org. (2009). From the Ground Up: The Evolution of the Telecentre Movement. Retrieved July 3, 2009, from http://ebook.telecentre.org/

Thatcher, A., & Ndabeni, M. (2005). HCI accessibility guidelines and illiteracy: developing a model of illiteracy and engagement with technology. *Ergonomics SA, 17*(1), 13–24.

The Gambia Population Secretariat (2005). Unpublished Draft Population Policy obtained from the Population Secretariat.

Thompson, R. L., Higgins, C. A., & Howell, J. M. (1991). Personal computing: toward a conceptual model of utilization. *Management Information Systems Quarterly, 15*(1), 124–143. doi:10.2307/249443

Thompson, J., & Guijt, I. (1999). Sustainability indicators for analysing the impacts of participatory watershed management programmes. In Hinchcliffe, F., Thompson, J., Pretty, J., Guijt, I., & Parmesh, S. (Eds.), *Fertile ground: The impacts of participatory watershed management* (pp. 13–31). London: IT Publications.

Tinio, V. L. (2003). *ICT in education*. Bangkok: UNDP-Asia Pacific Development Information Programme (APDIP). Retrieved September 1, 2008, from http://www.apdip.net/publications/iespprimers/eprimer-edu.pdf

Tong, D. (2001). Cybercolonialism: Speeding along the superhighway or stalling on a beaten track. In Ebo, B. (Ed.), *Cyberimperialism? Global Relations In The New Electronic Frontier* (pp. 1–6). Westport, CT: Praeger.

Tongia, R., & Wilson, E. J. (2007). Turning Metcalfe on his head: the multiple costs of network exclusion. *Telecommunications Policy Research Conference* (TPRC). September 2007. Retrieved October 2008 from http://web.si.umich.edu/tprc/papers/2007/772/TPRC-07-Exclusion-Tongia&Wilson.pdf

Tongia, R., Subrahmanian, E., & Arunachalam, V. (2005). *Information and communications technology for sustainable development*. Bangalore: Allied Publishers Pvt. Ltd. Retrieved on November 02, 2008 from http://www.cstep.in/docs/ict4sd.pdf

IFPRI. (2006). *Information and Communication Technologies for Development and Poverty Reduction: The Potential of Telecommunications* (Torero, M., & von Braun, J., Eds.). Washington, DC: Johns Hopkins University Press and IFPRI.

Toyama, K., Dias, M.B. (2008). Guest Editors' Introduction: Information and Communication Technologies for Development. *Computer*.

Trucano, M. (2005). *Knowledge maps: ICT in education*. Washington, DC: infoDev / World Bank. Retrieved November 22, 2008, from http://www.infodev.org/en/Publication.8.html

Turkle, S. (1984). *The second self: Computers and the human spirit*. New York: Simon & Schuster.

Turkle, S. (1995). *Life on the screen: Identity in the age of the Internet*. New York: Simon & Schuster.

Underwood, J. (2004). Research into information and communication technologies: Where now? *Technology, Pedagogy and Education*, *13*, 135–145. doi:10.1080/14759390400200176

UNDP. (1998). Information and Communication Technologies for Development. UNDP, New York. Retrieved June 20, 2005 from http://www.undp.org/info21/

UNDP. (2005) *UN Millennium Project: Investing in Development: A practical Plan to Achieve the Millennium Development, Goals. Overview*. Washington, D.C. UNDP. Retrieved June 20, 2008 from http://www.unmillennium-project.org/reports/index_overview.htm van Dijk, Jan (2005). Pitfalls of a Metaphor. Retrieved November 10, 2008 from http://www.gw.utwente.nl/vandijk/research/digital_divide/Digital_Divide_overigen/a_framework_for_digital_divide.doc/

UNESCO Institute of Statistics. (2006). *ICTs and education indicators: Suggested core indicators based on meta-analysis of selected International School Surveys*. Montreal: UNESCO Institute of Statistics. Retrieved October 15, 2008, from http://www.itu.int/ITU-D/ict/partnership/material/ICT_Education_Paper_Nov_2006.pdf

United Nation, Millennium Development Goals. (n.d.). Retrieved January 2009 from www.un.org/millenniumgoals

United Nations Conference on Trade and Development (UNCTAD), (2006). *The Digital Divide Report: ICT Development Indices*. United Nations, New York and Geneva. Retrieved June 20, 2008 from http://www.unctad.org/en/docs/sdteecb20061_en.pdf

United Nations Conference on Trade and Development (UNCTAD) (2008). *Information Economy Report; Science and Technology for Development; the new paradigm for ICT*. UNITED NATIONS New York and Geneva. Retrieved June 28, 2008 from: http://www.unctad.org/en/docs/sdteecb20071_en.pdf

United Nations Development Programme. (2000). Millennium Development Goals (MDG). Retrieved September 2009 from http://www.undp.org/mdg

United Nations Development Programme. (2001). *Evaluation Unit. Essentials: Information and Communications Technology for Development. Synthesis of Lessons Learned, no 5. September*. New York: UNDP.

United Nations. (UN) (2000), Millennium Development Goals (MDGs). Retrieved October 2009 from http://www.un.org/millenniumgoals/

Unwin, T. (Ed.). (2009). *ICT4D*. Cambridge: Cambridge University Press.

Unwin, T. (2009a). Blog. Retrieved October 2009 from http://unwin.wordpress.com/2009/04/27/reflections-on-ict4d-the-british-council-manchester

USK. (2008). Statistics by time. Retrieved July 3, 2009, from http://www.usk.stockholm.se/ internet/omrfakta/tabellappl.asp?omrade=0&appl=Tidserier&resultat=Andel&sprak=eng

Van der Vyver, A. G. (2006). Personal communication.

Van Dijk, J. A. G. M. (2006). *The network society. Social aspects of new media*. London: Sage.

Van Dijk, J. A. G. M. (2005). *The Deepening Divide: Inequality in the Information Society*. Thousand Oaks, CA: SAGE Publications.

van Dijk, J. (2001, 15-17 November). *The ideology behind "closing digital divides": Applying static analysis to dynamic gaps.* Paper presented at the IAMCR/ICA Symposium on the Digital Divide. Austin, Texas: University of Texas.

Van Leeuwen, G., & Vander Weil, H. (2003). Spillover Effects of ICT, *CPB Report*, 2003/3.

Van Rossem, R. (1996). The world-system paradigm as general theory of development: A cross-national test. *American Sociological Review*, *61*, 508–527. doi:10.2307/2096362

Van Wart, M., Rahm, D., & Sanders, S. (2000). Economic Development and Public Enterprise: The Case of Rural Iowa's Telecommunications Utilities. *Economic Development Quarterly*, *14*(2), 131–145. doi:10.1177/089124240001400201

Varian, H. (2006, January 12). American Companies Show an Edge in Putting Information Technology to Work. *New York Times*. Retrieved August 10, 2007 from http://www.topics.mytimes.com/top/reference/timestopics/people/v/hal_r_varian/index.html/?offset¼10&Vehovar, V., Sicherl, P., H¨using, T., & Dolnicar, V. (2006). Methodological Challenges of Digital Divide Measurements. *The Information Society*, 22, 279–290.

Vehovar, V., Sicherl, P., Hüsing, T., & Dolnicar, V. (2006, November-December). Methodological challenges of digital divide measurements. *The Information Society*, *22*(5), 279–290. doi:10.1080/01972240600904076

Veiga, J. F., Floyd, S., & Dechant, K. (2001). Towards modelling the effects of national culture on IT implementation and acceptance. *Journal of Information Technology*, *16*(3), 145–158. doi:10.1080/02683960110063654

Venkatesh, V. (1999). Creation of favorable user perceptions: exploring the role of intrinsic motivation. *Management Information Systems Quarterly*, *23*(2), 239–260. doi:10.2307/249753

Venkatesh, V., & Brown, S. A. (2001). A longitudinal investigation of personal computers in homes: adoption determinants and emerging challenges. *Management Information Systems Quarterly*, *25*(1), 71–102. doi:10.2307/3250959

Venkatesh, V., & Davis, F. D. (2000). A theoretical extension of the technology acceptance model: four longitudinal field studies. *Management Science*, *46*(2), 186–204. doi:10.1287/mnsc.46.2.186.11926

Venkatesh, V., & Morris, M. G. (2000). Why don't men ever stop to ask for directions? Gender, social influence, and their role in technology acceptance and usage behavior. *Management Information Systems Quarterly*, *24*(1), 115–139. doi:10.2307/3250981

Venkatesh, V., Morris, M. G., Davis, G. B., & Davis, F. D. (2003). User acceptance of information technology: toward a unified view. *Management Information Systems Quarterly*, *27*(3), 424–478.

Vishwanath, A. (2003). Comparing online information effects. *Communication Research*, *30*(6), 579–598. doi:10.1177/0093650203257838

Vodafone, (2005). Africa: Impact of Mobile Phones: Moving the debate forward. *Mobile Phone Paper Series* No. 3. Retrieved July 2, 2008 from http://www.vodafone.com/etc/medialib/attachments/cr_downloads.Par.78351.File.tmp/GPP_SIM_paper_3.pdf

Wagner, D. A., & Daswani, C. J. (2006). *Bridges to the Future Initiative: Project update and research report.* Philadelphia, PA: International Literacy Institute, University of Pennsylvania.

Wagner, D. A., Day, B., & Sun, J. (2004). *Information technologies and education for the poor in Africa (ITEPA): Recommendations for a pro-poor ICT4D non-formal education policy. Technical Report.* Philadelphia, PA: International Literacy Institute, University of Pennsylvania.

Wagner, D. A., & Day, B. James, T., Kozma, R.B., Miller, J. & Unwin, T. (2005). *Monitoring and evaluation of ICT in education projects: A handbook for developing countries.* Washington, DC: infoDev/World Bank. Retrieved July 24, 2008, from http://www.infodev.org/en/Publication.9.html

Waisbord, S. (2001). *Family Tree of Theories, Methods and Strategies in Development Communication.* Prepared for The Rockefeller Foundation, May 2001. Retrieved on July 2nd 2008 from: http://www.comminit.com/pdf/familytree.pdf

Waitayangkoon, P. (2004). *Thai project on the uses of low-cost technology in science and mathematics*. Paper presented at the International Conference on Educational Technology, Singapore.

Wakeford, N. (2003). The Embedding of Local Culture in Global Communication: Independent Internet Cafés in London. *New Media & Society, 5*, 379–399. doi:10.1177/14614448030053005

Wallerstein, I. (2005). After developmentalism and globalization, what? *Social Forces, 83*(3), 1263–1278. doi:10.1353/sof.2005.0049

Wallerstein, I. (1974). *The Modern World System*. Academic Press.

Wallerstein, I. (1979). *The Capitalist World Economy*. Cambridge: Cambridge University Press.

Walsham, G., & Sahay, S. (2006). Research on Information Systems in Developing Countries: Current Landscape and Future Prospects. *Information Technology for Development, 12*(1), 7–24. doi:10.1002/itdj.20020

Warscahuer, M. (2003). Dissecting the "Digital Divide": A Case Study in Egypt. *The Information Society, 19*, 297–304. doi:10.1080/01972240309490

Warschauer, M. (2004). *Technology and social inclusion*. Cambridge, Mass: MIT Press.

Warschauer, M., Knobel, M., & Stone, L. (2004). Technology and Equity in Schooling: Deconstructing the Digital Divide. *Educational Policy, 18*(4), 562–588. doi:10.1177/0895904804266469

Warschauer, M. (2006). *Tecnologia e inclusão social: a exclusão digital em debate* (Szlak, C., Trans.). São Paulo: Senac. (Original work published 2003)

Warschauer, M. (2002). Reconceptualizing the digital divide. *First Monday, 7*(7). Retrieved October 2009 from http://firstmonday.org/htbin/cgiwrap/bin/ojs/index.php/fm/article/view/967/888

Waverman, L., Meschi, M., & Fuss, M. (2005). The Impact of Telecoms on Economic Growth in Developing Countries. *The Vodafone Policy Paper Series, 3*, 10-23. Retrieved July 2, 2008 from http://www.vodafone.com/etc/medialib/attachments/cr_downloads.Par.78351.File.tmp/GPP_SIM_paper_3.pdf

Weick, K. (1995). *Sense making in organizations*. Thousand Oaks, CA: Sage.

Weil, M. M., & Rosen, L. D. (1998). *TechnoStress: Coping With Technology @work, @home, @play*. New York: John Wiley & Sons.

Wellman, B. (1986). Are Personal Communities Local? A Dumpterian Reconsideration. *Social Networks, 18*(3), 347–354.

Wenger, E. (1998). *Communities of Practice: Learning, Meaning and Identity*. Cambridge: Cambridge University Press.

Wenger, E. (2000). Communities of practice: The key to knowledge strategy. In Lesser, E., Fontaine, M., & Slusher, J. (Eds.), *Knowledge and communities* (pp. 3–51). Boston: Butterworth Heinemann. doi:10.1016/B978-0-7506-7293-1.50004-4

Werle, R. (2005). *The Dynamics of the digital divide*. Retrieved June 15, 2008 from http://www.mpi-fg-koeln.mpg.de/people/we/Links/Digital%20Divide%20Dynamics.pdf

West, A. R. (2006). Related Dangers: The issue of Development and Security for Marginalized Groups in South Africa. *The Journal of Community Informatics, 2*(3). Retrieved December 21, from http://www.ci-journal.net/

Wheeler, D. (2001). New technologies, old culture: A look at women, gender and the Internet in Kuwait. In Ess, C., Sudweeks, F., & Herring, S. C. (Eds.), *Culture, technology, communication: Towards an intercultural global village* (pp. 187–212). Albany, New York: Sunny Press.

White African. (2009). Spray against caterpillar. Retrieved September 2009 from http://whiteafrican.com/wp-content/uploads/2009/06/Caterpillar.jpg

Widrow, B., Hartenstein, R., & Hecht-Nielsen, R. (2005). 1917 Karl Steinbuch 2005. In *IEEE Computational Intelligence Society Newsletter, August* (p. 5). Eulogy.

Wilhelm, A. G. (2000). *Democracy in the Digital Age: Challenges to Political Life in Cyberspace*. New York: Routledge.

Williams, J., Sligo, F., & Wallace, C. (2004). What a difference it makes? The internet in the Everyday lives of new user families. In *Anzca04: making a difference annual conference of the Australian and New Zealand Communication Association*. University of Sydney. Retrieved September 18, 2008, from http://conferences. arts.usyd.edu.au/

Willis, K. (2005). *Theories and practices of development*. London: Routledge.

Wilson, G., & Heeks, R. (2000). Technology, Poverty and Development. In Allen, T., & Thomas, A. (Eds.), *Poverty and Development into the 21st Century*. Oxford: Oxford University Press.

Wilson-Grau, R. (2006). *Complexity and Evaluation in International Networks*. Toronto, Canada: International Development Research Centre.

Wolf, S. (2001). *Determinants and Impact of ICT Use for African SMEs: Implications for Rural South Africa*. Paper prepared for TIPS Forum.

Wolff, L. (1999). Costa Rica: Are computers in school effective? *TechKnowLogia*. Retrieved December 2, 2008, from http://www.techknowlogia.com/TKL_active_pages2/CurrentArticles/main.asp?IssueNumber=2&FileType=PDF&ArticleID=42

Wong, P.-K. (2002). ICT Production and Diffusion in Asia: Digital Dividends or Digital Divides? *Information Economics and Policy, 14*(2), 167–188. doi:10.1016/S0167-6245(01)00065-8

Wong, P.-K. (2001). The Contribution of Information Technology to the Rapid Economic Growth of Singapore. In Pohjola, M. (Ed.), *Information Technology, Productivity and Economic Growth*. Oxford: Oxford University Press.

Woodhill, J., & Röling, N. (1998). The second wing of the eagle: The human dimension in learning our way to more sustainable futures. In Röling, N., & Wagemakers, M. (Eds.), *Facilitating sustainable agriculture: Participatory learning and adaptive management in times of environmental uncertainty* (pp. 46–71). Cambridge: Cambridge University Press.

World Bank. (1999). *World Development Report: Knowledge for Development*. New York: Oxford University Press.

World Bank. (2003). *World Development Indicators*. New York: World Bank.

World Bank. (2004). *Monitoring and evaluation: Some tools, methods and approaches*. Washington, DC: The World Bank.

World Bank. (1998). *World Development Report*. World Bank, Washington, DC. Retrieved September 6, 2006 from www.g8.utoronto.ca/summit/2000okinawa/gis.htm

World Bank. (2000). Global development gateway project proposal draft. World Bank: Washington, DC. http://www. worldbank.org/gateway/ (accessed September 2000).

World Bank. (2005). Financing information and communication infrastructure in the Developing World: public and private roles. Draft for discussion. *Global Information and Communication Technologies Department (Gict)*. The World Bank. International Development Agencies: World Bank

World Bank. (2006). World development indicators. Retrieved December 2006 from http://www.worldbank. org/data

World Bank. (2007) World Development Indicators. Retrieved on October 13, 2007 from http://go.worldbank. org/k2ckm78cc0

World Bank. (2009a). Data & Statistics. Retrieved September 2009 from http://web.worldbank.org/WBSITE/EXTERNAL/DATASTATISTICS/0,contentMDK:20535285~menuPK:1192694~pagePK:64133150~piPK:64133175~theSitePK:239419,00.html. Accessed in September 2009.

World Bank. (2009b). Information and Communications for Development 2009: Extending Reach and Increasing Impact. Retrieved September 2009 from http://web.worldbank.org/WBSITE/EXTERNAL/TOPICS/EXTINFORMATIONANDCOMMUNICATIONANDTECHNOLOGIES/EXTIC4D/0,contentMDK:22229759~menuPK:5870649~pagePK:64168445~piPK:64168309~theSitePK:5870636,00.html.

World Development Report 2001 Forum on Inclusion, Justice and Poverty Reduction, prepared for the World Development Report 2001 Forum on 'Inclusion, Justice and Poverty Reduction'. Retrieved October 2008 from http://www.dfid.gov.uk/pubs/files/sdd9socex.pdf

World Factbook, C. I. A. (2009). Retrieved September 2009 from https://www.cia.gov/library/publications/the-world-factbook/

World Summit on the Information Society. (2005). Declaration of Principles; Building the Information Society: a global challenge in the new Millennium. Geneva, United Nations/International Telecommunications Union. Retrieved September 2009 from http://www.itu.int/wsis/docs/Geneva/official/dop.html

Wright, K. (2008). *What role for evaluation in the context of performance-based management? INTRAC Briefing Paper No. 22*. Oxford, UK: INTRACT.

Wu, J., & Wang, S. (2005). What drives mobile commerce? An empirical evaluation of the revised technology acceptance model. *Information & Management, 42*(5), 719–729. doi:10.1016/j.im.2004.07.001

Wynn, B. O., Dutta, A., & Nelson, M. I. (2005). *Challenges in program evaluation of health interventions in developing countries*. Santa Monica, CA: RAND.

Xiberras, M. (1996). *As teorias da exclusão: para uma construção do imaginário do desvio* (Rego, J. G., Trans.). Lisbon: Instituto Piaget. (Original work published 1993)

Xue, L., & Sheehan, P. (2002). China's Development Strategy. In Grewal, B. (Eds.), *China's Future in the Knowledge Economy: Engaging the New World*. Beijing: Tsinghua University Press.

Yamamura, K., & Streeck, W. (Eds.). (2003). *The end of diversity? Prospects for German and Japanese capitalism*. Ithaca, NY: Cornell University Press.

Yan, Y. (2002). Managed globalization: State power and cultural transition in China. In P. L. Berger & S. P. Huntington (Eds.), *Many Globalizations: Cultural diversity in the contemporary world* (pp. 19-47). Oxford: Oxford University Press.

Yoon, C., & Kim, S. (2007). Convenience and TAM in a ubiquitous computing environment: the case of wireless LAN. *Electronic Commerce Research and Applications, 6*(1), 102–112. doi:10.1016/j.elerap.2006.06.009

Young, J. R. (2001). Does 'Digital Divide' Rhetoric Do More Harm Than Good? *The Chronicle of Higher Education - Information Technology*. Retrieved December 20, 2008 from http://chronicle.com/free/v48/i11/11a05101.htm

Yu, L. (2006). Understanding information inequality: Making sense of the literature of the information and digital divides. *Journal of Librarianship and Information Science, 38* (229). London, Thousand Oaks, CA and New Delhi: Sage Publications. Retrieved November 29, 2008, from http://lis.sagepub.com/cgi/content/abstract/38/4/229

About the Contributors

Jacques Steyn holds a PhD in language and complex systems, and he received an award for excellence in science from the South African Association for the Advancement of Science (S2A3) for his Masters Degree. In 1999 he developed the first XML-based general music markup language (http://www.musicmarkup.info). He was member of the international ISO/MPEG-7 standards workgroup on metadata for interactive-TV and Multimedia. He was also member of the ISO/MPEG-4 extension workgroup for music notation (i.e. symbolic music representation). In 1999 and 2000 he was Associate Professor of Multimedia at the University of Pretoria. Since February 2005 he served as Head of the School of IT at Monash University's South African campus. Prior to that, for close to a decade, he was a private consultant in the field of new media, web technologies and multimedia. His interest in ICT4D began in 1999. In 2006 he established the International Development Informatics Association, which at the time of writing had its 3rd annual conference. The idea of this book was born from frustration with the scarcity of well-founded academic research in the field of ICT4D, where media hype seems to reign.

Graeme Johanson began professional life as a librarian, moving into academia after a decade of work experience. ICTs were in their infancy. His first academic qualifications were in history and law. His PhD research dealt with the hegemonic cultural and economic exchange of books around the British Empire, and their contributions to particular forms of development. In different universities he has taught and researched about disciplinary territories, information management, knowledge management, community informatics, community networks, learning commons, knowledge preservation, development informatics, e-research, migrant diasporas, and related themes. He has worked in faculties of Arts, Humanities, Communications Studies, Business, Education, and Information Technology. Multidisciplinarity has become a way of life!

* * *

Liliane Dutra Brignol is Ph.D. student at the Postgraduate Programme in Communications in Universidade do Vale do Rio do Sinos, Unisinos, Brazil, sponsored by CAPES (Coordenação de Aperfeiçoamento de Pessoal de Nível Superior) (2006-present). Master in Communications (2004, Unisinos, Brazil) and Bachelor in Journalism (2001, Universidade Federal de Santa Maria, UFSM, Brazil). Researcher of the Brazil-Spain Cooperation Programme (Comissão de Aperfeiçoamento de Pessoal de Nível Superior, CAPES, Brazil & Ministerio de Educacion y Ciencia, MEC, Spain, 2004-2008) and of the Media, Culture and Citizenship Research Group (http://midiaculturaecidadania. wordpress.com/).

Lecturer of Centro Universitario Franciscano (Unifra, Brazil, 2004-present). Affiliation: Universidade do Vale do Rio do Sinos (Unisinos) and Centro Universitario Franciscano (Unifra)

Matthew Clarke is Deputy Head of the School of International and Political Studies and Course Director of the International and Community Development postgraduate program at Deakin University, Australia. Associate Professor Clarke has published or presented over eighty academic journal papers, book chapters and conference papers. He has also authored or co-authored five books and edited or co-edited another 4. These publications have address climate change, the Millennium Development Goals, aid effectiveness, HIV/AIDS, sustainability and ICTs in development. Dr Clarke undertakes regular evaluations of community development projects in the Pacific and South-east Asia for various non-government organisations, with a particular interest in HIV/AIDS and health-related projects. Prior to working within the tertiary sector, Associate Professor Clarke worked with the international aid agency, World Vision, where he was responsible for designing and monitoring community development projects in the Southeast Asian region.

Denise Cogo is Ph.D. (2000) and Master (1995) in Communications (School of Arts and Communications, Universidade de Sao Paulo, Brazil) and Post-Doctoral Fellow at Department of Publicidad y Comunicación Audiovisual (Universidade Autonoma de Barcelona, Spain, 2007-2008), and Bachelor in Journalism (1985) and French (1989) (Universidade Federal do Rio Grande do Sul). Professor at Universidade do Vale do Rio do Sinos, Unisinos, and researcher of CNPq (Conselho Nacional de Desenvolvimento Científico e Tecnológico), Brazil and Visiting Lecturer at Universidade Autônoma de Barcelona (Spain, 2004-2008). Co-coordinator of the Brazil-Spain Cooperation Programme (Comissão de Aperfeiçoamento de Pessoal de Nível Superior, CAPES, Brazil & Ministerio de Educacion y Ciencia, MEC, Spain, 2004-2008) (www.intermigra.unisinos.br) and Coordinator the Media, Culture and Citizenship Research Group (http://midiaculturaecidadania.wordpress.com). Coordinator of the Special Interest Group in Communication for Citizenship of the Brazilian Association of Interdisciplinary Studies in Communications (Intercom, 2001-2006). Counsellor of CNPq (Conselho Nacional de Desenvolvimento Científico e Tecnológico), CAPES (Coordenação de Aperfeiçoamento de Pessoal de Nível Superior) and Fapergs (Fundação de Amparo à Pesquisa do Estado do Rio Grande do Sul).

Suely Fragoso is Ph.D. in Communications (Institute of Communications Studies, University of Leeds, England, 1998); Master in Communications and Semiotics (Pontifícia Universidade Catolica de Sao Paulo, Brazil, 1992) and Bachelor in Architecture and Urbanism (Universidade de Sao Paulo, Brazil, 1987). Professor at Universidade do Vale do Rio do Sinos, Unisinos, Brazil and sponsored researcher of The National Council for Scientific and Technological development (CNPq). Executive Coordinator of the Postgraduate Programme in Communications (Master and Doctorade levels) in the same University in 2005-2006, Coordinator of the Special Interest Group in Information and Communication Technologies of the Brazilian Association of Postgraduate Programmes (Compos) in 2004-2005, Founder and Coordinator of the Research Group Midias Digitais (http://www.midiasdigitais.org). Consultant for research sponsoring agencies (CNPq, CAPES, FAPERGS), scientific associations and journals.

Sara Ferlander is a researcher and lecturer at the Stockholm Centre on Health of Societies in Transition (SCOHOST), in the School of Social Sciences, Södertörn University. She holds a BA in sociology from Stockholm University and a PhD in sociology and psychology from the University of Stirling.

Prior to taking up her position in Södertörn University she was a research assistant at the Centre for eLearning Development in the University of Stirling. Her publications include papers on social inclusion, community and ICT and on the relationship between social capital and health in Russia.

Jasmine Harvey is a social, cultural and development informatics professional specialising in Information and Communication Technologies (ICTs) and their communities of practice. She has studied and worked in the ICT field for about 13 years and her particular areas of interest include ICTs for development, globalisation, the information society, and policy. Professional experience include ICT research, ICT training, database management, desktop publishing, web design and administration. Jasmine is currently a Research Fellow in the School of Community Health Sciences at the University of Nottingham working on a project that is evaluating ICT's impact in healthcare communities such as community pharmacies and general practices. She has also worked on a range of other ICT-related jobs including field work project management and coordination, Loughborough university; teaching and assessment of undergraduate degree students, Loughborough university; consultancy work on displaced peoples' needs with UNICEF Uganda; teaching basic software programs; database management and IT related duties for The Workshop conferences, Loughborough; and web design and authoring, Indygo New Media Ltd, London. Her education history includes a PhD in Human geography on: "Cyber and cellular cultures in the Gambia: socio-spatial perspectives on globalisation, development and the digital divide", Department of Geography, University of Loughborough; a Master's degree (MSc distinction) in Global transformations in Department of Geography, Loughborough University; and, a Bachelor's degree (BSc 2:1) in Information management and computing – Department of Information Science, Loughborough University. She also has two computing diplomas in Computer Programming; and, Computer Systems Design from West African Computer Science Institute (WACSI) and West London College (WLC) respectively.

Peter A. Kwaku Kyem is a Ghanaian who currently resides in the USA. Peter is a Professor of Geography at Central Connecticut State University, New Britain, Connecticut, USA. He holds a Ph.D. in Geography (1997) from Clark University, Worcester, Massachusetts, USA. He obtained an MA in Geography (1991) from Carleton University, Ottawa, Canada, and a Post-graduate Diploma in Applied Geomorphology from International Institute for Aerospace Survey and Earth Sciences, ITC (1987) Enschede, the Netherlands. Dr. Kyem attended the University of Cape Coast, Cape Coast, in Ghana for his BA degree in Geography and concurrently obtained a Diploma in Education in 1982. At Clark University, Peter worked in different capacities at Clark Labs (best known for its flagship product, the IDRISI GIS and Image Processing software). He was among the team of scholars at Clark Labs whose combined effort resulted in the development of Comprehensive Decision Support Tools in Idrisi GIS in 1993. Dr. Kyem followed this research with several publications on GIS and conflict management, Participatory GIS, and Information Communications Technology (ICT). His articles appear in books and reputable peer-reviewed journals such as the Annals of the Association of American Geographers, Cartographica - the International Journal of Cartography, and Transactions in GIS. Others journals include Applied Geographic Studies, the Electronic Journal on Information Systems in Developing Countries and the Journal of Planning Education Research. He has also presented a number of papers at various national and international conferences on Participatory GIS applications. Dr. Kyem's current research focuses on ICT adoption in Africa, the Digital Divide, Participatory GIS, and GIS applications in conflict management.

Chase Laurelle Knowles is currently earning a Ph.D. at Claremont Graduate University (CGU), where her research interests include the intersection of social psychology, religion, politics, culture, and new media technology. She previously studied at the University of California Los Angeles (UCLA), where she participated in a number of transdisciplinary research projects focused on the social implications of ICT. These included REMAPPING LA, the flagship project of the UCLA Center for Research in Engineering, Media and Performance, as well as an independent research initiative in which she tracked Islamist web activity. She is preparing herself for a career in academia, research, and consulting. All opinions expressed in her work are hers alone, and are not meant to be understood as representative of the views of any organization(s) she has been, or is currently, affiliated with.

Cristina Kiomi Mori is Ph.D. student in Social Policy (2007-2010) at University of Brasilia (UnB), with Bachelor (1994-1998) and Master's (1999-2003) degree in Media at University of São Paulo (USP). Since 2005, works as program manager for Digital Inclusion Policies at the Secretariat of Logistics and Information Technology in the Ministry of Planning, Budget and Management of Brazil. That includes coordinating public initiatives such as Computer for Inclusion Project, a national equipment refurbishing network that provides qualification to young people; Digital Inclusion National Observatory, a set of information organized for multiple uses at www.onid.org.br; Workshop for Digital Inclusion, annual event for public policy debate and improvement; and Telecentros.BR, a national program that supports digital inclusion in communities. From 2003 to 2004, worked in digital inclusion for local development in Amazon Forest communities, as project manager for the non-governmental organization Health and Happiness Project (Projeto Saúde & Alegria). From 2000 to 2003, worked for Cidade Escola Aprendiz, in São Paulo, as journalist, editor, project manager and youth educator. Also worked at Sydney Olympic Games, in year 2000, as press assistant. Previously, had worked for the web edition of Folha de S.Paulo newspaper, and as editor in websites and news agencies.

Meredith McCormac is currently a Project Specialist at the American Institutes for Research, where she manages large-scale education development projects in sub-Saharan Africa and conducts research on various education policy issues. Specifically, she is interested in the impact of both formal and non-formal education programs on the resiliency of marginalized or vulnerable youth, as well as the impact of state fragility on education and the possibilities for educational programs to mitigate fragility. Prior to joining the American Institutes for Research, Ms. McCormac coordinated student exchange programs on human rights education in Bosnia and Herzegovina, and conducted research on post-conflict transitional justice mechanisms for the Jennings Randolph Senior Fellowship program at the United States Institute of Peace. Ms. McCormac holds a B.A. in Religious Studies from the University of Oklahoma, a M.A. in International Peace and Conflict Resolution from American University, and is currently pursuing her Ph.D. in International Education Policy at the University of Maryland, College Park, where her research focuses on education policy in post-conflict environments as well as measurement and evaluation.

Saeed Moshiri is an assistant professor in the Department of Economics, STM College, University of Saskatchewan, Canada. He received his BA and MA in Economics from University of Allameh Tabatabaie and University of Tarbiat Modarres in Iran and his MA and PhD from University of Toronto and University of Manitoba in Canada. He has taught undergraduate and graduate courses in macroeconomics and econometrics in university of Manitoba, University of Winnipeg, Memorial University of Newfoundland in Canada and University of Allameh Tabatabaie in Iran. Saeed's research interests are applied econometrics, macroeconomics, economic growth, technological change, and energy economics. He has published 24 papers in refereed journals such as Journal of Forecasting, International Review of Applied Economics, Energy Journal, Iranian Economic Review, Information System in Developing Countries, Economic Journal, and Quarterly Iranian Economic Review in the areas of forecasting, energy, macroeconomics, and the effect of technological change on productivity and growth.

Don Schauder (BA DipLib Rhodes, MA Sheffield, MEd PhD Melbourne, FALIA, MACS) is Emeritus Professor of Information Management, and former Associate Dean (Research), in the Faculty of Information Technology at Monash University. He was a pioneer of Australian electronic publishing as founder of INFORMIT Electronic Publishing, and of community networking as co-founder of VICNET: Victoria's Network. He has been Director of several libraries, the first being the South African Library for the Blind and the latest RMIT University Library. As part of a Monash team he undertook commissioned research on knowledge management for the Olympics movement internationally. He served as a member of several advisory committees to the Government of Victoria on library and information policy, and of the Australian Government delegation to the UN World Summit on the Information Society. He is currently Honorary Chair of Monash's Centre for Community Networking Research (CCNR).

Somaieh Nikpoor is a PhD candidate in University of Ottawa, Canada. She received her BA and MA from Shahid Beheshti University and University of Allameh Tabatabaie in Iran, and now working on her PhD dissertation in University of Ottawa.

Mbongi Ndabeni holds a Masters degree in industrial psychology from Wits University. In his masters thesis he invesistigated the moderating effect of self-efficacy in the relationship amongst perceived competence, job stress and career commitment. Since graduation, he has been in involved in running a small business, part of which was community internet services in a rural town in the Eastern Cape (and has therefore a practical exposure to some elements of e-adoption from the perspective of rural communities). During this same period, he has been involved in short research projects – including human factors and mental models. Mbongi is currently lecturing HR, Org Behavior, Org Theory and Consumer Psychology at Rhodes University. He and is curently reading for for his PhD in industrial psychology looking at the concept of technology usability among illiterate communities. His research interests include: self-efficacy as it relates to learning and acquisition of organisational skills, career and organisational commitment, technology and usability amongst illiterate communities.

Fabio Nascimbeni has a Degree in Economics, with an international business management specialisation, and is finalising a PHD on ICT for Development in the Knowledge Society. In his actual position of Director of the MENON Network (www.meno.org), he is in charge of research coordination, business development, coordination of international working groups, policy advisory and strategic consultancy. He has been coordinating, in collaboration with the European Commission, a number of international collaboration actions, such as the International Stakeholders Component of the @LIS Programme, focusing on the cooperation of Europe and Latin America in the fields of e-learning, health, e-government, e-inclusion, the SINCERE Network, focusing on the collaboration of Europe, Latin America and South East Asia on Educational Research, the WINDS-LA project, focusing on Euro-Latinamerican and Caribbean collaboration in ICT research, and the VIT@LIS Network.

Kenneth Pigg is Associate Professor of Rural Sociology at the Univ. Of Missouri. He has been involved in the analysis of technological impacts on communities, especially rural communities, for 35 years. Recently his interest has turned to community informatics and the adoption process in rural communities with a concern for the factors that contribute to success in this process of adoption, deployment and use by local communities. He has recently completed a national study of this process and is currently advising several dissertations in related areas of research.

Ricardo Ramirez is a freelance consultant based in Guelph, Ontario, Canada. He has worked in communication for development for 25 years. His evaluation work in the field of information and communication technology (ICT) emphasizes participatory action research. He has worked with ICT projects by First Nations in remote communities in northern Ontario where applications like telemedicine are being implemented by Aboriginal organizations. Ricardo has worked with communication as a component of rural development projects through NGOs, universities, consulting firms and the United Nations. He was associate professor of Capacity Development and Extension in the School of Environmental Design and Rural Development, University of Guelph. He remains an Adjunct Professor of the same school. He has collaborated with the International Development Research Centre (IDRC) of Ottawa in applied research on M&E of ICT projects. In particular, he has been exploring the role of participatory and developmental evaluation approaches including Utilization Focused Evaluation, Most Significant Change and Outcome Mapping into the ICT world. Ricardo has written about the promise of these methods in light of the unpredictable dimensions of ICT-induced change. He advocates for multi stakeholder negotiation around what to measure to capture benefits as perceived by different actors. Ricardo was born and raised in Mexico. His Canadian university education began in agriculture, then moved to adult education and finally to information and communication technology for rural community development.

Nitika Tolani-Brown is currently a Research Analyst with the American Institutes for Research (AIR). Her main interests lie in program management, monitoring and evaluation within the social welfare, education and health sectors. Over the past ten years, she has developed programs and lead large-scale, policy-relevant mixed methods studies investigating the effects of persistent socioeconomic disadvantage and psychosocial traumas on cognitive, behavioral and psychological outcomes in children and adults from the desert villages of Rajasthan to the inner-city communities of New York. Dr. Tolani-Brown has also served as a technical advisor for a range of interventions in educational development, teacher professional development, psycho-social and emotional learning, youth empowerment and life skills, distance learning, and program evaluation (including quantitative and qualitative techniques). She received her Ph.D. in Developmental Psychology (with a concentration in International Educational Policy) and her M.A. in Applied Psychology from Columbia University. She received a B.A. in English and a B.S. in Psychology from Santa Clara University.

Andrew Thatcher is an Associate Professor in Psychology in the School of Human & Community Development at the University of the Witwatersrand where he is also Deputy Head of School. He holds a BSc, MSc and PhD in Psychology from the University of the Witwatersrand. His principal teaching interests are in the area of Industrial/Organisational Psychology (Engineering Psychology, Cognitive Ergonomics, Psychometric Assessment, Organisational Theory and Research Design). Andrew strives to integrate his teaching with his research interests and subsequently was the recipient of the 2004 Vice-Chancellor's Individual Teaching Award and the 2007 University e-Learning Award. He is currently the School Graduate Studies Chair overseeing postgraduate issues in the departments of Psychology, Speech Pathology and Audiology, and Social Work. His research interests are in the domains of the psychological influences of technology adoption, the cognition of technological devices, and computer supported cooperative work systems. His current research projects are looking at the feasibility of online conference systems and the psychological, cognitive aspects of technology adoption in illiterate people, moral disengagement mechanisms in software piracy, and attendance patterns in large class tertiary education classes. Andrew is registered with the Health Professions Council of South Africa as an Industrial Psychologist and is also a member of the Human Factors & Ergonomics Society and the Ergonomics Society of South Africa. He was the Chairperson of the Fourth International Cyberspace Conference on Ergonomics (CybErg 2005, he was also Chairperson of the Third CybErg Conference, and a member of the International Scientific Advisory Committee for the Second CybErg Conference), and is a member of the Scientific Advisory Panel of HCII2009, IEA2009, and CybErg 2008. He is the Chair of the Division of Engineering Psychology and Human Factors for the 30th International Congress of Psychology to be held in cape Town in 2012. He was an Associate Editor of the 'South African Journal of Psychology' until 2007, and is currently a Co-editor of 'Ergonomics SA'. He has reviewed for the journals Behaviour & Information Technology, International Journal of Industrial Ergonomics, Ergonomics SA, CyberPsychology & Behaviour, Computers in Human Behaviour, Information & Processing Management, The Open Ergonomics Journal, South African Journal of Industrial Psychology, Ergonomics, and the South African Journal of Industrial Psychology. He is also a member of the editorial boards of the journals Behaviour & Information Technology, Ergonomics, and The Open Ergonomics Journal.

Duncan Timms is Emeritus Professor of Applied Social Science in the University of Stirling and holds BA and PhD degrees from the University of Cambridge. He was Deputy Principal of the University of Stirling between 1978 and 1984, Acting Principal & Vice-Chancellor 1981-2 and Dean of the Faculty of Human Sciences from 1999-2006. From 1998-2006 he was Director of the Centre for eLearning Development. Earlier appointments included Senior Lecturer in Anthropology and Sociology in the University of Queensland and Professor of Sociology in the University of Auckland. His main research interests are social inclusion and social capital, the social implications of information and communications technologies and the sociology of mental health. He has directed a number of research and development projects, including SCHEMA (Social Cohesion through Higher Education in Marginal Areas), an EC-funded project under the auspices of the Telematics Applications Programme (1998-2001), and ODELUCE (Open and Distance Learning in University Continuing Education, funded under the EC MINERVA Programme 2001-2003. Research grants have included funding from the ARC, the ESRC and the Wenner Gren Foundation for research into urban social structure and the mental health and family background of a Swedish cohort and from the ESRC , the Swedish NFR and the EC Human Capital & Mobility fund for a series of international schools on comparative social research. Publications include books and papers on urban social structure, IT and social inclusion, and family background and mental health.

Roy Zimmermann is Deputy Director for Global Initiatives at the American Institutes for Research. In this position, he provides strategic and technical support to projects in the areas of Information Communication Technologies (ICT) including expertise in design, implementation and supervision of technology related projects in international developing contexts. In this capacity, he ensures implementation of ICT supports project goals and is contextually appropriate to achieve maximum benefit to target audiences. He works at the ministerial, regional, school and community levels to determine challenges and appropriate interventions. Roy's role at AIR also includes strengthening the organization's ties to the private sector and identifying opportunities for partnerships to leverage public and private sector resources for development projects. Prior to joining AIR, Roy was Senior Project Director at the Education Development Center (EDC). He managed USAID's $117 Million dot-EDU initiative for EDC which worked with USAID Missions around the world to develop and implement strategies for improving K-12 education at national, regional and local levels. Dot-EDU specifically sought to improve education systems in developing countries through the integration of appropriate technologies, which have included everything from low-tech radios, to computers, to cell phones and MP3 players. Roy was involved with designing, implementing, monitoring, evaluating and promoting dot-EDU projects. Prior to coming to EDC, Roy was Manager of the Educational Programming and Services department at the Corporation for Public Broadcasting where he was responsible for overseeing design, implementation and evaluation of education projects targeting some of the country's neediest children, through public broadcasting content and services. He worked closely with national producers of children's programming and with local PBS stations to design and implement outreach activities in their local communities, always targeting those most in need. He earned a Ph.D. in Education at UCLA where he also worked as a Research Analyst providing qualitative assessments of national and local education reform programs, including focus groups, interviews, and classroom observations. He was a teacher for six years, two overseas with the Peace Corps in Papua New Guinea and four in low income communities in Maryland and Arizona.

Index